Macroeconomics, Fiscal Policy,

and Economic Growth

Also by Norman F. Keiser

Introductory Economics

Macroeconomics, Fiscal Policy, and Economic Growth

Norman F. Keiser

Associate Professor of Economics

San Jose State College

John Wiley & Sons, Inc.

New York . London . Sydney

SECOND PRINTING, MARCH, 1966

Library of Congress Catalog Card Number: 64-20073
Printed in the United States of America

To Nancy, Cindy, Bruce, and My Parents

Preface

This text was written primarily for use in the Fiscal Policy half of the year course in Public Finance, although it should be easily adapted to other courses with a macroeconomic and policy orientation. An attempt has been made to bring together the wide variety of theory, ideas, and materials necessary for an understanding of fiscal policy.

Basically, I have attempted to (1) review the macroeconomic theory necessary to an understanding of fiscal policy; (2) apply this theory to the area of fiscal policy; (3) discuss the problems involved in and the procedures, conflicts, and specific techniques of fiscal policy; and (4) evaluate and suggest improvements in fiscal (and monetary) policy. It would be incomplete, however, to ignore monetary theory and monetary policy; therefore I have devoted considerable time to both these areas. I have made some evaluation of the policies of the Federal Reserve and Chairman Martin. The reader may not agree with my frank remarks about Chairman Martin, but he will not see much discussion of him elsewhere.

This text was not originally intended to carry out any underlying theme. As the work progressed, however, it became increasingly apparent that the most serious problem confronting the American economy for most of the 'fifties and the early 'sixties, and the most probable single cause of the resulting slow rate of economic growth, was the lack of sufficient demand. Consequently, if any theme appears repeatedly throughout the text it is the need for balanced economic growth.

Part I is devoted to a discussion of the background and goals of fiscal policy, the problems and conflicts inherent in the attainment of these goals, and the role of government in the economy. Part II covers the modern income theory prerequisite to an understanding of fiscal policy. Depending on the students' comprehension of income theory, this part of the book may be stressed or deemphasized. Chapters 8 and 9 use the algebraic (as well as the descriptive, graphic, and tabular) approach, but the level of the algebra is extremely rudimentary. About all the student has to know is how to substitute, transpose, and factor terms.

Part III spends considerable time on the determinants of economic growth, theory, empirical evidence, policy, and potential growth. Part IV covers the influence of fiscal and other policies on consumption and investment and discusses both tax and nontax policies. Part V is devoted almost exclusively to policy problems, although the necessary analysis is included at the appropriate places. The need for adequate economic analysis to precede the formulation of policy is stressed throughout this part. Included are the problems of budgeting, high unemployment, monetary policy, inflation, and suggestions for improving both fiscal and monetary policy. Part VI is devoted to a chronological analysis of the various policies used since 1930. Chapter 21 covers the Depression and World War II years and should help dispel some popular but mistaken ideas about the fiscal policy of these periods. Some instructors may, in fact, wish to assign Chapter 21 early in the course.

The necessary theory appears early in the book, and the principles developed there are applied in the subsequent policy and problem-oriented sections. In addition, a plentiful supply of empirical data have been incorporated into the text. Further, the text includes many practical applications of theory to the problems that are faced in fiscal policy.

In this area of economics particularly, differences of opinion on the proper policy to follow are bound to occur; similarly, different judgments are inevitable when one begins to evaluate the actions pursued. I have been fully aware of the political nature of fiscal policy but have not attempted to sidestep the issues. The instructor may not agree with all the conclusions, but at least the student will have been exposed to the issues.

Additional recommended readings have not been included at the end of the chapters since the large number of footnote references, and the comments therein, should give the reader a more than sufficient supply of extra materials.

Because of the large number of footnotes and mathematical formulas, I have used abbreviations in the notes. The key for these abbreviations is located after the table of contents.

At this point it is appropriate to make the usual acknowledgments. Professor Jesse Burkhead of Syracuse University read 18 chapters of the first draft of the manuscript, and Professor Harold M. Somers of the University of California at Los Angles read the entire manuscript. To both of these gentlemen go my sincere thanks for their extremely helpful suggestions and recommendations.

Norman F. Keiser

April 1964
Saratoga, Calif.

Contents

PART TWO

Macroeconomic Theory and Fiscal Policy

PART THREE

Problems and Theory of Economic Growth

PART FOUR

Fiscal Policy and Consumption and Investment

List of Abbreviations

1. *Am. Ec. Rev.* = *American Economic Review.* Unless otherwise noted the May issue is the Proceedings issue
2. *Am. Polit. Sci. Rev.* = *American Political Science Review*
3. CEA = Council of Economic Advisors
4. *Ec. J.* = *Economic Journal*
5. *Ec. Rept. Pres.* = *Economic Report of the President* (with year to be specified)
6. FR or *FR Bull.* = Federal Reserve or *Federal Reserve Bulletin*
7. JEC, *Ann. Rept.* = Joint Economic Committee, *Annual Report* (with year to be specified)
8. JEC, or JCER = Joint Economic Committee, formerly Joint Committee on the Economic Report
9. *J. Polit. Ec.* = *Journal of Political Economy*
10. NBER = National Bureau of Economic Research
11. NPA = National Planning Association
12. *Natl. Tax J.* = *National Tax Journal*
13. OBE, USDC = Office of Business Economics, United States Department of Commerce
14. *Ox. Ec. P.* = *Oxford Economic Papers*
15. *Q.J.Ec.* = *Quaterly Journal of Economics*
16. *Rev. Ec. & Stat.* = *Review of Economics and Statistics*
17. *Surv. Current Bus.* = *Survey of Current Business*
18. JEC, *Fed. Tax Pol.*, P or H = Subcommittee on Tax Policy, Joint Committee on the Economic Report, *Federal Tax Policy for Economic Growth and Stability:*
    P = Papers (Nov. 9, 1955), 1956
    H = Hearings (Dec. 5–9, 12–16, 1955), 1956
19. JEC, *Jan. 1955 Ec. Rept. Pres.*, H = Joint Economic Committee, *January 1951 Economic Report of the President*, Hearings (Jan. 24, 26–28, 31, Feb. 1–3, 8–10, 16, 1955), 1955
20. JEC, *Monet. Pol.: 1955–56*, H = Joint Economic Committee, *Monetary Policy: 1955–56*, Hearings (Dec. 10, 11, 1956), 1957
21. JEC, *Fed. Exp. Pol.*, P or H = Subcommittee on Fiscal Policy, Joint Economic Committee, *Federal Expenditure Policy for Economic Growth and Stability:*
    P = Papers (Nov. 5, 1957), 1957
    H = Hearings (Nov. 18–27, 1957), 1958
22. JEC, *Rel. Prices to Ec. Stabil. & Growth*, H, P, or C = Joint Economic Committee, *The Relationship of Prices to Economic Stability and Growth:*
    P = Compendium of Papers, 1958

H = Hearings (May 12–16, 19–22, 1958), 1958 and (Dec. 15–18, 1958) 1959

C = Commentaries (Oct. 31, 1958), 1958

23. JEC, *Jan. 1959 Ec. Rept. Pres.*, H = Joint Economic Committee, *January 1959 Economic Report of the President*, Hearings (Jan. 27–30, Feb. 2–6, 9, 10, 1959), 1959

24. JEC, *Empl., Growth, Price Levels*, H, SP, SR, or R = Joint Economic Committee, *Employment, Growth, and Price Levels:*

H = Hearings:

Part 1: "The American Economy: Problems and Prospects" (March 20, 23–25, 1959), 1959

Part 2: "Historical and Comparative Rates of Production, Productivity, and Prices" (April 7–10, 1959), 1959

Part 4: "The Influence on Prices of Changes in the Effective Supply of Money" (May 25–28, 1959), 1959

Part 6A: "The Government's Management of Its Monetary, Fiscal, and Debt Operations" (July 24, 27–30, 1959), 1959

Part 6C: Same title as 6A; "Answers to Questions on Monetary Policy and Debt Management," 1959

Part 7: "The Effects of Monopolistic and Quasi-Monopolistic Practices" (Sept. 22–25, 1959), 1959

Part 8: "The Effect of Increases in Wages, Salaries, and the Prices of Personal Services, Together with Union and Professional Practices upon Prices, Profits, Production, and Employment" (Sept. 28–30, Oct. 1, 2, 1959), 1959

Part 9A: "Constructive Suggestions for Reconciling and Simultaneously Obtaining the Three Objectives of Maximum Employment, an Adequate Rate of Growth, and Substantial Stability of the Price Level" (Oct. 26–30, 1959), 1959

Part 9B: Same title; "Materials Submitted by 12 Organizations at the Invitation of the Joint Economic Committee." 1959

Part 10: "Additional Materials Submitted for the Record," 1960

SP = Study Papers:

No. 1: "Recent Inflation in the United States," by Charles L. Schultze, 1959

No. 2: "Steel and the Postwar Inflation," by Otto Eckstein and Gary Fromm, 1959

No. 3: "An Analysis of the Inflation in Machinery Prices," by Thomas A. Wilson, 1959

No. 9: "The Share of Wages and Salaries in Manufacturing Incomes, 1947–56," by Alfred H. Conrad, 1959

No. 11: "A Brief Interpretive Survey of Wage-Price Problems in Europe", by Mark W. Leiserson, 1959

No. 14: "Financial Aspects of Postwar Economic Developments in the United States," by John Gurley, 1959

No. 15: "Profits, Profit Markups, and Productivity: An Examination of Corporate Behavior Since 1947," by Edwin Kuh, 1959

No. 16: "International Effects of U.S. Economic Policy," by Edward M. Bernstein, 1960

No. 17: "Prices and Costs in Manufacturing Industries," by Charles L. Schultze and Joseph L. Tryon, 1960

No. 19: "Debt Management in the United States," by Warren L. Smith, 1960

No. 20: "The Potential Economic Growth of the United States," by James W. Knowles, 1960

No. 22: "An Evaluation of Antitrust Policy: Its Relation to Economic Growth, Full Employment, and Prices," by Theodore J. Kreps, 1960

R = *Report* of the Committee (1960)

SR = *Staff Report* (Dec. 24, 1959), 1960 (Sometimes called the "Eckstein Report")

25. JEC, *Rev. Ann. Rept. FR, 1960*, H = Joint Economic Committee, *Review of the Annual Report of the Federal Reserve for 1960*, Hearings (June 1, 2, 1961), 1961

26. JEC, *Current Ec. Sit. & Short-Run Outl.*, H = Joint Economic Committee, *Current Economic Situation and Short-Run Outlook*, Hearings (Dec. 7, 8, 1960), 1961

27. JEC, *Jan. 1961 Ec. Rept. Pres.*, H = Joint Economic Committee, *January 1961 Economic Report of the President and the Economic Situation and Outlook*, Hearings (Feb. 9, 10, March 6, 7, 27, April 10, 1961), 1961

28. JEC, *Jan. 1962 Ec. Rept. Pres.*, H = Joint Economic Committee, *January 1962 Economic Report of the President*, Hearings (Jan. 25, 26, 30, 31, Feb. 2, 5–8, 1962), 1962

29. JEC, *State Ec. & Pol. Full Empl.*, H = Joint Economic Committee, *State of the Economy and Policies for Full Employment*, Hearings (Aug. 7–10, 13–17, 20–22, 1961), 1962

30. JEC, *Var. Private Invest.* = Joint Economic Committee, *Variability of Private Investment in Plant and Equipment:*
Part 1 (Investment and Its Financing), 1962
Part 2 (Some Elements Shaping Investment Decisions), 1962

31. JEC, *Jan. 1963 Ec. Rept. Pres.*, H = Joint Economic Committee, *January 1963 Economic Report of the President*, Hearings:
Part 1 (Jan, 28–31, Feb. 1, 4–6, 1963), 1963
Part 2 (Statements of Interest Groups), 1963

32. COF, S. *Investigation Finan. Cond.*, C, H, or A = Committee on Finance, *Investigation of the Financial Condition of the United States:*
H = Hearings:
Part 1 (June 18–21, 25–27, July 1, 2, 8–12, 1957), 1957
Part 2 (July 29–31, Aug. 1–3, 6–9, 1957), 1957

Part 3 (Aug. 13–16, 19, 1957), 1957
Part 6 (April 16–18, 22–25, 1958), 1958
A, or 7 = Part 7: Analysis of Hearings (Aug. 18, 1959), 1959
C = Compendium, 1958
33. WMC, HR, *Tax Revis. Comp.*, P = Ways and Means Committee, House of Representatives, *Tax Revision Compendium*, Papers (Nov. 16, 1959), 1959

Inasmuch as all government publications cited have been published by the Government Printing Office at Washington, D.C. this information has been omitted.

The following have been used to abbreviate the titles of other journals or organizations: J. (Journal), Ec. (Economic), Am. (American), Assoc. (Association), Rev. (Review), and Bus. (Business).

PART I

Introduction: Goals, Conflicts, and the Role of the Federal Government

1

Public Finance, Political Science, and Fiscal Policy

THE SCOPE OF PUBLIC FINANCE

Despite the fact that one secures a real understanding of an area of knowledge primarily by studying that field itself, it is logical to first attempt some definitions. Fiscal policy is closely associated with and is directly descended from macroeconomics, especially from the contributions of John Maynard Keynes. The teaching of fiscal policy, however, is generally done in college courses in public finance. This being the case we must first present a definition of public finance.

At this point we shall briefly mention the issues and problems that public finance deals with. (1) What should be the function and role of government in the economy? What should government do and what should private enterprise do? Of the activities government should undertake, which should be assumed by the federal, which by the state, and which by the local government? (2) In absolute dollars, what should be the level of government expenditures? How much for alternative programs? (3) What types of taxes should be imposed to finance these expenditures—property, income, excise, estate, etc.? (4) Under varying economic conditions, what should be the level (amount) of taxes collected? (5) What should be the rate structure of the taxes collected? Should they be progressive, proportional, or regressive? (6) Who really pays the taxes? To what extent are they shifted? (7) What is the impact of taxes and government expenditures on consumption and investment and therefore on national income? (8) How should the federal budget be developed? Should it be balanced? Should we have a capital budget? (9) How do we simultaneously attain full employment, economic growth, and overall price stability? (10) How large should the public debt be? How should it be managed? How much of a burden is it?

3

As a subdivision of public finance, fiscal policy is concerned with the impact of government tax, expenditure, and debt policy on the levels of production, employment, income, and prices. Although we shall later want to discuss its goals and objectives further, we can state for the time being that the conventional goals of fiscal policy are threefold—full employment, general price stability, and economic growth. In the late fifties a fourth objective came to the forefront—equilibrium in our balance of payments. We should note that the above definitions are not static. The role and responsibilities of the government will vary with the period being studied and the political theory of the times.

FISCAL POLICY AND POLITICAL SCIENCE

Inasmuch as fiscal policy deals directly with the role and policies of government, its relation to the field of political science is rather obvious. That the two areas overlap becomes quite evident when one considers constitutional grants of and limitations on the powers of governments to tax and spend for specific purposes; voting for and against taxes, or for and against school bond issues; and the close connection between one's conception of the role of government in the economy and one's political philosophy.

Over the years the role of the government in society has varied according to the prevailing political philosophy. As political theory has changed, so has the role of the government (and, naturally, so has the definition of public finance). As all students who have been exposed to the principles of economics know, the role of the government in Adam Smith's time was quite circumscribed. The historical change since then was well illustrated in the 1960 Presidential election campaign, where government policies relative to (1) speeding up economic growth, (2) spending more or less for missiles and defense, (3) inflation, (4) employment, (5) medical care, and (6) education were important issues. In each instance the issue was not whether the federal government should participate in the area but rather "how" and "how much" it should participate.

We should not be misled into believing that there is necessarily a consensus in society on the "proper" role of government. We all know that the views of the National Association of Manufacturers and the U.S. Chamber of Commerce differ radically from those of the AFL-CIO. Whereas the AFL-CIO supports government programs aiming at full employment, medical care for the aged, etc., a representative of the NAM on the other hand has gone so far as to state that:

The question suggests use of tax policy as a means for manipulating the economy. The approach is contrary to the policies of the National Association of Manufacturers, which follow the philosophy reflected in the statement of Secretary of the Treasury, George M. Humphrey . . . . "The power to tax is the power to destroy and revenue laws should be used only to equitably raise revenue, not for other indirect purposes."[1]

It is evident that the NAM does not subscribe to the theory that taxation should be used to influence the level of economic activity. But it is also evident that the NAM recognizes that taxes do affect economic activity (as was certainly understood by Justice Marshall, the author of the statement that "the power to tax is the power to destroy"). Nonetheless, contemporary economists do not simply recognize that taxes affect economic activity; they also feel that taxation and expenditures can and should be used to control the level of employment, production, prices, and the rate of economic growth.

THE DEVELOPMENT OF FISCAL POLICY

The Background

We have already noted that fiscal policy is generally considered a branch of public finance, even though it is directly descended from Keynesian macroeconomics. At this point we should note some of the major aspects of pre-Keynesian fiscal policy.

Classical economic theory and nineteenth-century laissez-faire ideology provided a limited role for fiscal policy. Classical theory maintained that full employment was normal, lapses from it being due to wage rates which are too high, monopoly, or similar causes. Laissez-faire ideology taught that the least government is the best government; the government's budget should always be balanced; the lowest levels of taxes and expenditures are the best levels; the individual citizen is best equipped to decide how to spend his income; the self-regulating free market is the best guide to the efficient allocation of the country's resources; as far as possible taxes should be "neutral" (not affect the prices or allocation of resources, or the distribution of income); every dollar spent by the government is offset by a dollar reduction in private expenditure (therefore, how could deficit spending ever create employment?); and that government expenditures are unproductive expenditures (but private expenditures are productive). Today, few economists subscribe to such views without considerable qualification. In fact, our experience has shown that most of these dogmas are generally incorrect, cannot possibly be pursued in today's world, or have been directly rejected at the polls.

[1] JEC, *Fed. Tax Pol.*, P, p. 200.

It is certainly true that a century and a half ago most governments were tyrannical, undemocratic, and suppressed civil liberties. Under these circumstances it is quite understandable why political theorists and economists desired to limit their role. But it is true in most Western countries today that governments are democratically controlled; further, it has often been the central government that has protected civil liberties and that has best represented the total populace rather than special interests. In addition, the current size of our federal budget is not a function of the "new" Keynesian fiscal policy but rather of the fact that close to 80 percent of our federal expenditures are directly related to past wars or the cold war, and in order to provide for national and individual survival the lowest levels of government taxes and expenditures are not necessarily the best levels. It is also true, as we shall demonstrate later, that the annually balanced budget may aggravate either inflation or depression, both of which society wishes to avoid. Similarly, government expenditures can raise the level of employment when we have unused resources, as was so forcefully demonstrated during the period 1938 to 1942. (See Chapter 21, the second section, and Tables 21-1, 21-2, and 22-3.)

Taxes and government expenditures are not, as Adam Smith taught, necessarily unproductive. Along these lines it is interesting to note that during the Middle Ages the physiocrats held that only agriculture was productive, and that town life could exist only because of, and was supported by, a productive agriculture (which at one time was true). Although Smith pointed out that the towns no longer lived off the country and that they provided productive manufactured goods, his argument maintained that only those producing material goods were productive, and that physicians, lawyers, clergymen, teachers, musicians, etc., were unproductive. Hence public-sponsored projects and services were, and often still are, considered to fall in the unproductive category. The illogic of the argument is obvious. Government expenditures most certainly can contribute to production and to economic progress: to wit, education, research and development, transportation systems and economic development, police and war expenditures (which protect our wealth and capital equipment), the development of natural resources and the furtherance of conservation, and the provision of public parks. As Alvin Hansen has often pointed out, these expenditures are productive in the sense that they (1) create income; (2) develop skills, techniques, and new products; (3) contribute to efficiency; (4) create capital; and (5) satisfy human wants for a great variety of services and goods (whether publicly or privately created).

All this does not mean that we have a simple or definitive set of criteria for allocating functions between government and private enterprise, for determining which programs government should pursue, or for concluding that governments are not wasteful. In fact, in contemporary American society the argument over the allocation of functions between private and public agencies is often at the heart of our political campaigns and controversies. Further, certain government projects may at one time be highly productive and at another time be extremely wasteful. To build a new superhighway when those in existence are more than adequate, and when at the same time there is a great need for expenditures on education or health, is to pursue a wasteful policy. Walter F. Stettner claims: "The decisive consideration must always be in terms of what is needed most in any given situation. The most productive pattern of expenditure is that which contributes most toward the achievement of the economic, political, and social aims of a particular time and a particular country."[2]

American economists are basically committed to the principle that the free market should decide what is to be produced. But they also recognize that certain goods and services can be efficiently provided through the free market only with considerable difficulty; for example, flood control, police protection, national defense, and basic scientific research. In addition, society feels that some products or services, such as education or medical care, should be available to all its citizens even though they cannot assume their full cost.

In the foregoing we have dealt primarily with the role of the central government in contemporary society. While the reader may feel that we have gone somewhat astray from our discussion of the development of fiscal policy, such a diversion was necessary to show the historical changes that in turn enabled fiscal policy to develop. Fiscal policy is the direct result of actions taken by the government during the Great Depression of the 1930's, and of John Maynard Keynes' devastating attack on the classical principle that the economy would automatically return to a position of full employment equilibrium. Keynes' *General Theory of Employment, Interest and Money* (1936) also provided an analytical framework for determining the level of national income and product and employment. It can be said that Keynes was the father of modern macroeconomics and contemporary fiscal policy, and that his theoretical structure provided the justification for the actions governments were

---

[2] W. F. Stettner, "Carl Dietzel, Public Expenditures, and the Public Debt," in *Income, Employment, and Public Policy: Essays in Honor of Alvin H. Hansen*, New York: Norton, 1948, p. 298. Hansen has almost identical discussions of this same problem in his *Fiscal Policy and Business Cycles*, New York: Norton, 1941, pp. 144–152, and his *Economic Issues of the 1960's*, New York: McGraw-Hill, 1960, pp. 97–104.

already taking to combat high levels of unemployment and greatly reduced production. It still remained, however, for other economists (primarily Alvin Hansen) to fill in the details and further spell out fiscal policies.

The Present Status of Fiscal Policy

In American society and elsewhere, Keynesian economics and therefore fiscal policy are not completely accepted. Both have come under severe fire from certain groups. The contemporary critics of Keynesian economics and fiscal policy base their criticisms on both political and economic grounds, and many of their arguments are based on or directly descended from nineteenth-century economic and political theory.[3] The political criticism still is that the use of fiscal policy means greater intervention in the economy, central planning, and restrictions on individual rights. The economic criticism usually is that fiscal policy will not work—an argument which does not withstand the tests of economic analysis or experience. It should be recognized that many groups have sincere reservations about giving the federal government a major role in the economy. To them, granting increased responsibilities to the federal government results in inefficiencies, extravagance and waset, and restrictions on free enterprise. But some individuals and groups condemn a greater role for the government for more personal and selfish reasons. On the other hand, some advocates of a greater role for the federal government are not simply interested in greater economic stabilization and growth but are doctrinaire in their approach.

It is interesting to note that data gathered by the Survey Research Center of the University of Michigan have shown that a large majority of Americans have favorable attitudes toward several important government programs.[4] The surveys have shown that the vast majority of Americans feel that the federal government can and should influence "the level of economic activity" and "the proper functioning of the economy." The programs and the percent of people who felt that the government should spend more, less, and the same (in this order) are as follows:

1. Help for older people (70–3–23) (i.e., 70 percent said spend more, 3 percent said spend less, and 23 percent said spend the same)

---

[3] For criticisms by economists see M. Friedman, *Essays in Positive Economics*, Chicago: Univ. of Chicago Press, 1953, and *Capitalism and Freedom*, Chicago: Univ. of Chicago Press, 1963; and H. C. Simons, *Economic Policy for a Free Society*, Chicago: Univ. of Chicago Press, 1948.

[4] Eva Mueller, "Public Attitudes Toward Fiscal Programs," *Q.J.Ec.*, May 1963, pp. 210–235. This article contains much valuable information on attitudes toward government, taxes, and expenditures.

2. Help for needy people (60–7–28)
3. Education (60–7–28)
4. Slum clearance and city improvement (55–9–24)
5. Hospitals and medical care (54–9–28)
6. Public works (48–11–31)
7. Defenses and rearmament (47–6–34)
8. Support for small business (37–11–31)
9. Highway construction (36–10–45)
10. Unemployment benefits (29–14–45)
11. Parks and recreational facilities (27–15–48)
12. Space exploration (26–32–28)
13. Support for agriculture (20–26–34)
14. Help to other countries (7–53–28)

(The surveys were made in 1960 and 1961. Questions 4, 6, and 8 were asked only in June 1961, and 7, 12, and 14 were asked only in November 1961. The time period no doubt affected the response.)

When the responses of "spend more" and "spend the same" are combined one finds a rather astonishingly high degree of acceptance of most of these programs. In addition, these surveys produced no evidence that the existing federal debt causes great concern or uneasiness.[5] On the other hand, a negative attitude toward additional deficits was found, which may conflict with the desire for more programs and which may reflect the traditional acceptance of the annually balanced budget.[5] Further, "no pronounced dissatisfaction with the prevailing level of taxation" was found.[6]

It should be noted that Keynes was not motivated by a desire to overthrow the capitalistic system; his desire was to save it. In this sense his policy recommendations are themselves conservative.[7] Fiscal policy has been regarded by many as the middle-of-the-road policy which could provide a minimum of government intervention and yet preserve the laissez-faire, capitalist system and so avoid the regimentation of our economy. Let there be no misunderstanding though—fiscal policy does mean greater government intervention, but those who advocate an active role for the federal government contend that this type of intervention (still referred to as regimentation by the contemporary critics) must be

---

[5] *Ibid.*, p. 217.   [6] *Ibid.*, p. 222.

[7] On these points see D. Dillard, *The Economics of John Maynard Keynes*, New York: Prentice-Hall, 1948, Chapter 12; R. F. Harrod, *The Life of John Maynard Keynes*, New York: Harcourt, Brace, 1951; the three chapters by J. A. Schumpeter, R. F. Harrod, and P. M. Sweezy, in S. Harris, ed., *The New Economics: Keynes' Influence on Theory and Policy*, New York: Knopf, 1947; and Robert L. Heilbroner, *The Wordly Philosophers*, New York: Simon and Schuster, 1961, Chapter 9.

balanced against the degree of "regimentation" which results from 15 million people being unemployed.

We have already commented on some aspects of the anti-fiscal policy groups. Other issues will be discussed in greater detail in Chapter 4; still others will come under consideration at various points throughout the text.

It is not easy to overstate the importance of the political element in the determination of both tax and expenditure policy: the committee structure in the Congress, the party in power, the party in control of the White House, the personalities and leadership abilities of both congressional leaders and the Chief Executive—all these political elements play an important role in determining the exact nature of the legislative acts which are adopted and hence in the fiscal policies pursued. There is common agreement that President Kennedy appointed Douglas Dillon, a member of the previous Republican Cabinet, as Secretary of the Treasury because Dillon, as a Wall Street man respected by the business community, would convey the impression of fiscal responsibility and financial integrity. This would dispel, so it was apparently hoped, the fear at home and abroad that the new Democratic Administration would adopt free-spending economic policies. There seems little doubt that President Kennedy was attempting to appear fiscally responsible when he squeezed out of his fiscal 1963 (administrative) budget a surplus of $500 million even though the level of unemployment in the economy at the time of his budget message was some 6 percent of the labor force.[8] According to CEA Chairman Walter Heller, there is no question that political considerations lay beneath the fact that President Kennedy did not request a budget deficit of more than $11.9 billion in January 1963 (for the fiscal 1964 budget). A larger deficit would have resulted in a larger drop in unemployment, but President Kennedy was not anxious to match or exceed the largest deficit of his predecessor.[9] Other examples dealing with both Democratic and Republican Presidents could be cited.[10]

The extent to which modern income theory and fiscal policy are accepted by economists is not shared by the U.S. Congress, and hence economists' fiscal policy recommendations are not always adopted by the legislative and executive branches. In fact, as we shall see in Chapters 21 and 22,

---

[8] For a discussion of how repressive this was in terms of the national income and product account budget see Chapter 14.

[9] See JEC, *Jan. 1963 Ec. Rept. Pres.*, H, Pt. 1, pp 37–38.

[10] On some of these issues see S. Harris, *The Economics of the Political Parties: With Special Attention to Presidents Eisenhower and Kennedy*, New York: Mamcillan, 1962. This book is written from a particular point of view but nonetheless it illustrates well the political aspects of fiscal policy, or what we might refer to as "fiscal politics."

the proper fiscal policies have seldom been adopted (or have been for-
tuitously adopted for the wrong reasons, as was the case when taxes were
cut in both 1948 and 1954.) The stability and growth record of the
American economy during the postwar period has not been the result of
enlightened and deliberate fiscal and other policies, but rather, at various
times during the postwar period, of the backlog of consumer demand,
the demand for investment goods, a high degree of liquidity and a willingness to spend, foreign aid programs, and the sheer size of the federal
budget. Therefore, the most important problem for fiscal and monetary
policy during the first postwar decade or so was to contain inflation.
During the succeeding period, however, the scene changed and the problems
of unemployment and adequate growth became of primary importance.
The extent to which these sources of demand decline (regardless of
whether the cause is the situation of markets, excessive tax rates, inadequate
investment opportunities, or something else) is the extent to which the
need for appropriate fiscal policy action becomes increasingly significant.

2

Social Goals, Economic Goals, and Fiscal
Policy Goals: The Problem of Conflict

SOCIAL GOALS

What do Americans want? What are their goals? The answers to
these questions, essentially value judgments, reflect the preferences and
desires of people. So do their economic and fiscal policy goals. This is
not the place to present an exhaustive examination of society's goals, but
it is useful to survey them and their relation to economic goals.

Sociological studies of the goals and values held in high regard by
Americans are complicated by regional, class, and religious differences,
and by the fact that we sometimes hold conflicting goals. Nevertheless,
the following would appear to be a fairly accurate description:[1]

1. Emphasis on the individual—the state serving his interests rather than
   vice versa

---

[1] R. Williams, Jr., *American Society: a Sociological Interpretation*, New York:
Knopf, 1954, pp. 388–442. In this respect the Report of the President's Commission
on National Goals (Nov. 27, 1960) is interesting. In sum, it stressed individualism
and personal freedom, equality, the democratic process, greater education opportunity
for all on all levels, greater stress on the arts and sciences, "the democratic economy"
(sic), faster economic growth, technological progress, a more prosperous agriculture,
better living conditions, better health and welfare programs, peace in the world,
freer trade and aid to less developed nations, the defense of the free world, disarma-
ment, and the strengthening of the United Nations. For the full text see *The New
York Times*, Nov. 28, 1960, pp. 22–23.

Of further interest is the statement issued by The Cabinet Committee on Price
Stability for Economic Growth on Aug 17, 1959 (mimeo.), Washington, D.C.: The
White House. This group of Republicans listed our economic aims as economic
growth, maximum employment opportunities, and reasonable stability of the price
level. Many other conditions or factors which should be provided by our economy
were also listed.

12

2. Achievement and success—getting ahead, going up the social and economic ladder
3. Private ownership of property
4. A high regard for science and technology—efficiency and practicality— an orientation toward the world here and now
5. Material comfort, which sometimes approaches a hedonistic indulgence
6. Progress
7. Equality—in the political, economic (in terms of opportunity), and social realms
8. Democracy
9. Freedom and civil liberties

ECONOMIC GOALS

Moving from the general social to the economic realm we find, naturally, considerable overlapping of values. It is generally agreed, however, that our economy should provide reasonably full employment and economic growth (these are necessary if progress and opportunity to "get ahead" are to be realized), a socially acceptable distribution of income, general price stability, and opportunity for new enterprise. In addition, there is general agreement that these goals should be achieved within the context of, or should be pursued through, consumer-guided allocation of resources, a maximum of individual free choice, a competitive industrial organization, and efficiency in the use of resources.

FISCAL POLICY GOALS

Full Employment

The goals of fiscal policy naturally follow from those for the whole economy, though they are not as extensive. As we have previously noted, contemporary fiscal policy is aimed at providing full employment, general price stability, and adequate economic growth. Since the employment objective was first spelled out in the Employment Act of 1946, we can state that fiscal policy "came of age" with its passage. It was, after all, in accepting this act that the federal government officially assumed the responsibility for promoting maximum employment. This piece of legislation is often erroneously referred to as the "Full Employment Act of 1946." There is currently general agreement that fiscal policy should be utilized to promote full employment, but the law itself states only that the federal government should "promote maximum employment."

The appropriate excerpt from the 1946 Act states that the federal government should

use all practicable means consistent with its needs and obligations and other essential considerations of national policy, . . . to coordinate and utilize all its plans, functions, and resources for the purpose of creating and maintaining, in a manner calculated to foster and promote free competitive enterprise and the general welfare, conditions under which there will be afforded useful employment opportunities, including self-employment, for those able, willing, and seeking to work, and to promote maximum employment, production, and purchasing power.

As noted above the Act does not guarantee full employment. On the other hand, the Congress apparently intended maximum to be synonymous with full employment, and that this was to be a goal to be aimed at.[2]

Price Stability

Much of the literature dealing with the problem of inflation appearing in recent years should be properly deposited in File 13, the garbage can. It has been very emotional and has contained inaccurate descriptions of the impact of price increases on various economic groups and on the economy and of the causes of price level increases. Many groups who are alleged to have incurred a serious deterioration of economic status because of inflation have received compensating adjustments (increases in income, in OASI payments, etc.). While the dangers and unfairness of inflation (especially, in recent years, creeping inflation) have been exaggerated, there is nonetheless need for concern. The fixed income groups are hurt, and there are other undesirable effects (discussed in the fourth section of this chapter). The following quote shows how the private saver whose assets are in fixed obligations is hurt.[3]

Even if we assume that his earnings and hence his savings rise with the price level, an annual rate of inflation of, say 3 percent, may shrink by 40 percent the real value of savings accumulated over his working life. This assumes savings of 10 percent of income, compound interest at 4 percent, and a 30-year span. If the inflation rate is 2 percent and interest is 3 percent the loss is 27 percent.

As a general rule, then, there seems good reason for society to accept reasonable price stability as one of its goals.

The goal of overall price stability, which allows for shifts in the prices of individual goods or services, is accepted as a responsibility of the fiscal and monetary authorities (the federal government and the Federal

---

[2] For a discussion of the significance of the words "maximum employment" see the study of the committee staff in JEC, *Rel. Prices to Ec. Stabil. & Growth*, H, pp. 1–5.

[3] R. A. Musgrave in JEC, *Empl., Growth, Price Levels*, H, Pt. 9A, p. 2759. For further discussion see W. L. Thorp and R. E. Quandt, *The New Inflation*, New York: McGraw-Hill, 1959, pp. 193–202.

Reserve Board), but it is not specifically provided for in the 1946 Act. Many economists argue that the reference in the act to maximum purchasing power was really a reference to avoidance of inflation so as to maximize real income. The current chairman of the Council of Economic Advisers, Walter W. Heller, has stated that the goal of price stability was "clearly implicit in the 1946 Employment Act."[4] Edwin G. Nourse, member of the CEA under the Truman Administration, has noted that neither "price stabilization" nor "price level" or even the word "price" appears in the act, but that three other factors could refer to it.[5] The first is the maximum purchasing power phrase we have quoted.[6] The second is the statement that maximum employment was to be attained "in a manner calculated to foster and promote free competitive enterprise." Nourse states that "free enterprise competition takes place in the market, and its outcome is price." The third is that the objectives of the act are to be pursued "with the assistance and cooperation of industry, agriculture, labor, and state and local governments." Nourse claims that for this to have meaning it must be interpreted in terms of "prices, wages, and the market process generally." It is difficult to accept Nourse's second and third points.

As one might expect, the argument that "maximum purchasing power" means a stable price level has not gone unchallenged. Professor Seymour Harris staunchly contends that the phrase really referred to maximum aggregate demand.[7] Even though Professor Harris may be correct, and it is likely that he is, there is no reason why this phrase cannot be reinterpreted today to include price stability. Many of the powers granted to Congress and many congressional laws have been reinterpreted over the years, although primarily through changes in court decisions.

The issue of the intent of the 1946 Act concerning price stability will probably never be settled. Although it is evident that when the act was passed the major fear was of a postwar depression and major concern was directed toward deflation rather than inflation, the fact is that every President since the act was passed has assumed that it was his responsibility to combat inflationary tendencies, the Board of Governors of the Federal Reserve System has vigorously accepted it (sometimes as its *major* goal), the problem has been discussed in most of the Presidents' *Economic Reports* and in CEA Reports, and certainly the Congress accepts the goal. There seems to be little doubt that, throughout most of the 1950's, the

[4] JEC, *Jan. 1962 Ec. Rept. Pres.*, H, p. 13.

[5] JEC, *Rel. Prices to Ec. Stabil. & Growth*, P, pp. 13–14.

[6] Chairman Martin of the Federal Reserve interprets "maximum purchasing power" to mean price stability. See the Appendix of Chapter 3.

[7] COF, S, *Investigation Finan. Cond.*, A, p. 2144.

Federal Reserve accepted the maintenance of price stability as its major responsibility, notwithstanding public statements to the contrary by Chairman Martin. References to the Federal Reserve's assumption of this goal are legion, but Chairman Martin's appearances before the Joint Economic Committee and his public speeches for years were dominated by this theme.[8]

The period 1955–1960 was one of great concern over the problem of inflation. Insurance companies, banks and other financial institutions, and private corporations spent tremendous amounts on advertising stressing the dangers of inflation, and generally the blame was placed on wage demands. There were, in addition, public statements and speeches by President Eisenhower, Chairman Martin of the Federal Reserve, Cabinet members, and countless newspaper editorials condemning inflation. Finally, in his January 1959 *Economic Report*, President Eisenhower recommended that the Employment Act of 1946 be amended to make "reasonable price stability an explicit goal of Federal economic policy." Accordingly, an administration bill was introduced which would make this change, but it was limited in its scope and did "not concern itself with the specifics of how to achieve price stability."[9]

Should the Employment Act be amended to include explicitly the goal of price stability? Many economists have answered this question in the affirmative,[10] and the proposal has had the support of such organizations as the American Bankers Association, the Committee for Economic Development, and the American Farm Bureau Federation.[11] Other groups support this principle but not the amendment because they feel that such an amendment is not necessary—that the point is already covered in the "maximum purchasing power" phrase of the original act.

The reasoning underlying the proposal generally is that the federal government should serve notice on all groups that it will not tolerate inflation, that the government has not pursued this objective forcefully, and probably also a conservative fear that a more liberal administration may adopt free spending policies and ignore this goal unless it is explicitly stated.

In support of the position against explicitly incorporating the price stability goal into the Employment Act it is generally argued that:

[8] For a specific comment see *ibid.*, Pt. 3, p. 1256.

[9] For a discussion of the bill and others which were much more extensive see *House Report No.* 539, 86th Cong., 1st Sess., June 12, 1959.

[10] See the comments of Joseph Ascheim and George Bach in JEC, *Rel. Prices to Ec. Stabil. Growth*, P, pp. 29, 31, 46; Neil Jacoby and Richard Selden in JEC, *Empl., Growth, Price Levels*, H, Pt. 1, p. 86; and Pt. 4, p. 726.

[11] JEC, *Empl., Growth, Price Levels*, H, Pt. 9B, p. 3071. CED, *Defense Against Inflation*, New York, July, 1958, p. 53; JEC, *Empl., Growth, Price Levels*, H, Pt. 9B, p. 3087.

1. The objective generally means stability of some index of prices, and that these have an upward bias in that they do not accurately reflect product quality improvement and new products. To tie our policy to such an index may mean a serious sacrifice of other goals—mainly full employment and economic growth. A mandatory, rigid price goal may "place the economy in a strait jacket and block economic growth"[12]

2. Depressions excepted, long periods of economic growth have generally (but not always) resulted in some price increases

3. Generally speaking, the expansion phase of the business cycle has resulted in price increases

4. The price stability goal may become a fetish

5. We may have to make a choice between price stability and high employment

6. With a price and wage structure which is downwardly rigid, price increases are necessary to bring about a reallocation of resources in the economy

We might also note that just as we allow 3 to 4 percent of our labor force to be unemployed, we should allow for some flexibility in the price level, especially if this is necessary to provide for a reallocation of resources in an economy in which prices are downwardly rigid.

Economists are not against a stable price level, but some of them do have serious reservations about the feasibility of securing stable prices, full employment, and economic growth simultaneously, especially with our price and wage structure; and they are concerned that price stability may be pursued to the exclusion of other goals.[13] On the other hand, many will accept writing the price goal into the Employment Act explicitly *if* it is done in an abstract and not a rigid manner, and if the law is written so that greater priority is placed on economic growth and full employment.[14] As we noted previously the current Chairman of the CEA, Walter W. Heller, takes the position "that the price stability objective . . . is clearly implicit in the 1946 Employment Act." While he does not feel that it is necessary to add this to the law, he admits

that there might be some psychological advantage in reemphasizing it in that way. On the other hand, the process of amendment of an act is a serious one.

[12] A. H. Hansen, *Economic Issues of the 1960's*, New York: McGraw-Hill, 1960, p. 27.

[13] See some of the excellent papers in JEC, *Rel. Prices to Ec. Stabil. & Growth*, P.

[14] On these points and those in the preceding paragraph see JEC, *Empl., Growth, Price Levels*, H, Pt. 7, comments of C. L. Schultze, H. P. Minsky, and A. M. Okun, pp. 2228–2230, and Pt. 2, comments of R. W. Goldsmith; and JEC, *Rel. Prices to Ec. Stabil. & Growth*, P, comments of Leo and Betty Fishman, pp. 70–73.

It is one that I think should be undertaken if there is a basic defect in the act. I don't believe that the act is basically defective in leaving out explicit mention of price stability.[15]

Economic Growth

Just as the price stability goal is not explicitly included in the Employment Act, neither is the economic growth goal. However, it is not at all difficult to reconcile the goal of full or maximum employment with economic growth. To attain full employment continually must result in economic growth since there will be yearly additions to our labor force and since some labor will be technologically unemployed. These people can be employed (or reemployed) only if the GNP increases each year, unless, of course, we all work fewer hours and thus divide up jobs.

The increased interest in economic growth and governmental avowal of this as a national goal involves something more than a simple yearly increase in the GNP, however. Economic growth is generally defined not only to require an increase in the GNP sufficiently large enough

1. To absorb new entrants into the labor force and
2. To absorb technologically displaced workers,

but also to include increased per capita income. (In both instances there may be no increase in per capita income.) The projected increase in the labor force over the period 1963–1975 is 17 million. The actual increase from 1950 to 1962 was slightly more than 8.8 million. (The absorbtion of 17 million new workers during the 1963–1975 period will be no small task.) This brings up the very controversial question of the appropriate rate of economic growth, which we deal with at a later point.

A further problem for fiscal policy results from an emphasis on the growth objective, namely that fiscal policy must now be concerned not only with securing a level of demand high enough to provide full employment, but also with the composition of demand and output. Sufficient output must be allocated toward capital formation so that we can attain the economic growth we so dearly want, but at the same time consumption must be maintained so that excess industrial capacity does not result in lower capital accumulation. A proper balance between consumption and investment is no small attainment. There are further questions of the appropriate roles of private and public investment (which sector should expand the most?), especially whether there is a need for a greater stock of capital or better technical knowledge, skills, and research. These are problems of economic growth which fiscal policy must face up to.

[15] JEC, *Jan. 1962 Ec. Rept. Pres.*, H, p. 13.

Why Economic Growth? We have already noted two of the more important reasons why we need economic growth; i.e., to accommodate those who are technologically unemployed, and to absorb new entrants into the labor force. But there are other reasons which we shall briefly review, some in greater detail than others.

3. An inadequate rate of growth reduces incentives to invest and innovate. Potential productivity increases are not realized, and the expansion of our stock of capital is slowed down.
4. Growth is also necessary to build up our military strength.

Here, however, it is not just the yearly increase in our GNP, etc., which is important, but the "usable military output which counts."[16] Conceivably every other sector of the economy could grow and the military sector remain constant (or become obsolete).

5. We are also concerned with raising the level of living of the large number of low income families and individuals in our society.

In 1946, for instance, we had $9\frac{1}{2}$ million family units with incomes of less than $2,000 per year. In 1954 the number was the same. Although the percent of families in this bracket declined, the number in comparable economic circumstances probably changed little because of the increase in the price level.

6. Economic growth is desired also simply because Americans want and expect to receive higher incomes and attain higher standards of living over a period of time. Growth is necessary to provide the necessary opportunities and incentives for advancement.
7. Inadequate growth tends to hurt teenagers disproportionately.

With a large number of teenagers unemployed social problems such as juvenile delinquency tend to become increasingly important.

8. A higher rate of growth tends to help alleviate other social problems.

Various groups are more compatible with each other if they can raise their incomes without taking anything away from each other. Furthermore, sociological studies have shown that the intensity of prejudice and discrimination increase as the level of economic activity worsens. Minority groups are more likely to be accepted for the better paying and more prestigous positions if there is a high demand for labor, as our unemployment statistics show.

9. Inadequate growth creates pressures to reduce the length of the work

[16] J. K. Galbraith, *The Affluent Society*, Boston: Houghton Mifflin, 1958, p. 166.

week and spread work even though people wish to work the normal week if only the jobs were available.

10. Rapid economic growth enables us to give help to other nations, not only in the form of more aid but also through trade and investments.

11. Some individuals and groups feel that we have neglected our social responsibilities and advocate more rapid growth so that more resources may be devoted to education, housing and urban development, hospitals, resource conservation and development, fighting water pollution, etc.

12. One economist has also stated that growth is needed, among other reasons, "to maintain, or regain, both moral and scientific leadership in the world."[17]

In this discussion of why we desire economic growth no attempt was made to list the various reasons in order of importance. The manner in which one ranks objectives, however, will influence the economic policies one advocates. If we have a greater concern over defense and help to the developing nations, for example, then we will not serve these ends by a policy of aggressively encouraging the production of luxury goods and services for American consumers.[18]

The Fourth Horseman: Balance of International Payments

From the foregoing it is rather evident that our list of objectives for fiscal policy may be added to or otherwise modified over a period of time. Since 1958 the balance of payments problem has assumed an importance equal to our other three objectives. Although monetary policy may be more directly related to the problems created by the deficit in our balance of payments, fiscal policy does have an important relevance.

There is a definite danger in not viewing the balance of payments problem in the proper perspective. In the first place, the deficit in the American balance of payments has existed (excepting 1957) since at least 1950, depending on whose definitions one uses. It is generally agreed

---

[17] W. W. Heller in JEC, *Empl., Growth, Price Levels*, H, Pt. 9A, p. 2989. See also the remarks justifying growth by the late Sumner Slichter, *ibid.*, Pt. 1, pp. 2–4; those of A. G. Hart (Pt. 9A), R. A. Musgrave (Pt. 9A), and F. Machlup (Pt. 9A); and J. K. Galbraith, *op. cit.*, p. 166.

On the migrant farm worker problem see A. H. Raskin, "For 500,000—Still Tobacco Road," *The New York Times Magazine*, April 24, 1960, pp. 14, 128–130, and Committee on Labor and Public Welfare, Senate, *The Migrant Farm Worker in America* (by D. H. Pollitt and S. M. Levine), 1960, and other publications of this committee. The solution to the migrant worker problem is much more than a simple matter of economic growth.

[18] See R. A. Musgrave in JEC, *Empl., Growth, Price Levels*, H, Pt. 9A, p. 2761, and the Machlup paper, *ibid.*

that the resulting redistribution of reserves (to the benefit of our West European allies) was a desirable reflection of the success of our policies to restore their productive capacities. Second, it should be noted that the competitive position of the United States has not deteriorated. Our exports have consistently exceeded our imports by a substantial margin. Third, the contention that high wages in the United States have caused the deficit is grossly overdone. The relative importance of different goods in any country's export-import account is not due so much to wage differentials as to the relative efficiency of its various industries. Our most important exports come from industries in which wages are the highest. It is true that the share of the United States in world exports of manufactured goods has declined. But the increasing importance of Western Europe and Japan in international trade is a reflection of the rebuilding of their productive capacity, the strengthening of their competitive positions, and the regaining of their traditional positions in world trade. This development appears to be coming to an end. Furthermore, wage and price trends in recent years have shown a good deal of stability in the United States, but a strong upward trend in Western Europe and Japan. Fourth, a good part of the deficit was caused by direct investment abroad by American firms. As American investments abroad are built up our capital outflow will tend to decline, as has already happened in Canada and Latin America. The significant buildup of the stock of capital goods, the decline in the rate of growth, and the adoption of policies designed to promote greater consumption rather than investment (which was vigorously promoted during the 1950's) in several European countries tend to indicate that the attraction for American capital will decline. Also, as the capital outflow declines earnings from these investments will continue their recent increase. Finally, there may be some though slight reduction in the pressure placed on our balance of payments by military grants and expenditures, economic grants, and other loans.

There is a danger that excessive concern with the payments deficit will result in higher interest rates and, what may be more important, an accompanying slow growth in the money supply resulting from the attempt to keep interest rates high. (An attempt is made to raise short-term interest for the purpose of preventing private short-term funds from moving out of the United States to countries paying a higher rate.) Another possible result is the failure to plan for federal deficits even though they may be fully needed because policy makers and the public fear they will cause inflation and thereby reduce the ability of American firms to compete in international markets, or hasten the gold outflow by creating a flight from the dollar as an international currency. There is no reason to assume that the balance of payments deficit is a permanent problem, or that policies other than those which adversely affect domestic growth are not available. In short, there is no reason why domestic economic needs and growth should be sacrificed at the altar of the payments balance.[19] Finally, a restrictive fiscal-monetary policy which retards our rate of growth of output and stock of capital and slows down productivity advances will also reduce relative competitiveness and increase our balance of payments deficit.

CONFLICTS OF GOALS AND POLICY RESOLUTIONS

Growth and High Employment versus a Stable Price Level[20]

Is it possible to attain both a high rate of economic growth and full employment on the one hand and general price stability on the other? In recent years economists have devoted much attention to, and the Joint Economic Committee has conducted exhaustive hearings and studies of, this problem. Unfortunately, it has no definitive answer. We can, however, discuss the characteristics of our economy that contribute to an upward bias in the price level with an eye to the reduction of frictions.

The first, and in the literature of fiscal policy the most widely discussed, factor contributing to this conflict is a high level of demand—generalized excessive demand—which is pushing against or exceeding our capacity to produce. Such a demand, however, can usually be controlled with appropriate tax, credit, and monetary controls.

A second factor that may contribute to a long-run upward trend in the price level is a policy of "guaranteed full employment." It follows, according to this argument, that organized labor is substantially more powerful than it was prior to the 1930's and that, with almost twenty

---

[19] Since 1958 much has been written on the payments problem, gold outflow, new payments systems, gold guarantees, the significance of short-term interest rates, the "twisting" of short- and long-term rates, etc. On the Triffin Plan see JEC, *Empl., Growth, Price Levels*, H, Pt. 9A, pp. 2905–2945, and SP No. 16. See also *State Ec. & Pol. Full Empl.*, H, the papers by foreign economists, pp. 374–388; and also pp. 458–449, 388–412, and 489–517, pp. 458–489, pp. 388–412, and 489–517. On the Bell-Gemmill thesis (that low interest rates and capital outflows are not correlated) see JEC, *Jan. 1962 Ec. Rept. Pres.*, H, Pt. 1, pp. 586–7, 606–615, and 625–627. Excellent papers can be found in JEC (Subcommittee on International Exchange and Payments), *International Payments Imbalances and Need for Strengthening International Financial Arrangements*, Hearings, May 16, June 19–21, 1961, and *Report*, 1961, and *Factors Affecting the U.S. Balance of Payments*, 1962. See also P. B. Kenen, *Giant Among Nations: U.S. Foreign Economic Policy*. Chicago: Rand McNally, 1960 and 1963.

[20] On this problem see JEC, *Empl., Growth, Price Levels*, H, Pt. 9A. The statements of R. Musgrave and R. A. Gordon have been drawn on here.

years of continuous wage increases, labor's (and often management's) expectations are based on an extension of this trend. Supporters of this argument usually assume that the wage demands are excessive and must be passed on in the form of higher product prices.

The third factor, related to the second one, is the fact that employers will grant (and often have granted) wage increases as the price they feel they must pay to maintain industrial peace. Generally, the elasticity of demand for their products and their degree of market power is such that the cost increase can be passed on in the form of higher prices. This situation is tied up with the phenomenon of administered prices and mark-up pricing practices (wherein the producer attempts to maintain a certain profit mark-up over and above his material and labor costs). Mark-up pricing practices need not be associated only with concentrated industries, however.

We have previously mentioned a fourth factor in this process—the downward rigidity of prices and wages. This process operates to exert an upward secular trend in the price level in two ways. First, with no depression in the last two decades, and with less serious recessions, the natural tendency of low levels of economic activity to lower prices and wages in the economy generally has been absent. [Two counter arguments should be noted: (1) this stability has been desirable, and (2) the mildness of postwar recessions and the fact that prices and wages have generally held up have helped restrain the development of a serious depression based on falling purchasing power, reduced profits, and the expectation of lowered returns, prices, and values.] Second, an expansion in a particular sector of the economy (a reallocation of resources) may take place only with an increase in the price to be paid for labor and capital in that sector. In itself this is not to be condemned, because it is merely an illustration of how we expect the price system to operate; but the rub comes when prices and wages do not decrease in the declining industries. The net effect is an increase in the overall price level.[21]

Many economists have argued that different rates of productivity increases may be the fifth factor contributing to price increases. With strong labor unions in industries that experience a greater-than-average productivity increase, and fairly tight labor markets due to a relatively high aggregate demand, there will likely be a wage increase. If one such industry sets the pattern for other industries, and if the "other" industries have less than average productivity increases, then wages, costs, and prices will rise in the other industries.

---

[21] There may also be an increase in prices in the declining industries due to lower production and an increase in unit costs (overhead or fixed costs become a higher proportion of unit costs).

Is inflation necessary for growth? Economists have attempted to answer the question of whether price increases (inflationary trends) are necessary for economic growth. The answer to this question apparently is that "it depends." In one sense price increases encourage the accumulation of inventories to beat price increases and other output increases, which in turn will stimulate investment via higher sales and profits. Capital investment may be further stimulated by the fear of higher capital costs in the future. In addition, inflation penalizes liquidity, and individuals are encouraged to convert dollars into real estate, etc., as a hedge against price increases. This does not mean that inflation is necessary for growth, however (nor does it mean that we should be unconcerned with the inequities and maladjustments that inflation creates even if growth results).

Does inflation impede growth? One school of thought maintains that inflation creates barriers to growth. This group argues as follows:

1. The existence and/or anticipation of inflation creates instability.

This occurs because of overspeculation in inventories to beat the expected price increases, and the resulting premature additions to plant capacity which may saturate the market. The result is inventory liquidation and reduced investment, which in turn reduce employment. The result of the ensuing instability is to reduce our average level of production. (It is true that inventory liquidation and reductions in investment have been major characteristics of our postwar recessions; however, other factors must also be evaluated—the role of declining industries, the cutbacks in defense spending, fiscal policy—especially the tax burden, monetary policy, etc.)

2. Inflation results in a misallocation of capital because it impairs management investment decisions, since various costs and prices move at different rates.

Hence between the time when cost comparisons and the decision to use certain productive techniques are made and the time when the new machines are installed, cost relationships may have changed significantly. Therefore the most efficient capital equipment may not be used.

3. Similarly, if a margin of excess capacity is maintained as an offset to higher capital costs in the future, firms may not be using the latest and more advanced productive techniques developed in the meantime. The result is lower productivity than would otherwise have prevailed.

4. Inflation hurts growth because it distorts the saving-investment process and encourages overspeculation in hedges against inflation (especially common stocks and real estate rather than productive investment).

Real saving is necessary to secure economic growth because resources must be released from consumption to be used for additions to productive capacity as population grows. When savings are placed in life insurance policies, savings deposits, savings and loan associations, etc., we have both an abstinence from consumption and a channeling of savings into areas in which the funds are directly accessible to corporations for investment purposes. If, however, inflation results in increased consumption, the necessary resources are not released for investment purposes (assuming full use of resources, naturally); and if savings are placed in hedges against inflation, such as common stocks and real estate, they may not be financing capital investment. (The tendency has been for a very small proportion of the funds consumers use to purchase common stock to be used for new investment and therefore for investment in plant and equipment.) The incentive to invest in new plant and equipment may be dulled by the fact that they can be depreciated only over long periods of time and do not promise quick inflation profits. A corollary to this development could be an increase in consumption financed by capital gains (in turn received by the sellers of the securities and real estate). These developments can, or may be, quite important during periods of extremely active exchanges of equities and real estate and large capital gains—developments which tend to be largely inflation-stimulated. Particularly hard hit may be the firms that find it necessary to rely heavily on borrowed funds for expansion, especially in industries which are growing rapidly and whose demands for the available supply of funds is large.

5. Further, people and corporations tend to borrow as much and on as low a margin as they can, thereby forcing the interest rate up.
6. Last, inflation can retard growth by creating a deficit in the balance of payments.

This is caused by price increases that price goods out of the world market. The loss of markets can reduce the rate of growth.[22]

As we note at a later point, in some periods of economic growth the

---

[22] See the statement of W. W. Riefler, assistant to the Chairman of the Board of Governors of the FR System, in JEC, *Empl., Growth, Price Levels,* H, Pt. 10, pp. 3368–3377; and also "Inflation and Economic Development," *Monthly Rev.,* FR Bank of New York, Aug. 1959, pp. 122–127. Both studies bring out some very important points. The latter also shows that those underdeveloped countries which experienced no or only moderate price increases had a steadier and higher (6 percent) rate of growth and those which experienced sustained inflationary pressures had a widely varying, sporadic, and lower average rate of growth (about 4 percent). It has not been proved that slower price level increases caused more rapid growth, however. The period covered was 1950–1957.

price level has remained relatively constant or actually declined. However, to deny that inflation is necessary to economic growth is insufficient proof that contemporary institutional arrangements and processes (sticky prices and wages, oligopolistic markets and administered prices, strong labor unions, mark-up pricing practices, etc.) will still not create upward pressures in prices. Neither should we accept the defeatist attitude that the problem is insoluble and that we should not attempt to innovate and experiment with new institutional programs. Finally, we should very carefully point out that these criticisms of inflation are directed primarily at periods of rapid price level increases rather than those of slow increases. The latter has been our major problem in the 'fifties and 'sixties.

"Does an Aggressive Full Employment Policy Also Stimulate Economic Growth or Retard It?"[23]

Sometimes one hears the argument that it is desirable to reduce the level of demand (and therefore the pressure of demand on labor and other resources), bring about a small increase in unemployment, and thereby reduce pressures on prices and immobilities in the efficient use and allocation of both labor and capital. It is argued that this can be done without adversely affecting the growth rate—perhaps even raising it.

On the other hand, American experience has indicated that too much slack in the economy and an inadequate growth rate cause many in-efficiencies, reduce the mobility of both capital and labor, retard the introduction of innovations and superior technological techniques, etc., as we noted earlier. There has been substantial agreement among American economists that the level of employment in the United States could have been considerably higher in the late 'fifties and early 'sixties without having adversely affected the rate of growth by increased inefficiency.[24] (Solow, for example, states that "There exists no conflict on these grounds [greater inefficiency due to higher demand] between the goals of full, or at least fuller, employment and rapid growth." He care-fully notes, though, that the opposite may be true for other countries.)

If a higher level of employment is achieved continuously and over a relatively long period of time, there will normally be fewer recessions. One can ask if occasional recessions (the "short" business cycle) and periods of unemployment are necessary conditions for economic growth. The postwar experience of Western Europe does not support an affirmative answer. These countries have generally experienced more rapid economic

---

[23] The question was posed in this matter by R. M. Solow, in M. D. Ketchum and L. T. Kendall, eds., *Conference on Savings and Residential Financing*, 1962 Proceedings, May 10, 11, 1962, Chicago: U.S. Savings and Loan League, 1962, p. 133.

[24] *Ibid.*, pp. 134–135.

growth and productivity growth than the United States without the recessions that have characterized the American economy. Demand has exerted a greater pressure against resources, and unemployment rates (adjusted to a basis comparable to ours) have been lower.[25] (Solow notes that this interpretation is clearly anti-Schumpeterian.) The fiscal and monetary policies pursued by these countries have played an important part in these developments. In particular, they have imposed or increased deficits as soon as their growth rates began to hesitate and *before* recessions could become serious.

Even though the experience of full employment over a longer period of time does not have to result in inefficiencies that reduce the level of potential output, and even though the short business cycle is not necessary for economic growth, the question still remains whether full employment will *raise* the rate of economic growth. It is sometimes argued, for example, that over the longer run the average level of investment may turn out to be the same whether we have steady full employment or the short business cycles. Presumably the investment lost during the downturn could be made up during the boom period. Certainly this is possible, but it is nonetheless likely that continuous high demand encourages investment and innovations. More important, continuous high demand reduces risk and probably also reduces the rate of return the business community will accept. Hence investment projects that otherwise might not be pursued will be undertaken. Furthermore, to the extent to which increases in capital stock reduce profit rates, a lower level of risk encourages a greater level of investment. The result is both higher capacity and greater demand.[26] Finally, even though the average rate of capital accumulation may be the same, there will necessarily be other sizable losses in private consumption, the production of public goods, and wealth, in addition to the restrictions on opportunities and the human suffering that will occur. It would certainly seem that, given the proper fiscal-monetary policies, steady full employment would raise the yearly average level of the GNP if not also the level of capital accumulation.[27]

Trading Full Employment for Price Stability: The Phillips and Samuelson-Solow Studies

In recent years some groups, but only a few economists, have argued for the imposition of an enforced level of unemployment of 4 to 6 percent

[25] *Ibid.*, p. 135.

[26] *Ibid.*, pp. 135–136.

[27] Fuller use should result in faster wearing out. But the same factors that lead to a higher utilization of capacity will also tend to raise the level of capital stock accumulated.

in order to keep the price level stable. More often than not these people are also strong advocates of a tight money policy.

A. W. Phillips[28] showed in a study for the United Kingdom that there was a correlation between the percent of unemployment and the percent change in wage rates. His conclusion was that with an unemployment rate of 5 percent wages would remain stable. Professors Samuelson and Solow[29] have made a study of this relationship for the American economy. For the period 1946 to 1959, the most relevant period for our purposes here, with the annual unemployment rate ranging from 2.5 percent (in 1953) to 6.2 percent (in 1958), the lower the unemployment rate the more rapid the increase in wages. The authors' data indicated that money wages would rise 2 to 3 percent per year with an unemployment rate of 5 to 6 percent. They also state that "one would judge now that it would take more like 8 percent unemployment to keep money wages from rising." The 2 to 3 percent figure would be in line with our historical productivity increases and hence would not be inflationary. To attain this price stability, however, we would have to be satisfied with 5 to 6 percent of our labor force being unemployed, according to these data. On the other hand, to achieve full employment with only 3 percent of the labor force unemployed would require an annual increase in the price level of 4 to 5 percent.

We should carefully note, as Samuelson and Solow do in a series of disclaimers and qualifications, that the data utilized are short-run. Furthermore, a low-pressure policy which results in an increasing rate of unemployment may mean that more and more unemployment is needed to maintain a stable price level. This could lead to particularly disastrous results—an intolerably high level of unemployment, a low level of investment, and a low rate of growth. On the other hand, it is possible that the experience of a low-pressure economy may sufficiently dampen labor's and other's expectations of what they can expect, so that in the long run we may be able to attain higher employment with greater price stability than the data suggest.[30] In addition, with unemployment rates of 7 percent (not yearly data) we still have had increases in the price level, one cause being an increase in wage rates based on the assumption of continued productivity increases, which did not occur because of a low or declining rate of growth and the consequent existence of excess capacity. (This problem is more fully dealt with at a later point. The

---

[28] A. W. Phillips, "Money Wages and Unemployment in the United Kingdom," *Economica*, Nov. 1958.

[29] P. A. Samuelson and R. M. Solow, "Analytical Aspects of Anti-Inflation Policy," *Am. Ec. Rev.*, May 1960, pp. 175–194.

[30] *Ibid.*, p. 193.

wage increases may well have been part of contracts signed in the previous year or period of prosperity and high profits.) Further, there is no reason why the unemployment rate cannot be 5 to 7 percent and there still be wage and price increases in areas where unions are particularly strong (as in the building trades) or in a sector where excess demand exists. We should also note that during some recent periods our growth rate was very rapid but the price level quite stable.

Joseph A. Pechman further points out that the Phillips thesis has been rather severely criticized for the data used and also for having exaggerated the correlation between changes in wages and unemployment in the U.K.[31] The Samuelson-Solow suggestions that the cost of price stability is an unemployment rate of 5 to 6 percent, and that a rate of unemployment of 3 percent is likely to bring a 3 to 4 percent price increase in the United States, Pechman notes, are not substantiated by our experience. He notes that of 5 years since 1947 with an unemployment rate of less than 4 percent, 2 years saw the implicit price deflator rise more than 5 percent; 1 year saw it rise less than 1 percent; and in 1 year it remained constant. For 8 years unemployment was more than 4 percent, but there was no apparent relationship between price level changes and the unemployment rate.[31] The level of unemployment is no doubt related to the price level, but so are many other factors, which complicate the picture and the relationship.

Another expression of the relationship between the level of unemployment and the price level can be found in a statement of the current Chairman of the CEA. In March of 1961, Dr. Heller said that: "Indeed, the history of our postwar period, while not conclusively proving this, seems to suggest that the 4 percent rate of unemployment has been approximately the point at which we strike a balance between a high level of output and reasonable price stability."[32]

The foregoing relationship between rather specific rates of unemployment, wage rates, and the price level has not been presented as fact but rather as a tentative, short-run analysis of historical relationships under given conditions. Few economists will deny that labor (unionized or not) and producers will be more successful in raising their wage rates and prices when they experience excessive demand, bottlenecks in the economy generally or in particular sectors, or when labor and/or management possess sufficient market power to realize their demands. But this is quite different from precisely defining the relationship between unemployment rates and the price level. Further, conditions do change and other things

---

[31] J. A. Pechman, comments on the Samuelson-Solow paper, *Am. Ec. Rev.*, May 1960, p. 219.

[32] JEC, *Jan. 1961 Ec. Rept. Pres.*, H, p. 407.

do not remain the same, particularly new institutional processes and arrangements to deal with these problems. We do not know the extent to which the postwar period was unique and hence an inadequate basis for predicting future relationships.

Finally, it is not easy to solve the age-old problem of whether wages pushed up the price level or were pulled up by it, and the existence of a statistical relationship does not present an answer. (At a later point, we shall discuss a possible important exception to this statement regarding the steel industry and the steelworkers' union.)

This same problem, in terms of the degree of excess capacity necessary to keep wage increases from exceeding productivity increases, has also been considered by a leading British economist, F. W. Paish.[33] He has suggested than an underutilization of capacity of 5 percent may keep wages from rising at a rate which cannot be absorbed by productivity increases. Here again, however, we cannot be certain of securing this result at this level of underutilization of capacity. The necessary level may turn out to be one at which the level of unemployment is intolerably high; the impact of excess capacity may reduce incentives to further increases in capacity, lower the realized growth rate, and bring stagnation or near stagnation.[34] Furthermore, the pursuance of such a policy means that a higher value is placed on price stability than on full employment and economic growth; and the adoption of such a policy precludes other approaches that might enable us to attain full employment, economic growth, and greater price stability.

At this point we should recognize some other possibilities. Samuelson and Solow have noted that the more perfect a labor market is the less the pressure on the price level may be. If the labor market is fractionated and imperfect, it may take a higher level of excess labor (unemployment) to keep prices from increasing. In a more mobile labor market, increases in the demand for labor in certain areas will be more rapidly satisfied because information will be transmitted more rapidly and more directly to those who are unemployed. Policies that improve the mobility of the labor market, then, will have an anti-inflationary effect. As we note again later, the wider cyclical swings in the economy are, the higher wage and price increases will be (with a given average level of unemployment over the cycle). This, too, has significant implications for stabilization policy.

---

[33] F. W. Paish, *Studies in an Inflationary Economy*. London: Macmillan, 1962.
[34] See R. F. Harrod's review of Paish's book in *Economica*, Feb. 1963, pp. 85–89. Harrod points out that "it is precisely because we may need to have a fuller use of capacity than [a low level which brings large unemployment]. . . in order to get the necessary incentive for growth, that opinion has come round to the need for an 'incomes policy'."

Further, the more rapid the recovery period, the more shortages and bottlenecks may develop and the greater the pressure on prices. Finally, Samuelson and Solow carefully point out that at this stage in our knowledge it is not possible to reject the demand-pull (or demand-shift) or cost-push hypotheses of price increases, and that probably both theories account for the behavior of prices in the postwar American economy.[35]

Price, Employment, and Growth Goals of the Federal Reserve

It appears that in the period 1955–1960 policy decisions of the federal government were made on the assumption that some choice had to be made between full employment and price stability. Further, the Federal Reserve has proceeded on the assumption that price stability was an indispensable condition for economic growth. Although the Chairman of the Board of Governors has stated that the Federal Reserve is legally obligated to support the Employment Act of 1946, and even though he and other members of the system would deny that they have placed a higher value on price stability, their policy actions indicate that they did make such a choice. A few excerpts from hearings conducted by the Senate Committee on Finance illustrate the problem of attempting to reconcile goals that are thought to conflict.

When asked directly, Chairman Martin stated that he placed a higher value on "stabilized maximum employment" than on a "stabilized value of the dollar." Mr. Martin's reply was qualified, however, by the statement that the Employment Act "intended jobs that could be sustained, not jobs that are temporary in nature." Somewhat concerned about Chairman Martin's reference to "sustained" and "not temporary" jobs, and his failure to cite authority in the Employment Act, Senator Kerr asked if all jobs were not temporary. Chairman Martin's reply was "no."[36] His ultimate reply to what he meant by "temporary jobs" was

---

[35] Samuelson and Solow, op. cit., pp. 190–191. See Chapter 18.

[36] Senator Kerr humorously retorted, "why, Mr Martin, even your job is [sic] temporary when it started and [is] getting more so every day." It should be noted that the late Senator Kerr could be a somewhat ruthless questioner. On the other hand, from the Chairman's testimony before this and other committees, one could perhaps be somewhat critical of his understanding of modern income and employment theory; his failure on many occasions to give direct, clear, and meaningful answers before congressional committees; and what appears to be an attempt to give a politically acceptable answer and yet qualify it so as to protect his own beliefs. It is also interesting to note that Mr. Martin refused to be committed to a specific unemployment rate as a policy objective. This is somewhat understandable since no figure is given in the Employment Act and since he was then serving under an Administration which also refused to cite a figure as a policy objective. On the other hand, Mr Martin tended to accept price stability unreservedly as a clear and definite policy objective. See also Chapter 3 and its Appendix and Appendix A of Chapter 17.

that they were jobs created out of borrowed money to provide "an expansion program that would not be self-sustaining and would not pay for itself [sic] and would collapse" (not very specific criteria for government tax and expenditure programs).[37]

Mr. Martin's conception of objectives of economic policy and his attempt to find some mutually compatible set of objectives were further revealed when he "had to admit that there must be some bloodletting in this system; in other words, monetary restraint was required in order to correct the abuses that had crept into the system."[38] The exchange between Senator Kerr and Chairman Martin follows:

SENATOR KERR . . . If you were faced with the choice between price stability and temporary cessation of economic growth on the one hand, or creeping inflation and continuing economic growth on the other hand, which would you choose?

MR. MARTIN . . . I do not want a recession of any sort at any time. I do not want any man to be unemployed in this country if it is possible to avoid it. But I think you have to come face to face with the reality *that under conditions of excess, extravagance, waste, incompetence, and inefficiency—under these conditions somebody has to take a loss*.[38] [Italics added.]

It would appear that Mr. Martin would like to realize a higher level of employment, but not at any costs. That is, he would like to secure full employment and price stability, an efficient allocation of resources, the greatest degree of individual choice possible, consumer-guided allocation of resources, and the greatest degree of freedom of market operation and private decision making possible. He would further like to avoid economic abuse by powerful corporate or labor groups. These objectives certainly reflect those mentioned at the beginning of this chapter. Despite this some rather serious questions may be asked about Chairman Martin's attempt to reconcile possible conflicts in policy objectives. We might ask if Mr. Martin meant to apply this rather vast description to labor who should be punished through a forced increase in the unemployment rate, or to businessmen via a lower growth rate and lower profits, or both? We might also ask what particular legislative mandate Mr. Martin has to take upon himself the responsibility for correcting such social and economic abuses?

A further indication of some of the difficulties encountered in attempting to realize rapid growth, full employment, and price stability, and perhaps the clearest indication that the Federal Reserve was willing to bring about some unemployment in order to maintain price stability appears in a statement of Mr. Martin's concerning escalator clauses, cost-plus contracts, and

[37] COF, S, *Investigation Finan. Cond.*, H, Pt. 6, pp. 1899–1907.
[38] *Ibid.*, Pt. 7, p. 2145, summary of Seymour Harris.

fringe benefits which were not justified by productivity increases:

> SENATOR KERR . . . In all of this, has the supply of money and credit been fully adequate to support these increasing demands?
> MR. MARTIN . . . I do not know whether it has been fully adequate to support them, but it is our intention to keep a steady flow of money, as steady a flow of money as we have. And if that flow of money does not cover the increases that are unwarranted, there should be no pressure on us to increase the money supply just to invalidate some imbalance which occurs in the economy which is not warranted by productivity.[39]

Mr. Martin's apparent justification for this statement is "that at all times when employment is rising at the expense of price stability, you are one step removed from deflation."[40] Aside from showing the problem of making our economic goals compatible, the foregoing also indicates that the Federal Reserve assumed that price stability took preference over full employment, and that the Federal Reserve considers price stability a prerequisite to full employment and economic growth. The historical record contradicts the latter point, and it cannot be shown that inflation inevitably leads to deflation, as Mr. Martin has so often maintained. Although the historical record shows some relationship, one cannot accept such a monistic explanation of the business cycle. Furthermore, in his definition Martin includes also creeping inflation, and again the record does not support him here. Finally, there have been periods of relative price stability which were followed by periods of deflation.

Our criticism of Chairman Martin and the Federal Reserve should be tempered with a sympathetic understanding of the political and economic position of the Federal Reserve; the seriousness of the problems to be tackled; the relative newness of the problem of an increasing price level when the unemployment rate and excess capacity are fairly high, and demand is not continuously or universally (throughout the whole economy) excessively high; the "relatively recent" emancipation of the Federal Reserve from the policy of having to support the price of government securities, and its attempt to find its "way"; the resurgence of interest in monetary policy but the lack of agreement as to its effectiveness; and the fact that Martin's attitudes generally reflected (or were compatible with) those of the Administration then in power. (A conflict between the Federal Reserve and the Administration did occur: It is discussed in Chapter 20.) Despite all this, however, at least two very important questions or issues remain. One might ask whether the Federal Reserve has the obligation or right to impose a policy aimed at restraining

[39] *Ibid.*, Pt. 3, p. 1310.
[40] *Ibid.*, Pt. 3, p. 1407.

"excessive" (unwarranted) price and wage demands (and what authority does it have for deciding which are excessive?), which may well result in greater unemployment, in order to attain its goal of price stability. Second, is it the responsibility of the Federal Reserve to attack these institutional rigidities via tight money, or should the Federal Reserve direct its attention to growth, full employment, and price stability, admit that under present institutional circumstances it cannot solve the problem by itself, and request that other action be taken to deal with the problem of price and wage rigidities? Should not the *goals* of full employment and economic growth be aimed for and other action taken, so that they are realized within the context of overall price stability insofar as possible? These problems must be considered by the Administration in power in the development of its overall policy position, but surely not by the Federal Reserve alone.

Some Costs of Unemployment

In the spring of 1962 President Kennedy forced certain steel firms to rescind their price increases. But nothing has been done to change institutional relationships to deal with the possible conflict between price level stability and full employment. If a choice between the two must be made in the future (and we have not proved that it must), and if nothing can be done by changing institutional arrangements or processes, then the voters should be made explicitly aware of the choice to be made. It is not the responsibility of economists to make the choice, but it is their responsibility to point out the relative costs of the two policies. GNP-employment relationships used in 1963 indicated that for every 1 million unemployed we lose about $15.5 billion in our GNP.[41] In May 1963, for example, the unemployment rate was 5.9 percent of the labor force and about 4.3 million were unemployed. An unemployment rate of 3 percent would have made 2.37 million jobless and the GNP about $33 billion greater. (This is a rough estimate. The figures do not allow for the increase in the labor force that would occur if we had greater job opportunities, for possible price increases which may occur when production is pushing against capacity, or for other factors.)

On the other hand, it should be carefully noted that it is not easy to arrive at a reasonable and satisfactory relationship between these two factors. If the GNP-employment relationship is viewed from the standpoint of the increases in employment associated with an increase in GNP (in constant dollars) during recovery periods (from the low to the high

---

[41] In 1962 the Department of Commerce used $10 billion. Letter from Louis J. Paradiso, Assistant Director-Chief Statistician, Office of Business Economics, June 11, 1962, to the author.

point), one finds some rather startling figures. During the 1954–1956 recovery, $10,725 was associated with each extra position; during the 1958–1962 and 1961–1962 recoveries the figure rose to $20,567 and $39,667, respectively.[42] This gives us a GNP-employment relationship of 1 million extra employed for $40 billion of extra GNP for the 1961–1962 recovery. In examining these relationships one must evaluate recent increases in productivity, the particular types of spending which have increased, and other factors. Productivity increases, for example, are higher during recovery periods, and the same increases in GNP would not be required per extra job after the rate of growth had leveled off or after the prosperity phase of the cycle was reached. In addition, when government expenditures contribute heavily to the recovery—as was true in 1961–1962, the changes in military technology (from traditional weapons to missiles, etc.), which require substantially fewer employees per dollar of expenditure, must be considered. One must estimate also the impact of an increase in government spending on the creation of jobs for those unemployed who have specific types of skill.

The average figure used by the Council of Economic Advisers in early 1963 was $15,500 (current dollars), as noted above. The CEA expected to apply this average figure to increments in the GNP during calendar 1963. It is adjusted for the fact that productivity increases are always greater during the early stages of recovery than during the later months of the recovery period. From the first quarter of 1961, for example, to the fourth quarter of 1962, the marginal GNP per job was $33,600, but during the second year of the recovery (1962) the marginal figure dropped to $13,200. The average GNP per job in 1962 was $7,800.[43]

As we noted in discussing economic growth, however, there are losses to society from unemployment other than those directly related to production losses. There is the impact on the incentive to invest, increase the stock of capital, and innovate; as a result productivity increases are held back; human resources are not fully developed because the social and economic advancement of minority groups and others is retarded; resistance to automated techniques, etc., is increased; and pressures to spread work and to reduce the work week are increased. There is also the undesirable impact on teenagers who cannot find work and whose careers may be disrupted; and conditions are more conducive to juvenile delinquency, and to racial prejudice and discrimination. The loss to society in output, employment, and growth seems to be substantially greater than the loss incurred with a 1 or 2 percent price increase. Further, lags in productivity increases due to excess capacity and high unit costs may cause

---

[42] These figures first came to my attention as a result of a study by N. Goldfinger.

[43] JEC, *Jan. 1963 Ec. Rept. Pres.*, H, Pt. 1, pp. 58–59.

a price increase of this amount even if unemployment is kept at the 5 to 6 or 7 percent level. It may be of some interest to note that most economists appearing before congressional committees, when asked for their private opinions, favor full employment over price stability. These opinions, of course, are value judgments.

3

Social Goals, Economic Goals, and Fiscal Policy Goals (Continued): The Problem of Full Employment

CONCERN OVER FULL EMPLOYMENT

Although it may be quite obvious to the reader why full employment is an important social, political, and economic objective in our society, it may still be useful to point out some reasons for concern. We are all familiar with the great financial suffering which some 25 percent of our labor force was forced to endure during the worst days of the Depression of the 1930's. Not only did these people lose current income; they also lost lifelong savings and possessions which, needless to say, were never recovered. The condition of unemployment created many psychological and social problems: Radicalism showed its head, education and technology suffered, capital deteriorated, and we suffered a great setback in the build-up of our capital stock; people could not afford higher education, and hence skills were not only unused but undeveloped. Even the birth rate declined!

Since the 1930's we have not experienced a similar depression; however, we have undergone four recessions since the end of World War II. Although some have a tendency to slight over our postwar recessions as not very serious and/or as inevitable, such is not the case. Recessions do have serious and undesirable effects on those unemployed and on our rate of growth; further, while our economy does not tend to grow in a straight line there is much that we can do, and could have done, to alleviate the seriousness of these recessions.

A study of the impact of unemployment in the 1958 recession[1] showed

[1] W. J. Cohen, W. Haber, and E. Mueller, *The Impact of Unemployment in the 1958 Recession*, Special Committee on Unemployment Problems, U.S. Senate, 1960.

that 17 percent of all members of the labor force were unemployed in the course of a year (73 percent of these were heads of families); and 14 percent of all family heads suffered unemployment in the course of a year (eliminating groups not subject to unemployment, such as the self-employed, 20 percent of the family heads experienced unemployment). If those who worked shorter hours are included, we find that 25 percent of families suffered from unemployment during the year. (Data are for the year October 1957 to October 1958.)[2] The same study analyzed the impact of this recession on the financial status of those unemployed and on their attitudes, expectations, and inclinations to buy. In addition to the losses we have noted, the Chairman of the CEA has estimated that our four postwar recessions have cost us $200 billion in potential output.[3]

WHAT DOES "FULL EMPLOYMENT" MEAN? (THE HANSEN, DOUGLAS, EISENHOWER, MARTIN, AND KENNEDY DEFINITIONS)

What is a socially, politically, and economically acceptable rate of unemployment? What allowance should be made for seasonal unemployment and frictional unemployment? The acceptable rate of unemployment has more or less run through a cycle. Hansen[4] in 1947 cited a number of unemployed which at that time would come to about 4 or 5 percent of the labor force. Senator Paul Douglas[5] stated that to use deficit spending to drive unemployment below 6 percent would probably result in inflation. Hansen, however, was writing before we had much postwar experience, and he (with Senator Douglas and others) has raised his sights considerably. In fact, both Hansen and Douglas would be extremely critical of any President who defined full employment as 5 percent of the labor force unemployed. Both would probably tend to favor a 3 percent figure.

In the early 1950's the 3 percent figure was apparently the most widely accepted figure, but the recessions of 1953–1954 and 1957–1958 seemed to revise the standard downward to 4 percent. The Kennedy Administration, which inherited a situation in which the unemployment rate was below 3.5 percent for only 1 month in the previous 2 years of recovery and in which the annual rates for 1959 and 1960 were 5.5 and 5.6 percent,

[2] *Ibid.*, pp. 4–8. See Chapter 2 and p. 34*ff.* for estimates of income losses during the recession.

[3] W. W. Heller in JEC, *Jan. 1962 Ec. Rept. Pres.*, H, p. 3.

[4] A. H. Hansen, *Economic Policy and Full Employment*, New York: McGraw-Hill, 1947, pp. 19*n.*, 107*n.*

[5] P. Douglas, *Economy in the National Government*, Chicago: Univ. of Chicago Press, 1953.

respectively, reluctantly established for itself an "interim objective" of 4 percent, with the clear implication that it considered a lower figure more desirable.[6]

One of the earliest to discuss the concept of full employment was Sir William Beveridge.[7] He defined full employment as "having always more vacant jobs than unemployed men." Under normal circumstances this meant a figure of about 3 percent for Great Britain. This figure was condemned by Beveridge's critics as being inflationary and probably attainable only by excessive government interference, governmental ownership of industry, and the suppression of individual liberties.[8]

During the immediate postwar years, the United States established goals varying between 3 and 4 percent. Under the Eisenhower Administration, however, no specific goals were set forth. In 1955, when asked to account for their omission, Arthur Burns, then Chairman of the CEA, replied that

. . . although 4 percent of the labor force is nowadays widely regarded as an approximate measure of the average amount of frictional and seasonal unemployment, the Council has not favored this or any other rigid figure to serve as a trigger to governmental action or as a measure of good performance.[9]

We have noted the "interim objective" of the Kennedy Administration. It would be interesting to know also the policy goal of the Federal Reserve. An attempt by the late Senator Kerr to secure this answer from Chairman Martin proved to be futile. Chairman Martin refused to give any percentage unemployment rate or actual numbers of unemployed as an acceptable goal. Mr. Martin did admit that at that time (1958) there were too many people unemployed, but he refused to state how many. Confusing the issue further, Mr. Martin stated that the minimum unemployment would be closer to 2 or 3 million, and that "we probably had full employment in 1955 and 1956. I do not remember the levels at

[6] W. W. Heller, JEC, *Jan. 1962 Ec. Rept. Pres.*, H, p. 10.
[7] Sir William Beveridge, *Full Employment in a Free Society*, New York: Norton, 1945.
[8] See James A. Maxwell's excellent discussion of the argument in his *Fiscal Policy*, New York: Holt, 1955, pp. 61–71. In his discussion, however, Professor Maxwell obviously assumes that the critics were correct; see p. 63: "Indeed, the suspicion is that Beveridge knew that his figure, if accepted, would bring either socialism or governmental control over the location of industry, over labor mobility, over investment, and over prices and wages."

See also the rather scathing criticism of E. G. Nourse, a member of the CEA under the Truman Administration in *Am. Ec. Rev.*, May 1957, p. 99.
[9] JEC, *Jan. 1955 Ec. Rept. Pres.*, H. For more on the argument over specifying goals see JEC, 1955 *Ann. Rept.*

that time."[10] Then he refused to "stand on that figure," and further qualified his statement by saying that we had "over full employment" during that period. (The reader will find the exchange between Senator Kerr and Chairman Martin reprinted in the Appendix of this chapter.) We should note that the rates of unemployment for 1955 and 1956 were 4.4 and 4.2 percent, respectively (and that the rate for 1957 was 4.3 percent). When pushed into estimating how much overemployment there was during 1955 and 1956 Mr. Martin suggested 1 million. This would have meant an unemployment rate of 5.7 and 5.4 percent, respectively, hardly very satisfactory unemployment rates by almost anyone's current standards. Some excuses for Chairman Martin's performance are perhaps possible, however; see this chapter's Appendix.

The foregoing illustrates once again the difficulty of arriving at a reasonable policy objective and the fact that maximum employment is not the only objective of the Employment Act. There are certain periods of recovery when a higher rate of unemployment must be temporarily accepted. This is because (1) attempts to push the rate down too rapidly may well create unwanted price increases, or because (2) there exists a substantial amount of structural unemployment for which policies other than the usual fiscal or monetary policies are called for. But these were not important considerations in a discussion of setting a "goal." At any rate, by current standards, one can hardly call Chairman Martin's recommended rate of 5.4 percent unemployed acceptable during the second full year of recovery (1956), for there was at this time no evidence that the number of structurally unemployed could possibly be so large. Last, it is extremely important to point out that full employment is an ideal, a goal, not a guarantee.

In the literature of economics full employment is generally defined as a situation in which all those who are "able, willing, and seeking to work" are employed, with due allowance for structural and frictional problems. (The reader will note that the quote is the same as in the Employment Act.) To most economists, as was intended in the act, full employment is a *goal* to be aimed at but not to be always realized. It is accepted that there will probably be temporary pauses or downturns in a dynamic economy, and that problems such as structural unemployment will be greater at one time than another. For these reasons it is difficult to quantify an acceptable unemployment rate, and it must be understood, as we have noted, that the goal will vary with the particular circumstances. This does not mean that we cannot quantify the goal, however. Perhaps the most widely accepted goal by economists working in this field today is 3 percent.

[10] COF, S, *Investigation Finan. Cond.*, H, Pt. 6, pp. 1901–1904.

Richard Musgrave, certainly knowledgeable, respected, and responsible in this area of economics, has stated that

> If everyone changes his job once a year, and if a week is required for transfer, about 2 percent of the labor force will be unemployed on this count. Given adequate market organizations, and a sustained level of high employment, 2 or 3 percent should suffice for . . . this purpose.[11]

Robert A. Gordon, of whom the same can be said, accepts the 3 percent figure and hopes for a long-run rate of 4 percent (lower because of recessions).[12] Abba P. Lerner, who has made important contributions to modern income theory over the years, and who generally advocates an aggressive full employment policy, suggests 2 percent as being sufficient "for the economy to operate efficiently." It "would consist of relatively painless short rests between jobs."[13]

Most economists would not, however, quarrel with the 4 percent interim figure set by the Kennedy Administration, because of the particular economic situation it inherited. But it should be noted that several years of restrictive fiscal and monetary policy force the acceptance, temporarily, at least, of a higher rate. We shall here accept the 3 percent figure as a goal. As for "full" and "maximum" employment, we shall use the terms interchangeably.

Dr. Arthur F. Burns has attempted to allow for structural, retraining, and similar problems by defining full employment as meaning "that the number of vacant jobs at prevailing wages is as large as the number unemployed, and that the labor market is so organized that everyone who is able, willing and seeking to work already has a job or can obtain one after a brief search or after undergoing some training." Burns recommends that the unemployment insurance program should be revamped so as to provide more effective aid to job seekers (use electronic computers to match vacancies and potential employees even though they are located in different communities, etc.), use the insurance program for job retraining, and withhold benefits from those who quit without good cause or who will not accept suitable work.[14]

MEASURING THE RATE OF UNEMPLOYMENT

In addition to the difficulties encountered in arriving at some concensus on an unemployment rate, there is the further problem of who should be classified as unemployed. In recent years there has been considerable

---

[11] JEC, *Empl., Growth, Price Levels*, Pt. 9A, p. 2759.   [12] *Ibid.*, p. 2958.
[13] *Conference on Savings and Residential Finance*, 1962, pp. 40, 42.
[14] *The New York Times*, July 18, 1963, p. 13, Western edition.

criticism from certain groups of the methods used to compute our rate of unemployment. They have questioned not only the validity of the collecting techniques, but also in some instances even the honesty of government statisticians. Some have charged that the official statistics exaggerate the seriousness of unemployment, others that they understate the seriousness of unemployment.

The most serious attack on the preparation of unemployment statistics appeared in an article in *Reader's Digest* (September, 1961) by a Mr. James Daniel. He charged that government officials had deliberately attempted to mislead the American people as to the seriousness of the unemployment problem, that the survey results been juggled and manipulated. These charges prompted an investigation by the Subcommittee on Economic Statistics of the Joint Economic Committee,[15] which found absolutely no basis whatsoever for the charges of dishonesty and manipulation by government officials. Testimony from both liberal and conservative groups before the subcommittee expressed complete confidence in the honesty, integrity, and devotion to objective, unbiased reporting of the government's technicians who compute the employment and unemployment statistics.[16] There is always room for improvement in the collection of statistics, and it is true that our method of computing unemployment rates differs from that used by most European countries, with the result that our rates are higher. On the other hand, experts generally agree that our employment-unemployment statistics are more complete, accurate, and reliable than those of any other country.

A major difference between the statistics of the United States and those of some European countries is that the latter count as unemployed only those receiving unemployment insurance, while we count in addition new

---

[15] *Employment and Unemployment, Hearings*, Dec. 18–20, 1961, 1962. Daniel's article is reprinted on pp. 73–76. See also Commissioner Clague's excellent statement, pp. 64–72, and statements by various groups (including the NAM) supporting the government, scattered throughout the hearings. Mr. Daniel was asked to testify before the subcommittee but he refused to appear or to send a representative.

[16] *Ibid., Report* of the Subcommittee, Feb. 2, 1962, p. 3. An interesting and capable analysis of the problem of computing unemployment may be found in the *Monthly Letter* of the First National City Bank of New York, Jan. 1962. The conclusion, however, is open to considerable criticism as quite one-sided (see the last paragraph, pp. 7–8).

A clear explanation of the procedures used in computing the employment and unemployment rates, with labor's point of view clearly noted, is found in *The Am. Federationist*, Nov. 1961, pp. 19–23. Finally, for excellent discussions, with examples of the questions used, see "Our Unemployment Yardsticks: Concepts and Measurements," *Monthly Rev.*, FR Bank of Kansas City, Sept.–Oct. 1962, pp. 3–9; and "Measuring Unemployment," *Monthly Rev.*, FR Bank of New York, March 1959, pp. 35–37.

entrants into the labor force. A technical analysis of the differences between the American and British systems has been made by Edward Kalachek and Richard Westebbe.[17] They note that in Great Britain many unemployed persons may not be counted because of (1) delays in registering for benefits, (2) the fact that married women, widows, and pensioners have the option of not being covered (it is estimated that some 3 million are not so covered), (3) many groups are temporarily unemployed and ineligible for benefits and therefore not counted as unemployed (new entrants and most re-entrants into the labor force), and (4) unemployed persons who are temporarily sick.

THE FULL-TIME EQUIVALENT PROBLEM

In recent years there was some pressure for the government to issue an unemployment series which converted part-time employment into a full-time equivalent. This information was eventually made available to the Joint Economic Committee and others who used it upon request. A series is now published in the *Monthly Report on the Labor Force* (U.S. Department of Labor), an example of which appears in Figure 3-1.

Our normal unemployment figure includes all those over 14 years of age who are looking for work. Those who have done any work at all as paid employees, as self-employed, or those who are unpaid but have done 15 hours or more for a business operated by a member of the family are all counted as *employed*. Those on vacation, ill, on strike, out due to bad weather, etc., are counted as *employed*. Those who did not seek work because they believed no work was available are classified as not in the labor force unless they volunteer such information (hence some unemployed go uncounted). Many of the criticisms of the unemployment figures are directed at the inclusion of teenagers in the labor force during the summer months, or the inclusion of working wives.

In Figure 3-1 the broken line represents labor force time lost through unemployment and part-time work. We see that the rate of unemployment on this basis for the trough of the 1960–1961 recession would have been about 8.5 percent instead of 7 percent (the solid line). The figure uses a 37.5-hour week for computing time lost. A variable standard (average hours worked each month by all workers, excluding economic part-time) for the same period would give an unemployment rate of 9.3 percent, and a 40-hour standard a rate of 9 percent. The use of a full-time equivalent unemployment figure gives us a more accurate and useful measure of the seriousness of unemployment, but it fails to tell us how

[17] "Rates of Unemployment in Great Britain and the United States," *Rev. Ec. & Stat.*, Nov. 1961, pp. 340–350.

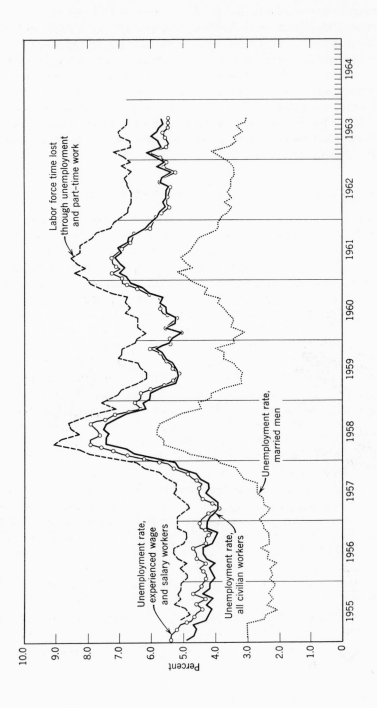

many hours the economic part-time workers *desired* to work, how many hours the unemployed workers wanted to work, and the hours that persons absent from their jobs all week generally work at their jobs. (Those who are sick, on strike, out because of bad weather or personal reasons are considered working, and are considered working the accepted number of hours.) The figure must be used with these qualifications, although they are probably not terribly serious.[18]

The suggestion has been made that if we are to count working time lost through involuntary part-time employment, we should offset this with the time worked in excess of a standard number of hours. But this computation is complicated by the fact that so many of those who work over the accepted standard are in the agriculture or nonfarm self-employed categories and their "extra" time is not available to partially or fully unemployed persons. "Even if, by Government edict, all persons would be prohibited from working longer than 40 hours, the extent to which

[18] For a thoroughgoing analysis see Subcommittee on Economic Statistics, JEC, *Unemployment: Terminology, Measurement, and Analysis*, 1961, pp. 33–48.

Figure 3-1. Selected measures of unemployment and part-time employment, January 1955–August 1963 (seasonally adjusted). *Source:* U.S. Department of Labor, *Monthly Report on the Labor Force*, Sept. 1963, p. 10.

Explanatory notes:

Labor force time lost represents the man-hours lost by the unemployed and those on part time for economic reasons, as a percent of total man-hours potentially available to the civilian labor force.

Man-hours lost are computed by assuming the unemployed lost 37.5 hours a week, and that those on part time for economic reasons lost the difference between 37.5 and the time they actually worked.

Man-hours potentially available (the base for the rate) are obtained by adding: (1) man-hours actually worked; (2) man-hours that could have been worked by employed persons with a job but not at work, assuming a 37.5-hour workweek; (3) man-hours lost.

Unemployment rate, experienced wage and salary workers, is based on unemployment and labor force figures that exclude those who never worked, self-employed, and unpaid family workers. All wage and salary workers are represented, including those in agriculture, domestic service, government, and all other nonfarm industries.

Unemployment rate, all civilian workers, is the standard seasonally adjusted rate of unemployment.

Unemployment rate, married men, represents the number of unemployed married men as a percent of all married men in the civilian labor force (employed plus unemployed). These figures exclude married men living apart from their wives. The rates for 1955 and 1956 are based on pre-1957 definitions of unemployment and employment.

this step would increase job opportunities for the partially unemployed or the unemployed is problematical."[19]

While there is room for improvement in our unemployment figures, the data cannot be labeled as misleading or inaccurate. Some concern may be expressed over the number of unemployed females who must be employed (women made up 29 percent of the civilian labor force in 1948, but 34 percent in May, 1962); the impact on the unemployment figures of the summer surge of teenagers into the labor force; and the number of men over 65, women 45 to 65, and others who are classified as unemployed but seek only part-time work—in other words, the problem of what have been called "secondary earners." On the other hand, data are available on unemployment rates by age, sex, marital status for both men and women, duration of unemployment (short-term and long-term), industry groups, occupational groups, color, and farm and nonfarm groups. There is, then, a rather comprehensive set of data available to those who wish to take the time to analyze it.

APPENDIX

What follows is an exchange between the late Senator Kerr and Chairman Martin of the Federal Reserve on what percentage rate of unemployment is an acceptable policy goal.[20] The reader is also referred to the comments in the text pages 31–34 and 38–41, and to footnotes 6, 7, and 36 of Chapter 2.

SENATOR KERR. What number do you think, in terms of unemployment, can exist and be consistent with the objective in this law [the Employment Act of 1946] which you say is addressed in part to the Federal Reserve System?

MR. MARTIN. I don't know what the figure ought to be on that, Senator.

SENATOR KERR. If you don't know, who does?

MR. MARTIN. I think we will have to—

SENATOR KERR. How long have you been in this job?

MR. MARTIN. I have been in the job 7 years.

SENATOR KERR. How long is it going to take you to find out?

MR. MARTIN. I am not sure I will ever find out. I am doing the best I can, and I have a lot to learn every day; I realize that.

SENATOR KERR. You mean you have been in this job for 7 years and you do not know what your objective is in terms of total unemployment to meet the requirements of this full [sic] employment act?

MR. MARTIN. My objective is very clear. How you attain it is not so clear, but my objective—

SENATOR KERR. What is your objective in terms of numbers of unemployed?

[19] *Ibid.*, p. 45. See pp. 45–46 for a discussion of reweighting the unemployment rate to reflect the relative risk of unemployment for different groups of the labor force. The results, as in the case of computing overtime, are insignificant.

[20] COF, S, *Investigation Finan. Cond.*, H, Pt. 6, pp. 1901–1904.

MR. MARTIN. I have no numbers of unemployed, but I want the men—

SENATOR KERR. If that is true, Mr. Martin, you would feel that you had met the mandate of this law with 10 million unemployed?

MR. MARTIN. I think that a figure of unemployed is not the—

SENATOR KERR. Is immaterial?

MR. MARTIN. No. I am concerned whenever 2 people, 1 person, is unemployed.

SENATOR KERR. Well, let's get back to this law. This law is a positive thing. It fixes an obligation on somebody.

MR. MARTIN. I pointed out in my last appearance before this committee that I have interpreted this law as I believe the law was intended to be. But I did point out at that time that it might be desirable to make explicit in the law instead of implicit in maximum purchasing power, as I read it, the responsibility for long-run price stability.

SENATOR KERR. That is one of the things.

It says to "promote maximum employment, production, and purchasing power." Yes.

MR. MARTIN. And those three merge together.

SENATOR KERR. Now then, I am trying to find out from you what degree of unemployment or what figure of unemployment, in your judgment, would be inconsistent with this objective.

MR. MARTIN. And I tell you I don't know.

SENATOR KERR. Well, make some estimate.

MR. MARTIN. I cannot make an estimate on that—

On that kind of thing. I am disturbed about the level of unemployment today.

SENATOR KERR. If you cannot make an estimate and you do not know, it would seem I can assume you would not know if 10 million unemployed created a situation inconsistent with it.

MR. MARTIN. The inconsistency here, Senator, is that what we are up against is the mistakes which were made 2 or 3 years ago—

SENATOR KERR. But, Mr. Martin, we are talking about this law, and you said the Federal Reserve Board has some responsibility under it.

MR. MARTIN. I am accepting that responsibility.

SENATOR KERR. How can you accept it if you do not know what it means.

MR. MARTIN. Well, if—

SENATOR KERR. If you cannot relate its mandate to you in terms of some figures, how are you accepting it.

MR. MARTIN. I do not know what figure I am going to—there is no figure written in the law.

SENATOR KERR. No; there is not, but there are words to promote maximum employment. Do you think we would have maximum employment if there was 10 million unemployed?

MR. MARTIN. No; I would not think we had maximum employment with 10 million unemployed. I do not think we have maximum employment at the present level of unemployment. That is why we are pursuing as vigorous an antirecession policy in the Federal Reserve as we are pursuing at the moment.

SENATOR KERR. I am glad you said "as vigorously as we are pursuing." I thought you were going to say as vigorously as you can, and then I was going to disagree with you.

MR. MARTIN. I was saying we were doing it as vigorously—

SENATOR KERR. As you are doing it.

MR. MARTIN. That is right.

SENATOR KERR. I think that is right. I want to tell you, I think it is a profound, accurate, and unchallengeable statement. You are pursuing it as vigorously as you are pursuing it.

MR. MARTIN. Nobody can quarrel with that.

SENATOR KERR. Not with its accuracy.

MR. MARTIN. That is right.

SENATOR KERR. Then you think the present number of unemployed is too many?

MR. MARTIN. I do.

SENATOR KERR. By how much?

MR. MARTIN. I don't know by how much.

SENATOR KERR. Then how do you know it is too many?

MR. MARTIN. Well, I have a feeling, and there are a good many points in these unemployment statistics which are not clear, but I have a feeling that frictional unemployment—

SENATOR KERR. Frictional?

MR. MARTIN. Well, the minimum unemployment in this country would be defined as closer to 2 or 3 million, and I would say we probably had full employment in 1955 and 1956. I do not remember the levels at that time.

SENATOR KERR. I think that is a leading statement. Did you just arrive at that conclusion? Did that just suddenly dawn on you here in your conversation with me?

MR. MARTIN. No.

SENATOR KERR. If it did, I may have made some contribution to your understanding of your responsibility.

MR. MARTIN. Well, I still would not want to stand on that figure.

SENATOR KERR. I do not want you to make statements here which you do not want to stand on.

MR. MARTIN. All right, Senator.

SENATOR KERR. Because that is not consistent with the dignity and prestige of your position. You know what the fact is. If you had to go back home and run for office, you would not make statements that you would not want to stand on.

MR. MARTIN. I am very much afraid I would not be elected; that I agree with you.

SENATOR KERR. You wouldn't right now. (Laughter.)

MR. MARTIN. I doubt if I would under any conditions.

SENATOR KERR. Well, I have seen the time when you would have done pretty good, but not now. (Laughter.)

Well now, you have made a statement here that is quite significant, and I wonder if I could persuade you to stand on it, that employment to the extent that not more than 2 to 3 million are unemployed reasonably, in your judgment, meets the mandate to promote maximum employment.

MR. MARTIN. I will stand on this: That in the period 1955 and 1956—we had a growing labor force all the time, of course—

SENATOR KERR. Yes.

MR. MARTIN. But in the period 1955 to 1956, it is my conviction that we had full employment.

SENATOR KERR. All right.

MR. MARTIN. And I would go one step further.

SENATOR KERR. Don't go just a bit further until we see what it was in 1955 and 1956.

MR. MARTIN. I just want to qualify it by one thing. I was inclined to think it was over full employment.

SENATOR KERR. How much?

MR. MARTIN. That is pretty hard to measure, but I would say by a substantial amount.

SENATOR KERR. Well how much would you say? You said a while ago you thought that in 1955 and 1956 we had what you would describe as reasonable full employment. Now you say that in your judgment we had overemployment. Which statement shall we accept as a basis to proceed on here?

MR. MARTIN. Well, you had better proceed on the basis that I have a conviction that the tendency was overemployment there. I was satisfied—

SENATOR KERR. If it was, Mr. Martin, tell me by how much.

MR. MARTIN. It would just be sheer guesswork.

SENATOR KERR. No, no. You can do better than guess. You can make a reasonable estimate.

MR. MARTIN. Well, let's say a million people.

It should be noted that the Chairman was being questioned by a not too friendly Senator. One might argue that Mr. Martin was reluctant to establish a goal of unemployment because the Eisenhower Administration had declined to do so. This defense is, however, complicated by the fact that the Chairman of the Federal Reserve is responsible (by Federal Reserve legislation) to the Congress, and not to the President.

One might also argue that it is difficult for one man to keep all the pertinent facts in his head. On the other hand, however, Mr. Martin's critics could point out that the period 1955–1956 was not in the distant past, and was so controversial that he should have been more familiar with the facts; that he had three economists with him who were no doubt thoroughly familiar with the figures, and that Chairman Martin no doubt had the necessary data with him, as do most witnesses appearing before such committees.

4

The Role of the Federal Government

STATISTICAL MEASUREMENTS

We are all aware of the very rapid growth in government expenditures, especially those of the federal government. A specific analysis of government expenditures will be presented in this chapter. We shall also attempt to break down these figures so that we may observe trends in certain lines of activity. After having done this, we discuss the "proper" role of the government in our economy, the Council of Economic Advisers, and criteria for the determination of government expenditures.

Presented in Tables 4-1 to 4-3 are data on governmental expenditures on three levels: (1) total government, (2) federal government, and (3) state and local government. Column 1 in Table 4-1 shows total government expenditures in current dollars; the trend is quite obvious. This figure, total government expenditures, includes all that the various levels of government have spent on (1) purchases of goods and services and (2) expenditures of other types which generally redistribute income, e.g., transfer payments such as OASI payments and unemployment insurance payments, interest on public debt, and federal grants-in-aid to state and local governments. In a highly interesting and informative little study, Francis M. Bator has classified the first category as "exhaustive" and the second as "nonexhaustive" expenditure. "Exhaustive expenditures" pertains to purchases of goods and services; they use up resources which in turn are no longer available for private consumption or investment. "Nonexhaustive" expenditures do not use up current output but rather redistribute income in the form of transfer payments, interest paid on debt, etc.[1]

---

[1] F. M. Bator, *The Question of Government Spending: Public Needs and Private Wants*, New York: Harper, 1960, pp. 11–12. Tables 4-1–4-3 are similar to Bator's, except that all data here are on the calendar year basis, and constant dollar data are

An examination of columns 1–4 reveals some interesting information. Columns 1 and 2 give us a quick idea of the significant increase in both total government expenditures and federal government expenditures. We see also that the federal government's share of total government expenditures has been increasing since 1930. In 1961 its share was about 68.5 percent, *but* its share of purchases of goods and services, or its exhaustive expenditure, was only 53 percent of the total. So the federal government accounts for about half of the total government claim on resources, which compares with a figure of 15 percent for 1929.

In column 4 we have total government nonexhaustive expenditures. Again we see a very large increase in total government expenditures for this purpose—from $1.7 billion in 1929 to $41.9 billion in 1961. Price level changes notwithstanding, this is a significant increase.

Columns 6–9 spell out federal nonexhaustive expenditures. Although this spelling out causes some difficulties, it does give us a rough approximation of the role and trend of nonexhaustive federal expenditures. (In particular, federal grants-in-aid and certain subsidies are earmarked for certain resource uses.) It can be seen from column 10 that there has been a significant increase in federal nonexhaustive expenditures (from $1.3 to $45.1 billion from 1929 to 1961). Even though the percent of nonexhaustive expenditures (column 11) has not changed significantly between 1929 and 1961, the magnitude of this increase is nothing to be scoffed at. The role of nonexhaustive expenditures as a percent of total federal expenditures has been distorted by the similarly dramatic increase in national security expenditures. To repeat, a figure of $45.1 billion is significant, even if corrected by price changes. (The reader should note that the major factor in federal nonexhaustive expenditure has been transfer payments—OASI, veterans', unemployment, railroad retirement payments, etc. Also important has been the increase in interest paid on the public debt, but federal grants-in-aid recently have assumed an equal importance.)

In 1929 state and local governments accounted for 75.4 percent of *total* government expenditures, but this figure dropped to 35.3 percent by 1961. State and local governments' share of exhaustive expenditures has also declined, from 85 percent in 1929 to 47 percent in 1961. Nonetheless, state and local governments still absorb almost half of all government expenditures on goods and services. Of particular significance in the state

---

in 1954 dollars while Bator's are in 1957 dollars. His technique of analysis is a real contribution and has been heavily relied on here.

A. C. Pigou was apparently the first to use the term exhaustive expenditures. See the discussion in K. E. Poole, *Public Finance and Economic Welfare*, New York: Rinehart, 1956, pp. 36–43, and note 4 on p. 38.

Table 4-1. Total Federal and State and Local Exhaustive and Nonexhaustive

	1	2	3	4	5
	Total Gov't Expenditures[a]	Federal Gov't Expenditures[b]	Total Gov't Purchases of Goods and Services[c]	Total Gov't Nonexhaustive Expenditures[c]	Federal Purchases of Goods and Services[c]
1929	10.2	2.6	8.5	1.7	1.3
31	12.3	4.2	9.2	3.1	1.5
32	10.6	3.2	8.1	2.5	1.5
33	10.7	4.0	8.0	2.7	2.0
35	13.3	6.5	10.0	3.3	2.9
36	15.9	8.5	11.8	4.1	4.8
37	14.8	7.2	11.8	3.0	4.6
39	17.5	9.0	13.4	4.1	5.2
41	28.8	20.5	24.7	4.1	16.9
43	93.4	86.0	88.6	4.8	81.2
45	92.9	84.8	82.9	10.0	74.8
46	47.1	37.0	30.5	16.6	20.6
47	43.9	31.1	28.4	15.5	15.7
49	59.7	41.5	40.1	19.6	22.2
51	79.4	58.0	60.5	18.9	38.8
53	102.5	78.1	82.9	19.6	58.0
54	96.8	69.6	75.3	21.5	47.6
55	98.5	68.9	75.6	22.9	45.3
57	112.2	79.6	86.2	26.0	49.4
59	131.7	91.4	97.2	34.5	53.6
61	149.3	102.1	107.4	41.9	57.0

[a] For 1929 to 1953, OBE, USDC, *National Income* (*1954 Edition*), 1954, pp. 172–173; for 1954 to 1957, OBE, USDC, *U.S. Income and Output*, 1958, pp. 164–165; for 1958 to 1961, *Surv. Current Bus.*, July 1962, p. 16.

[b] For 1929 to 1953, *National Income* (*1954 Edition*), pp. 172–173; 1954 and 1955, *U.S. Income and Output*, 1958, pp. 164–165; 1958 to 1961, *Surv. Current Bus.*, July 1962, pp. 16–17. The figures in this column include federal grants-in-aid to state and local governments.

and local nonexhaustive category is the increase in state and local transfer payments, which increased from $.22 billion in 1929 to $5.43 billion in 1961.[2]

In Table 4-2 we have some of the same data previously discussed in

[2] Data have been compiled by the author on state and local expenditure, purchases of goods and services, transfer payments, net interest, and nonexhaustive expenditures, on a calendar year basis for the years 1929 to 1961, and are available from him.

Expenditures, Selected Years (Billions of Current Dollars)

6	7	8	9	10	11
Federal Transfer Payments[d]	Federal Net Interest Paid[c]	Federal Grants in Aid to State and Local Gov'ts[c]	Subsidies less Current Surplus of Gov't Enterprises[e]	Federal Nonexhaustive Expenditure[f] Cols. 6–9	Col. 10 as a Percent of Col. 2
0.69	0.44	0.12	0.85	1.3	50
1.72	0.44	0.31	0.17	2.7	64
0.93	0.48	0.13	0.16	1.7	50
0.70	0.52	0.50	0.25	2.0	50
0.63	0.53	1.71	0.73	3.6	55
2.06	0.49	0.72	0.41	3.7	44
0.83	0.62	0.76	0.47	2.6	36
1.24	0.64	0.99	0.93	3.8	42
1.37	0.77	0.81	0.67	3.6	18
1.24	1.71	0.94	0.86	4.8	06
4.31	3.33	0.87	1.52	10.0	12
9.21	4.17	1.11	1.62	16.4	44
8.89	4.17	1.74	0.57	15.4	50
8.75	4.40	2.23	0.74	19.3	47
8.66	4.71	2.48	1.28	19.2	33
9.67	4.85	2.81	0.84	20.1	26
11.61	5.01	2.89	1.17	22.0	32
12.51	4.92	3.05	1.64	23.6	34
15.97	5.63	4.09	2.84	30.2	38
20.63	6.38	6.73	2.50	37.8	41
25.84	6.64	7.01	4.07	45.1	44

[c] For 1929 to 1945, *National Income* (1954 *Edition*), pp. 172–173; 1946 to 1957, *U.S. Income and Output*, 1958, p. 64; 1958 to 1961, *Surv. Current Bus.*, July 1962, pp. 16–17.

[d] *Ibid.* Net foreign transfer payments are excluded.

[e] *Ibid.* "Subsidies reflected consist of Government payments to farmers, payments for the exportation and diversion of surplus agricultural commodities, shipping subsidies, and subsidy payments to air carriers." *U.S. Income and Output*, p. 164.

[f] Computed by subtracting column 5 from column 2.

constant (1954) dollars. The adjustment of these figures for price level changes does not change the basic trends or the respective roles of the federal or state and local governments. On a per capita basis the same significant increase in per capita government expenditures on goods and services prevails (from $152 to $457 from 1929 to 1961). For the federal

Table 4-2. Total Government, Federal, and State and Local Purchases, per Capita Federal and State and Local Purchases, and Total Government Purchases as a Percent of GNP (Billions of 1954 Dollars)

	1	2	3	4	5	6	7	8
	Total Gov't Purchases of Goods and Services[a]	Federal Purchases of Goods and Services[a]	State and Local Purchases of Goods and Services[a]	Population[b] (millions)	Per Capita Gov't Purchases of Goods and Services	Per Capita Federal Purchases of Goods and Services	GNP[a]	Gov't Purchases as a Percent of GNP
1929	18.5	2.9	15.6	121.8	152	24	181.8	10.2
31	21.6	3.7	17.9	124.1	174	29	153.0	14.1
33	19.9	5.3	14.6	125.7	158	42	126.6	15.8
35	23.0	6.7	16.3	127.4	181	54	152.9	15.0
37	26.0	9.6	16.4	129.0	202	74	183.5	14.2
39	30.1	11.0	19.1	131.0	230	84	189.3	16.0
41	47.7	30.7	16.9	133.4	358	230	238.1	20.0
43	137.9	123.9	14.0	136.7	1009	906	296.7	49.8
45	131.2	117.1	14.0	139.9	940	845	314.0	41.8
47	37.2	19.4	17.8	144.1	258	134	282.3	13.2
49	47.2	25.3	21.9	149.2	310	170	292.7	16.1
51	63.3	39.3	24.1	154.4	410	255	341.8	18.5
53	84.3	58.8	25.5	159.6	534	368	396.0	21.3
54	75.3	47.5	27.7	162.4	464	293	363.1	20.7
55	73.2	43.5	29.7	165.3	443	269	392.7	19.1
57	75.5	42.7	32.2	171.2	441	249	408.6	18.5
59	80.1	43.9	36.2	177.3	450	248	428.6	18.0
61	84.0	44.5	39.4	183.7	457	242	447.9	18.8

[a] Data for 1929 to 1946 from OBE, USDC, U.S. Income and Output, 1958, pp. 118–119; for 1947 to 1961, Surv. Current Bus., July 1962, pp. 8–9.
[b] Data include total population, including armed forces abroad, except for 1929. Bureau of the Census, USDC, Statistical Abstract of the U.S., 1961. Data for 1961 from Surv. Current Bus., July 1962, p. S-12. Data as of July 1 of each year.

government the same generalization is again true, the increase being from $24 to $242 for the same years.

Perhaps the most interesting and revealing data are contained in Table 4-3. Here we have federal government purchases of goods and services for

Table 4-3. Federal Government Nondefense Purchases in Constant and Current Dollars, per Capita Constant Dollars, and as a Percent of Nondefense GNP in Constant Dollars (Billions of Dollars)

	1	2	3	4	5
	Federal Gov't Nondefense Purchases of Goods and Services[a]	Federal Gov't Nondefense Purchases (1954 dollars)[b]	Per Capita Federal Nondefense Purchases (1954 dollars)	Nondefense GNP (1954 dollars)[c]	Federal Gov't Nondefense Purchases as a Percent of Nondefense GNP (1954 dollars)
1939	3.9	8.3	63	187.1	4.4
40	4.0	8.5	64	201.2	4.2
41	3.1	5.6	42	213.0	2.6
42	2.4	3.9	29	166.1	2.3
43	0.8	1.2	8	173.6	0.7
44	0.4	0.6	5	180.1	0.3
45	−1.1	—	—	—	—
46	1.8	2.5	17	256.5	1.0
47	4.2	5.2	36	268.1	2.0
48	7.7	9.1	62	279.3	3.3
49	8.6	9.8	65	277.2	3.5
50	5.0	5.6	37	302.1	1.8
51	4.9	5.0	32	307.5	1.6
52	6.5	6.6	42	306.8	2.1
53	8.7	8.8	55	319.0	2.8
54	6.3	6.3	35	320.9	1.9
55	6.2	6.0	36	355.2	1.7
56	4.3	3.9	23	363.1	1.1
57	5.3	4.6	27	370.1	1.2
58	7.8	6.6	38	346.4	1.9
59	7.3	6.0	34	390.5	1.5
60	7.4	5.9	33	404.4	1.5
61	6.9	5.4	29	409.3	1.3

[a] *Business Statistics* (*1961 Edition*) p. 3, and *Surv. Current Bus.*, July 1962. This is the difference between (1) federal government purchases of goods and services (less government sales) and (2) national defense purchases. The government sales figures complicate the procedure followed here because all sales are not of the military type and a division is not available. Deducting this figure brings a negative figure for 1945. Bator has developed his own method for dealing with this problem, but whether the result is an improvement is not clear.

[b] Computed by dividing by the implicit price deflator for federal government purchases for each year and multiplying by 100. Implicit price deflators from the *Jan. 1961 Ec. Rept. Pres.*, p. 133, and *Surv. Current Bus.*, July 1962, p. 8.

[c] Computed by subtracting column 2 from total federal purchases of goods and services in 1954 dollars (*Jan. 1962 Ec. Rept. Pres.*, p. 211) and then subtracting this result from GNP in 1954 dollars (*ibid.*, p. 210).

nondefense purposes in constant dollars. For 1939 the per capita non-defense expenditure in 1954 dollars amounted to $63, rose to $65 in 1949, and in 1961 was only $29. This is indeed rather astonishing. In column 5 we see that federal nondefense purchases as a percent of nondefense GNP (in 1954 dollars) declined from 4.4 percent in 1939 to 3.5 percent in 1949, to 2.8 percent in 1954, and to 1.3 percent in 1961. It should be noted that there is nothing particularly significant in using 1939 as a base year, but it would not be logical to use 1929 either. (Bator has calculated the 1929 figure to be .6 percent.) The important point is, though, that there has been a significant downward trend during the postwar years, especially since the years 1949 and 1953 (see column 5, Table 4-3). In selecting any year as the basis for comparison, such things as the level of unemployment and potential GNP are significant. With a constant level of federal expenditures over, say, a 2- or 3-year period, an important decline in the GNP automatically makes the federal nondefense expenditure percentage higher, and vice versa. Furthermore, even though there is a tendency for government's role to increase in industrialized countries, the increase is certainly not automatic.

Along these same lines, Bator has shown that in 1957, for *all govern-ments*, we allocated (in constant 1957 dollars) almost exactly the same volume of resources "per head of population to civilian-type public use as in 1939 despite the fact that total (real) civilian output per capita had risen from $1,514 in 1939 to $2,281 in 1957."[3] (The per capita government nondefense purchase figure for 1939 was $233, and for 1957, $234. The 1929 figure was $155.) He further shows that the ratio of all-government nondefense purchases to nondefense GNP declined from 13.4 percent in 1939 to 10.3 percent in 1957.[4] The 1929 figure was 7.4 percent, and the 1948–1949 figure was 9.5. The ratio has been fairly constant, but the federal government's share has declined significantly, as shown in the following paragraph.

An important argument which Bator successfully destroys is that the federal government has been rapidly replacing the state and local govern-ments in the latter's civilian functions during the postwar period. He shows that from 1939 to 1957 the ratio of federal government nondefense to all government nondefense purchases declined from 32.3 percent to 12.2 percent. (The 1929 figure was 8.1 percent.) The continuous downward trend since 1953 is indeed significant (from 23.1 percent to 12.2 percent in 1957). It is of further interest to note that the 1948–1949 figure (fiscal 1949)

---

[3] Bator, *op. cit.*, p. 22.
[4] *Ibid.*, p. 139. The 1940 figure was 12.0 percent, and 1953 was 10.1 percent. Bator's figures up to 1947 are on a calendar year basis. Thereafter they are on a fiscal year basis.

was 28 percent. Bator uses other measures to show that the federal government is not necessarily the villain that it is so often made out to be. The ratio of federal nondefense purchases to nondefense GNP was .6 percent in 1929, increased to 4.3 percent in 1939, but delined to 2.7 percent in 1948–1949 and then to 1.3 percent in 1957. In absolute terms, per capita federal nondefense purchases (in 1957 dollars) declined from $71 in 1939 to $29 in 1957 (again with a very significant decline from 1954 to 1957).[5]

Summary

We have seen that there has been a very significant increase in both federal and state-local government expenditures. We have also seen that the federal government has increased its share of total government expenditures. However, when defense expenditures are excluded from our purchases' figures we see a drastic decline in the federal government's percentage and per capita shares during the postwar period; indeed, a rapid decline from 1953–1954 to 1957. This has occurred in spite of a rapid increase in the nondefense output (total and per capita) of the whole economy. As we noted above, there is nothing magical in using 1939 as the basis for comparison. Nonetheless, the data show that especially since the 1948–1949 and 1953–1954 periods the role of the federal government relative to state and local governments has declined, that the role of federal government has declined as a percent of nondefense purchases, and its role in terms of per capita nondefense purchases also declined.

CAUSES OF INCREASED GOVERNMENT EXPENDITURES

Wars tend to increase federal government spending significantly. After wars, a complete and permanent retreat from the wartime levels of spending does not occur because prices are inflated, interest on war-incurred debt must be paid, benefits to veterans are expanded, foreign economic aid becomes necessary, and the prosperity of war may encourage the adoption of additional social and economic programs. Moreover, cold war defenses become necessary.

Although the same forces are not at work on the state and local governments, their expenditures have also shown a rather consistent upward trend. The reasons for this are quite simple. First, we must expand our existing facilities to provide for a growing population (see Table 4-2, column 4). More important, however, our society has demanded more and better services from the various levels of government. It has been estimated that between 1913 and 1950 the population increase accounted for about 6.9 percent of the increase in government expenditures, but

[5] *Ibid.*, p. 143.

the increase in government services accounted for about 40.9 percent.[6]
One of the most important reasons accounting for this increased
demand for government services has been the increase in our GNP and
in our productivity. As we have become richer and have accumulated
more wealth we have demanded more luxury goods and more and better
products from the government—"schools, roads, hospitals, recreational
facilities, more adequate provision for the aged, unemployed, infirm, and
needy children, increased attention to our natural resources, more provision for public safety, etc."[7] To this list we could also add public housing
and increased expenditures for the regulation of business and labor. All
these factors, obviously, are related not only to increases and shifts in
population and a wealthier nation, but also to urbanization and technological change.

The growth of the social security program perhaps illustrates both the
influence of urbanization and technological change. Because of a very
rapid increase in the productivity of agriculture, the number of people
needed to produce agricultural products has greatly declined. These
individuals in turn have migrated to the urban areas which have, partly
because of technological influences, provided job opportunities. Moreover, the change from a predominantly agricultural to an urban society
has brought about changes in the structure of the American family. In
the old days the grandparents could live on the farm, which generally had
sufficient room for them, and they could contribute substantially to the
operation of the home (cooking, canning, sewing, gardening, etc.) but
in today's small, expensive, urban household which must purchase its
food, etc., there is no room for them, there is no productive economic role
for them to assume, and they are expensive to provide for. Further, they
are often not wanted since the orientation of the typical American family
tends to be toward the children and not the grandparents. In addition,
our standards of medical care have risen greatly, with a great increase in
the cost of medical services. Social security in both the economic and
sociological senses partially fills this gap.

MYTHS AND FALLACIES CONCERNING
GOVERNMENT'S ROLE

In Chapter 1 we noted that since there was not complete consensus
over the role the federal government should play in our economy there

---

[6] Percentages from A. M. Soloway, "The Growth of Government over the Past
50 Years: An Analytical Review," in JEC, *Fed. Exp. Pol.*, P, p. 23. See this essay for
an excellent analysis of the reasons for the growth of government expenditures.
Also of interest in the same volume are the articles by P. B. Trescott, pp. 60–83,
W. W. Heller, pp. 98–107, and A. G. Buehler, pp. 230–238.

[7] *Ibid.*, p. 26.

was not complete acceptance of the use of fiscal policy. Despite the fact that the federal government's share of nondefense GNP and nondefense all-government purchases has been declining significantly, and the fact that federal nondefense expenditures on a constant dollar per capita basis has also declined drastically, there are still many myths and fallacies concerning the "proper" role of the federal government.

One of the cries most often heard is that such and such a project should not be undertaken because we cannot afford it. It was strongly felt by many responsible economists that in 1954 and 1955 cuts were made in our defense spending not because world tensions had been relaxed, nor because we had adequate defense facilities and could look forward to a safe future, but rather because so many of us accepted the argument that we could not afford the current defense budget. There was absolutely no economic basis for this argument. It was sometimes held that we were cutting fat through these defense cuts,[8] but the facts seem to indicate that most of the cut was in muscle.

Similar arguments have been advanced to defeat greater aid to education, higher teachers' salaries, urban slum cleanups, etc.—this in spite of the repeated contention of recognized experts in these various areas, and even of the public itself, that these problems should be tackled. The pursuance of these projects involves, under conditions of full employment, the use of the economy's resources for public rather than private uses. The responsible politician will state the issue for what it is rather than hide behind such myths as that government is bad, and fallacies that we cannot afford more public services. Another example, which shows both the political and the economic aspects of the problem, follows.

The important point is that much of the current drive for cutting the budget is carried on under the banner that taxes must be cut because the current load is intolerable. I am not qualified to judge whether this is the case from a political point of view; and if so, what congressional leadership can do to persuade the people otherwise. However, I can judge the economic aspect of the matter, and I am convinced that the tax load is not intolerable in this sense. What seems to be the President's repeated nightmare—that we must walk a knife edge between military defeat abroad and economic disaster at home—is just a nightmare. It has no basis in fact, at least not in the present setting. To be sure, there could be a level of military expenditures which would set us back into a rigged economy of the wartime type, but current proposals are far below that. The gross national product in real terms is now about one-third above wartime levels, and we are looking back at a decade of unsurpassed prosperity. Far from being an impediment, the big budget has contributed to this prosperity.

If the Congress insists on severe cutbacks in the budget, let it be done for the right reasons: That is, not because economic necessity demands it, but because

[8] For an eloquent denunciation of this argument see P. A. Samuelson, JEC, *Fed. Tax Pol.*, H, pp. 223–224.

these outlays are considered less desirable than private uses of income. It is only fair to add, vis-a-vis our friends abroad, that these cutbacks need not be undertaken because the American taxpayer would starve lest his taxes be cut. Notwithstanding present levels of taxation, the American consumer has experienced a 55 percent gain (in real terms) in his income after tax since 1940, and a 20 percent gain since 1947. I expect these gains would continue, even though present rates of tax have to be maintained.[9]

Space does not permit an examination of the arguments that have been used to contain or reduce government spending. We can, however, briefly mention them. The creeping socialism argument is still widespread. In addition, contemporary opponents of government spending have spent millions attempting to prove that almost any government spending is inevitably inflationary, or that further spending will bankrupt the economy, destroy private incentive, or produce a recession that will "curl your hair." Still more recently they have argued that fiscal policy could not help the unemployed because they were structurally unemployed and not further employable; and now the argument is that policy aimed at reducing unemployment will necessarily aggravate our balance of payments problem.

Professor Horace Gray has perhaps best summarized the ideology which condemns government action and which, in his opinion, "has paralyzed the national will":[10]

1. Private spending always yields greater utility than public spending.
2. Private activity is always efficient, public activity always inefficient.
3. It is possible to "get something for nothing" by inflation or some other legerdemain, thereby escaping the hard choice of allocating scarce resources to alternative ends.
4. Diversion of resources from the private to the public economy will undermine and eventually destroy private enterprise.
5. Subsidized private business can serve the general welfare better than direct public action.
6. State and local governments can do all that is needful in the public economy.
7. The principal function of the Federal Government is to promote private business.
8. The Federal Government is not directly responsible for the public economy.
9. The public economy is a parasitic, nonproductive organism which feeds upon and saps the vitality of the private economy.
10. Strengthening the public economy will destroy individual liberty and eventuate in a socialistic regimentation.

[9] R. A. Musgrave in Subcommittee on Fiscal Policy, JEC, *Fiscal Policy Implications of the Economic Outlook and Budget Developments*, Hearings, June 3–7, 14, 1957, p. 155.

[10] H.M.Gray, "Private Affluence and Public Poverty," *Illinois Bus. Rev.*, September, 1951, reprinted in JEC, *Empl., Growth, Price Levels*, H, Pt. 10, pp. 3456–3460. For current expressions of the "conventional wisdom" read almost any editorial in the *Wall Street Journal* (or most other newspapers), or the publications of the NAM.

SHORTCOMINGS OF THE PROFIT TEST AND THE MARGINAL SOCIAL COST AND BENEFIT APPROACH

It is not the function of the economist to determine the proper role for the government. He can, however, point out the fallacies in the foregoing arguments. As we noted in Chapter 1, American economists are committed to the determination of output via the free market—they feel that it is the most efficient method. They recognize, however, that the free market does not operate efficiently for some goods and services. It is quite difficult, for example, for us to allocate individual purchases for national defense. Further, it is difficult to apply the profit test to such things as roads, public libraries and parks, TVA-type projects, foreign aid, and police and fire protection. It is true that in some of these areas costs could not be covered and private enterprise would not therefore undertake the project. (This helps explain the use of subsidies to airlines, railroads, and the shipping industry.) Furthermore, many economists and political scientists maintain that if the market (dollar purchases) is used to determine the production of public goods people will understate their desires for these goods. It is quite likely that they will not voluntarily contribute their fair share of the cost of public goods—that they will rely on "others" to assume a greater share of the cost.[11]

An optimum allocation of resources is attained in the private sector when (1) the marginal social benefit of each good equals the marginal social cost of each good; (2) the marginal social benefits and costs of all goods are equal; (3) marginal private benefit equals marginal social benefit; and (4) marginal private cost equals marginal social cost. Welfare theory assumes that perfect competition exists, firms produce at the lowest point on their long-run average cost curve, price is equal to marginal cost, firms attempt to maximize profits, the distribution of income is given, efficient production techniques are used, all benefits go to those individuals who purchase the goods, and all costs to society of producing goods are included in the firm's costs. Under these circumstances a different use of resources (a reallocation of resources) would not increase economic welfare (total consumer satisfaction).

Marginal social benefit measures the total benefit to *society* at large from the increment of output. Marginal social cost is the total cost to society (not just to producers) of producing the good (it includes such things as smog). Marginal social cost is also equal to the sacrifice of other goods which could have been produced with the same factors of production. Marginal private benefit is the benefit accruing to those individuals who

[11] See Bator, *op. cit.*, p. 98 ff., and the sources he cites. See also R. A. Musgrave, *The Theory of Public Finance*, New York: McGraw-Hill, 1959.

purchase the good. Marginal private cost is the cost of production of the good to the private producer. When the conditions set forth above are not met either too much or too little production of goods results. When optimality is not achieved, marginal social benefits may exceed marginal private benefits; marginal private cost may not equal marginal social cost; marginal social benefit may exceed or be less than marginal social cost; etc.

Note that the significance of these conditions, in terms of welfare theory, is that failure to attain them has been an important factor accounting for the intervention of government in the economy. Marginal social costs, for example, may be greater than marginal private costs. The cost to private enterprise of producing certain industrial products may be less than the cost to society because of the smog that results from the operation of the factories. The government may then step in and tax producers to the extent necessary to eliminate the hazards to health which the smog creates. Costs to society of the production of liquor are greater than the actual dollar cost to the producer. They include accidents, broken families, and partial or complete unemployment. It is then argued that it is reasonable for the government either to place a high tax on liquor or to sell it itself at a price in excess of its marginal private cost, in order both to restrict its use (reduce production) and to help pay for the "damages" (or extra costs).

Similarly, the benefits resulting from certain public projects may exceed those accruing directly to individuals. There are, in other words, benefits to society which are over and above those to the individual; that is, marginal social benefits are greater than marginal private benefits. Education provides a certain benefit to the individual who secures it, but it provides even greater benefits to society. The price charged in the market will be so high that only a limited number will have access to education, and greater social benefits, which in this case are of the indirect type, will not be realized. (There are limits to this, of course, as when marginal social cost exceeds marginal social benefits.) Under these conditions it is legitimate to set price below marginal cost to get greater use and make up the difference with taxes. Furthermore, we want people to have certain goods that they would not have at the prices which would have to be charged—for example, medical care.[12]

Figures 4-1 and 4-2 display the familiar models of pure and imperfect competition. In Figure 4-1 we see that, under pure competition, the

[12] It is not only impossible but unnecessary for the objectives of this book to go into the debate over these points. See R. A. Musgrave's *The Theory of Public Finance*, Chapter 3 and Part II, especially Chapter 7, and J. M. Buchanan and M. Z. Kafoglis, "A Note on Public Goods Supply," *Am. Ec. Rev.*, June 1963, pp. 403–414.

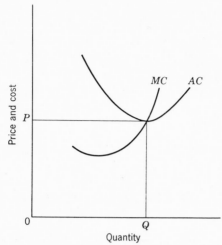

Figure 4-1. Marginal cost equal to price and average cost under pure competition.

producer will maximize his profit by increasing output up to the point at which marginal cost equals price. This is also the point at which average cost is the lowest. From the point of view of welfare economics this is the most significant advantage offered by purely competitive markets. In Figure 4-2 we have the typical imperfect competitor's downward-sloping demand curve. Following the rule that profits will be maximized by equating marginal cost and marginal revenue, the firm will produce at the output level at which price is greater than marginal cost. The real cost to society (the sacrifice of other goods) of producing more of this

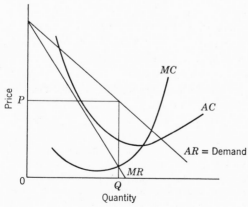

Figure 4-2. Price and output under imperfect competition.

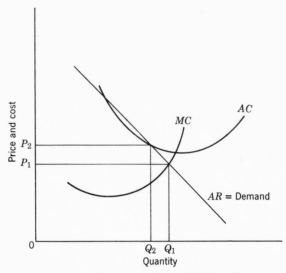

Figure 4-3. Marginal cost less than average cost under imperfect competition. $MC = P$ but AC is decreasing because MC is less than AC.

product is less than the price charged, and output is restricted. Under pure competition price would be less, output greater, and the firm would produce at the lowest point on its average cost curve.

Finally, there are cases in which marginal cost equals price but price and MC are less than average cost. The case in which marginal cost is less than average cost is usually the case of decreasing costs. This is illustrated in Figure 4-3.[13]

At certain lower levels of output in Figure 4-3 we see that price is higher than average cost. However, this is not the optimum output at which marginal cost equals price. Further, considerably more could be produced at lower costs because the AC curve is declining. The point at which $MC = P_1$ is a point at which the firm is not covering its average costs. If we raise the price to cover costs (to the level of AC), we must then reduce output from Q_1 to Q_2. On the other hand, if we are to maximize social welfare we should produce at the point at which $P = MC$. We should then have some industries producing at continuous losses.

---

[13] The diagram is after that of J. F. Due, *Government Finance*, rev. ed., Homewood, Ill., 1959, p. 426. See pp. 425–437 for an able analysis of these issues, and J. F. Due and R. W. Clower, *Intermediate Economic Analysis*, 4th ed., Homewood, Ill.: Irwin, 1961, Chapter 23. These two sources contain one of clearest introductory discussions to these topics. See also A. P. Lerner, *The Economics of Control*, New York: Macmillan, 1944, Chapter 6.

In the theory of public finance one principle used to determine the role of public expenditures has been the marginal rule. Social welfare is maximized when public spending is carried to the point at which the marginal social cost is equal to the marginal social benefit of each government project. In other words, when it is carried to the point at which the social satisfaction from the public expenditure is equal to the social satisfaction to be derived from private expenditure. Further, the marginal social benefits of all government activities should be equal to each other. That is, each marginal dollar spent on education should provide benefits equal to each marginal dollar spent on roads; if the marginal benefit from education is greater than that from roads, then expenditures on education should be increased and those on roads decreased until the two are brought into equality. There should therefore be an equality of social benefits between marginal dollars spent on private and public goods, and among the various types of public goods.

The marginal principle is acceptable theoretically but difficult to make operational. In particular, it makes certain unrealistic and untenable assumptions—that perfect competition exists; that the public knows what the alternatives are between the use of resources for private or public purposes, the costs and benefits of public programs, and the social or political costs (e.g., infringements on civil liberties) of public projects, and that the public is aware of the *costs of not undertaking* the public project; that the benefits of different public projects are similar; that costs and benefits can be adequately measured, and that people do not have dogmatic ideological positions which condemn any type of government program in spite of its demonstrated public value.[14]

Economists can demonstrate that in an important sense the private provision of many services can be quite inefficient. Returning to the case of decreasing costs, as illustrated in Figure 4-3, it is possible that a few firms which get the jump on the others will, because they expand rapidly, realize lower costs and drive their competitors out of business. The end result may be the establishment of an oligopoly (or a monopoly) in the industry. We now have a situation in which producers are able to set price. They will, if they are maximizing their profits, produce at the point at which marginal revenue equals marginal cost. Under conditions of imperfect competition marginal revenue and therefore marginal cost are less than price. As Figure 4-3 illustrates, if the firm were to produce at the point at which $MC = P$ it would not cover its average cost. Therefore, an optimal level of production is not achieved.

---

[14] A good list of criticisms can be found in K. E. Poole, JEC, *Fed. Exp. Pol.*, P, pp. 118–119.

In other projects the marginal cost to society, in terms of resources, of providing a service may well be zero (sending another letter through the mail, allowing another car to pass over a bridge, etc.). Hence price (or marginal revenue) must also be zero. Price therefore is again less than average cost, and what firm would stay in business under these circumstances? It should be clear that profit is not an adequate test of efficiency. In these cases of large-scale output, in which there are very high fixed or initial costs but very low variable costs, private enterprise would not pursue the project.[15] In other cases in which indirect benefits greatly exceed costs a subsidy may be justified.

What if the project is operated by a monopoly? Does this offer a way out? In this case we could assume that price would be set at such a level that the project would be profitable. But this, too, results in an inefficient allocation of resources since output (for example, bridge crossings) would not be at a point at which price equals marginal cost. If output is efficient, a loss is inevitable (because $P = MC$ but is less than AC). It would be possible here, under monopoly or oligopoly operation of a bridge (where MC = zero), to permit more cars to pass over the bridge without a corresponding reduction in the output of any other good or service. More people could pass over the bridge without denying anyone anything, but they do not because of the high price. This is inefficient in the sense that the output of bridge crossings could be much greater with no ill effects on anyone. In these areas of decreasing costs, in the price-output range we are dealing with, the free market fails. Generally speaking, when price is above marginal cost, an inefficient allocation of resources results.[15] When price is set equal to marginal cost but is less than average cost, a subsidy may be justified.

Pure public goods (sometimes referred to as pure collective consumption goods) are defined as goods "that, once produced, their enjoyment by each and every individual does not reduce their availability for the enjoyment of others."[16] Although it is difficult to find examples of pure public goods, since few government-provided goods or services are available equally and with the same cost to all, it is nonetheless true that in some areas the government is a more efficient producer than private

[15] See Bator, op. cit., pp. 76–112, for an extensive discussion.

[16] R. H. Stortz, Rev. Ec. & Stat., Nov. 1958, p. 329; and P. Samuelson, "The Pure Theory of Public Expenditures," Rev. Ec. & Stat., Nov. 1954, p. 387; and Samuelson's "Diagrammatic Exposition of a Theory of Public Expenditures," Rev. Ec. & Stat., Nov. 1955. On the problem of definition see W. W. Heller, JEC, Fed. Exp. Pol., P, p. 103.

For a criticism of the Samuelson approach, and an alternative, see G. Colm's comments, Rev. Ec. & Stat., Nov. 1956, pp. 408–412. See also S. Enke, "More on the Misuse of Mathematics in Economics: Rejoinder," Rev. Ec. & Stat., May 1955.

enterprise. In the case of the bridge just mentioned, additional services (crossings) simply would not be offered under private operation. There are, further, many areas where there are extensive indirect benefits from government services—public education (elementary, secondary, and university), public health, public housing and slum clearance, disease prevention, and public fire protection. If these services were sold in the market, their purchase would be limited to only a few and the price paid would underestimate their total benefits to the community. Price, therefore, is not an accurate guide to benefits provided.

In other areas the "external economies" provided by a government project may be great—e.g., the value to economic growth provided by an efficient transportation and communications system. There are also some areas in which indirect costs to society are likely not paid for or covered in the private firm's costs. Covering these costs via taxes (regulation, etc.) results not only in social benefits but greater productive efficiency. Smog control would be an example of this, for smog not only can reduce people's efficiency but can result in some workers locating outside the smog area and incurring extra transportation costs. And, of course, we should also count the social value of the elimination of eye irritation and the reduction of lung cancer. Again, is it likely that private enterprise would undertake its control? The elimination of water pollution and provisions for reforestation provide additional examples of this principle.

Government may be a more efficient producer of services in yet other respects. If, for example, all highways were to be privately owned and operated, consider the great administrative cost involved in collecting fees for our millions and millions of miles of highways.

POLITICAL AND ECONOMIC ASPECTS
OF THE ROLE OF GOVERNMENT

By now the reader may have concluded that the approach to determining the role of government spending is somewhat confused. To some extent he is right. Certain things may be said, however, and although we cannot exactly measure costs and benefits, we can note the questions to be asked and profitable procedures to follow:

1. What is the impact of the government tax or expenditure on (a) short-run stability, (b) long-run growth, (c) productivity in the economy, (d) consumption, and (e) investment?
2. What extra benefits do they bring to society? (For example, smog control, education, TVA, free bridges.) What extra costs?
3. What external economies do they create? (For example, the impact

of an efficient transportation and communications system on economic growth.)
4. Would the project be undertaken without the government?
5. Is the area one of large-scale output and decreasing costs?
6. What is the impact on civil liberties and individual liberties? (This argument has been grossly overworked.)
7. What would the impact be if the necessary tax had not been imposed? (For example, what would be the return to private investors if they had undertaken the project and had *not* been taxed?).
8. What is the cost to society of *not* undertaking the project?
9. What is the impact on income distribution?
10. What is the sacrifice that must be made in consumption or investment to use the resources for public purposes?

In our society it is the function of our political representatives to enlighten the public as to these costs and benefits in terms of resources, etc. The politician then must clearly and honestly present the issues and alternatives to the public and not hide behind myths, fallacies, irrelevancies, and shibboleths. It is the function of the economist not to make these decisions but rather to point out the areas where the market system fails to reflect peoples' choices accurately, to reveal total costs and benefits, or to allocate the use of resources efficiently; and, where possible, he should give some estimates of the cost and benefits of alternatives (public vs. private use of resources or use distributed among various possible public programs).

Decisions as to the role of the government will not be made solely on economic grounds. Social values, as we have stressed previously in earlier chapters, will govern this decision. But in making our decisions we should honestly attempt to set forth what facts we have on costs, benefits, and alternatives. Although we do not always have this information, because some of it defies measurement, we will at least have attempted a rational approach. It may still be that at some particular time it is unqualifiedly demonstrated that the governmental use of X number of dollars will provide far greater benefits to society than the use of the same X number of dollars for private purposes (automobiles, for example), but such government activity is not undertaken because society decides that it is not an appropriate function of government. The decision is made therefore on a strictly political, rather than economic, basis.[17]

Thus far in this chapter we have considered primarily the want-satisfying function of government. A second equally important function is the topic

[17] There has been, however, a decline in the debate over the "proper" role of government. See C. E. Lindbloom in JEC, *Fed. Exp. Pol.*, P, pp. 1–6; J. K. Galbraith, *Economics and the Art of Controversy*, New York: Vintage, 1961; and Chapter 2.

of the rest of this text—the economic stabilization function. A third function we have briefly mentioned, but we should now make it more explicit—the function of income redistribution. Income is redistributed either by means of progressive taxation and transfer payments, or by the provision of services (e.g., education) at less than cost. The extent to which it is pursued, however, is again a political and not an economic decision.[18] (We have not considered here the regulatory functions of government; for example, antitrust activity and the SEC. These activities nonetheless help to further explain the extent of government expenditures.)

Much has been said in recent years condemning the level of federal taxation and expenditures, but the level at which either becomes intolerable (either economically or politically) is unknown. Further, the level depends on the circumstances, and it is strongly influenced by the conditions existing in any society, especially by people's economic-political philosophy and their attitudes. No doubt the tolerable level is higher in periods of war than in peace. The knowledge at hand and the studies that have been done (e.g., on taxes and incentives or on new enterprise) strongly indicate that we have not yet reached the intolerable level.

As we previously noted, economists generally assume that their role is not to decide what the proper role for the government should be, but to provide the appropriate information to help society make its decisions efficiently. It is usually true, though, that some prefer to go futher and present their views to the public, particularly John Kenneth Galbraith in his *The Affluent Society*,[19] and Alvin H. Hansen in *Economic Issues of the 1960's*.[20] Galbraith contends that there has been an imbalance between the production of public goods and services on the one hand and of private goods and services on the other hand, the former being seriously shortchanged. Hansen's view is similar, and he goes on to argue that the partnership between private enterprise and government in our "Dual Economy" has strongly invigorated private enterprise. He maintains that public investment in scientific research, education, unemployment insurance, social security, rural electrification, and government programs (such as FHA) in the United States and the Western world generally have helped create a situation in which private enterprise "was never so strong or so secure as it is today throughout the free world."[21] (Even the late Sumner Slichter, who was not known for his

---

[18] These three functions are not necessarily incompatible. R. A. Musgrave has set forth a scheme for pursuing them simultaneously. See his *The Theory of Public Finance*, and his and W. W. Heller's statements in JEC, *Fed. Exp. Pol.*, P.

[19] Boston: Houghton Mifflin, 1958. See especially his Chapter 13, pp. 250–269.

[20] New York: McGraw-Hill, 1960.

[21] Hansen, *Economic Issues of the 1960's*, New York: McGraw-Hill, 1960, p. 46.

radical views, has maintained that over the long run the policies of the American government have been conducive to economic growth.[22]) In the final analysis, though, "what role for government" is still to be decided by the political process in our society.

THE EMPLOYMENT ACT OF 1946: THE ECONOMIC REPORT, THE JOINT ECONOMIC COMMITTEE, AND THE CEA

Although the argument over the role of the government in our economic life will continue, we have previously pointed out some of the areas in which rather definite commitments have already been made. We have noted in some detail the significance of the passage of the Employment Act of 1946 and the goals embodied in it. At this point we want to discuss some of the procedural aspects of the implementation of the law, mainly the CEA and the Joint Economic Committee (formerly called the Joint Committee on the Economic Report).

The 1946 legislation created both the CEA and the JEC. The particular significance of the establishment of the CEA in the Executive Office of the President was to elevate economic analysis and policy determination to a high level in our government. This also represented a momentous change in our economic ideology, for it was with this piece of legislation that the federal government formally accepted the responsibility for policies aimed at full employment, price stability, and economic growth.

The Economic Report of the President

The law requires the President to submit to Congress by January 20 of each year an economic report, which is to set forth

1. the levels of employment, production, and purchasing power obtaining in the United States and such levels needed to carry out the policy declared in section 2 [maximum employment, production, and purchasing power, etc.];
2. current and foreseeable trends in the levels of employment, production, and purchasing power;
3. a review of the economic program of the Federal Government and a review of economic conditions affecting employment in the United States or any considerable portion thereof during the preceding year and of their effect upon employment, production, and purchasing power; and
4. a program for carrying out the policy declared in section 2, together with such recommendations for legislation as he may deem necessary or desirable.

[22] See the concise but interesting discussion by B. R. Morris, *Problems of American Economic Growth*, New York: Oxford Univ. Press, 1961, pp. 241–246, especially p. 243.

The 1946 Act requires only that the President submit a January *Economic Report*, but during the first seven years of the act *Midyear Economic Reports* were also issued. Further, the usual procedure was for the *Report* to contain a report by both the President and the CEA. Under the Eisenhower Administration, however, the *Midyear Reports* were abandoned, and the *Report* became that of the President alone with a CEA report primarily on its activities.[23] The first (January 1962) *Report* of the Kennedy Administration reverted to the separate reports of the President and CEA, with a rather extensive analysis by the CEA. In fact, the President's statement covered 27 pages and that of the CEA 153 pages, plus an activities report of 6 pages and 93 pages of statistical tables. Kennedy's second report consisted of the President's statement of 20 pages and the CEA's analysis of 156 pages.

One important aspect of the presidential reports has been whether or not they should include quantitative estimates of the needed levels of employment and production to attain maximum employment, with policy proposals for attaining those goals. The earlier reports contained such estimates, but they were dropped beginning with the 1954 *Economic Report* (the first Eisenhower report). In the *Annual Report* of the JEC there was bipartisan criticism of this omission. Omission of these quantitative estimates in the *Economic Report* led to attempts to amend the Employment Act itself in 1959 to require their inclusion.[24] Such an amendment is unnecessary, however, for the original Act of 1946 clearly states that the *Economic Report* is to "set forth the levels of employment, production, and purchasing power *obtaining* in the United States and such levels *needed* to carry out the policy" of obtaining maximum employment, production, and purchasing power. (Italics added.) Furthermore, the *Report* is to set forth "current and foreseeable trends in the levels of employment, production, and purchasing power," a program for attaining maximum employment, etc., a review of the Administration's economic program, and certainly (by implication at least) an analysis of the impact of the Administration's economic program. It should be noted that the Treasury must and does make some of these estimates in order to arrive at its revenue estimates. In the January 1962 *Economic Report* these estimates were reintroduced. Many have argued that their previous

---

[23] For a review of the *Reports* see A. H. Hansen, *The American Economy*, New York: McGraw-Hill, 1957. On this and many other related matters see E. R. Canterbery, *The President's Council of Economic Advisers: A Study of Its Functions and Its Influence on the Chief Executive's Decisions*, New York; Exposition Press, 1961.

[24] See, e.g., *House Report No. 539*, 86th Cong., 1st Sess., June 12, 1959 (from the Committee on Government Operations).

omission was indeed a serious failure to carry out not only the spirit but also the legal mandate of the 1946 Act. One will have to speculate for himself as to why the omissions were made. It is also interesting, in terms of policy development, to note the element of prediction included in the requirement that the *Economic Report* set forth "current and foreseeable trends in the levels of employment, production, and purchasing power."

Dr. Arthur F. Burns, former Chairman of the CEA, has argued that the act may be interpreted as requiring a quantification of goals or otherwise (employment should be a "little higher," "substantially higher," etc.). He states that it would be unwise to publish numerical goals and estimates because (1) this might create the impression that government officials can reliably make these estimates, (2) economic forecasting is too inaccurate, (3) our statistical series are too inaccurate, and (4) such quantification would not improve the *Economic Reports*.[25] None are more cognizant than economists of the difficulties of both long- and short-term economic projections. When approached with a full understanding of the problems encountered, however, they can play a very important role in the development of goals and the altering of policy to attain these goals. We have more to say on this matter in a later chapter.

An additional controversy involving the *Economic Report* has been whether or not it should include a reasonably detailed statement on monetary policy. Again earlier *Reports* contained such statements but again the practice was, for all intents and purposes, discontinued. And again the practice of including such a statement was revived in the 1962 *Economic Report*. As in the case of quantification of goals, an attempt has been made to amend the 1946 Act to require the inclusion of a statement on monetary policy (and much more). This is discussed further in a later chapter.

The Joint Economic Committee

The 1946 Act also established the Joint Committee on the Economic Report, whose name was later changed to the Joint Economic Committee to reflect the fact that its studies and investigations were extending over almost the whole spectrum of economic issues and problems rather than simply an evaluation of the *Economic Report*. The committee is composed of eight members each from the House and the Senate, with the chairmanship (and vice-chairmanship) rotating each year between the House and

---

[25] JCER, *Jan. 1955 Ec. Rept. Pres.*, H, pp. 43–44. The Board of Governors of the FR System supports Burns. It gives reasons similar to those given by Burns plus some others which are meaningless. It says, for instance, that quantification of goals may "provoke debate about matters outside the area of control by Government action." See *House Report No.* 539, *op. cit.*, p. 19.

the Senate. The law states that the committee shall "make a continuing study of matters relating to the Economic Report," "study means of coordinating plans in order to further the policy of this Act," and file its report on the President's *Economic Report* no later than March 1 of each year. It is to evaluate the President's *Economic Report* and make other reports and recommendations to the House and the Senate as a guide to the other committees and Congress.

Although the Joint Economic Committee (naturally) has been greatly involved in partisan political issues (there is generally a majority and a minority report), it has produced some of the most worthwhile hearings to come out of the Congress, and it has supplied economists with a great many research studies that in quality are second to none. In addition, it has provided a vehicle for the public airing of many important economic issues, bringing them to the attention of the public (and of perhaps government officials and congressional committees also), and has perhaps even exerted a salutary pressure on officials of the Federal Reserve System. One may question whether all this could have been done without the guidance of Dr. Paul H. Douglas, former president of the American Economic Association, a recognized economist in his own right, and the senior Senator on the committee.

The CEA and Its Role

The 1946 Act stated that the CEA should "assist and advise the President in the preparation of the Economic Report"; gather data on current and prospective economic trends, and analyze the same in terms of section 2 (attaining maximum employment, production, and purchasing power, etc.); appraise government programs in terms of section 2 and make appropriate recommendations; "develop and recommend to the President national economic policies to foster and promote free competitive enterprise, to avoid economic fluctuations or to diminish the effects thereof, and to maintain employment, production and purchasing power"; and to make studies and recommendations on matters of federal policy and legislation as the President may request.

One of the most controversial aspects of the Employment Act has been the role of the CEA. Specifically, should it consist of an economic Supreme Court dispensing pure economic science, or should the CEA participate directly in the political process, freely testifying before congressional committees seeking support for the President's economic program, making public speeches in support of the President's program, etc.? Both points of view have been represented in the chairmanship of the CEA. Edwin G. Nourse, the first chairman, represented what has been called the "ivory tower" attitude of not wanting to testify, Burns was reluctant to, and Leon Keyserling went to the other extreme; he apparently desired to become rather deeply involved in politics.[26]

Those who feel that Council members should not become advocates of the President's program argue that good economists are not good politicans,[27] that "economic science" will be soiled with "politics,"[28] "that staff advisers close to the President should seek anonymity,"[29] or that the CEA would not want to reveal its differences with the President.

These arguments have not gone unchallenged, however. In the first place, the language of the act (as noted) clearly states that the CEA should directly participate in the development of national economic policy and the making of specific policy recommendations. This means much more than the mere provision of economic data. It means that the Council will participate in the development of goals, judgments concerning goals and policies, and alternative programs.

Critics of the anonymity argument point out that it was not the intent of the Employment Act to isolate Council members.[30] They note that Congress was well aware of the controversial nature of economics and felt that an examination of the methods of research and analysis of the CEA would be healthy and rewarding.[30] They have further stated that this examination by "seasoned legislators" has been helpful to the CEA, and to the Congress itself, in securing detailed information concerning the President's program. They have also pointed out that it is the Congress which makes the final policy decisions, and that many members of the CEA have felt that it would be inconsistent for the Council not to discuss analysis with the Congress.

Although members of the CEA must maintain the highest standards of professional performance, there is still room for some differences in analysis and policy recommendations. Further, since the CEA must also be concerned with value judgments and the appraisal of various public programs there may be differences between the President and the CEA.

It would perhaps be appropriate to note the ground rules for CEA appearances before Congress as developed by the Council under Dr. Heller's chairmanship.

[26] For Keyserling's point of view see Gerhard Colm, ed., *The Employment Act: Past and Future*, Washington, D.C.: NPA, 1956, pp. 66–73. For a strong argument supporting greater political participation by the Council, see S. K. Bailey, "Political Elements in Full Employment Policy," *Am. Ec. Rev.*, May 1955, pp. 341–350.

[27] See the comments of H. R. Bowen, *Am. Ec. Rev.*, May 1955, p. 354.

[28] See the discussion of these issues in B. M. Gross and J. P. Lewis, "The President's Economic Staff during the Truman Administration," *Am. Polit. Sci. Rev.*, March 1954, p. 116.

[29] *Ibid.*, p. 124.

[30] Gross and Lewis, *op. cit.*, pp. 124, 125.

1. The Council has a responsibility to explain to the Congress and to the public the general economic strategy of the President's program, especially as it relates to the objectives of the Employment Act. This is the same kind of responsibility that other executive agencies assume in regard to programs in their jurisdictions.

2. It is not appropriate or necessary for the Council to go into details of legislative proposals or of administrative actions which fall primarily in the domain of operating executive departments or agencies who can and do testify before the appropriate committees. Our concern is with the overall pattern of economic policy.

3. The program of the President is, of course, the outcome of a decision process in which advice, recommendations, and considerations of many kinds, from many sources, inside and outside the Executive, play a part. The professional economic advice of the Council is one element; it is not and should not be the sole consideration in the formulation of Presidential economic policy, or of congressional policy.

4. In congressional testimony and in other public statements, the council must protect its advisory relationship to the President. We assume that the committee does not expect the Council to indicate in what respects its advice has or has not been taken by the President, nor to what extent particular proposals, or omissions of proposals, reflect the advice of the Council.

5. Subject to the limits mentioned, members of the Council are glad to discuss to the best of their knowledge and ability as professional economists, the economic situation and problems of the country, and the possible alternative means of achieving the goals of the Employment Act and other commonly held economic objectives.

   In this undertaking the Council wishes to cooperate as fully as possible with the committee and the Congress in achieving a better understanding of our economic problems and approaches to their solution.

6. The Council is composed of professional economists, but economic policy, as the committee well knows, is not an exact science .... The Council is, and necessarily must be, in harmony with the general aims and direction of the President and his administration. A member of the Council who felt otherwise would resign. This general harmony is, of course, consistent with divergencies of views on specific issues.[31]

The position of the Heller Council is an attempt to face up to the problems confronting the members of the CEA in their multiple roles as professional economists, policy makers, presidential advisers, and advocates of the President's program. On the whole, the position of the Heller Council would seem to be realistic and reasonable. The primary function of the CEA is to provide and interpret technical economic analysis and advice, but it also has a responsibility in overall policy determination, and it must pass judgment on alternative policies, etc. It does seem reasonable that the Council members should explain the President's analysis and program to the public and to Congress, especially since the latter must, in the

[31] Testimony of W. W. Heller, JEC, *Jan. 1961 Ec. Rept. Pres.*, H, pp. 291–292.

final analysis, determine policy.[32] And as Gross and Lewis have argued, if a CEA member feels that honest, objective economic analysis is ignored by the President, or if he cannot closely enough reconcile his own policy judgments and values with those of the President, then he can hardly interpret the President's program adequately to the Congress, and he can hardly be effective as a presidential adviser. He then has only one choice— to resign.

Finally, the CEA is almost what the President makes it. He may give its role some lip service, but otherwise ignore it and permit others (personal friends or political cronies) to determine policy. Or he can pay attention to the advice of the Council, showing his respect for its analysis and suggestions by permitting it to participate in Cabinet meetings and other high-level discussions. The Council must rely on other executive departments for statistical data, and it has a responsibility to cooperate with them in planning, policy, and program development and in matters generally economic. If the President elects to ignore the Council, relegate it to the background, or otherwise give it only third-class status, then the rest of the Administration will do the same. The Council could not possibly operate effectively under these conditions.[33]

[32] See Alvin H. Hansen's interesting statement in G. Colm, ed., *The Employment Act: Past and Future*, pp. 92–97.

[33] See Neil H. Jacoby's discussion of his experience on the CEA and his idea of what role the CEA should play in *Can Prosperity Be Sustained?*, New York: Holt, 1956, pp. 53–59.

Literature on the CEA and its role is, to put it mildly, legion, especially during its earlier years. The usual periodical indexes will reveal a wealth of information.

PART II

Macroeconomic Theory
and Fiscal Policy

5

Income Theory (I): The Determinants
of Consumption, Saving, and Investment

Although all students nowadays are exposed to at least the most elementary ideas of national income analysis and income theory in their Principles courses, experience indicates that a review of basic concepts is not only called for but rewarding. This is our job in this and the following two chapters.

NATIONAL INCOME CONCEPTS

For the present the concepts we want to review are: the gross national product (GNP), national income (NI), personal income (PI), disposable income (DI), and net national product (NNP).

The Gross National Product

Our total production, the GNP, is not a difficult concept—it represents the total market value of the goods and services produced in our economy. The GNP is generally measured on a yearly basis, but the level at which it is running is also available on a quarterly basis. These goods and services are produced for and purchased by consumers, business, government, and foreigners. They consist mostly of finished goods and services, the exception being increases in inventories. That is, some products are produced in Year X (steel, for example) but not purchased by the potential user, and used in a final product. Therefore, if U.S. Steel has a net increase in its inventory of steel equivalent to $1 million in Year X, this amount is added into the value of the GNP. Similarly, consumer goods produced during the current period but not yet sold to consumers are included in the net increase in inventory. If we recall that the purpose of the GNP concept is to measure the value of our production, the logic for including this net increase in inventory becomes apparent: If we did not include this net increase in inventory, we would not have an accurate measure of our production. Similarly, if there is a decline in inventories, it is obvious that more steel was sold than produced and an appropriate deduction must be made.

In the preceding paragraph we showed how inventory adjustments were necessary to secure an accurate measure for GNP. In our computation of the GNP, however, we do not add up the value of every item produced in our economy. The example of the net increase in the value of inventory was a special case, for most of the steel produced each income period is used in other final products—automobiles, buildings, bridges, etc. That which was used in final products is already counted in the GNP.

Table 5-1. GNP Statement, 1963(2)^a (Billions of Dollars)

GNP = 579.6

(Goods and Services)

Purchased by (*Expenditures*):		*Purchase Price or Cost* (*Receipts*):	
Consumers	370.4	National income (factor cost)	474.6
Business (gross private		Capital consumption	
domestic investment)	80.7	(depreciation)	51.0
Government	123.8	Indirect business taxes	56.2
Net foreign balance	4.7	Statistical error	−2.2
	579.6		579.6

^{a} Second quarter, 1963. Some items estimated.

The value of the steel used in the production of your new automobile is included in the price of your new "machine." Therefore we attempt to avoid what economists call "double counting:" We do not count the value of steel as used twice.

The GNP then does not encompass all monetary transactions in the economy. A further example would be your purchase of a home in 1964 which was constructed in 1960. The home was not built in 1964 so its cost is not included in the value of the GNP. If, however, you purchased the home through a real estate agent, the value of his commission would be added into this year's (1964) GNP because he did provide a *service* during this period.

Who Buys the GNP? The GNP can be looked at in two ways—(1) who purchases it, and (2) its cost. The GNP is purchased by consumers, businessmen (in the form of gross private domestic investment), government, and foreigners (in the form of the net foreign balance). (See Table 5-1.)

Consumption expenditures are generally classified into (1) durable goods, (2) nondurable goods, and (3) services. *Gross private domestic investment* is classified into (1) producers' durable equipment (tools, machines, etc.), (2) construction (commercial buildings, plants, apartment buildings, private homes, etc.), and (3) net change in business inventories. Federal, state, and local governments purchase goods and services for (or of) schools, roads, banks, teachers, members of the armed services, etc. The *net foreign balance* is the difference between our exports and our imports.[1]

Receipts from the Sale of the GNP. The receipts from the sale of the GNP, or its cost, consist of three items: (1) national income, (2) capital depreciation, and (3) indirect business taxes. (See Table 5-1.) Why *national income* is a cost of producing the GNP is quite evident. We simply have to pay people to work to provide goods and services. NI, then, is income earned producing goods and services during the current productive period. It is further called "factor cost" for reasons which are again fairly self-evident. It is income going to the factors of production, although they appear in our national income accounts in a slightly different form than they generally appear in economics textbooks. (See Table 5-2.)

Table 5-2. The Components of National Income, 1963(2) (Billions of Dollars)

1. Wages, salary, and other labor income	338.7
2. Income of unincorporate businesses	50.6
3. Corporate profits	50.1
4. Rental income	12.0
5. Net interest	23.7
6. Statistical discrepancy	−2.5
Total	474.6

Item 1 is clearly labor income; 2 is a mixture of both labor income and return to capital; 3 is a return to capital; 4 is in practice a mixture of property income (a return to capital) and labor income (such things as rent from real property and royalties on oil, books, mines, etc., are included); and interest is a return to financial capital.

We see on the right-hand side of Table 5-1 an item called *capital consumption (depreciation)*. It is obvious that machines wear out or become obsolete and that this is a cost of production. Hence the businessman must make an allowance for these costs, and we must pay for them when we purchase goods in the market.

If we subtract from the GNP the allowance for capital depreciation, we have what is referred to as the *net national product*. NNP, then, is

---

[1] For an explanation of how it is computed see N. F. Keiser, *Introductory Economics*, New York: Wiley, 1961, pp. 192–193.

equivalent to the expenditures of consumers, business net investment, and government on our net product. While the NNP is an important concept for theoretical purposes, the manner in which it must be computed by the Department of Commerce creates many problems. (It is extremely difficult to arrive at accurate depreciation allowances, for instance.) Much use is made, therefore, of the gross private domestic investment (GPDI) and net private domestic investment (NPDI) concepts. We have already noted that GPDI consists of producers' durable equipment, construction, and net changes in inventories. NPDI is GPDI minus depreciation. This gives us some idea of the growth in our capital stock. As a measure of growth of capital stock, however, these concepts also present difficulties and a more accurate measure can be obtained by eliminating the value of inventory and private homes.

Indirect business taxes are paid by those who buy the GNP. Therefore they are considered to be a cost of producing it. The sales tax you pay, for example, is added on to the price of your purchase. It, however, does not go to a factor of production. Rather it is a source of income to government.

Personal Income

Although NI consists of income earned producing goods and services we do not receive all of it. If, for instance, the corporation in which you own stock decides not to pay out all its profits in dividends, you do not receive this part of NI. Nor do you receive what the corporation must pay in income taxes, or the amount of your income which you pay in social security taxes. On the other hand, you receive funds from other sources—that is, you have not earned these funds producing goods or providing services, and they are not a part of NI. The two main categories are transfer payments (such as veterans' payments, unemployment payments, etc.) and government interest. In Table 5-3 we can follow through the steps necessary to compute *personal income*.

Disposable Income

Personal Income consists of what we personally have a claim to but not what we can spend. We must deduct our personal taxes (mostly income taxes) before we can arrive at *disposable income*. The latter we may use for consumption or savings as we please. (See Table 5-3.)

The Circular Flow

Receipts from the sale of the GNP must be equal to expenditures on the GNP. Conceptually this must be so, for a dollar spent is received by someone even though, through the collection of statistics on the GNP, we must allow for statistical discrepancies. It is important to note that the level of the GNP, the production of goods and services, does not automatically occur at the same level at which we shall have full employment. A cursory examination of Table 5-1 will show that the activities of most of us appear on both sides of the T-account. That is, we produce goods and services for which we secure some of NI and then we turn

Table 5-3. Personal and Disposable Income for 1963(2)   (Billions of Dollars)

National Income		474.6
Less:		
Undistributed profits	9.2	
Corporate income taxes	24.2	
Social security taxes	26.0	
	59.4	59.4
Equals		415.2
Plus:		
Transfer payments	36.7	
Government interest	8.0	
	44.7	44.7
Personal Income		459.9
Less:		
Personal taxes		59.9
Disposable Income, which is used for		400.0
Consumption		370.4
Personal savings		29.6

around and spend that income on consumption goods. The same is true of businessmen. They receive income from corporate profits (and also borrow) for their expenditures on investment goods. And the government taxes the NI (both corporate and personal incomes), the sale of goods (excises, sales taxes, customs, etc.), and borrows as sources of its funds for expenditures. We have then a circular flow in which we earn (and borrow) and spend. If, from our current income, we (consumers, business, etc.) decide to spend less than we have received, the size of the GNP declines. If we spend more than we have received the size of the GNP increases, unless, of course, we have full employment of labor and capital, in which case we shall have inflation. (The monetary value of the GNP will increase, but the real production of goods and services will not.)

CONSUMPTION, SAVING, AND INVESTMENT

Consumption: Concepts and Determinants

The Average and Marginal Propensities to Consume. The relationships between consumption and income is expressed as the propensity to consume (or consumption ratio or consumption function). The average propensity to consume can be computed for individuals or for all consumers; i.e., on an individual or aggregate basis. If total disposable income is $250 billion and consumption is $225 billion, the aggregate average propensity to consume is

$$\text{APC} = \frac{\text{Consumption}}{\text{DI}} = \frac{225}{250} = 0.90$$

The marginal propensity to consume shows the relationship between an increase or decrease in DI and the subsequent increase or decrease in consumption. It, too, can be computed for either the individual or for all of society, as follows:

$$\text{MPC} = \frac{\text{change in consumption}}{\text{change in DI}}$$

The APC and the MPC then are *percentage* relationships. We might expect that a high income person would generally have a lower APC than a lower income person. Assume that the person with a $50,000 income spends $40,000 for consumption, and the $5,000 family man spends $4,900. Their respective APC's then are 80 and 98 percent. The high income person spends a lot more in absolute dollars but less as a percentage.

The average (or marginal) propensity to save is the complement of the APC (or MPC). Where the APC is 90 percent, the APS is 10 percent.

Determinants of Consumption. The major factor that determines the level of consumption is disposable income. This is readily illustrated in Table 5-4. We do not mean that there may not be autonomous shifts in consumption (that is, changes in consumption not related to changes in disposable income), for there may well be. But generally speaking, when people have the money they will spend it. (The causal relationship works in the other direction also, but to what extent it is not known. In other words, consumption depends on income, but income is also high because consumption is high. Some significance must be attached to the fact that the largest type of spending is on consumption goods.)

Other factors may and do affect the level of consumption—expected changes in prices, expected changes in income, the volume of liquid assets

Table 5-4. Disposable Income, Consumption, and Saving (1929-1963, Selected Years)

	1	2	3	4	5
	Disposable Income	Consumption	Personal Saving	Percent of Disposable Income Spent (Propensity to Consume)	Percent of Disposable Income Saved (Propensity to Save)
1929	83.1	78.9	4.2	95	5
1931	63.8	61.3	2.5	96	4
1933	45.7	46.3	−0.6	101	−1
1935	58.3	56.3	2.0	97	3
1937	71.0	67.3	3.7	95	5
1939	70.4	67.5	2.9	96	4
1941	93.0	81.9	11.1	88	12
1943	133.5	100.5	33.0	75	25
1945	150.4	121.7	28.7	81	19
1947	169.0	165.0	4.0	92	8
1949	188.2	180.6	7.6	96	4
1951	226.1	208.4	17.7	92	8
1953	250.4	230.6	19.8	92	8
1955	274.5	256.9	17.5	94	6
1957	307.9	284.8	23.1	92	8
1959	334.7	311.6	23.1	93	7
1961	364.4	336.8	27.6	92	8
1963(3)	404.4	374.3	30.1	93	7

Source: Data for columns 1 and 3 from *Surv. Current Bus.*, July 1959 and May 1960; OBE, USDC, *Business Statistics* (1955 biennial edition), p. 4; and *Economic Indicators*, Oct. 1963, p.1. Columns 2, 4, and 5 were calculated from these data.

consumers have, rationing, the availability of consumer credit, the distribution of income, past financial obligations, and demographic factors (size of family, area of residence—urban or rural, life cycle, etc.).

One of the difficulties encountered in fiscal policy is caused by inadequate knowledge of the MPC and how it may vary among income groups. The argument over which group has the highest MPC—low, middle, or higher income group—has particular relevance to tax cuts aimed at offsetting a recession. Since this question is primarily of a short-run nature, it is different from that which argues that, for purposes of long-run growth, taxes should be raised on those with a high MPC and lowered on those who save high percentages of their income so that investment will be stimulated. These problems are discussed in greater detail in subsequent chapters.

It is difficult to overstress the significance of the Keynesian consumption function for modern income analysis. Keynes argued that (real) consumption expenditures are a "fairly stable function"[2] of real income. He further argued that men will tend, "as a rule and on the average, to increase their consumption as their income increases, but not by as much as the increase in their income," "especially . . . where we have short periods in view."[3] In other words, the primary determinant of consumption is income, the MPC is less than one, and it may decline in the short run. Over the long run, as society becomes wealthier, the APC may decline. This has not happened, however. In a few brief paragraphs, which can hardly do justice to the volumes of research done on the consumption function, we shall attempt to summarize some of the current knowledge of the consumption function.

Studies of the aggregate consumption function for the 1930's and the postwar period do show (1) a very close and stable relationship between consumption and disposable income on a *long-run* basis, (2) the APC has been fairly constant, averaging (over several years, however) between 85 and 90 percent. On the other hand, it has been found that the MPC is lower than the APC, and that the *short-run* consumption function was one in which the APC declined when income increased. How then do we reconcile this with a relatively constant long-run APC?

Many students of the consumption function have attempted to show that the consumption function can be regarded as a schedule showing the relationship between income and consumption at a given period of time. Typically, we have a short-run consumption function like one of those shown in Figure 5-1. The flatter consumption functions are short run and cover a period, say, of 4 to 5 or 6 years. We have a series of them; each gives consumption at given income levels. Over a period of time, however, these short-run consumption functions have shifted upward as the economy has grown, so that we arrive at a long-run consumption function as shown by line C. The average income in period aa was Y_a and average consumption was C_a, and similarly for each short-run consumption function. Connecting points C_a, C_b, C_c, and C_d gives us line C, the long-run consumption function. Estimates of the short-run MPC have varied considerably. Gardner Ackley has calculated the functions covering periods of 4 to 6 years at .50 to .70.[4] For short-run

---

[2] See John Maynard Keynes, *The General Theory of Employment, Interest and Money*, New York: Harcourt, Brace, 1936, p. 95.

[3] *Ibid.*, p. 96.

[4] G. Ackley, *Macroeconomic Theory*, New York: Macmillan, 1961, pp. 258–265.

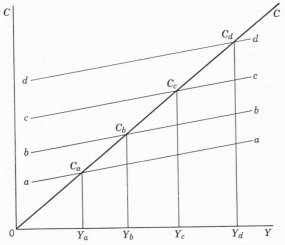

Figure 5-1. Short- and long-run consumption functions.

prediction Klein and Goldberger use .55 of employee compensation.[5] Estimates of the MPC for longer periods have also varied. Ackley computed that for 1946–1957 at .81, 1929–1941 at .73, and 1929–1940 at .79.[6] Ferber's estimates for 1929–1940 range generally from .80 to .85.[7] For an even longer period (1929–1940 and 1946–1958 combined) Ackley found the MPC to be .86.[8]

Econometric studies have produced equations that are very accurate in predicting the level of consumption on a longer-run basis, but they cannot accurately predict consumption on a very short-run basis; i.e., on a quarterly basis. From quarter to quarter the chances are just as great that consumption and income may move in opposite directions as in the same direction. Under these circumstances, then, more than income data are needed to be able to predict consumption. Under these circumstances a change in C is just as likely to change Y as vice versa. If, however, any change in income persists over a period of several quarters, then the income effect generally becomes quite clear again.

Saving

One of the more important ideas discussed in every elementary course in economics is that saving and investment are two different processes

[5] L. Klein and A. Goldberger, *An Econometric Model of the United States, 1929–1952,* Amsterdam: North Holland, 1955, pp. 8, 63–64, 90.

[6] Ackley, *op. cit.,* p. 252.

[7] R. Ferber, *A Study of Aggregate Consumption Functions,* New York: NBER, 1953, p. 47. See also Ferber's summary of earlier studies, pp. 8–9.

[8] Ackley, *op. cit.,* p. 248.

which, to a very significant degree, are carried out by two different groups in our society. Saving in our society appears in the form of *personal saving* (DI not spent for consumption), undistributed corporate profits, and business depreciation reserves.[9] For what reasons do people accumulate savings? The answer is fairly clear—for retirement, to buy a house, etc., for periods of unemployment, for insurance, for future income, and the like. It should be noted that in none of these instances does investment (in capital goods or inventories) occur.[10] This is a most important point—that personal saving is generally unrelated to investment; unrelated in the sense that the decisions to save and invest are separate and distinct decisions, and are made by different people. (The only exception is the individual proprietor or the partnership.) The significance of this for employment policy is that just because income is saved it does not automatically follow that it will be invested. The businessmen who do the investing then have to borrow these savings from those who have saved (or an equivalent amount from others) or the GNP will decline.

In the case of corporate depreciation reserves and undistributed profits there is a direct connection between saving and investment. Again, however, just because income is saved in these forms does not mean that it will be invested—even when both acts are carried out by the same party. The corporation will not replace machines, let alone add to them, in the face of a declining demand.

Investment: Short-Run and Long-Run Determinants

Investment is the most volatile factor on the expenditure side of our GNP statement. It can fluctuate widely, from very high to very low (even negative) levels. It has tended to lead both our booms and our declines. It has caused both inflations and deflations (as other forces have, too). But it is the factor about whose behavior we can write with the least confidence. Investment is important not only because of its volatility, but also because it consists of a sizable portion of aggregate demand, and because it is an important medium through which growth occurs.

In one important sense investment is limited by (1) the amount and kinds of goods that we produce, and (2) the amount of saving in the

[9] Most macroeconomic texts have extensive discussions of the factors influencing consumption. See, in particular, those of Joseph McKenna, Barry Siegel, Gardner Ackley, Wallace Peterson, and Dernberg and McDougall. Ackley's is the most thorough.

We shall ignore, for the time being, government saving.

[10] Purchase of a newly constructed home by a consumer is a special case. Since it would be counted in the investment account we see some connection between saving and investment; but the act of saving from current income is still separate and distinct from that of the purchase of a home so many years later.

economy. A society that has few skills in producing machinery, for example, is limited in how much of its national product it can invest in machinery. Similarly, we are limited here by the capacity of our capital goods industries to produce machinery. Continuing point (2), if we assume full employment then we must cut back our production of consumer goods, which means that we must save more in order to produce more capital goods.

In some respects, at least, discussions of investment are among the most esoteric in economics. We shall attempt here to discuss briefly the factors most generally accepted as influencing investment. When output and sales are growing and business firms are operating at, or close to, capacity output, we can expect net investment to occur. If output levels off, we can expect the rate of net investment to slow down or stop. If the level of output declines, net investment will also decline, and we may even have disinvestment. Also important in this sequence of events is the rate of profits. Their role, however, is not singular, but generally is accompanied by pressures on capacity and a high level of demand. This is the general pattern we might expect investment to follow.[11] Many other factors, however, will influence the direction of investment. The level of investment may increase, for example, for reasons unrelated to the current or expected level of demand. Such autonomous influences may be innovations (new products, more efficient productive techniques, or other factors).

When a firm makes a decision to purchase a capital good it must evaluate many factors, which will in turn influence its chance of receiving a reasonable return on the investment. These factors include future demand for the products of the firm, its current capacity, the current capacity of the industry, the market position of the firm, the supply of internal funds (cash flow), the availability and the cost of external funds, and the possible impact of new products or new productive techniques. Not only is the current level of capacity (and its rate of use) of the firm important; so are its age and technological characteristics. Other considerations are profit expectations, returns from other possible investments, the degree of present and future competition, wage rates, and tax and fiscal policies.[12]

Most of the previously noted factors influencing the investment decision of the single firm apply to the aggregate level of investment in the economy. Aggregate demand, capacity, cash flow and the cost of external funds, technology and innovations, wage rates, fiscal policy, and competitive

---

[11] See the discussion of JEC, *Var. Private Invest.*, Pt. 1, p. 59.

[12] *Ibid.*, Pt. 1, pp. 60–66. See Eisner's comments on the empirical evidence in *ibid.*, Pt. 2, pp. 32–34.

conditions all have a special aggregative significance and influence on the level of aggregate investment.

As we have noted previously, the level of investment has important autonomous effects on the economy and on the GNP. Conversely, the demand for investment goods is influenced by the level of aggregate demand in the economy. There is a correlation, for instance, between fluctuations in investment and the GNP (and firm output). Further, profits and cash flow are also correlated with investment, cash flow having a higher correlation than profits but not as high as GNP. Econometric studies have indicated that capacity (and its rate of utilization), demand, cash flow, and expected profits are the most important determinants of investment.[13] (The first three, of course, are also related to expected profits.)

Two interesting and informative discussions of quantitative research and the determinants of investment appeared in the May 1963 issue of the *American Economic Review*. They were by Edwin Kuh[14] and Robert Eisner.[15] Kuh notes that the empirical studies indicate that (1) "capacity accelerator motivation is more important than profits or internal funds in explaining the cyclical path of investment although profits still have a significant, if secondary, role to play"; (2) the capacity accelerator is a prime determinant of investment when long-run data are examined, and when capacity pressures are extremely high in the short run; and (3) when the pressure on capacity is less intense, profits and depreciation (which are related to cash flow) are more important than the accelerator influence. Kuh further notes that quarterly econometric models give some indication that interest rates are statistically significant determinants of investment.

Eisner's article makes similar points. He notes that investment demand depends on the rate of change of output; that capital expenditures (for the large firms accounting for most investment) is not "much affected by the rate of total profits"; that profit maximization is consistent with the rate-of-change-of-output idea; and that expected profitability "may or may not relate to total profits—past, current, or future." He further relates investment to permanent and transitory changes in demand, maintaining that the acceleration principle works when investment is related to a change in demand which the businessman thinks is permanent,

[13] For a review of the econometric studies on investment see Eisner and R. H. Strotz, "Determinants of Business Investment," in *Impacts of Monetary Policy* (for the CED) to be published by Prentice-Hall.

[14] Kuh, "Theory and Institutions in the Study of Investment Behavior," *Am. Ec. Rev.*, May 1963, pp. 260–274.

[15] Eisner, "Investment: Fact and Theory," *Am. Ec. Rev.*, May 1963, pp. 237–246.

and that investment will be less if he feels the increase in demand is temporary.

The various major influences on investment are generally classified as long-run and short-run. We shall examine them briefly.

An important long-run influence on the level of investment has been technology, which we can discuss in terms of (1) new productive techniques and (2) new products. We are all familiar with the long history of new techniques of production, from the introduction of new tools and techniques in simple agricultural societies thousands of years ago to the present-day adoption of highly complex, automated machinery. The labor-saving and capital-saving characteristics of these new techniques and machines have served to lower costs. Assuming a reasonable degree of competition, their adoption by one producer means that the latter's competitors must also adopt them or forego profits and their respective shares of the market.

The second type of technological progress, the development of new products, has also accounted for a substantial portion of our investment. The 1920's constituted an interesting era in which we experienced the exploitation of many innovations—the automobile, appliances, the radio, and motion pictures. The production of these products requires not only large direct investments, but also large subsidiary investments. In the case of the automobile, look at the subsidiary investment in plants and machinery to produce steel, glass, roads, service stations, etc.

We should note two additional characteristics of innovations—they have not been introduced at the same rate of speed but rather have tended to come in "clusters," and they may be "autonomous," that is, not dependent on the current rate of output.

It is not clear why innovations have, in the past (perhaps the distant past),[16] tended to come in clusters, but some influences stand out rather obviously. Wars and the research undertaken on their behalf hasten development, refinement, and introduction of new techniques and new products. A new scientific breakthrough, as in electricity, may lead to the introduction of a host of new products. The exploitation of an innovation is also dependent on whether business conditions are good or poor and whether businessmen want to undertake the risks; the availability of financing; and the willingness of consumers to accept the new product. Further, the rate at which new ideas are developed is also influenced by the sums of money devoted to basis research. The late Professor Joseph Schumpeter argued that innovations come in clusters and cause the business cycle. There is some evidence now, though, that the business

[16] See J. Schmookler, "Invention, Innovation, and Business Cycles," in JEC, *Var. Private Invest.*, Pt. 2, pp. 45–55, especially p. 47.

cycle itself creates innovations rather than the reverse. Some firms may withhold new products until the market for their "old" products is saturated, or until the economy declines and they want to raise their sales. Further, even though these factors may have tended to bring innovations in clusters, we should note that the sums business is willing to devote to research are considerably influenced by their financial status and the level of the GNP.

Technological innovations developed independently of the current level of our GNP are referred to as "autonomous" or exogenous. Investment of this type is not a function of an increasing level of consumption, subject to the qualifications we have noted, but rather of technological advance.

A second long-run influence on investment is the rate of population growth. An expanding population, in a society which has the means and resources to produce them, means new homes, schools, utilities, roads, automobiles, furniture, and other consumer goods. Greater private and public investment is needed to produce these goods and services. Further, population growth provides an increase in the labor supply. Without this the return to capital may decline, for a shortage of labor may mean higher wages.

A third long-run factor is territorial expansion. With the expansion of the frontier in the American West, as with population growth, came great increases in public and private investment in buildings, transportation systems, etc.

The fourth and last technological factor is resource development. Although the rate of resource use is a function of the level of current output, the development of and means of using resources depend on our technological knowledge. We use oil, coal, uranium, nickel, etc., because our technological knowledge provides uses for them.

In addition to the long-run influences on investment, there are several factors generally classified as influencing investment decisions in the short run. If aggregate demand is high, firms are operating at something close to full capacity, and profits are high, then conditions are conducive to further investment. The optimistic attitudes created by these favorable conditions may be projected into the future, creating further inducements to investment. By the same token, depressed demand, low profits, and excess capacity tend to dampen incentives to invest.

Like favorable or unfavorable profit and capacity factors, business expectations are important. Even if, for example, the level of output is high and profits are high, businessmen may not permanently add to their stock of capital because they feel that the current level of output is temporary. Since they expect it to decline eventually they refrain from investing in expensive capital and instead put on extra shifts or use up their inventories. On the other hand, we have seen in our postwar recessions that investment has been fairly well maintained. This is because businessmen expected that the declines would be only temporary. If during the temporary decline interest costs are lower, as they generally are, there may be an additional inducement to add to the stock of capital.

The firm's degree of liquidity will also exert considerable influence on investment decisions. Given a situation in which there are, according to the businessman's calculations, profitable investment opportunities, the firm will undertake these projects if it has the funds or can borrow or sell stock. The specific factors affecting the liquidity of a firm are depreciation reserves, profit levels, retained earnings, and the availability and cost of capital funds. Depreciation allowances are established by the Internal Revenue Bureau. Profit levels, corporate income taxes, and retained earnings are interrelated. Profit levels are influenced by the overall level of aggregate demand, the demand for the specific product of the firm, the efficiency and resourcefulness of the firm, its research program, the extent of concentration in the industry, etc. The corporate income tax is the result of a political decision, and beyond this the amount so paid depends on the level of profits. Retained earnings depend on profits, taxes, and the dividend policy of the firm (and possible stockholder pressure).

As far as specific fiscal policies are concerned we see that changes in the corporate income tax and in depreciation allowances, since they influence cash flow, will likely influence the rate of investment. This statement, however, is based on the assumption that profitable investment opportunities exist that would not otherwise be undertaken. If excess capacity exists, then higher depreciation allowances, investment tax credits, and lower corporate income taxes may result in nothing more than a redistribution of income through a redistribution of tax burdens.

The role of interest costs in investment decisions has been hotly debated in recent years. Interest is only one of several factors in the investment decision. As such it must be taken into consideration when investment projects are undertaken, but we shall postpone our discussion of interest-rate policy until a later chapter.

INVESTMENT, THE MULTIPLIER, AND THE ACCELERATION PRINCIPLE

Investment Theory (The Marginal Efficiency of Capital, the Investment Demand Schedule, the Supply of Funds, and Interest Rates)

We have noted previously that investment is important because it constitutes a fairly high proportion of expenditure on our GNP, because it is so volatile and has tended to initiate upward and downward movements in the economy, and because it is the process by which we add to our stock of capital. We also noted that the primary determinant of the level of investment is the expectation of profit, and that profit expectations are influenced by many factors. Keynes attempted to express this idea in theoretical terms with the development of the concept of the marginal efficiency of capital. The reader will note that the MEC has two meanings: It is defined as the rate of return over cost, and also as the rate of discount which makes the present value of the returns expected from a capital asset equal to the asset's supply price. Both definitions should become clear in the succeeding discussion.

The Marginal Efficiency of Capital. Since capital equipment has a life of a period of years, its value to a businessman depends on (1) the expected stream of income it will produce over its life (the result of sales of its output—its physical productivity, and the price at which its output can be sold, which in turn depend on future demand and competitive conditions), and (2) the supply price of the capital asset. (Other costs are incurred in the operation of the asset—materials, labor, an allowance for uncertainty, etc., and these too must be subtracted from the income to be produced by the capital asset. Usually the stream-of-income idea is considered as a net figure; that is, operating expenses are previously deducted.) Thus, for a businessman to purchase a new capital asset the stream of income he expects to realize must be in excess of what the asset costs him. When the expected income stream is in excess of the capital costs, a profit can be anticipated. This excess is called the MEC or the rate of return over cost.[17] If, for example, a capital asset costs $60,000 and the annual return (after costs) is $6,000, then the rate of return over cost is 10 percent.

This technique for relating the yield to the price of capital is called the marginal efficiency of capital (MEC). We should note that the term marginal is used because we are considering only the rate of return on *additions* to our stock of capital. The present rate of return on existing capital may be much higher or lower than the rate of return on additions to the stock of capital. Further, we are interested in determining incentives to further investment and we must therefore differentiate between the returns on present and additional capital facilities.

Mathematical formulas are available for the computation of the

[17] An extensive discussion can be found in A. H. Hansen, *A Guide to Keynes*, New York: McGraw-Hill, 1953, Chapter 5. See also G. Ackley, *Macroeconomic Theory*, New York: Macmillan, 1961, pp. 460–466, and W. C. Peterson, *Income, Employment, and Economic Growth*, New York: Norton, 1961, pp. 203–207.

MEC.[18] In our example we assumed that a capital asset cost $60,000 and yielded an annual income (after operational costs) of $6,000, or 10 percent. This capital asset has an MEC of 10 percent. A firm could borrow the necessary $60,000 or use its own funds to purchase the asset. As long as the rate of interest is less than 10 percent it is worthwhile to purchase the asset. Of course, if the interest rate is 10 percent the business man would be indifferent, and if the rate is greater than 10 percent he should lend out his money.

In somewhat more technical language, and our second definition, the MEC is defined as "being equal to that rate of discount which would make the present value of . . . the returns expected from the capital asset during its life just equal to its supply price."[19] Since discounting is a source of confusion to many, perhaps a few additional remarks will clarify the situation. When you receive a loan from your bank the bank may deduct from the face value of the note the interest to be charged. If this procedure is followed and you secure a loan for a year for $1,000 at an interest rate of 5 percent, then you will receive from the bank only $952. The present value of this loan then is $952. We might say that your payment at the end of the year to the bank of $1,000, when discounted to its *present* value is $952. If someone were to purchase this asset (your note on which the loan was based) he would not pay more than $952 for it. If he did his rate of return would be less than 5 percent.

The process of discounting is sometimes clearer if one remembers that it is the reverse of compounding. If you make a loan of $1,000 at 5 percent, a year from now you would get back $1,000 plus $1,000 times .05, or $1050. This may be stated alternatively as $1,000 (1 + 0.05) = $1,050$.

By letting A represent the amount of your loan, A_1 the value of the loan at the end of one year, and i the rate of interest, we obtain

$$A_1 = A(1 + i)$$

This states that the amount you receive at the end of the year is equal to the amount loaned plus the loan times the rate of interest.

Now this equation can also be solved for A, or the amount of the original loan. This is then the present value of a given sum that you could receive in a year. We can receive A_1 in a year, and we want to know the present value of A_1. If we solve for A we obtain

$$A = \frac{A_1}{1 + i}$$

[18] See H. E. Stelson, *Mathematics of Finance*, Princeton: Van Nostrand, 1957, Chapter 4. For more on the compounding approach see T. F. Dernburg and D. M. McDougall, *Macroeconomics*, New York: McGraw-Hill, 1963, pp. 91–97.

[19] J. M. Keynes, *The General Theory of Employment, Interest and Money*, New York: Harcourt, Brace, 1936, p. 135.

The present value of a loan of $1,000 for a year at 5 percent interest is computed as follows

$$A = \frac{1,050}{1 + 0.05} = \$1,000$$

Let us now assume that we have a capital asset that will yield an annual income of $1,000 for 3 years, and we want to determine its *present value*. The formula for discounting is

$$V(\text{present value}) = \frac{R_1(\text{expected income})}{1 + i(\text{current rate of interest})}$$
$$+ \frac{R_2}{(1 + i)^2} + \cdots + \frac{R_n}{(1 + i)^n}$$

R_1 and R_2 stand for the expected income in dollar amounts for years 1 and 2, and R_n for n years (future years). In the denominator, the powers of 1, 2, and n represent the years. Let us assume that the discount (interest) rate which the bank requires is 5 percent and substitute our known values into the discount formula:

$$V = \frac{\$1,000}{(1 + 0.05)} + \frac{\$1,000}{(1 + 0.05)^2} + \frac{\$1,000}{(1 + 0.05)^3}$$
$$V = \$952 + \$909 + \$862 = \$2,723$$

Present value then is $2,723. Or $2,723 compounded at 5 percent will grow to $3,000 in 3 years, and no one would pay more than $2,723 for this asset today.

We see from this that the longer the life of an asset (with a constant expected stream of income) the less its present value. This is as we might expect; if the bank lends you $1,000 for a 3-year period at 5 percent, then in order to secure $1,000 3 years from now it would give you only $862. If your note was for $1,000 for 1 year it would give you $952. The difference in the two loans is that $862 compounded for 3 years comes out to $1,000. Similarly with a capital asset—the longer the life the less the present value, given the income expected.

We next want to examine the supply or purchase price of the asset. This can be done with the proper substitutions in the formula as follows:

$$C(\text{cost}) = \frac{R_1(\text{expected income})}{1 + r(\text{MEC})} + \frac{R_2}{(1 + r)^2} + \cdots + \frac{R_n}{(1 + r)^n}$$

In this formula we know the values of C (cost) and R (expected annual income) and we want to compute r. (Expected returns, R, are the same in both equations.) *The MEC, or r, is the value that will make the present value of the expected stream of income* $(R_1 + R_2 + \cdots)$ *equal to C.* We are discounting the expected stream of income to make its value equal to C. What value of r will do this? When the MEC (the rate of return) has a value greater than that of i (the current rate of interest), then we would expect the firm to invest, and vice versa. This could occur, for example, if C were less than V. We can state, then, that investment will be forthcoming when the cost of the asset is less than its present value, or when i is less than r. Under the conditions given here investment will occur as long as r, the MEC, is greater than the current rate of interest, and we would expect investment to continue up to the point at which $r = i$, which also is the point at which $V = C$.

Assume that the supply price is equal to the present value $(V = C)$ or $2,723. If this is the case, then obviously $r = i$ (as noted), because R (expected income) is the same in both formulas. Assume now that C does not equal V but rather has a value of $2,500. In this case r would have to be greater than i (5 percent) because in the formula it would be necessary to divide a larger figure into R (which is the same in both equations) to get our lower figure of $2,500 rather than $2,723. This would be a good investment because $r > i$ and $V > C$. Finally, assume that $C = \$3,000$. Here r must be less than i in the formula in order to get a higher value of $3,000. This is not a good investment because $i > r$ and $C > V$.

The MEC Schedule. All other things given (technology, competition, consumer tastes, etc.) we can construct an MEC schedule which shows that *additional* investment results in a lower MEC. The MEC schedule in Figure 5-2 slopes downward and to the right. We see from this that there are, for the whole economy, many investment projects that will yield a high MEC, more that would yield a lower MEC, and still more that would

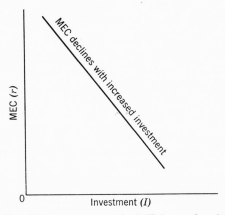

Figure 5-2. The aggregate marginal efficiency of capital schedule.

yield a still lower MEC. Or, to state the idea somewhat differently, we see that greater amounts of investment will reduce the rate of return or MEC. This is to be expected since greater investment will result in greater capital, which may result in diminishing productivity, greater output which must be sold at lower prices, and possible increases in the cost of capital as more capital is produced.

Before leaving this topic we should carefully note that at the base of computations of present value and the MEC is the *expected* stream of income. In other words, the MEC schedule is constructed on knowledge of factors which "is usually very slight and often negligible."[20] We should expect the MEC schedule then to be quite unstable and subject to shifts brought about by changes in the expectations of businessmen.

The Investment Demand Schedule. Figure 5-3 illustrates an aggregate investment demand function. It shows the relationship between the rate of interest and investment. In Figure 5-3 assume that the rate of interest is i_1. We see that investment expenditure will increase to point I_1. The reason is fairly obvious. To the left of point I_1 there exist investment projects with a rate of return which is above the given rate of interest. To the right of point I_1 the rate of return is below the rate of interest. Therefore the level of investment is I_1. If the rate of interest is raised, then investment will stop before it gets to I_1; if the rate of interest is lowered, then investment will increase beyond point I_1.

We could, in Figure 5-3, depict a shift in the investment demand schedule by drawing a line parallel to that in the figure. If the line were drawn to the right of the present line we would have an increase in investment, because at each MEC there would be a larger number of profitable investment projects. Similarly, if we drew a line parallel and to the left

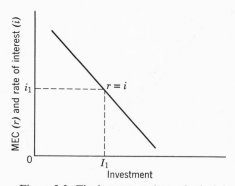

Figure 5-3. The investment demand schedule.

[20] *Ibid.*, p. 149.

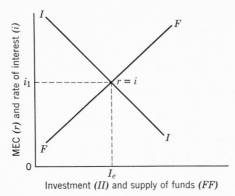

Figure 5-4. Equilibrium between investment and the supply of funds.

of that in Figure 5-3, there would be a decline in investment, because there would be fewer profitable investment opportunities at each MEC.

The Investment Schedule and the Supply of Funds. Figure 5-4 is the same as Figure 5-3 except that we have added a schedule for the supply of funds. We assume here that the supply of funds available for investment purposes increases as the rate of interest increases. This means that additional funds are forthcoming for additional investment only at increasingly higher interest rates. (This can be seen by going from zero investment to the right, and from zero funds to the right on the chart. As investment increases more funds are needed to finance it, but as the supply of funds increases the interest rate, measured on the vertical axis, increases.) Just as factors other than interest, which we have previously noted, affect investment, so they affect the supply of funds and the going rate of interest. Qualifications will be necessary at a later point.

Returning to Figure 5-4 we see that the rate of interest is set at the point of intersection of the two curves. We see also that businessmen will increase their investment expenditures to the point at which the two curves are in a position of equilibrium, or to the point at which the MEC is equal to i (the rate of interest). Again investment expenditures of less than I_e leave r (MEC) above i, and investment expenditures above I_e place i above r, an unprofitable position.

The dashed line in Figure 5-5 shows what can happen if we increase the supply of funds available for investment. In this case the FF curve shifts to the right (becoming $F'F'$), the rate of interest is lowered, and investment will be increased. The demand for funds for investment and the supply of funds for investment come into a new position of equilibrium at I_e'.

Investment and Interest Rates. In our analysis thus far we have assumed that investment was sensitive to the rate of interest. We have assumed that

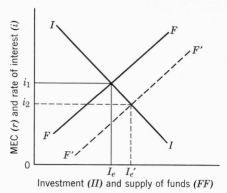

Investment *(II)* and supply of funds *(FF)*

Figure 5-5. An increase in the supply of funds available for investment.

simply by lowering the rate of interest we could increase the level of investment. But what if the investment demand schedule is *not* interest-elastic? If the current level of investment is below that which is necessary to attain full employment in the economy, then an increase in the supply of money by the monetary authorities will lower the interest rate and increase investment, but not enough to bring about full employment.

In Figure 5-6 we see that an increase in the supply of funds to $F'F'$ results in a lower rate of interest and an increase in investment from point I_1 to point I_f, the full employment level of investment. With an

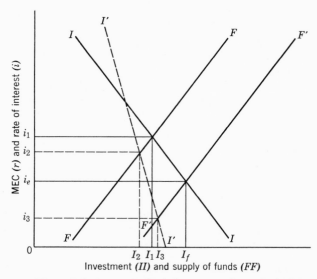

Investment *(II)* and supply of funds *(FF)*

Figure 5-6. A more inelastic investment demand schedule.

investment demand schedule of $I'I'$ an increase in the supply of funds from FF to $F'F'$ moves investment from point I_2 to I_3, and the interest rate is lowered from i_2 to i_3. It is true that there has been an increase in investment, but with an investment demand schedule like $I'I'$ it is impossible to increase the supply of funds sufficiently to bring investment to the full employment point.

We have noted previously that factors other than the rate of interest affect investment. It follows, then, that in some types of investment the rate of interest may not be very important in determining the level of investment. In recent years some empirical studies have noted that businessmen do not consider interest as important as economists had thought they did. Economists generally agree that the rate of interest is more significant for long-term investments, since in these cases the interest cost will be a much higher proportion of the purchase price of the capital asset. [Compare the difference in interest costs on an investment for (1) 3 years and (2) 25 years. Compare also the impact of a 1 percent change in the interest rate on these two investments.] It is for these reasons that it is argued that interest rate changes will affect residential, business, state, and local construction. But for other types of investment other factors assume an importance which is equal to or greater than interest rate changes. The growth of an industry, profit levels (if they are high a firm can afford to pay high interest), the availability of funds, competitive conditions, stylistic changes, etc., are often of greater importance. If other costs are very high, interest costs assume a very minor role. Many firms attempt to recover the cost of their capital equipment in a very short period of time, say 5 years. To the extent that they do this interest becomes a small part of total cost. Therefore changes in the interest rate become less important. On the other hand, interest charges above a certain level may rapidly reduce investment. Today, economists argue pretty much in terms of an investment demand schedule similar to that depicted in Figure 5-7. Below some rate, say 8 to 10 per cent, interest rate changes may not greatly affect investment. Above that level, however, the effect may be substantial.[21]

The Multiplier

The multiplier shows the relation between changes in investment and changes in income. We have previously stated that investment tends to initiate upward and downward movements in the economy. This is because of the amplified effect which changes in investment have on income. Let us assume, as in Table 5-5, that we have $10,000 of investment

---

[21] See A. H. Hansen, *Business Cycles and National Income*, New York: Norton, 1951, pp. 133–138.

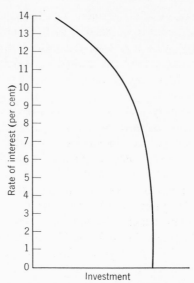

Figure 5-7. A more realistic investment demand schedule?

Table 5-5. The Multiplier Effects of $10,000 of Investment Spending (MPC = 75 Percent for All Parties)

Period	Income	Consumption	Saving
1	$10,000	$7,500	$2,500
2	7,500	5,625	1,875
3	5,625	4,218	1,407
4	4,218	3,163	1,055
5	3,163	2,372	791
6	2,372	1,779	593
7	1,779	1,334	445
8	1,334	1,000	334
9	1,000	750	250
10	750	562	188
11	562	396	166
12	396	297	99
13	297	223	74
.	.	.	.
.	.	.	.
.	.	.	.
Total	$40,000	$30,000	$10,000

expenditure. We further assume that all income recipients in our example have marginal propensities to consume of 75 percent. In period 1, then, these people receive $10,000, of which they spend 75 percent or $7,500, and save 25 percent or $2,500. Their expenditures become income to a second group which in turn spends and saves 75 and 25 percent, respectively. This process continues until total income from this initial investment expenditure of $10,000 is $40,000. The multiplier thus is 4. With a higher MPC the income effect and the multiplier would have been greater and vice versa. The formula for computing the multiplier is

$$k = \frac{1}{1 - \text{MPC}}$$

Although in this instance we have used an investment multiplier, we could have also used a multiplier that resulted from government expenditure. The multiplier is a useful concept in income analysis, although it is extremely difficult to predict its exact role. We do not all have the same MPC as we assumed in our example. Further, the MPC may vary from period to period as other conditions vary. In addition, it may not go into operation until there has been some lag.[22] Finally, for a permanent increase in income to occur there must be a permanent increase in investment (or other source of demand).

The Acceleration Principle

We have noted previously that one factor which affects investment demand is the level of current output—investment induced by changes in consumption and income. This leads us to the acceleration principle, which shows the relation between investment and the rate of change of current output. If a firm is operating at full capacity—no more shifts or no additional overtime is possible—then increases in the demand for its product will result in a magnified demand for capital goods. If, for instance, it takes $3 of capital goods to produce $1 of consumer goods, then under full capacity the increase in the demand for the firm's product will result in the firm's spending a greater amount on capital goods. The greater the increase in demand, the greater the induced investment.

This has some rather significant implications for both investment and employment in the economy. As long as demand is increasing at the same rate we can maintain employment in the capital goods industries, because we need capital equipment for both expansion and replacement. However, as soon as demand (and output) level off (cease to increase), we cease needing net investment. Investment then is only for replacement, it is

[22] See Table 16-5 for a hypothetical example of the multiplier effects of a tax cut.

lower, and employment in the capital goods industries is reduced. This is true even though the firm is still producing at a very high level. Similarly, it can be true for the economy as a whole; even though we are producing at a very high level, failure to continue to expand puts people out of jobs.

These points are illustrated in Table 5-6. We assume here that the capital-output ratio is 3/1 (that is, it takes $3 worth of capital to produce $1 in output), and that annual replacement costs are $30,000. In period 1 the firm can handle the demand for its product with its present supply of capital. Investment expenditures, therefore, are for replacement only. In period 2 the demand for the firm's output increases by 20 percent or

Table 5-6. The Acceleration Principle (in Thousands of Dollars)

Period	Output	Capital (Machines)	Additional Machines Required (New Investment)	Replacement (Depreciation)	Total Capital Expenditures (Gross Investment)
1	100	300	0	30	30
2	120	360	60	30	90
3	132	396	36	30	66
4	132	396	0	30	30
5	122	366	0	0	0

$20,000. The necessary investment for this period is then $90,000 ($30,000 for replacement and $60,000 to provide for the increased output). It is interesting to note that a 20 percent increase in the demand for the firm's output resulted in a 200 percent increase in additional capital expenditures. In period 3 the increase in demand (output) is 10 percent. This is still an increase in demand, but the declining rate of increase in demand (or the declining rate of change in output) results in a lower level of gross investment than in the previous period. This is true, and we have reduced employment in the capital goods industries, despite the fact that final output is still increasing. Next, look what happens in period 4, when output levels off at $132,000, which in itself is about 30 percent above the original level. Expenditures on capital equipment are cut to *less than half* of what they were in period 3—when output (demand) has merely leveled off. And finally, look at what happens when output declines somewhat, but not to its original lower level. Here we have enough machines (because of capital accumulation of previous periods) so that it is not even necessary to replace the machines that wear out. All this, again, points to the very interesting fact that as soon as the rate of change of output levels off or declines, investment in capital goods will decline even though output is still climbing.

We have assumed in our example that we were starting from a position of full capacity operation. If the firm is operating at less than full capacity an increase in output will not result in magnified increases in the demand for capital goods. In this case the firm can put on extra shifts or work its employees overtime. We also assumed that the capital-output ratio was constant, and that businessmen accepted the increase in output as permanent and invested accordingly. The relaxation of these assumptions weakens the acceleration principle.

The acceleration principle is still generally regarded as an unproved theory. However, it does contain a logical idea and most economists probably feel that it does offer some explanation for investment behavior.[23] It, along with the multiplier principle, show how changes in the economy can become cumulative and work on each other. The increase in investment will result in higher income which results in higher consumption which results in higher investment, and so on. Of course it can also work in the reverse. Naturally, the impact will depend on the values of the MPC and the capital-output ratio. When both have high values the cumulative effect will be greater.[24] Furthermore, models can be constructed using both the multiplifier and accelerator showing how their interaction can create self-generating cyclical movements in income.

[23] Eisner claims that failure to verify it is often due to the "failure to formulate that principle appropriately." "Investment: Fact and Theory," *op. cit.*, p. 237. Modified capacity accelerator models are widely used in econometric studies.

[24] See Table 16-6 for a hypothetical example of the multiplier-accelerator effects of a tax cut.

6

Income Theory (II): The Level of Income, Government, and Price Levels

In this chapter we want to bring together the various aspects of consumption and investment that determine the level of aggregate demand in our economy. In addition, we shall introduce the government into our theoretical framework. Finally, we shall examine some output-price relationships.

EQUILIBRIUM INCOME AND PRODUCT

The Total Demand Approach

The size of the national income in our economy depends on the expenditures of consumers, business for investment, the government, and the net foreign balance. At this point we consider only consumption and investment expenditures. We can represent our basic idea with the equation $Y = C + I$, in which Y represents income, C consumption, and I investment. For the time being let us assume that I is autonomous—that is, not dependent on the level of income. Further, let us assume a constant MPC—that each successive increase in disposable income results in the same percentage being spent on consumption. We also assume (1) that at some point total consumption will equal disposable income—that is, consumers break even; and (2) that at very low levels of income consumption will exceed disposable income. The last two assumptions are not unrealistic, as the actual figures for consumption in the United States show (see Table 5-4).

We have then a consumption function like that depicted in Figure 6-1. (Its equation is $C = a + cY = 50 + 0.75Y$.) On the horizontal axis we have national product and national income; on the vertical axis we have the total demand for goods and services, or $C + I$. The 45° line on

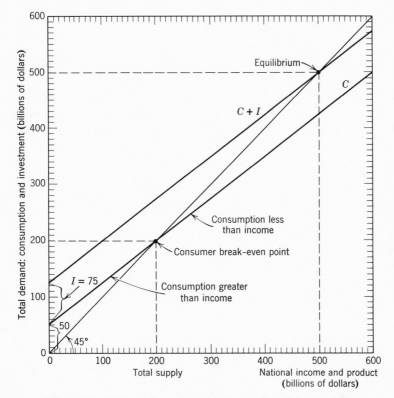

Figure 6-1. The total demand approach to income determination.

the chart cuts the 90° angle in half. This means that at any point on the 45° line total demand will equal total supply, or that we will have an equilibrium. If we look at consumption alone, we see that at $200 billion consumers break even. That is, the amount they receive as income is equal to the amount they spend. On our chart we see that the C line cuts the 45° line at this point and that the distances from this point to the horizontal and vertical axes are equal. If we select an income level, say $400 billion, where the C line lies below the 45° line, we see that we have saving of $50 billion, the vertical difference between consumption and the 45° line.

The $C + I$ line represents total consumption and investment expenditures. We note that the $C + I$ line is parallel to the C line, which means that investment is a constant $75 billion. This agrees with our assumption that I is autonomous and not dependent on the level of income.

The point at which the $C + I$ line crosses the 45° line is our equilibrium position. This is the point at which the distances to both the vertical and horizontal axes are equal—the point at which total supply is equal to total demand.

To point out the significance of this equilibrium we can ask two questions. What would happen if income were $400 billion? We know that investment is $75 billion, but what is consumption? Reading up the chart from the $400 billion income level we see that C is $350. Therefore $C + I$ comes to $425 billion. Total demand for goods and services is $425 billion and income and production are only $400 billion. Since businessmen are receiving $425 billion, they are selling $25 billion worth of goods more than they are producing. They will increase production and therefore employment and income will rise. This process continues until the equilibrium level of production is reached—that level at which the total demand for goods is equal to the total supply.

Table 6-1. The Equilibrium Position of Income and Employment

1	2	3	4	5	6	7
National Product (Total Supply) and National Income	Consumption	Saving	Investment	Total Demand $(C + I)$ and Amount Received by Business $(2 + 4)$	Business Surplus $(+)$ or Deficit $(-)$	Direction of Income Output and Employment
600	500	100	75	575	-25	down
500	425	75	75	500	0	Equil.
400	350	50	75	425	$+25$	up

The second question we can ask is: What happens if income is at a level of $600 billion? Here again investment is $75 billion. Consumption is $500 billion for a total spending of only $575 billion. Since businessmen are paying out $600 billion in income but receiving only $575 billion, they are producing more than they are selling. They will then cut back production and employment, and income will fall back to the equilibrium level. In Table 6-1 we have worked out these conditions.

The Saving-Investment Approach

In Figure 6-2 we have plotted an investment and saving schedule, in which the latter is a function of the level of income. The saving line slopes upward and to the right; it increases as income increases. The investment line, however, is at a constant level of $75 billion, in line with our assumption of autonomous investment. We see again that at an income of $200 billion consumers just break even, at $300 billion income they save $25 billion, at $400 billion income they save $50 billion, and at $500 billion they save $75 billion. At this point we have an equilibrium between saving and investment. This again is the equilibrium position for the economy—the point at which the economy produces the amount of goods and services that consumers and investors are willing to purchase.

To follow through with the two questions we asked previously, what will happen if income is $600 billion? Saving is $100 billion and consumption therefore is $500 billion. Total demand is then $575 billion or less than income paid out and less than the value of the product produced. Businessmen then cut production, employment, and income until the equilibrium between saving and investment is reached at the $500 billion level. Just the opposite occurs if income is $400 billion. Total demand is $425 billion ($C = 350 billion and $I = 75 billion), or $25 billion more than business is producing and paying out. Businessmen then increase their production and employment to meet demand, and income and saving increase until an equilibrium is reached at $500 billion. We see then that adjustments in income will take place to bring saving and investment into a position of equality. At this point the amount that consumers want to save is equal to the amount that business wants to invest. If our economy were such that consumers spent exactly 100 percent of their income, no more or no less regardless of the level of income, we would always have a position of equilibrium. (The C line would be the 45° line, and there would be no investment.) But people do want to save, and this means that someone else has to spend to offset this saving and to maintain the level of income. It is only when business invests the same amount as consumers save that the deficiency in expenditure on the national product can be made up and the level of income maintained.

This might be stated in somewhat different terms. We might say that only when consumers and business plan to save and invest the same amounts are they able to realize their plans. We noted that if consumers want to save $100 billion at a $600 billion income level, investment plans are for only $75 billion, and there must be a downward revision in saving. This will come about by the fact that business will reduce production and

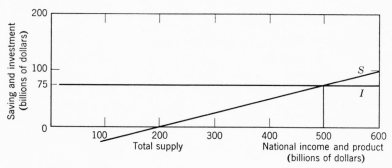

Figure 6-2. The saving-investment approach to income determination.

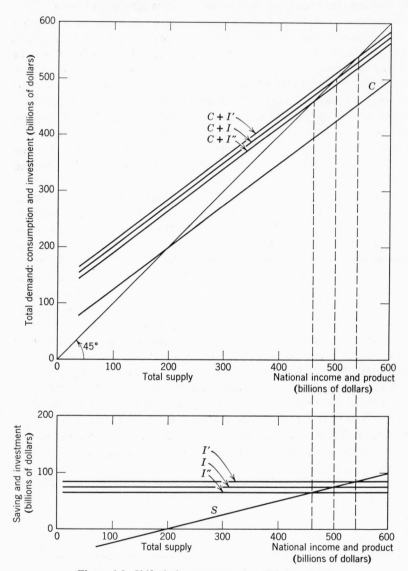

Figure 6-3. Shifts in investment and equilibrium changes.

employment and therefore income. With the decline in income consumers will be forced to save less. They will save less because they will not receive the $600 billion income. Just the opposite is true when saving plans are less than investment plans. Production, incomes, and saving all increase until the equilibrium is reached.

In summary then, when planned *I* and planned *S* are different, changes in production, employment, and income will occur and bring further changes in saving and investment. The direction of these changes will be toward a point of equality between *S* and *I*. *Planned* saving and *planned* investment can be different. But if they are different, changes in production, employment, and income will take place which force either consumers to alter their saving plans, or business to alter its investment plans (or both), until saving and investment are brought into equality. After the equilibrium point is reached, realized saving and investment will be equal.

Changes in the Equilibrium Level

As we all know, the equilibrium level of national income and product will change. These changes are due to either shifts in investment or shifts in consumption (saving). (Later we show how changes in government expenditures or revenues can also change the equilibrium level.) These shifts are analogous to shifts in either supply or demand schedules which result in changes in market price. In Figure 6-3 (bottom) we have an increase in autonomous investment of $10 billion, from *I* to *I'*. The new *I'* line intersects the *S* line now at an equilibrium level of $540 billion. In the top half of Figure 6-3 we see that the $85 billion of investment is depicted in the *C + I'* line, which also intersects the 45° line at an equilibrium level of $540 billion. We note in particular that the increase in investment was only $10 billion, but the increase in national income was $40 billion. The difference is accounted for by the multiplier, which in this case is 4.

The line *I''* (read *I* double primed) depicts a decline in investment of $10 billion. Again the multiplier works in reverse, bringing our equilibrium level of income and product down to $460 billion.

Figure 6-4 shows what happens when households decide to save more if at the same time business does not intend to invest more. The *S'* line reflects the decision to increase saving by $10 billion at each level of income. What happens to national income and product when people try to be more thrifty? It declines to about $420 billion, the new point of intersection of the *S'* and *I* schedules, and the new equilibrium for the economy. Here we have a situation in which planned saving and planned investment are out of kilter. Hence, changes in production must occur

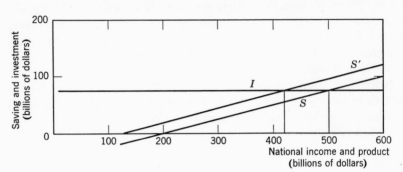

Figure 6-4. A shift in the saving schedule.

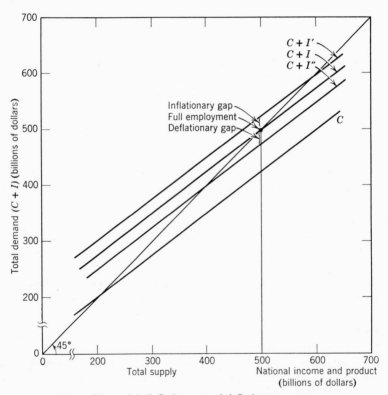

Figure 6-5. Inflationary and deflationary gaps.

for, at the original equilibrium ($500 billion), consumers suddenly decided to save more. Consumption became $415 billion and investment was $75 billion, for a total demand for goods and services of $490 billion while business was paying out $500 billion in income. It is not selling goods which it produced; hence the reduced production, employment, saving, and income. The moral of the story is that if we attempt to save too much, and business is not willing to match the increased saving with increased investment, we end up saving less because our incomes fall.

Inflationary and Deflationary Gaps

In Figure 6-5 let us assume that the $500 billion level of national income and product is again our equilibrium level, and that it is also our *full employment level*. (We should note, however, that just because total demand and total supply, or saving and investment, are in equilibrium does not mean that we shall also have full employment.) If we have an increase in investment of $25 billion we reach a new equilibrium at $600 billion. Since at the $500 billion level we have full employment of our human and productive resources, the new equilibrium can mean only that we have inflation—an increase in money income but not in real income.

Just the opposite occurs if we have a decrease in investment of $25 billion. Our equilibrium level now becomes $400 billion and we have lower production, employment, and income. Although we have demonstrated this idea with changes in investment we could also use changes in consumption, an upward or downward shift of which can cause either an inflationary or deflationary gap.

Induced Investment

Thus far we have assumed that investment was autonomous. Let us be more realistic and consider what happens to our analysis when we incorporate induced investment—increases in investment which are due to increases in the current level of income and production. In our discussion of the acceleration principle we noted that increasing sales of a firm's product will encourage it to expand its capital, and vice versa. Our investment-income schedule then probably somewhat resembles that shown in Figure 6-6. This more realistic approach to investment is incorporated into Figure 6-7. Here I_{a_1} represents our original autonomous investment of $75 billion, I_{a_2} autonomous investment of $100 billion, and I_{ai_1} and I_{ai_2} both autonomous and induced investment. We see that, without induced investment, the shift in autonomous investment from $75 billion to $100 billion caused national income and product to increase from $500 billion to $600 billion; but when we include induced investment

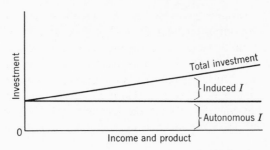

Figure 6-6. Induced and autonomous investment.

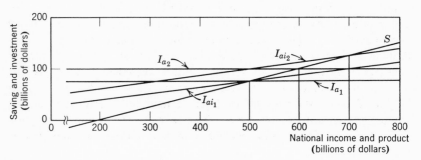

Figure 6-7. Induced and autonomous investment.

and show a shift from I_{ai_1} to I_{ai_2} the increase is from $500 billion to $700 billion. In the latter case the multiplier is greater. Again we should note that we are dealing here with hypothetical figures with the intent of showing tendencies in the economy.

GOVERNMENT AND INCOME DETERMINATION

We now complicate our model somewhat by adding the tax and expenditure activities of government. Just as changes in either consumption or investment will bring changes in output and income and create a new equilibrium level, changes in government expenditures and taxes will have the same result.

Change in Governmental Expenditure

In Figure 6-8 we assume that the government spends $20 billion and there are no taxes. This is represented by the $C + I + G$ line. (G is autonomous, as I is, and is added on to the $C + I$ line.) Our new equilibrium level is now $580 billion. This is the only point at which the three major types of expenditure ($C + I + G$) are equal to total supply. The same equilibrium level is shown in Figure 6-9. Here we add G to I and

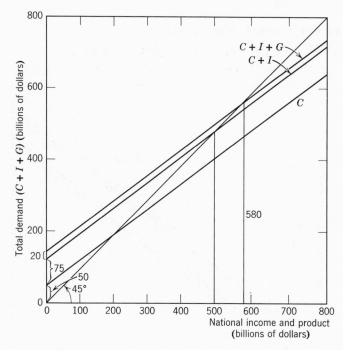

Figure 6-8. Government and income determination.

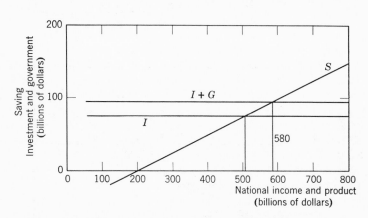

Figure 6-9. Government, investment, saving, and income determination.

find our new equilibrium at that point at which the S and $I + G$ schedules intersect. (I is still \$75 billion.)

Taxation and Income Determination

To discuss only changes in government expenditures is to show only one side of the coin. The other side is taxes, the effect of which will be to

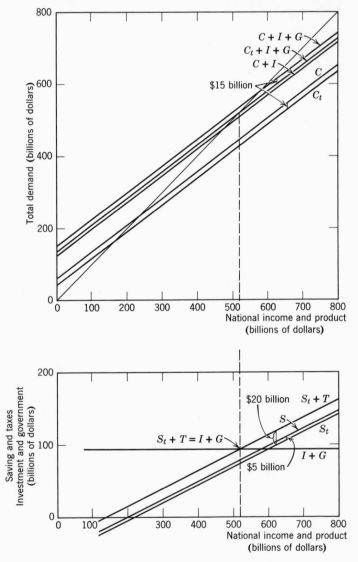

Figure 6-10. Taxes and income determination.

decrease both consumption and saving. If we impose taxes of $20 billion we can expect a $15 billion decrease in consumption and a $5 billion decrease in saving. We arrive at these figures through our knowledge of the MPC, which throughout our analysis has been assumed to be 75 percent. So if we have a drop in income of $20 billion we will consume of that figure $15 billion less and save $5 billion less.

Table 6-2. Income Determination with $I + G = S_t + T$

(Income)

Y	$I + G$	$S_t + T$
200	$(75 + 20) = 95$	$(-5 + 20) = 15$
400	95	$(45 + 20) = 65$
500	95	$(70 + 20) = 90$
520	95	$(75 + 20) = 95$
600	95	$(95 + 20) = 115$
800	95	$(145 + 20) = 165$

In Figure 6-10 (top) the impact of the imposition of a tax by the government is illustrated by the new line $C_t + I + G$, representing the impact of both government expenditure and taxes. The tax shifts the consumption function downward. At the $520 billion level of income consumption was about $440 billion. After the tax was imposed consumption dropped to about $425 billion. Consumption is now $15 billion less at all income levels. Our new equilibrium is $520 billion, which is higher than the original level of $500 billion despite the fact that both the tax and expenditure increases were $20 billion. In Figure 6-10 (bottom) we show that saving is reduced from the original S line by $5 billion (because of the tax) to S_t, which is $5 billion less at every income level. This is not all, however, because we must account for the tax withdrawal from the income stream. We recall from previous discussions that saving represents a withdrawal from the consumption of products which must be exactly offset by investment in order to maintain equilibrium. Similarly taxes represent a leakage. In Figure 6-10, then, the two leakages are S_t and T, and the two additions or offsets are I and G. Therefore, when $S_t + T = I + G$ we have reached an equilibrium. We see then that a change in C (or S), I, G, or T can bring about a change in equilibrium. A tabular presentation appears in Table 6-2. We see that at equilibrium $S_t + T = 95$ and $I + G = 95$ and the leakages offset the injections. The reader should also note that at equilibrium I need not equal S, because compensating adjustments can occur in T and G.

We should again emphasize that we are dealing with a simplified model. We have, for instance, assumed an autonomous I schedule; that is, that the tax impact was on consumption alone. This is not realistic because a tax which reduces consumption will also likely affect investment. Of course, the main impact of the tax may also be imposed on investment.

THE PRICE LEVEL AND AGGREGATE SUPPLY

During the postwar period the problem of price-output relations, in one way or another, has been one of the most controversial in economics and in economic policy. What happens when taxes are reduced? What happens when government expenditures are increased? Or when the government runs a deficit? What happens when the supply of money is increased? In all these cases does output or do prices increase? Or do they both increase? If not immediately, then at what point? What is the role of administered prices, costs, labor unions, etc., in this process? All these issues are related to price-output relations or what is generally referred to as the "aggregate supply function."

What is known as a simplified short-run aggregate supply function is illustrated in Figure 6-11. The ZZ' schedule, which relates the level of output to the price level, implies that increases in demand continue to increase output with only small increases in prices up to some point near the full employment level (designated by Q). If one assumes that wages and costs are constant throughout this range the curve would be flat up to the point referred to. After we have reached this point we then have a rather abrupt upward turn in our supply function, showing that increases in demand result primarily in increases in prices. Within this output

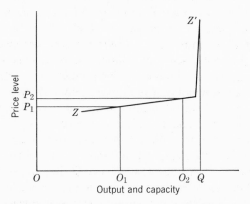

Figure 6-11. Simplified short-run aggregate supply function. From J. P. Lewis in JEC, *Rel. Prices to Ec. Stabil. & Growth*, P, p. 380. Q = full employment capacity, OO_1 = first level of demand, OO_2 = second level of demand, $OO_2 - OO_1$ = increase in aggregate demand, $P_2 - P_1$ = increase in price level.

range small increases in output are attained only at the expense of large increases in prices. When Keynes discussed this supply function he was using a very simple idea based on the assumptions that competition among the various factors of production would tend to keep price increases quite moderate up to the full employment level, and that the full employment was "fixed in a 'short run' that was long enough to be significant."[1]

As we noted, the aggregate supply function in Figure 6-11 was based on certain assumptions. It is questioned on the following grounds: (1) Many economists feel that capacity is not as fixed as the function assumes. Capacity does, under normal conditions in our economy, expand in the short run. This has the effect of moving the aggregate supply function to the right. Within a rather substantial range American industry has fairly constant unit costs, which means that substantial increases in production can occur without significant cost increases. Further, the addition of new capital is often more productive, and this operates to offset cost increases which do occur. (2) On the other hand, bottlenecks can occur, primarily because all firms or industries do not expand at the same rate, because they have different inventories on hand, etc. This factor tends to exert an upward pressure on prices. The price increases resulting from bottlenecks may not, however, become cumulative and continuous. They may be of the one-shot variety, and they may (in competitive industries) be temporary. (3) The assumption of the aggregate supply function in Figure 6-11 that wages, prices, etc., are generally set under competitive conditions is highly unrealistic. We do have the very important problem of rigid wages and prices. Temporary wage increases granted under conditions of high demand are no longer temporary. They are permanent, and further, they can and do occur at levels of employment which are less than full. In addition, businessmen are quite cost-oriented, and when possible they pass wage increases on in order to maintain their mark-ups. (They may, in some cases, also capitalize on the wage increase.) (4) Although bottlenecks and labor and industry actions place an upward pressure on prices, there is no reason to expect that the price level will, at some point, suddenly "take off" as in Figure 6-11. We would only expect this to occur under conditions of creation of excessive money supply (as in World War II and the postwar period). Furthermore, even though the economy is operating at something less than full employment and full capacity, the sudden imposition of a violent demand would create bottlenecks, shortages, and expectations of further shortages and price increases. (See Figure 6-13.) Obviously the rate of increase of demand (and output) has a considerable bearing on the rate of increase of prices. (5) We should note that the aggregate supply function tends to be nonreversible when we

[1] J. P. Lewis in JEC, *Rel. Prices to Ec. Stabil. & Growth*, P, p. 380.

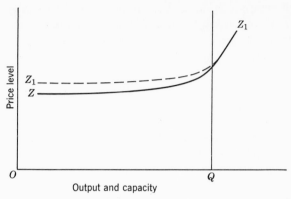

Figure 6-12. Possible aggregate supply functions: prices increase as full employment is approached.

have a decline in demand. This is because at the point of high demand and capacity, or near capacity, production wage rates and administered prices are rigid. Hence the economy does not slide back down the curve designated in Figure 6-12 as ZZ_1, but rather would be more likely to travel back down Z_1Z_1.

Figure 6-13 shows the generally accepted supply curve as ZZ_1. However, there may be a rather violent and sudden increase in demand which raises prices *before* full employment is reached. This is illustrated by ZZ_2, which shows that after the violent increase in prices the price-output relations may continue at the same rate as in ZZ_1, but on the higher plateau shown in ZZ_2.

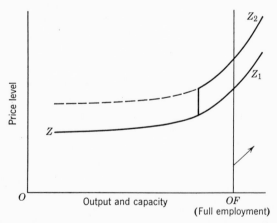

Figure 6-13. Possible aggregate supply functions: A large increase in demand pushes up the price level before full employment is approached.

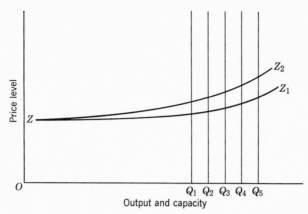

Figure 6-14. Possible aggregate supply functions: Expansions in capacity.

Once this new price plateau is reached, decreases in output will not take place along curve ZZ_1. Rather, because of price and wage rigidities, the backward direction will be along the broken line illustrated in Figure 6-13.

It is also possible to have a steady, nonviolent growth of both demand and capacity. The two curves shown in Figure 6-14 would be more ideal positions for the aggregate supply curve to take. ZZ_1 reflects the generally accepted policy goal, although some would want to make the curve even flatter in order to make price increases even smaller. While this is an ideal goal, it is not entirely unrealistic.

7

Income Theory (III): Monetary Theory
and General Equilibrium

Thus far we have utilized money primarily as a technique for measuring what was going on in the economy. We shall recall from our introductory economics course that money serves four basic functions—to act as (1) a medium of exchange, (2) a store of value, (3) a measure or standard of value, and (4) a standard of deferred payments. It is with the first two that we are primarily concerned in this chapter. In a very important way money has a role of its own to play which will influence what is going on in the economy. Put in other terms, events in the "monetary" sphere are such that they may exert considerable influence on the "real" goods sphere, which in turn affects our production and employment. We shall be concerned in this chapter with the factors determining the demand for and supply of money, and how equilibrium is arrived at in the monetary sphere.

THE DEMAND FOR MONEY

Strange as it may seem, it is not easy to define the term money. There is little doubt that currency in circulation (coins, Treasury bills, Federal Reserve bills) and demand deposits satisfy the basic requirement of money —acceptability. But what about time deposits, savings bonds and government securities generally, life insurance policy cash values, and reserve balances of member banks of the Federal Reserve System? These are all "near" money: That is, they can be easily and immediately turned into cash or demand deposits with no or little loss involved. There is not general agreement on which of these should be included in a definition of money, but it is fairly obvious that for some purposes items such as time deposits and member bank excess reserves should be included in our definition of money.

Since, if one prefers to hold money, he receives no return on it (no interest, etc., as compared with holding wealth in the form of a government security), why do people hold money?

The Transactions Demand for Money

One of the main reasons why money is held is to facilitate routine (and other) business and household transactions. Money is necessary for purposes of exchange, and generally speaking the higher the value of the GNP, the more transactions there are, and the greater the volume of money which will be held for this purpose. We would expect then that an increase in the GNP would require an increase in our supply of money for transactions purposes. Transactions balances could possibly be reduced by means of a high interest rate. Here the costs involved in going from cash to financial investments, such as bonds, and back to cash again within a very short period of time would be more than covered by the higher interest. But at lower interest rates the transactions demand for money is interest-inelastic.

The Precautionary Demand for Money

Some money will be held simply because people cannot predict what will occur in the future and feel that they want to be prepared to meet some future emergency (disability, unemployment, etc.) should it occur.

The Speculative Demand for Money

The speculative motive explains the holding of money balances for use at some future date. In particular, the holder is gambling on what happens in the market. If he decides to hold his wealth in the form of cash rather than bonds, he is gambling that he can get a better buy in the market in the future. Dealing first only with interest rates, if the current rate is, say, 12 percent and is not expected to go up any higher, then little would be held in cash balances. If, on the other hand, the interest rate is 2 percent but is expected to go up, people will increase their cash balances and the demand for money for speculative purposes will increase. If an individual did buy a long-term government security and interest rates declined, he would not only feel rather badly about his purchase, he would also have to hold the security until maturity, unless he were willing to suffer a sizable capital loss by selling. The possibility of people hoarding cash when interest rates are low was referred to by Keynes as the "liquidity trap." In this instance people are holding their assets in the form of cash, and the cost of holding money is the going (low) rate of interest. If the rate of interest goes up (and, therefore, the price of bonds goes down) we would expect that cash balances for speculative purposes would go down.

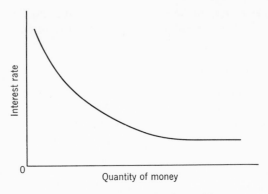

Figure 7-1. The speculative demand for money.

The demand for money for speculative purposes then is a function of the rate of interest.

The foregoing is illustrated in Figure 7-1. Here we see that the demand to hold money for speculative purposes increases as the interest rate drops, and decreases as the interest rate increases. At lower levels of interest the curve becomes perfectly elastic. Additional small declines in the interest rate will bring large increases in speculative holdings of cash because people would rather forego low interest, hold cash, and hope that the interest rate goes up. Further, the low interest rate means that the price of bonds is high and that they are not an attractive purchase.

The Total Demand for Money

Adding together the transactions, precautionary, and speculative demands for money we obtain the total demand for money, as shown in Figure 7-2. On the vertical axis we have the rate of interest and on the horizontal axis the demand for money. Here we see that at higher levels of interest only a small amount is held, and at lower rates more is held until we reach a very low rate where the demand for money is perfectly elastic. This is designated by the horizontal i_1, i_2, etc., lines showing the amounts to be held (demanded) at various rates of interest. The symbols Y_1, Y_2, and Y_3, represent different levels of income. The symbols L_1, L_2, and L_3 show the demand for money at these different levels of income. Y_1 might equal an income of $400 billion, Y_2 an income of $500 billion, etc. The whole L curve represents one constant income level. It shows us the demand for money at various interest rates at the given level of income. Hence we should expect that at income Y_2 the amount of money demanded is greater than at Y_1 at a given interest rate because at Y_2 the amount of money demanded for transactions purposes is greater.

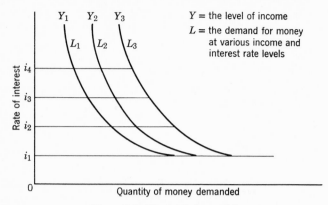

Figure 7-2. The total demand for money.

The Rate of Interest

We have noted thus far that the demand for money is dependent on both the level of income and the level of interest rates—the level of income in the sense that with higher incomes more is needed for transactions, and the level of interest because of its effect on the speculative demand for money. We have already introduced graphically the demand for money at various income and interest rate levels in Figure 7-2. We can now attempt to show equilibrium in the money market by introducing the supply of money. Again we point out that this is a difficult concept since we have so many "near" monies or "money substitutes." We shall be conventional, however, and restrict our definition of the money supply to demand deposits and currency. We will have reached an equilibrium when the demand for money for both transactions and speculative purposes is equal to the supply of money for these same two purposes. As we have noted, both income and interest rate factors must be taken into account in the determination of the equilibrium position.

We shall designate the supply of money as a fixed quantity since it is controlled almost completely by the monetary authorities. The autonomous supply of money then is shown by the vertical line MM in Figure 7-3, where the equilibrium position, as with supply and demand curves, is at the point of intersection of the L and M curves. (Remember that the L curves represent the demand for money at different interest rates at given income levels.) With an income level of Y_1 we have monetary equilibrium at the interest rate of i_1. If we have an increase in income the equilibrium interest rate *with the same money supply* increases to i_2. This is reasonable because at higher levels of income the demand for money for both transactions and speculative purposes would increase. The demand for speculative purposes would increase because of the uncertainty of future asset

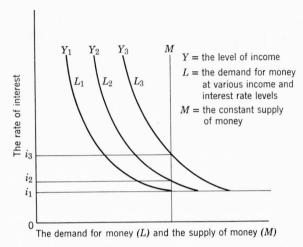

Figure 7-3. The determination of the rate of interest: equilibrium in the demand and supply of money.

values. With this higher level of income money will be put to use (people give up their liquidity) only if interest is raised sufficiently. It is of particular significance to note that at increasingly higher levels of income and production failure to increase the supply of money will result in higher interest rates.

What would happen if we increase the supply of money; that is, shift the M curve to the right? We would then attain monetary equilibrium at lower interest rates—at any particular income level the interest rate would be lower.

THE EQUILIBRIUM OF MONEY, INTEREST, AND INCOME

The *LM* Curve

In Figure 7-4 we have what is called an LM schedule. The LM schedule consists of a series of points each of which stands for an interest-income level at which the demand for money is equal to the supply of money. On the horizontal axis we show the level of income, and on the vertical axis the rate of interest. The LM curve is derived directly from Figure 7-3. It is drawn by plotting the various interest rate levels at which the demand for money equals the supply of money at given income levels. At income Y_1 we have a position of monetary equilibrium ($L = M$) at interest rate i_1; at income Y_2 at i_2; and at income Y_3 at i_3. Recalling that in our example the supply of money is *fixed*, at low levels of income the rate of interest is low because transactions demands are low. We would expect that a "relatively abundant money supply"[2] would result in lower interest. We note, however, that at the extreme left the *LM* curve becomes perfectly elastic with respect to interest. This lower limit to which the rate of interest will fall is the Keynesian "liquidity trap" which we mentioned previously.. As the level of income declines the demand for money for transactions declines. Hence a greater amount is available for idle balances but this does not result in lower interest because we have reached the lower limit to which interest will drop.

At higher levels of income the demand for money for transactions purposes will be higher, which will exert an upward pressure on interest rates. Again at a higher income level with a "relatively small money supply" we would expect a high rate of interest. It is particularly important to notice the shape of the *LM* function at the highest income level in Figure 7-4. This shape, which indicates that the curve becomes perfectly inelastic and no further increases in income (*Y*) will occur, is the result of the fixed money supply. At higher income levels the demand for money for transaction purposes increases. Since this money is secured from idle balances only by the payment of higher interest, interest rates are pushed up. Depending on the influence of interest on investment the higher interest rates may restrict further investment and a higher income. At the higher level of income then, with a fixed supply of money, the transactions demand for money is so high that interest rates are pushed up.

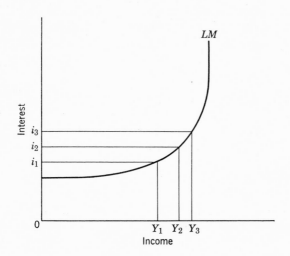

Figure 7-4. The *LM* schedule.

[2] A. H. Hansen, *Monetary Theory and Fiscal Policy*, New York: McGraw-Hill, 1949, p. 78.

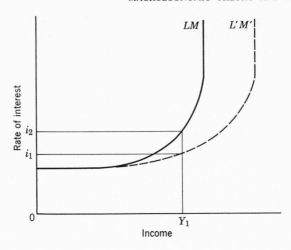

Figure 7-5. A shift in the *LM* curve.

This restricts investment. It may also be true that there simply is not enough money to finance the level of economic activity beyond a certain point.

A Shift in the *LM* Curve

In Figure 7-5 we have illustrated a shift in the *LM* curve by the dashed line *L'M'*. This shift in the *LM* curve can be caused by either an increase in the money supply or a decrease in liquidity preference (a decrease in the demand for money). (Increase the supply of money in Figure 7-3 and observe what happens to the rate of interest at each income level.) The result of this shift in the *LM* curve is, at the given income level of Y_1, the lower interest rate that will prevail with the increase in the money supply which shifts the curve to the right. The interest rate drops from i_2 to i_1 at income Y_1. Furthermore, both higher levels of income and higher levels of income at lower interest rates are possible than under the original *LM* curve.

The *IS* Curve

Thus far we have discussed the problem of equilibrium in the money market, but now we shall return to our discussion, in previous chapters, of equilibrium in the commodity market. We are concerned now with the problem of attaining equilibrium in both the money and commodity markets simultaneously. First we must examine the *IS* curve, which shows us a series of points at which saving equals investment at various income and interest rate levels.

Various graphical devices may be used to illustrate the derivation of the *IS* curve. In Figure 7-6a we have a saving curve in which saving increases as income increases, and a series of investment schedules at given rates of interest. Investment, therefore, depends on the rate of interest and the level of income. At each given level of interest the level of investment will rise as income rises. We have in addition several equilibrium positions shown by the intersection of the saving and investment schedules. The equilibrium positions, and hence saving and the level of income, are determined by the level of investment. In (b) we plot the *IS* schedule by marking the level of income at various rates of interest. Each point, like all others on this curve, represents levels of income at which saving equals investment at various rates of interest. At an interest rate of 5 percent investment is 50, saving is 50, and income Y_3. We continue on down to (b) and plot the income-interest point. This is done for each level of invest-ment, and the points are connected to secure the *IS* curve. As an "extra," we have drawn in a vertical line on which we may measure S and I. At each point $S = I$. We see then that the rate of interest determines in-vestment, investment determines income, and income determines saving. We see then the interrelationship between interest and investment, investment and income, and therefore interest and income. Of course, as we noted in a previous chapter, technology, the level of output, taxes,

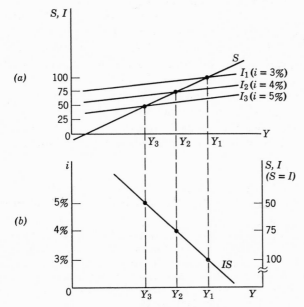

Figure 7-6. The derivation of the *IS* curve.

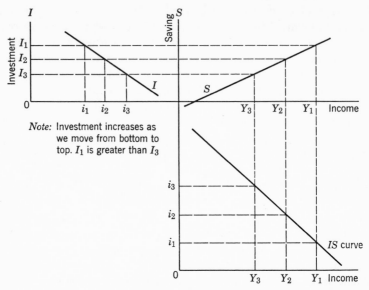

Figure 7-7. Investment, saving, and the *IS* curve. Adapted from L. V. Chandler, *The Economics of Money and Banking*, New York: Harper, 1959, p. 250.

labor and other costs, and other factors will strongly influence the return to capital and consequently the rate of investment.[3]

In Figure 7-7 we also illustrate the derivation of the *IS* curve. Again we have investment as a function of the rate of interest, saving as a function of income, and finally the investment-saving curve. Again, the *IS* curve shows us the various points at which S and I are in equilibrium at various rates of interest and levels of income. It shows us the various combinations of the rate of interest and income that will cause saving to equal investment. If income is Y_1, then at interest rate i_1, $S = I$. The *IS* curve slopes downward and to the right because as the rate of interest is lowered investment will increase and with the help of the multiplier, income will increase.

An Interest-Inelastic *IS* Curve

In Figure 7-8[4] we have an *IS* curve which is interest-inelastic. This means that reductions in the interest rate below a certain point will have

[3] For more on these matters and what follows see L. V. Chandler, *The Economics of Money and Banking*, New York: Harper, 1959, pp. 250ff., W. C. Peterson, *Income, Employment, and Economic Growth*, New York: Norton, 1962, pp. 371ff.; G. Ackley, *Macroeconomic Theory*, New York: Macmillan, 1961, pp. 360ff.; and other macroeconomic texts. See also F. Modigliani, "Liquidity Preference and the Theory of Interest and Money," in F. A. Lutz and L. W. Mints, eds., *Readings in Monetary Theory*, Homewood, Ill.: Irwin, 1951, pp. 201–204.

[4] See Hansen, *op. cit.*, pp. 79–80, or Peterson, *op. cit.*, p. 373, for more on this.

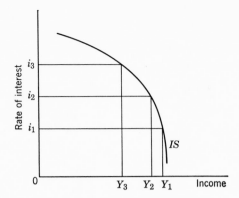

Figure 7-8. An interest-inelastic *IS* curve.

but little effect on investment. The drop in the rate of interest from i_3 to i_2 resulted in a significant increase in investment and income. But the drop from i_2 to i_1 has a much smaller effect on investment and income.

General Equilibrium: the Intersection of the *IS* and *LM* Curves

We shall now attempt to show equilibrium in both the money and commodity markets and how they are related by means of the rate of interest. In Figure 7-9 we see that at the point of intersection of the two curves the interest rate of i_e and income of Y_e are mutually determined.

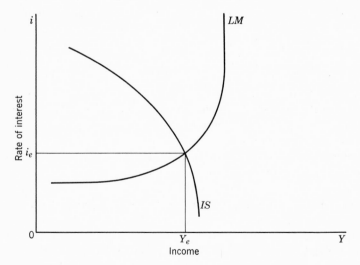

Figure 7-9. The simultaneous determination of the equilibrium rate of interest and level of income.

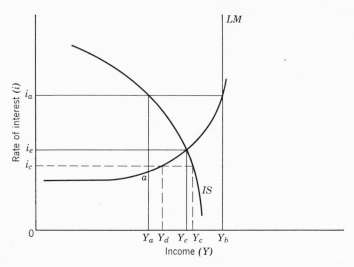

Figure 7-10. Continued from Figure 7-9.

At this point saving and investment are in equilibrium ($I = S$) and the demand for money is equal to the supply of money ($L = M$). We should note that with LM and IS functions given in the graph there can only be one point at which both are in equilibrium.

In Figure 7-10, if we assume an interest rate of, say, i_a, we find that we have an income level (Y_a) at which investment equals saving and another (Y_b) at which the demand for money is equal to the supply of money. But this is not a point of general equilibrium. Looking at the diagram first from the standpoint of the IS curve we see that we have a high rate of interest (i_a) and a low level of income (Y_a). In terms of the money supply and the demand for money, however, at this lower level of income interest must be lower. It will be at point a on the LM curve. At this lower income level the demand for money for transactions purposes is lower; hence with a given supply of money the rate of interest will be lower. There would be a tendency for the lower rate of interest to increase investment and income (and saving), and there is a movement toward the point of general equilibrium which raises the rate of interest.

On the other hand, if we follow through the i_a rate of interest to the LM curve and down to the income level of Y_b, we see that we have both a high rate of interest and a high level of income (Y_b). But the rate of interest is too high to sustain this high level of income. This high rate of interest will adversely affect investment, bringing with it a decline in income which in turn will reduce the transactions demand for money, which in turn will lower the interest rate. The direction of movement then will be backwards on the *LM* curve toward the general equilibrium income level of Y_e.

Let us now examine the diagram with a given interest rate of i_c. From the standpoint of the *IS* curve we have an income level (Y_c) which is higher than the equilibrium level (Y_e). But at this income level the demand for funds for investment and transactions is high and the rate of interest is high, as shown by the fact that at this income level L and M are in equilibrium at a higher rate of interest. Investment will therefore decline, income and saving will decline, and there will be a movement back toward the equilibrium level.

From the standpoint of the *LM* curve we have a lower level of income (Y_d). The lower level of interest will increase the level of investment, and income and interest are pushed up. There is a movement toward equilibrium again. Of course the higher demand for money for transactions as income increases also helps push up the interest rate.

Shifts in the *IS* and *LM* Curves

Thus far we have dealt with a fixed supply of money. What happens if we have an increase? This is shown in Figure 7-11 by the dashed line $L'M'$ function. Note here the impact of this increase in the quantity of money on IS_3. We see that the rate of interest is lowered, the level of aggregate demand increases because of increased investment, and the level of income therefore increases from Y_3 to Y_4. The equilibrium has shifted to the right. We have a new higher level of income because the IS_3 curve is relatively interest-elastic. Monetary policy now has its day.

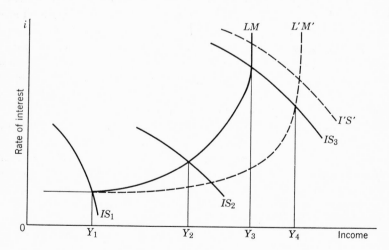

Figure 7-11. Different *IS* curves and shifts in the *IS* and *LM* curves.

We should note that the LM curve in this same range (where IS_3 intersects LM) is perfectly inelastic with respect to the rate of interest. What would happen if we should use fiscal policy instead of monetary policy to increase aggregate demand? (We could either cut taxes, or increase government spending, or both.) IS_3 would shift upward to $I'S'$ but with no increase in income. Income is still at Y_3. There is in fact no reduction in the interest rate; there is rather an increase. The attempt to increase aggregate demand would increase the transactions demand for money, which in turn would increase the rate of interest with no change in the level of income. We can assume that there are no more idle balances to be drawn regardless of now high the interest rate goes. Presumably any increase in spending is at the expense of some other type of spending. We have instead saving and investment in equilibrium at a higher rate of interest. This case and the one following show the importance of theory and model building to policy determination.

Look now at the point of intersection of the IS_1 and the LM curves. Now what happens with the increase in the supply of money? Nothing, at least as far as interest, investment, and income are concerned. There is no lowering of the rate of interest, and therefore investment and income are not affected. The extra money created is merely added to idle balances. This result is caused by the fact that in this range the LM curve is perfectly elastic. Similarly, the IS_1 curve is relatively interest-inelastic. At this point we have an illustration of the liquidity trap. This means that monetary policy will not be effective in reducing interest rates and fiscal policy will have to be used. This situation is descriptive of a fairly serious depression. On the other hand, because of the shape of the LM and $L'M'$ curves a shift to the right of the IS_1 curve can bring some increase in the level of income with an increase in the rate of interest. A shift to IS_2 results in a substantial increase in income with reference to the $L'M'$ curve with only a small increase in the rate of interest. Of course, if the curve were to rise more steeply the increase in the rate of interest would be greater. What would be the result of the increase in the money supply had the IS_1 curve been quite flat and intersected both the LM and $L'M'$ curves?

In the intermediate case of IS_2 either monetary or fiscal policy, or both, could be used. An increase in the supply of money would shift the LM curve to $L'M'$, lower the rate of interest, and raise the level of investment and income. A reduction in taxes, etc., would shift the IS_2 curve upward and to the right, thereby raising the level of income.

8

The Theory of Fiscal Policy

We have previously noted that in classical theory the functions of government were severely restricted and there should be no such thing as fiscal policy as we presently define it. The government could satisfy some social wants, but to use government expenditures or taxes to influence the level of output and employment, the system of income distribution, and to provide services such as those provided today—all these were precluded from the acceptable functions of government. Aside from the fact that fiscal policy, as defined currently, is widely accepted, two other facts stand out. First, the level and types of government expenditures and taxes will inevitably affect the level of income and employment; and second, there is a need in today's highly interdependent economy for the stabilizing pressures which can be exerted on the economy by fiscal policy. We have a long history of economic fluctuations in our society—of depressions and inflations of both short- and long-run duration. We have made the political decision to stabilize these fluctuations. Furthermore, given the impact of a large federal budget and concomitant tax and expenditure policies on the economy, why not use it to attain economically as well as socially and politically desirable ends?

SOME ELEMENTARY RULES

It might perhaps be advisable to review briefly some simple rules for fiscal policy at this point.

1. In the first place, during a period of unemployment we are interested in raising the level of aggregate demand to the point of full employment. This can be done by (*a*) an increase in government purchases of goods and services in the economy, (*b*) an increase in government transfer payments, (*c*) a reduction in taxes, or some combination of these actions (*abc*, *ab*, *ac*, or *bc*).
2. If we are experiencing a period of inflation, our objective is to reduce the level of aggregate demand—to sop up the excess demand in the

economy. This can be done by (*a*) an increase in taxes, (*b*) a reduction in government expenditures on goods and services, (*c*) a reduction in transfer payments, or by some combination of these (*abc*, *ab*, *ac*, or *bc*).

3. Once a high and acceptable level of employment and output is reached, we must attempt to attain an acceptable rate of economic growth so that the objectives of full employment and price stability may continue to be realized.

This means that we must strike a balance between consumption and investment so that one does not outpace or lag behind the other, creating conditions of insufficient productive capacity or stagnation, or so that either or both do not increase so rapidly that excess demand results. This most difficult problem in economic policy is really the one that has been at the heart of policy controversies since about 1957 or 1958. Capital formation is most necessary for economic growth, but there are times when emphasis must also be placed on consumption (and/or government expenditures), or a policy aimed at restraining consumption and encouraging investment will turn out to be self-defeating—both consumption and investment will decline. The problem is analogous to the "paradox of thrift." An attempt to save too much (voluntarily or through taxes) may create a situation in which we end up saving less, investing less, and consuming less. It seems to have taken many congressmen and other public policy-makers a long time to learn this simple lesson.

In addition to noting the impact of these alternative policies, we should again note the importance and impact of (1) the supply of money, (2) the sources of funds for government expenditure, and (3) the use of funds secured from a budget surplus.

We have already noted the importance of the supply of money on liquidity preference, the transaction demand for money, and hence on the rate of interest. With economic growth there is a need for a similar growth in the money supply. Failure of the money supply to grow could be offset by velocity increases, but there are limits to this.

Funds for government expenditures may be created simply by the government's printing dollars. This could have the most expansionary impact on the economy. Funds to support government expenditures may also be borrowed. Borrowing from the commercial banks, which have excess reserves, would be very expansionary (new money is created) but possibly less so than printing money depending on the subsequent pressures of the borrowing on excess reserves. The volume of excess reserves will depend in turn on Federal Reserve open market and reserve requirement policy. Funds may also be borrowed from private individuals, but the effect is less expansionary. Borrowing the idle funds of individuals would be more expansionary than borrowing funds which would have been spent. Further, the borrowing of a large volume of funds from private individuals (including now other financial institutions such as savings banks) would reduce the funds available for investment and also put greater pressure on the rate of interest (given a certain money supply). Of course, the government could also secure its funds from taxation, but this would have a restrictive impact on the economy.

The achievement of a budget surplus in itself has a restrictive impact on the economy. The use of the funds secured by the surplus also has varying effects. If the government taxes private individuals and uses the surplus to retire debt held by commercial banks, then an expansion in the money supply can occur, some downward pressure is exerted on the rate of interest, and additional funds are available (presumably) for investment. If it retires debt held by noncommercial banks and other financial institutions, no new money is created but some downward pressure on interest rates still results. If the government merely holds the surplus (in its accounts in Federal Reserve Banks, for example), then the most restrictive policy results.

In this chapter we discuss the theory of fiscal policy. Results are not easy to attain if we do not have complete knowledge, however, and this is the situation we find ourselves in with respect to both fiscal and monetary policy. On the other hand, we are often confronted with situations in which action must be taken even though our knowledge is imperfect—in both the natural and social sciences. Furthermore ". . . policy decisions cannot wait until knowledge is perfected."[1] Most certainly in these situations caution is called for, but, nonetheless, action must be taken. Decisions must be made not only concerning tax and expenditure adjustments, but also concerning the types of taxes and expenditures to be altered, even though the exact impact is not always known.

THE LEVEL OF INCOME AND GOVERNMENT PURCHASES OF GOODS AND SERVICES, TAXES, AND TRANSFERS

We shall at this point review our previous discussion of the impact of the government on the economy from Chapter 6. We noted in Figure 6-8 that government expenditures superimposed on the levels of consumption

---

[1] W. W. Heller, in JEC, *Empl.*, *Growth*, *Price Levels*, H, Pt. 9A, p. 2988. Chairman Paul Douglas' response was a quotation from Oliver Wendell Holmes: "Every year, if not every day, we have to wager our salvation upon some prophecy based on imperfect knowledge."

A more advanced and more theoretical approach is that of Bent Hansen, *The Economic Theory of Fiscal Policy*, Cambridge, Mass.: Harvard Univ. Press, 1958.

and investment result in an increase in equilibrium income from \$500 to \$580 billion. We further note in Figure 6-10 that taxes have the same impact on the economy as saving.

If we were to have an increase in government purchases of \$5 billion, not financed by an increase in taxes, we would have an increase in our equilibrium income level to \$600 billion. The increase in government expenditures is \$5 billion, but the increase in income is \$20 billion; hence the government purchases multiplier is 4. This can be demonstrated by adding \$5 billion to the government expenditures in Figure 6-8. The reader should note that from this point on government expenditures will be divided into government purchases (G_p) and government transfers (*TR*). This is because their impacts are generally different, as noted shortly.

We shall, at this point, attempt to simplify our analysis and make it more accurate by introducing some elementary algebra. Assuming that we have a closed economy (ignoring foreign transactions) we can represent the equilibrium position with the following identity.

$$Y = C + I + G_p \tag{8-1}$$

This simply states that income equals consumption C plus investment I plus government purchases G.

Consumption can be represented by the following:

$$C = a + cY \tag{8-2}$$

which states that consumption is equal to some constant amount a plus the marginal propensity to consume c times income Y. The a follows from the fact that at zero income consumption will be greater than zero (the point at which the C line intercepts the vertical axis, which is zero income, in Figure 6-1). By drawing the consumption function in Figure 6-1 as a straight line we have assumed a constant marginal propensity to consume.

The Multiplier

At this point we consider only the impact of government purchases on consumption; we assume that investment is autonomous and constant. Before we proceed with our analysis, however, we should illustrate the manner in which the multiplier is computed. We have previously noted that $Y = I + C$, excluding government. It follows then that an increase in income which is caused by an increase in investment will also increase consumption, as noted below.

$$\Delta Y = \Delta I + \Delta C \tag{8-3}$$

The delta (Δ) sign refers a change and in equation 8-3 to an increase. Hence the increase in income consists of an increase in both investment and consumption. The increase in consumption is dependent on the MPC, which we designated above with the letter c. Therefore ΔC is the same as $c\Delta Y$. Substituting $c\Delta Y$ (the MPC × increased income) for ΔC in equation 8-3, we obtain

$$\Delta Y = \Delta I + c\Delta Y \qquad (8\text{-}4)$$

which states that the increase in income is equal to the increase in investment plus the MPC times the increase in income ($c\Delta Y = \Delta C$). Transposing $c\Delta Y$ we now have

$$\Delta Y - c\Delta Y = \Delta I \qquad (8\text{-}5)$$

Taking out the ΔY's on the left side we find

$$\Delta Y(1 - c) = \Delta I \qquad (8\text{-}6)$$

Dividing both sides of the equation by $1 - c$ we get

$$\Delta Y = \frac{\Delta I}{1 - c} \qquad (8\text{-}7)$$

Dividing both sides of this equation by ΔI we now obtain

$$\frac{\Delta Y}{\Delta I} = \frac{1}{1 - c} \qquad (8\text{-}8)$$

Since the increase in income divided by the increase in investment gives us the value of the multiplier, and this is exactly what the left side of this equation says, the quantity $1/(1 - c)$ is also the value of the multiplier. The multiplier then is equal to the reciprocal of the marginal propensity to save.[2]

The Government Purchases Multiplier

The above multiplier applies to government purchases as well as to investment expenditures. Let us proceed now with our assumption that

[2] For more on the derivation of the multiplier see A. Hansen, *A Guide to Keynes*, New York: McGraw-Hill, 1953, Chapter 4, which has been followed here. An alternative derivation is as follows:

$$k = \frac{\Delta Y}{\Delta I} = \frac{\Delta Y}{\Delta Y - \Delta C}$$

If we now divide both the numerator and denominator by ΔY, we have

$$\frac{1}{1 - \Delta C/\Delta Y}$$

Since $\Delta C/\Delta Y = $ MPC we now get

$$\frac{1}{1 - \text{MPC}}$$

investment is autonomous and that we are dealing solely with an increase in government purchases, there being no additional taxes. We see then that the increase in income which results from the increase in government purchases is as follows:

$$\Delta Y = \frac{1}{1-c} \Delta G_p = k \, \Delta G_p \qquad (8\text{-}9)$$

which states simply that the increase in income is equal to the multiplier times the increase in government purchases of goods and services. This can be checked out in Figure 6-8, in which the multiplier is 4, the value of new government purchases is \$20 billion, and therefore the increase in income is \$80 billion. We should note that the government purchases multiplier (with no taxes, and autonomous investment) can also be stated as follows: $k_g = \Delta Y / \Delta G_p$.

The Government Transfer and Tax Multipliers

We have in the foregoing dealt with the government purchases (of goods and services) multiplier in a situation in which there was no increase in taxes and in which investment was autonomous (not affected by the new equilibrium level of income). We also have a multiplier that results from government transfer payments. It operates exactly as the multipliers which we have previously discussed, except that we can almost always expect that it will be less than the multiplier results of either government purchases or investment. In the case of investment or government purchases a \$1,000 expenditure results in a shift in either I or G by this amount. In the case of government transfers, however, disposable income increases by \$1,000 but the upward shift in the consumption function will be less than \$1,000. This follows from our assumption of a constant MPC. Hence, if the MPC is .75 then the increase in consumption resulting from transfers of \$1,000 will be \$750 and the multiplier will be smaller. Of course, if the recipients of the transfer payments have a MPC of 100 percent, then the multiplier (and the upward shift in the consumption function) will be the same as in the case of government purchases or investment. We would expect that different transfer payments would have different multipliers—for interest payments the multiplier would be much smaller than that for unemployment compensation payments.

We have thus far discussed the government purchases and government transfer multipliers. Of course, we must also contend with the tax problem, and at this point we complete our discussion of the government by showing both the transfer and tax multipliers. We should expect that the tax multiplier would be negative.

The impact of both taxes and transfers is shown later, but we must first define disposable income, Y_d, as follows:

$$Y_d = Y - T_x + TR \qquad (8\text{-}10)$$

This states that disposable income is equal to income minus taxes T_x plus transfers TR. (This means that at various levels of output and income Y on our aggregate demand graphs, disposable income may be greater or less than Y. The reader should keep this point in mind.) Therefore an increase in disposable income is represented by

$$\Delta Y_d = \Delta Y - \Delta T_x + \Delta TR \qquad (8\text{-}11)$$

The increase in consumption which results from the increase in disposable income is equal to the MPC times the increased disposable income. Therefore, we can write

$$\Delta C = c\,\Delta Y_d \qquad (8\text{-}12)$$

in which c is the MPC. Substituting our definition for disposable income (equation 8-11) for ΔY_d we obtain

$$\Delta C = c\,(\Delta Y - \Delta T_x + \Delta TR) \qquad (8\text{-}13)$$

$$\Delta C = c\,\Delta Y - c\,\Delta T_x + c\,\Delta TR \qquad (8\text{-}14)$$

We can at this point read certain things into equation 8-14. The impact of taxes is negative. Notice, however, that a tax of $100 will not decrease consumption by that amount. Rather, it will result in reduced consumption by an amount equal to the MPC times the tax. The impact of government transfers then is

$$\Delta Y = \frac{1}{1-c}\,(c\,\Delta TR) \qquad (8\text{-}15)$$

The increase in income is equal to the multiplier times the amount of transfers spent by their recipients. The transfer multiplier then is as follows:

$$k_{TR} = \frac{c}{1-c} \qquad (8\text{-}16)$$

The algebraic derivation of the transfer multiplier is

$$\Delta Y = \Delta C + \Delta I \qquad (8\text{-}17)$$

$$\Delta Y = c\,\Delta Y_d + \Delta I \qquad (8\text{-}18)$$

Dropping ΔI, since investment is autonomous, and substituting the value of disposable income in 8-18 we get

$$\Delta Y = c\,(\Delta Y - \Delta T_x + \Delta TR) \qquad (8\text{-}19)$$

$$\Delta Y = c\,\Delta Y - c\,\Delta T_x + c\,\Delta TR \qquad (8\text{-}20)$$

Since there is no increase in taxes we can drop the term $c \, \Delta T_x$.

$$\Delta Y = c \, \Delta Y + c \, \Delta TR \qquad (8\text{-}21)$$

$$\Delta Y - c \, \Delta Y = c \, \Delta TR \qquad (8\text{-}22)$$

$$\Delta Y(1 - c) = c \, \Delta TR \qquad (8\text{-}23)$$

$$\Delta Y = \frac{c \, \Delta TR}{1 - c} \qquad (8\text{-}24)$$

Dividing both sides of the equation by ΔTR we get

$$\frac{\Delta Y}{\Delta TR} = \frac{c}{1 - c} \qquad (8\text{-}25)$$

The tax multiplier is computed in exactly the same manner.

Again we note from equation 8-14 that an increase in taxes will not reduce consumption by the same amount as the tax. The impact of taxes then can be shown as

$$\Delta Y = \frac{1}{1 - c} \, (-c \, \Delta T_x) \qquad (8\text{-}26)$$

which states that the change in income will be equal to the multiplier times the MPC times the tax, and that the effect will be negative. The tax multiplier then can be stated as follows:

$$k_{T_x} = - \frac{c}{1 - c} \quad \text{or as} \quad - \frac{1}{1 - c} \, c \qquad (8\text{-}27)$$

A comparison of the multipliers for government purchases, transfers, and taxes shows that the last two are smaller because their immediate impact is smaller. An increase in government purchases of, say, $1,000 results in an immediate increase in spending and income of $1,000, but an increase in transfers results immediately in spending of MPC × $1,000. Hence the total effect must be less. An increase in taxes of $1,000 does not reduce consumption by $1,000, but rather by an amount equal to MPC × $1,000. The reason for this is that people pay part of their increased taxes from their saving; hence the impact of the tax is only partly on consumption, and therefore the tax multiplier will be less than the government purchases multiplier.[3]

The Balanced Budget Multiplier

From our foregoing discussion we may now note what happens in the case of the "balanced budget." Is there any net impact on the economy if the increase in taxes and government purchases are of an equal amount?

[3] The simplest discussion for the beginning student is probably that of J. P. McKenna, *Intermediate Economic Theory*, New York: Holt, 1958, pp. 280–283.

The answer is yes, for the reason that the reduction in spending resulting from the tax is not equal to what the government spends. Consumption is not reduced by the amount of the tax because part of the tax is paid out of saving. If we substitute MPC values into the government purchases and government tax multipliers we can see that the difference between the two is one. With an MPC of .75 the multiplier for government is $1/(1 - .75)$ and that for taxes is $- .75/(1 - .75)$; the difference between these two fractions is 1. This means that income will rise by 1 times the amount of increase in government expenditures. Since the transfer and tax multipliers are the same except for sign one would expect that an equal increase in transfers and taxes would just negate each other.

Our discussion of the balanced budget multiplier has rested on some rather rigid assumptions. (1) We should note that it refers to government purchases of goods and services and not transfer payments (whose multiplier would just offset that of the negative tax multiplier). (2) It further assumes that those who pay the taxes have the same MPC as those who sell their goods and services to the government. (3) It neglects the impact of both the government's purchases and taxes on investment. Different types of purchases could affect business differently, perhaps even encouraging plant expansion in some cases. Of course, the source of the increase in taxes could affect either investment or consumption differently. And the impact of either action on business psychology can either inspire confidence or create doubts.

These qualifications to the balanced budget multiplier typify many policy problems in fiscal and monetary policy. Further, the use of the balanced budget as a device for significantly expanding income in the economy is quite inefficient on other grounds. It means that a very large increase in government purchases would have to take place and this would entail a very sizable shift in the allocation of resources from private to public uses. This in itself may be neither necessary nor desired. In addition, it would require large, self-defeating, and unnecessary increases in taxes which may cause further difficulties.[4]

Summary

Let us at this point bring together the main ideas just presented. We stated that we could have equilibrium with

$$Y = C + I + G_p \tag{8-28}$$

which we can now write as

$$Y = (a + cY_d) + I + G_p \tag{8-29}$$

[4] The literature on the balanced budget multiplier is extensive. The more important studies are listed in R. A. Musgrave, *The Theory of Public Finance*, New York: McGraw-Hill, 1959, p. 43, note 1.

in which we have substituted the value of C. Since disposable income is equal to $Y - T_x + TR$, we substitute this into our previous equation and get

$$Y = a + c(Y - T_x + TR) + I + G_p \qquad (8\text{-}30)$$

which is the same as

$$Y = a + cY - cT_x + cTR + I + G_p \qquad (8\text{-}31)$$

We should note that the equilibrium position can also be written as

$$I + G_p = S + T_x - TR \qquad (8\text{-}32)$$

We can also represent an increase in income when both government purchases and taxes are increased as

$$\Delta Y = \left(\frac{1}{1-c}\Delta G_p\right) + \left(-\frac{1}{1-c}c\,\Delta T_x\right) \qquad \text{from 8-9 and 8-26} \quad (8\text{-}33)$$

which becomes $[1/(1-c)](\Delta G_p - c\,\Delta T_x)$.

INDUCED TAXES

Our previous discussion has dealt simply with what may be called lump sum taxes; that is, they are autonomously determined. They were independent of the level of income. We know, of course, that in reality the level of taxation is also influenced by the level of income—as income increases the tax take will go up and vice versa. The problem becomes even more complex because not only do total tax collections increase as income goes up, but the rate of the tax increases also. This is because of the progressive income tax. In Figure 8-1 we show how the tax rate

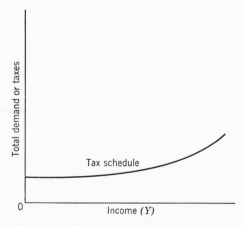

Figure 8-1. Tax collections and the tax rate increase as income increases.

increases as income increases. If the income tax were a constant percent, say 20 percent, of income then our tax schedule would be a straight line. However, since the tax rate increases as income increases, the tax schedule assumes the form of a concave curve. The primary significance of this is that the multiplier resulting from an increase in either government or investment expenditures will be less. This follows from the fact that each successive increase in income results not only in a tax being imposed, but in a tax whose rate increases as income increases. We have dealt previously with an autonomous, lump sum tax. Now we must deal with a tax which is dependent on the level of income.

The fact that taxes increase along with the increase in income is referred to as the "marginal propensity to tax." If we let d stand for our lump sum tax and t stand for our tax rate, then the total tax collection of government will be represented by $T_y = d + tY$. Note that we have assumed that the marginal tax rate is constant, not that it increases as income increases, which would be more realistic. If the marginal tax rate is 20 percent, then each successive increase in income is reduced by one-fifth. We can express this algebraically as follows, starting with equilibrium again:

$$Y = C + I + G_p \tag{8-34}$$

$$Y = a + cY_d + I + G_p \tag{8-35}$$

We know that disposable income is equal to total income minus taxes plus transfers (see equation 8-10), or $Y_d = Y - T_x + TR$. If we allow T_y to represent net taxes, or the difference between taxes and transfers, we get $T_y = T_x - TR$. Disposable income is then $Y_d = Y - T_y$. Next let us substitute $Y_d = Y - T_y$ in equation 8-35.

$$Y = a + c(Y - T_y) + I + G_p \tag{8-36}$$

Now substituting $T_y = T_x - TR$ for T_y we obtain

$$Y = a + c[Y - (T_x - TR)] + I + G_p \tag{8-37}$$

or, since $T_x = d - tY$, we obtain

$$Y = a + c\{Y - [(d + tY) - TR]\} + I + G_p \tag{8-38}$$

We can now either drop TR for the moment or subtract TR from d, in which case d becomes a net lump sum tax minus transfers item. In either case we secure the following:

$$Y = a + cY - cd - ctY + I + G_p \tag{8-39}$$

$$Y - cY + ctY = a - cd + I + G_p \tag{8-40}$$

$$Y(1 - c + ct) = a - cd + I + G_p \tag{8-41}$$

$$Y = \frac{a - cd + I + G_p}{1 - c + ct}, \quad \text{or} \quad \frac{1}{1 - c + ct}(a - cd + I + G_p) \tag{8-42}$$

Equation 8-42 represents our equilibrium position with a proportional tax which is levied on each successive increase in income. The increase in income is expressed as follows:

$$\Delta Y = \frac{1}{1 - c + ct} \Delta(I + G_p). \tag{8-43}$$

The multiplier for a change in C, I, or G_p when a proportional tax is included is

$$k_{gt} = \frac{1}{1 - c + ct} \tag{8-44}$$

The multiplier is computed as follows: The original level of income is

$$Y = \frac{a - cd + I + G_p}{1 - c + ct} \tag{8-45}$$

and the level of income after an increase in I or G is

$$Y + \Delta Y = \frac{a - cd + I + G + \Delta(I + G_p)}{1 - c + ct}$$

or

$$\frac{a - cd + I + G_p}{1 - c + ct} + \frac{1}{1 - c + ct} \Delta(I + G_p) \tag{8-46}$$

Subtracting Y from $Y + \Delta Y$ we get

$$\Delta Y = \frac{a - cd + I + G_p}{1 - c + ct} + \frac{\Delta(I + G_p)}{1 - c + ct} - \frac{a - cd + I + G_p}{1 - c + ct} \tag{8-47}$$

which becomes

$$\Delta Y = \frac{\Delta(I + G_p)}{1 - c + ct} = \left(\frac{1}{1 - c + ct}\right) \Delta(I + G_p) \tag{8-48}$$

which states that the increase in income is equal to $1/(1 - c - ct)$ times the increase in I and/or G. Therefore $1/(1 - c + ct)$ is the multiplier.[5]

It is significant to note again that this multiplier is considerably smaller than that without taxes, and that it will be smaller than if only a lump sum tax is used (because here we are using both the lump sum and the *proportional* income tax). The multiplier with a progressive income tax would become even smaller yet.

The impact of both the constant tax rate, which would be proportional, and the progressive tax rate can be shown with a few numerical examples.

---

[5] See B. N. Siegel, *Aggregate Economics and Public Policy*, Homewood, Ill.: Irwin, 1960, pp. 106–109, and T. C. Schelling, *National Income: An Introduction to Algebraic Analysis*, New York: McGraw-Hill, 1951, especially pp. 65–72, and pp. 37–38, 75, 91, 115.

First assume a MPC of .8 and a tax rate of .25. Without the tax the value of the multiplier $1/(1 - c)$ would be 5 [since $1/(1 - .8) = 5$]. With the tax the multiplier $1/(1 - c + ct)$ is reduced to 2.5 [since $1/(1 - .8 + .2) = 2.5$] the tax rate therefore has reduced this particular multiplier to half its original value. If we assume now that income is at a higher level, and that the rate of tax at this level is .30, then the value of the multiplier becomes 2.27. This is what we expect to happen in the economy because our tax system is progressive. The implications for fiscal policy are surely obvious.

THE SUPER MULTIPLIER

Our discussion thus far has included the multiplier effects on income and consumption of an increase in government purchases of goods and services, government transfers, lump sum taxes, and proportional and progressive taxes, and the most familiar investment multiplier. Up to this point we have assumed that investment was autonomous. What happens, however, when we include in our analysis the impact of the level of income on investment? Does not an increasing level of income result in induced investment? The answer is that it does.

If we assume that we have an increase in autonomous investment that raises the level of income and consumption, then it is likely (depending on the overall state of profits, plant capacity, and available funds for investment) that some induced investment will result also. We see then that we have a marginal propensity to consume and a marginal propensity to invest, both of which can together be called the marginal propensity to spend. We have therefore the following equation:

$$\text{MPS} = \text{MPC} + \text{MPI} \qquad (8\text{-}49)$$

which can be written in multiplier form as

$$k_s = \frac{1}{1 - (\text{MPC} + \text{MPI})} = \frac{1}{1 - \text{MPC} - \text{MPI}} \qquad (8\text{-}50)$$

in which k_s is the multiplier for MPS. The important point is that when conditions are conducive to induced investment we will have a larger multiplier.

The computation of the multiplier is as follows. Assume that there is no government and that income equilibrium is $Y = C + I_a + I_i$, which states that income is equal to consumption plus autonomous investment plus induced investment. We next have the increase in income resulting from the increase in autonomous investment as

$$\Delta Y = \Delta C + \Delta I_a + \Delta I_i \qquad (8\text{-}51)$$

which tells us that the increase in income is equal to the increase in autonomous I plus induced C and I. Our spending multiplier is

$$k_s = \frac{\Delta Y}{\Delta I_a} \qquad (8\text{-}52)$$

Now ΔI_a is equal to $\Delta Y - \Delta C - \Delta I_i$, which we substitute in the foregoing equation to obtain

$$k_s = \frac{\Delta Y}{\Delta Y - \Delta C - \Delta I_i} \qquad (8\text{-}53)$$

If we next divide both the numerator and denominator by ΔY we get

$$k_s = \frac{1}{1 - \Delta C/\Delta Y - \Delta I_i/\Delta Y} \qquad (8\text{-}54)$$

The second fraction in the denominator is the MPC and the third is the MPI, which we can substitute in the equation and obtain

$$k_s = \frac{1}{1 - \text{MPC} - \text{MPI}} \qquad (8\text{-}55)$$

It is common to specify the MPI by some letter, say m, with which the following results.

$$k_s = \frac{1}{1 - c - m} \qquad (8\text{-}56)$$

It appears that we have strayed a long way from our original simple multiplier. We have now a rather complex multiplier which must account for the impact of a change in income in terms of the MPC, MPI, government purchases, taxes, transfers, and autonomous investment.

At this point let us incorporate induced investment into our multiplier. Dividing investment into the two categories of induced and autonomous we have our equilibrium income as follows:

$$Y = a + c[Y - (d + tY)] + I_a + I_i + G_p \qquad (8\text{-}57)$$

Since induced investment is a function of the level of income, and we assume that m represents that portion of income, the I_i term becomes mY. We now have

$$Y = a + c[Y - (d + tY)] + I_a + mY + G_p \qquad (8\text{-}58)$$

which is the same as

$$Y = a + cY - cd - ctY + I_a + mY + G_p \qquad (8\text{-}59)$$

Transposing we have

$$Y - cY - mY + ctY = a - cd + I_a + G_p \qquad (8\text{-}60)$$

which becomes

$$Y(1 - c - m + ct) = a - cd + I_a + G_p \qquad (8\text{-}61)$$

or

$$Y = \frac{a - cd + I_a + G_p}{1 - c - m + ct} \qquad (8\text{-}62)$$

The level of income after an increase in I or G is

$$Y + \Delta Y = \frac{a - cd + I_a + G_p + \Delta(I_a + G_p)}{1 - c - m + ct} \qquad (8\text{-}63)$$

If we subtract Y from $Y + \Delta Y$ we get

$$\Delta Y = \frac{a - cd + I_a + G_p}{1 - c - m + ct} + \frac{\Delta(I_a + G_p)}{1 - c - m + ct} - \frac{a - cd + I_a + G_p}{1 - c - m + ct}$$

$$(8\text{-}64)$$

which becomes

$$\Delta Y = \frac{\Delta(I_a + G_p)}{1 - c - m + ct} \quad \text{or} \quad \frac{1}{1 - c - m + ct} \Delta(I_a + G_p) \quad (8\text{-}65)$$

which states that the increase in income is equal to $1/(1 - c - m + ct)$ times the increase in I_a and/or G_p. Therefore, $1/(1 - c - m + ct)$ is the multiplier, which may be designated as k_{gti}. In other words, the more that we have to subtract from 1 in the denominator the larger the multiplier will be; and the more we add to 1 in the denominator (see $+ct$) the smaller the multiplier will be.

We have not dealt with transfers explicitly here. We noted previously that we could adjust d to incorporate the impact of transfers or we could deal with them separately. If we prefer to deal with them separately, that is, making d equal only to the lump sum tax and introducing transfers (TR) explicitly, we obtain

$$Y = C + I + G_p \qquad (8\text{-}66)$$

$$Y = a + c[Y - (d + tY) + TR] + I_a + mY + G_p \qquad (8\text{-}67)$$

Here again induced investment is mY and government purchases are represented by G_p.

The derivation of the multiplier when transfers are introduced explicitly is

$$Y = a + c[Y - (d + tY) + TR] + I_a + mY + G_p \qquad (8\text{-}68)$$

$$Y = a + c[Y - d - tY + TR] + I_a + mY + G_p \qquad (8\text{-}69)$$

$$Y = a + cY - cd - ctY + cTR + I_a + mY + G_p \qquad (8\text{-}70)$$

$$Y - cY + ctY - mY = a - cd + cTR + I_a + G_p \qquad (8\text{-}71)$$

$$Y(1 - c + ct - m) = a - cd + cTR + I_a + G_p \qquad (8\text{-}72)$$

$$Y = \frac{a - cd + cTR + I_a + G_p}{1 - c - m + ct} \qquad (8\text{-}73)$$

$$Y + \Delta Y = \frac{a - cd + cTR + I_a + G_p}{1 - c - m + ct} + \frac{1}{1 - c - m + ct}$$
$$\times [\Delta(I_a + G_p) + c\,\Delta TR] \qquad (8\text{-}74)$$

$$\Delta Y = \frac{a - cd + cTR + I_a + G_p}{1 - c - m + ct} + \frac{\Delta(I_a + G_p) + c\,\Delta TR}{1 - c - m + ct}$$
$$- \frac{a - cd + cTR + I_a + G_p}{1 - c - m + ct} \qquad (8\text{-}75)$$

$$\Delta Y = \frac{1}{1 - c - m + ct} [\Delta(I_a + G_p) + c\,\Delta TR] \qquad (8\text{-}76)$$

Since there is no increase in I_a or G_p, the increase in income resulting from an increase in transfers is

$$\Delta Y = \frac{1}{1 - c - m + ct} (c\,\Delta TR) \qquad (8\text{-}77)$$

and the multiplier is

$$k_{TR_{ti}} = \frac{c}{1 - c - m + ct} \qquad (8\text{-}78)$$

Transfers have now been separately accounted for. The tax multiplier would be the same except that its sign would be negative.

On the one hand we have introduced several factors which serve to increase the value of the multiplier—induced investment (mY) and government transfers; on the other hand we have added a major factor which reduces the value of the multiplier, mainly taxes. We should note that at higher levels of income transfers may reduce the value of the multiplier since they will tend to decline. Unemployment insurance payments, for example, decline as income increases. Also, since we have omitted foreign transactions, we have failed to note that at higher levels of income our imports increase, serving to reduce our net foreign investment figure.

SUMMARY OF EQUATIONS

It is perhaps time to summarize the more important equations that we have dealt with so far. They are listed in Table 8-1.

GRAPHIC, TABULAR, AND ALGEBRAIC ILLUSTRATIONS

In Table 8-2 we have incorporated the variables discussed before. In Part A we have our simple equilibrium data, in Part B we raise government purchases by $20 billion, in Part C we add government transfers of $50 billion, in Part D we introduce a lump sum tax of $25 billion, in Part E we add induced investment as 5 percent of income, in Part F a proportional tax, and in Part G we add a progressive income tax. The marginal propensity to consume is assumed to be .80 throughout the table.

The data for Part A of Table 8-2 are illustrated in Figure 8-2. This is the simple case of $Y = C + I + G_p$. Here substituting the proper values for $C + I + G_p$ we have an equilibrium income of $450 billion. Aggregate demand should be compared with the income (output) level to see that the two are equal only at the $450 billion level. It will be recalled that column 5 is the sum of columns 2, 3, and 4. That the multiplier is 5 can be readily seen by noting that the addition of either $30 billion I or $30 billion G increases income by $150 billion. Or, since $C = a + cY$, we can state our equilibrium as follows:

$$Y = a + cY + I + G_p$$
$$Y - cY = a + I + G_p$$
$$Y(1 - c) = a + I + G_p$$
$$Y = \frac{a}{1 - c} + \frac{I}{1 - c} + \frac{G_p}{1 - c}$$
$$Y = \frac{30}{1 - .8} + \frac{30}{1 - .8} + \frac{30}{1 - .8} = \$450 \text{ billion.}$$

In Part B of Table 8-2 we raise government purchases by $20 billion, or to $50 billion. The $50 billion level of government purchases we designate as G'. Our new equilibrium is now $550 billion, and our

Table 8-1. Summary of Equations

1 Equation	2 Explanation or Comment	3 Description
$Y = C + I + G_p$		Equil. income (8-1)
$C = a + cY$	$a = C$ at zero income; $c = $ MPC	Consumption (8-2)
$k = \dfrac{1}{1-c}$	$\dfrac{\Delta Y}{\Delta I} = \dfrac{1}{1-c}$	Simple multiplier (8-8)
$\Delta Y = \Delta I + c\,\Delta Y$	$c\,\Delta Y = \Delta C$	Increased income via increased I (8-4)
$\Delta Y = \dfrac{1}{1-c}\Delta G = k\,\Delta G_p$	$k_g = \dfrac{1}{1-c}$	Gov't purchases multiplier same as simple investment multiplier (8-9)
$Y_d = Y - T_x + TR$	$T_x = $ taxes; $TR = $ transfers	Disposable income = income − taxes + transfers (8-10)
$\Delta C = c\,\Delta_d$		Increase in C = MPC × increase in disposable income (8-12)
$\Delta Y = \dfrac{1}{1-c}(c\,\Delta TR)$	$k_{TR} = \dfrac{c}{1-c}$, 1 less than purchases multiplier	Gov't transfers multiplier (col. 2) (8-15)
$\Delta Y = \dfrac{1}{1-c}(-c\,\Delta T_x)$	$k_{T_x} = -\dfrac{c}{1-c}$	Gov't tax multiplier (col. 2) (8-26)
$Y = a + c[Y - (d + tY)] + I + G_p$	$d = $ lump sum taxes (adjusted for transfers or not) $t = $ income tax rate	Equil. with lump sum and proportional income tax (8-38, 39)

$$Y = \frac{a - cd + I + G_p}{1 - c + ct}$$

Same as above (8-45)

$$\Delta Y = \frac{1}{1 - c + ct} \Delta(I + G_p)$$

$$k_{gt} = \frac{1}{1 - c + ct}$$

Multiplier with proportional income tax (col. 2) (8-48)

$$\Delta Y = \Delta C + \Delta I_a + \Delta I_i$$

I_a = autonomous investment; I_i = induced investment

Increase in income with induced investment (8-51)

$$\Delta Y = \frac{1}{1 - c - m} \times \Delta I$$

m = marginal propensity to invest

$k_s = 1/(1 - c - m)$

Multiplier (spending) accounting for induced investment (8-56)

$$Y = a + c[Y - (d + tY)] + I_a + mY + G_p$$

$$Y = \frac{a - cd + I_a + G_p}{1 - c - m + ct}$$

Equil. with induced I, lump sum and proportional income tax (8-59, 62)

$$\Delta Y = \frac{1}{1 - c - m - ct} \times \Delta(I_a + G_p)$$

$$k_{gti} = \frac{1}{1 - c - m - ct}$$

Multiplier with MPI and proportional income tax added (col. 2) (8-65)

$$Y = a + c[Y - (d + tY) + TR] + I_a + mY + G_p$$

G_p = gov't purchases; TR = gov't transfers

Equil. with transfers and gov't purchases designated separately (8-68)

$$\Delta Y = \frac{1}{1 - c - m + ct}(c \, \Delta TR)$$

$$k_{TR_{ti}} = \frac{c}{1 - c - m + ct}$$

Transfer multiplier with induced investment and proportional income tax (8-77, 78)

Table 8-2. Equilibrium Income with Different Variables (billions of dollars). MPC = .80

	Part A $I=30,\ G_p=30$ $k=5,\ a=30$				Part B $G_p'=50,\ I=30$ $k=5,\ a=30$		Part C $TR=50,\ I=30,\ G_p'=50$ $k_{TR}=4,\ a=30$				
Income	Consumption	Investment	Gov't	Aggregate Demand	Gov't	Aggregate Demand	Gov't Trans-fers of \$50 billion	Income	Disposable Income	Consumption	Aggregate Demand
Y	C	I	G_v	$C+I+G_p$	G'	$C+I+G_p'$	G_{TR}	Y	Y_d	C'	$C'+I+G_p'$
1	2	3	4	5	6	7	8	9	10	11	12
0	30	30	30	90	50	110	50	0	50	70	150
50	70	30	30	130	50	150	50	50	100	110	190
100	110	30	30	170	50	190	50	100	150	150	230
150	150	30	30	210	50	230	50	150	200	190	270
200	190	30	30	250	50	270	50	200	250	230	310
250	230	30	30	290	50	310	50	250	300	270	350
300	270	30	30	330	50	350	50	300	350	310	390
350	310	30	30	370	50	390	50	350	400	350	430
400	350	30	30	410	50	430	50	400	450	390	470
450	390	30	30	450	50	470	50	450	500	430	510
500	430	30	30	490	50	510	50	500	550	470	550
550	470	30	30	530	50	550	50	550	600	510	590
600	510	30	30	570	50	590	50	600	650	550	630
							50	650	700	590	670
							50	700	750	630	710
								750	800	670	750

Part D MPC = .80 **Part E**

Part D: $T_x = 25$, $TR = 50$; $I = 30$, $G'_p = 50$; $k_{Tx} = 4$, $a = 30$

Part E: $I_i = 0.05Y$, $I_a = 30$; $G'_p = 50$, $TR = 50$; $T_x = 25$, $a = 30$

Taxes	Income	Disposable Income	Consumption	Aggregate Demand	Induced Investment	Income	Disposable Income	Consumption	Aggregate Demand
T_x	Y	Y_d	C''	$C'' + I + G'_p$	I_i	Y	Y_d	C''	$C'' + I_a + I_i + G'_p$
13	14	15	16	17	18	19	20	21	22
25	0	25	50	130	0	0	25	50	130
25	50	75	90	170	2.5	50	75	90	172.5
25	100	125	130	210	5	100	125	130	215
25	150	175	170	250	7.5	150	175	170	257.5
25	200	225	210	290	10	200	225	210	300
25	250	275	250	330	12.5	250	275	250	342.5
25	300	325	290	370	15	300	325	290	385
25	350	375	330	410	17.5	350	375	330	427.5
25	400	425	370	450	20	400	425	370	470
25	450	475	410	490	22.5	450	475	410	512.5
25	500	525	450	530	25	500	525	450	555
25	550	575	490	570	27.5	550	575	490	597.5
25	600	625	530	610	30	600	625	530	640
25	650	675	570	650	32.5	650	675	570	682.5
					35	700	725	610	725
					37.5	750	775	650	767.5
					40	800	825	690	810
					42.5	850	875	730	852.5
					43.4	867	892	743.6	867
					45	900	925	770	855
					47.5	950	975	810	937.5
					50	1000	1025	850	980

Table 8-2 (*Continued*)

MPC = .80

Part F

Tax rate = 0.05
$I_i = 0.05Y$, $I_a = 30$, $G_v = 50$
$TR = 40$, $d = 25$, $a = 30$

(23) Tax Rate (Percent)	(24) Income Y	(25) Disposable Income Y_d	(26) Consumption C	(27) Aggregate Demand $C + I_a + I_i + G'_v$
0.05	0	25	50	130
0.05	50	72.5	88	170.5
0.05	100	120	126	211
0.05	150	167.5	164	251.5
0.05	200	215	202	292
0.05	250	262.5	240	332.5
0.05	300	310.0	278	373.0
0.05	350	357.5	316	413.5
0.05	400	405.0	354	454.0
0.05	450	452.5	392	494.5
0.05	500	500.0	430	535.0
0.05	550	547.5	468	575.5
0.05	600	595.0	506	616.0
0.05	650	642.5	544	656.5
0.05	684.2	675.4	570.3	684.2
0.05	700	690.0	582	697.0
0.05	750	737.5	620	737.5

Part G

Tax rate = as given in column 28
$I_i = 0.05Y$, $I_a = 30$, $G_v = 50$
$TR = 50$, $d = 25$ (lump-sum tax), $a = 30$

(28) Tax Rate (Percent)	(29) Income Y	(30) Disposable Income Y_d	(31) Tax (Income) tY	(32) Consumption C	(33) Aggregate Demand $C + I_a + I_i + G'_v$
0	0	25	0	50	130
0	50	75	0	90	172.5
0	100	125	0	130	215
0	150	175	0	170	257.5
0	200	225	0	210	300
5	250	275	15	250	342.5
5	300	310	17.5	278	373
10	350	357.5	40	316	413.5
10	400	385	45	338	438
15	450	430	72.5	374	476.5
15	481.5	434	82.5	377	481.5*
20	550	492.5	120	424	531.5
20	600	500	130	434	544
20	650	545	140	466	578.5
20	700	585	150	498	613
20	750	625	160	530	647.5
20	800	665	170	556	676
20	850	705	170	594	716.5

* Induced investment is $0.05Y \times 481.5$ or 24.08 billion.

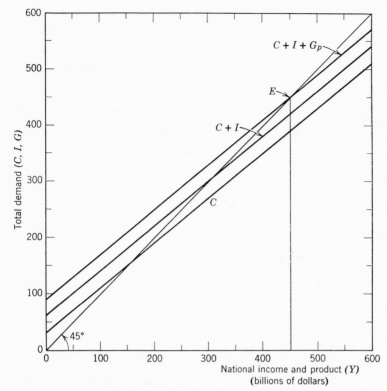

Figure 8-2. Equilibrium with $C + I + G_p$. (See Part A of Table 8-2.)

multiplier is 5 ($\Delta Y/\Delta G_p = 100/20 = 5$). Our equilibrium is as follows:

$$Y = C + I + G_p$$
$$Y = a + cY + I + G_p'$$
$$Y(1 - c) = I + G_p'$$
$$Y = \frac{a}{1 - c} + \frac{I}{1 - c} + \frac{G_p'}{1 - c}$$
$$Y = \frac{30}{1 - .8} + \frac{30}{1 - .8} + \frac{50}{1 - .8} = \$550 \text{ billion}$$

This is illustrated in Figure 8-3.

In Part C of Table 8-1 we introduce government transfers of \$50 billion. I is still \$30 billion and G_p' is \$50 billion. Our new equilibrium is now \$750 billion. Note that government transfers \$50 billion, but that the increase in income is only \$200 billion, giving a multiplier of 4. We noted that the government transfer multiplier is

$$c/(1 - c) = .8/(1 - .8) = 4$$

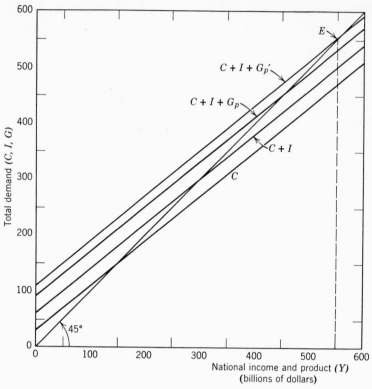

Figure 8-3. The impact of an increase in government purchases. (See Part *B* of Table 8-2.)

The multiplier in terms of increased consumption, however, is 5.

$$\Delta Y / \Delta C = 200/40 = 5$$

Our equilibrium in algebraic terms is

$$Y = C + I + G_p$$
$$Y = (a + cYd) + I + G_p'$$
$$Y = a + c(Y - Tx + TR) + I + G_p' \qquad \text{(we here compute } Yd\text{)}$$
$$Y = a + cY - cTx + cTR + I + G_p'$$
$$Y - cY = a - cTx + cTR + I + G_p'$$
$$Y(1 - c) = 30 - .8(0) + .8(50) + 30 + 50$$

$$\qquad\qquad\qquad (\textit{Note: } a = 30, \text{ since it is a constant})$$

$$Y(1 - c) = 150$$

$$Y = \frac{150}{1 - c} = \frac{150}{1 - .8} = \$750 \text{ billion}$$

In Part C we have added \$50 billion in transfers at all income levels. Hence we can no longer permit Y_d to be synonymous with Y, but must designate Y_d separately. Therefore disposable income (Y_d) is increased by \$50 billion at every income level. (See column 10.) In Figure 8-4 we note that the consumption function shifts upward by \$40 billion (80 percent of the increase in disposable income). It therefore shifts the $C + I$ and $C + I + G_p'$ lines upward by this same amount. This new consumption line is designated by C', and the new aggregate demand line by $C' + I + G_p'$. We should also carefully note that this increase in transfers did not affect government purchases of goods and services, but rather had its impact on disposable income and consumption. Since it is reflected in disposable income and since consumers have an MPC of .8, the initial increase in consumer expenditure is only \$40 billion.

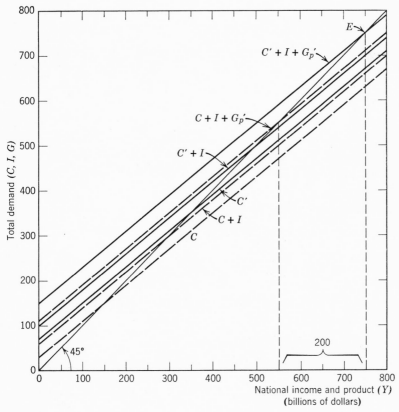

Figure 8-4. The introduction of government transfers and an upward shift in the consumption function. (See Part C of Table 8-2.)

In Part *D* of Table 8-2 we introduce a lump sum tax of $25 billion. We retain our transfers of $50 billion, G_p' of $50 billion, and I of 30. We know that an increase in taxes will not reduce consumption by the amount of the tax increase because part of the tax payment will come out of consumer saving. We further know that the reduction in consumption will be equal to MPC × tax, which is .8 × 25 or $20 billion. Therefore, consumption is reduced by $20 billion and saving by $5 billion. The consumption line is now depressed by $20 billion at every income level, as shown by the *C″* line in Figure 8-5, and by column 16 in Table 8-2. Income is reduced by $100 billion, to a new equilibrium level of $650 billion. In Table 8-2, Column 15, we see that disposable income is reduced by $25 billion, but the reduction in income is only $100, and therefore the multiplier is 4. We noted that the government tax multiplier is $-c/(1 - c)$, which gives us a value of -4. Our equilibrium level can

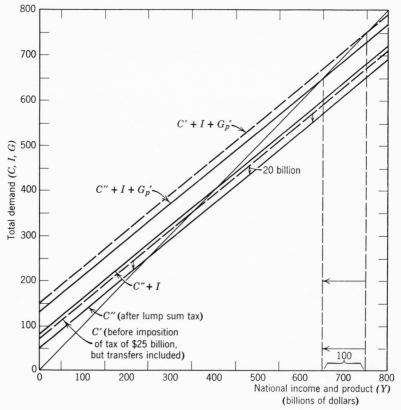

Figure 8-5. An increase in taxes of $25 billion shifts the consumption function downward by $20 billion. (See Part *D* of Table 8-2.)

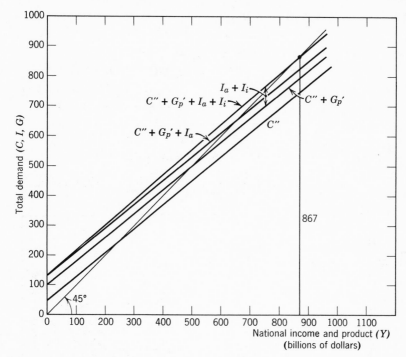

Figure 8-6. Equilibrium with induced investment. (See Part *E* of Table 8-2).

now be stated as follows:

$$Y = C + I + G_p'$$
$$Y = (a + cYd) + I + G_p'$$
$$Y = a + c(Y - Tx + TR) + I + G_p'$$
$$Y = a + cY - cTx + cTR + I + G_p'$$
$$Y - cY = a - cTx + cTR + I + G_p'$$
$$Y(1 - c) = 30 - .8(25) + .8(50) + 30 + 50$$

(*Note:* $a = 30$ since it is a constant)

$$Y(1 - c) = 130$$

$$Y = \frac{130}{1 - c} = \frac{130}{1 - .8} = \$650 \text{ billion}$$

In Part *E* of the table we introduce induced investment. It will increase with the level of income at the rate of $.05Y$. Taxes are still \$25 billion, G_p' \$50 billion, transfers \$50 billion, and I_a \$30 billion. Our new equilibrium is now \$870 billion. In Figure 8-6 we see that the I_i line, designating induced investment, is not parallel to the $C'' + G_p' + I_a$

line. Our algebraic statement is

$$Y = C + I + G_p$$
$$Y = a + cYd + I_a + I_i + G_p{'}$$
$$Y = a + c(Y - Tx + TR) + I_a + mY + G_p{'}$$
$$I_a = mY = .05Y$$
$$Y = a + cY - cTx + cTR + I_a + mY + G_p{'}$$
$$Y - cY - mY = a - cTx + cTR + I_a + G_p{'}$$
$$Y(1 - c - m) = a - cTx + cTR + I_a + G_p{'}$$
$$Y(1 - c - m) = 30 - .8(25) + .8(50) + 30 + 50$$
$$Y = \frac{130}{1 - c - m} = \frac{130}{1 - .8 - .05} = \$867 \text{ billion}$$

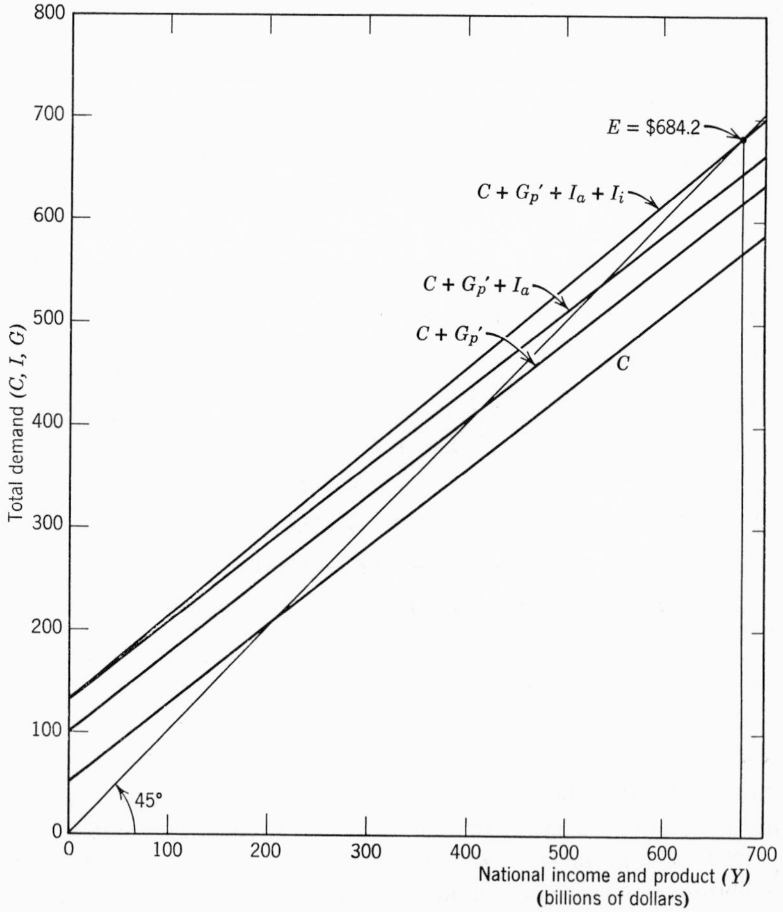

Figure 8-7. The impact of a proportional income tax. (See Part F of Table 8-2.)

In Part F we show the impact of a proportional income tax. Our equilibrium is

$$Y = C + I + G_p$$

$$Y = a + cYd + I_a + I_i + G_p'$$

$$Y = a + c(Y - Tx + TR) + I_a + I_i + G_p'$$

$$Y = a + c[Y - (d + ty) + TR] + I_a + I_i + G_p'$$

$$Y = a + cY - cd - ctY + cTR + I_a + mY + G_p'$$

$$Y - cY + ctY - mY = a - cd + cTR + I_a + G_p'$$

$$Y(1 - c + ct - m) = a - cd + cTR + I_a + G_p'$$

$$Y(1 - c + ct - m) = 30 - .8(25) + 30 + 50$$

$$Y = \frac{130}{1 - c + ct - m} = \frac{130}{1 - .8 + .8(.05) - .05}$$

$$= \frac{130}{.19} = 684.2$$

Equilibrium is depicted graphically in Figure 8-7.

In Part G, we show the impact of a progressive income tax. Our equilibrium in algebraic terms is

$$Y = C + I + G_p$$

$$Y = a + cYd + I_a + I_i + G_p'$$

$$Y = a + c(Y - Tx + TR) + I_a + I_i + G_p'$$

$$Y = a + c[Y - (d + tY) + TR] + I_a + I_i + G_p'$$

$$Y = a + cY - cd - ctY + cTR + I_a + mY + G_p'$$

$$Y - cY + ctY - mY = a - cd + cTR + I_a + G_p'$$

$$Y(1 - c + ct - m) = a - cd + cTR + I_a + G_p'$$

$$Y(1 - c + ct - m) = 30 - .8(25) + .8(50) + 30 + 50$$

$$Y = \frac{130}{1 - c + ct - m} = \frac{130}{1 - .8 + .8(.15) - .05}$$

$$= \frac{130}{.27} = \$481.5 \text{ billion}$$

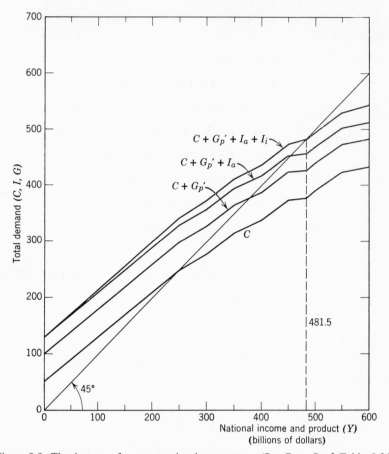

Figure 8-8. The impact of a progressive income tax. (See Part *G* of Table 8-2.)

In this computation we substituted the tax rate at the equilibrium level. Under ordinary circumstances this would not have been possible because we would not know the equilibrium level of income and hence would not possibly know the corresponding tax rate. The graphic presentation appears in Figure 8-8.

9

Using Fiscal Policy to Raise and Lower
the Level of Income

In Chapter 8 we noted the various policies that might be pursued to raise or lower the level of aggregate demand. If our objective is to raise aggregate demand we may increase the level of government purchases or transfers, or we may lower taxes, or use various combinations of these actions. Per dollar of revenue loss, however, the use of government purchases is the most efficient, because the multiplier for government purchases is greater than that for either increased transfers or reduced taxes. If the MPC is .8, for every $4 of increased government purchases we would have to reduce taxes by $5 or increase transfers by $5 to get the same impact. If the MPC is 2/3, for every $2 increase in government purchases we would have to increase transfers, or reduce taxes, by $3. Of course, if the *recipients* of the transfers, or those whose taxes were reduced, had an MPC of 100 percent, the impact would be the same. Furthermore, there may be little difference between an increase in government purchases and a tax reduction (or increase in transfers) if those who sell to the government have a low MPC. The qualifications noted in the previous chapter still hold.

Assuming the conditions we have stipulated, however, the increase in government purchases results in less deficit than the transfer increase or tax reduction. We could, in addition, use the balanced budget approach, but this would involve a substantially greater increase in both taxes and government purchases to attain a given increase in income. If we had a simple economy in which everyone paid the same taxes and in which everyone had the same MPC these computations would be much easier. However, we must deal with the problems of (1) a progressive tax rate, (2) different MPC's, and (3) different individuals paying different rates of taxes at a single point in time.

RAISING THE LEVEL OF INCOME

Although it is sometimes ridiculous to push to extremes ideas that are based on unproved assumptions—such as a constant MPC—it is nonetheless useful to do so as a point of departure in policy formation. We want, at this point, to utilize some of our analysis from the preceding chapter, showing additional purposes for which this information can be used.

Raise Government Purchases

We noted that our simple multiplier was $k = 1/(1 - c)$. From this we can determine the needed increase in government purchases necessary to raise income to a given figure, say $10 billion. Assuming that there will be no effect on investment—it is autonomous, in other words—that our MPC $= 2/3$, and that we are not going to raise taxes, we will find that our multiplier is 3. Therefore the required increase in government purchases is $3\frac{1}{3}$ billion (10/3). Or we can write

$$\Delta Y = \frac{1}{1 - c} \Delta G_p$$

which becomes

$$10 = \frac{1}{1 - 2/3} \Delta G_p$$

$$\Delta G_p = \frac{10}{3} = \$3\frac{1}{3} \text{ billion}$$

If, however, we have to contend with a proportional income tax, we must use the multiplier of $k_{gt} = 1/(1 - c + ct)$, which will give us a smaller numerical multiplier. We have the same assumptions as before, MPC $= 2/3$, investment is autonomous, there is no increase in lump sum taxes, and we have the added assumption of a tax rate of .20. Our multiplier is now 2.14 and the required increase in government purchases is $4.67 billion (10/2.14). Our appropriate equation to determine the required increase in government purchases is

$$\Delta Y = \frac{1}{1 - c + ct} \Delta G_p$$

which becomes

$$10 = \frac{1}{1 - 2/3 + 2/3(.20)} \Delta G_p = 2.14 \, \Delta G_p$$

$$\Delta G_p = \frac{10}{2.14} = \$4.67 \text{ billion}$$

Hence, with the proportional income tax (of rate .20) we need government purchases of $1\frac{1}{3}$ billion more to raise income by \$10 billion.

Raise Transfer Payments

The second alternative is to raise transfer payments, the multiplier for which is as follows: $k_{TR} = c/(1 - c)$. The value of the multiplier is 2, one less than the government purchases multiplier. Hence the increase in transfers required to raise income by \$10 billion is $10/2 = 5$. Or to find the required increase in transfers in our equation we write

$$\Delta Y = \frac{c}{1 - c} \Delta TR$$

which becomes

$$10 = \frac{2/3}{1 - 2/3} \Delta TR$$

$$\Delta TR = \frac{10}{(2/3)/(1 - 2/3)} = \$5 \text{ billion}$$

We have not included a proportional income tax. Its inclusion changes our multiplier to $k_{TRt} = c/(1 - c + ct)$. The value of the multiplier now is 1.43. Therefore, the increase in transfers necessary to increase income by \$10 is $10/1.43 = \$7$ billion. In equation form, assuming a proportional tax rate of .20, we have

$$\Delta Y = \frac{c}{1 - c + ct} \Delta TR$$

which becomes

$$10 = \frac{2/3}{1 - 2/3 + 2/3(.20)} \Delta TR = 1.43 \, \Delta TR$$

$$\Delta TR = \frac{10}{1.43} = \$7 \text{ billion}$$

Lower Taxes (a Reduction in the Lump Sum Tax)

The third situation involves a possible tax cut to raise income by \$10 billion. The multiplier for a cut in lump sum tax is $k_{T_x} = c/(1 - c)$, and our multiplier is the same as with transfers, or 2. (Transfers are often called negative taxes since the multipliers are the same except for sign.)

Again the cut in taxes would have to be $5 billion. In equation form we have

$$\Delta Y = \frac{1}{1 - c}(-c\,\Delta T_x) \quad \text{or} \quad -\frac{c}{1 - c}\,\Delta T_x$$

$$10 = -\frac{2/3}{1 - 2/3}\,\Delta T_x$$

$$\Delta T_x = -\frac{10}{2} = -\$5 \text{ billion}$$

With a proportional income tax our multiplier would be $k_{gt} = c/(1 - c + ct)$. Our equation, assuming again a proportional income tax rate of .20, is

$$\Delta Y = -\frac{c}{1 - c + ct}\,\Delta T_x$$

$$10 = -\frac{2/3}{1 - 2/3 + 2/3(.20)}\,\Delta T_x$$

$$\Delta T_x = -\frac{10}{1.43} = -\$7 \text{ billion}$$

Again, the addition of the proportional tax rate to our multiplier lowers the multiplier to 1.43 and the required lump sum tax reduction is $7 billion. We should note that we have assumed here that the proportional income tax rate t is the same before and after the lump sum tax cut.

[This can be demonstrated as follows. Let $G_p = 50$, $I = 30$, $d = 24$, $TR = 30$, $t = 0.20$, $a = 30$, and MPC $= 2/3$. Solve for equilibrium Y.

$$
\begin{aligned}
Y &= C + I + G_p \\
&= a + cYd + I + G_p \\
&= a + c[Y - (d + tY) + TR] + I + G_p \\
&= a + cY - cd - ctY + cTR + I + G_p \\
Y - cY + ctY &= a - cd + cTR + I + G_p \\
Y(1 - c + ct) &= a - cd + cTR + I + G_p \\
Y &= \frac{a - cd + cTR + I + G_p}{1 - c + ct} \\
&= \frac{30 - \frac{2}{3}(24) + \frac{2}{3}(30) + 30 + 50}{1 - \frac{2}{3} + \frac{2}{3}(.20)} \\
&= \frac{114}{1.4/3} = 244.29 \text{ billion}
\end{aligned}
$$

Now reduce the lump sum tax by \$7 billion, and solve for the new equilibrium Y.

$$Y = \frac{30 - \frac{2}{3}(17) + \frac{2}{3}(30) + 30 + 50}{1 - \frac{2}{3} + \frac{2}{3}(.20)} = \frac{118\frac{2}{3}}{1.4/3} = 254.29 \text{ billion}$$

We see then that a \$7 billion reduction in lump sum taxes raises income by exactly \$10 billion.]

Balanced Budget Expansion

A fourth possibility is to raise the level of income by a balanced budget expansion. In this case our increase in income is equal to k_g times ΔG_p minus k_{T_x} times ΔT_x, or we have

$$\Delta Y = \frac{1}{1 - c} \Delta G_p - \frac{c}{1 - c} \Delta T_x$$

We know that we want to raise income by \$10 billion. We also know that the multipliers for government purchases and lump sum taxes are 3 and -2, respectively;[1] and that ΔG_p is to equal ΔT_x. We can then write

$$\Delta Y = 3\Delta G_p - 2\Delta T_x$$

Since $\Delta G_p = \Delta T_x$ we substitute ΔG_p for ΔT_x.

$$10 = 3\Delta G_p - 2\Delta G_p$$
$$10 = \Delta G_p$$
$$\Delta G_p = \$10 \text{ billion}$$

Since $\Delta T_x = \Delta G_p$

$$\Delta T_x = \$10 \text{ billion}$$

With a proportional income tax we get

$$\Delta Y = \frac{1}{1 - c + ct} \Delta G_p - \frac{c}{1 - c + ct} \Delta T_x$$
$$\Delta Y = 2.143\Delta G_p - 1.43\Delta T_x$$

Since $\Delta G = \Delta T_x$ in a balanced budget expansion we substitute ΔG for ΔT_x

$$10 = 2.143\Delta G_p - 1.43\Delta G_p$$
$$10 = .713\Delta G_p$$
$$\Delta G_p = \$14.025 \text{ billion}$$
$$\Delta T_x = \$14.025 \text{ billion}$$

[1] With a given and constant MPC, k_g is one greater than k_{T_x}. Therefore, if we raise both G_p and T_x by 10 the net impact is 10.

Raise Government Purchases and Lower Taxes

We can also raise G_p and lower T_x in various proportions. Here our increase in income is equal to k_g times ΔG minus k_{T_x} times ΔT_x. Our equation is again

$$\Delta Y = \frac{1}{1-c}\Delta G_p - \frac{c}{1-c}\Delta T_x$$

If we assume a value for G_p of 2 and substitute this into our equation we obtain

$$\Delta Y = 3(2) - 2\Delta T_x$$

$$10 = 6 - 2\Delta T_x$$

$$2\Delta T_x = 6 - 10 = -4$$

$$\Delta T_x = -\$2 \text{ billion}$$

If we decide to raise G_p by 2 billion, then in order to get our desired increase in income we must lower taxes by \$2 billion. The deficit for this transaction is \$4 billion.

Let us perform this same procedure with a proportional income tax. Now our equation becomes (assuming a proportional tax rate of .20)

$$\Delta Y = \frac{1}{1-c+ct}\Delta G_p - \frac{c}{1-c+ct}\Delta T_x$$

If we decide on an increase in G_p of \$2 billion we see that

$$\Delta Y = 2.14(2) - 1.43\Delta T_x$$

$$1.43\Delta T_x = 4.28 - 10 = -5.72$$

$$\Delta T_x = -\frac{5.72}{1.43} = -\$4.0 \text{ billion}$$

This tells us that we may secure a \$10 billion increase in income with a \$2 billion increase in government purchases and a \$4 billion reduction in taxes. The reduction in taxes here would have to be in the lump sum tax. Otherwise, we would have to reduce the tax rate. The deficit for this transaction is, then, \$6.0 billion.

Reduce the Proportional Tax Rate

A somewhat more complicated method is to reduce the tax rate. If we use the data underlying Part G in Table 8-2, we have the values listed below.

Since we are using data from the table we necessarily have to use a more complex equilibrium equation.

$$a = 30 \qquad\qquad Y = 481.5$$
$$I_i = .05Y \qquad\qquad t = .15Y \quad \text{at} \quad 481.5$$
$$I_a = 30$$
$$G_p = 50$$
$$TR = 50 \qquad \text{(transfers)}$$
$$d = 25 \qquad \text{(lump sum tax)}$$
$$\text{MPC} = .8$$

We have then the following equilibrium equation in which $Y = 481.5$. Our purpose is to raise Y to 491.5. Therefore we have

$$Y = C + I + G_p$$
$$Y = a + cY_d + I + G_p$$
$$Y = a + c[Y - (d + tY) + TR] + I_a + I_i + G_p$$
$$Y = a + cY - cd - ctY + cTR + I_a + I_i + G_p$$
$$491.5 = 30 + .8(491.5) - .8(25) - .8t(491.5)$$
$$\qquad\qquad + .8(50) + 30 + .05(491.5) + 50$$
$$\qquad = 30 + 393.2 - 20 - 393.2t + 40 + 30 + 24.575 + 50$$
$$\qquad = 547.775 - 393.2t$$
$$t = \frac{56.275}{393.2} = .143$$

By substituting the value of t into our equation we can check our answer.

$$491.5 = 30 + .8(491.5) - .8(25) - .8(.143)(491.5) + 8(50)$$
$$\qquad\qquad + 30 + 24.575 + 50$$
$$\qquad = 30 + 393.2 - 20 - 56.2276 + 40 + 30 + 24.575 + 50$$
$$\qquad = \$491.5474 \text{ billion}$$

If we lower our tax rate to .143 we will increase income by \$10 billion.

THE MARGINAL PROPENSITY TO CONSUME AND THE MULTIPLIER

It would indeed be interesting and useful if we had more reliable information on the marginal propensity to consume; we could then be more exact in policy formulation. Various informed guesses have been made of the value of the investment and government multipliers and of the marginal and average propensities to consume. The postwar average propensity to consume in the United States has been about 93 percent; the postwar MPC at .81, but the short-run MPC at .50 to .70, the lower the estimate the shorter the time period. All things considered, the value of the multiplier is generally set at 2 or slightly more. (To this should be added the value of the accelerator.) These issues are further discussed in Chapter 16.

Many have felt that with higher levels of income the average propensity to consume would decline. If one takes, for example, data on the propensity to consume for pre-World War II years, and projects a consumption function into the postwar period, he would get a trend line which is below that of the actual consumption-disposable income relation. That is, during the postwar years there was an upward shift in the consumption function over that which would have been expected from pre-World War II data.[2] The consumption function over the long run has been fairly stable; however, it may and does fluctuate in the short run.

What of the effect of the distribution of income on consumption expenditures? Studies have shown that there are differences in the average propensities to consume among different income groups. That is, those individuals in the higher income groups tend, on the average, to have a lower average propensity to consume than those in the lower income brackets, on the average again. We say "on the average" because in *each* and *every* income group there are net savers and net debtors. (See Table 16-3.) While there is good evidence that the average propensity to consume varies in different income brackets, the same cannot be said for the marginal propensity to consume. Some economists have argued, especially during the 1930's, that since the average propensity to consume varies a redistribution of income downward would raise the level of consumption (and the average propensity to consume). This is based on the assumption that the *marginal* propensity to consume, like the average propensity, is higher for lower income groups. This assumption has been seriously challenged during the postwar years, and a definitive analysis of it is yet to come. Most economists apparently side with the challenge rather than the redistribution hypothesis. On the other hand, however, many economists (including some of those who question differences in the short-run MPC) feel that redistribution will work in the direction of greater consumption, especially if the redistribution is *permanent*. (This does not justify income redistribution, however.)

The issue of who has the highest marginal propensity to consume is of particular importance to fiscal policy. When a tax cut is called for to spur

---

[2] Graphs are to be found in most macroeconomic textbooks. See those of Ackley, *Macroeconomic Theory*, New York: Macmillan, 1961, and Peterson, *Income, Employment, and Economic Growth*, New York: Norton, 1961.

the economy, whose taxes should be cut? If one accepts the thesis that the marginal propensity to consume for all groups is the same, then it does not matter whose taxes are cut, because the impact will be the same (or everyone's could be cut). If one accepts the thesis that the lower income groups have the higher marginal propensity to consume, then a tax cut in these income brackets would be most effective.

We have noted that the redistributive effect may be influenced by whether or not the action is permanent. It seems quite definite that the effect of a permanent redistribution in favor of the lower income groups would raise the consumption function. If, then, a tax cut of a long-run nature is called for (as may well have been the case during the late 1950's and early 1960's), its impact would be greatest if it were to fall on the lower income groups (which include what is normally considered the middle income group). Even if the tax cut is limited to 6 months or a year, the result may be approximately the same. At any rate, there is little doubt that a permanent tax cut will be effective, since even those in the $10,000 to $15,000 income bracket have an average propensity to consume of 80.2 percent, and those above $15,000 one of 76.2 percent. (See Table 16-2.) We will return to this topic later.

There seems little reason to doubt that a reduction of personal income taxes will raise consumption. Other factors, however, must be considered. If we are to have, for example, an accompanying shift of the tax burden on to investment, there likely will be some adverse effects and contrary results. The nature of the impact will naturally be related to the magnitude of the shift in the tax burden, the extent to which the corporate income tax is shifted, the extent to which corporate retained earnings and dividends are affected, and the effect of changes in "confidence" (the "business climate") on investment.

ANTI-INFLATIONARY POLICY

When we are interested in stopping inflation we can raise taxes, lower government purchases or transfers, use some combination of higher taxes and lower government expenditures, or use an equal cut in both government expenditures and taxes. If we fear that inflation is forthcoming (as during the early days of World War II) we attempt to reduce aggregate demand by some x amount. If inflation is already under way, we are still interested in securing a reduction in aggregate demand by some x amount.

An Increase in Autonomous Investment

Reduce Government Purchases. Let us assume that prices are now stable, but that there is an increase in autonomous investment expenditures (as compared with induced investment, which is a function of income). We want to keep the level of income constant. In this case, since the multipliers for both government purchases and investment are the same we need only to reduce the level of government purchases by an amount equal to the expected increase in autonomous investment. Assuming the values given on the right, our equilibrium level of income would be $416.66 billion.

$$Y = C + I + G_p \qquad\qquad\qquad I = 30$$

$$Y = a + c[Y - (d + tY) + TR] + I + G_p \qquad a = 30$$

$$Y = 30 + .8(Y - .02Y) + 30 + 30 \qquad G_p = 30$$

$$Y = .8Y + .016Y = 90 \qquad\qquad MPC = .80$$

$$.216Y = 90 \qquad\qquad\qquad tY = .02Y$$

$$d = 0$$

$$Y = \$416.66 \text{ billion}$$

$$TR = 0$$

If, in these equations, autonomous investment increases by $20 billion, we can lower government purchases by exactly the same amount and secure our required result. If the recipients of income resulting from government purchases have an MPC different from those receiving the income from investment, then, of course, this would have to be taken into account. If the reduction in G_p is in an area (such as, say, expensive space expenditures) where actual employment provided is lower per dollar of G_p, income per employee is high, and business savings are high, the reduction in G_p may result in a reduction in income that is smaller than the rise in income caused by the increase in investment. It is impossible to avoid such micro-economic aspects of aggregate analysis.

Of very great importance is whether the resources released by the reduction in G_p can be used for investment. If different resources are involved, inflation will still result. That is, if the resources released as a result of lower government purchases cannot be used for business investment, then prices will still rise and another policy is called for.

Even though we have stabilized the level of demand by reducing G_p, the level of investment is still increasing. If the capacity of the capital goods industries was reached before the increase in investment (or is reached before the increase in I has spent itself out), then inflation may still result. If the capital goods industries are operating at full capacity, the only successful policy will be a direct assault on investment. *These same comments apply to the next three policy examples.* The situation may call for a selective tax or monetary policy.

Reduce Consumption. A second alternative is to raise the level of taxes. This can be done by either raising the lump sum tax or raising the proportional tax rate. In either case we are here reducing consumption. To reduce spending by increasing the lump sum tax we reverse the procedure followed on p. 167. Recalling that autonomous investment has increased by $20 billion, by how much must we reduce consumption to keep aggregate demand constant? (The example used here includes a proportional tax.) Placing the lump sum tax d back into the equation we have

$$Y = a + c[Y - (d + tY) + TR] + I' + G_p \qquad I' = 50$$

$$Y = a + cY - cd - ctY + cTR + I' + G_p$$

Since we want to solve for d we write

$$cd = a + cTR + I' + G_p + cY - ctY - Y$$

$$d = \frac{a + cTR + I' + G_p + cY - ctY - Y}{c}$$

Since we want to keep Y constant (at $416.66 billion) we get

$$d = \frac{30 + .8(0) + 50 + 30 + .8(416.66) - (.8)(.02)(416.66) - 416.66}{.8}$$

$$d = \frac{30 + 50 + 30 + 333.33 - 6.67 - 416.66}{.8} = \frac{20}{.8} = \$25 \text{ billion}$$

The lump sum tax then must be placed at $25 billion (it was zero) to offset the $20 billion increase in autonomous investment. This can be checked by substituting the value of d in our equation:

$$Y = a + cY - cd - ctY + cTR + I' + G_p$$

$$Y = 30 + 333.33 - 20 - 6.67 + 50 + 30$$

$$Y = 416.66 \text{ billion}$$

Now if we have an autonomous increase in investment of $20 billion and we want to keep income constant by raising the tax rate we get, from our original assumptions,

$$Y = 30 + .8(Y - tY) + 50 + 30$$
$$Y = 30 + .8Y - .8tY + 50 + 30$$
$$Y - .8Y + .8tY = 110$$
$$416.66 - .8(416.66) + .8(416.66)t = 110$$
$$333.328t = 26.268$$
$$t = .08$$
$$\Delta T_x = 33.33 - 8.33 = \$25 \text{ billion}^3$$

The tax rate must be raised from $.02\,Y$ to $.08\,Y$. The increase in taxes is again \$25 billion. This is much greater than the \$20 billion reduction in G_p in our previous example. The reason that the tax increase must be greater than the autonomous increase in I is that spending is not reduced by the amount taken in taxes because part of the tax payment comes from saving. This example can be checked out by substituting in our equation the new tax rate.

$$Y = C + I + G_p \qquad\qquad\qquad tY = .08\,Y$$
$$Y = a + c(Y - tY) + I' + G \qquad I' = 50$$
$$Y = 30 + .8(Y - .08\,Y) + 50 + 30 \qquad d = 0$$
$$Y - .8Y + .064\,Y = 110 \qquad\qquad TR = 0$$
$$.2Y + .064\,Y = 110 \qquad\qquad\quad G_p = 30$$
$$.264\,Y = 110$$
$$Y = \$416.66 \text{ billion}$$

Since in this case we have reduced consumption we must assume that resources can be shifted from the production of consumption goods to investment goods; if not, prices will rise. Even though resources are not transferable it may be argued that reduced consumption would have some restraining effect on investment. The difficulty with this, though, is that there may be such a long lag in the impact on investment that prices would still rise.

---

^{3} The answer can also be computed by using the multipliers. The investment multiplier is $1/(1 - c + ct) = 4.63$; the tax multiplier is $c/(1 - c + ct) = 3.7$. The increase in income resulting from the increase in investment is then $4.63 \times 20 = 92.6$. We can then ask the amount by which taxes must increase to offset this—the reduction in income is equal to 92.6.

$$\Delta Y = -\frac{c}{1 - c + ct}\Delta T_x$$
$$92.6 = -3.7\Delta T_x$$
$$\Delta T_x = -\$25 \text{ billion}$$

Increase the Tax Rate and Reduce Government Purchases. A third approach to offset the $20 billion increase in autonomous investment is to increase the tax rate and lower government purchases. It is possible to do this algebraically by setting taxes equal to government purchases. Our question then is, what tax rate will $T_x = G_p$?

$$Y = C + I + G_p \qquad\qquad\qquad T_x = tY$$
$$Y = a + c(Y - T_x) + 50 + G_p \qquad\quad T_x = G_p$$
$$Y = 30 + .8(Y - tY) + 50 + tY \qquad\quad I' = 50$$
$$Y = 30 + .8Y - .8tY + 50 + tY \qquad\quad TR = 0$$
$$Y - .8Y + .8tY - tY = 80 \qquad\qquad d = 0$$
$$416.66 - .8(416.66) + .8(416.66)t - 416.66t = 80$$
$$416.66 - 333.328 + 333.328t - 416.66t = 80$$
$$83.332 - 83.332t = 80$$
$$-83.332t = -3.332$$
$$t = .04$$
$$T_x = .04(416.66) = 16.6664$$
$$G_p = 16.6664 \text{ billion}$$

This can be checked by substituting as follows.

$$Y = C + I + G_p$$
$$Y = a + c(Y - tY) + 50 + 16.664$$
$$Y = 30 + .8[416.66 - .04(416.66)] + 50 + 16.664$$
$$Y = 30 + 333.328 - 13.333 + 50 + 16.664$$
$$Y = \$416.66 \text{ billion}$$

In other words, by raising the tax rate from .02 to .04 and by lowering government purchases from $30 to $16.664 billion we will be able to offset the multiplier effects of a $20 billion increase in autonomous investment.

Reduce Taxes and Government Purchases by the Same Amount. A fourth approach is an equal contraction in taxes and government purchases— what is known as a balanced budget reduction. Here we want to know the amount by which we must reduce both taxes and government purchases to offset the increase in autonomous investment. In the basic model which we have been using our equilibrium was 416.66, tax rate .02Y, and taxes (at this rate) = 8.33. It is not possible to use this model as an example of balanced budget contraction primarily because the level of taxation is not large enough to permit a reduction sufficient enough (coupled with a reduction in government expenditures) to offset the autonomous increase in investment of $20 billion. We shall, therefore, alter our assumptions as follows:

$$Y = C + I + G_p \qquad\qquad a = 30$$
$$Y = a + c(Y - tY) + I + G_p \qquad \text{MPC} = .6$$
$$Y = 30 + .6(Y - .20Y) + 60 + 60 \qquad G_p = 60$$
$$Y = 30 + .6Y - .12Y + 60 + 60 \qquad I = 60$$
$$Y - .6Y + .12Y = 150 \qquad tY = T_x = .20Y$$
$$.52Y = 150 \qquad TR = 0$$
$$Y = \$288.46 \text{ billion} \qquad d = 0$$

Our equilibrium income then is $288.46 billion. Let us assume that autonomous I increases by 20 so that $I' = 80$. Our aim is to have a balanced contraction in our budget. This means that we shall have equal reductions in both T_x and G_p. In our new equilibrium income statement then (where $I' = 80$) the new level of taxes will be equal to $t_1 Y - \Delta T_x$ (the original tax rate times income minus the drop in taxes), and the new level of government purchases (G_p') will be $G_p - \Delta T_x$ (since $\Delta T_x = \Delta G_p$). We then have

$$Y = C + I + G_p \qquad\qquad a = 30$$
$$Y = a + c[Y - (t_1 Y - \Delta T_x)] + I' + G_p' \qquad c = .6$$
$$Y = a + c(Y - t_1 Y + \Delta T_x) + I' + G_p' \qquad Y = 288.46$$
$$Y = a + cY - ct_1 Y + c\Delta T_x + I' + G_p' \qquad I' = 80$$
$$t_1 = .2$$
$$\Delta T_x = \Delta G_p$$
$$\Delta T_x = t_1 Y - t_2 Y$$
$$t_2 Y = t_1 Y - \Delta T_x$$
$$TR = 0$$

Substituting the values of a, c, Y, I', and G_p', we obtain

$$288.46 = 30 + .6(288.46) - .6(.2)(288.46)$$
$$+ .6\Delta T_x + 80 + (60 - \Delta T_x)$$
$$288.46 = 30 + 173.076 - 34.6152 + .6\Delta T_x + 80 + 60 - \Delta T_x$$
$$\Delta T_x - .6\Delta T_x = 30 + 173.076 - 34.6152 + 80 + 60 - 288.46$$
$$.4\Delta T_x = 20$$
$$\Delta T_x = 50$$
$$\Delta G_p = 50$$
$$G_p' = 10$$
$$t_2 Y = 7.692 \text{ billion (the new tax bill)}$$

Hence an equal reduction in T_x and G_p of $50 billion will offset the multiplier effects of an increase in investment of $20 billion *plus* the multiplier effects of the tax reduction. Since taxes originally were $57.692 billion ($t_1 Y = .20 Y = 57.692$), the new tax bill is $7.692 billion. Originally G_p was $60 billion, but now it is $10 billion. We can check our analysis by substituting the new tax and G_p values in our equation in which $I' = 80$.

$$Y = C + I + G_p \qquad\qquad I' = 80$$
$$Y = a + c(Y - T_x) + I' + G_p' \qquad G' = 10$$
$$288.46 = 30 + .6(288.46) - .6(7.692) + 80 + 10 \qquad T_x' = 7.692$$
$$288.46 = 30 + 173.076 - 4.6152 + 80 + 10$$
$$288.46 = \$288.46 \text{ billion}$$

Our new tax rate is $7.962/288.46 = .027$.

We can make a further check on our analysis by comparing the effect of our multipliers. The government purchases and the investment multipliers will be

$$\frac{1}{1 - c + ct} = \frac{1}{1 - .6 + .6(.027)} = 2.4$$

The tax multiplier will be $c/(1 - c + ct) = 1.441$. The reduction in taxes raises income; the increase in investment raises income; and the reduction in government purchases lowers income. The tax reduction raises income by 50×1.441, or 72; the increase in investment raises income by 2.4×20, or 48; but the reduction in government purchases lowers income by 50×2.4, or 120. Hence the reduction in income brought about by the reduction in G_p just offsets the increase in income resulting from lower taxes and higher investment.

An Increase in Government Purchases

An increase in government purchases can be offset by an increase in taxes. As we have previously noted, however, the increase in taxes[4] will have to be greater than the increase in government purchases. Let us return to our equilibrium model with the following assumptions:

$$Y = C + I + G_p \qquad\qquad a = 30$$
$$\qquad\qquad\qquad\qquad MPC = .6$$
$$Y = a + c(Y - tY) + I + G \qquad G_p = 60$$
$$\qquad\qquad\qquad\qquad I = 60$$
$$Y = 288.46 \text{ billion} \qquad T_x = tY = .20 Y$$

---

[4] The increase in taxes may also have a restrictive effect on investment. Because savings are reduced the supply of capital funds may be reduced and made more costly. This may be offset by making the increase in government saving available to investors by retiring bank held government debt.

If we have an increase in G_p of \$20 billion, we see that income will rise by

$$\frac{1}{1 - c + ct} \Delta G_p = \frac{1}{1 - .6 + .6(.2)} 20 = 1.923(20) = 38.46$$

To offset this we will have to raise taxes by \$33.33, which is $38.46 \div 1.154$, the latter being the tax multiplier. The change in income with a change in both G_p and T_x is

$$\Delta Y = \frac{1}{1 - c + ct} \Delta G_p - \frac{c}{1 - c + ct} \Delta T_x = 1.923(20) - 1.154 \Delta T_x$$

Since $\Delta Y = 0$, we obtain
$$0 = 38.46 - 1.154 \Delta T_x$$
$$\Delta T_x = \$33.33 \text{ billion}$$

Our total tax bill now is $tY = .20(288.46)$ plus 33.33, or 91. If we substitute this tax bill and $G_p{}' = 80$ into the last equation we can check our results.

Of course, we can compute the necessary increase in taxes by letting T_x be the unknown in our equilibrium equation. Letting T_{x_2} be our new tax bill, and t_2 our new tax rate, we have[5]

$$Y = C + I + G_p \qquad\qquad G_p{}' = 80$$
$$Y = a + c(Y - T_{x_2}) + I + G_p{}'$$
$$288.46 = 30 + .6(288.46 - T_{x_2}) + 60 + 80$$
$$288.46 = 30 + .6(288.46) - .6T_{x_2} + 60 + 80$$
$$288.46 = 30 + 173.076 - .6T_{x_2} + 60 + 80$$
$$.6T_{x_2} = 54.616$$
$$T_{x_2} = 91.027 = t_2 Y \qquad t_2 = \frac{91.027}{288.46} = .31446$$

An Upward Shift in the Consumption Function

Let us assume now that at every income level consumption is \$20 billion higher. This means that $a = 50$ instead of 30. The question is:

[5] The fact that $t_2 Y = .31556$ can be shown by substituting this value into the equilibrium equation:

$$Y = a + c(Y - T_{x_2}) + I + G_p{}'$$
$$Y = a + cY - cT_{x_2} + I + G_p{}'$$
$$Y = a + cY - ct_2 Y + I + G_p{}'$$
$$Y - cY + ct_2 Y = a + I + G_p{}'$$
$$Y(1 - c + ct_2) = a + I + G_p{}'$$
$$Y = \frac{a + I + G_p{}'}{1 - c + ct_2} = \frac{30 + 60 + 80}{1 - .6 + .6(.31556)} = \frac{170}{.589336} = \$288.46 \text{ billion}$$

By how much must we raise the lump sum tax or the proportional tax rate to offset this $20 billion autonomous increase in consumption? We can reduce investment, consumption, or government purchases by this amount. (The latter is extremely difficult in terms of political commitments and, even if accomplished, may involve too long a lag.) The necessary reduction in consumption could be attained in exactly the same manner as consumption is reduced under the first two schemes. In the immediately preceding example, in which taxes are raised to offset a $20 billion increase in G_p, consumption can be substituted for the increase in G_p and the same result will follow—the required tax increase will be $33.33 billion. Or the required tax bill, with the $20 billion shift in C, can be computed by solving for T_x as the unknown in the equilibrium equation. The tax increase can be either an increase in the lump sum tax or the proportional tax rate. Other policy combinations covered previously could also be used.

An Increase in the MPC

Let us assume that the MPC increases from .6 to .8. We now have a multiplier of

$$\frac{1}{1 - c - ct} = \frac{1}{1 - .8 + .8(.20)} = 2.8$$

which is higher than the multiplier of 1.92 with the MPC of .6. This can be offset by an increase in T_x, a decrease in G_p, or a balanced budget contraction.

One way by which we can keep the value of the multiplier at the earlier level of 1.92 is to double the tax rate (from .20 to .40). In other words, the original multiplier with an MPC of .6 and t of .2 was

$$\frac{1}{1 - .6 + .6(.2)} = \frac{1}{.52}$$

The new multiplier with a tax rate of .40 is

$$\frac{1}{1 - .8 + .8(.4)} = \frac{1}{.52}$$

Hence the increase in the MPC is negated. If we substitute the new MPC and t in our equilibrium equation we obtain

$$Y = C + I + G_p$$
$$Y = a + c(Y - tY) + I + G_p$$
$$Y = 30 + .8[288.46 - .4(288.46)] + 60 + 60$$
$$Y = \$288.46 \text{ billion}$$

The method used here to arrive at the tax rate was simple trial and error.[6] A quick glance at the multiplier will show the necessary increase in t in order to arrive at a value of $1/.52$, the same as the value of our original multiplier. We could also have computed the necessary tax to keep income at our equilibrium level by setting Y at 288.46, substituting the new MPC, and solving for T_x. It should come out to tY, or $.4(288.46)$, or 115.384.

To offset the increase in the MPC we could also lower government purchases.

$$Y = C + I + G_p$$

$$Y = a + c(Y - Tx) + I + G_p$$

$$Y = 30 + .8[288.46 - .2(288.46)] + 60 + G_p'$$

$$288.46 = 30 + .8(288.46 - 57.692) + 60 + G_p'$$

$$288.46 = 30 + 184.6 + 60 + G_p'$$

$$G_p' = \$13.86 \text{ billion}$$

Again this can be checked in the equation.

A third technique which may be employed to offset the higher MPC is a balanced contraction in both government purchases and taxes. As before, we would change our tax rate to decrease the tax bill. Our new level of taxes would be equal to $t_1 Y - \Delta T_x$ (the original tax rate times income minus the drop in taxes), and the new level of government purchases would be $G_p - \Delta T_x$ (since $\Delta T_x = \Delta G_p$). In the example in which equilibrium is 288.46 it is not possible to offset the increase in MPC by an equal reduction in T_x and G_p. This is because the level of taxes is not high enough to begin with to enable a sufficiently high enough reduction in G and T_x to offset the higher MPC. If the level of taxation had been higher, though, the procedure would have been the same as that used to offset the $20 billion increase in investment previously.

[6] The new tax rate, t, can be solved for in the equilibrium equation:

$$Y = C + I + G_p$$

$$Y = a + c(Y - tY) + I + G_p$$

$$Y = a + cY - ctY + I + G_p$$

$$288.46 = 30 + .8(288.46) - .8(t)(288.46) + 60 + 60$$

$$288.46 = 30 + 230.768 - 230.768t + 60 + 60$$

$$230.768t = 30 + 230.768 + 120 - 288.46$$

$$230.768t = 92.308$$

$$t = .4$$

CONCLUDING COMMENTS

If our wish is to raise the level of income we may (1) lower taxes, (2) raise government purchases, (3) raise government transfers, (4) raise both government purchases and taxes equally or in various proportions, or (5) use various combinations of these actions. Per dollar of revenue loss, however, an increase in government purchases is the most efficient (unless the direct recipients of transfers have a marginal propensity to consume of unity). To expand income by raising both taxes and purchases requires a significant increase in both items.

On the other hand, if one assumes that the level of government expenditures on public goods should be constant regardless of the level of economic activity, then items such as public works cannot be used for countercyclical purposes. Further, public works involve substantial lags and are not ordinarily subject to immediate initiation or cessation as countercyclical policy may demand. More and more resort may, therefore, be had to tax and transfer cuts and increases.

If our objective is to depress demand, we use the same tools in reverse gear. Again, however, greater reliance will likely be put on tax increases since it is extremely difficult to cut the expenditures of the federal government. This follows from the nature of federal budget expenditures themselves, most of which are on defense, foreign aid, interest, and similar items that are very difficult to dispense with. Further, it would be very inefficient to stop building a partially completed project for countercyclical purposes.

The multiplier has been at the heart of much of our analysis and a summary comment is due it. The addition of a tax factor, especially a proportional tax, to the multiplier significantly reduces its value. Its value may also be reduced by increased business saving and by an induced increase in imports as our income rises. On the other hand, its value is increased by the fact that investment will increase as income increases. The value of the multiplier will, however, be influenced by many prevailing factors. A high current stock of consumer durables may reduce it; considerable excess capacity even though income is high may reduce induced investment; consumers' and businessmen's expectations and their liquidity and cash flows may raise or lower it; the distribution of income raises or lowers it; etc. Because these factors influence the level of consumption and investment they determine the size of the multiplier. Our discussion did not consider the importance of business confidence, international transactions, monetary policy (interest rates and the financing of a deficit), income distribution, liquid assets, and other factors that may affect consumption and investment, and price level changes. These factors are generally treated elsewhere in the text, but we should note that their inclusion in any model introduces a greater number of unknowns and additional sources of possible error.[7]

It is not easy to measure the value of the multiplier accurately, although estimates at close to 3 have often been used. A recent guess is that the multiplier for government expenditures is 2.2 or 2.3, or larger.[8]

We should further note that we were dealing here with *changes* in T_x and G_p. We were, in other words, superimposing these changes on a budget perhaps running a surplus or a deficit. This means that we can raise or lower income by raising or lowering the surplus or deficit already in existence. Further, the size of the MPC and the marginal propensity to invest may and will vary over a period of time depending on whether we have a strong underlying demand in the economy, and depending on who receives the expenditures and who pays the taxes. It is possible then that even with a surplus we may expand income, again depending on who pays the taxes and their reactions to the taxes, and who receives the expenditures. Shifting the tax burden from consumption to investment would raise consumption, generally speaking, unless the increased tax on investment adversely affected it. This in turn may well be influenced by the existence (or lack) of excess capacity and the previous level of taxes on investment, and by how vigorous consumer demand is. Similarly, shifting the tax burden onto consumption will, generally speaking, reduce consumption unless consumers are intent on continuing their spending at a high rate and are willing and able to reduce their saving. Or, shifting the tax burden to those with a low MPC will enable consumption to remain high and perhaps even permit a budget surplus to be realized unless, of course, such tax shifting adversely affects investment either psychologically or through the supply of savings. In attempting to analyze the impact of the multiplier one must make some guesses concerning its impact under prevailing conditions and attitudes at any particular point in time.

We should point out that the size of the government budget will influence its restrictive or expansionary effects. The larger the budget the larger the impact, and vice versa. Similarly, in a given situation with a given government budget what is important is an increase or decrease in expenditures and/or taxes represented by the increase or decrease in the surplus and/or deficit.

[7] A concise but pointed criticism of the type of analysis used here is that of G. Ackley, *op. cit.*, pp. 344–346.

[8] This is Henry Wallich's guess, JEC, *Jan. 1962 Ec. Rept. Pres.*, H, p. 651. Econometric studies have also placed it in this range. Several other estimates are given in Chapter 16 and note 26 of that chapter. The consumption and investment aspects are discussed separately in Chapter 16.

Regarding changes in government purchases, taxes, and transfers, then, it is important to know:

1. Who is to receive the expenditures and their MPC,
2. the impact of government expenditures on the supply of capital funds,
3. the impact of government taxes on the supply of capital funds (on saving) and on consumption,
4. the impact of government borrowing on the supply of capital funds and on consumption, and
5. the impact of the repayment of debt on consumption and on the supply of capital funds.

It is possible then to have a balanced budget that is restrictive, neutral, or expansionary. It is further possible to have a surplus that is restrictive or expansionary (by means of taxing heavily idle balances, for example). And it is possible to have a deficit that is either restrictive or expansionary. The result and ultimate impact depends on the relative importance of the MPC of those who receive the payments and those who pay the taxes (or purchase government securities).[9]

---

[9] The excellent statement of H. M. Somers, JEC, *Fed. Exp. Pol.*, P, pp. 412–419, is required reading on this subject.

PART III

Problems and Theory
of Economic Growth

10

Economic Growth:
Facts, Theory, and Policy

THE NEED FOR GROWTH AND ITS MEASUREMENT

In Chapter 2 we noted the reasons why economic growth is a primary concern of the American people—to absorb new entrants into the labor force, to employ those who are technologically unemployed, to maintain and build up our military strength, to raise the standard of living, to alleviate social problems, to support foreign aid and investments, and to provide more and better public goods and services. It is for approximately the same reasons that almost all nations of the world, industrialized or underdeveloped, long for higher rates of growth.

A primary motive underlying the concern for economic growth is human welfare, as can be easily seen from the list of reasons why Americans want a more rapid rate of growth. Although there may be differences of opinion as to what constitutes welfare, it is interesting to note that the *Staff Report* of the Joint Economic Committee stated that: "The fundamental purpose served by the Nation's economic growth is to increase the welfare of its people."[1] The report stresses an increase in the total production of goods and services not only for private but also for public consumption. The share of increments in our GNP which should go to private and public uses has been, is, and will continue to be a matter of controversy. Most Americans, however, are willing to appropriate increased shares for defense and at least a minimal amount for public goods such as education.

MEASURING GROWTH

With few exceptions economic growth is discussed in terms of an increase in the productive capacity of a country. As we have noted in

[1] JEC, *Empl.*, *Growth*, *Price Levels*, SR, p. 2. Uses of growth are discussed on pp. 2–6.

previous chapters, however, there must also be an increase in aggregate demand—in the actual production of goods and services. We can have different rates of growth based on the particular proportions in which we allocate our resources annually to the production of consumer and investment goods. Nonetheless, we must have some degree of balance in their relative rates of growth or else we will end up (excepting central controls) growing less. Just as too much consumption can lower the growth rate because it preempts resources from use for investment, too slow a rate of growth of consumption will eventually retard the rate of growth of investment. No one knows exactly what these proportions should be or can be, and they no doubt vary under different circumstances.

Various concepts have been advocated to measure growth—aggregate or per capita GNP, aggregate or per capita consumption, aggregate or per capita NNP, per capita consumption for the poorest third (fourth, or fifth) of the population, and various productivity measures (such as NNP per worker or per hour of labor).[2] In addition, these measures can be stated in either constant or current dollars. The use to which the data are being put will influence the selection of the measure.

The use of the GNP as a measure of economic growth has been criticized because it omits many intangibles such as paid vacations, leisure via shorter hours, better working conditions, higher-quality goods and services (for example, drugs and medical services), and greater personal security; because it includes many imputed values (for example, services of owner-occupied homes);[3] and because of the importance of national defense expenditures in the GNP. Although we could argue that national defense expenditures do contribute to our (and others') welfare, the criticisms are still legitimate. A continuous increase in the GNP that is totally reflected in increased defense expenditures, for example, does nothing to *increase* material welfare. It is for this reason that the use of per capita consumption in constant dollars receives considerable support as one of the more important measures of welfare. Material welfare as measured in consumption data, however, does not include the important contribution of governmental expenditures on education and a great

---

[2] See F. Machlup in JEC, *Empl., Growth, Price Levels*, H, Pt. 9A, p. 2820.

[3] See the CEA statement in JEC, *Jan. 1961 Ec. Rept. Pres.*, H, p. 567; minority report in JEC, 1961 *Ann. Rept.*, pp. 61–62; the interesting comments of R. Patterson in JEC, *Fed. Exp. Pol.*, P., pp. 13–14; and the more extensive statement by G. Jaszi, "The Measurement of Aggregate Economic Growth," *Rev. Ec. & Stat.*, Nov. 1961, pp. 317–332; and the sources cited there. A very thoughtful statement on the meaning of growth, the problem of measurement, and the composition of growth is that of R. W. Goldsmith in JEC, *Empl., Growth, Price Levels*, H, Pt. 2, pp. 267–279. This paper is highly recommended.

many other items. The advantage of using constant dollars is obvious and does not require further comment.

Per capita figures are subject to the limitations of all averages. It is true, for instance, that total income or product may increase but that it may accrue entirely to certain privileged, high-income groups. In the

Table 10-1. Trend of GNP and Personal Consumption 1839-1959 (United States) (Percent Increase per year—Calculated from Values in First and Last Year of Period)

	Entire Period	40-Year Subperiods		
	1839– 1959	1839– 1879	1879– 1919	1919– 1959
A. GNP				
1. Aggregate, constant prices	3.66	4.31	3.72	2.97
2. Population	1.97	2.71	1.91	1.30
3. Per capita, constant prices	1.64	1.55	1.76	1.64
B. Personal Consumption				
4. Aggregate, constant prices			3.68	3.17
5. Consumers (equivalent adult males)			2.01	1.30
6. Per full consumer,[a] constant prices			1.64	1.85

	1919–47	1947–53	1953–59
C. GNP			
1. In constant 1958 dollars	2.6	4.6	2.3[b]
2. Per person	1.1	2.5	0.6[b]
3. Per person engaged in production	1.4	2.6	1.8[c]
4. Per unweighted man-hour	2.4	4.1	2.6[d]

Sources: JEC, Empl., Growth, Price Levels, H, Pt. 2, p. 271; and ibid., R. Parts A and B from R. W. Goldsmith's paper. See also his table in Pt. 10, p. 3456. Part C from the studies of John Kendrick and Solomon Fabricant.
[a] Goldsmith has allowed for differences in consumption requirements due to age and sex differences by estimating the number of equivalent full consumers.
[b] 1959 dollars.   [c] Series ends with 1958.   [d] Series ends with 1957.

meantime the average income has gone up but with no benefit to the "average" man. This may not be a problem in the United States but it can be a serious problem in smaller, underdeveloped nations.

In Table 10-1 we have data on the GNP and consumption in current and constant prices. The long-run growth record, covering a period of 120 years, is indeed rather impressive at the rate, in constant 1929 prices, of 3.66 percent per year. A comparison of the growth rate for 40-year periods does show a declining rate (4.31, 3.72, and 2.97 percent in constant prices). The per capita data (constant dollars), however, do not show the same declining trend, an absence due in part to different rates of population increase. Therefore, even though the rate of increase of the aggregate GNP during the 1839–79 period was the highest, in per capita terms it was less because this was a period of substantial population growth. This same reasoning in reverse accounts for the higher per capita increase in the 1919–59 period—that is, the rate of population increase was much lower, which helped raise per capita GNP. Limited data are also given for consumption.

In Table 10-1, Part C, we have similar data on a different period basis. The data include only GNP figures. We see that from 1919 to 1947 GNP in constant dollars grew at a yearly average of 2.6 percent, from 1947 to 1953 at 4.6 percent, and from 1953 to 1959 at 2.3 percent.

The *Staff Report* and the *Report* of the Joint Economic Committee (majority section, naturally) placed special emphasis on the low rate of growth from 1953 to 1959. The fact that this period happened to coincide with that of the Eisenhower Administration created quite a furor and a great deal of criticism of the *Staff Report* itself. This was indeed unfortunate because it detracted from what was otherwise a commendable performance by the staff of the committee and the committee itself.

The argument over growth rates was referred to as the "numbers racket," and emotions were stirred up on both sides of the political fence. An estimate of the rate of economic growth is dependent on the initial and terminal years selected. One could, for instance, pick the years 1945 to 1949 and come up with a −1.7 percent rate; 1945 to 1950 and a .3 percent rate; 1945 to 1952 and a 1.7 percent rate; or 1945 to 1959 and a 2.2 percent rate. The problem here is that we have included the postwar reconversion period—obviously an abnormal period when the GNP dropped drastically. One cannot use such data to smear the Truman regime. The Committee for Economic Development has published a table that gives the rate of growth for any year to year period from 1910 to 1959.[4]

The 1947–1953 rate (4.6 percent in constant dollars) was quite high and perhaps not sustainable since it included the pent-up demand of the postwar period and the Korean buildup. Nonetheless, the rates of growth between the peaks of the 1953–1957 and 1957–1960 recoveries were 2.3 and 2.7 percent, respectively. It is significant that these rates were *below*

---

[4] Reprinted in JEC, *Empl. Growth, Price Levels*, R, and reprinted and updated in E. F. Denison, *The Sources of Economic Growth in the United States*, New York: CED, 1962, p. 17.

the *long-term* average. (The rate for the 1948–1953 period was 4.7 percent.) Furthermore, the length of the periods of recovery (expansion) were shorter after each of the first three postwar recessions (45, 35, and 25 months). In addition, the unemployment situation had generally become worse, the rate of growth of employment becoming less from peak to peak in each period, and the average unemployment ratio becoming higher during each cycle. The rate of growth of real disposable income per capita had similarly declined successively in each period.[5] The problems of inadequate growth and high unemployment are illustrated in Figures 11-3 and 11-4.

The point here is not to indict the Administration which was in power, but to note that the rate of economic growth during the 1950's was under the long-term trend and a problem for great concern. Further, if the 1960's continue as they have been (under a different Administration) the record will not have been substantially improved. Small changes in the rate of growth make a substantial difference when they are compounded over several years. If the rate of growth from 1955 (fourth quarter) to 1960 (second quarter) had been 2.9 percent instead of 2.2 percent, the GNP would have been 30 billion dollars higher than it was.[6]

It is because of this low growth rate and its accompanying loss of employment and production that considerable concern has been expressed about the performance of the economy of the United States. This concern has been intensified by comparisons of our growth rate with that of other countries.[7] (See Table 10-2). In some respects, however, a comparison of this sort is not completely fair or reasonable. In an early stage of economic growth, when a country is busy building up its stock of capital, a large pool of unemployed (but reasonably skilled) labor is available, and many unexploited areas or demands exist, we can expect rather high rates of growth. Further, some countries (such as West Germany) have suffered extreme destruction of their capital. Both of these conditions differ from those in the United States.

An Acceptable Rate of Growth

What is an acceptable, reasonable rate of growth for the American economy? The problem of determining such a growth rate is not unlike

---

[5] JEC, *Current Ec. Sit. & Short-Run Outl.*, H, pp. 111–115.

[6] Pechman's estimate, *ibid.*, p. 114.

[7] Additional data on foreign growth rates are available periodically and annually from Organization for Economic Cooperation and Development and United Nations statistical surveys and publications.

It is difficult to make accurate price comparisons, but see footnote 47 in Chapter 19. Table 10-2 does not accurately reflect the recent good performance of the U.S.

the problem of arriving at a politically, socially, and economically acceptable level of unemployment. Governor Rockefeller (of New York) has
called for a 5 to 6 percent rate;[8] the AFL-CIO[9] and the Rockefeller

Table 10-2. Comparative Growth Rates (and Price Increases) (Average Annual
Growth and Price Rise, Percent)

	Growth Rate						
	1950–60			1955–60			
	Employment	Productivity	GNP	Employment	Productivity	GNP	Prices 1953–1959
Japan	—	—	—	—	—	6.3[a]	1.6
West Germany	2.2	5.2	7.5	1.7	4.3	6.0	2.3
Italy	1.6	4.3	5.9	1.9	3.9	5.9	2.0
Netherlands	—	—	—	—	—	4.5[a]	3.6
France	0.4	3.9	4.3	0.6	3.6	4.2	—
Norway	—	—	—	—	—	2.9[a]	3.7
Sweden	—	—	—	—	—	3.6[a]	3.2
Denmark	—	—	—	—	—	2.8[a]	3.0
United States	1.2	2.1	3.3	1.0	1.3	2.3	2.3
Belgium	—	—	—	—	—	2.5[a]	2.3
United Kingdom	0.6	2.0	2.6	0.3	2.3	2.7	3.0
Canada	—	—	—	—	—	3.2[a]	1.6

Sources: Advisory and International Committee, Am. Bankers Assoc., *International Financial Developments*, Fall 1960, p. 3; G. Colm and P. Wagner,
Targets for U.S. Economic Growth in the Early 60's, Planning Pamphlet No. 111,
Washington, D.C.: NPA, Feb. 1961, p. 9; *O.E.C.D. Observer*, Jan. 1963, p. 6,
and its *Policies for Economic Growth*.
   [a] 1953–1959.

Brothers' Fund[10] a 5 percent rate; Walter Reuther a 5 percent rate;[10]
Professor Robert Gordon of the University of California (Berkeley) a 4
percent (average annual) rate;[11] Gerhard Colm of the National Planning
Association a $4\frac{1}{2}$ percent rate;[12] the late President Kennedy a $4\frac{1}{2}$ percent

[8] *The New York Times*, June 2, 1960.   [9] *Labor's Ec. Rev.*, Dec. 1959.
[10] JEC, *Jan. 1961 Ec. Rept. Pres.*, H, p. 118.
[11] JEC, *Empl., Growth, Price Levels*, H, Pt. 9A, p. 2959.
[12] JEC, *Jan. 1961 Ec. Rept. Pres.*, H, pp. 523, 525.

rate for the 1960's;[13] Professors William Fellner of Yale and Paul
Samuelson and Robert Solow of M.I.T. a 4 percent rate;[14] and Professors
Arthur Smithies and Otto Eckstein of Harvard, who doubt that we can
rise above the long-run average of 3 percent, agree that we need a 4 or 5
percent rate.[15] In 1962, for example, the growth rate could be at least 6
percent for 3 years or so before the unemployment rate dropped to 4
percent. Over a period of time the rate of growth may be significantly
influenced by technical change and changes in the rate of population
growth. A slower rate of population growth and a slower increase in the
size of the labor force, for instance, would require a less rapid rate of
growth. With one or two exceptions, the rates cited, however, are
intelligent guesses over shorter-run periods by seasoned economists whose
opinions cannot be taken lightly. It would seem then, for reasons to be
subsequently discussed, that a rate of around $4\frac{1}{2}$ percent is perhaps a little
high, and that if we realize a longer-run rate of 4 percent we will have
done well.

THE CAUSES OF GROWTH

Economic and Noneconomic Factors in Economic Growth

We have noted the important role that increases in a nation's stock of
capital play in the rate of growth. We should also note that the increase
in capital not only raises productive capacity in the future but also creates
income in the present. This is because the capital goods are purchased in
the market and income is created when they are produced. In the long
run, however, employment and income must be maintained at a sufficient
level so that the additions to productive capacity will be utilized. Further,
even though a high rate of capital accumulation helps maintain the level
of employment, the higher the rate of growth of capital, the greater
becomes our productive capacity and the more difficult it will likely be to
attain full employment and full capacity production.

While the rate of capital accumulation is of central importance to
growth, growth is influenced by other factors. Of primary importance is

[13] *Jan. 1962 Ec. Rept. Pres.*, p. 9.

[14] Fellner in an unpublished paper prepared for the Commission on Money and
Credit, pp. 23–24; Samuelson in Am. Bankers Assoc., *A Symposium on Economic
Growth*, New York, 1963, p. 82; and Solow in *Conference on Savings and Residential
Financing*, Chicago: U.S. Savings and Loan League, 1962, pp. 133, 145. Solow feels
that the "three-percenters" are excessively pessimistic.

[15] JEC, *Empl., Growth, Price Levels*, H, Pt. 7, pp. 2427, 2436.

the prevailing system of values.[16] If it is progressive, challenges old ways of doing things, places a high value on technology and science, and emphasizes hard work, efficiency, and responsibility, then it is conducive to growth. Many other sociological, political, and economic factors and characteristics of a society are, of course, very important—the state of its technological knowledge; its level of educational attainment; the quality, quantity, and attitudes of labor; the quality and quantity of its natural resources; the absence or presence of a stable political system; its past and present attitudes towards saving; its present stock of capital; and its level and distribution of income. In our society, for instance, we have had an abundance of natural resources, a stable political system; a high level of educational attainment; well trained-scientists, engineers, and skilled labor; a healthy attitude toward work; a responsible labor force; an urge to "get ahead"; a willingness to undertake risks and a system of rewarding them; a healthy attitude toward saving and capital accumulation; and an adequate supply of labor. In short, we have had the attitudes abilities, resources, and social-political-economic characteristics that are conducive to growth.

Quantitative Estimates of Contributions to Growth and Raising the Growth Rate

Attempts have been made to measure the relative value of the various factors that have contributed to economic growth. Estimates are then made of the future importance of these factors and of adjustments which may be made in these factors in order to raise the growth rate. The important sources of growth are often classified as follows.

1. Labor force—the rate of employment, the length of the work week, vacations, better utilization of women workers and members of minority groups, and changes in the age and sex composition of the labor force;
2. technical progress—changes which bring about or affect improvements in production techniques, labor skills, managerial skills, innovations and scientific breakthroughs;
3. capital formation and resource development—changes in the stock of capital equipment; and

---

[16] The role of social values in social change is an interesting topic in itself. See E. E. Hagen, *On the Theory of Social Change: How Economic Growth Begins*, Homewood, Ill.: Dorsey, 1962. Hagen discusses how the stagnant traditional society is transformed into one characterized by technical and economic progress. He stresses, in particular, personality development, psychology, and social psychology.

C.E. Ayres (*The Theory of Economic Progress*, Durham, N.C.: Univ. of N.C. Press, 1944) attributes technological progressiveness to the weak hold of religion over society (pp. 132–135).

4. investment in human beings—education, training and retraining, mobility, and health.

In addition to the usual labor and capital inputs there are also what have been called the "unconventional inputs." The latter include expenditures on education, health, and research; changes in monopoly power and other restrictions that affect economical use of resources; and changes in economies of scale that result from the growth of all imputs. Because of the difficulty involved in making estimates of all the factors (especially the unconventional imputs) it is extremely difficult to arrive at a reliable conclusion as to their relative importance in calculating both growth rates and productivity changes. Much of what has been done on the sources of growth in the United States is admittedly based on shaky foundations.[17] The most detailed quantitative study is that of Edward F. Denison. Before proceeding with additional discussion of these factors it is first useful to briefly examine the relative importance of the sources of growth as estimated by Dr. Denison in his study for the Committee for Economic Development. The data are presented in Table 10-3.

Table 10-3 shows us the relative importance of increases in (1) labor inputs, (2) capital inputs, and (3) productivity increases in the growth of real GNP. The percentage increase in national product is given first. This is then followed by the "exact" percentage point amount by which each of these inputs contributed to the growth in national product. The percentage increase (Denison's estimate in column 2) of real national product for the period 1929–1957 was 2.93 percent. Of this 2.93 percent increases in total inputs accounted for 2.00 percentage points and productivity increases accounted for .93 percentage points. The contribution of the labor input was 1.57 percentage points; of the capital input .43 percentage points. The contributions of breakdowns of labor and capital inputs, as well as productivity increases (the unconventional inputs, also called "the Residual") are also given.

In Part *B* of the table we have estimates of the percentage contribution

[17] The more important studies include at least: J. Schmookler, "The Changing Efficiency of the American Economy, 1869–1938." *Rev. Ec. & Stat.*, Aug. 1952, pp. 214–231; F. C. Mills, *Productivity and Economic Progress*, New York: NBER, 1952; M. Abramovitz, *Resource and Output Trends in the United States Since 1870*, New York: NBER, 1959, reprinted in JEC, *Empl., Growth, Price Levels*, H, Pt. 2, pp. 283–339; S. Fabricant, *Basic Facts on Productivity Change*, New York: NBER, 1956; JEC, *Empl., Growth, Price Levels*, SP No., 20; J. W. Kendrick, *Productivity Trends in the United States*, New York: NBER, 1961; R. M. Solow, "Technical Progress, Capital Formation and Economic Growth," *Am. Ec. Rev.*, May 1962, pp. 76–86; and E. F. Denison, *op. cit.*

Many textbook discussions of the causes of growth are available. See also E. V. Domar, JEC, *Fed. Exp. Pol.*, H, pp. 142–143, and P, pp. 268–270.

Table 10-3. Allocation of Growth Rate of Total Real National Income Among the Sources of Growth[a]

| | Part A Percentage Points in Growth Rate | | Part B Percent of Growth Rate | | |
	1 1909–29[a] Commerce	2 1929–57	3 1909–29 Commerce	4 1909–29[a] Kendrick-Kuznets	5 1929–57
Real National Income	2.82	2.93	100	100	100
Increase in total inputs	2.26	2.00	80	71	68
Labor, adjusted for quality change	1.53	1.57	54	48	54
Employment and hours	1.11	0.80	39	35	27
Employment	1.11	1.00	39	35	34
Effect of shorter hours on quality of a man-year's work	0.00	−0.20	0	0	−7
Annual hours	−0.23	−0.53	−8	−7	−18
Effect of shorter hours on quality of a man-hour's work	0.23	0.33	8	7	11
Education	0.35	0.67	12	11	23
Increased experience and better utilization of women workers	0.06	0.11	2	2	4
Changes in age-sex composition of labor force	0.01	−0.01	0	0	0

Land	0.00	0.00	0	0	0
Capital	0.73	0.43	26	23	15
Nonfarm residential structures	0.13	0.05	5	4	2
Other structures and equipment	0.41	0.28	15	13	10
Inventories	0.16	0.08	6	5	3
U.S.-owned assets abroad	0.02	0.02	1	1	1
Foreign assets in U.S.	0.01	0.00	0	0	0
Increase in output per unit of input	0.56	0.93	20	29	32
Restrictions against optimum use of resources	NA	-0.07	NA	NA	-2
Reduced waste of labor in agriculture	NA	0.02	NA	NA	1
Industry shift from agriculture	NA	0.05	NA	NA	2
Advance of knowledge	NA	0.58	NA	NA	20
Change in lag in application of knowledge	NA	0.01	NA	NA	
Economies of scale					0
Independent growth of local markets	NA	0.07	NA	NA	2
Growth of national market	0.28	0.27	10	10	9

Source: E. F. Denison, *Sources of Economic Growth in the United States*, 1962, p. 266, by permission of the CED. Contributions in percentage points are adjusted so that the sum of appropriate details equals totals. Percents of the growth rate have not been so adjusted.

[a] "Commerce" and "Kendrick–Kuznets" headings refer only to the growth rate of total product. Contributions in percentage points under the Kendrick–Kuznets heading would be identical with those shown under the Commerce heading except for "real national income," 3.7; "output per unit of input," 0.91, and "economies of scale—growth of national market," 0.32.

of the various inputs to the growth rate. In column 5 we see that the increase in labor and capital inputs accounted for 68 percent of total growth between 1929 and 1957. Productivity increases accounted for 32 percent of the total growth. The increase in labor input accounted for 54 percent and the increase in capital input accounted for only 15 percent. It should be noted that Denison's estimate of the importance of capital is considerably lower than the other two estimates given. In the labor category we see that quality improvement due to higher levels of education contributed 23 percent to the growth of the national product. In the productivity category we see that by far the most important of the seven factors is "advance of knowledge." It is responsible for 20 percent of the 32 percent contribution of increases in productivity. Of further significance in this category is the increase in productivity due to economics of scale resulting from growth of the national market (9 percent).[18]

The factors that have been of outstanding importance in the past as sources of economic growth will not necessarily be of similar importance for the future growth of the economy. Estimates of potential growth in the economy and reasonably acceptable growth rates are based on considerations of the previously mentioned sources of growth. Let us briefly examine how several of these factors may be manipulated (or are not subject to manipulation, excepting significant social intervention) to raise the growth rate. (It should be noted that we are discussing potential increases in supply.)

As far as the rate of growth of the labor force is concerned, past births have been determined already. Three possibilities do remain, however: an increase in the labor force participation rate, a reduction in the decline of hours worked, and an increase in immigration. It is true that a higher average level of employment increases the participation rate (of women and elderly workers), but it is argued by Denison that the impact of an increase in the participation rate resulting from higher employment is not really great. A lower rate of unemployment also reduces the pressure for a reduction in hours worked, and Denison feels that a greater gain can be made here. The rate of immigration can certainly be increased, but even if it is doubled it would add only about .1 point to the growth rate.

If reliance is placed on increasing the rate of capital formation, there remains the further question of the proper use of fiscal and monetary

---

[18] An outstandingly able summary and evaluation of Denison's study, as well as the determinants of growth, can be found in Moses Abramovitz, "Economic Growth in the United States: A Review Article," *Am. Ec. Rev.*, Sept. 1962, pp. 762–782. A thorough reading of this article will impress one with the complexity of the problems of measurement.

policies to raise the level of investment, and of how significant a higher rate of capital formation is for the rate of growth.[19] It is Denison's opinion, and many economists differ with him on this point, that if we are to raise the growth rate by any substantial amount by raising the rate of capital accumulation, there would have to be an extremely large increase in the level of investment. A 1 percent increase in the growth rate would require that the ratio of net investment to national income be raised (at a minimum) 3.3 times.[20] To raise the growth rate .1 percentage points would require, over the next 20 years, that the ratio of net investment to national income be increased by 25 percent. These are, indeed, rather significant increases.

Concerning education, this may be a good example of a factor which has been very important in past growth but may not be so important in the future because of the substantial improvements which have already been made. Since the level of education has already increased by so much, it is not likely that similar increases will occur in the future and therefore that past increases in output due to higher levels of education will be repeated. Growth due to extended education is, in the long run, destined to fall. Denison's figures are quite convincing on this issue. All this does not mean that there is not room for improvement here but if an important contribution to the growth rate is to come from education in the future it will likely have to be by stressing those areas which contribute most to economic growth, selecting the most able students more successfully, and upgrading the quality of education.[21]

"Research and development" is often cited as an important source of economic growth. Denison estimates that the contribution of R and D to economic growth is very small. A major reason for this is that so much of the expenditure in this area is for product improvement and gadgetry rather than basic research; perhaps another reason is the high degree of concentration of R and D expenditures in a few industries. It is again quite true that substantial improvements can be made in this area, but also true that they may require considerable intervention to be realized.

Finally, Denison presents "A Menu of Choices Available to Increase the Growth Rate" (including those we have discussed) above $3\frac{1}{3}$ percent during the period 1960–1980. He here gives a quantitative estimate of the contribution to the growth rate of 27 factors, and suggested orders of

[19] *Ibid.*, p. 779.

[20] Denison, *op. cit.*, p. 116. The figure is 2.7 times if nonfarm residential construction is excluded. Allowances for economies of scale but not diminishing returns have been made. The latter would raise these figures.

[21] Abramovitz, *op. cit.*, pp. 778–779.

magnitude for 4 additional factors. It should be noted that (1) most of these factors would make an extremely small contribution to the rate of growth, and (2) many of them could be set into motion only as a result of drastic social action.

We return once more to our discussion of what would be a reasonable and acceptable growth rate. It is clear that Denison is not overly optimistic about raising the growth rate. It is for the reasons we have cited that many have questioned whether the United States can actually realize a long-run growth rate of 5 percent. But qualified professional judgment does indicate that the realization of a 4 percent rate would not require any drastic changes in economic policy. This may be a slightly more optimistic viewpoint than Denison would accept.

SOME FACTS ON PRODUCTIVITY INCREASES

Trends

The rate of productivity increase in the economy has been an important factor in our rate of growth, as we have noted. It simply means that we can produce more per man-hour, which in turn means that our incomes and standards of living will rise. It is of further importance as an offset to the yearly increases in wages demanded by labor in order to maintain prices at a reasonable level. In addition, it is of particular significance in international trade because it enables us to keep our costs down and our prices competitive.

Various measures of productivity are available. The average annual percentage increase in physical output per unweighted man-hour was 2.4 percent for the period 1889 to 1957, 2.0 percent from 1889 to 1919, 2.6 percent from 1919 to 1957, and 3.3 percent from 1945–48 to 1953–57. Physical output per weighted man-hour (higher-paid labor receives a heavier weight, presumably because of higher skills) rose, for the same periods, 2.0, 1.6, 2.3, and 2.9 percent respectively. Physical output per unweighted unit of tangible capital rose, during the same periods, 1.0, 0.5, 1.3, and −0.5 percent, respectively. The annual increase in physical output per weighted unit of labor and capital combined was, for the same periods again, 1.7, 1.3, 2.1, and 2.1 percent, respectively.

Thus the unweighted rate was higher after 1919 than before, with an even greater increase in the postwar period. When the index is weighted, the trend is approximately the same. When output is expressed in terms of combined labor and capital, there is a slower rise in productivity, because the rate of growth of capital was considerably greater than the rate of growth of labor. In fact, in the postwar period the increase in tangible capital was so large that the annual percentage change in output per unit of capital was negative.[22]

Changes in Output and Reduced Productivity

Data are available on increases in real output per man-hour in different sectors of the economy. (A readily available source is the *Economic Report of the President*, but see also the 1959 *Staff Report* of the JEC.) We are particularly interested here in the close association between changes in output and changes in productivity in manufacturing. An examination of the data will show a relationship between changes in the rate of productivity growth and the recessions of 1948–49, 1953–54, 1957–58, and 1960–61. (The 1956–57 period was also one of slow overall economic growth in the economy, which is reflected in productivity measures.) We see that when we have a reduction in the rate of growth of output we also have a slower rate of growth of productivity. This trend is not characteristic of only the postwar economy. It is typical of the whole period 1889–1957. Fabricant found that output per unweighted man-hour rose when output rose 44 times of a total of 51 rises in output during this period.[23] While this does not prove the previous point it does show the association. There is no question, though, of the high relationship between a rapid rate of growth and rapid productivity growth. This has been demonstrated on both an *aggregate* basis and an *industry* basis.[24]

This conclusion is important for at least two reasons. It shows that a sufficiently high rate of increase in aggregate demand is highly conducive to, if not necessary for, a high rate of productivity increase, and that recessions have a harmful effect on income growth not only because they reduce output and employment (if not absolutely, then relatively) but also because they reduce the rate by which productivity increases. Further, long-term labor contracts signed during periods of prosperity and high profits assume a continuation of these trends. A slowdown in the economy reduces the productivity increases needed to absorb these contractual increases in labor costs, firms' costs may go up, and prices may be raised.

---

[22] Fabricant, *op. cit.*, pp. 11, 39ff. See also JEC, *Empl., Growth, Price Levels*, SR, p. 44, H, Pt. 2, pp. 301, 328ff.

[23] Fabricant, *op. cit.*, p. 14. Productivity fell in 6 upturns and in 10 of 17 downturns. On a weighted basis it rose in 42 upturns and fell in 8, and rose in 8 and fell in 9 downturns.

[24] See JEC, *Empl., Growth, Price Levels*, SR, p. 93, and sources cited there. For more on this see *ibid.*, SP No. 15; C. L. Schultze, *Prices, Costs and Output in the Postwar Decade*, New York: CED, 1960, and his "Uses of Capacity Measures for Short-Run Economic Analysis," *Am. Ec. Rev.*, May 1963, pp. 293–308, especially pp. 301–304 for qualifications.

Table 10-4. The Share of Capital Formation in GNP (United States) (in Percent)

A. Current Prices

Period	Excluding Consumer Durables			Consumer Durables			Total		
	1 Gross Capital Formation	2 Capital Consumer Allowance	3 Net Capital Formation	4 Gross Capital Formation	5 Capital Consumer Allowance	6 Net Capital Formation	7 Gross Capital Formation	8 Capital Consumer Allowance	9 Net Capital Formation
1869–78	20.3	8.0	12.3						
1879–88	20.6	8.7	11.8						
1889–98	23.1	10.7	12.5						
1899–1908	22.8	10.5	12.4	6.3	5.0	1.3	29.1	15.5	13.6
1909–18	20.9	11.5	9.4	7.1	6.3	.8	28.0	17.8	10.2
1919–28	22.0	11.3	10.8	9.2	7.4	1.8	31.2	18.7	12.5
1929–38	15.5	13.4	2.1	8.0	8.2	–.2	23.5	21.6	1.9
1939–48	17.1	13.2	3.9	7.7	6.0	1.7	24.8	19.2	5.6
1946–55	21.9	14.2	7.7	9.1	6.3	2.8	31.0	20.5	10.5

B. Deflated Prices

Period	Excluding Consumer Durables			Consumer Durables			Total		
	1 Gross Capital Formation	2 Capital Consumer Allowance	3 Net Capital Formation	4 Gross Capital Formation	5 Capital Consumer Allowance	6 Net Capital Formation	7 Gross Capital Formation	8 Capital Consumer Allowance	9 Net Capital Formation
1869–78	23.4	9.5	13.9						
1879–88	22.9	9.8	13.1						
1889–98	26.0	12.1	14.0						
1899–1908	24.2	11.3	12.9	7.7	6.2	1.5	31.9	17.5	14.4
1909–18	22.6	12.3	10.3	8.0	6.9	1.1	30.6	19.2	11.4
1919–28	21.9	11.5	10.4	9.1	7.3	1.8	31.0	18.8	12.2
1929–38	14.4	12.6	1.8	8.9	8.2	.7	23.3	20.8	2.5
1939–48	15.9	12.1	3.7	8.8	7.0	1.8	24.7	19.1	5.6
1946–55	18.8	12.2	6.6	8.8	6.1	2.7	27.6	18.3	9.3

Source: JEC, *Jan. 1962 Ec. Rept. Pres.,* H, p. 528. Data of S. Kuznets and R. W. Goldsmith.

The "Human" Factor in Productivity Increases

We noted previously that capital has grown more rapidly than the labor force—about 2.6 percent per year. This raises output per man-hour because more capital per worker is available and because new capital embodies technological progress. But it is neither the only nor the most important factor. There is not a simple relationship between capital growth and labor productivity. In fact, Fabricant has estimated that, of the average 3.1 percent annual growth in physical output from 1919 to 1957, [25] increases in the supply of both capital and labor account for only 1 percent. (Denison estimated that increases in employment and hours accounted for 27 percent of total growth, and increases in capital input accounted for 15 percent—10 percent when inventories and nonfarm residences are deducted. These are 1929–1957 data.) The rest of the increase in output, which is estimated at about two-thirds, is accounted for in terms of our organizational and technical knowledge, which in turn is due to investment in research, education, and better health.[26] This represents the human factor in productivity increases.

Investment and the Growth of Capital

We have noted the role of capital in the process of economic growth, but what is the record of the American economy with respect to capital growth? In Table 10-4 we present data on the share of capital formation in the GNP. The data are arranged so that capital formation is given (1) excluding consumer durables, (2) for consumer durables, and (3) for both, on both a gross and net basis, and (4) in constant and current prices. If we look at *net* capital formation excluding consumer durables (column 3) we see that the long-run trend has been downward. *Net* capital formation as a percent of our GNP has declined significantly, regardless of whether constant or current prices are used to measure it. In column 6 we see an increase in net capital formation in consumer durables in both constant and current prices. If both are combined on a net basis, as in column 9, we see that the long-run downward trend has not been so serious, dropping from 13.6 in 1899–1908 to 10.5 in 1946–1955 in current prices.

If we examine *gross* capital formation excluding consumer durables in *current* prices (column 1), we see very little change. The same is true for *total gross* capital formation (column 7). (Both columns show a distinct

[25] See Fabricant, *op. cit.*, p. 19.

[26] See T. Schultz, "Investment in Man: An Economist's View," *The Social Service Rev.*, June 1959, and *Investment in Human Beings*, Universities—NBER Committee for Economic Research. Special Conference Vol. 15, published as a Supplement to the *J. Pol. Ec.*, Oct. 1962. See also Schultz's "Investment in Human Capital," *Am. Ec. Rev.*, March 1961, pp. 1–17.

downward trend in constant prices, though.) The data included in this table are those of Simon Kuznets and Raymond W. Goldsmith and have been compiled by Professor Goldsmith.[27] The study by Dr. Kuznets aroused quite a furor since it stressed the declining share of net capital formation in our economy. Kuznets further suggested that the main restraint on capital formation was an inadequate supply of saving and not a lack of demand for capital. Kuznet's statistics were immediately seized on as an explanation for the American economy having been in the doldrums since 1956. The cure was simple—lower taxes on investment and higher income groups. Dr. Kuznets' study, along with the high rates of capital formation in West Germany, Japan, and other countries which also had high rates of economic growth, was proof that a policy to induce investment was needed. We have previously noted, however, that some balance is needed between the rates of growth of both consumption and investment, and that saving is primarily a function of the level of income. If consumption is not high enough to cause a high rate of utilization of productive capacity, investment will decline. The American economy has had considerable excess capacity since 1957. (See Table 10-5.)[28] A more logical explanation of our failure to grow at a higher rate will perhaps be found in the built-in full employment surplus in our budget (the tax take, which may be thought of as a saving schedule, as the economy expands, is too great to enable consumption to get as high as it should), the lack of a vigorous underlying demand such as we had during the immediate postwar and Korean War periods, and perhaps also by a restrictive monetary policy. Those countries which have experienced high rates of economic growth have also been countries in which there have been high levels of demand. Also, there is no evidence that the rate of saving has been too low in the United States: Excess capacity has existed, there has been plenty of slack whereby real investment expenditures could have increased, and financial savings have been adequate. (See Chapter 15.)

It is very interesting to note that Professor Goldsmith has stated "that I am inclined to doubt the existence of a significant decline in the share of capital formation in national product over the past generation."[29] We should also note that the decline which has occurred may be explained in terms of the change in our aggregate production function. As we noted, increases in inputs of labor and capital have resulted in more than

[27] An appreciation of the complexity of the problem of measurement can be gained only by examining the Kuznets study itself. (*Capital in the American Economy: Its Formation and Financing*, Princeton, N.J.: Princeton Univ. Press for the NBER, 1961.) See the summary on pp. 8–11, and also the tables on pp. 64–65, 92–93, and 95–96.

[28] See the report cited in the table for a discussion of capacity indexes.

[29] JEC, *Jan. 1962 Ec. Rept. Pres.*, H, p. 530.

proportionate increases in output. This is due to the technological-human factor that we discussed earlier. Therefore, we may need less capital (relatively) to bring about the same, or even a greater, increase in output. Newer and better capital is capital-saving.

It is too often assumed that new capital is simply labor-saving; the extent to which it saves capital is ignored. More than output per unit of labor is involved. Output per unit of capital increases, or smaller quantities of fuel, power, and materials are used. There has been a relative stability of gross private investment in producers' durable equipment over the sixteen-year period 1947–1962 despite varying growth rates during this period. In particular, the Department of Commerce has estimated that the stock of business structures and equipment "has increased by only 2 percent per year over the past 5 years [1957 to 1962], compared with 4 percent a year in the period 1947–57."[30] (For total nonfarm equipment expenditures the figures, for the same periods, were .6 and 6.9 percent. For manufacturing alone the figures for equipment were 1.6 and 6.5 percent.) The fact that (according to CEA estimates) our rate of growth could have been 3.5 percent, or almost as high as that for the 1947–1957 period (which was 3.8 percent), even though the annual rate of growth of capital was much lower, supports the contention that capital has been capital-saving.

Of further interest is the observation of both Goldsmith and Kuznets "that the historical record does not disclose an obvious, regular, unchanging association between the intensity of capital formation and the rate of economic growth."[31] The same, they observe, is true for the assumed simple relation between the level of income and saving proportions and economic growth. We should note that these two conclusions pertain to the empirical evidence concerning these relationships. On the other hand, the evidence is consistent with our prior point that factors other than growth of capital significantly affect the rate of economic growth.

In addition to the points we have noted, we should take note of other considerations when evaluating Dr. Kuznet's study. (1) Capital consumption allowances (mainly because of obsolesence rather than wearing out) have grown rapidly, (2) the share of construction in gross capital formation has declined significantly, and (3) capital stock per member of the labor force has increased almost continuously.

---

[30] *Jan. 1963 Ec. Rept. Pres.*, p. 29. For a pointed statement on the capital-saving nature of new capital see Duncan Burn, "Why Investment Has Fallen," *Lloyds Bank Rev.* April 1963, pp. 8–11.

[31] *Ibid.*, p. 532. See the table on p. 530 for a summary of the empirical evidence. See C. L. Schultze's capable detailed, evaluation and criticism of the implications of Kuznets' study in *Am. Ec. Rev.*, Sept. 1962, pp. 814–821.

Table 10-5. Measures of the Rate of Utilization of Capacity for Total Manufacturing as Shown by 5 Organizations 1947–1962

As Reported
(Percent of Capacity)

Year	Federal Reserve Board	Wharton School[a]	National Industrial Conference Board[b]	*Fortune* magazine[c]	McGraw-Hill[d]
1947	90	95	—	98	—
48	87	93	—	96	—
49	78	83	—	88	—
50	88	90	—	99	—
51	91	92	—	102	—
52	90	91	—	101	—
53	93	94	100	104	—
54	83	86	—	94	84
55	90	94	97	102	92
56	89	95	91	100	86
57	85	93	88	96	78
58	76	84	87	87	80
59	84	92	94	97	85
60	84	92	93	96	77
61	82	90	92	95	83
62—1st quarter	85[e]	94[e]	—	—	—
2d quarter	—	—	—	100	—

			Adjusted[f]		
1947	90	91	—	86	—
48	87	89	—	85	—
49	78	79	—	78	—
50	88	86	—	88	—
51	91	88	—	90	—
52	90	87	—	89	—
53	93	90	93	92	—
54	83	82	—	83	84
55	90	90	90	90	92
56	89	91	84	88	86
57	85	89	82	85	78
58	76	80	81	77	80
59	84	88	87	85	85
60	84	88	86	85	77
61	82	86	85	84	83
62—1st quarter	85	90[e]	—	88	—

The first point may indeed be very significant, for if it is then we should be more concerned with gross than with net capital formation. Professor C. L. Schultze points out that new ideas are incorporated into production processes mainly through investment in capital goods, that short-lived producers' equipment is increasingly important relative to long-lived plant, and that this implies a faster turnover of capital stock. In addition, the average age of capital stock has declined, which implies a faster rate of adoption of new technology and a "larger rate of increase in output per man-hour, per unit increase in the net capital-labor ratio." This infers that the stability of gross investment in GNP may be much more important than the decline in net investment that Kuznets and others have found alarming. Schultze is also very critical of Kuznets' saving argument.

Full Employment versus Full Capacity

The foregoing leads to another point of some significance. Failure of the economy to grow results in a slower rate of growth of capital equipment. If this trend persists over a very long period of time, it is possible that we may reach a stage at which we have something close to full employment of capital equipment but not full employment of our labor resources. We should therefore note that full employment output may not be the same as full capacity output. We may have either one and not the other.

Notes to Table 10-5

Source: Hearings on *Measures of Productive Capacity* before the Sub-committee on Economic Statistics of the JEC, May 14, 22, 23, and 24, 1962.

[a] Covers total industrial production as measured by the FR Board index and therefore includes mining and utilities in addition to manufacturing.

[b] Rate of capacity utilized at peak of operations in each year. Covers all manufacturing except newspapers. Data were supplied too late to be included in the printed record of the hearings.

[c] Data are for the unrevised *Fortune* series for all manufacturing and were received after the hearings had been printed. *Fortune* is now engaged in a check-up and revision of their series which may change some of these rates given in this table. The series shown was arrived at by dividing an index of output by an index of capacity, both of which were computed with 1956 equal to 100. Therefore, the rate of utilization has an arbitrary value of 100 for the year 1956.

[d] McGraw-Hill data are for the end of each year and are therefore not strictly comparable to the other series shown which are averages for the year.

[e] Preliminary.

[f] The data in the bottom half of the table have been adjusted so that they all have an arbitrary value of 90 percent of capacity in the year 1955 in order to reveal differences in relative movements. The McGraw-Hill series was not adjusted in any way since its value of 92 for the end of 1955 would appear to be roughly comparable to a value of 90 for the average of the year used by the other indexes.

INCREASES IN PRODUCTIVE CAPACITY
AND ECONOMIC GROWTH

Our income analysis discussed previously was primarily of the static Keynesian type. It was static because it attempted to determine the equilibrium level of income at a given point in time. Since it dealt with a given point in time it assumed that the supply of labor, labor skills, the quantity of capital, the productivity of capital, the existing organizational and technological techniques, the degree of competition, and the tastes and habits of consumers were given or constant. If we know the capacity of the economy, the supply of labor, and other factors, then the level of demand will give us the level of production and employment. We know that this level of aggregate demand may bring an equilibrium at less than full employment, at full employment, or greater than full employment (in which case we experience inflation).

The level of aggregate demand we have referred to is the result of the level of consumption and investment (dropping government and foreign trade). If we know consumption, then we know the level at which investment must be to attain full employment. If we assume that all investment is for replacement, then with a constant labor supply and technique we can continue at this level. However, some portion of gross private domestic investment is generally *net*. It results in a net addition to—an increase in—our stock of capital. We therefore have changed one of the conditions in our static Keynesian model (the assumption of a given supply of capital) and are now dealing with a dynamic factor. The net increase in the stock of capital means that the productive capacity of the economy has increased. (It also generally means some displacement of labor—technological unemployment.) Therefore, in order for our resources to be fully utilized in the next period, our level of output and employment must rise.

When we discuss the Keynesian model in net terms we see the problem even more clearly. The level of income is determined by the level of consumption and net investment. This level of net investment, we can assume, was sufficient to offset net saving and sufficient to attain a full employment level of production. This net investment then increased income up to the full employment level, but it *also* increased our productive capacity. If, in the next period, the level of income (spending) does not also increase, then (1) unemployment will result because those technologically displaced could not be employed, (2) the level of (even a constant) income will decline because the increased productive capacity goes unused, which dampens incentives for further (net) investment.

The theory of economic growth has been a matter of concern for economists since the days of Adam Smith. In recent years it has been the object of increased interest and attention. Many economists have developed models for dealing with economic growth, but the most widely used are those of a British economist, Roy Harrod,[32] and an American economist, Evsey Domar. We shall follow their models here.

Domar's Growth Model

Given the fact that net investment increases productive capacity, Domar asked the question: At what rate does demand have to grow to assure the use of the new capacity and maintain full employment?[33] In his model, Domar assumes a constant marginal propensity to save, α (alpha), and a constant average capital-output ratio. The average capital-output ratio tells us how much stock of capital, on the average when fully used, is needed to give us one unit of output. This ratio is generally designated as K/Y, the ratio of capital to output. The *marginal* capital-output ratio relates net investment (an increase in our stock of capital) to increased output and is represented by $\Delta K/\Delta Y$. This ratio tells us by how much we must increase capital, ΔK, in order to increase output by a given amount, ΔY, in the next period. Assuming an increase in technology the capital-output ratio would decline. (It is generally assumed that the capital-output ratio for our economy is about 3.)

The Increase in Potential Output (ΔYp). The average productivity of capital can be expressed as Y/K, the reciprocal of the capital-output ratio. Using the capital-output ratio cited, the average output-capital ratio (average productivity) would be $\frac{1}{3}$ or 0.33. The productivity of the *increase* in capital stock is then $\Delta Y/\Delta K$. This shows us the increase in output which can accompany an increase in capital. Domar points out that the ratio $\Delta Y/\Delta K$ (the productivity of net investment), which he designates as s, will likely be greater than the productivity of the total stock of capital Y/K.

When net investment I_n occurs, the productive capacity created by *this* investment will be $I_n s$ dollars per year (net investment times its productivity or its output-capital ratio), which is also equal to ΔY. If we assume that $I_n = \$60$ billion and $\Delta Y/\Delta K = 1/2.7$, then the productive capacity of this investment is \$22.22 billion. Total capacity however, will not increase by the ΔY of the ratio $\Delta Y/\Delta K$, or by $I_n s$ dollars per year. The reason is

[32] "An Essay in Dynamic Theory," *Economic Journal*, March 1939, pp. 14–33, and *Towards a Dynamic Economics*, London: Macmillan Co., 1948, pp. 63–100.

[33] "Capital, Expansion, Rate of Growth, and Employment," *Econometrica*, April 1946, pp. 137–47; "Expansion and Employment," *Am. Ec. Rev.*, March 1947, pp. 34–55; "The Problem of Capital Accumulation," *Am. Ec. Rev.*, Dec. 1948, pp. 777–94. All these essays have been reprinted in Domar's *Essays in the Theory of Economic Growth*, New York: Oxford Univ. Press, 1957.

that the new capital does not represent an equal addition to capacity: It will be replacing some existing capital.[34] This means that the increase in capacity is less than s times net investment. Domar represents the increase in productive capacity by $I_n\sigma$. Productive capacity per dollar of investment increases by σ, the symbol σ (sigma) representing "the *potential* social *average productivity of investment*."[35] Clearly then the increase in production of the net investment is ΔY (or $I_n s$). This, however, is a separate concept from, and is greater than, the net increase in productive capacity $I_n\sigma$.

With the net investment which serves to maintain income in the economy, then, we have an increase in our productive capacity. This increase in capacity, σI_n, can be written as ΔY_p and is equal to potential productivity times net investment:

$$\Delta Y_p = \sigma I_n \tag{10-1}$$

In Domar's words this "is the increase in output which the economy can produce"; it is "the supply side of our system."[36] If the economy is to utilize this extra capacity and also maintain full employment, aggregate demand must grow by an amount equal to ΔY_p. If aggregate demand does not grow, the increase in capacity will not be used. This means a reduction in net investment, employment, and output.

The Required Increase in Aggregate Demand (ΔY_a). The increase in aggregate demand which is required to use the extra capital can be stated as

$$\Delta Y_a = \Delta I_n \times \frac{1}{\alpha}, \quad \text{or} \quad \frac{\Delta I_n}{\alpha} \tag{10-2}$$

which is net investment times the multiplier. [Since $\alpha = mps$, $1/\alpha$ is the same as $1/(1 - MPC)$.] Domar carefully notes that "an increase in national income is not a function of investment, but of the *increment* in investment."[36] We noted previously that a constant level of net investment will not raise the level of income. It is necessary that net investment be greater in each successive period in order for the net investment of the immediately preceding period to be utilized and therefore justified.

The question arises why the increase in demand must come from the increase in net investment. The reason is that both the government and

----

[34] See Domar, *Essays in the Theory of Economic Growth*, pp. 89–90. This is a confusing point. Even though we are talking here about *net* investment Domar still maintains that "the operation of new capital will take place, at least to some extent, at the expense of previously constructed plants . . . ." See also pp. 73–74.

[35] *Ibid.*, p. 89. The whole discussion is in net terms, but the productivity of replacement capital raises an interesting question concerning the value of σ. Presumably σ could be adjusted to account for this.

[36] *Ibid.*, p. 90.

international sectors are excluded, and consumption is made a function of income (since the propensity to save is made a constant). These are indeed highly restrictive assumptions, none of which can be made in reality, and the elimination of which makes the attainment of a full employment growth rate vastly easier to achieve.

Equilibrium. The equilibrium rate of growth is the rate at which the increase in aggregate demand is equal to the increase in productive capacity. It can be represented as[37]

$$\Delta Y_p = \Delta Y_a \tag{10-3}$$

or

$$\sigma I_n = \frac{\Delta I_n}{\alpha} \tag{10-4}$$

Since σI_n is the increase in capacity (the output-capital ratio or the productivity of capital times net investment), $\sigma I_n = \Delta Y_p$. Since $\Delta I_n/\alpha$ is the required increase in aggregate demand (the increase in net investment times the multiplier), $\Delta I_n/\alpha = \Delta Y_a$. Therefore $\sigma I_n = \Delta I_n/\alpha$. The left-hand side of both equations 10-3 and 10-4 represent supply (potential), and the right-hand side of both equations represent demand (required).

In the last paragraph we set the increase in potential capacity equal to the required increase in demand. By doing this we secure what Domar calls his "fundamental equation" (equation 10-4). Domar solves this equation by multiplying both sides by α and dividing both sides by I_n:

$$\sigma I_n = \frac{\Delta I_n}{\alpha}$$

$$\alpha \sigma I_n = \alpha \frac{(\Delta I_n)}{\alpha} = \Delta I_n \qquad \text{(multiply by } \alpha\text{)}$$

$$\frac{\alpha \sigma I_n}{I_n} = \frac{\Delta I_n}{I_n} \qquad \text{(divide by } I_n\text{)}$$

$$\frac{\Delta I_n}{I_n} = \alpha \sigma \tag{10-5}$$

The left side of equation 10-5 states the rate of growth of net investment. To maintain full employment this rate must be equal to $\alpha \sigma$ (the MPS times the productivity of capital). This is the rate at which investment must grow to assure that potential capacity will be used so that, in turn, we may attain full employment through time.

[37] *Ibid.*, pp. 90–91, and 74–75.

The rate of increase in income must be the same. This can be shown algebraically as follows:

$$\Delta Y_a = \sigma I_n$$

In equation 10-4

$$\Delta Y_a = \Delta Y_p$$

In equation 10-1

$$\Delta Y_p = \sigma I_n$$

Therefore

$$\Delta Y_a = \sigma I_n$$

Now

$$I_n(\text{net investment}) = \text{MPS}(Y)$$

assuming that saving is invested. Y is also equal to Y_a because income equals aggregate demand or aggregate expenditure. Therefore we can write Y as Y_a.

Since $I_n = \alpha Y_a$, we substitute αY for I_n:

$$\Delta Y_a = \sigma(\alpha Y)$$

$$\Delta Y_a = \sigma \alpha Y \qquad\qquad (10\text{-}6)$$

$$\frac{\Delta Y}{Y} = \sigma \alpha$$

We see then that net investment must increase by a constant percentage rate (given the assumptions we have used) in order to attain full employment. Notice, however, that although this is a constant percentage, in absolute terms income and investment increase each period. In each succeeding period net investment in absolute dollars must be larger than in the previous period to assure that the increased capacity resulting from the net investment of the previous period is used. This is so because the increase in demand will not come from an upward shift in the consumption function. (We have assumed a constant MPC.) Hence the extra demand must be in the form of investment. Of course, consumption will increase because of the increase in investment, but only at a constant rate. (There are no shifts in the consumption schedule. We move along the schedule as income increases.) We will not attain full employment if investment is merely increased by a constant dollar amount. It must be increased by a certain rate, and this amount must increase in absolute terms each year. This further means that it is not sufficient for investment of tomorrow to equal the saving of today. It must exceed today's saving. Investment, and therefore output and income, must grow rapidly enough or idle capacity will result.

A Numerical Example of Growth Theory. In Table 10-6 we have a numerical example of the type of economic growth which we have been discussing. We assume the value of σ (the output-capital ratio) to be .30 and the value of α (the propensity to save) to be .20. Since the required rate of growth of income is $\Delta Y/Y = \sigma\alpha$, the rate is .06. We need in each period an increase of 6 percent in our net national product and income.

Table 10-6. The Growth of Income and Investment (Billions of Dollars)

$\alpha = .20; \quad \sigma = .30; \quad \sigma\alpha = .06 = $ required rate of growth of I and Y

1	2	3	4	5	6	7	8	9
								$I_n\sigma$ Capacity Increases
	Capital		ΔC		ΔI_n		ΔY	from I_n of
Period	Stock	C	$.8 \times \Delta Y$	I_n	$.6 \times I_n$	Y	$.6 \times Y$	This Period
1	1,667	400		100		500		30
2	1,767	424	24.00	106	6.0	530	30.0	31.8
3	1,873	449.4	25.44	112.4	6.36	561.8	31.8	33.7
4	1,985.4	476.4	26.96	119.1	6.74	595.5	33.7	35.7
5	2,104.5	505.0	28.58	126.2	7.14	631.2	35.7	37.9

If our initial level of income is $500 billion, an annual growth rate of 6 percent will raise income in successive periods to $530, $561.8, $599.5, and $631.2, as shown in column 7. The increase in C, shown in column 3, is a constant percent of the increase in income—80 percent. In column 5 we see that net investment increases at a constant rate (6 percent). However, each level of net investment is a constant rate of an increasing absolute volume of investment. Therefore, in each income period the actual dollar volume of net investment is greater than in the previous period. Saving in each income period is equal to $Y - C$, and is assumed to equal investment. This means then that investment in each succeeding period must be greater than the saving of the previous period. And since I_n expands in each income period, Y must also expand if we are to attain full employment. Column 9 gives the amount by which capacity increases in each period as a result of the investment *of that period*. This means that in the next period output and income may increase by the amount of the increase in capacity in the previous period. In the first period, when $I_n = 100$, the increase in capacity was $30 billion ($100 \times 0.3$). In the second period, then, income can increase by this amount, or to $530 billion.

We could construct other models showing how different values for α and σ result in different required rates of growth. If the MPS (α) is higher, for example, then investment will have to be higher to maintain full employment. When I_n is higher, capacity increases more rapidly. Because of this the rate of growth of income must be greater. Assume that α has a value of .25 instead of .20, and that σ is still .30 as before. The rate of growth now is $\alpha\sigma = .25 \times .30 = 7.5$ percent. If the value (of the output-capital ratio) increases we reach the same result—an increase in the required rate of growth. If both α and σ increase, the result is even further magnified. The increase in capacity will be greater, and the required rate of growth in income will be greater. As we noted previously the increase in consumption will be a constant percent of the increase in income. The rest of the increase in demand must come from an increase in net investment.

Under the conditions we have stipulated here the absolute volume of investment must increase. If it increases by more than it should, inflation results (under full employment conditions). If it does not increase enough (to raise demand), we will have excess capacity and reduced investment and income. Since we have precluded an autonomous increase in consumption, the cure for excess capacity is greater investment.

The conditions under which Domar's model is presented are strict—a constant and unchanging MPS, and a constant output-capital ratio. Of course, the government has been omitted also. Even though it is not true that all groups have the same MPS or that it will not be subject to change, or that all industries will have the same output-capital ratios, changes in these variables do not change the basic point Domar has tried to make—that it is essential that the economy grow year after year . . . . Is it likely, for instance, that the MPS will drop as income grows? In the long run it is not likely, if past income-saving relationships have any validity. Further, there is the very real possibility, based on both theory and evidence, that in the shorter run the MPS will rise. This will raise the required rate of investment and of income. If the output-capital ratio decreases, the capacity-creating effect of investment would not be as great, and the required rate of growth would be smaller. As we noted previously, however, the productivity of capital, in the long run, has increased, although the trend of the postwar period is not entirely clear.

Professor Harrod and the Actual, Warranted, and Natural Rates of Growth

As a prelude to our discussion of Harrod's theory of economic growth we can make a few introductory remarks concerning the ideas and goals Harrod had in mind.

1. Professor Harrod discusses three different rates of growth: (a) the actual rate, which gives the increment in production attained during

any period; (*b*) the natural rate, which is set by the growth of the labor force and technological improvements, and which may be called the full employment rate; and (*c*) the warranted rate, which is the rate entrepreneurs counted on and, if it has been realized, are willing to repeat. Each is discussed in more detail as we proceed.

2. Harrod is attempting to show how steady (equilibrium) growth may occur in the economy.

3. He shows how, once this steady rate of growth is interrupted, cumulative factors tend to perpetuate this divergence, the result of which may be either secular stagnation or secular exhilaration.

4. Harrod's theory is based on the acceleration principle as an explanation for the level of investment and the extra investment required to produce extra output. (This follows from the capital-output ratio.)

5. Under Harrod's warranted rate of growth there is an equilibrium rate of growth between (*a*) saving and investment and (*b*) total supply and total demand. Both of these equilibrium rates are crucial to his theory. Once realized investment exceeds or is less than planned investment the warranted rate of growth will be interrupted.

6. Under the warranted rate net investment is equal to the amount necessary to produce the increased output of the period.

7. Finally, under the warranted rate of growth production decisions are made and *then* investment is undertaken to satisfy these production decisions. Thus, in a sense, production is assumed to create its own demand.

The Actual Rate of Growth. Professor Harrod expresses the actual rate of growth with the equation[38]

$$GC = s \qquad\qquad (10\text{-}7)$$

G represents the rate of growth, $\Delta Y/Y$, for any given period, and C represents the ratio of net investment I_n or the ratio of the increase in the

---

[38] Domar's necessary rate of growth was $\alpha\sigma$, where $\alpha = aps$ and $\sigma =$ the output-capital ratio. The similarity between the approaches is shown below:

$$GC = s$$

$$G = \frac{s}{C}$$

$$G = \frac{S}{Y} \div \frac{I_n}{\Delta Y} = \frac{S}{Y} \times \frac{\Delta Y}{\Delta K}$$

The ratio S/Y is the same as the *aps* in Domar's equation, and the $\Delta Y/\Delta K$ ratio is roughly equivalent to Domar's σ. The techniques used to arrive at these rates differ however. The reader is further advised that there is room for different interpretations of Harrod's work—he was not always explicit in his assumptions or statements.

stock of capital to the increase in output ($I_n/\Delta Y$ or $\Delta K/\Delta Y$). The s stands for the propensity to save, S/Y. The equation states that the rate of growth times the appropriate incremental capital-output ratio gives the necessary rate at which capital must increase for the actual rate of growth to be realized. This rate of growth of capital in turn must be equal to the actual ratio of saving to income S/Y. This means that saving must equal investment.

Harrod describes equation 10-7 as a truism, the meaning of which becomes more obvious if certain substitutions are made. As noted above, $G = \Delta Y/Y$, $C = I_n/\Delta Y$, and $s = S/Y$, which when substituted in equation 10-7 gives us

$$\frac{\Delta Y}{Y} \times \frac{I_n}{\Delta Y} = \frac{S}{Y}$$

By canceling out the ΔY terms we obtain

$$\frac{I_n}{Y} = \frac{S}{Y}$$

This states that *ex post* saving equals *ex post* investment (both terms are net), which is what we expect in any past period.[39] For illustrative purposes the reader may substitute numerical examples in equation 10-7. He will readily observe that, with C constant, a higher growth rate means that the growth of capital must be larger (in order to produce more goods), and that saving must have been higher because income is higher and/or because full employment is assumed. Also, with a given growth rate, the higher C is, the greater the growth of capital (and saving) must be. This is because more capital is required per unit of output.

Harrod's equation has been criticised for placing excessive reliance on the acceleration principle. As we note later, he does stress the point that businessmen will attempt to invest to reflect changes in output. To offset this criticism Harrod adds a term to his equation by which he can subtract "current additions to capital the worthwhileness of which is not deemed to have any immediate relation to current requirements." This is "the capital outlay of a long-range character, capital outlay which no one expects to see justified or not justified within a fairly short period."[40] By this Harrod means investment intended to satisfy a demand which will be realized only over a long period of time, and autonomous investment.[41]

[39] For definitions of terms see Harrod's *Towards a Dynamic Economics*, pp. 77–79. The C term, which is often a source of confusion, is defined on pages 80 and 85.

[40] *Ibid.*, pp. 79–80. The new equation is $GC = s - k$.

[41] See his "Essay in Dynamic Theory" as reprinted in A. Hansen and R. V. Clemence, *Readings in Business Cycles and National Income*, New York: Norton, 1953, p. 213.

It is of further interest to note that net investment "need not consist exclusively or even mostly of capital goods."[42] Hence an important role may be ascribed to inventory accumulation, a point that will be of some importance in the following discussion.

The Warranted Rate of Growth. It is important to note that the concept of the warranted rate of growth is related primarily to the behavior of businessmen. This rate of growth is the rate "at which producers will be content with what they are doing."[43] It is the "entrepreneurial equilibrium; it is the line of advance which, if achieved, will satisfy profit takers that they have done the right thing."[44] An entrepreneur will continue to produce (and purchase inventories) at the same rate this period as last if he has been able to sell his goods. Harrod discusses this in aggregate terms—some markets will expand and some contract, the two balancing out so that the rate of advance in the present period will equal that of the last period. The warranted rate of growth is the rate at which demand is high enough to enable entrepreneurs to sell the goods they have produced (and the inventories they have bought). If this happens businessmen are happy, and we shall have a repeat performance in the next period: That is, businessmen will produce at the same percentage rate of growth. Businessmen then decide to produce so many goods and invest the necessary amount to produce these goods. We have a sequence then of production decisions, investment, and income creation for consumers. If actual sales and investment are what had been planned, their warranted rate will have been achieved, and we can expect the same percentage rate of growth in the next period.

If the warranted rate of growth is realized, then *ex ante* (planned) and *ex post* (realized) investment, and *ex ante* saving and investment are in equilibrium. Since we are discussing rates here, the absolute volume of saving and investment will be growing, but they will be in equilibrium from one period to the next if the warranted rate prevails. If output grows enough so that investment equals saving, the warranted rate will prevail. Or, in Harrod's words, "if the advance is to be maintained . . . the quantity of the addition to capital actually accruing must be what is needed."[45]

The equation for the warranted rate is as follows:

$$G_w C_r = s$$

[42] "It is merely the accretion during the period of all goods" (less those goods which are included in k).

[43] Harrod, *Towards a Dynamic Economics*, p. 81.

[44] *Ibid.*, p. 87.

[45] *Ibid.*, p. 85.

Again the warranted rate can be represented by $\Delta Y/Y$. C_r is analogous to C, except that in the equation expressing actual growth C was an *ex post* term which gave us net investment and the ratio of increased capital to increased output. The term C_r is an equilibrium term which gives us our requirement for new capital, or the required capital coefficient. It is the ratio of the addition to capital which is needed to produce the additional output ($\Delta K/\Delta Y = I_n/\Delta Y$). It is then a marginal concept whose value may not be equal to the value of the capital coefficient for the economy as a whole. Harrod, however, assumes that the two ratios are the same and therefore that the capital-output ratio is constant, or more accurately that capital-reducing innovations are offset by those which require greater capital.[46] If we are to have an even rate of growth, then the actual rate of growth must equal the warranted rate of growth. The significance of this statement should become clear in the next section.

The Actual and Warranted Rates Compared. In comparing the two growth equations $GC = s$ and $G_wC_r = s$ it is necessary to first point out certain characteristics of the equations. In the equation which represents actual growth we see that, with a given value of s, the higher G the lower C must be. If both equations are equal to the same thing (s), then it follows that if the actual rate of growth G is greater than the warranted rate of growth G_w, then the ratio of increased capital to increased output C and therefore net investment must be below C_r, the required increase in capital necessary to produce the additional output. This point can be clarified by a numerical example, setting s equal to 12, and letting $G = 3$, $C = 4$, $G_w = 2$, and $C_r = 6$:

$$G > G_w$$

therefore $C_r > C$;

$$G \times C = s$$
$$\downarrow \quad \downarrow$$
$$3 \times 4 = 12$$

$$G_w \times C_r = s$$
$$\downarrow \quad \downarrow$$
$$2 \times 6 = 12$$

Again, actual growth exceeds warranted growth. Inasmuch as warranted growth is the factor which is crucial to how much capital and inventories are produced, it is clear that when $G > G_w$ shortages result. "There will be insufficient goods in the pipe-line and/or insufficient equipment . . . ."[45] This means that planned investment is greater than realized investment, inventories have been depleted, and orders increase. This divergence of

[46] *Ibid.*, pp. 83–84.

the actual and warranted growth rates creates a very unstable condition in a growing economy and forces are at work which cause "the system to depart further and further from the required line of advance."[47] The fact that planned investment exceeded realized investment means that aggregate demand exceeded aggregate supply. There is not enough capital to supply this demand; businessmen attempt to make up for this deficiency by raising investment. This increase in investment leads to further increases in income and demand, which lead to further increases in investment to match the increased demand. Then income and demand increase and investment goes up again (and so on) in a cumulative departure from the equilibrium rate of growth. Clearly such a situation would be highly inflationary. The only way in which the process may be curtailed is through an increase in the value of s (the propensity to save), but Harrod does not feel that significant variations in the saving ratio will occur. Finally, because of the great number of people involved in the decisions which determine G, there is no reason to assume that the value of G will automatically equal that of G_w.

Of course, just the opposite of the above process may also occur: That is, the actual may be below the warranted rate of growth. Following the procedure used above we see that C is greater than C_r. That is, if in our equations ($GC = s$ and $G_w C_r = s$) G_w exceeds G, then it follows that C must be greater than C_r, or that the ratio of actual net investment to the increment in income is greater than the ratio of net investment to output necessary to satisfy the equilibrium or warranted rate of growth. Using the same procedure as before we can clarify the point by setting s equal to 12 again.

$$G_w > G$$

therefore $C > C_r$;

$$G \times C = s$$
$$\downarrow \quad \downarrow$$
$$2 \times 6 = 12$$
$$G_w \times C_r = s$$
$$\downarrow \quad \downarrow$$
$$3 \times 4 = 12$$

This means that net investment was too high, or that realized investment exceeded planned investment, or that the total output of goods was not sold. This further means that excess capacity results and that investment and income will decline in the next period. Again, once the pattern of the warranted rate of growth is disturbed by either too little or too much investment, it is difficult to get the economy back in the same pattern even

[47] *Ibid.*, p. 86.

if there is a return to the warranted rate itself. That is, even after disturbances are corrected the levels of income which should have otherwise been attained will not be attained during the same time periods. The path of growth will be different from that which would have resulted had the actual growth rate been the same as the warranted rate.

Professor Harrod's Natural Rate of Growth. The natural rate of growth "is the rate of advance which the increase of population and technological improvements allow." To recapitulate, the actual rate of growth describes the actual increment in total production, the natural rate describes the "full employment" rate,[48] and the warranted rate "is the entrepreneurial equilibrium" in which "profit takers" are satisfied with their own behavior. It is possible that unemployment may exist (and grow) under the warranted rate, but that industrial capacity is fully utilized. The equation for the natural rate of growth is as follows:

$$G_n C_r = \quad \text{or} \quad \neq s.$$

Here G_n represents the long-run maximum average rate of growth. It is of course true that G may exceed G_n during the recovery from a recession but this condition will soon cease to exist because of the limit established by population increase and technological improvements.

The relation of the natural rate of growth G_n to the warranted rate of growth G_w is of great significance in determining whether the economy will tend toward secular (or long-run) exhilaration or secular stagnation. If the actual rate G exceeds the warranted rate G_w secular exhilaration will tend to result, and vice versa. The former results because demand (and planned investment) were greater than supply (and realized investment); the latter because supply (and realized investment) were greater than demand (and planned investment).

Harrod points out that if the warranted rate G_w is greater than the natural rate G_n there will be a tendency for secular stagnation to develop. This certainly seems paradoxical because one would ordinarily think it a good thing for businessmen to be pushing ahead at a rate which is greater than labor and productivity growth permit. When G_w exceeds G_n the actual rate G must on the average and over a period of time be below G_w because the upper limit to the actual rate G is set by the natural rate G_n. When G_w lies above G_n investment goods which have been created go unused because of a shortage of labor. The shortage of labor in turn places a limit on the rate at which the level of output can increase. The rate of increase in output then is not equal to G_w, machines therefore lie

---

[48] In Harrod's words, "it excludes the possibility of 'involuntary' unemployment." *Ibid.*, p. 87.

idle, and excess capacity results. This dampens investment incentives. Under these conditions saving is a vice—"a force making for depression."[49] It should be noted that this case gives results similar to the previously discussed case in which G_w was greater than G. This is because when $G_w > G_n$, G_w is also greater than G as explained above.

If G_n exceeds G_w there is a tendency for secular exhilaration to develop. This may occur when labor is plentiful and inexpensive. Profits may be high, a fact which induces businessmen to invest at a rate which is in excess of the warranted rate. The result may be inflation; the more G_w is below G_n the greater the potential inflation. In this case realized investment is less than planned investment and businessmen continue to attempt to increase their stock of capital. Under these conditions saving becomes virtuous because it can raise G_w. The case in which $G > G_w$ is similar to that in which $G_n > G_w$ because if the warranted rate is below the actual rate it *must* also be below the natural rate since the limit to the actual rate is set by the natural rate.

There is no reason why the warranted rate of growth should turn out to be equal to the full employment or natural rate of growth. It would be most advantageous for society, however, if the warranted rate of growth turned out to be the same as the natural rate of growth (in which case $G_n = G_w = G$). If, however, G_w is greater than G_n, steps can be taken to lower the rate of saving, and raise the level of expenditure and reduce the level of investment (which had become too high and redundant). If G_n exceeds G_w steps can be taken to raise the rate of saving. Since under these conditions businessmen may push the actual rate of growth beyond the warranted rate price increases result. An increase in saving permits the warranted rate to increase and releases resources for use in the production of capital goods.[50]

Neither Harrod nor Domar would argue that one should or could take their formulas and arrive at the necessary rate of growth for the United States. Their primary purpose is to pinpoint and stress certain crucial factors which characterize the growth process. It may be argued that production plans are less likely to determine investment (and aggregate demand), as Harrod's theory maintains, than an increase in aggregate demand. On the other hand the expectations of businessmen are an important factor in the economy (which fact does not necessarily justify the use of Harrod's explanation, however).

[49] *Ibid.*, p. 89.

[50] Harrod has refined his analysis somewhat in a later article ("Second Essay in Dynamic Theory," *Ec. J.*, June 1960, pp. 277–293). The analysis is essentially the same except that the discussion is primarily in terms of the rate of saving. See also Harrod's "Domar and Dynamic Economics," *Ec. J.*, Sept. 1959.

We may also question the contention of Harrod that just because the warranted rate has been realized businessmen will automatically increase output by exactly the same *percentage* in the next period. It is seemingly more logical to argue that if the production plans of businessmen have been justified by sales, they would then be more likely to merely produce that same output again rather than necessarily and automatically increase it. Finally, these theories are very narrow[51] in their approach—many of the previously discussed determinants of growth are abstracted away, government is excluded, and other rather rigid assumptions are made (as with the capital-output ratio, the APC and the MPC, for example). Moreover, the historical evidence shows that output and capital have not increased at the same rate. Solomon Fabricant's study on productivity has shown that from 1889 to 1957 output increased by about ten times and capital about five times.[52]

SOME POLICY CONSIDERATIONS

Fiscal Policy Considerations

In line with our discussion of the Harrod and Domar theories of growth there are some rather specific fiscal policy measures which may be employed to alter the rate of growth. (1) If the actual rate of growth is less than that which is justified by the increase in the labor force and the increase in productive capacity, then we have unemployment. Fiscal policy actions should be taken then to raise the level of aggregate demand—lower taxes, higher government purchases, or higher transfers. (2) If a situation should develop in which we have unemployment but no particular excess capacity then we must "go easy." That is, we do not want to raise the level of aggregate demand at a rate which is in excess of the capacity of the economy to produce the goods. To do so would be inflationary. Here we should increase demand but not as much as in (1). Fiscal and other policies should be directed toward raising investment and capacity in general. (But we should note that a prolonged period of relatively high unemployment can adversely affect the growth of capacity.) (3) If we have a situation in which the rate of growth is very high and unsustainable, demand is greater than supply, employment is high, and there are upward pressures on prices. If the cause is a very high level of consumption, action can be taken to reduce it by reducing disposable income. We can

---

[51] Joan Robinson (*Economic Philosophy*, Chicago: Aldine, 1962, p. 105) has, perhaps unkindly, expressed her concern over this narrowness: "The formula has made a great negative contribution to the development of economics. . . ."

[52] Arthur Smithies ("Productivity, Real Wages, and Economic Growth," *Q.J. Ec.*, May 1960, pp. 189–205) attempts to account for this.

again raise personal taxes, reduce transfers, and reduce government purchases. If, however, the high level of spending is caused by investment, policy is not so clear. If it is true that in this situation the warranted rate is not as high as it should be because of insufficient investment, we could increase saving and raise investment *if* such action does not place undue pressure on or create excess demand or bottlenecks in, the capital goods industries. Our policy then is partially dependent on the productive capacity of the firms that manufacture capital goods. If, on the other hand, the exuberance of the economy is due primarily to a high and excessive level of investment, then tax policy should be directed toward reducing the level of investment. In this case selective, direct controls may be needed, especially since we have not been particularly successful with restricting investment by means of monetary policy.

Other Government Actions to Raise the Growth Rate

We have previously noted that economists, private citizens, and various politicians have been concerned with the performance of the American economy during the late 1950's and early 1960's. If one accepts a 3 or 4 percent employment rate as a desirable social goal, an examination of the rate of unemployment and the rate of growth justifies this concern. The rate of growth can be raised, and the primary requirement in the minds of many economists is to raise the level of demand. This can be done by reducing taxes and the full employment surplus in the federal budget (as will be noted at a later point), or by raising the level of federal expenditures (or state and local expenditures via federal grants-in-aid).

There are many projects on which the federal government may raise its expenditures (directly or indirectly via grants) before we reach the point at which such expenditures have a lower marginal utility than private expenditures. In terms of the production of private goods our record has been unmatched and our volume great.[53] But in the opinion of many we are starving the public sector. (In this respect we should recall the trend of federal government per capita nondefense purchases and the federal government's declining share of the nondefense GNP discussed in Chapter 4.) Although we have private affluence, education is in need of greater financing, hospitals (and the nation generally) are short of nurses, staff, and physicians, our streams and bays go polluted when they could be used for extensive recreational purposes, slums proliferate, many highways are either terribly congested or unsafe, urban

---

[53] For more on this see J. K. Galbraith, *The Affluent Society*, and A. H. Hansen, *Economic Issues of the 1960's*.

transportation has lagged, water supplies are growing shorter in some areas, public parks are often more crowded than city streets, etc.[54]

There is not here an unqualified acceptance of the main thesis attributed to Galbraith's *Affluent Society*—that the great level of production has been sufficient. Certainly, there are many very low income groups whose income we should like to see raised, as Galbraith himself would note. Nor is there an acceptance here that we should have "full employment at whatever cost." There may well be times when the cost is very high in terms of price increases, the inefficient subsidization of declining industries, and under similar circumstances. The rate of growth will likely not be even in a dynamic society characterized by shifts in demand and the rise of new and the decline of old industries. On the other hand, present evidence indicates that we need not accept great fluctuations in output and employment as a necessary cost of economic growth. Many things have changed to make the economy stronger and more resistant to declines. (They are discussed later.) For those ups and downs which are not avoidable, those who are unemployed should have the protection of an improved unemployment compensation system.

Another important point should be noted in this context. The short-run stabilization of the economy, unless unwise policies are adopted, can be conducive to long-run growth. Recessions not only lower the average growth rate—they also lower the level of investment. Policies that reduce the number and depth of recessions are not only conducive to a high rate of long-run growth, they are necessary for it. (See the discussion in Chapter 2.)

Have Government Policies Encouraged Growth?

A devoted reader of publications like the *Wall Street Journal* may feel that everything the federal government does is wrong. But evaluations of the policies of the federal government over our history support the thesis that, on the whole, these policies have been conducive to growth. We can cite a few examples here: aid to canals, railroads, steamship lines, and airlines; provisions for support of land-grant colleges and universities and other support for education; TVA and similar flood control and power projects; the promotion of a *laissez faire* economy; monetary reforms; banking legislation and credit programs (such as

[54] See the very interesting article by E. L. Dale, Jr., *The New York Times*, March 13, 1960, p. E5, and Leon Keyserling, "Public Weal—and Private, Too," *The New York Times Magazine*, Aug. 21, 1960, pp. 22ff. The Committee for Economic Development, an organization of businessmen concerned with vital economic issues, has called for federal aid to poorer states in the field of education. See Ralph Lazarus, *We Can Have Better Schools*, New York: CED, 1960.

FHA and the FDIC); the conservation and development of natural resources; the highway program; urban renewal and development programs; tariff policies; the unemployment insurance program; and research programs.

One of the more significant contributions of the federal government during the postwar period has been its policy of support of research, which accounts for about two-thirds of all the research and development programs in the country. This includes research and development in universities, research institutes, government, and other nonprofit organizations, the dollar value of which was $14 billion in 1960. The sum expended on research performed in industry alone, but supported by government and private sources, was $10.5 billion.

Unfortunately, but of necessity, the lion's share of the government's R and D expenditures is on defense. Of even greater concern is the very small amount of expenditures on *basic* research. Of the $10.5 billion spent in industry only 8 percent ($382 million) was for basic research in 1960.[55] Business spends far too much on applied science and far too little on basic research. Nonetheless, the research expenditures of the federal government have significantly contributed to growth. It has been argued that expenditures and research involving new products and increases in productivity should be supported on a larger scale by the government since business expenditures are too low and too sensitive to changes in the level of income. According to Vandermeulen, the main areas involved are education and skills of labor, the quantity and quality of natural resources, and the stock of pure and applied scientific technological expenditures.[56]

The support for government promotion of basic research has been strong. In fact, it has been recommended that serious consideration be given to the establishment of national productivity centers similar to those which the United States encouraged in other countries under the Marshall plan to stress in particular new techniques in low-productivity industries. The success of federal research in agriculture is cited as evidence of the potential results. Presumably, considerable effort would go toward productivity increases in industries consisting of small, competitive units, unable to support research themselves.[57]

[55] JEC, *Ann. Rept.*, 1962, pp. 74–76; D. M. Keezer, "The Outlook for Expenditures on Research and Development During the Next Decade," *Am. Ec. Rev.*, May 1960, pp. 355–369, and the extensive analysis in *Reviews of Data on Research and Development*, National Science Foundation, No. 26, Feb. 1961.

[56] D. C. Vandermeulen, "Federal Expenditure and Economic Growth," in JEC, *Fed. Exp. Pol.*, P, pp. 308–318.

[57] JEC, *Empl., Growth, Price Levels*, SR, p. 59. It should not be concluded that only oligopolies are capable of supporting research.

One type of federal expenditure to promote growth which has received wide support from economists is federal support of education. The reasons usually cited are (1) the important relationship between skills, productivity, and income and education; (2) the large number of highly (and otherwise) qualified students who do not attend college—a great many of whom do not have the opportunity;[58] (3) the extremely low quality of education in many states due to the inability or refusal of many states to provide at least for a minimum standard for all students; (4) the fact that the long-run race with the Soviet Union may ultimately be decided on the basis of the relative quality of our educational systems; (5) the extremely high correlation between family background and college graduation;[59] and (6) the fact that skills and knowledge may be the most important factor in productivity increases.

In short, the government can contribute to economic growth by reducing the depth and incidence of recessions, by increasing its productivity-increasing expenditures, and by curtailing those policies and practices that create inefficiencies or result in a misallocation of resources (such as percentage depletion and the consequent overexpansion of oil capacity, and in agriculture). In other specific areas incentives are perhaps dampened because of high marginal tax rates, the inability to average income for tax purposes, etc. It would be helpful if we could revise these and similar policies, but changes in the high marginal tax rates would have an extremely limited effectiveness. (The available evidence simply does not support the popular notion that high marginal tax rates provide the greatest drag on investment. The impact on incentives is exaggerated; moreover, the rates push people into riskier investments so as to realize capital gains. These are other reasons, however, for reducing the high marginal rates.) In addition, the government can pursue many specific expenditure programs, such as in education and slum removal. Many who feel that public services have been slighted argue that an increase in the rate of economic growth will raise government revenues to a level which will automatically cover the cost of these additional services.[60] This, of course, depends on the rate of growth of government programs. If the programs which many people feel should be undertaken are pursued, the increased revenue will probably not cover the increased expenditures.

[58] Some 40 percent of high school graduates with an IQ of 125 or over do not go on to college, and some 38 percent in the upper 20 percent of their graduating class and with an IQ of 145 or over do not either. See the statistics cited by Evsey Domar in JEC, *Fed. Exp. Pol.*, P, pp. 270–272.

[59] *Ibid.*, p. 276.

[60] Arthur Smithies suggests this in JEC, *Fed. Tax Pol.*, P, p. 34. Kenyon Poole challenges it in JEC, *Fed. Exp. Pol.*, P, p. 124, as does Alvin Hansen in *Economic Issues in the 1960's*.

SAVING AND THE RATE OF GROWTH AGAIN

The rate of growth can be increased under conditions of full use of our resources if we reduce consumption and release resources for use for further investment, subject, of course, to all our previous qualifications concerning the contribution of increases in capital to the rate of growth. This can be done by reducing the degree of progression in the personal income tax and increasing taxes on consumption via a general sales tax, and/or by reducing the corporate income tax and increasing the personal income tax or consumption taxes. There must, however, be sufficient investment outlets for this policy to be successful. And if it is successful there will probably have to be selective controls on investment so that it does not proceed at a rapid, inflationary rate. This policy is more likely to succeed when prosperity prevails since the existence of unused capacity dampens investment except for autonomous and some productivity-increasing investment. And it is the type of policy we should follow if we decide that we want to raise our growth rate under conditions of prosperity. It is questionable whether such a policy would meet with much success when unused resources and excess capacity existed. We must admit, however, that we are not certain of the effect of tax reduction on private investment. In pursuing this policy it should be noted that the American public is probably not favorably disposed toward the redistribution that would occur if such a tax program were carried to the point of having a substantial impact. A possible alternative to such income inequality is an easy monetary policy (low interest and available credit) combined with a reasonable degree of fiscal restraint.

This question is raised again here with regard to the level of saving. Much has been written in recent years about insufficient saving being the cause of insufficient investment. This in fact was the October, 1962 theme of the Chairman of the Board of Governors of the Federal Reserve System. Is it true that saving is insufficient or is likely to be so in the future? If what we learned in the first course in economics has any validity, our answer is "no." The American economy has experienced neither the pressures on capacity nor on prices which would call for a policy of greater saving. Probably the best way to raise the rate of saving and the level of investment in our economy under these conditions is to raise the rate of growth and the level of income. In other words, with a higher level of income saving will likely take care of itself. If at that higher level of income we want an even higher rate of growth, then we should pursue the policy just noted. But many fear that if we follow the advice of Mr. Martin to raise our rate of saving under the conditions of the late 'fifties and early 'sixties we shall fall smack into the "paradox of thrift."[61]

[61] We have not dealt with the problem of monopoly and monopolistic practices and their relation to economic growth. The standard arguments condemning monopoly restrictions on output and capital expansion and hence on national income and consumption can be found in almost any introductory and intermediate theory text. See also the excellent and pointed statements by J. Markham, J. P. Miller, and D. Hamberg in JEC, *Empl.*, *Growth*, *Price Levels*, H, Pt. 7; and E. V. Rostow, "Market Organization and Stabilization Policy," in Max F. Millikan," ed., *Income Stabilization for a Developing Democracy*, New Haven: Yale Univ. Press, 1953, pp. 439–513.

11

Potential Economic Growth
of the American Economy

The concern over the performance of the American economy in recent years has been motivated by the realization that our *potential* growth was considerably higher than our actual growth.[1] In this chapter we shall examine the potential growth of the American economy and the factors which determine that growth. Needless to say, the main emphasis here will be on the supply side. We recognize, however, that an increase in demand is equally important—a point which we have emphasized in previous chapters. There is a particular value in noting the relevance of both supply and demand in the same context though. That is the fact that actual growth is determined by whichever is smaller—the growth of demand or the growth of supply in each time period. If either factor fails to grow when the other does, then it (the factor which does not grow) will be the *limiting factor* for that time period.[2]

CAPACITY, ACTUAL GROWTH, AND POTENTIAL GROWTH

Discussions of potential growth should point out the fact that potential output and capacity output are not generally considered to be the same thing. The concept of potential growth is used to refer to a rate of growth which is "optimum"—an average, sustainable, yearly growth rate. It represents an acceptable and reasonable rate of growth which results in a good performance for the economy without incurring significant fluctuations in prices, output, or employment. It further represents a stable

---

[1] And concern over the rate of unemployment and other factors discussed in previous chapters.

[2] See JEC, *Empl.*, *Growth, Price Levels*, SR, p. 97.

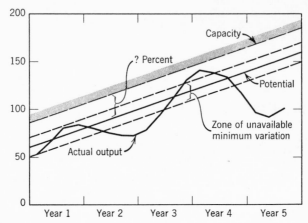

Figure 11-1. Capacity, actual, and potential output: an explanatory sketch. From JEC, *Empl., Growth, Price Levels*, SP No. 20, p. 6.

and reasonable level of capacity utilization.[3] It is a rate of growth whose attainment would satisfy the requirements of the Employment Act. In addition, because of the great problems surrounding the measurement of capacity, there has been an attempt to express potential output in terms of "something approaching the economy's notion of a least-cost combination of inputs."[4] The unemployment rate used in the study by the Joint Economic Committee Staff in computing potential growth was 4 percent. The staff carefully points out that it does not recommend or accept that rate, but uses it as a more realistic reflection of the economy's performance during the late 1950's.[5]

It is necessary to keep in mind the fact that it may not be possible to have full employment because capacity (the stock of capital), for reasons noted in the previous chapter, may not be great enough. It is necessary to keep this in mind when examining "gaps" in potential output, including the gaps in output so widely publicized by the CEA.

The concepts of capacity output, actual output, and potential output are illustrated hypothetically in Figure 11-1. The potential output is shown by the solid straight line. The broken lines above and below it represent tolerance zones, fluctuations between which may not be desirable

[3] JEC, *Empl., Growth, Price Levels*, SP No. 20, p. 6. No attempt is made to quantify this concept. (An earlier study by the JEC Staff was *Potential Economic Growth of the United States During the Next Decade*, 1954. This report contains a summary of other similar studies, pp. 21–23.) The reader should remember that capacity may be so small that even though it is fully used unemployment is very high.

[4] *Ibid.*, p. 7. This also means least cost per unit of ouptut.

[5] *Ibid.*, pp. 9 and 48–49. The interested reader should examine the analysis of the complete study.

but which do not violate the intent of the Employment Act. Actual output is shown by the solid fluctuating line. When it rises above the tolerance zone it pushes against capacity and creates inflationary pressures. This level may also be unsustainable. When it is below the tolerance zone we have a recession and serious unemployment. Naturally, we would like to work toward two goals in this respect. We would like (1) to push the potential closer to the capacity line without having inflation, and (2) by better use of policy, to be able to narrow the tolerance zone. The use of the potential output and potential rate of growth concept is justified as an instrument to judge the extent to which the objectives of the Employment Act are being realized, and as a standard against which the actual performance of the economy can be evaluated.[6]

In the measurement of potential growth the more important factors cited by Knowles and Warden (Study Paper No. 20) and the *Staff Report* are the size of labor force, the accumulated stock of capital, the availability of natural resources, current technology, and the rate of introduction of new products and new techniques. Additional factors of considerable importance are trends in productivity and the average age of capital, the ratio of the labor force to population, the length of the work day and week, the amount of output devoted to net investment, rising levels of educational attainment and health, managerial skills, the rate and character of scientific research, the extent to which efficiency is stimulated by both domestic and foreign competition, and numerous social and political environmental factors.[7]

It would be useful if we could measure potential output and its rate of growth in terms of capacity. A measure of actual output as a percent of capacity over a period of years would be useful in the development of a standard for desirable performance of the economy. Then the actual performance could be judged against this standard in terms of percent of capacity used, percent of labor employed, the rate of growth of capacity, and the stability of prices. The standard developed above would be the desired potential output.[6]

It is not possible to do this adequately because of the lack of a good measure of capacity for the whole economy. The technique used then involves a variation of the production function,[8] which, as we know, gives the relationships between the factors of production and the output of the economy. It must, therefore, contain measures of the labor available for work, the stock of capital, the age of capital, and some estimate of

---

[6] *Ibid.*, p. 7.

[7] *Ibid.*, pp. 9–10. (See also JEC, *Empl., Growth, Price Levels*, SR, pp. 97–98.)

[8] See *ibid.*, p. 17, for a discussion of the characteristics of a desirable production function.

other factors such as managerial skill, technological progress, and health and education. It is no easy task to project potential output into the future since certain estimates and assumptions must be made concerning these variables. Of course, heavy reliance on historical trends and relationships is necessary in the development of the assumptions underlying the projections.[9]

ALTERNATIVE PROJECTIONS

Knowles and Warden have made projections of potential growth for the period 1959–1975 for the JEC. These projections, shown in Table 11-1, represent alternative but realistic potential growth rates that the American economy could realize. There is a high (A), a medium (B), and a low (C) projection of potential output and its rate of growth. Trends of population, the labor force participation rate, unemployment, hours of work, changes in the capital stock, and the average level of prosperity are all reflected in the projections.

Projection A is based on the assumption of a high level of prosperity. Occasional but minor recessions might occur, but a prolonged depression is excluded. The types of policy required to attain this growth rate are not specified. Unemployment is assumed to be about 3 percent,[10] which means that sufficient opportunities will exist to draw a large percentage of the population into the labor force. The number of average annual hours of work is assumed to decline at the annual rate of 0.4 percent per year, which is less than the rate of the past half century. The rate of growth of the gross capital stock is assumed to be 3.2 percent per year. The trend of composition of demand is similar to that of past periods of strong growth. The share of services in the GNP is about the same as that of 1955–1957 (with a rise in private housing and government and a decline in other consumer services), durables somewhat above the 1957 share, and construction and nondurables down moderately. Under Projection A the growth rate over the period of 1959–1975 as measured from the actual 1959 rate would be 5.2 percent, and 4.6 percent from the 1959 potential.

Medium Projection B assumes an average unemployment rate of about 4 percent. Participation rates are based on present trends. The gross

[9] Historical potential and actual rates and different projections for 1975 are charted in *ibid*, p. 36.

[10] Denison (*The Sources of Economic Growth in the United States*, New York: CED, 1962, pp. 63–65, 283) does not accept Knowles' assumption that the size of the labor force is inversely related to the level of unemployment. Denison, furthermore, does not think that differences in the unemployment rate—"as between, say, 3, 4, or 5 percent"—will make as large a difference in the rate of growth as Knowles calculates.

stock of capital is assumed to increase at the rate of 2.7 percent per year. There is the further assumption that a serious depression will not occur. Changes in the composition of demand have only a slight impact on the growth rate. Under this medium projection the growth rate from 1959 actual would be 4.7 percent per year, and from 1959 potential 4.0 percent.

Table 11-1. Selected Indicators of Economic Growth Potentials 1959–1975 (Percent Increase per Year[a])

Indicator	Rate of Growth 1909–1958	Projected Potential Growth Rates, 1959–1975		
		A	B	C
Total labor force	1.4	1.9	1.7	1.5
Total employment including Armed Forces	1.4	1.9[b]	1.7[c]	1.5[d]
Average annual hours of work	−0.6	−0.4	−0.5	−0.6
Total man-hours	0.9	1.6	1.2	0.9
Stock of private plant and equipment in constant prices	2.4	3.2	2.7	2.2
Average age of capital stock	0.3	0.2	−0.1	0
Composition of demand	0.1	0.015	0.001	−0.005
GNP, in constant prices	2.9	—	—	—
From 1959, actual (preliminary estimates)	—	5.2	4.7	4.2
From 1959, potential	—	4.6	4.0	3.5

Source: JEC, *Empl., Growth, Price Levels*, SP No. 20, p. 40.

[a] Computed by compound interest formula, using initial and terminal years.
[b] Assumes 97 percent of the labor force employed in 1975.
[c] Assumes 96 percent of the labor force employed in 1975.
[d] Assumes 95 percent of the labor force employed in 1975.

Projection *C*, which is low, "assumes a continuation of public and private policies in such mixture that there will be fairly frequent interruptions to growth, inadequate mobility of capital and labor, and more slack on the average . . . ." Unemployment is to average 5 percent, the participation rate will be down, average annual hours of work decline at the average rate of about 0.6 percent per year (about the average of the past half century), and the rate of growth of gross capital stock is 2.2 percent (lower because of more excess capacity). The growth rates under this low projection would be, from 1959 actual and potential, 4.2 and 3.5 percent, respectively.

It is significant to note that Knowles and Warden claim that the assumptions used in these three projections are conservative. There is no reason to question their judgment. In fact, since historical relationships have been used as the basis for the data used, and since the historical data include a very long period of depressed economic conditions, it is possible to have even higher growth rates. Knowles and Warden have been particularly conservative in their use of the "time trend" factor. The time trend factor (analogous to the unconventional inputs noted in Chapter 10) includes a large variety of forces which have a significant impact on growth but which are not measurable—educational progress, research and development, the speed of introduction of improved production techniques, and similar forces. The acceleration of research and development, managerial use of greater productive efficiency (and this varies widely within each industry even today), and a higher level of skills could significantly influence the growth rate.

It is interesting to note that even the lowest growth rate in the projections (3.5 percent) is above the long-run average of 3 percent for the past 50 years. The reason for this is the assumption in all three projections that there will be no deep, prolonged depressions as there was during the period 1929–1941. As we have noted previously, increased stability significantly raises the average growth rate and tends to raise the rate of growth of the labor force, lower the rate of decline in the hours of work, raise the rate of capital accumulation, raise the rate of use of new technology in production techniques, and to change the composition of demand more rapidly. In particular, a larger labor force, a greater stock of capital, and new capital have important impacts on the rate of growth.

Table 11-2 shows Denison's projected rate of growth for the period 1960–1980 to be 3.3 percent, not a very optimistic projection. Of this 3.3 percent he expects that 2.19 percentage points (or 66 percent) will come from an increase in inputs. The labor input (adjusted for changes in quality) is estimated at 1.70 percentage points (51 percent), and the capital input is estimated at 0.49 percentage points (15 percent). The increase in output per unit of input is set at 1.4 percentage points (34 percent). In Denison's estimates only five factors will be significantly different from their contributions to the 1929–1957 rate of growth. (1) Employment will increase at a much more rapid rate and the rate of reduction of hours worked will be reduced. (2) A larger stock of capital will raise the contribution of capital. (3) Factors that restrict the optimum allocation and

Table 11-2. Allocation of Growth Rate of Total Real National Income Among the Sources of Growth

	Percentage Points[a] in Growth Rate 1960–1980[b]	Percent of Growth Rate 1960–1980[b]
Real National Income	3.33	100
Increase in total inputs	2.19	66
Labor, adjusted for quality change	1.70	51
Employment and hours	0.98	29
Employment	1.33	40
Effect of shorter hours on quality of a man-year's work	−0.35	11
Annual hours	−0.42	−13
Effect of shorter hours on quality of a man-hour's work	0.07	2
Education	0.64	19
Increased experience and better use of women workers	0.09	3
Changes in age-sex composition of labor force	−0.01	0
Land	0.00	0
Capital	0.49	15
Nonfarm residential structures	NA[c]	NA
Other structures and equipment	NA	NA
Inventories	NA	NA
U.S.-owned assets abroad	NA	NA
Foreign assets in U.S.	NA	NA
Increase in output per unit of input	1.14	34
Restrictions against optimum use of resources	0.00	0
Reduced waste of labor in agriculture	0.02	1
Industry shift from agriculture	0.01	0
Advance of knowledge	0.75	23
Change in lag in application of knowledge	0.03	1
Economies of scale		
Independent growth of local markets	0.05	2
Growth of national market	0.28	8

Source: E. F. Denison, *The Sources of Economic Growth in the United States*, 1962, p. 266. Reprinted by permission of the Information Division of the Committee for Economic Development.

[a] Contributions in percentage points are adjusted so that the sum of appropriate details equals totals. Percents of the growth rate have not been so adjusted.

[b] Growth rate based on high employment projection.

[c] NA: Not available.

use of resources will not subtract from the growth rate as they did during the 1929–1957 period. (4) The shift in the use of resources away from agriculture will not contribute as much to the growth rate as previously. (5) The contribution resulting from the advance of knowledge is increased significantly. Denison's projection assumes a "high-employment national product" over the 1960–1980 period. This assumed rate of growth implies that national income per person employed will increase at the rate of 1.62 percent as against a rate of 1.60 percent from 1929 to 1957.

The Short-Run Projections of the Council of Economic Advisers

Beginning in early 1961 and continuing through 1962, considerable discussion was aroused by the emphasis placed on the gap between the potential and actual levels of production of the economy by the CEA. In its statement before the Joint Economic Committee on March 4, 1961, the CEA presented a chart showing the gap between potential and actual production, and a chart showing the GNP gap as a percent of potential.[11] These same charts were included and updated in the *January 1962 Economic Report of the President*.[12] In the latter it was estimated that in the first quarter of 1961 [also written 1961(1)] a gap of $51 billion (1961 prices) existed, by 1961(4) the gap was $28 billion, the average for 1961 as a whole was a gap of $40, and the production potential for 1962 was estimated to be $580 billion. For the 1961 gap the $40 billion increment in output was divided as follows: $15 billion due to lower unemployment, $4 billion due to labor force response to greater demand, $5 billion due to longer hours of work per man associated with higher utilization, and $16 billion due to greater productivity per man-hour associated with higher utilization.[13] The assumed rate of unemployment was 4 percent.

The gap between potential and actual GNP is shown in Figure 11-2. It is interesting to note that the gap has not been closed since 1955. It widened sharply during the 1957–1958 recessions, and even though the recovery from the recession was quite rapid we did not get back to the potential level. At the peak of the 1960 recovery the gap was still about 5 percent.

[11] See JEC, *Jan. 1961 Ec. Rept. Pres.*, H, pp. 323, 373–377. For a criticism of the CEA's analysis of the computation of potential output see W. Reuther, JEC, *Jan. 1962 Ec. Rept. Pres.*, H, and JEC, 1961 *Ann. Rept.*, Minority Report, pp. 63ff. In a speech at the University of Chicago on April 21, 1961 (reprinted in *The Morgan Guaranty Survey*, Morgan Guaranty Trust Company, May, 1961, and in slightly revised form in *The New Leader*, June 19, 1961), Dr. Arthur F. Burns, former chairman of the CEA, condemned the use of the CEA's projections and labeled their analysis as secular stagnation. The CEA countered with a rather forceful answer (see *The New Leader*, July 3 and 10, 1961, and *The Morgan Guaranty Survey*, August, 1961, which also contains Burn's second thoughts.)

[12] *Jan. 1962 Ec. Rept. Pres.*. p. 52.   [13] *Ibid.*, pp. 49–50.

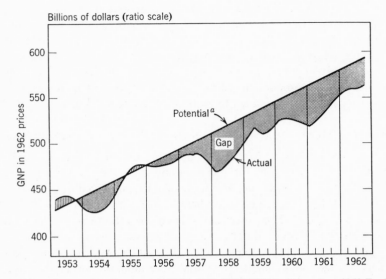

Figure 11-2. Actual and potential GNP, 1953–1962 (CEA). From *Jan. 1962 Ec. Rept. Pres.*, p. 52.

a $3\frac{1}{2}$ percent trend line through middle of 1955.

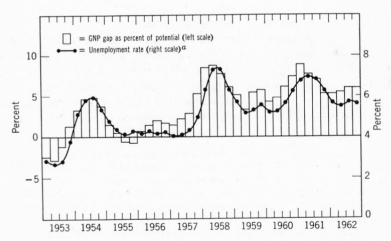

Figure 11-3. Unemployment rate and GNP gap as a percent of potential GNP, 1953–1962. From JEC, *Jan. 1962 Ec. Rept. Pres.*, H, p. 27.

a Unemployment as a percent of civilian labor force, seasonably adjusted.

Figure 11-3 gives the gap as a percent of potential GNP and also the unemployment rate. The general correlation between the two is not surprising. Note that the rate of unemployment was still about 5.6 percent in the last quarter of 1962 in spite of the recovery. This was due to the relatively high rate of unemployment during the recession and the rapid increase in productivity during the recovery. (The increase in productivity has been estimated to be between 6 and 9 percent.)[14]

THE NATIONAL PLANNING ASSOCIATION PROJECTIONS

The National Planning Association has been one of the leaders in the development of projections for the economy on a long-run basis. The first NPA report[15] of this type, which incidentally produced quite a furor and some considerable criticism for being too optimistic, was published in December, 1952.[16] The procedure followed was the same as that used by Knowles and Warden; that is, a range of estimates were made of labor force growth, the rate of unemployment, average weekly hours, productivity changes, and changes in capital accumulation and in the composition of demand. Instead of three projections, however, the NPA presented six.[17] The six different models were based on various combinations of high consumption and high taxes, high consumption and moderate taxes, high domestic investment and moderate taxes, high domestic and foreign investment and moderate taxes, very low taxes, high government purchases and moderate taxes. None of these models was felt to be economically sustainable in the sense that it represented a balanced economic expansion which was socially desirable and politically acceptable.[18] An adjusted model for full employment in 1960 was made therefore, with a projection in terms of 1960 prices of a GNP of $505 billion. The actual level of GNP was $503 billion (first 9 months), but the rate of unemployment averaged 5.5 percent rather than the 4 percent assumed by the NPA in its *full employment* projection.[19]

[14] The preliminary estimate for the whole year for manufacturing (for which the estimate for the index of man-hours was below that for 1960) was 4.6 points. During the recovery period alone the rate was no doubt much higher. *Ibid.*, p. 244.

[15] To my knowledge the 1952 report was the first of this type from the NPA. The NPA had done considerable work on the National Economic Budgets since at least 1945, however.

[16] G. Colm and Marilyn Young, *The American Economy in 1960*, Planning Pamphlet No. 81, Washington, D.C.

[17] *Ibid.*, p. 31.

[18] In the very low tax model, for instance, consumption is high but investment is set a rate which is quite low, which seems quite unrealistic. See Model F, *ibid.*, p. 31.

[19] The NPA cites these figures in NPA, *Looking Ahead*, Dec. 1960, p. 4. Since the original model was for a 1960 full employment model of $425 billion the assumption made in the text above that the original model was expressed in terms of 1960 prices must be true.

The second NPA report on long-run projections appeared in 1959. This was an attempt to bring up to date the projections which had been made in 1952, and estimates were made for 1965 and 1970. The data are shown in Table 11-3, and in graphic form in Figure 11-4. In Figure 11-4 the three broken lines represent the projections with the top and bottom lines the upper and lower ranges of the reasonably probable future rate of progress. The line in between these limits represents the NPA's judgment of the most useful trend line. This figure also shows the alternative trends in per capita GNP.

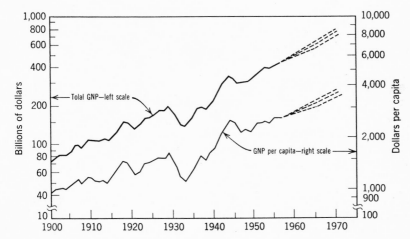

Figure 11-4. Total and per capita gross national product, 1900–1970 in 1958 prices (NPA estimates). From NPA, *Long-Range Projections for Economic Growth: The American Economy in 1970*, Planning Pamphlet No. 107, Washington, D.C., Oct. 1959, p. 3.

The third projection by the NPA appeared in February 1961, and was shorter-run, being directed toward the year 1965.[20] The NPA plotted the actual GNP for the years 1955–1960, the projected *full employment* GNP from 1955 to 1965, and alternative GNP projections for the period 1960–1965. Two of the NPA's three projections assumed an average rate of growth of 4.1 percent to 1965, which would result in an unemployment rate of 4.0 percent at that time. Of particular interest was the NPA's projection of an unemployment rate of 13.2 percent by 1965 if the country continued to plod along at a 2.5 percent growth rate.

[20] G. Colm and P. Wagner, *Targets for U.S. Economic Growth in the Early 60's*, Planning Pamphlet No. 111, Washington, D.C.: NPA, 1961, p. 13. See also NPA, *Looking Ahead*, Dec. 1961, p. 3.

Table 11-3. Selected Indicators of Economic Growth, 1965, 1970 (NPA) (1958 Prices except as Noted)

Projections

	1965		1970	
Indicator	Judgment	Range	Judgment	Range
GNP ($, billion)	630	390–650	790	735–820
Private GNP ($, billion)	579	536–595	727	674–753
Index of industrial production (1947–49 base)	209	199–215	259	238–270
Consumer expenditures ($, billion)	405	375–440	515	485–570
Investment expenditures ($, billion)	100	80–105	120	95–125
Gov't expenditures ($, billion)	125	100–155	155	115–180
Net exports ($, billion)	5	5–5	6	6–6
Population (millions)	196	196	214	214
Civilian labor force (millions)	76.6	75.4–77.4	83.6	81.7–84.8
Civilian employment (millions)	73.9	73.1–74.3	80.7	79.2–81.4
Private employment (millions)	66.3	64.3–67.4	72.7	69.7–73.8
Armed services	2.4	2.0–3.3	2.3	1.7–4.4
Average weekly hours of work	39.0	39.0–40.0	37.5	37.5–38.5
Unemployment ÷ civilian labor force (%)	3.5	3.1–4.0	3.5	3.1–4.0
Labor force ÷ working age population (14 and over)	57.2	56.5–57.9	57.0	55.8–57.8
Private stock of plant and equipment (billions of 1955 dollars)	768	750–780	935	897–952
Ratio of private stock of plant and equipment to private GNP	1.45	1.42–1.53	1.41	1.38–1.46

Source: NPA, *Long-Range Projections for Economic Growth: The American Economy in 1970,* Planning Pamphlet No. 107, Washington, D.C., Oct. 1959, pp. 6–7.

THE USE OF SHORT-RUN AND LONG-RUN PROJECTIONS

The projections noted in this chapter do not claim to predict exactly what the level of the GNP or its components will be 10 or more years in the future. They do, however, give an acceptable range of possibilities and the direction of the trend in the economy. As such they are useful in the planning which businessmen and government must do. Of course, yearly revisions must be made to incorporate recent developments. The businessman, in particular, will have to take into account current data on orders, inventories, capacity, competition, new markets and techniques, and price-cost developments.[21]

The projections have particular significance for fiscal policy and federal policy in general. Projected increases in the population mean similar increases in residential construction, consumer expenditures, capital stock, and government services. Regardless of whether or not there should be a proportionate increase in government services there will be an increase made necessary by the growth in population. These necessary expenditures are separate and distinct from those resulting from an increasing role for government. Of course, the projections, particularly of the short-run forward type, are also useful as a standard against which we can measure the extent to which the economy achieves the objectives of the Employment Act.

[21] See NPA, *Long-Range Projections for Economic Growth*, *op. cit.*, pp. 9–11.

PART IV

Fiscal Policy and
Consumption and Investment

12

Consumption and Fiscal Policy

CONSUMPTION AND TAXES

In this chapter we want to review briefly the policies that may raise or lower the level of consumption. We shall examine taxes first and then go on to other policies.

We can raise the level of consumption by lowering excise and sales taxes or by lowering personal income taxes. It is generally argued that reductions in excise and sales taxes have important stimulative effects on consumption because these taxes are regressive. The assumption, obviously, is that the marginal propensity to consume among the lower income groups is high. Available evidence supports this assumption, but it is not strictly necessary if the sales or excise taxes are fairly wide in their coverage. Since consumption consists of the largest type of expenditure on our GNP, the tax reduction will likely have a considerable impact.

It is interesting to look at reductions in the rates of excise and sales taxes in terms of their price elasticities of demand. Consider first lowering the tax rate on those products for which demand is price-elastic. The removal of the tax on the product lowers the price and total spending increases. Consider next lowering the tax on those products for which demand is price-inelastic. In this case the lower price on these products results in consumers purchasing not much more than they had before removal of the tax. But total expenditure on these products will decline and release income which may be spent on other products. It follows, therefore, that total consumer expenditure may increase even though the tax reduction falls on items with price-inelastic demands. It is possible that a tax reduction on price-inelastic products actually results in a larger stimulus to the economy than a tax reduction on products the demand for which is price-elastic.

Alternatively, personal income tax rates may be lowered (exemptions raised, or the definition of the base narrowed) so as to raise disposable income and stimulate consumption. The impact on consumption expenditures depends on the size of the rate reduction; whether the reduction is for high or low income groups or an across-the-board straight percentage reduction; whether the reduction is by means of increased exemptions or splitting the first bracket, etc. Similarly, a comparison of the relative effectiveness of excise and income tax reduction depends on the manner in which the income tax is reduced. It is often argued that excise tax reduction has a greater impact. This is not necessarily true, especially if the reduction is in lower income groups whose MPS is very low.

If the object is to lower or restrain further increases in consumption, these policies would be reversed. Of particular significance, though, would be an increase in the excise tax rate on those products for which demand is price-inelastic, for there would be an absorption of purchasing power. In the case of the price-elastic products the higher price resulting from the increased tax will actually reduce total spending on them. Hence little anti-inflationary effect is achieved. The larger the volume of consumption of the price-inelastic product, the greater the anti-inflationary impact of the tax rate increase.

The impact of an increase in, or the imposition of, a sales tax is similar to that of a wide use of excises, except that the sales tax has the advantage of not being as discriminatory. The sales tax effectively penalizes spending, encourages saving, and absorbs purchasing power. An important difficulty with sales taxes is that they lead to demands for higher wages because the impact of the tax increase is to raise the price level. But this must be excluded from the Consumers Price Index; if it is not, escalator clauses will raise wages and incomes and the tax increase will be partially offset.

Again, if the intent is to exert a deflationary influence, income taxes may be raised. There is little question that this tax will absorb a good deal of income that would otherwise have been spent. Further, the rates can be raised or lowered easily, rapidly, and inexpensively. But the exact effect of the increase in the tax rate will depend on the marginal propensity to consume. This is because part of the tax increase would be paid out of reduced saving, as we noted previously, or some may spend from accumulated savings. In this respect the sales and excise tax increase is superior to the income tax. In addition, raising the tax rate on personal incomes will likely produce some disincentive effect whereas the increase in the excise tax acts as a reward to saving. If you save you do not pay the tax.

Some other comparisons between the personal income tax and taxes on consumption can be made.

1. If there is an announcement that consumption taxes are to increase, the immediate effect will likely be to increase consumption so as to

beat the tax. This can only be avoided if consumers do not have sufficient liquid assets to purchase goods, especially durables, and if prior arrangements have been made for considerable tightening of the terms of consumer credit.

2. If the tax is considered temporary, then the effect may be to postpone consumption expenditures and increase saving. If the policy aim is to reduce consumption for only a stipulated or expected period of time there is nothing wrong with this effect. It is unlikely that the consumption tax would be terribly long-run if only occasional recessions and flexible fiscal policy were part of the picture.

3. If consumers have a money illusion and continue to spend the same amount, their real purchases decline and the purpose of the tax has been satisfied.

4. If consumers do not have a money illusion and increase their dollar expenditures so as to maintain their real consumption, the purpose of the tax has been frustrated.

It is probably true that if there is no money illusion a consumption tax is more effective in reducing consumption than an income tax. This statement assumes that consumers do not reduce their saving rate, that the tax is completely shifted to consumers, and that total dollar consumption expenditures remain the same before and after the tax is imposed. (These may be unduly restrictive assumptions.) It also assumes that if the income tax is imposed part of the tax payment comes from saving; therefore consumption is not reduced by the amount of the income tax. With these assumptions it follows that per dollar of revenue the consumption tax has a greater impact than the income tax. If the comparison is between an income tax on groups with a low MPC and a consumption tax on low income groups with a high MPC, the difference between the two taxes is magnified—the consumption tax greatly represses consumption and the income tax only partially represses consumption.[1] On the other hand, if an income tax is imposed on lower income groups whose MPC is unity then the results should be the same. If they save zero income, they cannot cut into their saving to maintain consumption.

Many economists consider a spending tax—a tax on one's consumption expenditures—to be most ideal. Such a tax falls directly on consumption from either current income or past savings. It can exempt a minimum amount on necessities; it can be highly progressive and therefore highly effective; and it encourages saving. Unfortunately, the administrative difficulties in enforcing it present almost insurmountable barriers.[2]

[1] E. C. Brown, "Consumption Taxes and Income Determination," *Am. Ec. Rev.*, March 1950, pp. 74–89.

[2] Some additional comments will be made on taxes on consumption at the beginning of the next chapter.

OTHER POLICIES TO INFLUENCE CONSUMPTION

The National Dividend

One policy aimed at raising the level of consumption that received considerable attention in the immediate postwar period was the proposal for the declaration of a national dividend. This involved more than the reduction or forgiveness of taxes; it was an outright payment to the consumer.[3] This device has also been called a consumer dole. A payment of this type to all consumers or all heads of households (the latter may be necessary in order for the program to be politically acceptable) could be varied countercyclically, and imposed or stopped almost immediately. It can place funds in the hands of those who will spend them. It further leaves the allocation of resources in the hands of consumers, avoids governmental decisions on types of expenditures to be undertaken, can be easily varied in size, and involves no great problem of expert knowledge or coordination. It is, in other words, a very simple and easily administered proposal.[4]

Such a proposal runs the risk of being labeled socialistic, but what is the difference if we permit every taxpayer to deduct $100 from his tax bill or give them each a $100 bill? (There is some difference in coverage because not all recipients of the dole would pay taxes.) There are also the charges that such a proposal would become a political football, the dole would be used to bribe votes, it would destroy the incentive to work, it is politically unacceptable, etc., which have been effectively answered elsewhere.[5]

The Redistribution of Income

During the 1930's, when it was felt that the system of income distribution was too unequal and that there were large differences in the propensity to consume among high and low income groups, there developed some support for policies that would redistribute income downward for the purpose of raising the level of consumption. In this context we should note that Keynes himself thought that it was necessary to use the progressive income tax to cut saving, raise consumption, and therefore

[3] One of the most widely publicized proposals was that of John H. G. Pierson, *Full Employment and Free Enterprise*, Washington, D.C.: Public Affairs Press, 1947.

[4] See R. A. Dahl and C. E. Lindblom, "Variation in Public Expenditure," in Max F. Millikan, ed., *Income Stabilization for a Developing Democracy*, New Haven: Yale Univ. Press, 1953, pp. 384–386.

[5] *ibid.* Their statement concerning these charges is very well put.

raise the level of employment and output. Keynes, however, was only willing to go "so far" in this direction: He was no egalitarian. (In fact, Keynes' justification of capitalism and inequality was the fact that the latter, given the Puritan ethic, resulted in the accumulation of capital goods.)

As everyone knows, the progressive income tax has been adopted in the United States, and some degree of redistribution of income does take place through the tax-transfer mechanism and through government expenditures. The exact amount of redistribution which takes place is a matter of conjecture, but it is widely recognized that there is a substantial gap between the statutory and effective rates of the federal income tax and that the total impact of taxes of all levels of government is roughly proportional up to about $10,000.

The success of the further adoption of such policies would depend upon the relative size of the high income groups, the impact of such policies on expectations and on investment, and the MPC of those who receive the transfers (or who have more to spend because a service which they previously paid for is now provided free). It is accepted that not too much is to be gained from redistribution, mainly because there simply is not that much to take from the very high income groups.

Regardless of the size of the higher income group and of different marginal propensities to consume in the high and low groups, such policies should probably be ruled out on other grounds. It would be more useful socially, economically, and politically, under conditions of higher unemployment, to give the lower income groups direct payments (financed by printing new money or debt) and/or to adopt other policies which would enable the lower income groups to raise their incomes. The adoption of the latter policy would require that greater reliance be placed on other policies to raise consumption and investment during a general recession or depression, and more specific educational and training programs for those who are permanently in the low income brackets. In either case the point is that it would be better to increase the size of the pie rather than to create all the problems involved in redividing the pie.

Unemployment Compensation Payments

One of our most important lines of defense against recessions is unemployment insurance. This program, unfortunately, has fallen behind in terms of the size of payments. Furthermore, the techniques used to finance it have resulted in inadequate funds for even the fairly mild postwar recessions, a fact testified to by the need for the federal government to come to the aid of the states during the past three recessions.

There seems to be little question that this program has important counter-cyclical effects and that a strengthening of it is highly desirable. The program is further discussed in Chapter 20.

Public Works

A time-honored proposal for raising the level of income and consumption is to increase public works expenditures. (The Egyptians did it.) Public works projects, however, have not been used in a countercyclical manner, and it is further doubtful if they can ever play a very important role in short-run stabilization policy.

In the first place they lack flexibility. Too often they have been reduced during periods of recession and depression and expanded during periods of prosperity and inflation. Public works projects take time to (1) plan, (2) secure legislative authorization for, (3) implement, and (4) complete. By the time the projects are well under way the depression may be quite deep or the recession passed, in which case they may actually turn out to be inflationary. Given the usual lag between authorization and the actual expenditure of funds all our postwar recessions would have been over by the time public works funds were poured into the economy.

If one considers the total number of steps involved in public works from the passage of an act (after hearings are held!) through to the establishment of a new organization to set up new procedures, etc., and finally on to the completion of a project, as many as 8 years may have passed. This was actually what happened in the case of the public housing aspects of the Housing Act of 1949. In this case the Korean War interrupted the process, but even correcting for this the time span between authorization and completion of the first year's program was $4\frac{1}{2}$ years. Further, the physical construction lag from the start to the completion of the project was about 20 months.[6]

A further difficulty encountered in the use of public works is that public projects may not use the resources left idle by insufficient private demand. The assumption is often made that public works projects merely replace private construction projects and use the same resources. This is not necessarily true, as is shown by at least one important study of the problem.[7] To the extent that it is not true we may have rather serious

---

[6] See S. Maisel, "Varying Public Construction and Housing to Promote Economic Stability," in JEC, *Fed. Exp. Pol.*, P, pp. 382–397. See also his "Timing and Flexibility of a Public Works Program," *Rev. Ec. & Stat.*, May 1949. For an earlier statement see H. S. Perloff, "Dynamic Elements in a Full Employment Program," *Income, Employment, and Public Policy: Essays in Honor of Alvin H. Hansen*, New York: Norton, 1948, pp. 213–215.

[7] J. Margolis, "Public Works and Economic Stability, *J. Pol. Ec.*, Aug. 1949, pp. 293–303.

dislocations in specific markets. Quite generally the specific materials for the usual public projects are different from those used in private projects. Hence there would be pressures on some industries to expand, and pressures on other declining industries to contract even more.

There is no doubt that some speeding up of public works projects could be done. The rate of progress of those under way, for instance, could be increased. (This has been done in recent recessions with the federal highway program and other projects.) Better planning ahead of time would facilitate the initiation of the projects when the need arose to use them. Some European countries, for example, have a plentiful supply of public works projects on the shelf ready to go into operation immediately. Such a shelf of public works projects, however, would have to be periodically revised in terms of the more important changes in the needs and wishes of society. Inventories have been made of the public construction needs of the United States,[8] and it has been suggested that these schedules be used as the basis for guiding future public works expenditures. The public needs, in the areas of highways, educational construction, housing, hospitals, water systems, sewage systems, recreational facilities, rapid transit systems, and urban renewal, are fairly evident to most of us.

Even though improvements can be made in the national selection of public works projects, in their planning, and their speed of initiation, the lags are still too long for them to be used as antirecession tools. Similarly, public works projects are difficult to cut off during periods of inflation; in fact, cutting them off may be quite wasteful. Their use in a prolonged depression is, however, both logical and valuable. On the other hand, their use does not necessarily have to be limited to a depression. There may be times of normal declines and increases in the economy during which the unemployment rate persists in remaining at a fairly high rate even during the peak of the recovery. Under these conditions public works projects may be undertaken, although not on the same massive scale as during a full-fledged depression. In 1961, then, with a $50 billion or so differential between our potential and actual GNP, we probably could have successfully undertaken public works projects and lowered the level of unemployment without creating inflationary pressures.[9] It is further true that some special public works projects may be subject to rapid introduction and therefore useful for combating

[8] See E. J. Howenstine, Jr., "An Inventory of Public Construction Needs," *Am. Ec. Rev.*, June 1948, p. 365, and R. A. Freeman, "Public Works—Fond Hopes and Harsh Realities," JEC, *Fed. Exp. Pol.*, P, pp. 1087–1106, esp. p. 1098.

[9] See, for example, W. W. Heller's comments in JEC, *Jan. 1961 Ec. Rept. Pres.*, H, p. 397.

recessions. And last, certain projects can be speeded up, as we have noted.

A POSTSCRIPT ON TAX POLICY

We have noted previously the difficulty of arriving at accurate conclusions on the impact of various taxes. We have also noted that it is easy to exaggerate differences in the relative impact of different taxes on consumption or investment. Further, there is not common agreement among economists on the value of using various taxes for the attainment of specific goals. Richard Musgrave would advocate that in our tax system we stress primarily the problem of equity and then vary the levels of taxation (and transfers) according to the needs of stabilization policy. Although we shall more closely examine Musgrave's theory of budgeting in Chapter 14, it is perhaps appropriate to conclude this chapter with a quote from him.

I would say that differences between the impact of various taxes on consumption spending, excepting perhaps the corporation tax, are a good deal less than might be thought. Moreover, in a prosperous economy the impact of various taxes on total spending, including consumption and investment, differs less than might be thought. Thinking about tax legislation I would therefore concern myself primarily with the objective of obtaining an equitable tax structure and one that meets my objectives of social policy, and I would not let this be interfered with too much either by the consideration that we ought to tax this fellow more or less because we want to have a certain import [impact] on consumption, or that we ought to tax this fellow more or less because we want to have a certain impact on investment.

Basically, the objective of taxes is to hold down private demand, because if we didn't want to hold down private demand we could print money and finance Government expenditures that way.

We think that would be inequitable because of the inflation that results, so we do it through taxes. Therefore let's not blame taxes for holding down private demand because that basically is what they are there for.

That is why we impose them, so I would say the main consideration by and large in tax policy ought to be that of obtaining an equitable tax structure, sticking to it and being very skeptical about arguments which demand from us to interfere [sic] with these considerations of equity, because we want to induce consumption or investment.

Now, for instance, with regard to consumption, I would dislike an argument which says that in the depression we ought to have highly progressive taxes because this would hurt consumption less, and then by virtue of the same reasoning come to the conclusion that we should have a regressive tax system in the boom. Rather, we ought to be for progressive, proportional, or regressive taxes depending upon our social ideas, if you want our views of social justice. In other words this is essentially an equity and social justice concept on which the economist has no particular opinion. Having decided on what we want, we should set up the tax structure accordingly and then stick to it, and get our effects on economic policy primarily by lowering the level of taxation in the depression and by raising it in the boom.[10]

[10] R. A. Musgrave, JEC, *Fed. Tax Pol.*, H, p. 75. The discussion of Musgrave's theory in Chapter 14 differs somewhat from his statement here, which was not prepared and which appeared a few years before his book. In particular, he talks here of raising and lowering taxes, whereas he later states that taxes should be used to fight inflation and transfers to fight deflation. On the equity issue see Chapter 13, footnote 47. For more on these issues see the many excellent papers included in the volume cited above. See especially those of P. Samuelson (and his comments in the Hearings), W. Fellner, and R. Musgrave, and C. S. Shoup, "Taxation and Fiscal Policy" in Millikan, *op. cit.*, Chapter 6. See also N. Ture, "Economic Growth and Federal Tax Policy," National Tax Association 1958 Proceedings, 1959, pp. 388–401, and C. A. Hall, Jr., *Fiscal Policy for Stable Growth*, New York: Holt, Rinehart and Winston, 1960.

13

Investment and Fiscal Policy

SOME GENERALIZATIONS ON THE IMPACT OF TAXES

Expenditure versus Personal Income Taxes

It seems appropriate at this point to review briefly some of the characteristics of the relative incidence of various taxes on consumption and investment, and the results obtained when these taxes are substituted for each other. Unfortunately, our information on the relative impact of taxes is not at all satisfactory. We can, however, show some tendencies as far as the direction of impact is concerned.

One of the main reasons why income and consumption (or expenditure) taxes have received considerable concern has been the assumption that the latter is more conducive to greater personal saving and economic growth. We can reasonably assume that if a given tax burden (a constant yield regardless of source) is shifted from the personal income tax to an expenditure tax, there will be an increase in the personal saving ratio. The burden will now fall on low savers because as they spend (consume) they are taxed.[1] There is fairly common agreement on this principle but not necessarily on its extent, for two main reasons. (1) The statement assumes that those on whom the burden of the personal income tax has been reduced, and whose disposable income now increases, will save a high proportion of their marginal income. (If most groups have the same MPC, as some economists claim, the substitution of a tax on consumption for the personal income tax should not greatly affect aggregate saving. Goode, however, feels that those who have a high APS will also have a high MPS.) (2) Furthermore, both the expenditure and personal income taxes are paid by both the high and low savers. In addition, since over 90 percent of disposable income is used for consumption, it is argued

[1] R. Goode, "Income, Consumption, and Property as Bases of Taxation," *Am. Ec. Rev.*, May 1962, pp. 327–330.

that the substitution of an expenditure for a personal income tax will not greatly affect the proportion of the tax revenue which comes from potential saving when taxes have a wide coverage. In spite of this it is still maintained that since the personal income tax does more adversely affect potential saving, a relaxation of the burden on incomes can mean a sizable increase in aggregate personal saving when taxes are high.[1] In other words, while it is accepted that the expenditure tax is more favorable to private saving, the difference between its impact and the impact of the income tax on private saving is not great unless tax rates are high. Furthermore, the most important determinant of saving is the level of income, plus the fact that most economists feel that there would be little change in saving (and the rate of growth) if present income tax rates were lowered and replaced by an expenditure tax.

As far as the comparison between the impact of the expenditure and personal income taxes on investment is concerned, it is generally argued that the income tax adversely affects investment incentives *unless* the income tax contains extremely liberal loss offsets, flexible amortization, and averaging.[2] It is also logical to argue that a reduction in the corporate income tax would increase private saving and corporate saving. But if an expenditure tax is introduced to fill the gap, other factors must be considered—the social and political consequences, and the volume of investment opportunities. Just because personal and corporate saving has increased does not mean that investment automatically increases.

INVESTMENT AND TAXATION

The concern over the performance of the American economy in the late 'fifties and early 'sixties has been reflected in a concern over the rate and volume of investment. During the postwar period many countries attempted to increase investment by means of special depreciation allowances and special tax concessions. The United States has also used these devices—the increase in depreciation allowances in 1954 and 1962, and the investment tax credit in 1962. It is with these special devices that we are concerned in this section.

Present Value and the Rate of Interest

We previously noted, in Chapter 5, the variables involved in arriving at an investment decision. In that discussion we noted that the business-man, in one manner or another, attempts to make some estimate of the

---

[2] *Ibid.*, p. 331. See also the quotation from Musgrave at the end of Chapter 12, and the discussion in the fifth part of Chapter 10.

present value of a stream of net receipts from an investment project. Of course, the expected stream of income is uncertain. But he must make some estimate (allowing for uncertainty, deducting taxes, interest charges, and operational costs) so that he can then compare the present value of that stream of income with the cost of the capital asset. If the present value exceeds the cost of the asset he should undertake the investment project.

What changes can be made in fiscal and other policies that will increase or decrease present value and therefore investment? If the present value and the purchase price of a capital asset are equal, then a reduction in interest rates should raise the present value above the purchase price and therefore induce investment expenditures. We noted before that a discount in present value must be made for uncertainty. If the discount for uncertainty is high, then the increase in present value resulting from the lower rate of interest will not be as great as if the discount for uncertainty had been lower. Moreover, the longer the life of the asset the greater the increase in present value because of the reduction in the interest rate.[3]

Present Value, Cash Flow, and Lower Taxes

We noted that the expected stream of income is net of taxes. Hence a reduction in taxes will also raise present value. It is presently agreed by some economists, though, that it is the cash flow which is important. (Cash flow is defined as "the amount of cash which a firm has left over at the end of any time period . . . from its receipts during that period after it has paid all the bills, including taxes, presented during the time period."[4]) If one approaches the investment situation from the standpoint of cash flows, then future cash flows are just as important as present cash flows. This is because the amount of cash flow produced by the purchase of a new investment good determines the profitability of the project. From this point of view, then, the project that creates the largest cash flow, or the earliest cash flow, is the most profitable.

From the standpoint of fiscal policy, then, government policies that increase present and future corporate cash flow can stimulate investment by (1) making more funds available for investment, and (2) making the investment project more profitable. From this Bodenhorn argues that it is not the impact of any particular policy on profits, depreciation, inventory valuation, or asset values in general which is important, but the impact

---

[3] E. C. Brown, "Tax Incentives for Investment," *Am. Ec. Rev.*, May 1962, p. 337.
[4] D. Bodenhorn, "Taxes, Cash Flow, and Investment," in JEC, *Var. Private Invest.*, Pt. 2, p. 37.

on cash flows. Therefore a tax reduction will increase *current and future* cash flows and profits and stimulate investment.[5]

Accelerated Depreciation and Cash Flow: Advantages and Criticisms of Accelerated Depreciation

If the government increases depreciation allowances it reduces the tax burden on a firm. In this case the firm's costs have increased and its tax liabilities have decreased. Even though the firm's costs have increased because it is charging off greater dollar amounts for depreciation it may still have the same "book" profit. Cash flow, however, has increased because the tax burden has been reduced (for the time being at least).

This device for stimulating investment has been used during war periods and was also introduced during 1954. Accelerated depreciation has also been used to stimulate investment by the United Kingdom, Sweden, Australia, Canada, the Netherlands and other countries. There is not, however, a wholehearted endorsement of its use among American economists.[6]

As we have noted, accelerated depreciation means that for tax purposes a firm charges off higher costs, which results in a lower tax base and a lower tax burden for the present period. Thus depreciation allowances are concentrated in the early years of an asset's life. If the accelerated depreciation is to apply to only investment as of a current date, the effect should be to stimulate new investment since the tax break is for new investment.

Various devices or methods may be used to accelerate depreciation. The United Kingdom, for example, gives an initial allowance in addition to normal depreciation, the rate for which is also varied.[7] In the United States we have used the sum of the digits and other methods such as a complete write-off in 5 years of defense facilities.

Advantages of Accelerated Depreciation. Accelerated depreciation may not reduce the total, long-run tax burden of the firm—it may merely postpone the payment of the tax—but it does result in an interest-free

[5] *Ibid.*, p. 38.

[6] This is not meant to imply that it is universally accepted among foreign economists.

[7] Evaluations of the British system can be found in R. M. Bird, "Countercyclical Variation of Depreciation Allowances in the United Kingdom," *Natl. Tax J.*, March 1963, pp. 41–55; J. Black, "Investment Allowances, Initial Allowances and Cheap Loans as a Means of Encouraging Investment," *Rev. Ec. Studies*, Oct. 1959, pp. 44–49; Committee on the Working of the Monetary System (Radcliffe Committee), *Principal Memoranda of Evidence*, London: H.M. Stationery Office, 1960, Vol. I; and D. P. Barrit, "Accelerated Depreciation Allowances and Industrial Investment," *J. Indust. Ec.*, Vol. 8 (1959), pp. 80–98. The last three are cited by Bird.

loan. That is, since the firm *does not* pay the tax in the immediate period, it has the use of an additional supply of funds (greater cash flow) interest-free, which it would not have without accelerated depreciation.[8]

It is also true that accelerated depreciation means that the firm will be able to pay off the investment project in a short period of time. This means a significant reduction in risk and uncertainty, which both increase with the life of the asset. This factor should serve to stimulate investment by raising the cash flow, and by lowering the discount for uncertainty and raising present value.

Since accelerated depreciation increases cash flow and provides funds for investment, small firms that experience difficulty securing funds from the capital market (even though they are "deserving") and other firms (including large ones) that do not care to go to the capital market, should be induced to invest. Certainly, if profitable investment opportunities exist, the increase in cash flow should increase the investment of these firms over what it would have been without the available funds.

The effectiveness of accelerated depreciation is also influenced by the present and expected future tax structure. Generally speaking, the higher tax rates are, the more a business firm can gain from accelerated depreciation. If, as may be the case, the firm expects that tax rates will go down in the future, it would be anxious to have the higher depreciation allowances now so as to reduce its current (and therefore total long-run) tax bill. This should have a stimulating effect on the firm's investment plans. If tax rates are expected to increase in the future, accelerated depreciation would be less attractive. If this is the case, the certainty of the tax increase must be estimated, and a comparison must be made between present tax and interest savings under accelerated depreciation and the future increase in the tax bill. Further, in the future the firm will still have depreciation allowances as long as it has a stable level of investment, and greater depreciation allowances if it is a growing firm.

Another factor determining the advantage to the firm of using accelerated depreciation is whether or not it has sufficient taxable income against which the extra depreciation may be charged. If the depreciation allowance is greater than taxable income, there obviously is no tax saving. If the firm can carry a loss backward or forward and charge it against taxable income, the advantage of accelerated depreciation can be realized. To the extent that we have liberal provisions in our tax laws to carry these accounting losses (not necessarily real losses) forward or backward (averaging losses and profits), the effectiveness of accelerated depreciation

---

[8] This aspect has been bitterly criticized by several economists. See W. Adams and H. Gray, *Monopoly in America: The Government as Promoter*, New York: Macmillan, 1955, pp. 84–94.

is increased. If accelerated depreciation is *mandatory* during a period of depression the effect may actually be to decrease investment because the firm will postpone its investment expenditures until it has a profit against which the depreciation charges may be made. If the firm has the option of using or not using accelerated depreciation, this effect would not develop.[9] It has been suggested that the firm be allowed to carry depreciation credits forward and backward.

For a growing firm (a firm that increases its investment expenditure each year) accelerated depreciation results in a permanent reduction in the effective tax rate. As the first asset is fully depreciated, others come along to maintain and increase the depreciation allowance.

Criticisms of Accelerated Depreciation. Accelerated depreciation is most advantageous to the firm when it has taxable income against which the depreciation allowances can be charged. This is most likely to occur during periods of prosperity, or some degree thereof, when profits are high and lower tax burdens are important. On the other hand, during depressed conditions its use may actually worsen the depression (especially if its use is mandatory) since firms may postpone investment until they have profits against which the depreciation charges can be made. Accelerated depreciation then will likely be cyclically perverse—intensifying both booms and depressions. If large profits are reduced by accelerated depreciation during the boom, profits will be understated. Further, profits will be overstated during the slump because the firm does not now have the depreciation charges available to it. Domar argues, however, that the measure encourages growth, that growth is the best way to avoid depressions, and therefore this is not a sufficient basis on which to reject the use of accelerated depreciation.[10] To offset the cyclically perverse nature of accelerated depreciation Domar and many others have advocated its modification or complete suspension during periods when inflation is a threat. Projects started under accelerated depreciation, however, would be permitted to continue under it until completed.

The manner in which accelerated depreciation schemes have worked has meant that they have favored capital-intensive industries over labor-intensive industries. If it were true that the former were the sources of greater growth, or of the type of growth we want, then there would be no problem. But the former also include industries in which there is a heavy

[9] This and the previous points are rather thoroughly explored by R. Goode, "Accelerated Depreciation Allowances as a Stimulus to Investment," *Q. J. Ec.*, May 1955, p. 191–220. See also E. D. Domar, "The Case for Accelerated Depreciation," *Q. J. Ec.*, Nov. 1953, pp. 493–514, also reprinted in his *Essays in the Theory of Economic Growth*, New York: Oxford Univ. Press, 1957.

[10] Domar, *op. cit.*, p. 510.

investment in steel, brick, and mortar. These industries then get a substantial tax break while those relying heavily on intangible capital and brainpower go unaided.[11] Heller has suggested that a general reduction in the corporate income tax rate of several points would aid both tangible and intangible capital. Further, greater discretion (by corporate managers) in the use of funds results under accelerated depreciation than under a tax cut because in the latter case the reinvestment of the greater net earnings is at least challengeable by stockholders.

Heller is also critical of this device because it further insulates investment from the impact of monetary policy by granting an interest-free loan. (The evasion of monetary policy is twofold: the firm gets the funds and it gets them without paying interest.) In addition, the 1954 liberalization of depreciation allowances no doubt contributed to the capital boom and to the inflationary pressures of 1955–1957.[12] Instead of the stimulating effect of accelerated depreciation, we should have had temporarily lower depreciation allowances. Heller, we should note, has been extremely critical not only of accelerated depreciation, but of all special tax devices that give preferential income tax treatment. "Tax preferences pull resources away from the optimal uses to which they would be channeled by the free workings of the market mechanisms—and optimal use means maximum value output per unit of input, which is the royal road to economic growth."[13]

Some have been critical even of the effectiveness of accelerated depreciation. That is, the claim has been made, and it is not easily refuted, that studies of the effectiveness of the 1954 liberalization are not conclusive because there may have been a high rate of investment anyway.[14] Of course, a rational evaluation must show that accelerated depreciation makes investment more attractive and more likely because it increases cash flow, amounts to an interest-free loan, reduces the payoff period of an investment and therefore reduces risk and increases present value, and may actually reduce the firm's tax bill. If the investment boom would have occurred anyway, the question is whether the loss of revenue and possible price level increases were worth the extra investment resulting from accelerated depreciation.

---

[11] W. W. Heller, "Some Observations on the Role and Reform of the Federal Income Tax," WMC, HR, *Tax. Revis. Comp.*, P., p. 181ff.

[12] Others have condemned the inflationary effects of accelerated depreciation during the 1955–1957 period. See O. Eckstein in JEC, *Rel. Prices to Ec. Stabil. & Growth*, P, p. 370.

[13] Heller, *op. cit.*, p. 189. Domar defends the preferential treatment, "The Case for Accelerated Depreciation," *op. cit.*, p. 512.

[14] W. W. Heller, JEC, *Jan. 1961 Ec. Rept. Pres.*, H, p. 413.

E. Cary Brown has argued that the 1954 liberalization probably had little effect on the incentive to invest. He found that over a fairly wide range of asset lives and of rates of discount, the tax saving was about 5 percent of the initial cost of an asset. This is comparable to increasing yield after tax about 5 percent, which means that a 10 percent yield would become a $10\frac{1}{2}$ percent yield and a 20 percent yield a 21 percent yield, etc.[15]

Brown's estimates are for the life of the asset. If one examines the interim influence, the tax advantage is much greater. J. Fred Weston has estimated that a comparison of the straight-line method with the sum-of-year digits method for an asset with a life of 5 years gives a 65 percent larger tax deduction in the first year, a 45 percent advantage in the second year, and a 31 percent advantage in the third year. Under this method after 2 years an asset is 60 percent depreciated whereas only 40 percent would be depreciated under the straight-line method.[16]

Brown also points out that for a growing firm the postponement of taxes becomes virtually permanent. At the time the tax is due on one asset the firm purchases another asset which it can depreciate. As long as the firm continues to purchase assets at a constant rate (and value) the tax never comes due. If the firm increases its rate of investment the permanent tax postponement grows.

We noted earlier that if the effect of accelerated depreciation on investment is not substantial a judgment should be made between the advantages of the increased investment on the one hand and the reduction in revenue and the possible inflationary pressures on the other. Any estimates of the annual revenue loss must be based on projections of the future rate of investment and are therefore only estimates. Brown, however, estimated that at a rate of growth of investment of 3 percent the revenue loss (under the 1954 bill) would be over $2 billion in 5 years, over $4 billion in 10 years, nearly $4 billion in 15 years, over $2 billion in 20 years, and thereafter the revenue loss would grow at 3 percent per year.[17]

It was on this basis that Brown concluded that the 1954 action was "a costly method of getting a modest investment stimulus."[18] Brown suggested as an alternative a cut in the corporate income tax rate of $2\frac{1}{2}$ percentage points which, he claims, would have provided the same

[15] E. C. Brown, JEC, *Fed. Tax Pol.*, P, pp. 497–498, and "The New Depreciation Policy Under the Income Tax: An Economic Appraisal," *Natl. Tax J.*, March 1955, p. 92.
[16] J. F. Weston, "Accelerated Depreciation and Opportunities for Tax Avoidance," WMC, HR, *Tax Revis. Comp.*, P, pp. 801–805.
[17] E. C. Brown, JEC, *Fed. Tax Pol.*, P, pp, 497–498. Eisner's estimates were higher. See *ibid.*, H, p. 473.
[18] *Ibid.*, P, p. 498.

investment stimulus with a smaller loss in revenue. (It would increase yields after tax by 5 percent.)[19] He estimated that the revenue loss would be about $1 billion per year and would grow to less than $2 billion in 20 years with a 3 percent growth rate. The 1954 depreciation change would reduce corporate taxes by approximately $30 billion more than a corporate tax rate reduction over the first 20 years.[20]

Other criticisms of accelerated depreciation follow. (1) If it is used in the firm's accounts and in the firm's business decisions it may raise prices through artificially overstating costs.[21] Quantity produced may decrease because of higher prices and investment may decline. The higher prices, with or without a reduction in quantity purchased at higher prices, may adversely affect aggregate demand, especially consumption. (2) The interest-free loan and the tax savings have been criticized as unnecessary subsidies.[22] (3) If taxes are raised in other areas to offset the decline in revenue the alternatives may be regressive or otherwise reduce demand and growth.[23]

Summary. There seems to be fairly wide agreement that accelerated depreciation will raise the level of investment. The impact will be greater, though, during periods of prosperity than under depressed conditions when the impact actually may be to postpone investment. This is because of the increase in cash flow, the tax saving, the interest-free loan, and the increase in present value due to faster payoff and reduced risk.

On the other hand, accelerated depreciation is cyclically perverse, may result in higher prices and lower aggregate demand, favors capital-intensive industries, tends to insulate investment from monetary policy even more than it is insulated from it now, may really be inflationary during boom periods, takes more investment out of the hands of market-guided allocation, and may "unfairly" shift the burden of taxes onto other groups. The 1954 action was particularly condemned as an unnecessary tax reduction, the stimulative effects of which could have been realized more efficiently by a $2\frac{1}{2}$ percent corporate tax reduction. On the other hand, Richard Goode (in discussing accelerated depreciation generally, not just the 1954 liberalization) claims that accelerated depreciation has advantages over both tax reduction and interest rate reduction—the

---

[19] *Ibid.* The rate reduction for corporations subject to the 30 percent rate would have to be $3\frac{1}{2}$ rather than $2\frac{1}{2}$ percentage points.

[20] *Ibid.*, pp. 498–499. Tax revenues would be less under the 1954 depreciation in virtually every year.

[21] *Ibid.*, p. 503. Eisner dwells on this in his criticism of Domar's paper, *Q. J. Ec.*, Nov. 1955, p. 285.

[22] A. Hansen, JEC, *Fed. Tax Pol.*, P, p. 14ff.

[23] R. Eisner, JEC, *Fed. Tax Pol.*, H, p. 473.

former because it applies only to new investment and is not a tax reduction on the return to *all* capital, over the latter because there would have to be a large decrease in interest rates to achieve the same impact.[24] Brown recognizes that tax cuts will not have the same effect as some of the more extreme forms of accelerated depreciation.[25]

AN ALTERNATIVE TO ACCELERATED DEPRECIATION: THE TAX CREDIT

The 1962 Tax Credit Law

Brown has supported tax credits which would be over and above normal depreciation as a device to achieve the same incentive effect as accelerated depreciation. A tax credit can be granted in the year in which an asset is purchased, or it can be spread over several subsequent years. It would not affect business accounts and distort business decisions as accelerated depreciation might. It could be varied from time to time as economic conditions require without adversely affecting business accounting policies. It can be applied only to expenditures on capital in excess of normal depreciation. This means that a firm must spend more than that amount necessary to maintain the book value of its assets in order to get a tax credit. Therefore, only growing firms would benefit and it would pay (tax-wise) to grow.[26]

It is of particular interest to note that in 1962 action was taken on both tax credits and depreciation. The revision of depreciation schedules, however, was done to "bring them up to date" rather than to adopt a policy of accelerated depreciation. The tax credit, introduced in 1961 was finally passed and signed as part of a tax revision bill in October, 1962. The tax credit, it should be carefully noted, has as its primary purpose the raising of the level of investment (substituting investment for consumption in the opinions of some) not the raising of the level of income (although, if effective, it will have some impact here, too). The authors of the original bill were Richard Musgrave and E. Cary Brown.[27]

[24] R. Goode, "Accelerated Depreciation Allowances as a Stimulus to Investment," *Q.J. Ec.*, May 1955, pp. 210–204. For a comparison of various methods of accelerated depreciation, see pp. 211–218.

S. Davidson in WMC, HR, *Tax Revis. Comp.*, P, p. 810, compares our depreciation rates with those of the United Kingdom, Sweden, the Netherlands, and Denmark. This same volume contains other comparisons. A comprehensive comparison of corporate tax rates, depreciation, and initial and other investment allowances in the United States and other countries can be found in JEC, *State Ec. & Pol. Full Empl.*, H, pp. 670, 693–719.

[25] E. C. Brown, JEC, *Fed. Tax Pol.*, P, p. 503.

[26] *Ibid.*, pp. 503–504.

[27] JEC, *Jan. 1962 Ec. Rept. Pres.*, H, p. 503.

The 1962 tax credit is retroactive to January 1, 1962 (to July 1, 1961 for firms on a fiscal year basis), and permits businessmen to subtract up to 7 percent of the cost of new investment in machinery and equipment, both new and used. The Treasury estimated that the tax credit (referred to as investment credit) would reduce business tax liabilities by $1 billion in 1962 and by the same amount in each future year. It would seem, though, that in spite of the limitations on the credit, the loss to the Treasury should increase each year, depending on the increase in the number of business firms and the degree of prosperity.

Although the exact details of the investment credit are yet to be worked out, the overall picture is something like this: A firm can receive a credit against tax of up to 7 percent of the cost of new machinery and equipment and up to a $50,000 purchase of used machinery and equipment. Buildings are excluded, and the property must be depreciable and must be for use in trade or business to produce income. To secure the 7 percent credit against cost the asset must have a life of at least 8 years. If the life is from 6 to 8 years the credit is 7 percent of two-thirds of the cost of the property. If the life is 4 to 6 years the credit is 7 percent of one-third of the cost of the asset. For an asset with a life of less than 4 years there is no tax credit. In addition, the credit will be against the first $25,000 of tax and against 25 percent of tax in excess of $25,000. This is the maximum for any 1 year.

If a firm invests a large amount and its tax is large, the 7 percent of its investment may be much more than the amount it is allowed to deduct from its tax. The unused portion of the tax credit can be carried forward as much as 5 years. In addition, it can eventually be carried back 3 years; there are no carry-backs for credits on the 1962 tax, but a 1-year carry-back will be allowed for 1963, a 2-year for 1964, and a 3-year for 1965.

An example should help clarify the new law. If a firm earned $1 million in 1962, it would regularly pay about $520,000 in federal income tax. The limit of its investment credit is $25,000 plus .25($520,000 − 25,000) = $25,000 + $123,750 = $148,750. If the firm purchases $2 million in new equipment it takes 7 percent of this and arrives at a figure of $140,000. This is within the allowable tax credit. It subtracts $140,000 from $520,000 to arrive at a tax bill which it must pay of $380,000. If this firm had invested a larger amount (with a life of 8 years or more) and if it had had an unused credit, it could carry this forward and deduct it from subsequent tax bills under the conditions noted.[28] In general the basis for depreciation is reduced by an amount equal to the credit.

[28] *The New York Times*, Western edition, Oct. 22, 1962, pp. 17, 18; *Wall Street Journal*, Pacific Coast edition, Oct. 17, 1962, p. 3.

Tax Credit, Accelerated Depreciation, Lower Interest, and Lower Corporate Taxes Compared

E. Cary Brown has compared the investment credit with interest rate cuts, accelerated depreciation, and corporate income tax rate cuts.[29] Under his assumptions Brown concludes that interest rate reduction will be the most efficient in stimulating investment per dollar of revenue loss. There would be no loss in revenue to the government, and in fact the government's transfers might actually go down because of lower interest costs on the public debt. Brown eliminates from his policy choices this alternative, however, because of the possibility of its further aggravating our balance-of-payments problem.

Brown further argues against the application of accelerated depreciation, tax credits, or rate reductions to existing as well as new assets, because this "would be an enormously costly way to achieve a given substitution effect." The result would be sizeable lump sum transfer payments based on the volume of current assets held. Since it would be impossible to divide profits into two categories for tax purposes (those from old and those from new assets), the income tax rate reduction is also ruled out. From the standpoint of securing the greatest stimulus from given revenue losses the choice then boiled down to accelerated depreciation or tax credits.[30]

A comparison of the revenue losses under the tax credit with those under accelerated depreciation can be very complex because it rests on certain assumptions concerning the lives of assets, the rate of discount, the rate at which investment grows, and the tax rate. The problem is further complicated by the fact that so many different types of accelerated depreciation may be used. Brown attempted some comparisons for assets with 15-year lives, further assuming that business firms would be certain about their depreciation deductions. He concluded that, with an interest rate of 8 percent, an initial depreciation allowance of about 40 percent, a tax credit of 8 percent, and a corporate tax rate of 50 percent, the incentive effect of both would be equal. Under the 40 percent initial allowance the annual revenue loss would "steady down" to almost 3 percent of current investment with a growth rate of investment of 2 percent, and so on, as shown on page 268.

With a rate of growth of investment of about $7\frac{1}{2}$ percent or less, the annual losses from the initial allowances would catch up with those from the investment credit (assuming an investment credit of 8 percent). "For

[29] E. C. Brown, "Tax Incentives for Investment," *Am. Ec. Rev.*, May 1962, pp. 335–345.

[30] *Ibid.*, p. 341.

Revenue Loss as a　　　　With a Growth Rate
Percent of Investment　　　of Investment of

3%	2%
5	4
7	6
Over 8	8
Nearly 10	10

growth rates of 2, 4, and 6 percent, the *annual* losses would be equal under the two methods in ten, eleven, and thirteen years, respectively."[30] (Italics added.) If the growth rate were zero, it would take 9 years to catch up. With growth rates over $7\frac{1}{2}$ percent the revenue loss under the initial allowance would always be greater than those under the investment credit (both annually and in the aggregate sense).

If one aggregates the relative losses of the two methods, then a considerably longer time period would be involved than when annual losses are equated. The higher the rate of growth of investment, the longer the time period. The aggregate losses would be equal at 19 years with no growth in investment, and with growth rates of 2, 4, and 6 percent at 21, 25, and 33 years, respectively.[31]

It appears then that the investment credit is less costly unless the growth rates of investment are very high.[32] Even though this is true, the accelerated depreciation device provides that firms will secure no extra deduction in income unless current investment is greater than normal depreciation, after the large initial allowance is taken and the government has absorbed the large temporary revenue losses. A straight tax credit is applicable to both growing and stable firms. If a firm's investment is less than its past average it will still receive a tax credit. If the tax credit is amended to apply only to the amount of investment which is greater than depreciation the tax then will apply only if growth occurs. It then becomes a device which pays only for the growing firm—it becomes a growth-stimulating device. Further, if this condition is made[33] the base for the credit is narrowed, revenue losses are reduced, and there can be a large increase in the size of the tax credit to be granted. Brown loudly applauds this growth-stimulating condition.[34] Depending on the size of the tax credit granted the revenue loss should be less. (Official Treasury estimates place

[31] *Ibid.*, pp. 341–342.

[32] Brown notes that under certain circumstances the investment credit could be more costly.

[33] President Kennedy recommended this in the 1962 bill, but it was omitted.

[34] E. C. Brown, "Tax Incentives for Investment," *Am. Ec. Rev.*, May 1962, pp. 342–343. The reliance on Brown's article in this section should be obvious to the reader.

the annual revenue loss at $1 billion for 1962 and the same for subsequent years for the 7 percent tax credit, as noted above.)[35]

Issues in the 1962 Tax Credit

It is very difficult to evaluate the impact of the 1962 tax credit. Theoretical considerations indicate that it will have some effect, but the size of the impact is a matter of controversy. One problem that has bothered many critics has been the dampening effect of excess capacity on investment. One author of the original tax credit suggested that simultaneous action should be taken to raise the level of demand in the economy so as to work off some of the excess capacity.[36] Nonetheless, there should be some impact on marginal projects, there will likely be some impact because of the speeding up of investment since the longevity of the tax credit is uncertain, and there will be some impact since all industries and all firms probably are not equally plagued with excess capacity.

It is interesting to note that the business community was only lukewarm (to say the most) to the tax credit plan. This, coupled with the fact that it was opposed by some who considered it a tax windfall to corporations,[37] those who felt that business already had sufficient cash flow for investment,[37] those who felt that priority or equal weight should be given to tax cuts to stimulate consumption,[38] those who felt that it might not be at all necessary if demand could be raised,[38] and those who criticized it as cyclically perverse,[39] caused it to have some trouble getting through the Congress. (There is no question that the tax credit will benefit higher income groups. In fact some calculations have been made of its effect on stock prices. There is also no question that some windfalls will occur,

---

[35] The reported tax saving actually was slightly greater than $1 billion. The tax saving resulting from the 1962 revision of depreciation schedules was $1.25 billion. *The New York Times*, Western edition, July 10, 1963.

[36] Musgrave made this comment. See JEC, *Jan. 1962 Ec. Rept. Pres.*, H, p. 503. It is probable that Brown would agree with Musgrave. Both have repeatedly stressed the need for a high demand in the economy.

[37] W. Reuther, *ibid.*, pp. 774–778. Reuther's comments on General Motors' and Ford's cash flows and his data from *Fortune* and *Forbes* are very interesting. Reuther called for a tax on uninvested and undistributed corporate profits. See p. 751. Organized labor generally condemned the tax credit. See also the discussion of and table on cash flow in Chapter 15.

[38] G. Colm, *ibid.*, p. 526.

[39] Senator William Proxmire, JEC, 1962 *Ann. Rept.*, pp. 115–118. He condemned it vigorously as inequitable—a tax loophole for business, cyclically perverse, and ineffective—and maintained that it would not raise investment. He was further concerned over the fact that it was of little benefit to small business (but the same is true of accelerated depreciation). See JEC, *Jan. 1962 Ec. Rept. Pres.*, H, p. 509–515, esp. p. 515.

that some firms do have adequate cash flow—retained earnings and depreciation allowances, and that some of the tax cut will go into dividends. It is hoped, however, that the aggregate leakage from investment will be small.) Presumably, the business community was holding out for accelerated depreciation and/or a cut in the corporate income tax rate. We should note, however, that business did get a revision and updating of their depreciation allowances in the summer of 1962. It was estimated that the revenue loss from this would be $1.8 billion per year,[40] but the actual figure was $1.25 billion.

The tax credit will raise the rate of return on capital, increase the cash flow of corporations, and reward new investment rather than raise the return to both new and old investment as a corporate tax rate reduction would do. It is a better incentive to investment and economic growth than corporate tax rate reduction (although less equitable). Further, it is much more efficient (in terms of its goals) than dividend credit and exclusion.[41] It remains to be seen how significant the economic impact of the tax credit will turn out to be.[42] During periods in which excess capacity is a problem though, it does seem logical to ask for policies that will also raise the level of demand.

It is widely felt that businessmen require a rate of return before taxes of 25 to 30 percent or more. If the tax credit is successful in reducing the required rate of return, it will increase the level of investment. It is not clear, however, exactly how strong this incentive will be because firms can already charge off the losses on one venture against the gains of another, and thereby reduce taxable income. In other words, the government is already sharing in the risk.

Other possibilities must also be recognized, but they too are difficult to evaluate properly.[43] Part of the tax credit may result in lower prices and in effect go to consumers (this would not be particularly objectionable except in so far as the direct purpose is to raise the growth rate via higher investment but it does seem unlikely), to dividends as we have noted, to

[40] This is a preliminary estimate of the JEC 1962 *Ann. Rept.*, p. 82. The evidence is far from overwhelming that our depreciation allowances were way out of line as far as replacement is concerned. See JEC, *Fed. Tax Pol.*, H, pp. 454–461.

[41] Musgrave's comments are very instructive. See JEC, *Jan. 1962 Ec. Rept. Pres.*, H, p. 509ff.

[42] For an alternative proposal, in which taxes would be based on value added, and an exemption from taxes or a tax rebate based on the firm's percentage growth of the firm's value added on sales (which is compared with the firm's value added of the preceding year), see K. Knorr and W. J. Baumol, eds., *What Price Economic Growth?*, Englewood Cliffs, N.J.: Prentice-Hall, 1961. This program was apparently adopted in Canada in 1962. See also Baumol's comments in JEC, *Empl., Growth, Price Levels*, H, Pt. 9A, p. 2792ff.

[43] See J. Duesenberry's statement in JEC, *Fed. Exp. Pol.*, P, p. 285ff.

greater advertising or sales expenditures, to higher wages, or partly to raise retained earnings, in which case firms may borrow less and not raise their level of investment.

Policy Problems of Tax Credit and Other "Subsidies"

The lowering of taxes on investment by means of the tax credit may, if one considers the prevailing system of taxes desirable, normal, etc., in so far as the overall level of the burden and the distribution of the burden between consumption and investment is concerned, be called a subsidy.[44] We have already noted some of the problems of the tax credit: (1) How effective will it be? Will it result in an increase in investment over what it would have been? Will it require simultaneous stimulation of consumption? (2) Should it be on the value of investment in excess of depreciation allowances or on gross investment?

Other policy problems are: (3) Should it include operating expenditures, especially where they may be quite important to particular types of firm? Should increases in inventory be included? (4) Should purchases of existing capital goods be included? (5) Should the President have discretionary power to start and stop the tax credit as economic conditions warrant? (6) If so, what criteria should be used to introduce or stop the tax credit? (7) What should be the percentage rate of the tax credit? (8) How long should the tax credit be in effect in order to allow for the planning and completion of investment projects?[45]

Countercyclical Accelerated Depreciation

Some economists have advocated that depreciation allowances be varied with economic conditions. That is, they want them raised during

[44] The subsidy aspects of the 1962 tax credit are discussed in J. Wiseman, "Public Policy and the Investment Tax Credit," *Natl. Tax J.*, March 1963, pp. 36–40. The effect of the credit is to raise the firm's income by 14 percent of the cost of the asset. Taxable earnings would have to increase by $14 to secure a similar gain with a 50 percent corporate income tax. Depreciation allowance is 93 percent rather than 86 percent of the cost of the asset. The net result is that the firm gets a "tax-free gift of $3\frac{1}{2}\%$ of the qualified investment, plus a diminishing interest-free loan beginning at $3\frac{1}{2}\%$ of cost and reducing to zero over the depreciation period." In other words $100 is invested, a taxable subsidy of $14 is secured, and $7 returns to the government in the year of subsidization. After this "depreciation at 93 percent of cost causes $7 more to show up as income than would have appeared in the absence of the measure." The firm therefore pays $3.50 more in taxes and is better off to the extent of a tax-free gift of $3.50 plus the interest-free loan.

[45] See Ralph S. Brown, Jr., "Techniques for Influencing Private Investment," in Max F. Millikan, ed., *Income Stabilization for a Developing Democracy*, New Haven: Yale Univ. Press, 1953, pp. 420–428. While Brown applies these questions to slightly different proposals they are still pertinent to the tax credit. Brown's points are very well stated.

periods of lower economic activity so as to encourage investment, and lowered during periods of prosperity to retard investment.[46] This action was taken in Canada in August, 1951 (and lasted until December, 1952), and in West Germany in March, 1960, when depreciation rates were cut from 25 to 20 percent and further. It has also been used in the United Kingdom. There seems little doubt that such action would have some impact, because the result is to raise the firm's tax bill in the immediate period (presumably an inflationary period) and lower it in the next period when profits are lower. In the Canadian case, however, the postponement of depreciation was for *nonessential* investment projects only. This presents a rather imposing problem in tax administration since it must be determined which assets are "essential." Further, there is additional discrimination here in favor of business firms that acquired assets just prior to the enactment of the law, and against firms whose assets were just wearing out during the postponement period. The disadvantage of designating essential and nonessential assets can be eliminated merely by eliminating this requirement, but the discrimination which results because of the time at which a firm's assets wear out cannot be eliminated. Considerations of equity rank high in any tax scheme. Eisner has criticised accelerated depreciation on these grounds; he also challenges most of the claims made for it.[47]

OTHER TAX PROPOSALS AND INVESTMENT

Carry-Forward and Carry-Back Provisions

Another tax proposal which has a positive impact on investment is the carrying back or forward of business losses. If the law is written to include only the carrying back of losses it would discriminate against new firms. The latter would have nothing against which it could apply losses it experiences in the current taxable period.

[46] Hansen advocates this in *Economic Issues of the 1960's*, New York: McGraw-Hill, 1960, pp. 51–52.

[47] R. Eisner, "Effects of Depreciation Allowances for Tax Purposes," WMC, HR, *Tax Revis. Comp.*, P, pp. 793–799. See, in the same source, Musgrave's statement on pp. 22–23; Musgrave's statement in JEC, *Jan. 1962 Ec. Rept. Pres.*, H, p. 499; and Musgrave's "Growth with Equity," *Am. Ec. Rev.*, May 1963, pp. 323–333, which contains many pertinent points.

The literature on accelerated depreciation is voluminous. The articles of Domar, Eisner, and Goode previously cited contain many references, and the *Tax Revision Compendium* contains many recent articles. For a recent review of the issues and some of the literature see D. D. Ray, "Some Economic Aspects of Depreciaton Accounting," *The Quarterly Review of Economic and Business*, Feb. 1962, pp. 59–69.

If current losses cannot be carried forward, then the current losses of the new firm can never be used as an offset against taxable income. In the meantime, however, its competitors have been in a more favorable financial condition. If the economy is undergoing a recession and all firms in the industry are experiencing losses, the new firm's competitors could be receiving tax rebates on the application of current losses to past profits.

If the law is written to include only carrying forward of losses it would be disadvantageous to established firms with current losses about to close down. Another disadvantage of including only a carry-forward provision would be the impact on risk since businessmen would be less certain that such a provision would be continued in the future. Further, if the carry-forward period is short (say, 2 years) and we have an extended period in which losses are sustained (say, 4 years) then losses for only half the period are deductible from profits. Carry-forward provisions can also be inflationary since recession or depression losses may be used to reduce current high profits. (This depends on the length of the carry forward and assumes a rapid recovery. Therefore the disadvantage may not be very serious.)

The carry back can have a desirable countercyclical impact since current losses can be deducted from past profits and thereby improve the financial condition of the firm. Carry forwards and carry backs of losses are both desirable fixtures of our tax law. Under present circumstances losses can be carried forward for 5 years and back for 3 years.

Other Proposals

Other proposals are generally aimed at increasing the supply of funds for venture capital. They include more liberal provisions for capital losses to be subtracted against ordinary income, averaging of personal income, and lower personal and capital gains taxes. There is little question that income averaging would improve interpersonal equity in the tax system. Those who receive fluctuating incomes are unfairly hurt by the present tax schedule as compared with those who receive the same income at a constant rate over the same period. Similarly, there is common agreement that the extremely high rates of the personal income tax should be lowered, but not necessarily for economic reasons, as noted previously. As far as capital gains are concerned, however, it is widely known that they serve as a device for reducing the high personal income tax rates. Hence all sorts of devices are developed to convert ordinary income into capital gains so that the tax rate will be lower. It is not easy to predict the impact of these changes on investment. There are many and complex problems and issues of tax avoidance, loopholes, and equity which become terribly involved. Where changes can be made that increase the incentive to invest (or work) and are still in line with our social and political concepts of progression in the tax laws, equity, revenue needs, and administrative feasibility, these changes should be made. These problems involve an examination, evaluation, and revision of the whole tax structure; considerable attention has been paid to them in recent years.[48] About all we can say here is that, in the *aggregate*, the tax laws have not been as vicious as many have pictured them, that they have not seriously restricted investment and incentives to work, and that they have not seriously restricted the flow of savings or venture capital. These comments pertain to our postwar experience, but they do not exclude individual inequities, cases of misallocation of resources (as in oil), the fact that the overall level of taxation may be somewhat high to generate sufficient demand under current economic circumstances, or that desirable changes should not be undertaken.

The Swedish Selective Policy of Investment Reserves

Sweden has been a forerunner in the development and use of fiscal devices aimed at attaining full employment and economic growth. In the period between the two world wars, for example, Sweden introduced very liberal rules for inventory valuation and liberal (rapid) depreciation schedules on machinery and equipment. Although the purpose was to strengthen the financial position of business firms during periods of economic decline the procyclical nature of these policies became quite evident. These regulations on depreciation and inventory evaluation were tightened somewhat in 1955, and during the 1952–1953 and 1955–1957 boom periods special investment levies of 10 and 12 percent (respectively) were imposed. It has been reported that the latter were able "to hold back the increase in business investment." This levy was looked on as a mixed blessing, however, because it increased the cost of investments and therefore weakened the competitive ability of those companies which had to invest during the boom period.

Reliance has therefore been placed on the investment reserve device as a means of influencing the timing of business investments. Actually, the device was introduced in 1938, but it was plagued by such complicated regulations that it was difficult to apply and was not very successful.

---

[48] Many collections of essays or proposed revisions in the tax laws are available. The previously cited *Fed. Tax Pol.*, H, P, and *Fed. Exp. Pol.*, H, P, of the JEC; WMC HR, *Tax Revis. Comp.*, P, and WMC, HR, *President's 1961 Tax Recommendations*, Hearings (May and June 1961), 1961. See also H. Brazer, *A Program for Federal Tax Revision*, Ann Arbor: Univ. of Michigan, 1960; and H. Stein and J. A. Pechman, *Essays in Federal Taxation*, New York: CED, Dec. 1959 (from *Tax Revision Compendium*).

The revision of the regulations in 1955 has substantially increased the importance of the investment reserves program.

The program is designed to use tax credits and tax reductions to enable firms to build up reserves of investment funds which can be used for investment during recessions. The amount firms may place in investment reserves per year apparently varies with the legal form of organization and industry, but under 1962 regulations "joint-stock companies and economic associations" could allocate, tax-free, 40 percent of their annual profits to investment reserves.

If the firm deducts this amount or less from its profits it cannot hold all of these funds. In 1962 it had to deposit 46 percent of its allocation in a noninterest-bearing account with the Riksbank (the Bank of Sweden). The remaining 54 percent would be retained by the firm as working capital "without any obligation to hold it in liquid assets."

What is the tax benefit to the firm under this system? It depends upon (1) when the fund is used and (2) the area in which funds are invested (buildings, machinery, inventories, or forestry). The main regulations are as follows. (a) The main determinant of the tax benefit is the fact that the investment reserves (the amount deposited with the Riksbank and the amount held) can be used only in recession as decided by the Labour Market Board. (b) When permission is so granted the firm is granted a special additional investment allowance of 10 percent of the amount invested. (c) In addition, the government has the authority to grant special permission for the reserves to be used over longer periods for the purpose of speeding up development in certain areas. (d) There is a time limit on how long the government may tie up these investment reserves. Failure to release them within 5 years means that the firm may use 30 percent of them without special permission. (e) Use of the funds without special permission means that the firm will pay tax on 110 percent of the amount used. In addition, the firm may not make new allocations to its investment reserves during that year. (f) The Labour Market Board has the authority to direct a corporation to use all or a part of its investment reserve.

By allocating part of its profits to the investment reserve a firm receives an immediate tax reduction. When the funds are invested under the rules established, they are not restored to taxable income. On the other hand, the basis of assets purchased with the reserve funds is reduced correspondingly. Further, a special investment deduction of 10 percent is granted on this amount of reserves so used.

The first major drawing on these funds occurred during the 1958–1959 recession, at which time about Kr.1,000 million were released. The corresponding increase in industrial investment during this period is indicative of the stimulative effect the reserve fund had. There was one difficulty, however; the period during which the funds were released was not clearly defined, with the result that some of its funds were still being paid out during the boom period in 1960. A much shorter payout period was used during the spring of 1962 when concern was expressed over unemployment in the building industry for the winter of 1962–1963.

The investment reserve fund can be used in combination with other policies to secure the necessary results. During 1960 and 1961, for example, special tax benefits were offered if a firm's entire allocation to investment funds was paid into the Riksbank. The policy resulted in substantial payment into the Riksbank and a corresponding large decrease in the liquidity of firms and banks.[49]

OTHER NONTAX TECHNIQUES FOR INFLUENCING INVESTMENT

One of the important ways in which the government has stimulated investment is in the provision of credit by means of direct loans to users, loans to other credit agencies, or insuring or guaranteeing loans. The importance of FHA, GI, and other guaranteed mortgages on the housing industry (and their use of the amortized mortgage) in the maintenance of a high level of demand in the economy is significant.[50] The establishment of the Federal National Mortgage Association has added to the attractiveness of these mortgages to banks since, if a bank feels that it has too large a portion of its portfolio in FHA mortgages, it may sell some of them to FNMA. Other credit programs have been set up for apartment houses, public housing projects, farmers' homes, and the construction of college and university buildings.

In the area of agriculture special loans are available not only for the construction of homes but also for the purchase of farms and land, livestock, and equipment. The Central Bank for Cooperatives provides funds to cooperatives on commodities, for operating capital, and for long-run facilities. There is in addition the Rural Electrification Administration which extends to cooperatives whose purpose is to extend the use of electricity to farm areas. This organization has been cited as an example of an area into which the government was forced by the failure

---

[49] This section was drawn almost exclusively from *Index*, Svenska Handelsbanken Economic Review, No. 9, Stockholm, 1962.

See also E. Mildner and I. Scott, "An Innovation in Fiscal Policy: The Swedish Investment Reserve System," *Natl. Tax J.*, Sept. 1962, and a comment by L. G. Sandberg in the March 1963 issue, pp. 107–108.

[50] It is also true that these programs have at times had some inflationary influences and caused higher wages and costs in the construction industry.

of private interests to pursue it. The financial record of the REA has been respectable, and its socioeconomic achievements have been highly praised.

The Reconstruction Finance Corporation was set up in 1932. At first it aided banks and railroads but later it was authorized to make loans to businesses that experienced difficulty securing credit through normal channels. It offered aid in particular to small and medium-sized businesses of an intermediate-term type (5-and 10-year loans). This partially filled a gap in the credit structure that was quite serious during the 1930's. The RFC has been replaced by the Small Business Administration which also makes direct loans to small business and insures private loans to a deserving firm which cannot secure funds elsewhere at reasonable rates of interest.

Some government programs have likely contributed to inflationary pressures during the postwar period (particularly in the housing industry). Further, private credit institutions do not look with favor on the rate competition or general competition for loans of government credit agencies. On the other hand, there is little doubt that these programs have increased the liquidity of both the borrowers and the lender (where loans are insured by the government), resulted in lower risks for lending institutions (when the loans were insured again), have increased the level of investment in the economy, and have provided credit to many individuals and regions unable to secure it otherwise. Furthermore, large volumes of government funds have not been utilized by these credit agencies since the most important federal action is to insure loans. The continuation of the insured type of loan is probably one of the most acceptable policies in our economy. There is much to be said, though, for the formation of some overall federal agency to reconcile lending operations with the state of the economy and the level of investment.[51] In other words, some degree of coordination and flexibility should be introduced into the program.

ANTI-INFLATIONARY POLICY AND INVESTMENT

Investment, we have noted, can be the main source of inflationary pressures. Investment certainly contributed to the inflation of the immediate postwar period and, in the analysis of many economists, played a major role in the 1955–1957 price increases. An important factor in this process is the capacity of the capital-producing industries. If they are able to expand their production to meet the increased demand for

---

[51] It is possible that certain programs should be pushed in spite of their inflationary tendencies because they involve important social priorities.

equipment, the situation is not serious. But if they have a somewhat limited capacity, and they apparently do, we can expect important price increases such as occurred in the 1955–1957 period. On this point a quotation from Professor Schultze's study is particularly appropriate: ". . . the capital goods and associated industries accounted for two-thirds of the rise in industrial prices during the period, but in these same industries prices rose substantially more than wage costs. Profits per unit of output rose in the capital goods industries, although for the economy as a whole they declined."[52]

Just as the results of proposals for strengthening investment are clouded by uncertainty, especially if some excess capacity exists, proposals for restraining investment have not met with a high degree of success (short of outright rationing, licensing, and price controls). The usual prescription for restraining investment has been a tight money policy which (1) raises the rate of interest, and (2) limits the availability of credit which can be used for investment. Postwar attempts to restrain investment, at least to the degree desirable to restrain price level increases, have not been very successful. Large corporations rely a great deal on retained earnings for investment and these are not affected by a restrictive monetary policy. Further, these corporations have access to the stock market and can sell their securities at favorable prices since we are discussing here a period of prosperity; and they generally have first preference for loans from banks and other financial institutions.

A desirable feature of an antirecession policy is that it be thoroughly countercyclical—that it be completely reversible. The new tax credit of 1962 does not have this feature, nor do the changes in depreciation granted in 1954 and 1962.

The plain fact is that we have no discretionary fiscal tools for restricting investment. We must, therefore, fall back on a restrictive monetary policy, which apparently did not work in 1955–1957, take legislative action to raise the corporate income tax, or develop some type of selective control over investment.

One further possibility should be noted. If it is not feasible to restrict investment, what about further restriction of consumption as a means of reducing overall demand? This policy is not without its difficulties either. (1) In the first place little is accomplished in the way of reducing pressure on the capital goods industries, since resources are not easily transferable from the production of consumer to the production of capital goods. (2) The only impact would be indirect (through the acceleration principle, for example), and this would probably not be very effective because by the time consumption was restricted, the orders for capital goods would have

[52] JEC, *Empl., Growth, Price Levels*, SP No. 1, p. 2.

probably already been made. (3) We do not now have the comprehensive controls over consumer credit that we had during World War II—controls over down payments and repayment periods. (4) This also involves a social decision to restrict consumption and raise investment. Actually, however, this problem is probably not very serious because the reduced consumption can likely be made up in a very short period of time.

PART V

Policy Problems
in Fiscal Policy

14

Problems and Issues of Federal Budgeting

THE FORMULATION OF THE BUDGET

The primary responsibility for developing the budget lies with the Chief Executive. In this role, the President is aided by the staff members of his executive office, department and agency heads, and the Bureau of the Budget. It is his responsibility to propose the budget with the programs and projects it contains to the legislative branch, and it is his responsibility to supervise its execution. The final responsibility for total and specific appropriations, however, rests with the Congress.

The preparation of the budget begins in various bureaus and agencies a year or more before the fiscal year in which it will be effective. Shortly thereafter the agency receives from its departmental budget office a policy statement which serves as a guide to its request for funds. This information is utilized by the various agencies in the preparation of their requests. These requests go to the departmental budget office. Discussions are then held between the Bureau of the Budget and the departments and their subdivisions on the latter's requests and needs.[1]

In about June of the year before the next fiscal year begins, the Bureau of the Budget pieces together the various requests. It then secures from the Treasury Department a statement on its revenue estimates. It may also check the economic forecasts of the Treasury against those of the CEA, the Department of Commerce, or the staff of the Board of Governors of the Federal Reserve.[1]

Conferences are then held between the Director of the Bureau of the Budget and the President and his staff so that the President's program intentions are defined and to advise the President on conflicts which must ultimately be resolved by him. It is at this point that a preliminary consideration of complete budget expenditures and revenue is made and

---

[1] This information is from J. Burkhead, *Government Budgeting*, New York: Wiley, 1956, pp. 88–94.

283

the President's fiscal policy emerges. In the opinion of one expert on budgeting, fiscal policy is not handed down as a program in and of itself, but rather "emerges and crystallizes as decisions are made."[2]

At this point the Director of the Bureau of the Budget issues a policy statement covering the expected levels of national income, price developments, possible recommendations on public works projects that should be expanded or postponed, and budget ceilings for many departments and agencies. The latter are subject to review just as are requests that may fall below their ceilings.[2]

Before September the agencies and departments intensively analyze their budgets in terms of ceilings or policy announcements. Their budgets are then sent to the Bureau of the Budget for examination. Usually the department receives a communication dealing with important questions concerning its budget. Next come the hearings in the Bureau of the Budget in which the agency or department is required to defend its requests.[3]

After the hearings, recommendations are sent to the Director of the Bureau by the budget examiners. After some further consultation with his examiners and the department or agency heads, he holds a formal review usually conducted by himself and his chief subordinates. An unhappy agency may make an appeal for more funds at the Director's Review, or it may also appeal directly to the President. At this point, the Bureau of the Budget again has an opportunity for an overall view of the financial estimates of the various branches of government. At approximately this same time the President is reviewing the budget, and the writing of his budget message is undertaken.[4]

At the same time final revenue estimates are made by the Treasury. These are to be included in the budget document. It is at this point that the Bureau, the Treasury, and the CEA can recommend last-minute policy suggestions and changes to the President in order to increase or decrease the budget deficit or surplus.[5]

The budget message and the budget are generally submitted to the Congress in the third week in January. Although revenue bills may originate only in the House, appropriations bills may originate in either body. In practice, however, there is a tendency for the House to take the initiative in appropriations bills also, with the Senate starting later and acting to modify the actions and decisions of the House. The House and Senate appropriations committees and their subcommittees hold hearings

---

[2] *Ibid.*, p. 91.
[3] *Ibid.*, pp. 91–92.
[4] *Ibid.*, pp. 92–93.
[5] *Ibid.*, p. 93.

at which the requests of the various agencies and departments are defended by the agencies themselves, not the Bureau of the Budget. The subcommittees make their recommendations to the House and Senate Appropriations Committees and from here action is taken in each body. Generally, the final action of the Senate committees comes after that in the House, which means that the Senate committee often acts as a court of appeal for the restoration of budget cuts made by the House. When differences occur between the House and the Senate, a conference committee is set up to work out some type of compromise.[6]

THE BUDGET AS AN ECONOMIC DOCUMENT[7]

Congress does not have a technique for an overall evaluation of the President's budgetary policy. Similarly, there is no opportunity for the Bureau of the Budget to defend the President's overall program. The appropriations are made in piecemeal fashion by the various subcommittees without an eye to the relation to the rest of the appropriations to be made or to the overall impact on the economy. Neither is there any effective overall evaluation of the Administration's program of both expenditures and revenues and their impact on the economy. The only exceptions to this are the hearings and report of the Joint Economic Committee which, in recent years has heard testimony from the CEA, the Director of the Bureau of the Budget, the Secretary of the Treasury, and the Chairman of the Board of Governors of the Federal Reserve (who officially has nothing to do with the formulation of the budget). The only power the Joint Economic Committee has, however, is to make recommendations to other House and Senate committees.

The budget has not been a useful economic document. It has not provided information concerning choices among alternative economic policies, the impact of government policies on the use of resources, the level of employment, economic growth, or the allocation of resources within the private economy. Furthermore, we really have three budgets. The conventional budget (the one that receives the widest use) is short on information, and the information it gives can be terribly misleading as far as the impact of the government budget is concerned. In past years policies of a countercyclical nature generally have not been mentioned in the budget, economic assumptions have been generally omitted, and

---

[6] *Ibid.*, pp. 93–94.
[7] Some 35 pages of the May 1963 issue of the *Rev. Ec. & Stat.* were devoted to a symposium on federal budgetary concepts and problems. The articles are very informative but were received too late to incorporate into this chapter.

allocations were and still are made now which may not be spent for 3 years.[8]

Some changes were finally made in the budget for fiscal 1963. Its size was reduced from something like a metropolitan telephone directory of over 1,000 pages weighing more than 4 pounds to "book size," details were printed in a special budget appendix, other changes were made so as to separate and consolidate certain items to make the document more useful and more digestible, and several changes designed to give a more accurate picture of the actual economic impact of the budget were made. Data on new obligational authority (which gives a more accurate picture of the timing of the budget impact) rather than expenditures, special analyses of public works, grants-in-aid, credit programs, etc., and some Department of Commerce national income and product account data were all included.

Probably one of the main reasons why the budget has not been a useful economic document in the past is that it has been developed more with an eye toward legislative control and administrative management. Hence the procedures involved in the preparation of the budget and the final document itself have been in direct conflict with the objectives of fiscal policy. Many of these points of conflict, of course, are unavoidable, since fiscal policy must be subservient to other national objectives. The size of the budget and increases in the budget have been determined primarily by defense needs and foreign policy objectives. These changes have generally come during periods when the economy was already experiencing a high level of prosperity. At the least, an evaluation should be made of the repercussions of such changes in the private economy. Similarly, it does not make much sense to postpone all urgent public works programs such as school buildings just because we have several successive years of prosperity. Such a policy implies that private expenditures have a higher social priority than public expenditures. "It would be absurd to argue that the people must wait for a depression before they can obtain urgently needed services of public undertakings."[9]

    [8] An excellent analysis of the shortcomings of the present budget can be found in Roy E. Moor, *The Federal Budget as an Economic Document*, for the JEC, Subcommittee on Economic Statistics, 1962, pp. 19, 31–43, 55, 59, 65, 67, 78–81, 87–89, 97–106, 110–113, 117–120, 129–136, 131–132, 136–137. See in particular Chapter 8. See also the subcommittee's hearings of April, 1963, and the full committee's *Report*, August 14, 1963.

    [9] G. Colm, "Fiscal Policy and the Federal Budget," in Max F. Millikan, ed., *Income Stabilization for a Developing Democracy*, New Haven: Yale Univ. Press, 1953, p. 240.

THE ADMINISTRATIVE BUDGET, THE CONSOLIDATED CASH BUDGET, AND FEDERAL RECEIPTS AND EXPENDITURES IN THE NATIONAL INCOME ACCOUNTS

The Administrative or Conventional Budget

The administrative budget receives the most publicity and is the most widely cited in the press. In many respects, however, it comes close to being a hodge-podge and is not reliable as a basis for judging the impact of the federal government on the economy. The form of the administrative budget has developed along present lines primarily because it is most useful to the appropriations committees of Congress.[10] For this reason certain items are included, certain are excluded, some items are net, some are gross, and most items are on a cash basis but a few are on an accrual basis.[11] The total impact of expenditures and receipts for the Post Office Department and other public enterprises, for instance, is not shown because all that is included is a net figure. The government then contributes funds mainly to cover net deficits. Other operations (such as trust funds) are almost completely ignored since the government is making no contribution of funds.[12]

That the three different types of budgets measure different things can be readily seen by a comparison of the expected surplus under the three types. For fiscal 1963 they were $0.5, $1.8, and $4.4 billion, respectively, under the administrative, cash consolidated, and national income and product account budgets—a substantial difference![13] Other comparisons can be made in Tables 14-1 and 14-3.[14]

In Table 14-1 the budget expenditures are estimates based on expectations of future economic developments, new legislation, and other factors. These expenditures are by function; and some agencies (trust funds) are entirely excluded and others included on a net basis, as we have noted. The vast majority of the expenditures are on an estimated "checks issued" basis. The obligations may have been incurred in a previous budget year and the goods may not have been received when the checks are issued.

[10] JEC, 1962 *Ann. Rept.*, p. 34.
[11] Moor, *op. cit.*, p. 110.
[12] JEC, 1962 *Ann. Rept.*, p. 35.
[13] The expected deficits in the administrative, cash, and national income accounts budgets for fiscal 1964 were, respectively, $ −11.9, $ −10.3, and $ −7.6 billion.
[14] In the national income account for fiscal 1963 federal expenditures were estimated at $111.19, purchases of goods and services at $64.2, and receipts at $116.3 billion.

Table 14-1. Administrative Budget (Excludes Trust Funds)

(Fiscal Years, Billions of Dollars)

Description	1963 Estimate	1964 Estimate
Budget expenditures		
National defense	52.7	55.4
International affairs and finance	3.0	2.7
Space research and technology	2.4	4.2
Subtotal	58.1	62.3
Interest	9.4	10.1
Domestic civil functions		
Agriculture and agricultural resources	5.8	5.7
Natural resources	2.3	2.5
Commerce and transportation	2.5	3.4
Housing and community development	0.8	0.3
Health, labor, and welfare	5.1	5.6
Education	1.5	1.5
Veterans' benefits and services	5.3	5.5
General government	2.0	2.2
Subtotal, domestic civil functions	25.4	26.7
Civilian pay reform	0.2	0.2
Allowance for contingencies	0.2	0.2
Deduct interfund transactions	0.7	0.7
Total	92.5	98.8
Budget receipts, total	93.0	86.9
Budget surplus (+) or deficit (−)	+0.5	−11.9
Public debt, end of year	294.9	

Source: Tables 14-1–14-4 are all from the JEC, *Jan. 1962 Ec. Rept. Pres.*, H, pp. 76–79, and 102, and 70, 74.

The treatment of government enterprises is different from the treatment generally given government agencies. These enterprises appear on only the expenditure side as a net positive or negative expenditure. That is, neither the total receipts nor the total expenditures of the enterprise appear. The difference between expenditures and receipts appears as a negative expenditure if receipts exceed expenditures, and as net deficit if expenditures exceed receipts.[15]

[15] Moor, *op. cit.*, p. 113.

Table 14-2. Trust Fund Summary

(Fiscal Year, Billions of Dollars)

Description	1963 Estimate
Trust fund receipts	
Federal old-age and survivor's insurance trust fund	14.2
Federal disability insurance trust fund	1.2
Unemployment trust fund	4.2
Railroad retirement account	1.2
Federal employees' retirement funds	2.1
Highway trust fund	3.4
Veterans' life insurance funds	0.7
Other trust funds	1.0
Subtotal	28.0
Deduct interfund transactions	0.5
Total, trust fund receipts	27.5
Trust fund expenditures	
Federal old-age and survivors' insurance trust fund	14.3
Federal disability insurance trust fund	1.2
Unemployment trust fund	3.9
Railroad retirement account	1.1
Federal employees' retirement funds	1.1
Highway trust fund	3.4
Veterans' life insurance funds	0.7
Federal National Mortgage Association trust fund, net	0.5
Deposit funds and all other trust funds	1.0
Subtotal	27.1
Deduct interfund transactions	0.5
Total, trust fund expenditures	26.6
Net accumulation	0.9

We noted that some activities are excluded entirely from the conventional budget. Certain enterprises "sponsored" by the government (such as the FDIC or Federal Home Loan Banks) are assumed to be independent of it, and their receipts and expenditures are not included even in a net form. If, however, the government makes a loan to such a sponsored enterprise, this is listed as an expenditure by the government.[15]

Let us turn now to the item listed in Table 14-1 as "budget receipts." These are not itemized, but they consist of receipts from individual income taxes, corporate income taxes, excise taxes, estate and gift taxes, customs,

Table 14-3. Consolidated Cash Budget (Includes Administrative Budget and Trust Funds' and Some Other Federal Transactions; and Eliminates Intragovernmental Transactions)

(Fiscal Year, Billions of Dollars)

Description	1963 Estimate
Receipts from the public	
Budget receipts	93.0
Trust fund receipts	27.5
Less:	
Intragovernmental transactions	3.9
Receipts from the exercise of monetary authority	*
Total receipts from the public	116.6
Payments to the public	
Budget expenditures	92.5
Trust fund expenditures	26.6
Government-sponsored enterprise expenditures (net)	.3
Less:	
Intragovernmental transactions	3.9
Accrued interest and other noncash adjustments (net)	.8
Total payments to the public	114.8
Excess of receipts (+) or payments (−)	+1.8

* Less than $50,000,000.

and "miscellaneous budget receipts." The figure given in Table 14-1 represents expected income based mainly on a projection of future economic conditions and expected congressional action on tax laws. The receipts figures are net after estimated refunds. Employment taxes are not included in total receipts at all and parts of some excises are also excluded (mostly for the highway trust fund). "Miscellaneous receipts" include seigniorage, interest payments, and payments of earnings given to the Treasury from government enterprises (not total receipts nor total profits of enterprises), and payments from the Federal Reserve System. Some items appear twice—as an expenditure and as a receipt to the Treasury (such as interest paid by the Export-Import Bank, which appears as an expenditure of this agency and as a receipt to the Treasury), and these are accounted for by the deduction for "interfund transactions."[16]

[16] *Ibid.*, pp. 110–112.

The Cash Consolidated Budget

The cash budget includes some items not included in the administrative budget and excludes other items which would be counted twice because of these additions. It follows then that some of the shortcomings of the administrative budget are repeated. Gross cash receipts are not included since all receipts are net after refunds, and many enterprises are again on a net basis as before. Again, the cash budget fails to reflect the total flow of cash into and out of the government.[17]

The cash budget totals are generally explained by starting with the conventional budget and then indicating the changes. The items added are the trust funds and trust enterprise funds.[18] Since some double counting results with these additions, deductions must be made where sums appear both as conventional budget receipts and as trust fund expenditures, as both trust fund receipts and as conventional budget expenditures, and certain transfers among the trust funds.[19] Another rather complicated step includes the addition of certain figures which are somewhat similar to the net surplus or deficit of certain government-sponsored enterprises.[20] Again the figures are not total cash receipts or expenditures.[21]

The Federal Budget in the National Income Accounts

The national account budget attempts to show how the economic activities of the federal government are included in the national income and product data issued quarterly by the Department of Commerce. In many respects this approach gives a more accurate picture of the impact of government programs on the economy and on the government's use of resources. The data are available on a fiscal or calendar year basis, and are actual rather than estimated. If we examine the budget figures in the national income accounts, we note that certain taxes are listed on an accrual basis, which is before they are actually due. The corporate income tax is listed as such even though it may not fall due until a much later date. This is economically justifiable since it gives an accurate estimate of liabilities. The same is true of most personal taxes, indirect business taxes, and social security taxes.[22]

Some use is also made of the accrual concept in expenditures. In other

[17] *Ibid.*, p. 114.

[18] These two categories include trust funds for federal disability insurance, old-age and survivors' insurance, federal employees retirement, railroad retirement, unemployment, veterans' life insurance, the highway trust fund, and others.

[19] See Moor, *op. cit.*, p. 118, Table 39, Table 40; and p. 119, Table 41.

[20] *Ibid.*, p. 117, and Table 42, p. 119.

[21] See *ibid.*, p. 120, for further detailed refinements.

[22] *Ibid.*, p. 123.

words, even though government payments have not yet been made, if some construction has occurred an estimate is made of the accrued liabilities. This again is justifiable since it records the value of the resources used and the impact of the government program at that particular time. Most other expenditures are on a cash flow basis. Federal lending activities are omitted, which many feel is its most important shortcoming.

By way of contrast with the administrative and cash consolidated budgets, federal expenditures in the national income accounts were (in fiscal 1963) estimated to be $111.9 billion. Of this amount $64.2 billion were for purchases of goods and services and $47.7 billion for "other" expenditures (transfer payments $29.0; grants in aid $8.4; net interest $7.2; and subsidies less current surplus of government enterprises $3.1). Estimated receipts were placed at $116.3 billion for a surplus of $4.4 billion.

This treatment of the federal budget on a national income basis should not be confused with all government purchases of goods and services in the GNP statement. Transfers, grants in aid, and the current surplus of government enterprises are excluded from this account because the intent is to show the impact of government expenditures on resource use.

A Restatement of the Differences

In summary then, the particular method of compiling the *administrative budget* makes it of only limited use for the purpose of judging the impact of the federal government on the economy. Aside from the use of many net figures that do not show total impacts, and the use of the "checks issued" concept, which shows payment after the impact may have occurred, it completely omits the trust fund expenditures.

The *cash consolidated budget* attempts to give a more complete picture of all the financial activities of the government by including the trust fund transactions. Other changes are made, again with the aim of presenting a more accurate picture of the cash transactions between the government and the public. Employment taxes, for example, which are paid to the social security trust funds, and the payment of social security benefits are included. It excludes transactions between agencies of the government (interest payments between the Treasury and trust funds, for example). This budget has, in past years, showed larger surpluses than the administrative budget mainly because the receipts of the trust funds have been greater than their payments.

The *income-and-product account budget* data are on an accrual rather than a cash basis—the impact then is registered as it accrues rather than when taxes are paid or checks are issued for expenditures. This is particularly important for the corporate income tax because tax collections for it lag behind accrual by 6 or 7 months. This budget also attempts to measure the impact of the federal government on resource use—on production and income, and therefore purely financial transactions are omitted.[23] The first time that the national income account budget was included in the budget document was in connection with the fiscal 1963 budget.

Probably the most important shortcoming of the national income-and-product budget is that it eliminates the lending activities of the government. It is also true that certain items such as the Post Office and the Commodity Credit Corporation are included as net figures. Including them as gross figures would involve considerable double counting, however; and this issue has not been resolved.

If we return to the three different surpluses shown in the different budgets we are again struck by the difference between the surpluses of the administrative and national income account budgets. The $4 billion difference is accounted for by three factors: the inclusion of trust funds in the national income account, which was expected to run a slight surplus, the fact that the credit transactions in the administrative budget resulted in a net outflow of funds, and an expected increase in corporate profits and corporate taxes which were to accrue more rapidly than they are paid into the Treasury.[24]

Considerations such as these are no doubt upsetting to staunch advocates of the annually balanced budget. In particular, which budget is to be balanced? These considerations have also led to demands for reform of present budget practices. Suggestions for reform include the establishment of a Joint Committee on Fiscal Policy made up of the leading members of the financial committees and the Joint Economic Committee to give an overall evaluation of the President's budget, to lay down guidelines for policy relative to expenditures, appropriations, taxation, and borrowing based on the needs and capacity of the country, and to provide "a unified consideration of budgetary policy."[25] The Committee for Economic Development has recommended a similar body (the "Joint Budget Policy Conference") to consider the same problems.[26] Other proposals would consist of a wholesale reform of both budgetary process and procedure.[27]

[23] A good short statement of the differences in the various budgets is that of D. Bell, former Director, Bureau of the Budget, in JEC, *Jan. 1935 Ec. Rept. Pres.*, H, pp. 123–124.

[24] See W. W. Heller, in *ibid.*, p. 72.

[25] A. Smithies, JEC, *Fed. Exp. Pol.*, P, 555.

[26] CED, *Control of Federal Government Expenditures*, New York: CED, 1955.

[27] See Moor, *op. cit.*, Chapters 6 and 7. See also A. Smithies in JEC, *Fed. Exp. Pol.*, P, pp. 551–557; and, in the same source, the papers in section VII. Smithies' book, *The Budgetary Process in the United States*, New York: McGraw-Hill, 1955, contains more extensive suggestions in Chapters 8 through 10 and elsewhere with reference to specific types of expenditure.

Budgets of Other Governments

Table 14-4 gives some data on deficits and surpluses in other countries and the United States. The data are approximately on a cash consolidated

Table 14-4. Central Government Surpluses and/or Deficits for Recent Years for Four Countries (Calendar Year Basis)[a]

Calendar year	England (millions of current £)	France (billions of current new francs)	Germany (millions of current DM)	United States (billions of current dollars)
1950	611	*	*	0.5
1951	−55	−2.40	*	1.2
1952	−464	−6.27	*	−0.6
1953	−628	−7.94	*	−7.2
1954	−74	−7.56	*	−1.1
1955	−42	−8.32	2,221	−0.7
1956	150	−11.72	1,331	5.5
1957	−175	−12.21	−2,926	1.2
1958	−101	−9.36	−1,755	−7.3
1959	−282	−5.48	−3,881	−8.0
1960	−453	−3.24	−200	3.5

Source: This table was prepared by Andrew H. Gantt II for Harvard University and financed by the Brookings Institution.

[a] The figures in this table differ from the usual "budget" deficit or surplus figures printed by these countries, which usually do not express adequately the surpluses or deficits for which their central governments are responsible. For instance, in the United States, the trust funds and other items are excluded from the budget figures. The figures in the table are on a basis analogous to the "Cash receipts from and payments to the public" of the United States, which encompass the entire operations of the central governments of these countries, including trust funds, government owned and sponsored enterprises, etc. It should be noted, however, that no attempt has been made to include exactly the same operations in each country. If the central government of the United Kingdom operates her radio stations and they run a deficit, this deficit is included above, even though the U.S. Government has nothing to do in an operational way with the radio stations here.

* Figures not available at this time on the same basis.

basis and are subject to the qualifications noted. The table shows that, on this basis, the United Kingdom had a deficit in 9 of the last 11 years, West Germany in 4 of the past 6 years, France in all of the last 19 years, and the United States in 6 of 11 years.[28] The results of this study have created some pressure for the establishment of a separate capital budget for the United States. The use of the capital budget would mean that long-term capital-type projects would not appear in the regular budgets and hence our surpluses would be greater or our deficits smaller. Many economists, however, feel that there is no need for such a division under normal conditions, although there might be some psychological advantage under depression conditions,[29] or if excessive reliance is placed on saving for growth, deficits are therefore necessary, and the public refuses to accept them.

It is of interest to note the conditions under which interest in foreign budgets was aroused. Many international, foreign private, and foreign central bankers have been extremely critical of the deficits in our budget in recent years. Some Senators and Representatives have become somewhat miffed at this, especially since they have been concerned about the low rate of growth of the economy, the high level of tax rates and the consequent full employment surplus which results, and their desire for tax cuts (in the past) to fight recessions and (more currently) to raise the growth rate. The high respect that has been accorded these foreign bankers by many economic groups in our society has helped frustrate their legislative programs. The more or less official publication of the figures lends support to what they have been arguing all along—that our deficits have not been more serious (even "as serious") as those of most countries in which these bankers reside.

[28] As noted in Table 14-4 the data were taken from publications of the Joint Economic Committee. Gantt has since published an article in which he notes the problems involved in making such comparisons. He also presents data on the ratio of the deficit or surplus to each country's GNP (yearly basis), and the cumulative surplus or deficit balance as a percentage of cumulative GNP. Although all countries experienced a deficit, that of the U.S. was the smallest.

Some critics of Gantt's figures have claimed that his analysis is misleading because France and the U.K. make large loans to nationalized industries for fixed capital formation (as the U.S. does not), a fact that supposedly implants a bias toward deficits in these foreign budgets. Gantt points out that if net government loans to nationalized industry are substituted for private borrowing then the figures should be deleted. Gantt subtracts these net loans from the surplus or deficits of France and the U.K. and finds that France's position is relatively unchanged but that of the U.K. changes radically from deficits in 9 of 10 years to a surplus in 9 of 11 years, and to a cumulative surplus. See Andrew H. Gantt, II, "Central Governments: Cash Deficits and Surpluses," *Rev. Ec. & Stat.*, Feb. 1963, pp. 34–46. This point is discussed in Chapter 15.

[29] A good analysis of the issue is that of J. Burkhead, *op. cit.*, pp. 203–210. Burkhead also surveys the use of the capital budget on the state and local level, and its use in Sweden. See Chapter 8. Another recent survey is that of Moor, *op. cit.*, Appendix, pp. 149–185.

It is very interesting to note that almost every one of our deficits resulted from recessions. They were, then, deficits by default rather than deliberate deficits. Hence their stimulative effect was much less than it would have been had the deficits been planned, as obviously most of those of foreign countries were. This, along with other factors previously covered in the text, helped account for the higher foreign growth rate.

There is nothing particularly sacrosanct about the wisdom of foreign bankers. Some economists claim that we could expect many of them to show little more insight into economic analysis than many of our own bankers and businessmen, whose experience in fields other than their specialty is very limited (as with most of us), who are themselves victims of the traditional economic ideology, who are working to save the country from the "staggering burden of taxation," inflation and high wages, and whose record in economic policy-making leaves a great deal to be desired.[30] Arthur Smithies argues that much of this is the fault of economists themselves.

FURTHER CONSIDERATIONS IN BUDGETARY POLICY— CRITERIA AND MEASUREMENT

Criteria and Measurement

We have previously (in Chapter 4) suggested various questions which may be posed in the consideration of the role of the federal government in the undertaking of various projects. It would seem appropriate at this point to add further questions to our list, especially those which have a bearing on fiscal policy. A partial listing follows:

1. What are the specific economic assumptions on which the budget expenditures and receipts are based? What are the assumptions regarding the anticipated levels of the gross national product, employment, prices, etc.?
2. What is the expected impact on production, employment, and resources of both tax and expenditure policies? Will the government programs draw people away from private employment? What are the direct and indirect impacts on private resource allocation?
3. What are the expected short-run and long-run impacts on disposable income, consumption, and investment?
4. In what ways does the budget contribute to short-run stability and long-run growth?
5. What is the impact on the distribution of private incomes?
6. What is the impact, if any, on the efficiency of private resource use?
7. What are the noneconomic effects of the budget?[31]

[30] Smithies' comments on this are instructive. See JEC, *Fed. Exp. Pol.*, P, p. 553.
[31] All these points are discussed in Moor, *op. cit.*, Chapters 6, 8, and 9.

It is not at all easy to judge the total impact of the federal government's budget on the economy. We have already noted that, depending on the source of taxes and the types of expenditures, budget surpluses, deficits, and the balanced budget may have widely varying impacts from those which simple logic would seem to imply. (See Chapters 8 and 9.) Not only are simple surpluses and deficits important; so are the total size of the budget, the direction of budget change, the size of the budget change, and the nature of the budget change and how it affects private incomes— the composition of both the tax source and the expenditures. Are the taxes mostly on funds that would be used for consumption, on idle funds, or on funds that would assuredly be used for investment? The impact of an increase in expenditures on the products of an industry in which inventories are currently high, for example, would be much less than the impact in the same industry if inventories were low.

One additional area in which difficulties arise is in the relationship between obligational authority and budget expenditures. In short, the impact on the economy of a government program generally comes *before* the government spends its money; obligational authorities bring about increases in private activity, but there may be no change at all in the level of government expenditures. This follows from the fact that as soon as a contract is signed (sometimes before) the private contractor purchases resources and raw materials, hires labor, and secures a loan to produce the goods long before the goods are produced and long before he is paid. Often the lag is 2 or 3 years. Therefore, the major impact on the economy tends to be when the order is placed.[32]

In the national income accounts, though, the increased economic activity appears as an increase in gross private domestic investment (inventories) and nowhere appears as a part of government expenditures. When the goods are delivered to the government we see an increase in the government account as a purchase (and a simultaneous decline in GPDI). If government purchases are of existing inventories, however, there may be no impact on production. On the other hand, other government expenditures such as transfer payments, grants to states, and loans may lead or coincide closely with the impact.[32]

Dr. Weidenbaum applied this idea to developments during the Korean War and came up with a very interesting conclusion that was contrary to the results of other studies. These studies had indicated that since the increases in spending during this period were in the private sector, the federal government was cleared of any blame for the inflation of the period. His analysis indicates that the doubling of the rate of placement

---

[32] M. L. Weidenbaum, *The Economic Impact of the Government Spending Process*, Univ. of Houston *Bus. Rev.*, Spring 1961. (See also his articles in the *American Journal of Economics and Sociology*, Jan. 1961, and in JEC, *Fed. Exp. Pol.*, P, p. 500ff.)

of military orders did contribute to the inflation.[33] He further notes that credit restriction and other curbs on private spending may have frustrated the production of war goods.

The lead series in this process are new obligational authority and obligations incurred. Expenditures lag or are, at times, coincident. These measures, then, can be very useful in forecasting the trends in the economy when government expenditures are significant factors.[34] An indication of the significance of these measures is shown in Table 14-5.

Table 14-5. **Relationship of Measures of Federal Spending to Changes in Economic Activity**

Percent Changes from Previous Period

Fiscal Year	GNP	New Obligational Authority	Obligations Incurred	Budget Expenditures
1951	+19	+68	+92	+11
1952	+18	+10	+25	+15
1953	+4	−12	−6	+14
1954	+1	−24	−23	−9

Source: M. L. Weidenbaum, *op. cit.*, p. 39, from *Surv. Current Bus.*, July 1956, pp. 26–27.

Professor Musgrave's Budget

Musgrave's unconventional approach to the budget really consists of three different budgets—one that deals with the provision for social wants, one that deals with the distribution of income, and one that deals with stabilization policy. The first two would generally be balanced, but the third will fluctuate between periods of deficit and surplus.

The first budget is handled by the Allocation Branch and involves the problem of determining the amount of resources which will be allocated for the satisfaction of social wants. These wants should be satisfied regardless of the level of income and employment. The release of resources can be attained by use of taxes if necessary. (Musgrave recognizes that some countercyclical variations in the satisfaction of social wants may occur.)[35]

The second budget is handled by the Distribution Branch. The amount of redistribution to occur is a decision that society must make. Once this

---

[33] *Ibid.*, p. 41.   [34] *Ibid.*, pp. 41–43.

[35] R. Musgrave, *The Theory of Public Finance*, New York: McGraw-Hill, 1959, pp. 6–26; and "Principles of Budget Determination," in JEC, *Fed. Exp. Pol.*, P, pp. 108–115. For exceptions to his principle that public services should not be varied countercyclically, see pp. 517–520 of his text.

decision is made, taxes must be levied on some high income people and transfers made to low income people. Taxes are to be collected on the ability-to-pay and equal-sacrifice basis.

The third budget is handled by the Stabilization Branch. Its purpose is to maintain a high level of income and employment and a stable price level. Taxes are to be raised if demand is too high and transfers raised if demand is too low. Both taxes and transfers would not be used together. Taxes are to prevent inflation and transfers to prevent deflation.[36] The Stabilization Budget is either a surplus or deficit budget. It will be balanced only when both taxes and transfers are zero—when private and Allocation Branch expenditures are high enough to secure full employment without the aid of the Stabilization Branch.[37] Musgrave apparently prefers the use of transfers to secure expansion in the economy. Since the satisfaction of public wants is the function of the Allocation Branch, the Stabilization Branch will not raise or lower public expenditures on goods and services. Since the second budget takes care of distributional goals, the taxes and transfers of the Stabilization Branch "will be proportional to the proper distribution of income as determined by the Distribution Branch."[38]

It does not seem very likely that Musgrave's budget will be adopted by the American Congress either now or in the foreseeable future. Nonetheless, his approach is a very useful contribution to clear thinking about the federal budget. It effectively separates for individual consideration certain social and economic goals, objectives, and policies which are too often confused.

---

[36] The use of taxes to prevent inflation implies that they would be dropped when the danger is past.

[37] See pp. 25–26 of his text.

[38] *Ibid.*, p. 25.

15

Determining the Basis for Policy:
Fiscal Policy and Unemployment
in the 'Fifties and 'Sixties

Much concern was expressed in our society during the late 'fifties and early 'sixties over the relatively high rate of unemployment, as anyone even vaguely acquainted with political discussions, business magazines, and newspapers must know. Many individuals and groups have expressed their opinions about the causes of our problems, the most important causes set forth probably being the structural transformation thesis, the inadequate saving-investment argument, and the "full-employment surplus"–aggregate demand theory.[1] In this chapter we shall examine each of these arguments. Furthermore, this chapter should illustrate the need for adequate economic analysis before policy is determined, and the problems encountered in arriving at a consensus on what the real causes of a problem are.

Figure 15-1 shows the trend of unemployment from 1948 to 1963. The peaks in the unemployment rate occurred during the 1949, 1953–54, 1957–58, and 1960–61 recessions. The highest peak was reached in 1949, but it was of extremely short duration. The 1953–1954 peak was not as high but was of longer duration. Further, the level of unemployment during the following recovery and "prosperity" period was substantially higher. Even during the rather prosperous periods of 1955, 1956, and most of 1957 the unemployment rate averaged 4.4, 4.2, and 4.3 percent, respectively.[2] The unemployment rate during the 1957–1958 recession

[1] The reader should note that the system of income distribution and the possibility of a misallocation of capital funds (via high levels of retained earnings, etc.) as causes of inadequate demand are not discussed here directly.

[2] *Economic Indicators*, Sept. and Oct., 1962, p. 9.

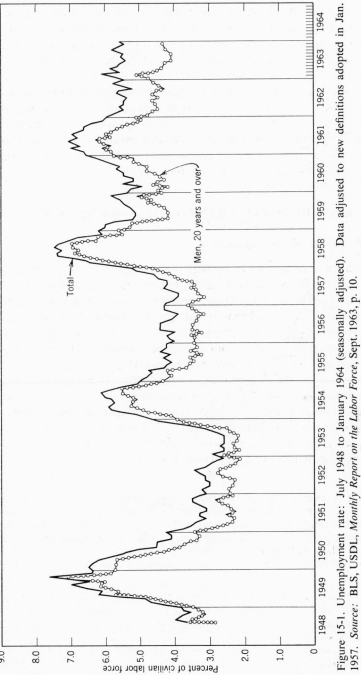

Figure 15-1. Unemployment rate: July 1948 to January 1964 (seasonally adjusted). Data adjusted to new definitions adopted in Jan. 1957. *Source*: BLS, USDL, *Monthly Report on the Labor Force*, Sept. 1963, p. 10.

was significantly higher than during the previous recession. Furthermore, the rate during and after recovery was again significantly higher than during the same period following the 1953–1954 recession. The rates during 1959 and 1960 averaged 5.5 and 5.6 percent, respectively. For the first 9 months of 1963 the rate averaged 5.7 percent. From these statistics we see that the average rate of unemployment has been higher after each of the first four postwar recessions, and thus that the unemployment situation has been progressively worse after each recession.[3] But another very important trend can be observed: The periods of recovery (the period from one trough to the next) have also become progressively shorter, except for the 1961–1964 recovery.

THE STRUCTURAL TRANSFORMATION THESIS

The Nature of the Argument

The structural transformation thesis argues that the unemployment of the late 'fifties and early 'sixties has not been caused by a lack of total demand in the economy (and a resulting lack of employment opportunities), but rather has been caused by "technological changes which are currently reshaping the American economy at an unusually rapid pace."[4] The argument is that white-collar occupations and service-rendering industries have risen in importance while there has been a simultaneous reduction in the importance of blue-collar occupations and goods-producing industries. There has been, then, an increase in employment opportunities in the first category and a relative decline in employment opportunities in the second category. Directing their attention toward the higher rates of unemployment since 1957, the structural transformationists' explanation for this runs as follows:

(1) A faster rate of technological change has led to a higher rate of displacement of labor; (2) the average worker, once displaced, experiences a number of weeks of unemployment while hunting for a new job; (3) most of the displaced workers possess blue-collar backgrounds. Automation has reduced the demands for workers with their type of skill and experience. Consequently, blue-collar workers who have lost jobs in recent years have, on the average, experienced

---

[3] The period of recovery following the 1949 recession brought very low unemployment rates. The causes were the increase in defense expenditures associated with the Korean buildup and the limited growth of the civilian labor force due to the increase in the size of the armed forces.

[4] Subcommittee on Economic Statistics, JEC, *Higher Employment Rates, 1957–60: Structural Transformation or Inadequate Demand*, pp. 6–7.

longer spells of unemployment than similar workers earlier in the postwar period.[5]

Those who accept the structural transformation thesis argue that the definition of full employment must be revised downward. That is, full employment will occur at a higher rate of unemployment than in the postwar period. It is their position, then, that fiscal and monetary policies of an expansionary sort will "lead to inflation long before the unemployment rate approaches 4 percent." The reader should note the relationship of this statement to the discussion of the Phillips' and Samuelson-Solow studies in Chapter 2.

The structural transformation theory is often confused with, or identified with, structural unemployment. The staff of the Joint Economic Committee, however, argues that these are two different types of unemployment. In the foregoing definition of structural transformation they stress the increase and decrease in different types of occupations—white-collar and service versus blue-collar and assembly-line jobs. They do recognize the factors of technological change and changes in the relative importance of various industries. On the other hand, they define structural unemployment as displacement "from particular jobs by technological change, or geographic migration of industry, or by some other long-run influence..."[6] The emphasis here obviously is on long-run factors. But the distinction is not sharp. Hyman L. Lewis[7] of the staff of the Bureau of Labor Statistics, after a thorough analysis of the literature in the field, defined structural unemployment as due to dynamic changes (such as technology, consumer tastes, plant location, and in the composition, distribution, and uses of labor and other resources) which "are massive, extensive, deep-seated, amounting to transformation of economic structure, i.e., the production functions or labor supply distribution. More specifically, it refers to changes which are large in the particular area, industry, or occupation." The emphasis, therefore, is on *shifts* and not on absolute decreases. Also

[5] *Ibid.* It is perhaps a bit unfair to quote the theory from a source which has concluded that the theory has only a limited value. On the other hand, there is absolutely no reason that I know of to question the integrity of the committee staff (which prepared the report). In fact, the evidence indicates that the staff should be commended for the quality of its work.

Furthermore, the presentation of the theory in the statements of its advocates is often far from being very clear. Better statements can be found in the comments of (particularly) Representative Curtis and Senator Proxmire in various JEC Hearings and *Annual Reports* of recent years.

[6] *Ibid.*, p. 7.

[7] Subcommittee on Economic Statistics, JEC, *Unemployment: Terminology, Measurement, and Analysis*, 1961, pp. 6–7. The study was prepared for the JEC by the Bureau of Labor Statistics.

included in recent years, according to Lewis, are changes in the composition of the labor force (number of unskilled workers, for example),[8]
"the inability or reluctance of individuals, communities, or industries to
make adequate and relatively quick adjustments to changing economic
conditions."[9]

The emphasis in the *structural transformation thesis*, then, is on different
occupations; the emphasis in *structural unemployment* is on long-run
factors and shifts in the relative importance of areas, industries, or
occupations. (The qualifications added to each definition, however,
create confusion and considerable overlap.) The staff of the Joint
Economic Committee states that "structural" should be used to refer to
technological change (automobiles replacing horse buggies), geographic
migration of industry, or other *long-run* factors, and not to particular
workers or groups of workers.[10]

The structural transformationists have developed their theory as the
basis for criticism of the aggregate demand theorists, who argue that,
during the late 1950's and early 1960's, expansionary monetary and fiscal
policies could have increased job opportunities and reduced unemployment to somewhere around 4 percent. It is particularly important to note
that the different theories call for different policies. The policy we have
noted of increasing aggregate demand would result only in price level
increases if the problem were that of structural transformation. The
reason is that the unemployed are unemployable because they lack the
proper skills, and the increase in demand would not result in an increase in
output. More money would be buying the same volume of goods and
services and prices would rise. Hence a level of unemployment of greater
than 4 percent is unavoidable unless other action is taken. The policy
prescription would be an increase in the mobility of labor, movement out
of labor surplus areas, a more effective Employment Service, and
retraining.

We should note that these policies are not exclusive with the structural
transformation thesis—some of them apply to aggregate demand and the
encouragement of efficiency in the placement of labor under any and all
conditions. We should also note that some structural and some structural
transformation unemployment will always occur in a dynamic economy.
Further, a sufficient rate of growth of the economy is still necessary
regardless of the cause of unemployment. Unemployment caused by
structural changes is more easily dealt with under conditions of more rapid
growth. In the discussion that follows it will be apparent that both the

---

[8] *Ibid.*   [9] *Ibid.*, p. 19.
[10] Subcommittee on Economic Statistics, JEC, *Higher Unemployment Rates, 1957–
60: Structural Transformation or Inadequate Demand*, 1961, p. 7.

structural demand and structural transformation theses can be considered on the one hand and the aggregate demand theory on the other.

Structural Transformation Arguments, Assumptions, and Expectations

Those who support the structural transformation thesis claim that since mid-1957 we have had "adequate overall demand forces" and sufficient job opportunities. The persistence of unemployment in the face of these two "facts" is to be explained by the following conditions.

1. An acceleration of the *overall* rate of technological change has caused improvements in output per man-hour and has displaced labor. If the increase in productivity in an industry is greater than the average, labor will be displaced if demand for the product is price-inelastic and if prices are not decreased so that income may be used to increase demand in other areas.
2. An increased *concentration* of productivity increases, without a simultaneous acceleration of the overall rate, will also reduce employment if demand in the high productivity areas is price-inelastic and prices are not reduced so that demand is increased in other industries.
3. A change in the *qualitative impact* of productivity increases that reduces the demand for semiskilled blue-collar workers can increase the unemployment rate. These people find it difficult to find employment in the more rapidly growing trade, government, and services sectors because of their skills, color, education, or temperament. There is an imbalance between the skills of the blue-collar workers and the types of position open. This is the most often cited cause of "structural unemployment."
4. It is also argued, or at least implied, that labor mobility has decreased because the unemployed are less likely to seek employment in other industries, occupations, or geographic areas. The reasons given are increased home ownership, unvested pension plans, seniority programs, vacations based on years of service, and unemployment compensation and supplements. The assumption apparently is that rather than change jobs (occupationally or geographically) the person prefers to stay where he is with the hope of reemployment and retention of these benefits.

The result of all this should be that unemployment is concentrated in certain industries, occupations, and areas—especially blue-collar occupations and goods-producing industries. Since the theory argues in terms of the developments of the late 1950's and early 1960's, the rate of unemployment among these groups should have been "higher relative to the overall employment rate than it was earlier." Further, there should be a strong demand for other workers since it is assumed that final demand is high enough to employ the employable. Greater job vacanices, longer average work weeks, economizing on the services of professional personnel (more assistants for the high-priced engineer, etc.), an inadequate supply of professional and highly skilled labor—all these should result.

Evidence and the Structural Transformation Thesis

The first question, in line with the assumptions noted in the preceding section, is: "Have increases in output per man-hour shown any signs of acceleration?" The rate of increase during the postwar period (in manufacturing, railroad transportation, the private nonfarm sector, and agriculture) has been more rapid than the average for the period 1909–1960. But, when compared with a similar period of expanding employment and mild recessions such as the 1920's, the postwar rates have not been particularly high. In fact, in manufacturing, the postwar rate of advance has been slower than in the 1920's. A comparison of overall rates for the 1948–57 and 1957–60 periods reveals no significant difference.

The second question becomes: "Would an acceleration of increases in output per man-hour necessarily lead to higher levels of unemployment?" This question is debatable. A more rapid rate of productivity increase can certainly displace more labor, but this does not mean that the unemployment rate must increase. This is because technical progress also can and does increase both consumption and the demand for investment goods. There is no statistically significant short-run relationship between changes in productivity and changes in man-hours, but the long-run relationship is positive.

The third question can be asked in two related parts. "In recent years, have increases in productivity become more concentrated in a select group of industries? Have consumers, producers, and government agencies become more fickle in their purchasing patterns?" Were there significant shifts in demand during the 1957–1960 period? We noted that there has been no significant upward trend during the postwar period as compared with the 1920's and that the rate of productivity increase was higher in manufacturing during the 1920's than during the postwar period. During the same time periods the only areas in which some acceleration occurred were agriculture and railroad transportation.

When comparisons are made within the postwar period we see that the largest increases in output per man-hour for both the farm and nonfarm sectors of the private economy occurred during the 1948–1953 cycle. The annual rates during the 1953–57 and 1957–60 cycles were about the same, and were lower than that of the 1948–53 cycle.[11] In nonmanufacturing

[11] *Ibid.*, p. 30.

industries the increases in output per man-hour during the 1957–60 and 1953–57 cycles were lower than in 1948–53.[12] The gains in productivity in railroads and mining were higher in the 1957–1960 period than in the two earlier postwar cycles. Public utilities showed the opposite pattern. In manufacturing it was found that the productivity gains (on the basis of man-hours) were higher during the 1957–60 period than the 1948–53 and 1953–57 periods. Based on the Federal Reserve index of manufacturing production, the figures were, respectively, for *all* employees 3.5, 3.1, and 3.7 percent, and for production employees 4.1, 4.2, and 4.6 percent. Based on the real-product estimates of the Labor and Commerce Departments, the figures were, for all employees, 3.4, 1.9, and 3.9, and for production workers 4.0, 3.1, and 4.9 percent. Because of the increased dependence on nonproduction workers in manufacturing it is probably best to use the all employee figures, although the ranking of the periods does not change significantly regardless of which measure in used.[13]

In addition, "there has been no autonomous increase in the variability of employment changes in manufacturing, either since the 1920's or since 1957."[14] In other words, with the overall change in manufacturing employment given, there has been no tendency over time for large increases or decreases in employment to become increasingly concentrated in a small number of industries.[15] If consumers had become more fickle in their purchasing patterns, employment changes in specific industries should show a greater divergence from the average rate of change, but they did not.

The fourth question is: "How significant has been the down-trend in employment among workers in blue-collar occupations and goods-producing industries?" The whole of the twentieth century has seen a continued transformation in the occupational and industrial composition of the labor force. In the 1950's it has taken the form of a rapid growth in professional workers and a comparatively slow rate of growth of nonfarm blue-collar workers. These divergent trends between goods and service industries were also true of the 1920's. If, after mid-1957, this trend had been the cause of higher unemployment rates, the evidence should show up in much higher rates of unemployment among blue-collar occupations and in goods-producing industries.

In view of the assumption of high and sufficient aggregate demand of the structural transformation thesis there should also have been (after mid-1957) higher levels of unfilled job vacancies, higher than average

---

[12] Based on household survey estimates. Establishment payroll estimates show a different pattern, but they were not adjusted as yet. See *ibid.*, p. 29.

[13] *Ibid.*, pp. 25–32.

[14] *Ibid.*, p. 77.   [15] *Ibid.*, pp. 35–36.

increases in the civilian labor force, and longer work weeks in non-manufacturing industries. The staff of the Joint Economic Committee found, however, that:

(a) Unemployment rose among all groups of workers between 1957 and 1960, regardless of industrial or occupational attachment.

(b) Changes in unemployment between 1957 and 1960 duplicated the patterns which have occurred during recession periods.

(c) Independent investigations indicate the existence of an extraordinary amount of interindustry mobility. Many workers cross the barrier of industrial classifications with comparative ease. A sharply rising level of educational attainment has facilitated the flow of younger workers into white-collar occupations and service-rendering industries. Higher educational levels among young labor force entrants, together with mobility among experienced workers, permit the labor force in specific occupations and industries to adjust to differential changes in the demand for labor, provided sufficient job opportunities are available.

(d) Available evidence indicates that the number of nonfarm job openings was lower in 1959–60 than in 1955–57 in every major occupational category.

(e) The overall labor force participation rate declined between 1957 and 1960. The participation rate for women continued to rise but at a slower rate than in 1953–57.

(f) The increase in man-hours was noticeably smaller than in 1948–53 or 1953–57. The average length of the workweek in nonmanufacturing industries was shortened, but not as appreciably as in the 1948–57 period. However, average hours worked in nonmanufacturing industries appear to be influenced by institutional changes more than by fluctuations in output.[16]

Structural Transformation vs. Inadequate Demand: A Final Comment

Studies of this type are always subject to the limitations of the data. Some of the data are at best intelligent guesses and subject to error. Further, this study is still subject to independent statistical verification. Nevertheless, it seems safe to state that the staff used the best available data and carefully evaluated the events of the periods studied. In addition, they approached the problem from several points of view.

Little evidence was found to support the structural transformation thesis or the structural unemployment thesis. On the other hand, the failure of aggregate demand to grow rapidly enough to absorb those who are normally structurally unemployed in a dynamic economy has meant severe hardship due to unemployment, the necessity of taking lower-paying positions, and a lowered standard of living. Higher unemployment rates have not been influenced significantly by the lack of jobs in goods industries and in blue-collar occupations; but the lack of sufficient demand has hit those who were displaced. There has not been a sufficient number of jobs available elsewhere.

[16] *Ibid.*, p. 78.

Furthermore, the evidence offered to disprove the structural transformation thesis tends to confirm the inadequate demand theory—a slower
rate of economic growth in 1957–60 than in 1948–57 even though productive capacity continued to grow; a low level of nonfarm openings;
the rise of unemployment in all occupational and industrial groups; a
sharp rise in unemployment among inexperienced workers; the absence
of any unusual concentration of unemployment in 1957–1960; a reasonably high rate of interindustry mobility; and a high level of geographic
mobility. Finally, even if there is an important shift toward the expansion
of trade, services, and government, the rate of unemployment should still
decline to around 4 percent if the level of aggregate demand is adequate
because former industrial workers are generally capable of performing
many of these jobs. On the other hand, if jobs are highly concentrated in
highly skilled occupations there should be a very sharp rise in unfilled
job vacancies.[17]

The study of the staff of the Joint Economic Committee was preceded
by that of the Council of Economic Advisers and was no doubt prompted
by it. In its evaluation of what it called the "hard-core" unemployment
argument, the CEA compared unemployment rates for 1957 (and other
years) with those for 1960 on the basis of the age, sex, color, marital
status, and educational, industrial, and occupational composition of the
labor force. Its conclusion was that the changes occurring in the composition of the labor force were small and were not the cause of a higher
level of unemployment. They found, as the staff study found later, that
the unemployment of 1960 was not unusually concentrated in particular
compartments of the labor force.[18] They further found that, even though
depressed economic areas suffer more when unemployment rates are
higher, the depressed areas accounted for no more of the unemployment
problem than they did in two early business cycles. The question here is
not whether the composition of employment and the labor force has been
shifting against the unskilled and semiskilled. Rather it is whether recent
increases in the incidence of unemployment among these groups were out
of line with the experience of other occupational groups. It apparently
was not. (Ever since 1940 these groups have experienced relatively higher
rates of unemployment than other occupational groups. It was the change
in the relationship that the CEA was interested in.)[19]

In a follow-up study released in the fall of 1963 the CEA challenged the

[17] See *ibid.*, p. 13.
[18] Reprinted in JEC, *Jan. 1961 Ec. Rept. Pres.*, H, pp. 378–382. James Tobin was
apparently primarily responsible for the analysis. (See p. 481.) The JEC staff study is
much more comprehensive.
[19] *Ibid.*, p. 570.

commonly heard argument that automation is eliminating jobs at a dangerous rate, that the unskilled and semiskilled "blue-collar" workers were hit hard by atomation, and that the sectors most affected were manufacturing, mining, and transportation. The Council's analysis of unemployment by category of worker and by industry, for the 1948–1957 period and the period 1957–1962, found (1) a regular relationship between the jobless rate in these categories and in the trend of overall employment, (2) that for a majority of the "technologically vulnerable" workers "actual unemployment in 1962 seems to have been somewhat lower than would have been estimated from the projection of the 1948–57 experience." If automation had been significant the unemployment rate in the worker category and industries so affected should have been *higher* than in the 1948–1957 period.[20]

Needless to say, not all policy-makers accept these conclusions. The most important critic has probably been Chairman Martin of the Board of Governors. In his testimony before the Joint Economic Committee on March 7, 1961 he unequivocally accepted the structural unemployment and structural transformation thesis. Further, he confused cyclical with structural unemployment.[21] Mr. Martin was presented with an opportunity to refute the results of the CEA study[22] but apparently neither he nor any member of the Federal Reserve has done so.

All the foregoing should not convey the impression that programs designed to give aid to depressed areas, retain and relocate workers, etc., are to be precluded. These programs are needed and should be stepped up in the normal course of events to reduce the unemployment rate and ease the transition from one job to another, and for other social and political reasons. It is also extremely important to recognize that the chronically unemployed will become a larger group and a more serious problem if aggregate demand does not increase at a rate rapid enough to absorb them into other jobs. The evidence indicates that most of those referred to as structurally unemployed would be quickly employed if job opportunities were plentiful. We had a great deal of structural-type unemployment during the 1930's, and these people quickly adjusted to the job requirements of World War II. Further, many European countries (Sweden, England, Denmark and others) have apparently successfully combated structural-type unemployment.[23]

[20] As reported in *The New York Times*, Nov. 18, 1963, Western edition, p. 17.

[21] JEC, *Jan. 1961 Ec. Rept. Pres.*, H, p. 470. Much of the unemployment in the industries he cites has been cyclical. He does not differentiate between the two. See also pp. 486–487.

[22] See his added statement, *ibid.*, pp. 486–487. See the CEA's courteous refutation of Martin's position on pp. 570–571.

[23] See JEC, *Economic Programs for Labor Surplus Areas in Selected Countries of Western Europe*, 1960.

THE FULL EMPLOYMENT SURPLUS

Tax Rates, the Tax Take, Inflation, Demand, and the Level
of Government Expenditures

The Problem. The basic idea underlying the full employment surplus
argument is that the federal budget has been set up to yield a gigantic
surplus at full employment levels of production and income. As the
economy expands, too great a share of the increases in income are drained
out by the tax system. Hence we never attain that level of full employment
at which the surplus is so great. Another way of stating the idea is that
we have attempted to balance our budget at less than full employment—
say 5.5 or 6 percent unemployment. The result is that the tax drain is too
high ever to attain full employment which, if attained, would produce a
surplus of 10 billion dollars or more.[24] These figures reflect the budget
of the late 'fifties and early 'sixties. The exact level of unemployment and
surplus will obviously vary with each budget.

Demand, Tax Rates, and Inflation. A few other comments should be
made about the economic circumstances which are related to the full
employment surplus. (1) This situation has developed at a time when
there was not a vigorous underlying demand in the economy. Had we
experienced such a vigorous demand as (say) after World War II, or as is
developing in the area of consumer durables and other lines in Europe,
the situation might not have developed, or at least would not have been
as serious. Up until about 1957 several factors helped maintain demand
and/or offset the built-in surplus: the vigorous consumer and investment
demand in the earlier postwar period, the Korean War expenditures and
large deficits, the continued high rate of investment and residential
construction, the automobile sales of 1955, the Suez Canal crisis in 1956,
and (sporadically) government expenditures. (2) Present (1963) tax rates,
except for some changes relating mostly to investment and investment
income made in 1954,[25] were designed to combat the inflationary developments of the military buildup during the Korean conflict. Personal,

[24] The reader should also note that the average propensity to consume has been
somewhat lower than in 1948 (95 percent), 1949 (96 percent), and 1950 (94 percent).
A recent study of the full employment surplus and other problems discussed in
this text, but published as the present text was going to press, is that of M. E. Levy,
Fiscal Policy, Cycles and Growth, New York: National Industrial Conference Board,
1963.
[25] Rates for a married person with no dependents can be found in National Industrial Conference Board, *The Economic Almanac*, 1958, pp. 435–436, or in P. E.
Taylor, *The Economics of Public Finance*, 3d ed., New York: Macmillan, 1961, p.
365. The year in which the rates are enacted and the year in which they become
effective are sometimes confused.

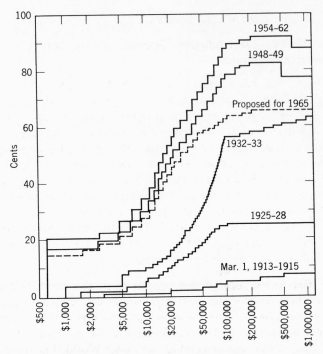

Figure 15-2. Taxation of one additional dollar of income as related to net income (logarithmic scale for net income brackets). The 1965 curve does not allow for proposed arbitrary increase in taxable income (in the amount of 5 percent of adjusted gross income) for persons itemizing deductions; this would be equivalent to an increase of more than 5 percent above scheduled tax rates as shown in the chart for 1965. The 1925–28 curve does not allow for limited earned income credit. *Source:* First National Bank of New York, *Monthly Economic Letter*, Feb. 1963, p. 18.

corporate, and other tax rates were raised at that time and have remained high since then. The tax system is set up to combat a high-demand, "high pressure" economy in which inflation is a serious threat.

An illustration of the marginal rates appears in Figure 15-2. The rates were raised to over 50 percent during World War I and then cut in 1922 and 1925 to a top rate of 25 percent on income over $100,000. During the depression of the 1930's they were raised to very high levels (63 percent over $1,000,000 in 1932 and 79 percent over $5,000,000 in 1936 for the top rate). In 1942 the top rate went to 88 percent over $200,000 and in 1944 to 94 percent over $200,000. In 1948 the rate structure was reduced to 16.6 to 82.13 percent over $400,000. During the Korean War the range was set at 22.2 to 92 percent over $400,000. The 1954 rate was put at 20 to 91 percent over $400,000. These rates are for the net income of a married couple filing jointly. The rates in effect at the end of World War II and for the Korean War are not shown in Figure 15-2, but they would fall very close to those for the 1954–1962 period.

(3) In addition, our income tax dips into the lower income ranges, and hits fairly hard the middle income people. By far the biggest portion of the revenue from the personal income tax comes from lower and middle income brackets rather than from upper income groups. This is simply because there are not very many people in the upper income groups.

(4) Further, inflation has raised all of our money incomes since 1950, which has placed some of us in higher income tax brackets. The amount of tax actually paid then has increased, for some absolutely and for others also percentage-wise. The impact of both inflation and the slightly higher tax rates in 1962 (as compared with 1950) on disposable income is shown in the example which follows. Since 1950 the consumer price index has gone up approximately 26 percent (from 83.8 as the 1950 average to 105.5 in August 1962). This means that a couple with a taxable income in 1950 of $5,000 and whose income increased in direct proportion to the price level increase (which would give them a 1962 income of about $6,300) paid a tax in 1962 of $1,306 rather than $896 as in 1950. This is a sizable increase. The couple's disposable income then increased by only $890 ($4,994 − 4,104) rather than $1,300 ($6,300 − 5,000), while their real income actually declined. In 1950 dollars their real income in that year was equal to their disposable income of $4,104 ($5,000 − $896). It is true that their dollar income rose but part of this they paid in extra taxes, and the purchasing power of their *total* remaining income was about 26 percent less. Their real income after taxes in 1962, expressed in 1950 dollars, was $3,963, whereas it was $4,104 in 1950 (we divide $4,994 by 126 to arrive at $3,963.) This is what we should expect, for their income has increased in proportion with the price level increase, but their taxes are greater. If we had selected a case in which the inflation-caused increase in income placed the individual in a higher tax bracket the percentage reduction in real income would have been even greater.[26]

(5) Also accounting for an increase in the annual tax take is the natural upgrading of and growth of the labor force, which means an increase

[26] Actually, the Korean War tax rates did not go into effect until 1951. The rate in 1950 in the first bracket was 17.4%, in 1951, 22.2%, and in 1954, 20%. In each case the first bracket was $0–4,000 and for a married couple filing jointly.

The example above is in terms of taxable income, which would no doubt also be lower in 1962 because of higher deductions due to the fact that inflation has also raised property taxes, etc. Also average family income rose more than the price level, as did wage rates. Finally, it is probably more than a coincidence that more and more people are itemizing deductions.

in the number of people working and paying taxes at high rates and in inflated dollars. Total income will move up but the tax structure remains the same. (6) Had there not been attempts to balance the budget with 5 and 6 percent unemployed, either taxes would have been reduced or expenditures increased. Obviously, expenditures have not increased enough to offset the tax drain. (7) Finally, a relatively tight money prevailed during the upswings of the middle and late 1950's.

Perhaps the more important aspects of the full employment surplus are that (a) tax rates based essentially on war and excess demand conditions have been retained, (b) the rate of increase in government expenditures has not been at a high enough rate to offset the preceding, and (c) there has not been a strong enough underlying demand in the economy, and (d) inflation has raised incomes and the amount of income drained out in taxes has increased. In other words, the progressive personal income tax structure is likely only a part of the problem.

Background. It is not easy to determine who is primarily responsible for pointing out the implications of the increasing size of the full employment surplus over a period of time. The Committee for Economic Development in 1947 did recommend that the federal tax rates and expenditures be set so as to produce a surplus at full employment, but this is different from recognizing the drag effect of the tax system on income and production. In early 1954 or 1953 Herbert Stein of the C.E.D. anticipated that economic growth would permit substantial tax reductions by about 1958.[27] There was some recognition of the surplus problem in some of the papers which were presented to the Joint Economic Committee in its investigation of *Federal Tax Policy for Economic Growth and Stability* in 1955.[28] This recognition appeared in the form of an assumption that as the economy grew more tax revenue would be available either for greater government projects or tax reduction. In 1960 David Lusher of the CEA made a study pointing out the great size of the full employment surplus. This study was presented to a seminar on the implications of national defense for private business at the University of California (Los Angeles)

[27] *Problems in Anti-Recession Policy*, New York: C.E.D, 1954, p. 100.

[28] See the papers of G. Colm, especially pp. 27–29, and W. Fellner, especially p. 212.

One of the more important studies in which this type of analysis was used is that of E. C. Brown, "Fiscal Policy in the Thirties: A Reappraisal," *Am. Ec. Rev.*, Dec. 1956, pp. 857–879. Brown's computations of the state of the budget show that, for the 'thirties, the budget would have been in balance or run a surplus. Hence his conclusion that this was not a case in which fiscal policy did not work, but rather one in which it was not really tried. Unfortunately, there is no evidence that any of the studies in this chapter drew upon Brown's important article.

on May 4–5, 1960.[29] In December of 1960, Charles Schultze also charged that the economy was and had been going down the road of "high-level creeping stagnation."[30] Schultze's statement was apparently the first published which used the concept of the "full employment surplus" and discussed it in some detail. The next extensive discussion of the problem was by the CEA before the Joint Economic Committee on March 6, 1961.[31] This was followed by the inclusion of a fairly comprehensive study by James Knowles of the Joint Economic Committee in the 1961 Annual Report of the committee.[32] Other statements on the problem by the CEA appeared in 1962.[33]

Data on the Tax "Take." Although studies of income taxes have not shown that the average tax rate has increased, it is true that the ratio of taxable income to personal income has risen from 0.355 in 1948 (it was .369 in 1950) to .434 in 1959.[34] The increase in taxable income was more than 50 percent of the increase in total personal income. The reason why the average rate has not increased even though the taxable income–personal income ratio has increased is probably because so much of the taxable income falls in the first bracket. As Lewis has pointed out, the couple with three children taking only the standard 10 percent deduction

[29] Published in slightly revised form in J. A. Stockfisch, ed., *Planning and Forecasting in the Defense Industries*, Belmont, Calif.: Wadsworth, 1962, Chapter 3.

[30] JEC, *Current Ec. Sit. & Short-Run Outl.*, H, pp. 114–122. Other economists recognized the tightness of monetary and fiscal policy in 1955–56 and 1959–60.

[31] JEC, *Jan. 1961 Ec. Rept. Pres.*, H, pp. 296, 330–336. See also pp. 572–573, and the discussion of H. Stein, pp. 209–226.

[32] See pp. 119–125. The staff of the JEC recognized the importance of lowering tax rates in its 1954 study of *Potential Economic Growth in the United States During the Next Decade*, pp. 10–11.

[33] *Jan 1962 Ec. Rept. Pres.*, pp. 77–82. It is noteworthy that the CEA did not make a point of the restrictive effects of the large surplus ($4.5 billion on the national income and product basis) in the fiscal 1963 budget in the hearings before the JEC. See JEC, *Jan 1962 Ec. Rept. Pres.*, H, esp. pp. 6, 9, 16, and 73–74. The full employment surplus was computed by the CEA to be about $9 or $10 billion. The surplus was used as a basis for action in 1961 but seems to have been slighted over in early 1962 apparently because of Kennedy's determination to present a balanced budget to the Congress. Did Dr. Heller and other CEA members really think that the Administration's goals would be realized during calendar 1962? Certainly many members of the Joint Economic Committee were doubtful. Does the CEA's statement exemplify the political role which it must assume at certain times? On the other hand, it was fully aware of the optimistic nature of its expectations, and the administration requested standby authority to cut taxes and increase public works spending in case they were not realized.

[34] See W. Lewis, Jr., *Federal Fiscal Policy in the Postwar Recessions*, Washington, D.C.: Brookings Institution, Dec., 1962, pp. 44, 294. The average tax rate declined by approximately one percent from 1948 to 1959. There may be causes other than those noted such as an enlargement of loopholes, greater itemizing of deductions, etc.

can have an income up to almost $7,800 and be taxed at first bracket rates.[35] There is then plenty of room for movement up the income scale before one falls into a higher bracket. This is particularly important since the lower incomes consist of a very large portion of all incomes.

Table 15-1, column 9, gives total government receipts as a percent of national income. Relative to the full employment surplus it is important

Table 15-1. **Federal Government Receipts on a National Income Basis, Receipts Receipts as a Percent of National Income**[a] **(Billions of Dollars or Percent)**

	1	2	3	4
Fiscal Year	Total Federal Receipts	Personal Tax and Nontax Receipts (Federal)	Corporate Profits Tax Accruals (Federal)	Indirect Business Tax and Nontax Accruals (Federal)
1948[a]	43.7	20.0	11.2	8.0
1953	69.9	31.5	19.8	11.0
1954	65.9	30.4	17.1	10.7
1955	67.0	29.9	18.4	10.4
1956	76.3	33.5	21.0	11.2
1957	80.9	36.7	20.4	12.1
1958	77.8	36.3	17.3	12.0
1959	85.9	38.7	21.1	12.3
1960	95.5	43.1	21.8	13.9
1961	95.5	44.0	19.8	13.6
1963[c]	104.0	47.6	21.8	14.5

[a] All data are on a national income and product basis; from *Business Statistics*, 1961; Jan. 1954, 1962, and 1963 *Ec. Rept. Pres.*; *National Income* (1954); *U.S. Income and Output* (1958); *Economic Indicators* (June 1963); and JEC, *State Ec. & Pol. Full Empl.*, H, p. 212. Column 9 and other data for 1948 are on a calendar year basis. Other data are on a fiscal year basis.

[b] State and local revenue from federal government excluded.

[c] Estimated first quarter.

to note that total government receipts as a percent of national income have increased from 27.8 percent in 1948 (fiscal year) to 35.2 percent in 1963 (first quarter estimated). This is indeed a significant increase. Total federal receipts as a percent of national income increased from 20.6 percent to 23.4 percent over this same period; and federal personal tax

[35] *Ibid.*, p. 45.

and nontax receipts as a percent of national income increased from 9.48 to 10.69 percent. It is also interesting to note that total government receipts were $101.4 billion in 1955, but by 1962 (preliminary) were up to $158.2 billion—a substantial increase of $56.8 billion.

Personal income rose from $405.4 billion in 1961(1) to $442.6 billion in 1962(3), or by $37.2 billion. Federal personal tax and nontax receipts,

and Personal Taxes as a Percent of National Income, and Total Government

5	6	7	8	9
Contributions for Social Insurance (Federal)	National Income—Fiscal Year	Total Federal Receipts as a Percent of NI	Federal Personal tax and Nontax Receipts as a Percent of NI	Total Gov't Receipts as a Percent of NI
4.6	212.6	20.6	9.48	27.8
7.6	302.0	23.2	10.43	32.2
7.7	301.5	21.8	10.08	30.5
8.3	313.2	21.4	9.54	30.3
10.5	342.0	22.3	9.80	32.1
11.7	360.7	22.2	10.17	28.9
12.3	363.8	21.4	10.00	31.4
13.8	386.9	22.2	10.00	32.0
16.7	408.7	23.4	10.56	34.0
18.1	418.4	22.8	10.52	36.4
19.8	445.2	23.4	10.69	35.2[c]

indirect business tax and nontax accruals, and social security taxes rose by $11 billion. This indicates a marginal tax rate of 29.6. The average rate for 1961(1)—these items divided by personal income for 1961(1)—was 18.3 percent, and for 1962(3) it was 17 percent. The average rate for these same items for 1948 was 15 percent, but for all of 1962 was up to 19.2 percent (calendar year basis), and for 1963(3) was 19.6 percent. If one adds to the federal items above corporate taxes, and to personal income corporate profits (and inventory valuation adjustment), he will secure a marginal tax rate of close to 45 percent. The high corporate tax rate is the more important factor in the high marginal tax bite.

If one calculates the amount by which total government receipts (tax and nontax receipts or accruals) increased as a percent of the increase in the GNP over this same period he comes out with a figure of 38.8 percent.

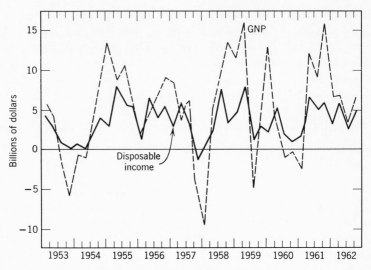

Figure 15-3. Quarterly changes in GNP and disposable income. *Source:* CEA, *Jan. 1963 Ec. Rept. Pres.*, p. 68.

(The average for 1962–63 was 28.7 percent.) If undistributed corporate profits are added to this the drainage per extra dollar of GNP will be about 47 percent.[36] This means that, after saving, each dollar increase in GNP will generate about 50 cents in additional consumer expenditure.[37] Finally, the CEA estimates that for each extra dollar of GNP 30 cents goes to extra federal receipts, 6 cents to state and local government revenues, and 10 cents to corporate retained earnings. Disposable income, then, is roughly 54 cents. This is a total figure from which transfers are not deducted. Calculations like these must be used with caution, and tempered with a consideration of the rate at which government expenditures are increasing relative to the rate at which taxes are draining income out the income stream.

Perhaps the easiest way to see how automatic stabilizers work in the economy (1) to keep disposable income from declining as much as GNP, and (2) to keep disposable income from rising as much as GNP, is in Figure 15-3. In a growth-oriented economy, then, the automatic stabilizers have become an "ambiguous blessing." The point of all this is that increases in disposable income lag behind increases in GNP by a substantial amount.

[36] For further discussion see the testimony of members of the CEA, JEC, *Jan. 1963 Ec. Rept. Pres.*, H, pp. 7, 14, 17.

[37] The breakdown is given in *ibid.*, pp. 17–18.

Professor Schultze's Statement

Schultze estimated the full employment surplus to be a whopping $11 to $12 billion. He pointed out in his statement that under these circumstances private income and therefore demand would not be high enough to purchase the output of the economy were full employment to be realized. Of course, if full employment is not reached, and its chances of being realized (under demand conditions existing then) with such a restrictive budget were very slight, then tax revenues will not rise as much and the large surplus implicit in the 1960 (and other) government budget, could not be reached. If, as we noted previously, we have a large and vigorous private demand, then it may be possible to realize both full employment and the surplus. But there have been no signs of such a vigorous demand in the American economy for some time. Under the conditions which characterized demand in the economy in these years the size of the surplus or deficit consistent with full employment will be relatively modest. It is possible, as implied in the previous statement, that we may even have to run a budget deficit to attain full employment if we experience somewhat lower private demand. Further, the tighter monetary policy is, the greater the budget deficit will have to be. Schultze took special pains to stress that his main concern was not to measure the impact of fiscal policy with the actual budget surplus but rather with the implicit full employment surplus. He castigated the Congress for failing "to look at the implications of budget policy in a full employment context" and vigorously recommended "that the annual and midyear budget estimates be accomplished by a full employment budget calculation."[38]

The CEA's January 1961 Analysis

The fact that the revenue collections of the federal government are highly sensitive to the level of the GNP is shown in Figure 15-4. As the size of the GNP increases, federal revenues increase rapidly. Although the CEA was careful to point out that this chart is based on certain assumptions, it does rather vividly point out the problem. If full employment had been realized in fiscal 1962, then the level of federal receipts would have been $92 billion. The expected and projected level of expenditures based on the Budget Message of January 16, 1961 was $81 billion dollars (shown on the horizontal line in Figure 15-4). Hence the budget surplus at full employment would have been $11 billion dollars. According to CEA computations, with the 1961 tax structure, an annual growth rate of $3\frac{1}{2}$ percent would increase federal revenues by $3 to $3\frac{1}{2}$ billion per

[38] Schultze, in JEC, *Current Ec. Sit. & Short-Run Outl.*, H, pp. 120–121.

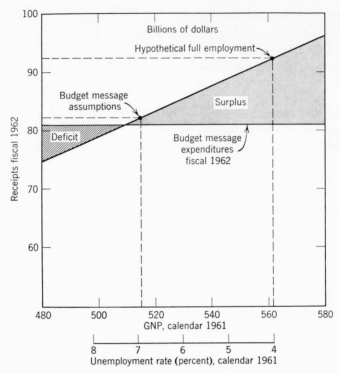

Figure 15-4. Federal budget receipts increase as the GNP rises. With a given level of expenditures a large surplus would result at full employment. (Revenue figures are estimated.) "Budget message" is that of Jan. 1961. *Source:* CEA in JEC, *Jan. 1962 Ec. Rept. Pres.*, H, p. 333.

year. We might ask the question: What would happen if budget expenditures were raised to $92 billion? At this point the budget would presumably be in balance and full employment would prevail.[39]

The Knowles Study[40]

To compute the level of federal revenue collections at full employment we must first compute an estimate of the size of the GNP at full employment. In other words, an estimate must be made of potential output. The procedure Knowles used is similar to that used in the computation of potential output in Chapter 11. In Table 15-2 Knowles presents data on potential output with full employment (defined as 4 percent unemployed), and estimates for federal budget expenditures and revenues. The difference

[39] JEC, *Jan. 1962 Ec. Rept. Pres.*, H, pp. 331–333.
[40] JEC, 1961 *Ann. Rept.*, pp. 119–125.

between the actual and potential levels are also given in actual dollar value and as a percentage of potential GNP. Actual federal expenditures are presented, as are the level of federal expenditures at potential GNP, and potential federal expenditures as a percentage of potential GNP. The same data are given for federal receipts. Finally, the actual surplus

Table 15-2. Illustrative Budgets at Potential Output, Selected Calendar Years, 1954 to 1965

(National Income and Product Account Basis, Billions of Dollars)

	1954	1957	1958	1960	1961	1962	1965
GNP–Current prices							
Actual	363.1	442.8	444.2	503.2			
Potential	369.2	458.9	484.8	541.1	568.0	595.0	690.0
Actual less potential	−6.1	−16.1	−40.6	−37.9			
Percent of potential	−1.7	−3.5	−8.3	−7.0			
Federal budget on GNP basis							
Expenditures							
Actual	69.6	79.7	87.9	92.3			
At potential	69.1	79.5	85.6	90.0	96.0	101.0	110–115
Percent of potential GNP	18.7	17.3	17.7	16.6	16.9	17.0	15.9–16.7
Receipts							
Actual	63.8	81.8	78.6	95.3[a]			
At potential	65.8	87.7	94.1	108.0	114.0	120.0	143–146
Percent of potential GNP	17.8	19.1	19.4	20.0	20.1	20.2	20.7–21.2
Surplus (+) or deficit (−)							
Actual	−5.8	+2.1	−9.3	+3.0			
At potential	−3.5	+8.2	+8.5	+18.0	+18.0	+19.0	28–36
Percent of potential	−0.9	1.8	1.8	3.3	3.2	3.2	4.1–5.2

Source: JEC, 1961 *Ann. Rept.*, p. 120.
[a] Preliminary.

or deficit and the surplus or deficit at potential GNP is given in dollar value, and the potential as a percent of potential GNP.

Knowles then notes certain characteristics of both federal revenues and expenditures. With respect to revenues (1) they swing up and down more than NI or GNP because the marginal tax rate on changes in incomes or profits is larger than the average rate. Under 1954 tax provisions "the average take out of the *cyclical* difference between actual and potential output has been about 36 percent." (Italics added.) In other words, this is the amount which would have been collected in taxes if full employment had prevailed measured as a percent of the difference between actual and potential output. (2) On the other hand, Knowles' figures show that "as the economy grows along the full employment or potential trend,

Federal revenues rise by about one-fourth or 25 percent of the rise in potential GNP." In other words, the increase in potential GNP from 1960 to 1961 was $26.9 billlion and the rise in potential taxes was $6.0 billion. The increase in potential taxes in this case was 22.3 percent. (3) Potential federal receipts as a percent of potential GNP have risen for each year shown, increasing from 17.8 to 20 percent in 1960. The tax take is less than that computed previously in this chapter, and less than more recent CEA estimates, but it is still a fairly significant increase.

Knowles has made certain assumptions about federal expenditures in the table. (1) Increases in defense occur solely for reasons of security and are not correlated here with changes in actual or potential GNP. (2) "Federal nondefense spending is separated conceptually into two parts: one . . . includes longer run programs not sensitive to cyclical fluctuations in output; the other includes the countercyclical items, especially unemployment compensation programs." (3) "Potential expenditures are estimated by adding to the defense and noncyclical nondefense items an estimate of the countercyclical items corrected to correspond to an unemployment rate of 4 percent." Knowles uses the 4 percent unemployment rate as the basis for the computation of his full employment potential output.

Based on the data given in the table, the deficit at potential GNP in 1954 was $3.5 billion or about 1 percent of potential GNP. However, by 1960 the full employment surplus was $18.0 billion, or about 3.3 percent of GNP. By 1965 the expected surplus would be in the neighborhood of a grand $28 to $36 billion dollars! This would be 4 to 5 percent of the GNP. Knowles estimates were before the 1962 investment tax credit and depreciation schedule revision. Even though his data rest on estimates, a large margin of error (say, even of as much as 25 or 30 percent) would not alter the fact that the tax structure is exerting a large drag on the economy. As noted previously, a lower rate of growth will lower the surplus. For the surplus to be as low as 1.5 percent of potential GNP in 1965 the growth rate in current prices could not exceed 3.2 percent per year (1954 to 1964), or expenditures would have to rise by about $18 billion to $133 billion in 1965. Knowles notes that "the growth rate of actual GNP in current prices has been about 5 to 6 percent per year since 1947 and has averaged about 4 to 5 percent per year since 1953." In other words, the 3.2 percent growth rate in current prices is not at all very high in terms of prices of the recent past. The average price increase since 1954 was 2.3 percent per year and Knowles assumed a 1 percent per year rise in the GNP deflator from 1960 to 1965.

In Figure 15-5 Knowles shows his estimates of the yield of the federal tax structure for a period of 16 years following its enactment. This is

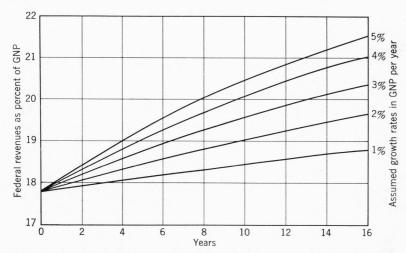

Figure 15-5. Hypothetical yield of the Federal Revenue structure, first 16 years from enactment, calculated as a percent of potential GNP, assuming selected growth rates of GNP per year. (National income and product accounts basis.)

calculated as a percent of GNP at various rates of growth for the economy ranging from 1 to 5 percent. It is apparent from the graph that the average effective rate of taxation rises as the economy grows. The only condition under which it would not rise would be if output remained constant (unless there was a significant change in income distribution). The faster the rate of growth, the more rapidly the average tax rate rises. After a period of time, for all rates of growth the rate of increase in the average tax rate declines. Year 0 on the chart roughly represents the 1954 tax structure. The basis for projecting the trends over a period of years is the data in Table 15-2. (In the table Knowles attempted to use revised budget estimates for 1961 and 1962. His estimate for 1965 assumes a substantial increase in expenditures but not in the ratio of federal expenditure to GNP.)

In its 1954 study of *Potential Economic Growth of the United States During the Next Decade*, the staff of the Joint Economic Committee assumed that reductions in the federal tax rates would occur over the 10-year projection period. The assumed tax reductions were spread out among all federal revenues except social security taxes. A balanced budget was assumed for the federal government for 1965, but the state and local governments were assumed to have a $2 billion deficit. It is significant to note that this study assumed that total federal, state, and local revenues would be reduced by about 15 to 20 percent (at potential GNP) below what they would have been under the 1954 tax law. Since state and local taxes have risen since that period, the assumed reduction in federal taxes would have to be somewhat greater than the assumed 15 to 20 percent. Further, the 1954 study did not take into account the fact that inflation increased the revenue take significantly.

By now it should be rather apparent that the steadily rising potential surplus exerts a serious drag on the economy. This surplus, by 1965, will be in the range of 4 to 5 percent of the GNP or $28 to $36 billion. This is a large and significant increase from about 3 percent in 1960, especially in view of the changing demand conditions. (The conservatively estimated surplus for 1970 would be $34.1 billion dollars according to David Lusher.)[41] While these represent estimates only, and are based on certain assumptions relative to federal expenditures, this large a potential surplus "almost certainly threatens an inseparable barrier to the achievement of full employment,"[42]

The 1962 *Annual Report* of the CEA

The January 1962 *Economic Report of the President* contained a separate report by the CEA in which they worked out a somewhat different diagram illustrating the full employment surplus.[43] This is shown in Figures 15-6

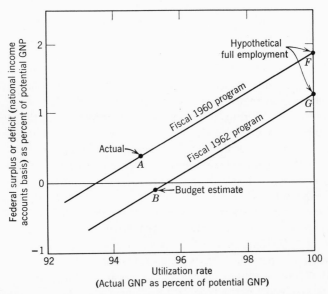

Figure 15-6. Effect of level of economic activity on federal surplus or deficit.

[41] Lusher, in J. A. Stockfisch, ed., *op. cit.*, p. 41.
[42] JEC, 1961 *Ann. Rept.*, 1961, p. 125. These data do not include the 1962 investment tax credit or depreciation schedule revision, or the 1964 tax reduction.
[43] See pp. 78–82 of the *Jan. 1962 Ec. Rept. Pres.*

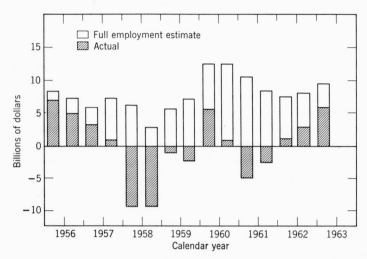

Figure 15-7. Federal surplus or deficit: actual and full employment estimate (national income accounts basis). The rates are seasonally adjusted and annual; the data are for half years. The actual surplus or deficit is estimated beginning with the second half of 1961.

and 15-7. Again, the CEA notes that federal tax revenues vary automatically with the level of economic activity, increasing as it increases and declining as it declines. (The same is true for some government expenditure programs such as unemployment compensation.) Given the level of expenditures, the level of budget surplus or deficit is dependent on the level of economic activity. In Figure 15-6 the federal surplus or deficit is given as a percent of potential GNP on the vertical axis. The fact that the deficit declines and the surplus increases as the economy grows is shown by the slanted lines. This figure gives estimates of the trend of deficit or surplus for the budget program for both fiscal 1960 and fiscal 1962. Point A shows the actual budget position for 1960—a surplus of $2.2 billion or 0.4 percent of potential GNP. At this point the GNP was 5 percent below its potential level, according to CEA calculations. At full employment the budget surplus would have been $10 billion. The anticipated line for fiscal 1962 was below that for 1960, yielding smaller surpluses or larger deficits at the same levels of economic activity.

In Figure 15-7 the full employment surplus is given for every 6 months from 1956 to 1963. The year that turns out to have had a very high surplus was 1960, a fact which played a part in the premature leveling of the recovery of 1959 and 1960. It is of further interest to note that the full employment surplus increased from about $3 billion in the second half of 1958 (expenditures were higher during the 1957–1958 recession) to about

$12½ billion in 1960. It is noteworthy also that the *actual* deficit-surplus trend made a big swing during the last 6 months of 1959 and the first 6 months of 1960—from about $−2.5 billion to about $+6 billion.[44] Again, the leveling off of the economy in 1960 was not retarded by this development. Further, there was the usual Eisenhower attempt to balance the budget at less than full employment. Of course, Kennedy's policies in fiscal 1962 and 1963 did not represent a great change from those of Eisenhower. (But there was a great difference in understanding of the problem, and a desire to eliminate it. President Kennedy's failure to do more was based on the political necessity of recognizing congressional, banker, business, and other attitudes toward deficits.)

The CEA has estimated that tax revenues at full employment are growing under tax laws in effect in early 1962, by about $6 billion per year. Of course, this rate will grow over time if tax rates remain constant. The full employment surplus will grow or decline according to changes in tax rates and expenditures.[45]

The Significance of the Surplus

In late 1962 the CEA estimated that the full employment surplus for fiscal 1963 would be $7 to $8 billion dollars on a national income and product basis.[46] The increasing acceptance of economists of the full employment surplus theory has several implications. (1) This concept is becoming more widely accepted as a more accurate measure of the impact of fiscal policy on the economy. (2) A reevaluation of the lag of federal expenditures behind revenues at full employment (or, what is the same thing, of the lead of revenues ahead of expenditures) needs to be done. (3) A new estimate of the needed anti-inflationary surplus at full employment in order. (4) A reconsideration of the rather convincing argument that a tax reduction will bring a higher actual surplus than present tax rates which prevent any surplus from being realized, or result in a lower surplus. In other words, the "price" of the tax cut, contrary to usual expectations, is probably (an eventual) positive surplus. (5) A reevaluation of the "need for greater saving" argument which comes from the ardent investment advocates. (6) A recognition of the fact that there is no theoretical or actual reason why total demand may not drag behind total supply and hence retard growth. Some of us have forgotten that

[44] Gerhard Colm, in 1955, stated that a tax reduction of $5 to $6 billion dollars was necessary for 1960. See JEC, *Fed. Tax Pol.*, P, pp. 27–29.

[45] The criticisms of estimates such as these are similar to those of potential output noted in Chapter 11. See also the statement of H. Wallich in JEC, *Jan. 1962 Ec. Rept. Pres.* H, pp. 620–626.

Another analysis of the full employment surplus is that of Daniel Hamburg, "Fiscal Policy and Stagnation since 1957," *Southern Ec. J.*, Jan 1963, pp. 211–217.

[46] JEC, *State Ec. & Pol. Full Empl.*, H, p. 115.

a necessary balance between consumption and investment (or between total supply and total demand) is necessary for balanced growth. (See Chapter 10.)[46a]

THE INADEQUATE SAVING-INVESTMENT THESIS

The Issues and the Argument

If one were to read the hearings of the Joint Economic Committee during the late 'fifties and early 'sixties he could easily become confused over what has been the real cause of the slowdown in our rate of growth. Various groups have come forward with their pet theories. For the NAM, the Chamber of Commerce, and similar organizations, and most leaders in the Eisenhower Administration, the problem has been a lack of sufficient saving and investment, and structural transformation. For the AFL-CIO and Leon Keyserling's Conference for Economic Progress it has been inadequate demand generally and insufficient consumption specifically. Chairman Martin of the Federal Reserve has generally sided with the first group. He has claimed that saving has been too low, investment too low, and corporate taxes too high, and he has criticized the inadequate demand group and defended (but without any evidence) the structural transformation thesis. The Kennedy Administration has worked to raise both demand and investment.

We have already noted that American policy-makers have come under considerable fire from many Europeans and from various domestic groups for running so many deficits in the federal budget during the last decade, and also that most of the European governments have run more deficits than we have. At any rate, the deficits that we have run and the rate of saving have been combined in one argument as an explanation for our low rate of economic growth. In fact, the presentation has taken the form of an overconsumption-underinvestment argument. We shall review one of these presentations, that has received considerable attention and publicity and attempt to evaluate it in this section.

An article appeared in late August of 1962,[47] at a time when many economists and politicians (from both parties) were arguing for a tax cut

[46a] On Feb. 26, 1964 the tax reduction bill was passed. The rate, for heads of households, was lowered to 16 percent and the marginal rate on income over $200,000 was lowered to 77 percent. On Jan. 1, 1965, the tax rates are to fall to 14 percent on income up to $1000, and to 70 percent on income in excess of $180,000. A minimum standard deduction was also allowed and the corporate income tax was reduced.

It has been estimated that *net* tax collections from individuals will decline by $6.5 billion.

[47] Mathew J. Kust, "Deficits and Economic Growth," *The New Republic*, August 27, 1962.

to counteract the declining growth rate, and at a time when President Kennedy was considering whether or not he would ask Congress to cut taxes, which questioned the use of deficits as a vehicle for the realization of a higher rate of growth in the United States. The author, M. J. Kust, argued that deficits of European countries have yielded high rates of growth because there is more government ownership of industry there and that consequently government deficits have resulted in investment in productive facilities. In the United States, however, our deficits result in greater consumption since a large proportion of our federal expenditures are for military purposes. Kust further maintained that one of our problems is that too great a percentage of our national income goes into wages and salaries, which further depresses economic growth since wages and salaries are largely consumed. Saving and therefore investment are reduced. He was also critical of our higher corporate and personal income tax rates. And last, he cited Simon Kuznets' study on capital formation, implicitly condemning the trend in our economy toward reduced saving and investment and greater consumption. He concluded with a restatement of his thesis that "perhaps" our economic troubles are due more to overconsumption than to underconsumption. It should be noted that Chairman Martin of the Federal Reserve in the fall of 1962 took up these arguments also.[48]

We have already discussed the problem of striking a reasonable balance between the growth of total demand and total supply and between consumption and investment. We have also noted that increased saving at high levels of unemployment may further reduce demand. We shall, therefore, limit our comments on this form of the underinvestment-overconsumption argument to a brief statement.

Active vs. Passive Deficits, and Productive vs. American Deficits

The first question is: To what extent were the respective European and American deficits planned to combat economic declines, and to what extent were they the result of recessions? In other words, to what extent were the respective deficits "active" or "passive"? In Table 14-4 we saw that the United States incurred deficits in 1952 ($6 billion), 1953 ($7.2 billion), 1954 ($1.1 billion), 1955 ($.7 billion) 1958 ($7.3 billion), and 1959 ($8.0 billion). It is clear that the major cause of these deficits has been recessions. When we have a recession in our economy our tax collections automatically drop, thereby creating a deficit. The impact of this deficit by default is different from that of a deliberately planned deficit aimed at offsetting the decline before the economy drops to a low level, or one

---

[48] In addition to the many references cited previously, see the series of articles on Chairman Martin in *The Christian Science Monitor*, Sept. 1962, Western edition.

imposed on an economy that is experiencing a rapid rate of growth. If, at the first definite signs of a recession, a deficit is planned, the evidence indicates that the size of this deficit will be much less than that which is incurred by default. Consequently, the longer we wait to take action to combat an ensuing recession the larger the deficit required to bring about recovery. The seriousness of the situation is further aggravated by the fact that if the vehicle of lower taxes is used to bring recovery the larger the tax cut will have to be for full employment to be attained and the larger the tax increase will have to be when full employment is reached.

On the other hand, the growth rate in Germany has been very steep and continuous, and for France, although not so steep, certainly respectable. There has been absolutely no leveling off of the growth rate in either country during the period covered in this analysis. It is not entirely clear which European deficits were incurred to stimulate their economies and which deficits were imposed on an economy with a growth rate that was already reasonably high. But these nations have been known to take antideflationary action *before* the decline became serious, and to rely on greater use of discretionary action rather than to place primary reliance on automatic stabilizers as we have done so often. When their rate of advance merely hesitated they acted. The motivations for, and the causes and timing of these "active" deficits were no doubt vastly different from our recession-caused deficits by default.[49] Their deficits were deliberate and at times undertaken for specific antirecession purposes. Under these circumstances we would naturally expect that their deficits, brought about primarily for different reasons and used for different purposes, would not have the same results. It should be fairly clear why our "passive" deficits have given our economy less "boost."

It has been argued that part of the deficits of European countries goes into nationalized industries (and capital formation) and is therefore more productive; and that this gives their budgets a bias toward a deficit compared with the United States' budget. This is a complicated issue, but it can be asked if the loans to nationalized industries were substituted for borrowing from private sources. If the answer is yes, then there was no net increase in increase in investment; if not, then additional investment occurred. On the other hand, if the government loans were a substitute for private loans, why was such subsidization necessary? A. H. Gantt, who analyzed the foreign budgets, deducted net loans to nationalized industries in France and the United Kingdom. (See Table 14-4 and the accompanying text.) France still had a deficit in each year, but the United Kingdom in only 3 of 11 years (and ended up with a cumulative

---

[49] Since this was written further justification for the statements was provided from a short analysis by Walter W. Heller, See JEC, *Jan. 1963 Ec. Rept. Pres.*, H, p. 42.

surplus), and replaced the United States as the leader in smallest deficits for the period. Also, the United Kindom has not experienced as high a growth rate as the other European countries; it has been closer to that of the United States. The result of deducting net loans to nationalized industries is to support the thesis that deficits still occurred, that they were active, and that they helped raise the growth rate. Even if the deficits had been caused by loans to nationalized industries, we should still expect that they would have an expansionary impact aside from the extent to which they increase capacity. They were, in other words, *active* deficits.

These considerations lead to several questions. Should the United States also subsidize more industry to raise its level of capital formation, and if we did would this type of deficit be more acceptable to the American public? Is it really possible to determine the total impact of deficits or government expenditures on capital formation? There is no reason to assume, as Kust's argument does, that *deliberate* deficits incurred by either government consumption or investment have substantially different expansionary influences. Further, even if foreign deficits do raise the level of capital formation the fact is irrelevant to our economy, in which there has been excess capacity. What of the impact on capital formation of federally sponsored research in the United States as compared with both government-sponsored research and subsidization of nationalized industry abroad? Or of the productivity-increasing expenditures of all levels of government, or of the impact of other government expenditures on capital formation? Finally, and most important, an "active" deficit which raises the level of demand by raising consumption alone could surely induce a higher level both of income and of capital formation. This is the most important point—not overconsumption, productive deficits, high wages, or undersaving as Kust would have us believe. Although some multiplier differences between various types of government expenditure may be found, there is no question of the potency of a deficit which results from either a tax cut or expenditure increase. So many questions may be asked about the so-called more productive European deficits, and the evidence contradicts the point anyway, that the burden of proof of the argument that active deficits will not work in the United States falls on Kust's and Martin's shoulders.

Business and Government Sector Deficits and Credit Expansion

All students of economics are aware of the role of an increasing supply of credit in a growing economy.[50] An important technique by which

---

[50] On public credit as the basis for the whole credit structure of the economy, see W. F. Stettner, "Carl Dietzel, Public Expenditures and the Public Debt," in *Income, Employment, and Public Policy: Essays in Honor of Alvin H. Hansen*, New York: Norton, 1948, pp. 276–99 esp. 282ff.

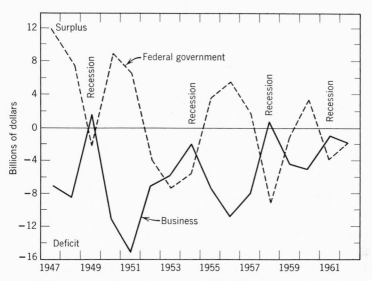

Figure 15-8. Federal Budget and business capital account: Surpluses or deficits. Federal government: surplus (+) or deficit (−) on national income accounts basis. Business: excess of gross retained earnings (excluding depreciation on nonfarm residential property) over gross private domestic investment (excluding residential construction), or excess of GPDI over gross retained earnings (−). *Source: Jan. 1963 Ec. Rept. Pres.*, p. 76.

money is created is the simultaneous creation of debt. Debt creation, money creation, and economic growth are related. Although the federal debt and monetary policy will be discussed in some detail in later chapters, it is important to point out the apparent relation between surpluses and deficits of the federal government on the one hand and surpluses and deficits of the business sector on the other. This is done in Figure 15-8.

Since in national income accounting a dollar spent is a dollar received, when one sector's spending exceeds its income another sector must be receiving more than it has spent. The deficit of the former will equal the surplus of the latter.[51] It has been normal for the business and federal government sectors *combined* to show a deficit which offsets the total surplus of other sectors. But the surpluses and deficits of these two sectors are highly dependent on the relative level of economic activity. As Figure 15-8 shows, the deficits and surpluses of the business and federal government sectors are inversely related to each other, at least for 12 of the 15 years shown. During years of recession or slow growth the business sector shows surpluses or very small deficits. In years of greater prosperity the

[51] A good explanation of these relationships among all sectors can be found in *Jan. 1963 Ec. Rept. Pres.*, pp. 74–77.

business sector has very large deficits, supported by borrowing the surpluses of other sectors in the capital markets. It is to be expected that in recession years incentives to invest are less and less borrowing takes place.[52]

As we would expect from the operation of the automatic stabilizers, the federal government experiences deficits during depressed years and surpluses during more prosperous years. (There has been some influence here from discretionary policies also.) Federal surpluses have tended to occur when the unemployment rate averaged (yearly) about $5\frac{1}{2}$ percent (except for 1952 and 1953, because of the high level of Korean War expenditures, and 1960, when expenditures were purposely cut and a surplus aggravated the already high unemployment rate and retarded the recovery from the 1957–1958 recession).

The CEA has also noted that during years when the unemployment rate exceeded $5\frac{1}{2}$ percent there was an average deficit in the business sector of less than \$2 billion, and an average deficit of \$9 billion when unemployment was less than $5\frac{1}{2}$ percent. (These are not static numerical examples; they rather illustrate the relations noted above.) Debt, deficits, and surpluses then have an important bearing on the level of economic activity. Business sector deficits have an expansionary impact, business sector surpluses (or smaller deficits) a contractionary impact, federal surpluses a contractionary influence, and federal deficits an expansionary impact.[53] The federal deficits, however, have tended to be passive (resulting from lower economic activity). It should be quite apparent now that federal deficits (active rather than passive deficits) superimposed on sizable business deficits, would have a substantial expansionary effect.

Growth Rates, Taxes, Wages, and Investment

Kust points out that West Germany and France devote a larger proportion of their GNP's to investment in new machinery and equipment. We have previously asked, is it not a bit unfair to compare our growth rate with that of Western Europe, particularly Western Germany? Because of the devastation caused by World War II Germany has had to devote more of its available resources to building up its industrial plant. To a considerable extent, then, Western Europe has been "catching up" with us. This factor also helps explain why a smaller proportion of the national

---

[52] Like the expectation of profit, the availability of credit is an important factor. High levels of business borrowing then raise income, which raises saving (surpluses) in other sectors (as well as business). As income increases so does the federal surplus (or the federal deficit declines) because tax revenue increases. The discussion in the text is essentially in *ex post* terms.

[53] Subject, naturally, to the qualifications noted at the end of Chapter 8.

income of Western Europe has gone to wages and salaries. Controls on wages and salaries were certainly helpful in restraining consumption when these countries were building up their supplies of capital goods, but this trend will surely reverse itself. In addition, many of these countries are now experiencing a great increase in the demand for consumer durables— automobiles, home appliances, etc. For these two reasons there is, then, a vigorous demand in Western Europe, which is not true of the United States. There is no doubt that our postwar backlog of demand for both consumer and investment durable goods has been satisfied.

As for Kust's comments on our personal and corporate income tax rates, this is a terribly complicated problem. But again some interesting questions may be raised. Taxes to restrain consumption and encourage investment in European countries have without doubt played an important role in policies aimed at increasing their stocks of capital. But it has been reported that some countries are abandoning their special tax concessions, and no less an economist than Richard Musgrave has expressed the feeling that they "have been handled in a way which made them very wasteful and inequitable, and gave rise to wealth and income distribution effects which are undesirable."[54] Referring to faster depreciation Paul Samuelson has said: "Let us face it, they are deliberate bribes to coax out faster growth" and "*cannot* be justified as a return to fair recognition of true economic depreciation (inclusive of obsolescence) needed to measure true *money income*."[55]

Few economists disagree with proposals for tax reform but the elimination of existing tax concessions accompanied by overall tax reduction is just as important as the addition of further tax concessions. Most economists, for example, favor reduction of the high personal income tax rates, but for Kust to say that "an income tax . . . provides no incentive for personal savings" is a rather powerful statement which neglects the problem of effective rates, a large body of contrary evidence, income as the main determinant of saving, and other social as well as economic goals of taxation in our society. To be sure, additional sales taxes may be necessary in order to provide additional social services but the tone of the article under discussion makes one wonder how far the author is willing to go in this direction. On this same topic it may be significant to point out that the total tax burden as a percent of GNP is in West Germany 34, France 33, Austria 33, Finland 32, Norway 31, Luxembourg 30, Sweden 29, Italy 29, Netherlands 29, Britian 28, and the United States 26.[56]

[54] JEC, *Jan. 1962 Ec. Rept. Pres.*, H, p. 499.
[55] Am. Bankers Assoc., *A Symposium on Economic Growth*, New York, 1963. p. 91.
[56] JEC, *Jan. 1963 Ec. Rept. Pres.*, H, p. 57.

The author cites Simon Kuznets' study on capital in the United States as evidence that we have had undersaving and overconsumption in our economy. We have already noted that the Kuznets study and the discussion of the role of capital in economic growth in recent years has led to an exaggerated emphasis on budget surpluses and special incentives to saving and investment. Economists most certainly do point out that saving and investment are important, indeed necessary, for economic growth. We also pointed out, however, that there is a need for a balanced growth of both consumption and investment in the economy, and over-emphasis on either one can be self-defeating. With the excess capacity that has characterized our economy in recent years one may well question whether a higher saving-investment ratio is the proper short-run goal. Under different circumstances, full employment and capacity production for example, the encouragement of saving and investment is an appropriate goal to pursue in order to raise the growth rate. Finally, the fact that gross corporate saving exceeded corporate investment in both 1961 and 1962 does not support the inadequate saving thesis.[57]

Furthermore, in addition to the fact that more mature economies may need to allocate a smaller proportion of their GNP to investment and the capital-saving nature of new capital, one's interpretation of Kuznets' figures varies with the measure of capital formation one uses. Raymond M. Goldsmith has shown that if one includes consumer durables in un-deflated values in his definition of capital we have had only a slight decline in the ratio of net capital formation to national product from 1888 to 1950. (See Table 10-4.) Perhaps even more significant is Kuznets' own conclusion that the simple assumed high correlation between saving and growth and capital formation and the rate of growth are not substantiated in the long-term records.[58] Goldsmith's investigations in industrial countries support Kuznets' conclusions. The relationship is neither simple nor consistent. (This does not mean that it does not exist, however.)

One may also ask the question of whether we need as much capital investment today as we did in the past, as discussed in Chapter 10. The fact that our rate of growth of output per head in recent years has been as high as when our capital formation ratio was higher certainly indicates a change in our aggregate production function. Because of vast tech-nological improvements it simply takes less capital to produce the same amount or more goods today. In recent years our increases in output apparently have been caused not by mere increases in labor and capital; rather, they have been primarily the result of technical progress. We can,

[57] *Jan. 1963 Ec. Rept. Pres.*, p. 34.
[58] S. Kuznets, *Economic Development and Cultural Change*, July 1961, pp. 55–56.

therefore, have the same rate of economic growth with a smaller invest-ment-output ratio. We should not leave this discussion without pointing out that both theoretical and empirical considerations indicate that the best policy for raising our level of saving and investment may well be to reduce unemployment and boost income to higher levels. (The current emphasis on higher interest as an incentive to higher saving is also mis-guided. Furthermore, higher interest rates have a relative restraining effect on investment.)[59] One may also question the assumption that depreciation allowances have been grossly inadequate and that our industrial plant is "old and obsolete." There is no doubt room for improvement here, but even the comparisons of the age of our machinery with that of West Germany and England do not prove by a long shot that we are in such bad straights, especially when one considers the rapid capital growth and catch up in the European countries.

The Profit Squeeze

Those who stress the inadequate saving–inadequate investment argu-ment are often dismayed by statistics which show the profit squeeze—that profits after taxes per dollar of sales, or that annual rates of profit after taxes on stockholders' equity have declined during the 1950's. The con-tention is that lower rates of return impede investment and restrain more rapid growth in the economy, and that lower taxes on investment are called for.

The first part of the previous sentence is certainly true in a free enterprise economy, but the second part does not automatically follow for three reasons. In the first place, profit rates are highly correlated with capacity utilization, as shown in Figure 15-9.[60] In the second place, corporate profit rates have been artificially reduced by higher depreciation allow-ances which have increased rather than reduced cash flow. In the third place, to compare profit rates of more recent years with those of the immediate postwar years, when they were at an all-time high for the past 60-year period because of the very high rate of demand and of inventory profits (with inflation profits are raised by a higher value of inventories), and to understate the cost of capital which was being consumed is to exaggerate profit figures for those years. (See Table 15-3.) Profit rates are a matter of concern in a free enterprise economy, but their trend should also be kept in the proper perspective from the standpoint of public policy.

There is no question that corporate profits in the late 'fifties and early 'sixties showed a downward trend in terms of sales and stockholders'

---

[59] The necessity to keep interest rates higher to restrain an outflow of gold is another issue.

[60] *Jan. 1962 Ec. Rept. Pres.*, p. 55.

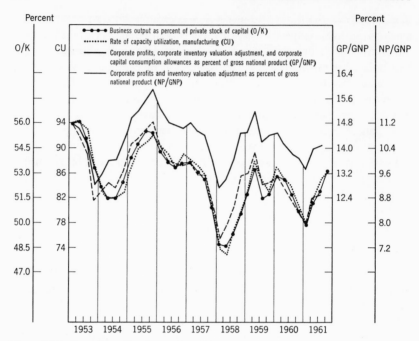

Figure 15-9. Capacity utilization and profits. *Source: Jan. 1962 Ec. Rept. Pres.*, p. 55; CEA (based on data of Department of Commerce and Board of Governors of the Federal Reserve System).

equity. In addition to the three points noted in the last paragraph, there is some evidence of a return to more normal relationships during the late 'fifties and early 'sixties.[61] A presentation of profit rates without consideration of these factors is sterile and very misleading. The factors have led some analysts to use the concept of "cash earnings" in preference to pure profit rate. Cash earnings are equal to corporate profits after tax plus depreciation charges. In column 3 of Table 15-4 we can see the very large increase in depreciation allowances resulting from (a) more liberal depreciation policies of the Korean War and the Revenue Act of 1954 (the 1962 revision of depreciation schedules will raise this more), and (b) the continuing relatively high level of investment (for cost cutting and modernization as well as expansion), and (c) increases in the price of capital goods. Because of the increase in cash earnings the financial strength and liquidity of corporations has been substantially improved, and the financing of purchases of new capital assets has been made less

[61] Based on a study by the First National Bank of New York on the rate of return on net worth, for leading manufacturing corporations, for the years 1925–1961 as reprinted in *Jan. 1962 Ec. Rept. Pres.*, p. 332.

Table 15-3. Corporate Profits in Relation to Depreciation Accruals and Capital Outlays, 1946–1962
(In Billions of Dollars)

Year	1 Corporate Profits after Taxes	2 Depreciation and Amortization Allowances	3 Cash Earnings[a]	4 Plant and Equipment Outlays	5 Net Cash Earnings[b]	6 Corporate Dividends	7 Corporate Saving[c]	8 Plant and Equipment Outlays plus Inventory
1946	$13.4	$4.2	$17.6	$12.5	$5.1	$5.8	$11.4	$23.7
1947	18.2	5.2	23.4	17.0	6.4	6.5	16.6	24.1
1948	20.5	6.2	26.7	18.8	7.9	7.2	18.6	23.0
1949	16.0	7.1	23.1	16.3	6.8	7.5	14.7	12.7[d]
1950	22.8	7.8	30.6	16.9	13.7	9.2	20.2	26.7
1951	19.7	9.0	28.7	21.6	7.1	9.0	19.0	31.4
1952	17.2	10.4	27.6	22.4	5.2	9.0	17.8	23.7
1953	18.1	11.8	29.9	23.9	6.0	9.2	19.7	24.7
1954	16.8	13.5	30.3	22.4	7.9	9.8	19.8	20.8[d]
1955	23.0	15.7	38.7	24.2	14.5	11.2	26.6	30.9
1956	23.5	17.3	40.8	29.9	10.9	12.1	27.8	37.5
1957	22.3	19.1	41.4	32.7	8.7	12.6	28.0	34.8
1958	18.8	20.3	39.1	26.4	12.7	12.4	26.0	24.0[d]
1959	24.5	21.6	46.1	27.7	18.4	13.7	31.1	34.3
1960	23.0	23.1	46.1	30.8	15.3	14.4	30.4	33.4
1961	23.3	24.8	48.1	29.6	18.5	15.0	32.1	30.4
1962	26.0	26.2	52.2	32.3	19.9	15.9	35.3	34.8

Sources: J. H. Langum, JEC, State Ec. & Pol. Full Empl., H, pp. 331–339; Jan. 1956 Ec. Rept. Pres., p. 227; Jan. 1963 Ec. Rept. Pres., pp. 246, 250.

[a] Cash earnings equal reported earnings plus depreciation charges, or the sum of columns 1 and 2.
[b] Net cash earnings are cash earnings less plant and equipment outlays.
[c] Depreciation and amortization allowances plus retained profits and depletion allowances.
[d] Inventories were negative.

costly (ignoring opportunity costs) and much easier. The increase in cash earnings from $39.1 billion in 1958 to $48.1 billion in 1961 is extremely high. The same can be said for "net cash earnings" (cash earnings less plant and equipment outlays, in column 5). Operation at a higher rate of capacity should raise these figures considerably.[62]

These comments are further supported by other data. If the ratio of depreciation charges to corporate sales (instead of corporate profits after taxes to sales) is examined, it will be found that the ratio rose from 1.77 percent in 1947–1951, to 2.46 percent in 1952–1956, and to 3.01 percent in 1957–1961. Langrum has pointed out that the increase in the ratio is equivalent to all the decline in the ratio of corporate profits after taxes to total corporate sales during the last 10 years of this period. The ratio of cash earnings to corporate sales averaged 6.66 percent in 1946–1951, 6 percent in 1952–1956, and 6.11 percent in 1957–1961. Of further interest is the correlation one will find between cash earnings and business capital outlays.[63] The point of all this is that the long-term decline in corporate profit rates during the postwar period only tells part of the story and therefore is not as significant as many in the business and banking communities have claimed.

A comparison of the relation between gross corporate saving (retained earnings and depreciation allowances essentially) and corporate expenditures on plant and equipment and inventory can be found in columns 7 and 8 of Table 15-3. The reader should carefully note that these data are for corporations, not all business firms.

Summary and Conclusion

If, those who argue the inadequate saving thesis concentrated on the restrictive nature of a high surplus federal budget, they would present a more acceptable argument for tax reduction. Given the lack of vigorous underlying demand in the economy, a generally restrictive monetary policy, and the general sopping up of the excess liquidity which characterized the postwar economy, attempts to balance the budget at 6 percent unemployment results in neither a balanced budget nor full employment. As we have noted, our attempts to balance the budget at such high levels of unemployment would produce huge and repressive budget surpluses at full employment levels. Under these conditions a surplus of this size

[62] Interesting questions are: To what extent did corporations invest in cost-cutting equipment purchases because they had the funds to do so under conditions of loss than optimum capacity operation? To what extent would the expenditures have been an increase to capacity had demand been higher? And to what extent could this have been done without having much impact on productivity trends?

[63] Ibid., p. 338, and the tables on pp. 332–333.

would tend to choke off the recovery before an acceptable level of unemployment was reached. The contentions of this group that active deficits brought about by increased government expenditures or a tax reduction are ineffective finds no support in theory or in experience; that greater saving will automatically be converted into capital is contradicted by what we know about the determinants of saving (as a function of the level of income) and the existence of excess capacity; that higher interest will significantly raise the level of saving is misguided and would reduce the level of demand and further reduce the growth rate under conditions of the last decade; that the squeeze on corporate profits is to blame for our troubles ignores cash flow and the high correlation between profits and the rate of capacity utilization. In addition, they may be seriously ignoring important changes in our production function and may, therefore, be placing too much emphasis on the role of capital in economic growth.

DEPRESSED ECONOMIC AREAS

For some time now the Department of Labor has periodically published a list of "areas of substantial labor surplus." Persistent unemployment in major labor market areas has tended to be concentrated particularly in Pennsylvania and Massachusetts, although Indiana, Michigan, New Jersey, North Carolina, Rhode Island, and West Virginia have appeared on the list. Other states have often appeared on the list, but generally under the category of smaller rather than major labor market areas. When recessions have occurred, these areas have experienced substantially higher levels of unemployment. During recovery periods they experience much smaller gains in employment. In 1959 (a year of recovery) they experienced unemployment rates 50 percent or more above the national average. Further, workers in these areas tend to exhaust their unemployment benefits.

The economies of these areas have been heavily dependent on manufacturing, or upon one or two nonmanufacturing industries (such as railroads or coal). In 1959, of the seventeen major labor market areas classed as labor surplus areas, twelve were single-industry towns. Further, the absolute level of employment in these areas has been declining, and they have had a fairly high ratio of skilled and semiskilled workers.[64]

The commodities involved in the 1959 study were transportation equipment, primary metals (mainly steel works and rolling mills), and machinery (electrical and nonelectrical). Part of the unemployment in certain geographical areas has been due to (1) increased productivity (it is

[64] I. Lubin, "Reducing Unemployment in Depressed Areas," *Am. Ec. Rev.*, May, 1960, pp. 162–163.

estimated that the automobile industry offered 130,000 less jobs in Detroit than it did a decade ago), (2) technological change and the subsequent decline of certain industries, (3) the switch in defense production from tanks, etc., to missiles, (4) firm decentralization (such as in automobile production), and (5) the relocation of all of or substantial segments of certain industries (as in textiles).[65] Technological change has eliminated the need for the big railroad repair yards (Altoona, Pennsylvania has been a substantial surplus labor area for about 10 years); industrial relocation has moved the textile mills from the Northeast to the South; and the shift from coal to oil has left Johnstown, Scranton, Wilkes-Barre, and Hazelton, Pennsylvania in a terribly depressed state.

This situation confronts one with the problem of whether he should attempt to move people to jobs or jobs to people. Of course, it is impossible to move people to jobs if a high level of employment does not exist in the economy generally. Although fiscal and monetary policies are limited in what they can do to relieve unemployment of this type, the realization and maintenance of full employment is certainly a prerequisite. We cannot assume that all the people in these areas are characterized by obsolete skills. Even in the case of farm laborers, many of whose skills are quite limited, these people have migrated from the farms at a rather rapid pace when employment opportunities existed elsewhere. Also, our experience has shown that depressed areas adjacent to other more prosperous areas have more easily reduced their unemployment rates.

Of course, the mobility of people in depressed areas is retarded by family attachments, costs of moving, home ownership (and big losses when houses are sold), ignorance of employment opportunities in other geographical areas, skills that are not easily adapted to other occupations, and age. The person over forty-five has a particularly difficult time securing a new position.

On the other hand, it is difficult to bring industry to these people because of the market—rather than resource—orientation of so much of our industry. Furthermore, the competition to bring in new industry is extremely keen among both states and communities. Last, those states and communities which have gone all out to bring in new industry have not been very successful. The result is that probably both approaches will have to be tried—that is, bringing people to jobs and jobs to people.

Frankly, there are no easy solutions to this problem. High on the list of policies advocated by those who have studied depressed areas is high-quality education that will turn out well-educated and well-trained

[65] *Ibid.*, pp. 163–165.

graduates whose aspirations will motivate them to seek out good employment and income opportunities.[66] Many feel that these same educational opportunities should be extended to the low income sections of the urban areas, and to the several minority groups, especially Negroes. Other programs include retraining, loans and grants for various public projects and plants for use by private firms, and technical assistance (all of which are included in the Area Redevelopment Act of 1961)[67] for both rural and urban areas. Needless to say, unemployment of this type involves a terribly high cost to the nation in the form of unrealized production. Finally, we should not feel totally pessimistic about this problem; rather we should recognize that since World War II our labor force has displayed a high degree of mobility. The reduction in the number of people living on farms is an important case in point.[68]

Although the automation problem has been related to that of depressed areas, it is primarily a separate problem. Total employment in manufacturing had declined by 1.2 million, and employment in the service industries increased by over 5 million between 1953 and 1961. Within the service industries, transportation and public utilities were down by 400,000; wholesale and retail trade up 1.2 million; finance, insurance, and real estate up by 600,000; service and miscellaneous up by 1.6 million, and government up by 2.2 million. Within the service industries,

[66] H. S. Perloff, "Lagging Sectors and Regions of the American Economy," *Am. Ec. Rev.*, May 1960, p. 229. In the same issue see also Eleanor M. Snyder, "Low Income in Urban Areas," pp. 243–250; F. J. Welch, "The Evolving Low-Income Problems in Agriculture," pp. 231–242; and the comments of the panelists.

[67] For a summary of the program see the statement of Luther H. Hodges, Secretary of Commerce, JEC, *Jan. 1962 Ec. Rept. Pres.*, H, pp. 428–430.

[68] An appreciation of the problem of depressed areas can be secured by a quick reading of some of the cases and statements included in Committee on Banking and Currency (Subcommittee), *Area Redevelopment—1961*, Hearings (Jan. 18, 19, 26, Feb. 20, 1961), 1961.

W. H. Miernyk has written much on both foreign and American experience. His articles appear in the following: *Industrial and Labor Relations Rev.*, Oct. 1958; *Monthly Labor Rev.*, June 1955; in *Studies in Unemployment* (see below); Proceedings of the Twelfth Annual Meeting, Industrial Relations Research Association, December 28, 1959; *Monthly Labor Rev.*, March, 1957. See also CED, *The Little Economies*, May 29, 1958, and its *Distressed Areas in a Growing Economy*, June 1961.

Two volumes, in addition to extensive hearings of the Special Committee on Unemployment Problems (Senate) offer good coverage of the problems: *Readings in Unemployment*, 1960, and *Studies in Unemployment*, 1960. See also the *Report* of the Committee, March 30, 1960.

A summary of the approach of many countries is found in JEC, *Economic Programs for Labor Surplus Areas in Selected Countries of Western Europe*, 1960. See the discussion of criteria for eligibility, loans, grants, tax incentives, site improvement and building construction, and administrative organization on p. 12ff.

though, there has been a shift away from the blue-collar worker. Non-supervising class I railroad employment has dropped from 1.2 to 0.7 million—by 500,000.

It is not easy to assess accurately the role of automation in the unemployment in recent years. This is particularly true because much unemployment is blamed on automation that would not exist if we had had a higher rate of growth to reabsorb the unemployed into the employed portion of the labor force. This is not an attempt to present full employment as a cure-all for all our economic problems, but rather to point out that some of the technological unemployment would have disappeared if we had had a higher rate of growth. The actions already taken will help alleviate the situation, but many experts feel that this is a national problem which requires federal retraining, support of education, financing a worker's movement to other industrial areas, and better employment services and similar aid. Some industries (meat packing and steel, for example) have already established their own private retraining programs.[69]

---

[69] For a well-balanced statement on automation see JCER, *Automation and Technological Change*, Report, Jan. 5, 1956, and the accompanying Hearings. See also JEC, *Instrumentation and Automation*, Hearings (December 12, 13, 14, 1956), 1957, and Bureau of Labor Statistics, U.S. Department of Labor, *Impact of Automation*, Bulletin No. 1287, Nov. 1960.

16

Special Problems in Fiscal Policy

THE PROBLEM OF TIMING IN FISCAL POLICY

Time Lags in Recognition, Consideration, Action, and Impact

Policy-makers are confronted with rather imposing problems of the timing of action in both fiscal and monetary policy. First of all, there will inevitably be some lag between the actual need for policy changes and recognition of this need. There will also be a lag between the recognition of the need to change policy and the actual change of policy. Further, there will be a lag between the imposition of the policy change and the impact of the policy change on the economy. The first two lags are themselves rather time consuming, because of the lag in the collection of a suitable stock of significant statistics. At this stage there is the further problem of identifying where the trouble is, and whether the economy is temporarily hesitating or permanently faltering. It may be that the slowdown is temporary and that the economy will bounce back. If this is the case, there is the added danger of overcompensating and causing aggregate demand to swell too much, exerting upward pressures on prices. Hence there is a great need for flexibility and reversibility in policy.

Some Initial Policy Actions

In the case of a decline in the economy, certain gradual steps may be taken until sufficient information is available to assess more accurately the depth, seriousness, and areas of greatest trouble in the downturn. The President, for instance, has certain inherent powers to speed up or slow down spending. Typically, the Executive has directed government agencies to accelerate their purchases of goods and services. The Department of Defense has often speeded up the letting of contracts, and other departments have accelerated expenditures on various public works projects; tax refunds have been paid more rapidly; payments under grant-in-aid programs have been stepped up; and federal credit agencies have encouraged more loans at (in the case of private homes) lower down payments, longer repayments periods, and lower interest. A former member of the CEA has estimated that the use of these discretionary powers by a determined Administration could increase total demand by $3 to $5 billion within a period of 9 to 12 months (apart from actions of the Federal Reserve).[1] Of course, we would expect that the Federal Reserve would at the same time increase excess reserves and ease the availability and terms of credit.

In the case of inflation, these steps could be reversed, although this power should be exerted with the same degree of caution. Just as it is sometimes difficult to ascertain whether a rather deep recession is setting in and therefore how moderate initial policy changes should be, so it is difficult to determine the seriousness of a price level increase. If there is, for example, a sudden one-shot increase in prices, substantial action may seriously limit the needed expansion of aggregate demand. It is unlikely that we shall ever be able to control moderate shifts completely, because the economy is dynamic and autonomous changes are possible. Changes of this type could be controlled only with rather complete central control of prices and wages, which control would itself involve not only an economic cost in terms of efficiency, but other political and social costs. This is all the more reason why we should strengthen the unemployment system as one of our first lines of defense against downturns (aside from humanitarian considerations).

Time Lags, Monetary Policy, Unemployment Insurance, and Discretionary Tax Cuts

It is sometimes argued that monetary rather than fiscal policy should be used for short-run stabilization purposes. The impact of monetary policy, however, is not agreed upon. Further, estimates of the time lag in monetary policy range from 9 to 18 months; and even if the lower figure is accepted, this represents a terribly long lag and additional human suffering from depression or loss of real income from inflation. On the other hand, changes in tax and expenditure policies are potent tools for fighting both inflation and deflation, but budgetary changes also have a long time lag (the budget is prepared at least a year before it goes into effect), and congressional changes in tax and expenditure policies also involve long lags. As we note later, discretionary tax changes by the President have much to offer on this basis. It would further be desirable if the policy actions were sufficiently flexible so that initially, when the full impact of the change in private spending has not yet revealed itself in the available statistics, gradual steps could be taken which could be either reversed or speeded

[1] Neil Jacoby, *Can Prosperity be Sustained?*, New York: Holt, 1956, pp. 52–53.

up as the statistics indicate and the situation demands. Naturally, any improvement in the collection of useful statistics would be helpful.

There are obvious dangers in acting too rapidly—the dangers of over-compensating—but there are also dangers in waiting too long. By the time the action has been taken the need may have passed. This would be particularly true of action following extended congressional studies, hearings, and debates on a tax reduction during a recession. Further, if a more serious decline is under way, by the time the policy becomes effective it may be inadequate to deal with the difficulty although it would have been sufficient at an earlier stage. Last, if we wait too long after we have sufficient evidence to show that a recession is under way, the cost of inaction will be a larger budget deficit.

It is true, of course, that the automatic stabilizers, especially income taxes and unemployment compensation, do operate in a countercyclical manner. They represent valuable improvements which contribute to the stability of the economy, but they are not sufficient to offset inflationary movements (as history has shown) or to substantially offset sizable recessions. (See the fourth section of this chapter.) On the other hand, the unemployment insurance program is important in that it helps fill the gap and enables us to wait somewhat longer until sufficient statistical evidence is available to take stronger action. This, in itself and aside from other considerations, is sufficient basis for the improvement of the system. (See the end of the third section of Chapter 20 for shortcomings of and improvements in the system.) We do not want to be accused of taking the ivory tower approach here, but the Congress, jealous as it is of its prerogatives in the field, must eventually come to realize that if it is serious about a flexible and effective short-run stabilization policy it will have to recognize that this goal can probably be best achieved by delegating to the President the power to use a discretionary tax program.

FORECASTING

Techniques

Since the Congress has not yet seen fit to delegate to the President limited discretionary tax authority, the need for forecasting becomes imperative. Of course, forecasting is necessary for other reasons—it is the basis for yearly budgetary programs, longer-range development of the economy and developments in certain sectors or areas of the economy, and for use in the determination of both anti-inflationary and anti-deflationary programs generally. Furthermore, the federal government must compile its budget expenditures and examine its expected revenue each year. It should not make these decisions without an understanding of their probable impact on the economy.

Everett E. Hagen has stated that a usable forecasting method must possess great accuracy, and its accuracy must be demonstrable.[2] The number of forecasting techniques used in the past has been large. Many were based on single or exclusive causes (sun spots, changes in the quantity of money, the price of steel scrap, stock prices, etc.), or the assumption that business fluctuations are rhythmic, and have been cast aside when they did not withstand the test of time.[3]

The National Bureau of Economic Research publishes on a monthly basis its list[4] of leading (coincident, and lagging) economic indicators, which have had a rather high degree of success. The leading indicators, secured by the NBER from other sources, are now thirty in number. They include such factors as the average work week in manufacturing, accession rate, nonagricultural placements, layoff rate, unemployment insurance claims, new orders, construction contracts, and business failures. The NBER indicators, however, have shortcomings of their own, as the NBER itself recognizes. (1) The approach is symptomatic rather than causal. It further assumes the continuation of certain relationships in the economy. Since the technique is not causal it tends not to point to the needed remedial action. (2) It is useful for short-run forecasts only.[5] (3) It is possible that the leading indicators will go in different directions, revealing no clear trend. Sometimes they wiggle or hesitate before finally turning. (4) The whole series is not consistent—some may accurately indicate the trend and others may never reveal it.

Other techniques currently in use are polling of (1) executives or (2) sales forces of their expected sales (which methods have a very wide margin of error); econometric projections (which are still in the developmental stage); the special surveys of businessmen's intentions to spend on plant and equipment (the Department of Commerce-SEC and the McGraw-Hill surveys), of consumers' financial status and intentions (Federal Reserve-Survey Research Center of the University of Michigan), and others. Finally, the most widely used technique is probably that of model building in the framework of the national income and product accounts.

[2] In Max F. Millikan, ed., *Income Stabilization for a Developing Democracy*, New Haven: Yale Univ. Press, 1953, pp. 175–176. Hagen's paper, even though a decade old, is still an excellent statement on forecasting.

[3] See R. C. Turner, "Problems of Forecasting for Economic Stabilization," *Am. Ec. Rev.*, May 1955, pp. 329–340.

[4] These are included in the Department of Commerce's *Business Cycle Developments* (published monthly). Geoffrey Moore of the NBER has recently published a two-volume study on the indicators.

[5] Turner, *op. cit.*, p. 335.

This latter technique is basically what was used in the computations of potential yearly output and projections of potential growth. This technique enables the forecaster to incorporate the important data provided by other indicators and surveys. It is worth noting that the data of the Survey Research Center have substantial predictive value,[6] and that the Commerce-SEC survey has "an impressive record of predictive accuracy."[7] (The McGraw-Hill survey of investment plans is also quite reliable. It seems to have a slight upward bias whereas the SEC-Commerce survey has had a downward bias.)[8] Although these surveys are still of the symptomatic type, they can be tested against empirical data of the causal type such as (in the case of investment surveys) profits, sales, and excess capacity. Other data which have a bearing on investment can also be integrated into this technique. In construction, for instance, data are available on monetary policy, the availability of capital, interest rates, the inventory of family units (apartments) and homes (and the "vacancy ratio"), the rate of family formation, financing terms such as required down payments, and wages and building material costs. In addition to profits, sales, and excess capacity, other factors influencing investment are the cost and availability of credit, inventory-sales ratios, and price and wage trends and expectations. In the area of consumer expenditures data are available on disposable income, the distribution of income, financial status, consumer expectations, consumer credit terms, personal taxes, and consumer holdings of durable goods. Of course, in any of these areas an unexpected development may occur, as with the increase in consumer expenditures in 1950, which was caused by an expected fear of shortages.

In other words, the important advantage of the income and product approach "is that it encompasses the entire gamut of economic activity. The method itself requires the forecaster to consider, in as much detail as is practical and necessary for the purpose, all of the components of the totality of demand."[9] Similarly, an analysis of potential supply must also be made. Obviously, undue emphasis is not likely to be placed on a single variable. Again, if we are concerned with the ratio of production to capacity, as we should be, a computation of potential output must be made. This, as we have noted in previous chapters, gives a much better measure of performance than an absolute dollar figure for the GNP. 1962 may be the best year yet for the GNP, but it still may be $30 billion below potential output.

[6] Cf. the statement of George Katona in JEC, *State Ec. & Pol. Full Empl.* H, p. 69.
[7] A. M. Okun, "The Predictive Value of Surveys of Business Intentions," *Am. Ec. Rev.*, May 1962, p. 219.
[8] See FR Bank of New York, *Monthly Rev.*, Aug. 1960, pp. 140–143.
[9] Turner, *op. cit.*, p. 336.

We have previously noted that under the Eisenhower Administration the CEA was reluctant to set "forth . . . the levels of employment, production, and purchasing power . . . needed to carry out the policy" of the Employment Act. We have noted that in answer to the Joint Economic Committee's inquiry as to why this had not been done, Dr. Burns said that the forecasts were inaccurate, the statistical data open to criticism, and that it may not be good for people to think that economists could be that accurate. Another reason is probably found in the natural conservatism of the Eisenhower Administration, its excessive concern with price stability, and its reluctance to indulge in what in its opinion might be considered an overly-activist employment program.[10] Failure to include such data in the *Economic Reports* raises the serious question of whether the Administration is carrying out not only the spirit and intent but also the word of the law. At any rate, it is inevitable that forecasts will be made within the Administration even if they are not made public or included in public documents and statements. The Treasury Department, in particular, does much forecasting.

In effect, then, it is desirable if not necessary, to have forecasts of (1) potential output, income, and employment, (2) likely output, income, and employment, and (3) output, income, and employment after the adjustments which have been incorporated into the budget program go into effect, and (4) output, income, and employment after the budget changes have been made and after discretionary executive authority (if any) has been applied. Some have argued that the CEA should not, because of its official capacity, make forecasts. They would appear, so it is argued, to be "authoritative," which certainly they would be. The assumption underlying this argument is that the feedback effect, especially of a pessimistic forecast, would be highly undesirable. Any good forecaster must, and will, take this into account. We must also consider the fact that, even if a pessimistic forecast is made, a forthright and definite statement by the government, backed up with proof in the form of action, can have a favorable impact on the economy. Furthermore, emotional and sensational statements of the forecast can be avoided. A statement which is calm and dispassionate does not have to have an undesirable effect.[11] Some think that the most important danger here is that the government's forecast is too pessimistic and programs are adopted which have inflationary consequences. Of course, just the opposite could also happen—a forecast of

[10] Paul Samuelson adds also the scientific temperament of CEA members, in G. Colm, ed., *The Employment Act: Past and Future*, NPA: Washington, D.C., 1956, p. 133. But surely Samuelson would not say that the members of the CEA under Walter Heller were less scientific. See also Jacoby's defense of the CEA's actions in Jacoby, *op. cit.*, p. 77.
[11] See Turner, *op. cit.*, p. 334.

prosperity, the adoption of anti-inflationary policies, and a government-caused downturn.[12]

The income and product model building approach is not without its own shortcomings. It is possible that one may place undue emphasis on the aggregates and overlook important changes in component parts; the projections may too often be pessimistic because of their emphasis on existing and past factors which determine demand and possibly neglect new and unanticipated demands; the method is extremely time-consuming and involves a large mass of data; it tends to emphasize static rather than dynamic factors in the economy; and cumulative factors (such as the accumulation of capital or liquid assets) may be neglected.[13]

Despite these criticisms this technique is still widely used. Of course, its users incorporate information from the NBER leading indicators, the SEC-Commerce and McGraw-Hill surveys of investment plans, and the consumer surveys, and other data and surveys. In addition, the econometric method, though often in modified form, is used. The net result is a fairly strong feeling that present forecasting on a short-run basis is quite accurate.[14] Some forecasters claim that they can be quite accurate (within 1 percent) for a period of at least 6 months.[15] Turner attributes the high degree of success to the great improvement in economic science of the last twenty-five (or so) years, the high degree of predictability of government policies (due in part to the Employment Act), greater economic understanding of Congressmen, and greatly improved data (economic statistics and the surveys we have noted).[16]

It is obvious that greater problems are encountered in longer-range forecasts, but even here the record has not been so terribly bad. The problems encountered are greater because the unknowns are greater. But important studies have been made which have provided data related to the possible growth of total supply, which we noted in Chapter 11 in our discussion of potential growth. Furthermore, it is not as imperative that

[12] See Hagen, in Millikan, ed., *op. cit.*, pp. 208–210. The fact is that this type of forecast was legion under Eisenhower.

[13] For criticisms of this approach, see Turner, *op. cit.*, p. 337; R. A. Gordon, "Stabilization Policy and the Study of Business Cycles," *Am. Ec. Rev.*, May 1957, pp. 118–119; and A. G. Hart, "'Model-Building' and Fiscal Policy," *Am. Ec. Rev.*, Sept. 1945, reprinted in Smithies and Butters, eds., *Readings in Fiscal Policy*, Homewood, Ill.: Irwin for Am. Ec. Assoc., 1955, pp. 307–334. See Hart's article for suggestions for improvement.

[14] Both Gordon and Turner agree on this point, and Okun agrees for the SEC-Commerce survey of planned investment. See also the statement of Paul Samuelson in G. Colm, ed., *op. cit.*, p. 133, and Neil Jacoby, *op. cit.*, p. 68.

[15] See T. Anderson, JEC, *Fed. Tax Pol.*, H, p. 80. See also the statement of G. C. Smith in JEC, *Jan. 1961 Ec. Rept. Pres.*, H, pp. 15–23.

[16] Turner, *op. cit.*, p. 338.

we be as accurate with long-range forecasts, since in some important ways we are more able to affect long-run supply and demand factors.

We noted that a rather high degree of reliability is claimed for 6-month predictions. Actually, however, predictions of longer periods have had a fairly high degree of success. Many economists (as high a percentage as 90 in 1960) accurately forecast the 1957–58 and the 1960–1961 recessions, although most of these were predictions of the general rather than the exact magnitudes of the recessions.[17] Finally, we should also point out that President Kennedy's proposal to stagger tax cuts over a twelve-month and longer period is open to considerable criticism on the ground that we would not know what economic conditions would be at that time.

A Note on the Econometric Method[18]

Econometricians attempt to develop a set of simultaneous mathematical equations which will express the relationships among "a system of essentially measurable quantities: prices, costs, incomes, savings, employment, and so on." Even though the behavior of individual households or firms may vary considerably, an attempt is made to develop averages over a long period of time and over large numbers so that more stable relationships may be arrived at.

After the relationships have been established in equation form, historical data are sought, and the expressions are stated in numerical form by use of appropriate statistical methods. The final result is to represent the economic system with a set of numerical equations containing variables of two kinds; (1) knowns, such as population, public expenditures, tax rates, and price supports, which influence the level of economic activity but which are not significantly influenced by what is going on in the economy; (2) unknowns, such as income, consumer expenditures, saving and employment, which are determined by the level of economic activity. If the model is complete and accurate, the future level of economic activity can be determined by substituting the values of the knowns and solving for the unknowns. Various forecasts can be made which incorporate alternative public policy decisions.

[17] G. C. Smith, *op. cit.*, pp. 15–16. We should not leave this section without mentioning the forecasts for the post-World War II period when so many economists were far from their target. For a review of these forecasts of what would happen after World War II, see M. Sapir, "Review of Economic Forecasts for the Transition Period," Conference on Research in Income and Wealth, *Studies in Income and Wealth*, Volume XI, Princeton: Princeton Univ. Press, 1949, pp. 275–367.

[18] See D. B. Suits in JEC, *Empl., Growth, Price Levels*, H, Pt. 8, pp. 2492–2498, and M. H. Spencer, C. G. Clark, and P. W. Hoguet, *Business and Economic Forecasting: An Econometric Approach*, Homewood, Ill.: Irwin, 1961. Suits' statement has been drawn on heavily here.

Some idea of the accuracy of econometric forecasts can be found in Tables 16-1 and 16-2. The direction in which the economy was to go was predicted correctly and, with some exceptions, the actual level was predicted quite well. Generally, the predicted level of the GNP was closer to its actual level than the predicted levels of its components.

Policy Action Before or After the Fact

The question is often asked, should action be taken on the basis of forecasting or after the statistics show a change? Those who argue that policy action should be based on forecasting want to anticipate and minimize the impact of the expected deflationary or inflationary movement in the economy. Those who argue that we should wait maintain that forecasting is not sufficiently accurate and that predetermined policy action enhances the possibility of overcompensating in one direction or the other. The most practical approach would probably use both techniques. There is, for instance, fairly wide agreement that we can predict with a high degree of accuracy for at least 6 months ahead (and longer with reasonable accuracy).

Certainly countercyclical action can be taken by the Congress even though there is a long lag in the budget process. If the President uses his inherent powers, the Federal Reserve acts, *and* the President has and uses discretionary tax authority (to operate in both directions), and if these actions are not sufficient, the Congress can take further action, which (in this case) would be after the fact. Furthermore, our periods of both inflation and recession have lasted sufficiently long that Congress has been in session and could act on remedial programs. In many of these cases it has been quite apparent that the inflationary pressure (as, say, during the Korean War) would exist for a period of 2 years or more, because the increase in defense expenditures was known. Certainly, in cases such as this (and in other cases in which significant changes in the economy are known factors) both the long-run forecasting and after-the-fact bases for policy determination are used.

We should note again that CEA forecasts can be conditional; that a reasonable degree of discretionary tax authority should be delegated to the President so that adjustments may be made in order to correct the degree of error in the forecast; that the Congress could avoid wasting precious time if it would do this, and could spend its time on more serious changes in tax and expenditure policy; that the delegation of tax authority (within limits) would with little doubt result in smaller deficits (which when large are so terribly bothersome to so many Congressmen); that the Congress should pay more attention on a continuing basis to the impact of its expenditure and tax policies; that the Federal Reserve, or some

Table 16-1. Review of Forecasts, 1953–1959 (Billions of Current Dollars)

| | 1953 | | 1954 | | 1955 | | 1956 | | 1957 | | 1958 | | 1958 Prices | 1959 Prices |
	Fore-cast	Actual	Fore-cast	Actual	Fore-cast	Actual	Fore-cast	Actual	Fore-cast	Actual	Fore-cast	Actual	Fore-cast	Actual
GNP	364.3	363.2	361.8	360.6	364.8	390.9	413.2	414.7	438.8	434.4	438.6	437.7	456.7	482.7
Personal consumption	229.9	230.5	237.8	236.5	235.9	254.0	263.3	267.2	280.1	280.4	285.9	290.6	295.4	313.5
Gross private domestic investment	57.1	50.3	52.2	52.0	54.1	60.6	71.8	65.9	69.3	74.4	62.7	54.4	61.2	72.7
Employee compensation	165.2	172.8	170.4	171.8	206.2	223.2	235.1	241.4	255.6	254.4	257.8	253.8	261.0	278.5
Nonfarm, nonwage income	72.1	71.9	74.7	69.5	76.0	78.5	93.8	85.3	91.1	93.1	90.0	92.6	103.0	

Source: D. B. Suits, JEC, *Empl., Growth, Price Levels*, H, Pt. 8, p. 2493. Data for 1959 added.

Table 16-2. Review of Forecasts, 1960–1962 (Billions of 1954 Dollars)

	1960		1961		1962	
	Fore-cast	Actual	Fore-cast	Actual	Fore-cast	Actual[a]
GNP	432	439.2	450.1	447.9	474.3	471.5
Consumption	287.1	296.8	304.3	304.3	318.6	318.1
Automobiles	16.7	15.6	14.6	15.5	18.8⎫	45.1
Other durables	25.2	25.2	25.1	26.1	26.7⎭	
Nondurables	138.9	141.9	144.7	143.3	148.0	148.5
Services	106.3	113.7	119.9	119.4	125.1	124.5
Private gross capital expenditure	62.4	60.5	61.3	57.8	61.1	62.9
Plant and equipment	40.5	39.3	39.0	37.7	38.6	40.5
Residential construction	19.7	18.0	19.9	18.2	17.8	19.6
Inventory:						
Durable goods					2.6	
Nondurable goods	2.2	3.2	2.4	2.0	2.1	
Gov't purchase of goods and services	83.7	80.3	84.7	84.0	92.3	90.2
Net exports	−1.3	1.6	0.2	1.8	2.3	0.4
Civilian employment (millions)	65.5	66.7	67.0	66.8	68.9	67.8
Unemployment (millions)	4.4	3.9	4.3	4.8	3.6	4.0
Percent of labor force	6.3	5.6	6.0	6.7	5.0	5.6

Source: JEC, *State Ec. & Pol. Full Empl.*, H, p. 24. Data for 1962 added.

[a] Preliminary.

comparable agency—preferably one over which the Executive has some control—should be given standby authority over consumer credit; and that it may be necessary to develop a more effective selective control over inflationary pressures arising from investment expenditures. There is little reason to assume that we shall not again have a strong inflationary pressure from investment such as that of 1955.

TECHNIQUES, SIZE, AND IMPACT OF A DISCRETIONARY TAX CUT

The case for the discretionary tax cut (or increase) has already been stated: It is effective; its impact is immediate; it is flexible; and it avoids lengthy congressional debates, hearings, and other delaying tactics. To this may be added the point that in the recovery from the 1960–1961 recession federal purchases rose some $7 billion, mostly because of what was felt to be a need for greater defense and space exploration expenditures, that this was largely coincidental, that a similar need may not exist during the next recession, and that at that time we may have to face up to the need for a substantial tax reduction.[19] There are, on the other hand, some problems: Congress is hesitant to increase the authority of the executive branch. How large should the tax cut be? Should the tax cut be across the board (proportional)? Should the first bracket be split and the rate in just the new or both lower brackets be reduced? Or should exemptions be increased? Should the corporate income tax be included? What range of authority should be granted to the President? What criteria should be used to guide tax changes? For what period of time should the tax cut be effective? (Although major attention is usually directed toward a tax cut, any such delegation of authority to the President should also include the power to raise taxes.)

The Problem of Delegating Discretionary Tax Authority and Tax Reform

The delegation of authority to the President to vary tax rates within explicit statutory limits may be difficult to get through the Congress since the latter is jealous of its prerogatives in this area, jealous of the increases in executive power which have already occurred, and (in many cases, at least) suspicious of greater executive authority. Since the authority to levy and collect taxes is vested in the Congress by the Constitution, the delegation of such authority to the President would have to be within clearly defined, probably not too permissive limits. There is also the possibility that the tax authority may be used to lower taxes before an election. But we must assume some degree of responsibility in the Executive's use of tax power, as in the use of other powers. Furthermore, any irresponsibility can be restricted by the criteria under which the tax cut could become effective, and the option of a congressional veto.

There seems to be no question that a limited delegation of tax authority would be constitutional. Furthermore, the proposal would constitute an important step forward toward the realization of the goals of the Employment Act, for reasons noted previously. Many of the Congress' fears of the proposal can be adequately dealt with. In the final analysis, whether or not the proposal will be adopted by the Congress must depend on how serious the Congress is about attaining a more stable economy.

---

[19] See the statement of R. Musgrave in JEC, *Jan. 1962 Ec. Rept. Pres.*, H, p. 465.

In recent years there has (justifiably) been much talk of major tax reforms. This, however, should be separated from the issues of discretionary tax cuts and overall tax reduction.[20] To separate the issues of equity in taxation and stabilization policy would be a highly desirable development, if it is at all possible.

Musgrave has argued that taxes for stabilization policy should be proportional to the system of distribution of income (which has already been decided on and realized). He has also recently stated that "monetary ease is not likely to have a significant effect on the level of consumer expenditures, the very component of demand which needs to be strengthened when investment begins to slacken."[21] There is no intent here to point out any inconsistency in Professor Musgrave's statements but rather to point out that proportional tax cuts may not be the most efficient way to bring about an increase in spending per dollar of revenue loss. A proportional tax cut, for instance, is not as likely to increase spending as much as a tax cut, say, in the first income bracket. On the other hand, a proportional or some type of across-the-board tax cut is perhaps the only politically acceptable one. Similar, but not equally significant, comments could be made about including a reduction in the corporate tax rate in a program of temporary tax reduction.

The reform of the tax structure, then, the overall reduction in the tax structure in order to reduce the full employment surplus, and the delegation of discretionary authority to the President to cut or raise taxes are three separate issues.

Various alternatives have been proposed to secure the direct delegation of discretionary tax authority to the President. The CEA has suggested that procedures be established whereby the President's proposal to change the tax rates should be voted on by both houses of Congress within (say) 60 days of its presentation. Professor Henry Wallich of Yale, a member of the CEA under Eisenhower, has suggested that Congress decide on the type of tax cut that would be appropriate in a recession, and then the President make his proposal when the occasion arose; thus Congress would quickly vote on it without amendment.[22] Either proposal would speed up action and prevent the tax reduction issue from becoming

---

[20] In 1963 President Kennedy attempted to argue that the "price" of a tax cut would be tax reform. He was rather strongly criticized for doing this by the CED and other organizations and individuals. Later, when he apparently felt that reform was a dead issue and pushed for only tax reductions, he was criticized by *The New York Times* in many editorials. See JEC, *Jan. 1963 Ec. Rept. Pres.*, H, Pt. 2, for the CED's statement.

[21] See JEC, *Jan. 1962 Ec. Rept. Pres.*, H, p. 466.

[22] *Ibid.*, pp. 621–622.

bogged down in arguments over whether it should be across-the-board, permanent or temporary, on consumption or investment, etc.

The 1962 Discretionary Tax Authority Proposal

Shortly after his election President Kennedy appointed Paul Samuelson chairman of a special task force on economic conditions in the United States. Their report[23] was made public on January 6, 1961; it included a suggestion[24] that, if the recession then under way became worse, Congress could reduce the tax rate 3 or 4 percentage points in March or April to continue to the end of the year. Congress might then "grant to the Executive the right to continue such a reduction for one or two 6-month (or 3-month) periods beyond that time (subject to the actions being set aside by joint resolution of Congress) with the clear understanding that the reduction will definitely expire by the end of 1962." It is clear that this involves only a limited delegation of authority to the President to cut taxes. During the next recession the process would have to be initiated all over again, subject to all the delays and debates inherent in additional hearings and new bills. The Samuelson proposal, however, seems to represent a diplomatic attempt to prod Congress into action and at the same time avoid the issue of a permanent grant of greater discretionary authority to the President.

The January 1962 *Report* of the President[25] contained a proposal that the President be granted the power to reduce the rates in the individual income tax as follows:

1. The President should make a finding that such action is necessary to meet the objectives of the Employment Act.
2. He would propose to Congress a uniform reduction not to be more than 5 percentage points lower than the permanent rates.
3. The proposal would go into effect 30 days after submission unless rejected by a joint resolution of Congress.
4. It would remain in effect for 6 months, subject to revision or renewal by the same process or extension by a joint resolution of the Congress.
5. If the Congress were not in session a Presidentially proposed tax adjustment would automatically take effect but would terminate 30 days after the Congress reconvened. Extension would require a new proposal by the President, which would be subject to Congressional veto.

[23] Reprinted in JEC, *Jan. 1961 Ec. Rept. Pres.*, H, pp. 703–711. (A copy may also be found in the *New York Times* shortly after its release.)

[24] This is not the first time such a proposal to grant discretionary tax authority to the President has been made. It has been discussed by economists for years. Representative Patman introduced a bill in the 86th Cong., 2d Sess., H.R. 12360, to give the President authority to raise or lower the income tax by as much as 10 percent. A copy will be found in *ibid.*, pp. 225–226.

[25] *Jan. 1962 Ec. Rept. Pres.*, p. 18.

It should be noted that the authority is not to be granted for an increase in taxes to combat inflationary influences. From the point of view of both short- and long-run stability and growth, this is to be lamented. Otherwise, the procedures as proposed should do little or no damage to congressional prerogatives.

The Impact of the 1962 Discretionary Tax Reduction Proposal

It has been estimated that (for 1962) the *annual rate* of tax collections would be reduced by $2 billion per percentage point. For a year the maximum reduction would be $10 billion and for 6 months, $5 billion. On a 6-month basis the reduction would be $1 billion, per percentage point.[25] The Chairman of the CEA, Walter W. Heller, suggested that out of the $5 billion or 6-month reduction perhaps 75 percent would be spent on consumption. Using a multiplier of 2, which he felt was reasonable, we find that the total stimulus would be approximately $7.5 billion during the 6-month period.[26] The impact on the deficit would be somewhat more difficult to compute. In the first instance income taxes are reduced by $5 billion. If we assume that about 75 percent is respent on consumption and that the multiplier is 2, we have about a $7.5 billion increase in income (Heller's estimate). If we assume that approximately 30 percent of this is paid in income taxes (or about $2.25 billion), the net increase in the

---

[26] JEC, *Jan. 1962 Ec. Rept. Pres.*, H, pp. 70–71. Otto Eckstein used the same multiplier. See JEC, *State Ec. & Pol. Full Empl.*, H, p. 199.

Using the tax multiplier, $k = c/(1 - c + ct)$, MPC = .75, and t = .30, a multiplier of 1.58 will be arrived at. This gives us an increase in income of $7.9 billion *if* we can assume that the impact occurs within a 6-month period, and can ignore the drains of corporate profits, social security taxes, and state and local taxes. If a drainage from these factors of 50 percent is used, which is high, a multiplier of 1.2 is arrived at. It is usually assumed that 6 or 7 expenditure rounds take place in a year, but that only 50 percent of a tax cut's impact occurs in a year. This alters the figures in the text.

The Office of Business Economics of the Department of Commerce has estimated the multiplier to be about 2. This includes only a slight increase in investment since it is assumed that under conditions of excess capacity there would be little impact on investment. The accelerator was then practically eliminated. JEC, *Jan. 1963 Ec. Rept. Pres.*, H, Pt. 1, pp. 246–247. For longer-run effects it agreed on a multiplier-accelerator (with its own definition of the latter) of 2.5.

Gerhard Colm has long used a multiplier of 2, and a multiplier of 3.5 when induced investment is included. *Ibid.*, p. 461 and 469. Colm presents an arithmetic example of the tax multiplier in *ibid.*, pp. 476–477. The JEC arrived at a super multiplier of 4.0; *ibid.*, p. 20.

Paul Davidson's study ("Multipliers and the Price Level," *Am. Ec. Rev.*, Dec. 1962) came up with a money income multiplier of 2.11. He also found different employment multipliers depending on whether or not the money wage rate increased. Other economists have also used a multiplier of 2.

deficit would be approximately $2.75 billion.[27] This, however, would have to be judged against the decline which would occur (under recession conditions) if the tax reduction were not undertaken in the first place, which in turn is likely to reduce revenue by an amount greater than $2.75 billion. There are at least three further considerations: (1) The tax reduction for 6 months will mean that income will be greater also in the following 6 months than it would have been without the tax cut. This means a further reduction in the no-tax-cut deficit. (2) There will undoubtedly be some increase (or less decline) in investment, which further reduces the deficit. (3) The impact of the tax cut may take much longer than was assumed here.

Other questions might be raised about President Kennedy's proposal. (1) Was it enough to do the job? Some critics would answer that a more potent technique would be a 100 percent tax remission for, say, 1 or 2 months. Others suggested that a greater impact may be secured by lowering only the first bracket rate, raising exemptions, etc. (2) What happens after the tax cut expires? In view of the size of the full employment surplus and the repressive impact of the total tax structure of this period, this was a most important question. If the analysis of the full employment surplus is approximately correct (and other vigorous demands do not develop) then, during the period in which the temporary tax cut is in effect, policymakers should have been working on a permanent tax reduction.

Criteria for Discretionary Tax Authority versus Formula Flexibility

Clearly the criteria for the imposition of discretionary tax changes should be reasonably flexible; it is for this very reason that formula-flexible techniques are not adequate. Under the formula-flexible proposal a stipulated tax reduction (or increase) would *automatically* (rather than on the basis of a decision of the President) go into effect if unemployment reached a stipulated level (say, 6 or 7 percent) or if the Consumers Price Index rose a stipulated amount (say, 5 percent) within a stipulated period of time. The use of formula-flexible stabilizers has been advocated by those who will tolerate some use of the tax system for stabilization purposes but who distrust delegation of tax authority to the executive branch, or those who feel that the Congress will not delegate discretionary authority and that formula flexibility is better than nothing—better than what we have had in the past.[28] We should note also that formula-flexible stabilizers

[27] D. B. Suits uses a figure of 40 percent, which seems a bit high for the federal government alone. (JEC, *State Ec. & Pol. Full Empl.*, H, p. 26.) Eckstein, *ibid.*, p. 199, estimates the tax recovery at 25 to 33⅓ percent.

[28] Hansen has justified their use on the latter grounds. See JEC, *Jan. 1962 Ec. Rept. Pres.*, H, pp. 647–648.

have been recommended to include, in addition to automatic tax cuts and tax increases, increases or decreases in public works or other expenditures (such as unemployment compensation)—all of which would be altered on the basis of a previously determined change in a statistical series.

The use of formula flexibility assumes that we can predetermine the remedy for the trouble that develops in the economy. In a dynamic economy the source of difficulty may well vary from one period to another. The automatic imposition of a tax increase following a one-shot increase in the Consumers Price Index, which in turn was caused by some autonomous force, may serve only to depress the level of economic activity. Even when the automatic increase in taxes is justified, what shall be the criteria for its removal? A 6-month period of general price stability? It may be that the additional tax is just sufficient to restrain inflation and its automatic removal would be harmful. The formula-flexible stabilizers are no substitute for sound economic judgment in this case.

On the other hand, what if there is a high level of activity in the economy and the unemployment rate increases because of problems in a certain sector of production or a certain regional area? Would a tax reduction be the best policy under these circumstances? The criticisms of automatic increases in expenditures for public works are that society should have what it needs and desires in this area regardless of stabilization needs, their cessation would be wasteful, their imposition may be in areas where resources are scarce, they may be outdated by the time they are used. These situations are not terribly unique: The economy is simply too complex for us to expect perfection with the use of formula-flexible stabilizers.[29]

It is for exactly these same reasons that the criteria for the use of discretionary stabilizers must be flexible. Everett E. Hagen has suggested that an attempt should be made first to ascertain the cause of a recession before action is taken. If the recession is caused by a reduction in business inventories, it is likely that the decline will be neither deep nor prolonged. If, on the other hand, a significant decline in plant and equipment expenditures is under way, residential construction has declined sharply, etc., then a prompt tax reduction would be appropriate. Hagen has suggested that if unemployment reached a certain level and stayed there for 3 successive months, a tax reduction would probably be safe since the unemployment is likely due to more basis causes (then inventory reduction) which will not reverse themselves quickly. It would be appropriate to include criteria such as these in any law delegating discretionary authority to the

---

[29] A good discussion of formula flexibility, somewhat more optimistic than this, is that of E. E. Hagen in JEC, *Fed. Tax Pol.*, P, pp. 62–66. A pessimistic discussion can be found in R. A. Musgrave, *The Theory of Public Finance*, New York: McGraw-Hill, 1959, pp. 512–517.

President, but it would be equally appropriate to require the President to examine the total economic picture before he took action. If the Congress felt that the President's approach was too conservative, that he would not take action when he reasonably should in view of prevailing economic conditions, it could include a clause whereby it could initiate the tax reduction by a joint resolution or other constitutionally acceptable means.

Alternative Programs and Their Impact

We have already noted that President Kennedy's 1962 proposal would reduce income tax collection by a maximum of $5 billion for 6 months, or $10 billion for a year. Others have proposed a 100 percent tax remission for 1 or 2 months. It is not easy to determine the impact of this proposal, but it would be useful to know (1) how much consumption would result, (2) how much of the tax cut would go into saving, (3) if the large revenue loss would be worth the gain, and (4) whether the proposal will have any inflationary impact. Individual income tax collections averaged almost $4 billion per month in 1961. If a 100 percent tax remission were undertaken for 2 months, the tax cut would be approximately $8 billion, for 3 months $12 billion, etc.

The question of how potent the impact of a discretionary tax cut would be has been answered variously. Some observers argue that most of the tax cut would go into saving.[30] Admittedly, we do not have highly accurate data on the *marginal* propensity to consume in different income brackets, although it is true that the lower income brackets have an *average* propensity to consume which is much higher than that of the higher income brackets. See Table 16-3, which compares several studies.[31] The differences in the studies are due primarily to sampling variations and differences in the treatment of components of saving (excluding or including equity in corporate pension funds, etc.) Of the older studies the Friend-Schor data are generally thought to be the most reliable.

Most economists who have commented on the impact of a tax reduction on consumption in recent years are in agreement that the tax cut would be potent. It is interesting to note, however, that there has been some change of attitude among economists on the effectiveness of a tax cut—that is, whether it would be spent, and whether is makes any difference if the cut is on low or high income groups. On the first point it had been, and still is, argued by some that a large proportion of the tax cut would be saved. On the second point it was often assumed that the marginal propensity to

---

[30] See the statement of Senator Proxmire, JEC, *Jan. 1962 Ec. Rept. Pres.*, H, p. 71.

[31] For a detailed analysis of 1950 data by income tenths, positive and negative saving by tenths, etc., see Keiser, *Introductory Economics*, Wiley, New York, 1961, p. 209.

consume varied little among income groups. These issues have not been finally settled, but during the years 1958 and 1961–1963 a great many economists supported the idea that a tax cut would be effective, and some that it would be more effective if primarily for the benefit of low income people. One major point which they relied on was the long-run average propensity to consume. That is, consumers have tended to spend over

Table 16-3. Estimates of Saving-Income Ratios, by Income Class, 1950 and 1960–61

Saving-Income Ratios (percent)

Income after Taxes	FR—Michigan (Total U.S.)	FR—Michigan (Urban)	BLS—Wharton (Urban)	Friend— Schor (Urban)	Michigan Survey Research Center 1960–61
Under $1,000	−55.2	−48.9	−105.5	−81.7⎫	⎫
$1,000–1,999	−0.2	0.9	−13.5	−6.2⎭	−5.2
$2,000–2,999	0.1	−0.7	−5.0	−1.7⎫	⎫
$3,000–3,999	5.6	4.9	−0.7	2.4⎭	3.9
$4,000–4,999	9.1	7.7	1.7	4.5	6.2
$5,000–5,999⎫				⎰ 6.5	8.8
$6,000–7,499⎭	12.7	12.9	5.2	⎱10.01	11.6
$7,500–9,999	28.4	30.1	12.3	16.3	13.6
$10,000 and over	33.1	29.6	26.4	30.7	—
$10,000–14,999	—	—	—	—	19.8
$15,000 and over	—	—	—	—	23.8
All	8.6	9.2	4.3	8.2	

Source: JEC, *State Ec. & Pol. Full Empl.*, H, p. 673; JEC, *Jan. 1963 Ec. Rept. Pres.*, H, p. 335.

90 percent of annual additions to income. This has been relied on as having been "clearly predictable."[32]

Certainly, the relationship between income and consumption has been established beyond doubt, even though there are many factors affecting consumption and even though there will be individual differences. But supporters of the 1963 tax reduction proposal were clearly relying on the MPC as the basis of their predictions of the bill's effectiveness. We noted in Chapter 5 that the short- or intermediate-term MPC is apparently somewhere between .50 and .70. Since the long-run APC is around 90 percent the impact of an $11+ billion tax cut will no doubt be felt, but perhaps not as soon as many expect. In addition to the possibly lower MPC there is also the very high likelihood that some of the steam of the

[32] See Dr. Heller's statement in JEC, *Jan. 1963 Ec. Rept. Pres.*, H, 1, p. 7.

1964 tax cut may have been already released in 1963. That is, many businessmen invested during 1963 in anticipation of a 1963 tax cut. (The progress of the economy during 1963 was unexpectedly good and this is one reasonable explanation.)

Some have argued that the tax cut will be ineffective because it consists of only a few dollars in a weekly paycheck. There is no theoretical or empirical justification for assuming this, however, and the impact should be the same even if the tax cut is relatively small. It is the aggregate effect which is important.[33] (See Table 16-3, last column.)

After consumer tax liabilities were reduced in 1948 and 1954 the ratio of consumption to disposable income actually rose, if the data are analyzed on a quarterly basis. There may have been other influences at work here (during periods of reduced income we expect the APC to rise) but the evidence certainly does not contradict the argument that the tax reduction will be spent. There is a strong feeling that increased disposable income resulting from lower taxes will be spent just as if it had come from increased wages or salaries. The sociological evidence indicates that Americans are just as interested in raising their standard of living as those who live in low income countries, and that the middle (and some upper) income people are just as interested in raising their standard of living as those with lower incomes. Finally, the Institute of Social Research at the University of Michigan has produced evidence to the effect that each increase in their living standard motivates them to move further up the scale.[34]

For illustrative purposes only, estimates (made by Roy Moor of the JEC staff) of the tax savings in dollar amounts and by percent for various income classes are shown in Figures 16-1 and 16-2. Also illustrated are the tax savings which result from alternative methods—reducing the rate in half in the first bracket, increasing the personal exemption by $200, and reducing the first bracket 4.6 percentage points.[35]

The total tax reduction on which these figures are based is 6 billion dollars. The top section of Figure 16-1 shows the income gain resulting

[33] A good statement in these matters is that of John Lintner in *ibid.*, pp. 551–560. See also the more extensive statements on the impact of previous tax cuts in *ibid.*, p. 7.

[34] See the paper by Paul McCracken in *Am. Bankers Assoc., A Symposium on Economic Growth*, New York, 1963, especially p. 24.

[35] Estimates of the impact of several different types of tax cut on different income groups can be found in JEC, *State Ec. & Pol. Full Empl.*, H, pp. 179–180, and COF, S, *Investigation Finan. Cond.*, A, pp. 1992–1993.

In August 1963 President Kennedy sent a new proposal to the Congress. The major change was that greater reductions were to be granted to higher income groups than previously. The new rate structure was to range from 14 to 71 percent; current statutory rates were 20 to 91 percent. A description, with the tax saving for each income group, is found in *The New York Times*, Western edition, Aug. 13, 1963, pp. 1, 5. [The bill was finally passed in February, 1964. See p. 327, note 46a.]

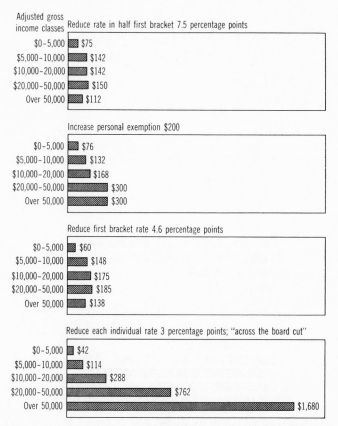

Figure 16-1. Average tax savings per individual under various methods of making a $6 billion reduction in individual income taxes. Estimated for 1962 on basis of 1960 data of Internal Revenue Service. *Source:* JEC, *State Ec. & Pol. Full Empl.*, H, p. 223.

from splitting the first income tax bracket. This would establish a new income bracket, and all the tax cut would apply to it. Individuals with adjusted gross income of less than $5,000 would on the average experience a net gain of $75. This is to be compared with a gain of $76 for this same group if we raise the personal exemption from $600 to $800, a gain of $60 if all the tax cut is in the present first bracket, and a gain of $42 if the tax cut is of the across-the-board type. It is interesting to note that the gain to the highest income bracket is generally very high (relative to the gain of the lowest bracket) in all but the first method. The across-the-board cut benefits them greatly. An examination of the percentage gains in income under the various methods reveals that the greatest gain to the highest income group also comes under the across-the-board cut.

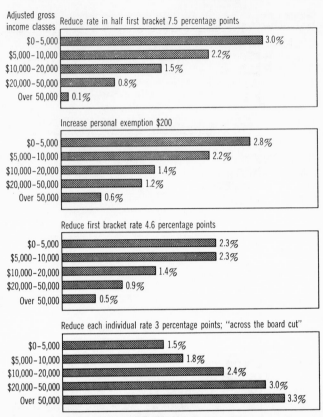

Figure 16-2. Percentage increase in taxable incomes, after taxes, of the different income classes under various methods of making a $6 billion reduction in individual income taxes. Estimated for 1962 on basis of 1960 data of Internal Revenue Service. *Source: JEC, State Ec. & Pol. Full Empl.*, H, p. 224.

An estimate of the percent of total tax reduction that would go to the various income groups is shown in Table 16-4. We see that, under the "across-the-board cut," even though the tax saving in dollar amount and percent is greater (Figures 16-1 and 16-2) in the highest income groups, they (as a group) will not secure the greatest percentage of the total tax reduction. This is because there are relatively few people in the income group above $10,000 (12 percent of the returns). Nevertheless, a $6 billion tax reduction means that they will receive $2.4 billion of it if the across-the-board method is used.

It is rather apparent that the across-the-board tax cut would stimulate consumption the least. It is probably true that President Kennedy presented his proposal in this form for political reasons. It would, however, be less efficient per dollar of revenue loss. It is difficult to place a value judgement on this action. Musgrave's agrument that tax cuts for stabilization purposes should be "proportional to the system of income distribution" has the great advantage of avoiding arguments every time a tax cut is needed, but is of limited help because we have not in our society explicitly rendered a decision on the question of income distribution.

Table 16-4. Distribution of Tax Savings by Income Classes under Alternative Tax Reduction Methods

Percent of Total Tax Reduction

Income Group	Percent of Total Returns	Across-the- Board	First- Bracket	Split First- Bracket
$0–$5,000	39.1	12.7	18.1	23.1
$5,000–$10,000	48.9	47.6	63.0	61.9
Above $10,000	12.0	39.7	18.9	15.0
Total	100.0	100.0	100.0	100.0

Source: JEC, 1962 Ann. Rept., p. 41.

Musgrave has himself, on one occasion, established the following criteria:

1. The best approach may well be that which gets us the quickest action.
2. Those changes should be made which will be most effective in raising private expenditures promptly.
3. The tax cut should be such as to facilitate rather than hinder a later return to higher rates if and when needed.
4. Tax reduction should improve, or, in any case, not damage the long-run equity of the tax structure.[36]

Musgrave stressed that his most important point was to get quick action. In this context, which also included the delegation of executive authority to change the tax rates, he suggested that the changes should come in the first bracket.[37]

Some may argue that it is good to reduce taxes on higher income groups as these taxes are already too high. Most economists would agree, but it should be done as an explicit tax reform action, not by means of stabilization policy. Furthermore, this method increases the incomes of those who already have plentiful loopholes as well as those who do not, and

[36] JEC, Fiscal Policy Implications of the Current Economic Outlook, Hearings (April 28–30, May 1, 1958), 1958, p. 110.
[37] Ibid., p. 111.

further magnifies and compounds the inequities in the tax structure. Moreover, what of the inequities arising from failure to raise the personal exemption in line with inflation? Finally, it should be remembered that a first-bracket tax reduction (by splitting or mere rate reduction) applies to all.

It is very tempting under these circumstances and because tax reduction has already been granted to higher income groups in the form of higher depreciation allowances and the 7 percent tax credit, to recommend either of the first-bracket approaches. It is perhaps especially noteworthy that the Commission on Money and Credit, which was far from a liberal organization, recommended a reduction in the first bracket.

A reduction via the increase in exemptions is usually criticized by economists for the following reasons, which are primarily noneconomic. (1) The low income groups should in a democracy contribute something (even though the applicable rate may be very low) for political and socio-logical reasons. (2) They constitute a very high percent of our total tax base and no tax at all reduces not only revenue but also the impact of countercyclical measures. There is reason to believe that our long-run revenue requirements will be high. (3) If they are not taxed by the more equitable income tax, they may well be taxed by the regressive sales tax. (4) It would mean that millions of taxpayers would be taken off and put back in the tax rolls which, it is argued, is likely to be confusing and not good on psychological grounds. We should note in closing that tax relief goes only to those who are paying income tax, which excludes those un-employed. Hence the unemployment compensation program should not be ignored.

The Multiplier, the Accelerator, and the Effects of a Tax Cut

An interesting experiment in fiscal policy occurred with reference to the proposed 1963 tax cut. That is, the CEA spelled out to the Congress and the public the manner in which a tax reduction would affect the economy. (Although the proposed tax reform reduction program of 1963 was intended to go into effect over a period of time, what follows assumes that all the reduction is immediate.)[38] Attempts to quantify multiplier and accelerator effects of a tax cut are fraught with dangers. The size of the multiplier will depend on the value of the consumption propensities of those whose disposable income increases with the tax cut and other

---

[38] Data on the size of the proposed 1963 tax cut by income groups can be found in JEC, *Jan. 1963 Ec. Rept. Pres.*, H, Pt. 1, pp. 13, 14, 17, 19, 21–23, 25, 638; Pt. 2, pp. 719 and 721; and in the committee's 1963 *Ann. Rept.*, pp. 15, 42, and pp. 45–55. It should be noted that the 1963 proposals were very comprehensive in that they en-compassed both tax reform and tax reduction.

factors. The effect of the accelerator will depend on the existence and distribution of excess capacity relative to the areas in which demand is increased. The impact of the accelerator will be further influenced by factors which influence investment.

Another difficulty is the manner in which a marginal dollar of GNP is distributed. To allow for various leakages the CEA used the figure of a 50-cent increase in consumption resulting from each extra dollar of GNP. The CEA estimates that from each added dollar of GNP (1) net federal receipts increase by approximately 30 cents. This 30 cents is divided as follows: (a) 12 cents for corporate profits; (b) 8 or 9 cents, at the new tax rate, for increased individual income tax collections; (c) 2 to 3 cents for indirect business taxes; (d) 3 to 4 cents for additional social insurance contributions; and (e) a reduction in transfer payments, primarily unemployment insurance payments, of about 3 cents.

These estimates are based on the movement of the economy toward the full employment level. In a period of expansion they would necessarily be higher than average figures on a yearly basis. The remainder of the 50-cent leakage per dollar of extra GNP is divided as follows: (2) corporate retained earnings, 10 cents; (3) net state and local receipts, 6 cents; and (4) personal saving, 4 cents.[39]

The size of the leakage is of obvious importance in the determination of the value of the multiplier. In his estimate of the multiplier for the Joint Economic Committee, Roy Moor noted that consumption as a percentage of GNP per year varied by less than 1 percent from 65 percent for the years 1954 to 1962. (The ratio of increased consumption to increased GNP over these years, however, varies greatly. These ratios actually varied from 0.53 to 4.70.) In the computation of his multiplier resulting from the increased consumption resulting from the tax cut Moor used a leakage factor of slightly more than 35 percent. Assuming a tax reduction of $8 billion dollars (and $.5 billion increase in dividends, after taxes, resulting from corporate tax reduction) this would bring an increase in GNP of $16 billion under the CEA assumptions, and $20.24 billion under Moor's assumptions. (Moor assumed only an $8 billion tax reduction.) Under 1963 conditions it would seem that the CEA's assumptions were somewhat more realistic. We should also note that the CEA (and Moor) assumed that approximately 50 percent of the stimulus would occur within a year.

The impact of the CEA analysis is illustrated in Figure 16-3. We see first that the $8.5 billion increment to disposable income is assumed to occur immediately. (See columns a and b.) Personal saving is $0.5 billion and personal consumption is $8.0 billion (column c). In other words, the

[39] Testimony and statement of the CEA, JEC, *Jan. 1963 Ec. Rept. Pres.*, H, Pt. 1, pp. 12–18.

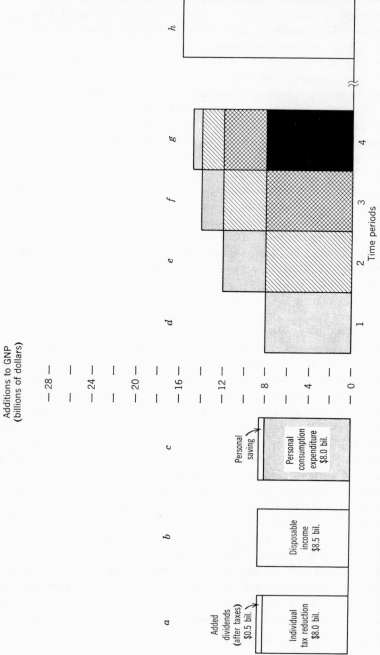

Figure 16-3. Effect of tax reduction on consumption and GNP (CEA). *Source:* CEA in JEC, *Jan. 1963 Ec. Rept. Pres.*, H, Pt. 1, p. 13.

propensity to consume out of this increase in disposable income is 94 percent. Column *d* shows the increased consumption for period 1 at $8 billion. It is important to note that the CEA assumes a *permanent* lump sum tax reduction. Therefore the addition to income of the 8.5 billion tax reduction is continuous. Your income is permanently increased by this amount and you (it is assumed) will continue to spend the extra 94 percent on consumption in each successive period. If the tax reduction were temporary there would be the $8 billion increase in consumption during the first period, and the consequent stimulating effect resulting in an increase in consumption of only $4 billion in the second period. However, since the tax reduction is permanent the second period is characterized by the $8 billion increase in consumption plus the $4 billion increase in consumption resulting from the original, first period consumption increase of $8 billion.

In column *d*, then, consumption has increased by $8 billion. Therefore, GNP and income increase by this amount. Since about 50 percent of this (because of the various leakages) will be spent on consumption we have a further increase of $4 billion in period 2. This $4 billion increase in output and income generates further spending to the extent of about $2 billion. In period 3 (column *f*), then, consumer expenditures are $8 billion higher because of the tax cut, $4 billion higher because of the increased consumption of period 1, and $2 billion higher because of period 2's $4 billion, raising GNP by a total of $14 billion for period 3. The grand total is $16 billion. This is where the impact should level off; a permanent increase in GNP of $16 billion. This is the pure "consumption effect," the impact on investment being ignored.

Figure 16-4 shows how the CEA incorporated into its analysis the impact on investment. The figure shows the increased consumption resulting from the tax cut, the impact of the increased consumption on investment, and the further impact of increased investment on consumption. Following through the original consumption effects again, starting in the lower left part of the figure, we see the resulting $16 billion increase in GNP. Starting with period 2 we see the first original increase in consumption of $8 billion, the increase of $4 billion resulting from the $8 billion increase in consumption of period 1, and the level of induced investment of $2 billion. In period 3 we see (reading up the column) (*a*) original consumption of $8 billion, (*b*) induced consumption of $4 billion, resulting from the $8 billion, (*c*) induced consumption of $2 billion resulting from the $4 billion, (*d*) induced investment of 4 billion, and (*e*) further induced consumption resulting from induced investment of $1 billion. In period 4 we have, added to all this, further induced investment. The total impact is not shown exactly, but it is in the neighborhood of $28 to 31 billion.

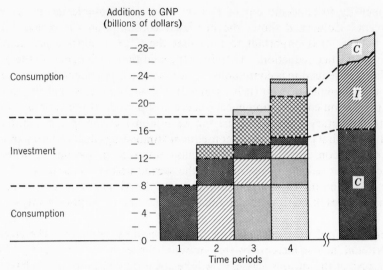

Figure 16-4. Effect of tax reduction on consumption and GNP including stimulus to investment. *Source:* JEC, *Jan. 1963 Ec. Rept. Pres*, H, p. 25.

In Table 16-5 we have another example of the possible increase in consumption resulting this time from a tax reduction of $10 billion. (The MPC = 93 percent of disposable income.) In this case, however, the tax reduction is not permanent. Therefore, we do not have the cumulative impact as in the previous examples. Instead, we should expect the GNP to return to its previous level after the impact of the tax cut has worked itself out. The point is quite clear if one compares the last column in Table 16-5 with either of the CEA figures discussed. Table 16-5 is that of Roy Moor and is subject to the assumptions he uses, as noted before. One advantage of this table is that each step is carefully spelled out, and the leakages can be easily followed through. It is for this reason, rather than because of its predictive accuracy, that it has been included here.

For purposes of analysis rather than because of its predictive accuracy, we have also included Moor's illustration of both the accelerator and the multiplier operating together, during a period of rising GNP. The example, of course, is subject to all the limitations previously noted and the assumptions underlying the table. One point to be noted is the manner in which the level of investment is determined. Ignoring many other influences on investment Moor noted that the ratio of investment to consumption during the peaks of the postwar cycles *averaged .225C*. When the peak of the cycle is reached after the tax cut of Table 16-6 then investment will be 22.5 percent of consumption. (390.18 × .225 = 87.79). From this an accelerator can be computed.[40]

[40] For Moor's computation see JEC, 1963 *Ann. Rept.*, p. 52.

Table 16-5. Hypothetical Increase in Consumption Demand From 1-Year Tax Cut
(In Billions of Dollars)

Period	Tax Reduction	Increases in GNP	Increases in Nonpersonal Income (22.5 Percent of GNP)	Increases in Personal Income	Increases in Personal Tax (13 Percent of Personal Income)	Increases in Disposable Incomes	Increases in Personal Savings (7 Percent of DPI)	Increases in GNP
1	10.00	—	—	—	—	10.00	0.70	9.30
2	—	9.30	2.09	7.21	0.94	6.27	0.44	5.83
3	—	5.83	1.31	4.52	0.59	3.93	0.27	3.66
4	—	3.66	0.82	2.84	0.37	2.47	0.17	2.30
5	—	2.30	0.52	1.78	0.23	1.55	0.11	1.44
6	—	1.44	0.32	1.12	0.15	0.97	0.07	0.90
7	—	0.90	0.20	0.70	0.09	0.61	0.04	0.57
8	—	0.57	0.13	0.44	0.06	0.38	0.03	0.35
9	—	0.35	0.08	0.27	0.04	0.23	0.02	0.21
10	—	0.21	0.05	0.16	0.02	0.14	0.01	0.13
11	—	0.13	0.03	0.10	0.01	0.09		
·	·	·	·	·	·	·	·	·
·	·	·	·	·	·	·	·	·
·	·	·	·	·	·	·	·	·
Approximate totals		24.97	5.62	19.35	2.52	26.83	1.88	24.97

Source: JEC, 1963 Ann. Rept., p. 48.

Note: Assumes no change in (1) demand for imports; (2) private investment or government expenditures; (3) distribution of income; and (4) effective tax rates after tax reduction.

Table 16-6. Hypothetical Operation of Combined Multiplier-Accelerator with Increasing GNP (Seasonally Adjusted Annual Rates)
(Billions of Dollars)

| Period | GNP | Consumption | Investment | Changes in Consumption Associated with Tax Cut in Period | | | | | | | | Changes in Investment |
| | | | | 1963 | | | | 1964 | | | | |
				1	2	3	4	1	2	3	4	
1962: 4	562.00	363.50	75.00	—								—
1963: 1	575.92	372.80	79.62	9.30	—							4.62
2	584.90	378.86	82.54	5.83	9.53	—						7.54
3	590.87	382.87	84.50	3.66	5.98	9.68	—					9.40
4	594.48	385.39	85.59	2.30	3.75	6.07	9.77	—				10.59
1964: 1	596.94	387.07	86.37	1.44	2.35	3.81	6.13	9.84	—			11.37
2	598.51	388.15	86.86	0.90	1.47	2.39	3.84	6.17	9.88	—		11.86
3	599.71	388.97	87.24	0.57	0.92	1.50	2.41	3.87	6.20	9.90	—	12.24
4	600.24	389.33	87.41	0.35	0.58	0.94	1.51	2.43	3.89	6.21	9.92	12.41
	.	.	.	0.21	0.36	0.59	0.95	1.52	2.44	3.89	6.22	—
	.	.	.	0.13	0.22	0.37	0.60	0.95	1.53	2.44	3.90	—
	.	.	.	—	—	—	—	—	—	—	—	.
Approximate levels	601.46	390.18	87.78	—								12.78

Source: JEC 1963 Ann. Rept., p. 54.

The starting point in Table 16-6 approximates the economic conditions of 1962(4). In addition, government expenditures are held constant at $123.5 billion; the constant term in the consumption function is assumed to be $363.5 billion, autonomous investment is assumed to be $75 billion, and the tax cut is permanent. The increase in consumption resulting from the tax cut is shown at a quarterly rate over a 2-year period. Similarly, induced investment is shown in the last column.[41]

In Table 16-6 taxes are reduced by $10 billion, disposable income increases by this amount, and 93 percent of this is spent on consumption. Therefore $C = \$9.3$ billion in 1963(1). There is in addition the impact of increased consumption on investment via the accelerator, and $\Delta I = \$4.62$ billion. The total increase in GNP equals $\Delta C + \Delta I = 9.30 + 4.62 = 13.92$.

In 1963(2) C is $15.36 billion greater than in 1962(4). The $9.30 billion increase in C raised GNP by $9.30 billion. However, 22.5 percent of this went into nonpersonal income (see Table 16-5), and 13 percent of the remaining personal income goes for personal taxes, leaving increased disposable income of $6.27 billion. Of this 93 per cent or $5.83 billion is spent. This is not all, however; there is a further increase in C of $9.53 billion, due to the fact that the tax cut is *permanent*. We note that 9.53 is greater than 9.30; the lower tax rate (which brought the $10 billion tax reduction) is now applied to a greater aggregate income. Hence DI and C are both greater.

The impact of the accelerator, or induced investment, is shown in the last column. Moor made no attempt to show the further impact of induced investment on consumption. A more complete model, of course, would do this.

INSTITUTIONAL AND AUTOMATIC STABILIZERS

Although the tone of many of the preceding chapters may appear somewhat pessimistic, it must be recalled that we have spent considerable time measuring the performance of the economy against its *potential* output and growth rate. The overall performance of the economy since World War II, on an historical basis, has been favorable. An important factor in this development has been the role of both institutional and automatic stabilizers.[42]

---

[41] See *ibid.*, p. 54 for a discussion of Moor's assumptions and computations.

[42] Discretionary tax cuts on excise taxes, it is generally argued, would be too upsetting to business. They are not discussed here although they would either increase expenditures on items so taxed, or release income to be spent on other items.

We have not discussed the impact of the tax on purchases of consumer durables. It is sometimes argued that the tax reduction will be used to pay off installment debt

The Institutional Stabilizers

The institutional stabilizers (or "bulwarks") are institutional changes that tend to strengthen the economy and insulate it against both deflationary and inflationary movements. Among them are: the Federal Reserve system which, with its expanded powers, can exert a stabilizing and counter-cyclical influence on the supply of money and interest rates; the FDIC, which contributes to the stability of the banking system; the Securities and Exchange Commission, which contributes to the stability of the stock exchanges; the sheer magnitude of government expenditures, which has assured the turnover of funds and a larger generation of income; the growing power of organized labor, which makes it more likely that wage rates will rise with productivity increases and help maintain the level of income, and which will exert political pressure on the federal government to take action during recessions and depressions; the relative absence of cyclically aggravating short-term mortgages; the introduction of mort-gage insurance and guarantees; the revision of the tax structure and the use of the progressive income tax; the so-called institutionalization of research by oligopolistic business firms; the fact that so many people are in effect on a guaranteed annual wage (millions of civil service and educa-tional positions), and the relative increase in salaried as compared with wage positions; the acceptance by the federal government of the principles embodied in the Employment Act; greater rigidity of wages and prices; and the more equal distribution of income which has resulted from many of these things. It should not be assumed that these changes have been made primarily for stabilization purposes; rather, their stabilization characteristics are largely by-products of other goals for which they were established.[43]

The Automatic Stabilizers

Automatic stabilizers may be defined as provisions which (1) create a government deficit during a slump and a surplus during prosperous times, (2) expand the public's stock of money and near money during a slump and reduce it during prosperity, and (3) go into effect "automatically" rather than on the basis of discretionary action.[44] The more important

---

and not for the purchase of additional durables. On the other hand, there is some evidence that the tax cut will encourage consumer durable expenditures, and further create additional confidence.

[43] For further discussion see the sources cited in Keiser, "The Development of the Concept of 'Automatic Stabilizers,'" *J. Finance*, Dec. 1956, pp. 427–8.

[44] See A. G. Hart, *Money, Debt, and Economic Activity*, New York: Prentice Hall, 1953, p. 462, and W. P. Egle, *Economic Stabilization*, Princeton: Princeton Univ. Press, 1952.

automatic stabilizers are the individual income tax, unemployment insurance, and the corporate income tax. Also included are excise taxes and the OASI program.[45]

Although many studies have been done of the effectiveness of automatic stabilizers, we have cited only the most recent here.[46] Clement found the most important stabilizers to be the corporate and personal income taxes and unemployment insurance. In an investigation of the 1948–49 and 1953–54 recessions he found that with a $10 billion increase in national income disposable income would increase only by about $7.2 billion. The stabilizers, in other words, would offset almost 30 percent of the increase in national income. A fall in national income of $10 billion would result in a decrease in disposable income of $5.1 billion less than without the stabilizers. In other words, the $10 billion decrease in national income would decrease disposable income by only $4.9 billion. As for the impact on consumption, Clement estimated that, with the $10 billion drop in income, consumption would fall by $7.1 billion without the automatic stabilizers, but by only $2.7 billion with the stabilizers. Consumption is kept about $4.4 billion or 62 percent higher than it would otherwise have been (4.4/7.1). In the case of the increase in income consumption is held down by $2.6 billion or 33 percent—without the stabilizers the increase in disposable income would have been $10 billion, and the increase in consumption about $7.9 billion; but with the stabilizers the increase in disposable income is $7.2 billion, and the increase in consumption is only $5.3 billion. Professor Clement is careful to note it is not easy to determine the quantitative impact of the automatic stabilizers; that is, it will vary from cycle to cycle. This is particularly significant to policy makers.

The Individual Income Tax. Other studies (covering the period 1948–1953) have found that approximately 62 percent of increases in adjusted gross income show up as taxable income ($\Delta TI / \Delta AGI$); the average rate

[45] See Keiser, "The Development of the Concept of 'Automatic Stabilizers,'" *J. Finance*, Dec. 1956, p. 425, and M. O. Clement, "The Concept of Automatic Stabilizers," *Southern Ec. J.*, Jan. 1959, pp. 304–312.

[46] For a list of studies of the impact of automatic stabilizers see the Keiser article cited in footnote 45, p. 438; and the recent study by M. O. Clement, "The Quantitative Impact of Automatic Stabilizers," *Rev. Ec. & Stat.*, Feb. 1960, pp. 56–61, for other references. See also L. Cohen, "An Empirical Measurement of the Built-In Flexibility of the Individual Income Tax," *Am. Ec. Rev.*, May 1959, pp. 532–541; and K. E. Poole, "Built-in Flexibility and the Experience of the Fifties," pp. 2331–2344; E. R. Rolph, "Built-in Flexibility and Monetary Management," pp. 2345–2355; and E. Cary Brown, "The Personal Income Tax as an Automatic Stabilizer," pp. 2357–2362: all in WMC, HR, *Tax Revis. Comp.*, P. See also the estimates of the role of the automatic stabilizers of B. Hickman, "Federal Spending and Stability of the Postwar Economy," JEC, *Fed. Exp. Pol.*, P, pp. 369–373.

of taxation (Tax/AGI) has been 25 to 26 percent (and it did not change much during the years 1943–1953 even though total taxable income increased); and the marginal rate $\Delta T/\Delta TI$ has varied from 18 to 31 percent. The built-in flexibility, defined as $\Delta T/\Delta AGI = (\Delta TI/\Delta AGI)(\Delta T/\Delta TI)$, has varied from 10.8 to 19.3 percent and averaged about 14 percent.[47] This means that the change in tax liabilities associated with a change in total adjusted gross income was about 14 percent. With a given increase in adjusted gross income tax yield would increase by 14 percent.

The Individual Income Tax and Inflation. The role of the individual income tax in offsetting inflation was apparently not very significant during our most inflationary postwar period. During the 1946–1948 period the individual income tax yielded in constant prices almost a constant amount. The tax yield kept up with inflation but that was all.[48]

Increasing the Cyclical Sensitivity of the Income Tax. Brown maintains that the yield response of the tax can be changed by altering the basic rate or the level of exemptions, but that "tinkering with the progressive rate structure will be of relatively little consequence for its yield sensitivity."[48] (This comment is based, of course, on studies by Brown and others.) In a study covering a period of time longer than that of most other studies, Professors Brown and Richard J. Kruzinga found the yield sensitivity to be about 12 percent of personal income under 1953 rates and exemptions, and about 13 percent under the post-1954 structure. By raising exemptions and compensating for the revenue loss by increasing the initial tax rate yield, sensitivity can be raised to 14.5 or 15 percent. In other words, if the exemption is $600 and the tax rate is about 20 percent, yield sensitivity is about 14 percent; if the exemption is $800 and the rate 22 percent, yield sensitivity is 14.5 percent; and if the exemption is $1,000 and the starting rate 24 percent, yield sensitivity is 15 percent.[49] Even this, however, results in only a moderate change in yield sensitivity, which leads Brown to conclude that rather drastic changes would have to be made in the tax to increase significantly its yield sensitivity.

We noted above that the average tax rate has not been much affected by changes in income. This is because the distribution of taxable income in each bracket has been relatively stable. Logic indicates that if there were more brackets at the lower end of the taxable income scale, yield sensitivity would increase. A progressive rate structure at the top of the income scale is not too useful for the simple reason that there is not that much

[47] Cohen, *op. cit.*

[48] See Brown, "The Personal Income Tax as an Automatic Stabilizer," *op. cit.*, p. 2359.

[49] *Ibid.*, p. 2360.

income up there. The introduction of greater progressivity in the lower brackets would place the progressivity where the bulk of the taxpayers are. Brown has suggested that the first two brackets be sliced into $500 sizes.[49] This change should not be made without an evaluation of equity and other considerations, however.

Of course, the sensitivity of the income tax can be increased if rates are automatically increased or decreased to offset inflationary or deflationary movements. Brown has expressed a willingness to accept rate increases or decreases on a formula-flexible basis.[50]

The Automatic Stabilizers and Economic Policy

Economists welcome the built-in flexibility which is provided by the automatic stabilizers—as far as it goes. The automatic stabilizers are helpful during mild economic downturns, but they will not reverse a real depression movement. If the latter should develop, other remedial policies would have to be undertaken. Furthermore, the automatic stabilizers may have done us an injustice in one important sense: They may have contributed to a smug sense of economic security; they may have encouraged the acceptance of the idea that they will stop a depression from developing; they may have created the attitude among policy-makers that other action is not necessary; and they certainly have reduced the possibility of appropriate discretionary action being taken. During 1953–1954 recession, considerable pressure was exerted to reduce the the income tax. During the 1957–1958 recession, the pressure was even greater. One has only to leaf through congressional hearings during and after this period to see how economist after economist recommended a tax reduction to counteract the recession. Instead, the Administration and the Congress took a wait-and-see attitude. During the 1960–1961 recession, which turned out to be fairly mild anyway—due in part, at least, to discretionary actions being taken, the Congress was still waiting.

Other programs have been developed which have, in essence, embodied the principles either of the automatic stabilizers or formula-flexible stabilizers, but particularly emphasizing the latter.[51] Again, a major motivation underlying these schemes represents a distrust of the use of discretionary policy by the President, the fear of a bias toward full employment and inflation, the difficulties of forecasting, and the snail-like speed

---

[50] *Ibid.*, pp. 2360–2361. For a list of suggestions for improvement, see the Keiser article on automatic stabilizers cited previously, pp. 439–440.

[51] See the CED's "stabilizing budget policy" in *Taxes and the Budget: a Program for Prosperity in a Free Economy*, New York, Nov. 1947, and the many statements (and amendments) in later CED publications; and M. Friedman, "A Monetary and Fiscal Framework for Economic Stability," *Am. Ec. Rev.*, June 1948, pp. 245–64.

of revisions in taxes by the Congress and the Chief Executive. Further, they are subject to all the shortcomings of formula-flexible schemes, whereby the predetermined changes in taxes (or expenditures) may not be the appropriate remedy for the problem, and they are further suspect in that they often assume a serious economic decline to be precluded from the scene.[52]

[52] See W. W. Heller's review and evaluation of the CED program in "CED's Stabilizing Budget Policy After Ten Years," *Am. Ec. Rev.*, Sept. 1957, pp. 634–651, and A. Hansen's critique of the program in *Monetary Theory and Fiscal Policy*, New York: McGraw-Hill, 1949, Chapter 13.

17

Monetary Aspects of Fiscal Policy

In this chapter we examine some of the relationships among monetary, fiscal, and debt management policy. Such relationships are important because the type of monetary policy used with a given fiscal policy will result in greater or less expansion or contraction in the economy. The same statement can be made about the relationship between debt management and fiscal policy.

It is often advocated, for example, that a tight fiscal policy (higher taxes on consumption and lower taxes on investment) and an easy monetary policy would have the effect of increasing our stock of capital and our rate of growth. The function of lower taxes on investment and available credit and low interest rates is to encourage capital formation, while the purpose of higher taxes on consumption is both to release resources for use for investment and at the same time to restrain inflationary expenditures. By imposing a high tax rate on the economy, and at the same time restricting expenditures, we have come close to pursuing such a policy, except that monetary policy has also been tight during the relevant periods, (1956, 1957, 1959, and 1960). We have seen in Chapter 15, however, that the policy which was followed did not work, but rather was apparently stymied by the setting in of the paradox of thrift.[1] The existence of excess capacity, lower profits, and inadequate demand have restrained our rate of growth. All this, however, does not necessarily mean that a policy of tight fiscal and loose monetary control cannot be made to work.[2]

Our first business in this chapter is to review and discuss the techniques of monetary policy, expansionary and contractionary monetary policies,

---

[1] By virtue of an attempt to tax too much, which is to save too much, since each represents a leakage. Scheduled or planned saving (taxes) were too great.

[2] Whether or not it will work depends on investment demand, which in turn will be affected by innovations, consumption, and profits generally. The tight fiscal policy may result in imbalanced growth. On the other hand, inflation may result under conditions of strong investment demand unless consumption is strongly restrained.

and monetary policy and economic growth. We next discuss debt management and stabilization policy. Finally, we examine the effectiveness of monetary policy, in which context we cover offsets to monetary policy and the impact of monetary policy on various sectors of the economy.

MONETARY POLICY[3]

The traditional techniques of monetary control are (1) open market operations, (2) changes in reserve requirements, (3) the discount rate, and (4) moral suasion. (1) Open market operations involve Federal Reserve purchases and sales of (primarily) government securities from commercial banks, other financial institutions, corporations, private individuals, etc.[4] (2) Reserve requirements refer to the percentage of demand deposits and time deposits which a member bank must have on reserve at its respective Federal Reserve Bank. (3) The discount rate is the price member banks must pay for borrowing from the Federal Reserve. (4) Moral suasion concerns the actions of the central bankers to encourage commercial bankers to be more or less lenient in making loans, determining the cost and repayment of loans, and similar matters. Its use has apparently not been very effective in the United States, mainly because the Federal Reserve has not followed up its policy recommendations with threats of punitive action for noncompliance.

If an easy money policy is to be pursued, it can be realized by all or any combination of the following: Open market operations should consist of purchases of securities to place money in the hands of sellers and to lower interest rates; reserve requirements should be lowered so as to create or add to the volume of excess reserves; the discount rate should be lowered; and banks should be encouraged to make more loans, at lower interest, and with longer repayment terms. A tight money policy would call for the opposite of all these steps.

[3] For good accounts of monetary policy and theory from World War II to the present see W. L. Smith, Chapter 9 in JEC, *Empl., Growth, Price Levels*, SR; R. Freeman in *Postwar Economic Trends in the U.S.*, New York: Harper, 1960, Chapter 3; and A. Achinstein, *Federal Reserve Policy and Economic Stability, 1951–57*, Senate Committee on Banking and Currency, 1958. See also *Rev. Ec. & Stat.*, Aug. 1960, for short articles by S. E. Harris, J. W. Angell, W. Fellner, A. H. Hansen, A. G. Hart, Hans Neisser, R. V. Roosa, P. A. Samuelson, W. L. Smith, Woodlief Thomas, J. Tobin, and S. Weintraub. See also *ibid.*, Feb. 1963 Supplement, "The State of Monetary Economics" (Part I: Monetary Economics; Part II: The Report and Staff Papers of the Commission on Money and Credit). See texts on money and banking, such as those of A. G. Hart and P. Kenen, and L. V. Chandler. Finally, see H. G. Johnson, "Monetary Theory and Policy," *Am. Ec. Rev.*, June 1963, pp. 335–384; and L. Tarshis' review article, "Money and Credit," same issue, pp. 472–480.

[4] Other types of security may be included, but they are numerically small.

An Expansionary Monetary Policy: Financing a Deficit

In financing a deficit, the government may secure funds in any of the following ways:
1. Print new money.
2. Borrow directly from the Federal Reserve.
3. Borrow from commercial banks from excess reserves supplied them by means of open market purchases or lower reserve requirements.
4. Borrow from the commercial banks.
5. Borrow from the public generally.

For the most part, and for reasons to be subsequently discussed, these policies are listed in order of decreasing importance relative to their expansionary impact. For example, printing new money to finance a deficit is the most expansionary. (Its expansionary impact would be increased if, at the same time, the government were also to retire outstanding debt by issuing new money.)

1. Let us assume that we pursue a budget policy in which there is a deficit financed by printing new money. We can expect an impact on consumption which may be divided into the income and wealth effects. The income effect results from the fact that the government spends and consumers receive income. The wealth effect results from the fact that savings accumulate as income increases, creating greater security (and building up assets) and an attitude conducive to some further increase in consumption.

But this is not all: There is also an income and interest rate effect on investment. The fact that consumption increases will, assuming that income and consumption continue to expand for a long enough period, induce increases in investment. Furthermore, the fact that the deficit was created by means of printing new money keeps interest rates low, which should also encourage an increase in investment expenditures (unless, of course, the investment schedule is interest inelastic). If the government borrowed from commercial banks or other financial institutions some upward pressure may be exerted on financial institutions, depending on the amount of borrowing relative to the supply of available funds.

2. Borrowing from the Federal Reserve directly and **(3)** borrowing from the commercial banks from excess reserves supplied to them by means of open market purchases or lower reserve requirements gives similar results. In all three cases, the money supply is increased, the income and wealth effects operate on both consumption and investment, and there should be little or no pressure exerted on interest rates.

4. Borrowing from commercial banks with no increase in excess reserves is potentially less expansionary because the act of government borrowing may preclude later business loans for investment purposes, and there may also be created some upward pressures on interest rates, depending on the initial level of reserves. Nonetheless, the money supply is still increased, and the income and wealth effects should still operate on both consumption and investment. If the current level of reserves is low and is not enlarged as needed for growth, this policy will become unduly restrictive.

5. Borrowing from the nonbank public is still likely to have a substantial income effect. Such borrowing is not likely to reduce consumption significantly for the simple reason that those who purchase government securities would probably not spend these same funds on consumer goods anyway. There will, therefore, still be the income and wealth effects on consumption, the income effect on investment, but a possible adverse interest rate effect on investment. The potentially more restrictive impact on investment than that of policy 4 is the result of the fact that there has been *no* increase in the money supply. A further possible result of both policies 4 and 5 is an adverse reaction on consumer borrowing (and purchases) because of the unavailability of funds. Under recession or depression conditions, however, there should be little reason to be concerned over this possibility.

We have already noted that in policies 1 through 4 we have an increase in the money supply. Further increases in the money supply will occur as the initially created money is redeposited in and borrowed from commercial banks. We should also note that in policies 2 through 5 an increase in government debt has taken place. Further increases in private debt are likely to occur also as business and consumers increase their borrowing during the cyclical upswing.

The potential increase in the money supply is the same in the first three policies, but the net increase in assets is not the same. In policies 1 and 2 there is an immediate net increase in assets to the extent of the increase in the money supply. Policy 3 can go in either direction: If excess reserves are created by lowering reserve requirements there is a larger net increase in assets (government debt increases *and* the money supply increases), but if excess reserves are created by open market purchases, there is initially only an exchange of assets (the value of the securities purchased = to the excess reserves = to the size of the deficit). In this case, it is true, there has been an increase in the money supply, but this (initially) merely offsets the value of securities sold by the commercial banks or others. In policy 4 banks exchange excess reserves for government debt and there is no increase in net assets. Again, however, there is an increase in the money supply, which has important income and wealth effects. Similar results occur under policy 5.

In the midst of the discussion of the effectiveness and advisability of a substantial reduction in federal taxes in the summer of 1962, Chairman Martin of the Federal Reserve stated that the resulting deficit in the federal budget would have to be financed from current saving, not from "bank money." By this he apparently meant that the financing of the deficit would have to come from current saving from the current income of private individuals. Some feared that Mr. Martin meant (1) to reduce free reserves to zero, and (2) to force the banks to substitute government securities for private loans. As we noted, this is the most restrictive policy to follow. In the fall of 1962, Mr. Martin is reported to have modified his attitude; he most certainly must have done so, because he was reappointed Chairman of the Board of Governors for another 4-year term in February, 1963. For more on Mr. Martin's attitudes, see Appendix A of this chapter.

We have assumed that a budget deficit was a desirable policy to pursue. The expansion in the economy comes from the fact that income is increased and the multiplier begins to operate, and from the fact that as income increases saving and wealth increase, which tends to encourage some additional spending. Further, the greater the reliance placed on the creation of money to finance the deficit, the lower interest rates will be. Lower interest rates could mean that the deficit necessary to attain a given increase in income may be smaller because the lower interest rates may stimulate investment spending.

A Contractionary Monetary Policy

If a budget surplus is the goal of fiscal policy and it is realized, the question arises of what to do with it. The government can hold it itself (in, say, Federal Reserve Banks), hold it in the commercial banks, hold it in other financial institutions, or use it to pay off part of the public debt. Clearly the most restrictive policy is for the government to hold the surplus in the Federal Reserve Banks (or purchase securities from only Federal Reserve Banks). If it leaves the surplus on deposit in commercial banks the latter will increase loans (and create a multiple expansion of the money supply). If it places the funds in other financial institutions, the major portion of them will be loaned out. If it pays off the debt, it exchanges its money for its debt held by other people, corporations, financial institutions, etc., and again adds to the money supply (or reserves) which can result in further spending for investment or consumption goods, or both.

By following the most restrictive policy—holding the surplus in the

Federal Reserve Banks, or purchasing securities from only the Federal Reserve—it reduces the money supply, which in turn raises the interest rate and reduces the supply of funds, which in turn should have an adverse effect on investment. Further, and probably most important, is the restrictive effect of the surplus on consumption via the reduction in disposable income.

If the policy-makers are intent on restricting what is already a rapid growth of consumption but amenable to an increase in investment (or, in other words, are stressing a growth policy) then a surplus combined with the retirement of debt would be an acceptable policy. In and of itself such a policy may not be sufficient to both reduce consumption and raise investment at the same time unless further steps are taken to make certain that the funds so released are directly channelled into investment and not into consumer credit. Some control over the allocation of loans into these two areas may be necessary. Such a policy will likely work during a period of high prosperity, but caution must be taken to avoid a virtual explosion of investment spending and consequent inflation. On the other hand, care must also be taken to insure that investment demand is strong enough to maintain employment over the longer run.

Monetary Policy for Economic Growth

While it is true that a given supply of money can support a growing economy by means of an increase in velocity, it is also true that there is an upper limit. As we noted in our discussion of *LM* and *IS* curves (see Figure 7-11) a given supply of money will support an income level of a certain magnitude and no more. Eventually a point will be reached at which further attempts to increase investment (upward shifts in the *IS* curve) will be fruitless. Furthermore, as velocity increases the interest rate will rise. It is possible that higher interest (or the limitation of funds for investment) may adversely affect investment and reduce the rate of growth that we so dearly want. It is apparent, then, that an expansion in the money supply is a prerequisite to economic growth.

The expansion in the money supply can come through a reduction in reserve requirements, printing new money, or monetizing outstanding government debt. The latter could be accomplished by means of government printing of money and purchasing its own securities directly, or by Federal Reserve purchases of these same securities, which it would turn over to the federal government.[5] One may be inclined to state that there is only so much government debt outstanding and that there is therefore

---

[5] Under Sec. 14(b) of the Federal Reserve Act, the Federal Reserve can purchase securities directly from the Treasury. This, however, is intended to be a limited and emergency measure.

an upper limit to the amount of money which can be created by debt monetization. Such a conclusion would not be strictly correct, however, because the government would at times be issuing new debt. The circumstances under which this would occur would include periods when a deficit was necessary and the decision was made to finance the deficit with debt rather than the printing of new money, or situations in which the government pursued a policy of placing debt in the hands of the public and banking institutions as an anti-inflationary precaution.[6]

DEBT POLICY AND STABILIZATION POLICY

Interrelationships among Monetary, Debt, and Fiscal Policy: Buying and Selling Debt, Short- and Long-Term Debt, and Interest Charges

Debt management, fiscal policy, and monetary policy are all interrelated. The distinction between fiscal and monetary policy should be reasonably clear, but a clear-cut definition of debt management is not as easy to come by, especially since the three different policies are all related to sales and purchases of government securities. One well-known monetary economist has offered the following comment on policy differences:

We shall define *debt management* to include all actions of the Government, including both the Treasury and the Federal Reserve, which affect the *composition* of the publicly held debt. When defined in this way debt management includes: (1) decisions by the Treasury concerning the *types* of debts to be issued to raise new money, (2) decisions by the Treasury concerning the *types* of debt to be issued in connection with the refunding of maturing securities, (3) decisions by the Federal Reserve concerning the *types* of debt to be purchased and sold in the conduct of open market operations.

It should be noted that under this definition of debt management, the *amount* of new securities to be sold by the Treasury to cover budget deficits or to be retired with the proceeds of budget surpluses is not a matter of debt management but of fiscal policy. Moreover, decisions by the Federal Reserve which change the publicly held money supply, including changes in reserve requirements and the *amount* (but not the composition) of open market purchases and sales, fall under the heading of monetary policy.[7]

In using debt and monetary policy as integral parts of stabilization policy, decisions must be made as to when government securities should be bought or sold or new money printed. Policies actually used could,

---

[6] The interested reader may want to examine J. Aschheim, *Techniques of Monetary Control*, Baltimore: Johns Hopkins Univ. Press, 1961.

[7] W. L. Smith, JEC, *Empl., Growth, Price Levels*, SR, p. 411. See also Musgrave, *The Theory of Public Finance*, New York: McGraw-Hill, 1959, Chapters 22 and 24.

and probably should, be a mixture of these possibilities. The criteria that should be followed in the determination of this policy are the least cost per benefit received, the degree of liquidity desired, and the impact on economic stabilization.[8]

If the policy need is to expand the money supply, and the least-cost principle is accepted, this should be done by the monetization of some portion of the outstanding debt. We noted that this could be done by the direct printing of money to purchase government securities outstanding, or by Federal Reserve purchases of government securities (which the latter can turn over to the federal government). Many economists strongly feel that if the debt is not monetized under these conditions there should be strong reasons for not doing so, because outstanding debt creates important interest charges for the government to pay.[9]

If it is desired to soak up excess liquidity in the economy, government debt should be sold. This is, then, the justification for paying interest on the debt—the purchase of illiquidity. Interest charges are therefore certainly legitimate. We can go even farther than this and note that interest charges above current statutory limits are not necessarily objectionable *if* they result in a commensurate reduction of liquidity. The interest charge itself must be balanced against the amount of illiquidity secured. It is possible, for example, to sell the same dollar volume of short- and long-term securities, but a much higher degree of illiquidity will be purchased if the long-term securities are sold by the government. Although the interest charge is usually higher on long-terms, the total interest cost may not be, because less debt would have to be sold to secure a given degree of illiquidity.[10] These comments are not intended to convey the impression that interest charges should be slighted over. Quite to the contrary; it would be wise to keep them as low as possible because they have been running at a rate of about 11 percent of the federal budget. This, in turn, means that government funds used to pay interest charges are not available for other important and valuable social services.

In an inflationary (or potentially inflationary) situation, the type and extent of free reserves in the banking system influence the type of policy selected. Under these conditions, some combination of sales of debt, taxation, and increased reserve requirements can be used. If a very large volume of free reserves is outstanding, it is doubtful that any single policy would be used.

The primary responsibility for carrying out monetary policy falls on

[8] Musgrave, *op. cit.*, pp. 582–583.
[9] *Ibid.*, p. 582. The banker point of view, that preference should be given to the reduction of reserve requirements, is discussed in the next section.
[10] *Ibid.*, p. 583; W. L. Smith, *op. cit.*, pp. 418–419.

the Federal Reserve. Actions of the Treasury in its management of the debt and the structure of the debt, can, however, influence monetary policy.[11] These actions of the Treasury which affect the amount of debt outstanding and the structure of the debt may in turn influence interest rates and liquidity. These latter changes may then influence the level and types of private expenditures in the economy. Changes in debt management policy that result in changes in the composition of the debt may affect expectations relative to prices, employment, or yields which in turn result in changes in aggregate expenditure. To the extent that changes in debt management result in different supplies of debt or in yields, capital values, costs of borrowing, and the distribution of income are affected. There may, in addition, be changes in portfolios which in turn result in greater or less aggregate expenditures in the economy, or which may result in reallocation of expenditures.[12]

Traditional debt management theory has maintained that the maturity structure of the debt should be lengthened during periods of prosperity; that is, the Treasury should attempt to sell long-term securities during prosperous periods. The reasoning underlying this policy recommendation is that such sales will reduce the volume of funds available for investment and also reduce liquidity. The counterpart of the traditional theory is that short-terms should be sold during recessions to increase liquidity and to disturb as little as possible the available funds for long-term investment. In recent years, however, the Treasury has not been able to follow these traditional rules and has, in fact, found it necessary or advisable to sell long-terms during recessions.

We have previously noted that a conflict may develop between the goals of interest-cost minimization and economic stabilization. Sales of long-terms, for instance, generally involve a substantially higher interest cost, but they may also bring a substantially higher degree of illiquidity. We have noted, though, that the Treasury has found it very difficult to sell long-terms during periods of prosperity. Many economists have concluded, therefore, that a case can be made for the sale of long-terms

---

[11] It should be noted that there are several concepts of the federal debt. "Total gross debt" refers to *all* federal securities outstanding. Sizable portions of this gross debt are held by government trust funds, etc., and by the FR. Many monetary economists argue that our major concern should be the resulting publicly held debt, which has averaged about 70 percent of the total gross debt in recent years. As a percent of the GNP the publicly held debt has declined from 86.9 to 44.2 percent from 1947 to 1958. W. L. Smith, *op. cit.*, pp. 410–411.

[12] See B. C. Hallowell and K. M. Williamson, "Federal Debt Management, 1953–58," *Rev. Ec. & Stat.*, Feb. 1963, pp. 47–54. Also of value should be James Tobin's CED paper, "An Essay on Principles of Debt Management," to be published by Prentice-Hall.

during recessions for the purpose of keeping interest costs down. They would at the same time, however, have the Federal Reserve step in to counteract any undesirable impact that Treasury sales may have. It would be possible under these circumstances to sell long-terms during recessions and at the same time save the Treasury a substantial sum of money. Furthermore, with Federal Reserve cooperation again, it would be possible for the Treasury to sell short-terms during periods of prosperity. It would not be necessary for the Federal Reserve to support Treasury sales of short-terms, or to let up on its tight money policy, because the demand for short-terms is generally sufficient to assure their sales. It may be necessary, however, for the Federal Reserve actually to sell some long-terms because of stabilization considerations.

Improving the Management of the Debt

Several steps have been suggested for reducing the interest cost of the debt, increasing or reducing liquidity as policy needs dictate, and making it easier for the Treasury to handle the debt. (1) It has been argued by many that too much reliance has been placed on monetary policy, driving up interest rates and the cost of financing and refinancing the federal debt. A more balanced mix of fiscal and monetary policy, so it is argued, will ease monetary policy and result in lower interest rates generally, increase taxes on consumption, produce surpluses, and therefore reduce the rate of growth of the public debt and reduce interest costs to the Treasury. Some who support this approach have argued that fiscal policy has been too easy. The alleged easiness of fiscal policy during the late 'fifties and early 'sixties did not exist, however, as we have previously indicated in our discussion of the full employment surplus. Nonetheless, the above policy is feasible under the proper circumstances.

(2) The successful use of selective controls could also result in an easier monetary policy and smaller interest costs to the Treasury. (3) The secular expansion of the money supply by means of open market purchases rather than by reduced reserve requirements would reduce both the size of the publicly held debt and interest costs. The Federal Reserve has placed great emphasis on lower reserve requirements as its method of expanding the money supply and open market operations for short-run stabilization purposes, and it has not raised reserve requirements since 1951. (The use of reserve requirements to expand the money supply does mean larger bank profits,[13] and a slightly greater leverage effect. On the other hand, one may also ask the question of whether or not there should be reserve requirements at all since the FDIC now serves the original function of

---

[13] Purchasing securities from banks merely involves an exchange of assets, whereas lower reserve requirements create a net increase in bank assets.

reserves. Exclusive reliance could be placed on open market operations.) All things considered, perhaps some combination of open market purchases and lower reserve requirements could be used. The savings to the Treasury and the taxpaying public are certainly significant, and any direct purchases by the Federal Reserve result in *cumulative* savings to the Treasury.

It has been estimated, assuming a 3 percent yearly growth in our money supply, that with FR purchases of securities rather than lower reserve requirements about one quarter of the public debt could be retired in 10 years and all of it eliminated in about 30 years. A 4 percent yearly increase in the money supply could retire one third of the debt in 10 years. Such a rapid rate of reduction would, of course, create other problems, especially for financial institutions.[14] Bankers, on the other hand (and former Secretary of the Treasury Anderson), feel that current reserve requirements are unjustifiably high—that they are a "burden" on member banks.[15] Chairman Martin has stated that if exactly the same amount of money was created by lowering reserve requirements and by open market purchases, the latter would be inflationary.[16] Such a technique for expanding the money supply is, in his mind, equivalent to "printing press money." Further, in his opinion it is not the function of the Federal Reserve to help taxpayers and the Treasury by expanding the money supply in this manner.[17]

Other suggestions include (4) lengthening the term structure of the debt so that fewer securities would be sold during periods of tight money, and reducing the number of occasions on which the Treasury would have to go into the market and perhaps interfere with Federal Reserve policy; (5) greater use of the auction technique whereby sales are to the highest bidder and interest costs are therefore the lowest possible; (6) frequent small offerings so that the Treasury could more regularly draw on current

[14] For a defense of the use of lower reserve requirements see the statements of Secretary Anderson and of the American Bankers Association, both in JEC, *Empl., Growth, Price Levels*, H, Pt. 10, starting, respectively, on pp. 3337 and 3484.

[15] The "burden" idea is former Secretary Anderson's. For an analysis of the sources of funds for commercial banks see FR Bank of New York, A. J. R. Smith, "Sources and Uses of Member Bank Reserves, 1914–52," 1953, as cited in *ibid.*, p. 3244 and reprinted in Part 6A, pp. 1300–1306. The study notes that a very small portion of reserve funds have been invested by the commercial banks themselves.

[16] *Ibid.*, pp. 1243–1245.

[17] *Ibid.*, p. 1244. For other statements of the advantages and disadvantages and the interest savings involved see the comments (or studies) by Chairman Martin, O. Eckstein, J. Kareken, Senator Douglas, and Rep. H. Reuss in *ibid.*, pp. 1286, 1290, 1455, 1464, 1251–1253; JEC, *Empl., Growth, Price Levels*, R, p. 45; JEC, *Jan. 1961 Ec. Rept. Pres.*, H, pp. 439, 478–479, 485, 487–488, 501, *Rev. Ann. Rept. FR*, 1960, H, pp. 76, 78, 170–172. See also A. Hansen, "Bankers and Subsidies," *Rev. Ec. & Stat.*, Feb. 1958, pp. 50–51.

saving;[18] (7) effective underwriting by the Federal Reserve, which would resell the securities in small lots over a period of time; (8) the creation of a more efficient selling organization, especially to small investors and smaller financial institutions located away from the traditional financial centers of the country; (9) greater Federal Reserve help in the elimination of meaningless, erratic, and unnecessary but disturbing fluctuations in the prices of government securities (the events of early 1958 which seriously distorted interest rates could have been avoided or considerably offset with help from the Federal Reserve); (10) greater use of advance refunding for the purpose of reselling debt to those who tend to dispose of liquid, soon-to-mature securities; and (11) the greater use of call features so that the Treasury is in a position to take advantage of favorable interest rates in future years (as is done with corporate bonds).[19]

THE EFFECTIVENESS OF MONETARY POLICY: FLEXIBILITY IN THE MONEY SUPPLY AND OFFSETS TO TIGHT MONEY

The Issues

One of the most hotly debated topics of the 1950's was the proper role and impact of monetary policy. The following questions have been asked about monetary policy: Have higher interest rates reduced investment expenditures? consumption expenditures? What has been the impact on FHA and GI mortgages? Has there been a discriminatory impact on different borrowers? Has big business, with its access to funds from various sources, really been hurt in the sense that it has been denied investment funds? Has a 2 or 3 percent increase in interest rates been an effective deterrent to investment? What has been the impact of a restrictive monetary policy on the rate of growth of the economy and on the unemployment rate? If higher rates have not been effective in deterring spending, especially investment expenditures, has an undesirable distribution of income resulted?[20] Along these same lines, what of the necessity for the

---

[18] Small offerings should not disturb FR policy, by the very fact of their smallness.

[19] This entire section leans heavily on W. L. Smith's excellent chapter, *op. cit.*

[20] Not much has been written on the impact of tight money on income distribution. The answers would be influenced by many variables, including the degree of tightness of monetary policy (the extent to which it creates unemployment, for example). For some discussion of incidence see Musgrave, JEC, *Rel. Prices to Ec. Growth & Stabil.*, P, pp. 601ff; and O. Brownlee and A. Conrad, "Effects Upon the Distribution of Income of a Tight Money Policy," *Am. Ec.Rev.* May 1961, pp. 74–85. It could be noted that interest income has seen a fairly substantial increase from 1952 to 1962.

federal government to pay higher interest on its debt? Have commercial bank (and other financial institutions') holdings of government securities really been "locked in"? To what extent has tight money been offset by velocity increases and the use of what previously has been idle money balances? Finally, has the tight money policy worked—has it stopped upward price movements? Have the price increases of the 1950's been of the type which is sensitive to a restrictive monetary policy? Or have they been due to such factors as structural rigidities, administered prices, shifts in the composition of demand, higher costs due to lower output, and the profit-wage-contract problem brought about by very uneven growth rates? We cannot possibly expect to give definitive answers to this complex set of questions, but we can attempt to throw some light on them, recognizing that monetary specialists are in wide disagreement about many aspects of monetary policy. (They disagree, for example, on how the money supply shall be defined,[21] how tightness and looseness of monetary policy is measured, the role of free reserves, etc.)

It is fairly widely agreed that there is some degree of flexibility in our monetary system, provided by the presence of various types of liquid assets (such as government securities) and the use of various techniques (such as mercantile credit,[22] where the manufacturer extends credit to a retailer by sending him goods without immediate payment). Further, the income velocity of money has increased significantly during the 1950's, which were dominated by a tight money policy. We should carefully note that in an advanced monetary economy like ours, some degree of flexibility is provided in the monetary system by such things as near money and other highly liquid assets. It is probably true that monetary policy, if pushed far enough, could stop any inflation. It is also probably true that to apply such an extreme and stringent monetary policy would seriously reduce the level of employment and income. The point is that some degree of flexibility is likely the inevitable result of our type of economy and that some moderate price fluctuations are the price that must be paid to be free of complete price and wage controls. Price increases based on "scare" buying like that in 1951, for example, are probably inevitable and un-avoidable. Finally, some economists have argued that we were fortunate in having the degree of flexibility we did have during the middle and late 1950's, or the impact of tight money would have been much more serious.[23]

---

[21] Chairman Martin has often made the comment that he and his staff are not certain of how the money supply should be defined. See JEC, *Jan. 1961 Ec. Rept. Pres.*, H, p. 483.

[22] See A. H. Meltzer, *Rev. Ec. & Stat.*, Nov. 1960. Meltzer also did a study for the Commission on Money and Credit on this same topic.

[23] W. L. Smith argues this way; *op. cit.*

The Money Supply, Velocity Increases, and the Business Cycle

An examination of the money supply and the income velocity of money reveals several important points. (1) Business declines since 1909 have been preceded by a reduced rate of growth in the money supply. The average lead has been about 12 months. The degree of reliability of this lead period for monetary policy under conditions in which inflation is already a fact is of rather obvious significance. (2) As the rate of growth of the money supply declines, income velocity increases. In other words, increased velocity *is* an offset to a tight money policy.[24] During the 1950's, for example, the monetary equivalent of the rise in income velocity was greater than the increase in the money supply itself. It is this change in velocity which acts as an offset to monetary policy. (During a recession, as the money supply grows velocity continues downward until the trough of the business cycle is arrived at. Hence it again acts as an offset to the goal of monetary policy.) There is in addition a lag between an increase in the money supply and recovery, although it is shorter than the lag between a change in the rate of growth of the money supply and downturns in the economy.

Increases in velocity are made possible because people economize on their cash balances. But there must be an upper limit to this as we noted previously. If additional economizing on cash is impossible, and if consumers and businesses hold relatively fewer liquid assets (than, say, during the late 1940's and early 1950's), total spending declines or fails to expand. (See Appendix B of this chapter for some important data on liquid assets.) The corporate liquidity ratio has declined during the 1950's,[25] and individual holdings of savings bonds (from December, 1947 to November, 1962) have remained approximately the same while individual holdings of other government securities have actually declined. The latter developments spell a rather sharp decline in this type of liquidity per household. On the other hand, there has been a substantial increase in commerical bank time deposits (the bulk of which are held by individuals), mutual savings bank time deposits, and savings and loan shares, the latter two

---

[24] *Ibid.*, p. 344ff. See B. W. Sprinkle, JEC, *Rel. Prices to Ec. Stabil. & Growth*, C, p. 76ff; and R. T. Selden, JEC, *Empl., Growth, Price Levels*, H, Pt. 4, pp. 688–699; "Cost-Push Versus Demand-Pull Inflation, 1955–57," *J. Polit. Ec.*, Feb. 1959; and *The Postwar Rise in the Velocity of Money*, New York: NBER, 1962. See also M. Friedman, JEC, *Rel. Prices to Ec. Stabil. & Growth*, P, pp. 241–256; and L. S. Ritter, "Income-Velocity and Anti-Inflationary Policy," *Am. Ec. Rev.*, March 1959, pp. 120–129.

[25] See R. W. Storer, "Some Factors Influencing the Monetary Economy in the 1960's," *Q. Rev. Ec. & Bus.*, May 1961, p. 28.

consisting almost entirely of personal savings of individuals.[26] Adjusting liquid assets for price and population increases may show little change in the amount held per family. There may have been a significant change, however, in the distribution among income groups since 1950 or since the immediate postwar years. In addition to the reduced liquidity as idle money balances are used and other balances are lowered, the pressure on the money supply created by a high demand for loans pushes up the rate of interest. This may adversely affect investment.

(3) The available evidence indicates that there is a positive correlation between the degree of change in the growth of the money supply and in the size of the GNP. Our most severe depressions have also been periods of severe contractions in the money supply.

One group of monetary economists in the United States strongly feels that the money supply tends to be the most important causal factor in the direction in which the economy moves. In the words of one member of this school, "in the absence of monetary change, there will not be a rapid expansion in the level of income. In the presence of monetary change, there will be a rapid expansion in the level of income."[27] Even though changes in the supply of money are recognized as being important, not all economists would unqualifiedly accept the previous statement. There is disagreement on when changes in the money supply cause changes in the economy, and when they reflect them. Certainly money is not the only factor, as an examination of growth and the theory of income determination shows.

We have noted that the Federal Reserve can bring about changes in the money supply by manipulating reserve requirements or through its open market operations. Although it may create excess reserves for commercial banks there need be no immediate or automatic increase in the money supply. The increase in the money supply occurs when people demand cash and borrow *and* when the banks decide to make loans. The same is true with a contraction in the money supply: More people are paying off loans than are taking them out. The preceding means that increases and decreases in the money supply are also a function of the demand for

---

[26] Savings and loan shares in 1950 were $14 billion and in 1961 $70.5 billion! Mutual savings bank time deposits in 1950 were $20.1 billion and $38.3 billion in 1961; time deposits in commercial banks in 1950 were $36.6 billion and $82.5 billion in 1961. See "Selected Liquid Assets Held by the Public" in the *1962 Supplement to Economic Indicators*, pp. 100–101.

Liquid assets as a percent of the GNP have declined significantly throughout the postwar period. See JEC, *Empl. Growth, Price Levels*, SP No. 14, p. 5.

[27] Paper and statement of A. H. Meltzer, JEC, *Jan. 1963 Ec. Rept. Pres*, H, Pt. 1, pp. 595–602, and 603. Quantity theorists have done much empirical work, which may have given them something of a headstart on other groups.

money and the demand for loans, as well as of Federal Reserve and commercial bank policy. In other words, a natural expansion and contraction in the money supply follows the trend of the business cycle and the expectations accompanying it. An expansion or contraction in the money supply, in other words, is not necessarily caused by changes in Federal Reserve policy.

On the other hand, high liquidity preferences on the part of people, an outright refusal of banks to make loans even though their excess reserves are plentiful, or open market sales and higher reserve requirements can restrict the supply of money and the expansion and growth of the economy. Hence the expression that a tight money policy can definitely be effective but an easy money policy not necessarily so. (An easy money policy is sometimes referred to as pushing a string!)

Even though monetary specialists are still arguing over many aspects of tight money policy (including how such a policy is measured) it would still seem that the late 1950's have been characterized by a relatively tight money policy. The very significant increase in the income velocity of money,[28] the long-run upward trend in both short- and long-term interest rates (they have never returned to their previous lows after any contraction),[29] the unavailability of loans to many groups in our society who would not necessarily be classed as poor risks,[30] the failure of the money supply to increase in 1956 and 1957; the ratio of the money supply to the GNP (which has dropped from about 50 per cent in 1945 to about 26 percent in the third quarter of 1962), and the performance of free reserves—all these are evidence of a tight money policy.[31] (See Figure 17-1.)

Free Reserves—An Accurate Measure of Tightness?

Free reserves are often used as a measure of the degree of tightness of monetary policy. They represent the difference between member bank excess reserves and member bank borrowing at the Federal Reserve Banks. We should note, though, that there is no common agreement that free reserves represent an acceptable measure of the degree of tightness of

[28] There are other measures of velocity, but they all point toward tightness of money. See the studies, *op. cit.*, of Selden and Ritter. Income velocity rose to a very high level in 1956 and then jumped to an even higher level in 1957. This fact may well have borne some relationship to the recession which started in 1957.

[29] See Figure 17-1.

[30] On the availability thesis see Ira O. Scott, "Availability Doctrine: Theoretical Underpinnings," *Rev. Ec. & Stat.*, Oct. 1957; D. R. Hodgman, "Credit Risk and Credit Rationing," *Q. J. Ec.*, May 1960.

[31] For a unique measure of the "tightness" of an individual bank see G. L. Bach and C. J. Huizenga, "The Differential Effects of Tight Money," *Am. Ec. Rev.*, March 1961, pp. 52–80.

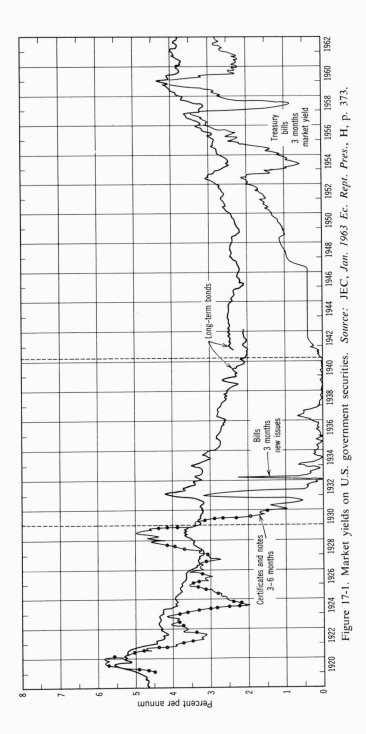

Figure 17-1. Market yields on U.S. government securities. *Source:* JEC, *Jan. 1963 Ec. Rept. Pres.,* H, p. 373.

395

monetary policy. Free reserves can result from Federal Reserve policy actions *or* from a decline in the demand for credit (or banker refusal to make loans). The free reserve figure does not distinguish between free reserves that result from a decrease in the demand for loans and those that result from deliberate Federal Reserve policy.[32] The free reserve figure, however, has been an important guide to Federal Reserve policy. The Federal Reserve generally takes credit for having leaned against the wind and therefore for having "created" (or reduced) these free reserves, but this is not completely true, for the reasons noted.[33]

It is possible that banks may sell government securities to parties other than the Federal Reserve and create free reserves in this way. It is also possible that banks will hold on to their securities and borrow from the Federal Reserve if the interest rate on the securities is higher than the Federal Reserve discount rate. There is, in fact, evidence to indicate that the size of free reserves is closely related to the Treasury bill rate and the discount rate.[34] (The large city banks seldom carry free reserves; they use them to purchase treasury bills or deal in the Federal Funds market.) In both cases there will be changes in the volume of free reserves independent of Federal Reserve action unless, of course, the latter takes steps to counteract these bank actions. Lerner's study, however, has shown that in the three recessions of the 1950's (1953–54, 1957–58, and 1960–61) the easing of credit conditions during the early months of the depression was the result of a reduction in the demand for credit rather than an increase in the supply of credit.[35]

Another difficulty with free reserves is that they do not accurately reflect what level of reserves are actually free or are over and above the level which banks want to hold. If the free reserve level is $400 million and if banks want to hold $300 million, then true free reserves are only $100 million.

[32] On this matter see E. M. Lerner, "A Criticism of Free Reserves," *Rev. Ec. & Stat.*, May 1962, pp. 225–228; A. J. Meigs, *Free Reserves and the Money Supply*, Chicago: Univ. of Chicago, 1962; and J. M. Culbertson, "The Use of Monetary Policy," *Southern Ec. J.*, Oct. 1961, p. 135.

On the other hand, for some evidence that the volume of free reserves is positively related to employment see the statement of Rep. Reuss, JEC, *Jan. 1962 Ec. Rept. Pres.*, H, pp. 184–185 and 230.

[33] In Feb. 1963 Chairman Martin renounced the placing of primary emphasis on free reserves as the (or a) major measure of tightness in the money market. See his testimony in JEC, *Jan. 1963 Ec. Rept. Pres.*, H, Pt. 1, p. 357. Governor Mitchell prefers to use interest rates and borrowings. *Ibid.*, p. 397.

[34] E. M. Lerner, *op. cit.*, points out that the discount rate tends to lag behind the bill rate during contractions as well as expansions. "When the bill rate falls, borrowing is discouraged and free reserves rise."

[35] *Ibid.*, p. 228.

A further difficulty of the free reserve measure is the fact that the reserves are generally unevenly distributed. The largest portion tends to be in the country banks, which tend to hold larger reserves for security purposes anyway. An examination of free reserves since 1950 shows that they were negative for the following years: 1950, 1955, 1956, 1957, 1958, and 1959. Free reserves for the New York City banks were negative for the years 1951 through 1959 and in 1961. The same pattern prevailed in the Chicago area, with the addition of the year 1960. Other reserve city banks had negative free reserves for the years 1951 through 1959. Country banks had sizable positive free reserves for all these years.[36] Banks short of reserves can borrow from the Federal Reserve or from each other in the federal funds market, of course, but this involves an interest cost which would not be present if additional reserves were secured by means of lower reserve requirements, plus the fact that it is unknown if the supply of federal funds is adequate.

Commercial Bank Sales of Securities

At one time many individuals felt that during periods of prosperity when interest rates were high (and bond prices low) bankers would be reluctant to sell their securities because they did not want to suffer capital lossess. The actual pattern, however, is one of commercial banks purchasing government securities during recession and selling them during prosperity. At the same time investors have been selling when commercial banks were buying, and buying when banks were selling, and the Treasury has been running deficits and selling when banks were buying, and running a surplus and retiring debt when banks were selling.[37] (It would be interesting to know the extent to which banks reject sound loan applications so as to invest in federal securities.) Although it is true that bank sales to other investors can reduce the money supply, it is more accurate to state that the deposits eliminated by these sales are likely to be idle deposits, while those created when the bank makes a loan are active, income-creating, and, therefore, potentially more inflationary.[38] Banks have been willing to sell securities at a loss (in 1959 losses on securities amounted to $750 million).[39] Beginning with the year 1950, and up to 1959, commercial banks suffered net losses on securities "sold or redeemed" in 1951, 1952, 1953, 1955, 1956, 1957, and 1959. This pattern has been encouraged by the fact that banks may deduct capital losses from ordinary income—their

[36] *FR Bull.*, Jan. 1963, pp. 28–29. All data are as of December of each year.
[37] W. L. Smith, *op. cit.*, p. 357. This section, and those following, draws heavily on Smith's chapter.
[38] W. L. Smith, *ibid.*
[39] W. L. Smith, *ibid.*; Am. Bankers Assoc., *Banking and Monetary Developments*, New York, 1961, Chart 28.

"tax savings on the capital losses exceed the tax liability on the capital gains which will accrue when security prices rise at a later time." It should be apparent then why bank holdings of government securities as a percent of total loans and investments has declined significantly throughout the 1950's.

The Financial Intermediaries

The phenomenal growth of financial institutions other than commercial banks since the end of World War II has brought with it considerable controversy over their role. Financial intermediaries cannot increase the supply of money. They can, however, exert a destabilizing influence on the economy and increase the supply of credit by (1) encouraging people to switch funds from demand deposits to savings and loan deposits, etc., where reserve requirements are much lower, or (2) selling government securities to holders of idle cash balances. To some extent financial intermediaries did behave in this fashion.[40]

Other ingenious devices, in addition to these offsets to monetary controls, have been developed to enable the public to get "more financial mileage out of the existing supply of funds."[41] This is to be expected in such a highly developed and sophisticated system as ours. These devices include the federal funds market, the diverse and complex lines of credit finance companies have set up, state and local government policies of keeping previously idle funds invested, loans on a wider geographical basis by life insurance companies, and the secondary market for FHA and VA mortgages.[42]

THE EFFECTIVENESS OF MONETARY POLICY (II): ITS IMPACT

Plant and Equipment Investment

As we have noted earlier the traditional view of monetary policy has been that its primary impact on the economy is through its influence on investment. The increase in the rate of interest to a level above the marginal

[40] W. L. Smith claims that most of their funds came from current saving though; *op. cit.*, p. 354.

[41] *Ibid.*, p. 359.

[42] For a description of these techniques see *ibid.*, pp. 358–359. Smith defends these developments on the grounds that they increase the mobility of funds, reduce interest rate differentials, and more efficiently allocate capital. Much has been written on financial intermediaries in recent years. The footnotes in Smith's chapter provide a good start.

Along these same lines see "Banking Structure and Reactions to Monetary tringency or Ease," *Monthly Rev.*, FR Bank of Kansas City, March–April 1963, pp. 9–15.

efficiency of capital supposedly makes investment expenditures unprofitable. As we have previously noted, however, the influence of the interest rate on many types of investment spending is extremely weak. In the first place, business expenditure on plant and equipment and interest rates have moved in the same direction.[43] Second, the major sources of funds for business investment are internal funds (capital consumption allowances and retained earnings).[44] Third, a change in the rate of interest of 1, 2, or 3 percent is likely to become quickly submerged in an investment picture where future demand, current capacity of the firm and the industry, the market position of the firm, possible substitute products or new productive techniques, wage rates, raw material prices, and as fast a payoff period as possible are important considerations. In other words, several factors, including current profit margins, reduce the importance of the rate of interest for many types of investment. Fourth, interest costs are deductible under the corporate income tax. Fifth, prices may be increased to recapture interest costs in certain concentrated industries. Sixth, an industry may deliberately set its prices so that a major part of its expansion is paid for from retained earnings (as the steel industry supposedly has done). Seventh, large firms have first claim to the funds banks do have available. Eighth, large firms can easily sell stock during such periods.

It appears, then, that during periods of explosive economic activity, increasing profits, and plentiful investment opportunities, higher interest rates, and reduced credit availability will restrain the total volume of credit and induce credit rationing but will not substantially restrain major investment.[45] They do not appear to have done so during the investment boom of 1955–1957. Furthermore, in those studies in which interest rates do play an important role, the existence of a lag of 1 year until the interest rate does have an effect means that the impact may be very poorly timed or that those who determine monetary policy will have to be expert forecasters.[46]

It is, of course, possible that a restrictive policy which restrains other

---

[43] From 1955(1) to 1957(3) plant and equipment expenditures were up 46 percent, and interest rates on high-grade corporate bonds were up 41 percent. *Ibid.*, p. 369.

[44] Internal sources of funds ranged from 82 to 124 percent of total plant and equipment outlay for the period 1955 to 1958. *Ibid.*, p. 371.

[45] Bach and Huizenga, *op. cit.*, conclude that tight money was more restrictive than Smith does.

[46] F. Gehrels and S. Wiggins, "Interest Rates and Manufacturers' Fixed Investment," *Am. Ec. Rev.*, March 1957, pp. 79–92; T. Mayer, "The Inflexibility of Monetary Policy," *Rev. Ec. & Stat.*, Nov. 1958, pp. 358–374, and W. H. White, "The Flexibility of Anticyclical Monetary Policy," *Rev. Ec. & Stat.*, May 1961, pp. 142–147; and W.L-Smith, "On the Effectiveness of Monetary Policy," *Am. Ec. Rev.*, Sept. 1956, pp. 588. 606.

types of spending can indirectly affect investment by reducing corporate sales and therefore can have an important lagged effect.[47] It is also to be expected that in areas where investment expenses are recovered over a long period of time, where marginal business firms exist, and among small businesses, higher interest rates will have a restraining influence. Studies in the public utility field are inconclusive, perhaps because the utilities expect an increase in interest costs to be passed on in a rate increase. Similarly, the alleged discrimination against small business has not really been settled,[48] although a priori reasoning would indicate that small firms would suffer as long as large firms are able to secure funds from internal sources and have the first claim on funds from banks and the stock market.

Residential Construction

Residential construction has probably been the area hardest hit by a tight money policy. The period beginning in 1953 when tight monetary controls were really used shows that housing construction has been clearly anticyclical. When money has been tight, there have been large and significant declines in housing starts. When credit has been more easily available, housing starts have increased sharply, although with some lag.[49] Housing starts dropped almost continuously from a peak in December 1954 of 1,443,000 units to 918,000 units in March 1958 during a period of increasing credit tightness, and then increased again until April 1959 when the impact of high interest and tight credit set in.

The anticyclical performance of housing has been primarily attributable to the ceiling on FHA and VA loans. The traditional argument is that high interest restrains investment. In the housing fields, however, the failure of interest rates to rise has reduced the availability of funds and forced expenditures to be cut back. As the yields on other investments such as government securities and corporate bonds increase, funds flow away from government-guaranteed mortgages into these other securities. This pattern characterizes a high level of economic activity. On the other hand, when the economy is in a recession, interest rates on these investments decline and funds flow instead into FHA and VA mortgages. Similarly, during periods of prosperity the proportion of conventional mortgages increases because interest rates will rise on them. If, however, conventional loans become an increasing proportion of total mortgages then expenditures on housing will tend to become less anticyclical.

---

[47] See Gehrels and Wiggins *op. cit.*, and John R. Meyer in JEC, *Empl., Growth, Price Levels*, H, Pt. 8, p. 2488, who strongly stress this point.

[48] But see Bach and Huizenga, *op. cit*,

[49] The statistical evidence can be found in W. L. Smith, JEC, *Empl., Growth, Price Levels*, SR, pp. 364–368.

Some observers have argued that the interest rate ceiling on government-guaranteed loans should be removed. If this were done it is likely that housing would be procyclical, unless, however, the demand for housing should turn out to be quite interest-elastic. There is also the consideration that higher interest rates commit more disposable income to an expenditure that can be classified as a contractual saving. This in itself may be undesirable. Last, there is the related ethical question of the impact of higher interest rates on income distribution. A tight money policy that reduces employment (such a policy may have caused some of our unemployment of the 1950's) and at the same time increases interest rates *tends* to redistribute income upward.[50]

Consumer Durables

During the postwar period consumer credit has contributed to the general instability of the economy by going through alternate periods of rapid acceleration and deceleration. The studies of Professor Warren L. Smith have indicated that the problem is not in the high average rate of growth of consumer credit in itself but in the rather extreme fluctuations in this growth. Consumer purchases of durables are done largely with the use of consumer credit, and as we know consumer durable purchases tend to fluctuate in a manner similar to that of business investment. Professor Smith has noted that fluctuations in consumer credit can contribute to economic instability in the following ways:

1. It increases the demand for consumer-durable goods and enlarges the sector to which the acceleration effect is applicable.
2. The tendency of lenders to ease credit terms in upswings and tighten them during downswings because of changes in the attitude toward the risks of consumer loans may increase the amplitude of the swings
3. The attitudes of consumer borrowers toward incurring debt to buy durable goods (as distinct from their attitudes toward the goods themselves) may shift in a destabilizing fashion over the business cycle.
4. Required repayment of outstanding debt may constitute a severe drag on the shrinking total of consumer purchasing power during a period of declining activity.
5. If consumers are overburdened with debt when income falls and are forced to default, the solvency of financial institutions may be imperiled.[51]

In addition to these problems of the use of consumer credit, there is the further possibility of autonomous shifts in consumer expenditures. It is widely felt that such a shift explains the behavior of consumer automobile

---

[50] Many other variables enter into the situation: the degree of unemployment, the extent to which prices are kept down, the impact on corporate profits, etc. versus the degree of inflation which may otherwise occur.

[51] W. L. Smith, JEC, *Empl., Growth, Price Levels*, SR, p. 389.

purchases in 1955. There is, furthermore general agreement that automobile purchases are characterized by greater instability than purchases of other durables.

The instability of consumer durable purchases and in consumer credit we have noted would seem to be good reason for the application of monetary controls to this sector. The general controls we have used, however, have apparently had little impact. Consumer loans to people (who are deceived by the phrase "low bank rates") are very profitable for commercial and other banks to make. The true annual interest rates on these loans are so much above the yields of government securities that banks are happy to sell the latter even if they must suffer a capital loss so that they can make more consumer loans.

Other factors encourage the expansion of loans to consumers: the pressure put on the banks by appliance and automobile dealers, the ingenious ability of sales finance companies to secure funds from various sources and avoid the impact of tight money,[52] and consumer ignorance of (or lack of concern over) the interest rates they really pay. Smith has concluded that general controls have some effect on consumer credit, but he feels that they are not very significant.

Our discussion should not leave the reader with the impression that effective controls over both consumer credit and mortgage credit cannot be developed. They can, especially through the control of the required down payment and the length of the repayment period.

State and Local Expenditures

It is not easy either to measure or to judge the impact of tight money on state and local expenditures, especially since it is impossible to know how many potential bond offerings were rejected or not made because of high interest rates or because of fear of inability to raise funds. It is further difficult to judge the extent to which taxpayers have become more interest-cautious (or expenditure-cautious) and have turned down bond issues. It does appear, however, that monetary policy has had some impact in this area, especially in restricting school construction. Further, inasmuch as most state and local projects are long-term, the level of the interest rate becomes increasingly important. It is too early to offer a conclusive statement on the actual impact, however.

Inventories

Periods of increasing economic activity are characterized by rapid and very large inventory buildups. Periods of declining economic activity, on

---

[52] For a possibly important qualification see W. L. Smith's comments, *ibid.*, p. 390, on the following: Paul Smith, "Response of Consumer Loans to General Credit Conditions," *Am. Ec. Rev.*, Sept. 1958, pp. 649–655.

the other hand, are characterized by rapid disinvestment in inventories. These fluctuations serve to exaggerate and amplify fluctuations in the economy, and economists have long hoped that they could control inventory changes by means of monetary controls. But the available evidence indicates that inventories are little affected by these controls. Inventories are held for short periods of time, which fact serves to reduce the importance of the interest rate, and the fact that prices are likely to rise offsets the interest cost in any case. It is true that devices with the objective of realizing greater control over inventories, could be used, but many practical problems still remain. Perhaps one of the most encouraging developments has been the use of computers, which has enabled firms to carry smaller inventories. This may (or may not because of the price speculation motive underlying much inventory accumulation) reduce the extreme fluctuations in inventories that characterize our business cycles.

CONCLUDING STATEMENT

It is impossible to determine the extent to which monetary policy may have adversely affected the growth rate of economy during the 1950's. It would seem, however, that much of the excess liquidity characterizing the immediate postwar years has been soaked up; that, on balance, restrictive monetary policies have not been offset by easy money policies; that the secular upward movement in both short- and long-term interest rates (which have resulted) should be halted (if not reversed); that the potential severness of monetary policy has been offset by velocity increases; that, aside from the impact on residential mortgages, the impact may not have been severe but the degree of tightness coupled with the full employment surplus may have had an adverse impact on the economy; that monetary policy has not been successful in restraining inflation; that selective controls and other approaches should be more closely examined; that monetary policy was perhaps too easy in 1954; that the Federal Reserve moved much too slowly after the 1957 decline started; that monetary (and fiscal) policy was too tight in 1956 and 1957; that a tight money policy was imposed much too early during the recovery from the 1957–1958 recession; that during this period monetary policy could have been less restrictive without at the same time being inflationary; that monetary policy in the early 1960's may have been too restrictive;[53] and

[53] For assertions that monetary policy in 1960 was not really very easy see the statement of John Gurley, JEC, *Rev. Ann. Rept. FR 1960*, H, pp. 12, 112, 117, 120–121; and also 128–129 (James Knowles' comment).

We could not begin to cite the multitude of articles which have been written in condemnation of monetary policy. See, however, most of the *Annual Reports* of the

that in the absence of inflationary pressures, and the possibility of higher liquidity preferences on the part of consumers, banks, business, and other groups, an easier monetary policy may be necessary for the remainder of the 1960's.

Because of the possible lags between changes in monetary policy and their impact on the economy, concern over the long-term upward drift in interest rates, the apparent stickiness of interest rates, the feeling that the growth in the money supply (and in productivity, output, and employment) has been inadequate, the fact that monetary policy may have actually raised costs (by restricting increases in output and therefore in productivity in 1956 and 1957), the feeling that monetary policy may have played a more important role in recent recessions than is generally recognized (or known), and the poor timing of monetary policy (easing very slowly in 1957 when the economy turned down, for example, and tightening very rapidly during the recovery in 1959), and for other reasons, many economists have recommended that we move somewhat more cautiously in the monetary realm and rely somewhat more on fiscal policy. The use of fiscal policy for expansionary purposes assumes, however, that a reasonably loose monetary policy will accompany it. (It may be questioned whether we could successfully expand output and employment with a policy of reduced taxes and really tight money.) Finally, it should be noted that since the accord of 1951 monetary policy has only recently come into its own as far as modern economic analysis is concerned. Something must have been learned from the experiences of the last twelve years.

JEC; *Am. Ec. Rev.* (W. L. Smith, Sept. 1956; W. W. Heller, Sept. 1957); *Q.J.Ec.* (H. Minsky, May 1957; E. Miller, Feb. 1956); A. H. Hansen in his *American Economy*, chapter 4, and in the *Rev. Ec. & Stat.*, May 1955; Sproul's testimony before the Subcommittee of the JCER, *U.S. Monetary Policy: Recent Thinking and Experience* (Dec. 6, 7, 1954), Hearings, 1955; Asher Achinstein, *Federal Reserve Policy and Economic Stability, 1951–57*, Committee on Banking and Currency, 1958. The comments of individual economists in the hearings of the Joint Economic Committee over the last ten years are simply too numerous to mention.

Some members of the JEC feared that monetary policy was not easy enough during 1960–1962. In addition, the free reserve figure dropped abruptly in mid–1963 and money rates had previously moved up. For an analysis concluding that there was sufficient liquidity in the economy to support a continued rise in the level of economic activity during 1963, see FR Bank of Cleveland, *Monthly Bus. Rev.*, March 1963.

Governor Mitchell of the FR has classified monetary policy in 1962 as not actively expansionary—velocity increased and interest rates increased. JEC, *Jan. 1963 Ec. Rept. Pres.*, H, Pt. 1, pp. 381–383. On the other hand, the failure of interest rates to rise as sharply as during previous recovery periods, the trend of other monetary measures, and the fact that banks went heavily into the tax exempt and real estate fields seems to indicate that pressure for consumer and business loans was not unduly great. See J. A. Gorman, "Capital Formation, Saving, and Credit," *Surv. Current Bus.*, May 1963, pp. 10–17.

APPENDIX A

Mr. Martin on Economic Analysis and Deficit Spending

Mr. Martin's economic philosophy as he has stated it has been quite different from that of the Kennedy Administration. He has stated that recent unemployment has been caused by inflation, that we cannot reduce unemployment merely "by just spending more money," that we cannot spend ourselves rich, and that the unemployed will not be helped by "flooding our economy with a stream of easy money" (instead we should "concentrate on fundamentals that permit the forces of the market to operate,"); and he condemns deficits and questions their use during recessions.[54] He has further stated that he believes deficits are "wrong in principle."[55] These points are almost diametrically opposite to the economic program advocated by the Kennedy Administration. Since one must assume that President Kennedy would not reappoint Mr. Martin to the Chairmanship of the Board unless there was at least a reasonable agreement on policy, one must also assume that Mr. Martin only carries out his personal beliefs when an Administration is in power which holds a similar outlook. All this indicates that the Board of Governors tends to cooperate with the Administration in power, especially if its failure to do so might result in a direct challenge from the Administration. One is only openly defiant if he thinks he can succeed. (See also Chapter 20.)

The problem of forcing the Federal Reserve to present a detailed public analysis for its prescriptions is another issue and is as yet unsolved.

Mr. Martin's Policy for Reducing Unemployment

Mr. Martin's policy prescription to reduce unemployment in 1962 consisted of a program aimed at (1) increasing productive efficiency, (2) introducing new products, (3) achieving stable prices, and (4) bringing about a balance of international payments. Further he noted that consumer demand should be increased by lowering prices and introducing new and better products, and that we should meet world competition by greater capital investment and increased productivity. He further questioned the validity of the CEA's study on "hard core" unemployment and the study of the JEC staff on Structural Transformation or Inadequate Demand.[56]

[54] JEC, *Empl., Growth, Price Levels*, H, Pt. 10, pp. 3385–3388, and Pt. 6A, 1243–1245, 1251–1253, 1280–1290, 1455–1464.
[55] COF, S, *Investigation Finan. Cond.*, H, Pt. 3, p. 1317.
[56] See JEC, *Jan. 1962 Ec. Rept. Pres.*, H, pp. 192ff.

Mr. Martin on Financing a Deficit

In the chapter we noted that Martin made the statement that the anticipated deficit from a possible 1962 tax cut would have to be financed out of current saving, but later qualified it. The impact of Mr. Martin's original statement is, of course, dependent on the reserve position of commercial banks. If there is no increase in total reserves in the economy, the financing of the deficit and the demands on the money supply resulting from an expanding economy would tend to tighten credit and push interest rates up. If the money supply is kept constant the pressures are obvious. Mr. Martin later distinguished between "total bank credit *expansion* and that portion of it which can be traced to the *creation* of money and credit." Mr. Martin's point apparently is that people should save by placing funds in savings accounts and that banks can then use these funds to purchase government securities. Hence the deficit is financed out of real saving rather than "money creation." But further "money creation" to meet the needs of a growing economy is "legitimate." "Additions to banks' holdings of government securities due to additional flows of savings through this particular intermediary or to normal growth in the money supply do not represent the financing of government deficits with bank-created or 'printing press' money." *Regardless* of the meaning of this qualified statement the impact can be quite restrictive. Perhaps Mr. Martin was inferring that reserves were adequate to finance the deficit and would be kept so, and that there would be no wholesale or large expansion in reserves. But who suggested that this would occur anyway? Senator Douglas' pointed questions no doubt cleared up some of the semantic difficulties. Further, Dr. Heller indicated that cooperation from the Federal Reserve was forthcoming. Governor George Mitchell's clear statement[57] gets right to the heart of the matter.[58]

Mr. Martin on the Determination of Interest Rates in a "Free" Market and "Operation Nudge"

Federal Reserve officials have often denied that they affect interest rates. Under the Eisenhower Administration, Chairman Martin argued that

---

[57] JEC, *Jan. 1963 Ec. Rept. Pres.*, H, Pt. 1, p. 382.

[58] On the matter of timing and the need to borrow *prior* to creating income see the discussion of E. J. Swan (President of the FR Bank of San Francisco) and Senator Douglas, *ibid.*, pp. 390–391. See also Mr Martin's statement in JEC, *State Ec. & Pol. Full. Empl.*, H, pp. 604ff; and the comments in JEC, *Jan. 1963 Ec. Rept. Pres.*, H, Pt 1, by W. Heller and G. Ackley of the CEA, p. 30; Douglas Dillon, p. 284; Mr Martin, pp. 342ff.; Senator Douglas, pp. 367–370; Governor Mitchell, pp. 379–382; and E. J. Swan, pp. 387–390, and the following discussion.

interest rates were set by the supply of and demand for funds in a free market, but under the Kennedy Administration he was cooperating in "Operation Nudge," an attempt to nudge long-term rates down to induce greater domestic investment and simultaneously maintain short-term rates to impede the outflow of foreign deposits (and gold).[59]

Mr. Martin had this to say about "Operation Nudge":

In much of this discussion . . . there has been a mistaken overemphasis placed upon the levels of interest rates, as if some particular level of rates could be in themselves [sic] an objective of monetary policy. This is not the case. What the Federal Reserve is seeking to do is not to set some particular level of rates for either short- or long-term securities, but rather influence the flow of funds in international and domestic channels.[60]

Variations in interest rates, of course, would not affect this flow of funds between countries!

Rouse had claimed that the purpose of open market operations is to affect bank reserves, and that there may be an incidental effect on interest rates. Rouse further stated that Federal Reserve purchases of long-terms were for the purpose of again affecting reserves, although the effect on interest rates "would be a desirable byproduct."[61] In the same source Martin states that the Federal Reserve should not be asked to force interest rates up or down, talks often in terms of a free money market governed solely by supply and demand, "natural" developments, etc. It seems time that the never-never land was abandoned. There should be little doubt that the Federal Reserve is in a position to exert a potent influence on interest rates. Furthermore, comments about the supply and demand for funds setting the rate of interest, as above, can only be made within the context of Federal Reserve increases or decreases in bank reserves.[62] Federal Reserve officials therefore must have some idea of the interest rate they want to exist when they purchase or sell securities in the open market. Martin has also said: "In a private enterprise economy they [interest rates] are established by the interplay of market forces."[63]

---

[59] For references to the FR and similar positions, criticisms of Mr. Martin's position, and caustic exchanges between Chairman Martin and members of Congress, see Warren L. Smith, JEC, *Empl., Growth, Price Levels*, SP No. 19, p. 121 and footnote 12; *ibid.*, H, Pt. 6A, pp. 1099, 1101, 1315–1316, 1491; and Pt. 10, pp. 3363–3364, 3277, 3387, and 3445.

[60] JEC, *Rev. Ann. Rept. FR 1960*, H, pp. 13, 16.

[61] *Ibid.*, p. 18.

[62] *Ibid.*, pp. 16–18, 33–34, 57–61, 89, 91, 118, 120, 150–153, 155, 162. See also JEC, *Jan. 1961 Ec. Rept. Pres.*, pp. 571ff, 603.

[63] JEC, *Empl. Growth, Price Levels*, H, Pt. 10, p. 3387.

APPENDIX B

Some important data on liquid assets appear in the table below. In the immediate period following World War II liquidity was abnormally high. The extent to which the subsequent decline was desirable is not obvious.

Selected Liquid Assets Held by the Public 1946, 1957, and 1960–1962 (Billions of Dollars)

	1946	1957	1960	1961	1962[a]
Liquid Assets	Billions of Dollars[b]				
Total selected liquid assets[c]	239.1	356.0	399.2	424.6	458.7
Money supply[d]	108.5	133.5	138.4	142.6	144.8
Money supply and time deposits at commercial banks[b]	142.4	191.0	211.5	225.1	242.2
	Percent of GNP				
Total selected liquid assets[c]	113	80	79	82	83
Money supply[d]	51	30	27	27	26
Money supply and time deposits at commercial banks[b]	68	43	42	43	44

Source: Jan. 1963 Ec. Rept. Pres., p. 56.

[a] Preliminary estimates by Council of Economic Advisers.

[b] Seasonally adjusted, end of year.

[c] Money supply time deposits at commercial banks and mutual savings banks, Postal Savings System, savings and loan shares, U.S. Government savings bonds, and U.S. Government and federal agency securities maturing within 1 year.

[d] Demand deposits and currency.

The fact that the ratios of "total selected liquid assets" and "money supply and time deposits at commercial banks" to GNP were approximately the same for the years 1957 and 1962 does not indicate that the 1962 ratios were appropriate. Those of 1957, for instance, may have been low enough to affect the economy adversely.

18

Inflation

In this chapter we attempt to (1) place recent inflation in some historical perspective, (2) discuss the war and postwar movements of the Consumer Price Index and the Wholesale Price Index, (3) review several theories of inflation, (4) attempt to apply these theories to the inflation of the past decade, and (5) discuss some of the policies for dealing with inflation. Other techniques of an anti-inflationary nature are discussed in Chapter 19.

PRICE LEVEL FLUCTUATIONS: THE EXPERIENCE

The Long-Run Picture

We have noted previously that the 1950's were characterized by an excessive concern over the problem of price stability. If the 1950's are placed in some historical perspective, however, we see that our record for these years was not really so bad. An examination of the Wholesale Price Index for the period 1720 to 1958 shows rather clearly that the major factor contributing to very large upward movements in this price index has been war. The Revolutionary War, the War of 1812, the Civil War, and World Wars I and II all showed large increases in the WPI. Estimates of the Consumers Price Index, which are available back to 1800, reflect exactly the same pattern. The major difference between the experience of previous wars and World War II, however, is that in the years following every previous war there was a substantial decrease in the price level. Such was not the case following World War II, although it should be noted that the decrease in the CPI following World War I was less than that following previous wars.[1]

The Behavior of the Wholesale Price Index

An examination of Table 18-1 shows that the WPI increased 14.9 points or 35 percent during the period 1940–1945. If, however, one uses 1929 as

[1] The data are presented in both tabular and graphic form in JEC, *Empl.*, *Growth*, *Price Levels*, H, Pt. 2, pp. 394–404. They were prepared by Ethel D. Hoover and George R. Taylor.

Table 18-1. Wholesale Price Indexes 1929–1962

$[1957-59 = 100]^a$

Year	All Commodities	Farm Products	Processed Foods	All Commodities Other than Farm Products and Foods (Industrials)				
				Total	Textile Products and Apparel	Chemicals and Allied Products	Rubber and Rubber Products	Lumber and Wood Products
1929	52.1	63.9	54.3	51.7	67.8	NA^b	57.6	26.4
1930	47.3	54.0	49.5	48.1	60.3	NA	50.4	24.1
1931	39.9	39.6	41.6	42.4	49.8	NA	42.8	19.6
1932	35.6	29.4	33.9	39.7	41.2	NA	37.1	16.9
1933	36.1	31.3	33.7	40.2	48.6	46.6	39.0	20.0
1934	41.0	39.9	39.6	44.2	54.7	48.8	45.5	23.5
1935	43.8	48.0	48.3	44.0	53.3	50.9	45.8	22.6
1936	44.2	49.4	46.4	44.9	53.7	51.2	49.4	23.6
1937	47.2	52.7	48.6	48.1	57.3	53.6	58.1	27.9
1938	43.0	41.9	42.3	46.1	50.1	51.0	57.1	25.4
1939	42.2	39.9	40.2	46.0	52.3	50.7	59.3	26.1
1940	43.0	41.3	40.4	46.8	55.4	51.6	55.3	28.9
1941	47.8	50.1	46.7	50.3	63.7	56.1	59.6	34.5
1942	54.0	64.6	54.8	53.9	72.8	62.3	69.4	37.5
1943	56.5	74.8	57.2	54.7	73.1	63.1	71.3	39.7
1944	56.9	75.3	56.0	55.6	73.9	63.8	70.4	42.8
1945	57.9	78.3	56.4	56.3	75.1	64.2	68.3	43.4
1946	66.1	90.6	71.7	61.7	87.3	69.4	68.6	49.7
1947	81.2	109.1	91.1	75.3	105.7	92.2	68.3	77.4
1948	87.9	117.1	98.4	81.7	110.3	94.4	70.5	88.5
1949	83.5	101.3	88.8	80.0	100.9	86.2	68.3	81.9
1950	86.8	106.4	92.6	82.9	104.8	87.5	83.2	94.1
1951	96.7	123.8	103.3	91.5	116.9	100.1	102.1	102.5
1952	94.0	116.8	100.9	89.4	105.5	95.0	92.5	99.5
1953	92.7	105.9	97.0	90.1	102.8	96.1	86.3	99.4
1954	92.9	104.4	97.6	90.4	100.6	97.3	87.6	97.6
1955	93.2	97.9	94.3	92.4	100.7	96.9	99.2	102.3
1956	96.2	96.6	94.3	96.5	100.7	97.5	100.6	103.8
1957	99.0	99.2	97.9	99.2	100.8	99.6	100.2	98.5
1958	100.4	103.6	102.9	99.5	98.9	100.4	100.1	97.4
1959	100.6	97.2	99.2	101.3	100.4	100.0	99.7	104.1
1960	100.7	96.9	100.0	101.3	101.3	100.2	99.9	100.4
1961	100.3	96.0	100.7	100.8	99.7	99.1	96.1	95.9
1962^c	100.6	97.7	101.2	100.8	100.6	97.5	93.3	96.5

Hides, Skins, Leather, and Leather Products	Fuel and Related Products, and Power	Pulp, Paper, and Allied Products	Metals and Metal Products	Machinery and Motive Products	Furniture and Other Household Durables	Nonmetallic Mineral Products	Tobacco Products and Bottled Beverages	Miscellaneous Products
56.6	61.5	NA	44.1	NA	56.4	53.4	67.4	NA
52.0	58.2	NA	39.7	NA	55.5	53.2	67.8	NA
44.7	50.0	NA	35.7	NA	51.1	49.7	67.2	NA
38.0	52.1	NA	32.8	NA	45.0	46.5	63.3	NA
42.0	49.3	NA	33.6	NA	45.1	49.2	56.6	NA
44.9	54.3	NA	37.1	NA	49.0	52.6	59.2	NA
46.5	54.5	NA	37.0	NA	48.6	52.6	59.1	NA
49.5	56.5	NA	37.8	NA	49.3	52.7	59.0	NA
54.3	57.5	NA	43.2	NA	54.7	53.9	59.5	NA
48.2	56.6	NA	41.6	NA	53.4	52.2	59.4	NA
49.6	54.2	NA	41.2	43.7	53.2	51.2	59.4	NA
52.3	53.2	NA	41.4	44.2	54.4	51.2	60.1	NA
56.1	56.6	NA	42.2	45.8	57.8	52.4	60.8	NA
61.1	58.2	NA	42.8	47.7	62.5	54.5	61.5	NA
61.0	59.9	NA	42.7	47.4	62.1	54.7	64.6	NA
60.5	61.6	NA	42.7	47.4	63.8	55.8	64.9	NA
61.3	62.3	NA	43.4	47.8	63.9	58.1	66.7	NA
70.7	66.7	NA	48.5	53.6	67.8	61.8	69.8	NA
96.5	79.7	75.3	60.2	61.8	77.8	69.1	75.6	108.7
97.5	93.8	78.6	68.5	67.5	82.5	74.7	78.2	111.2
92.5	89.3	75.2	69.0	71.2	83.8	76.7	79.6	103.5
99.9	90.2	77.1	72.7	72.6	85.6	78.6	80.5	104.1
114.8	93.5	91.3	80.9	79.5	92.8	83.5	85.1	113.1
92.8	93.3	89.0	81.0	81.2	91.1	83.5	87.0	116.7
94.1	95.9	88.7	83.6	82.2	92.9	86.9	89.8	105.4
89.9	94.6	88.8	84.3	83.2	93.9	88.8	93.8	110.5
89.5	94.5	91.1	90.0	85.8	94.3	91.3	94.6	99.1
94.8	97.4	97.2	97.8	92.1	96.9	95.2	95.1	98.1
94.9	102.7	99.0	99.7	97.7	99.4	98.9	98.0	96.6
96.0	98.7	100.1	99.1	100.1	100.2	99.9	99.7	101.5
109.1	98.7	101.0	101.2	102.2	100.4	101.2	102.2	101.9
105.2	99.6	101.8	101.3	102.4	100.1	101.4	102.5	99.3
106.2	100.7	98.8	100.7	102.3	99.5	101.8	103.2	103.9
107.4	100.2	100.0	100.0	102.3	98.8	101.8	104.1	107.3

Source: Department of Labor, *Jan. 1963 Ec. Rept. Pres.*, pp. 220–221.
 [a] This does not replace the former index (1926 = 100) as the official index prior to January 1952. Data beginning January 1947 represent the revised sample and weighting pattern. Prior to January 1947 they are based on the month-to-month movement of the former index.
 [b] NA: Not available. [c] Preliminary.

a base for measuring the war-caused increase in prices, we find only a 5.8 point increase, or an increase of 11 percent. This illustrates again the difficulty of selecting base years for the purpose of making comparisons. The year 1929 does not reflect high pre-Depression prices but rather the lowest WPI level of the 1920's. It does not seem unreasonable to attribute part of the price rise of the earlier war period to a recovery to pre-Depression levels. If this is done the increase in the WPI during the war years does not appear so serious.

Further examination of Table 18-1 shows a postwar upsurge in the WPI up to 1948, a decline in 1949, and another upturn during recovery from the recession and the Korean War. A comparison of the level of the WPI in 1952 with that of 1962 shows an increase of 6.6 points or a total increase of 7 percent and a yearly increase of .7 percent. Use of the year 1953, however, gives a 9-year increase of 7.9 points, a total increase of 8.5 percent, and a yearly increase of .9 percent. The years 1952 to and including 1955 were years of virtual stability in the overall WPI. The data shows that in only 2 years were there significant increases in the WPI in the whole period 1951–1962. These years were 1956 and 1957, when the yearly increases were 3 and 2.8 points, respectively. (The increase from 1957 to 1958 was 1.4 points.) Of considerable significance is the stability of the WPI for the 7-year period 1957 through 1962. (The index stood at 99.0 in 1957, and 100.6 in 1962, and 100.3 in September of 1963.)

The Behavior of the Consumer Price Index

An examination of the CPI for the period 1940 to 1945 shows an increase of 13.9 points or 28 percent. (See Table 18-2.) If 1929 is used as a basis for comparison we see an increase of only 3 points or 6 percent. (The price index for 1929 was 73.3; the lowest for the 1920's was 71.6 in 1921 and the highest 75.6 in 1926, using 1935–1939 as the base period.) As in the WPI, a significant increase in the CPI occurred during the immediate postwar period with the removal of price controls. By 1948 the index was up to 83.8. After a slight decline due to the 1947–1948 recession another significant increase appeared during the Korean War. From 1952 to 1962 the CPI climbed 14.9 points, and from 1953 to 1962 it climbed 12.2 points. The years 1952 to 1955 were years of relative stability, however, and significant increases in the CPI came in the years 1957 (up 3.3 points) and 1958 (up 2.7 points). Other years saw moderate increases (1956, 1.4 points; 1959, .8 point; 1960, 1.6 points; 1961, 1.1 points; and 1962, 1.2 points). The average yearly increase for the period 1952 to 1962 works out to 1.29 points or 1.4 percent. Although a breakdown of the CPI will show that most items have moved up during the 1952–1962 period, the particularly

Table 18-2. Consumer Price Indexes, by Major Groups, 1929–1962

For City Wage-Earner and Clerical-Worker Families [1957–59 = 100]

Year	All Items	Food	Housing Total	Rent	Ap-parel	Trans-porta-tion	Medi-cal Care	Per-sonal Care	Read-ing and Recrea-tion	Other Goods and Services
1929	50.7	55.6	NA^a	85.4	56.2	NA	NA	NA	NA	NA
1930	58.2	52.9	NA	83.1	54.9	NA	NA	NA	NA	NA
1931	53.0	43.6	NA	78.7	50.0	NA	NA	NA	NA	NA
1932	47.6	36.3	NA	70.6	44.3	NA	NA	NA	NA	NA
1933	45.1	35.3	NA	60.8	42.8	NA	NA	NA	NA	NA
1934	46.6	39.3	NA	57.0	46.8	NA	NA	NA	NA	NA
1935	47.8	42.1	56.3	56.9	47.2	49.4	49.4	42.6	50.2	52.7
1936	48.3	42.5	57.1	58.3	47.6	49.8	49.6	43.2	51.0	52.6
1937	50.0	44.2	59.1	60.9	50.1	50.6	50.0	45.7	52.5	54.0
1938	49.1	41.0	60.1	62.9	49.8	51.0	50.2	46.7	54.3	54.5
1939	48.4	39.9	59.7	63.0	49.0	49.8	50.2	46.5	54.4	55.4
1940	48.8	40.5	59.9	63.2	49.6	49.5	50.3	46.4	55.4	57.1
1941	51.3	44.2	61.4	64.3	51.9	51.2	50.6	47.6	57.3	58.2
1942	56.8	51.9	64.2	65.7	60.5	55.7	52.0	52.2	60.0	59.9
1943	60.3	57.9	64.9	65.7	62.3	55.5	54.5	57.6	65.0	63.0
1944	61.3	57.1	66.4	65.9	67.7	55.5	56.2	61.7	72.0	64.7
1945	62.7	58.4	67.5	66.1	71.2	55.4	57.5	63.6	75.0	67.3
1946	68.0	66.9	69.3	66.5	78.1	58.3	60.7	68.2	77.5	69.5
1947	77.8	81.3	74.5	68.7	90.6	64.3	65.7	76.2	82.5	75.4
1948	83.8	88.2	79.8	73.2	96.5	71.6	69.8	79.1	86.7	78.9
1949	83.0	84.7	81.0	76.4	92.7	77.0	72.0	78.9	89.9	81.2
1950	83.8	85.8	83.2	79.1	91.5	79.0	73.4	78.9	89.3	82.6
1951	90.5	95.4	88.2	82.3	99.7	84.0	76.9	86.3	92.0	86.1
1952	92.5	97.1	89.9	85.7	98.7	89.6	81.1	87.3	92.4	90.6
1953	93.2	95.6	92.3	90.3	97.8	92.1	83.9	88.1	93.3	92.8
1954	93.6	95.4	93.4	93.5	97.3	90.8	86.6	88.5	92.4	94.3
1955	93.3	94.0	94.1	94.8	96.7	89.7	88.6	90.0	92.1	94.3
1956	94.7	94.7	95.5	96.5	98.4	91.3	91.8	93.7	93.4	95.8
1957	98.0	97.8	98.5	98.3	99.7	96.5	95.5	97.1	96.9	98.5
1958	100.7	101.9	100.2	100.1	99.8	99.7	100.1	100.4	100.8	99.8
1959	101.5	100.3	101.3	101.6	100.7	103.8	104.4	102.4	102.4	101.8
1960	103.1	101.4	103.1	103.1	102.1	103.8	108.1	104.1	104.9	103.8
1961	104.2	102.6	103.9	104.4	102.8	105.0	111.3	104.6	107.2	104.6
1962	105.4	103.6	104.8	105.6	103.1	107.1	114.1	106.4	109.5	105.3

Source: Department of Labor, *Jan. 1963 Ec. Rept. Pres.*, p. 224.

^{a} NA: Not available.

^{b} Jan.–Nov. average.

dramatic increase in the prices of services stands out. As of December 1960 services received a weight of 36.3 percent of the CPI.

Some Observations on Price Behavior

The purpose in reviewing these price level statistics is to place the inflation of recent years in some perspective. Clearly, the price increases of World War II, immediate postwar, and Korean War years can be explained in terms of demand. The years 1951 to 1955 (or 1956) were years of reasonable price stability for both the WPI and the CPI. In fact, the only 2 years in which the WPI moved adversely after 1951 were 1956 and 1957. It is also interesting to note that, from 1952 to 1962, significant increases in the WPI were experienced in three major categories: (1) metals and metal products, (2) machinery and motive products, and (3) nonmetallic mineral products. (See Table 18-1.) [If one looks at the WPI from the standpoint of "stage of processing" the three areas with substantial price increases are (1) materials for durable manufacturing, (2) components for manufacturing, and (3) producer finished goods.]

While the behavior of the WPI since 1958 has not given us need for concern, the CPI since 1955 has reflected consistent yearly increases; they have averaged 1.87 percent. Consequently, the CPI has been the cause of the concern about inflation in recent years. On the other hand, some individuals contend that far too much confidence is placed in the CPI, that it fails to account accurately for changes in consumer tastes and increases in the quality of products and services, and that it is computed on too narrow a basis (the costs of noncity living are omitted). Some economists prefer to use the WPI or the GNP price deflator[2] over the CPI. Despite all this, however, a comparison of the levels of unemployment realized during this period with these price level changes may create a question as to which problem was really more serious.

PRICE LEVEL FLUCTUATIONS: POSSIBLE CAUSES

The recent literature dealing with inflation is more than voluminous. It simply is not possible to review all this information here, let alone present a definitive statement. Our procedure is to discuss briefly some possible theories of inflation and then attempt to make some applications to recent years.

Excess Demand: Cumulative and Noncumulative Aspects

Examples of excess (aggregate) demand inflation can be found in the price increases of World War II, the immediate postwar years, and the Korean War. During World War II the large increases in government expenditures were not offset by equal increases in taxes which would release sufficient resources for government use. The part of government expenditures that was not paid for by taxes (the deficit in other words) was financed through Treasury sales of government securities. In turn,

[2] The GNP implicit price deflators can be found in the *Economic Reports of the President.* In the 1963 *Report*, see pp. 178–179.

the Federal Reserve supported the price of government securities (and therefore kept interest costs down). The result was a large increase in the money supply. This substantial increase in the money supply was not fully reflected in price increases because of rationing and price controls.

During the immediate postwar years the Federal Reserve continued to support the price of government securities. Continual sales by commercial banks and other holders of securities then meant further increases in the money supply. Finally, largely because of the efforts of Senator Paul Douglas, the famous "accord" of 1951 between the Federal Reserve and the Treasury Department was "formulated." Thereafter the Federal Reserve was permitted greater freedom in controlling the supply of money and interest rates.

A graphic illustration of excess demand was presented in Figure 6-5, where we noted that an increase in demand occurs at the full employment level of output. This places total demand at a level greater than total supply. Consequently, prices and wages will rise, but by how much? Will there be a one-shot increase, or will there be a continuous upward spiral? Further, what will be the effect on aggregate demand? It is possible that after the initial price increase, total demand and supply will again be in equilibrium. The initial price increase in itself may be large enough to absorb and just offset the excess demand, and the price level will now remain steady. Or, it is also possible that the initial disequilibrium continues and prices (and wages) keep going up.

One thing that is not likely to happen is that the increases in prices will reduce real demand. This is because increases in prices are equivalent to increases in income. The prices of goods which the consumer purchases increase but so does his income; the prices of investment goods rise, but so do the prices of goods produced by capital goods; the businessman's wage bill may be rising, but so are the prices of the goods he sells. Generally speaking, then, we should expect no change in real demand when we have a generalized increase in the price level.

In the last paragraph we used the term "generally." The actual cumulative or noncumulative nature of inflation will tend to vary with whatever the net effect of certain influences on spending turns out to be. These influences are usually recognized as (1) the type of policy adopted by the monetary authorities, (2) the impact of the "Pigou effect," (3) the effect on the distribution of income, (4) the reaction in the foreign trade sector, and (5) income tax effects.

1. As we noted previously, price increases mean income increases; therefore, real aggregate demand is not reduced. Also, as long as the money supply increases (as during World War II) there should be no increase in interest rates which would reduce investment and therefore demand. If, however, the money supply is held constant, or increases only slowly, the rate of interest should rise, investment should fall, and so should consumption, because the multiplier would now be working in reverse. We have previously noted that erratic interest rate effects result during prosperous periods. It may be then that the unavailability of funds,[3] or the inability of a given supply of money to support a level economic activity beyond a certain point,[4] play a more important role in restraining the expansion of demand than interest rates. Finally, we should note that even if the money supply should remain constant, prices may still increase because of velocity increases, the use of money substitutes and the amount of monetary slack that will normally exist in the economy.

2. Pigou argued that an increase in the price level will reduce the real value of the wealth of consumers. In an attempt to preserve the real value of their assets, so it is argued, saving may increase and aggregate demand be reduced. As far as net creditors and net debtors in the private sector are concerned, however, the effects should cancel each other out. With an increase in the price level the position of creditors is damaged, while that of the debtors is enhanced; the tendency should be for the former to increase saving and the latter to increase consumption. It is also argued, relative to the debtor-creditor relationship between the public and private sectors, that the price level increase reduces the value of the debt of the public sector held by the private sector, which should have the effect of reducing consumption. Nonetheless, the overall empirical significance of the Pigou effect is difficult to measure and is generally questioned by economists.[5]

Of greater significance than the Pigou effect (the effect of current prices on consumption) is the effect of future price expectations. Clearly, if businessmen expect prices to increase, their reaction will be to attempt to raise investment (especially in inventories), which will worsen the inflationary situation. A similar result could occur when consumers are counting on a price increase.

[3] Due to the failure of the money supply to increase, or banker policy, etc.
For another demand-pull approach the reader may want to consult Bent Hansen, *A Study in the Theory of Inflation*, London: Allen and Unwin, 1951, especially Chapter 1; and also M. Bronfenbrenner and F. D. Holzman, "Survey of Inflation Theory," *Am. Ec. Rev.*, Sept. 1963, pp. 593–661.
[4] The second point could, of course, result from the first.
[5] See T. Mayer, "The Empirical Significance of the Real Balance Effect," *Q. J. Ec.*, May 1959, pp. 275–291; A. H. Hansen, "The Pigovian Effect," *J. Pol. Ec.*, Dec. 1951, pp. 535–536; and D. Patinkin, "Price Flexibility and Full Employment," *Am. Ec. Rev.*, Sept. 1948, pp. 543–564.

3. The result of a redistribution of income that is caused by inflation is similarly difficult to measure. If the major part of the price increases go to profits, and if the recipients of profits have a lower propensity to consume than the recipients of wage income, then real consumption will decline. If, however, the price increases go to wage earners, and if they have a high propensity to consume, then consumption will increase. Although these are real theoretical possibilities, such evidence as we have does not indicate that the effects will be strong in either direction.[6] Furthermore, even though wage increases may lag behind price and profit increases, there is little reason to expect that wages will not soon catch up and demand be further increased.[7]

4. To the extent that domestic prices increase relative to foreign prices, pressures are exerted to reduce demand. This is because imports will increase and exports will decline. (The usual pattern during recoveries from recessions in the United States is for the size of our favorable balance of trade to decline because imports increase.) If foreign prices are increasing, however, this effect should not result. In addition, the impact of foreign sales here may not be nearly as important as is often assumed because foreign merchants may charge high prices for goods sold here (thereby profiting by the higher price level here) as long as they can maintain a satisfactory share of the market. Although it is true that this behavior on their part does little or nothing to reduce the domestic price level, some of the pressures on our resources are relieved by these purchases of foreign-made goods.

5. As we have previously noted, a progressive tax structure may tend to increase tax revenues at a rate greater than the price increase. The increase in real tax collections should reduce consumption (shift the consumption function downward). We also noted that transfer payments tend to decline at high levels of income. Of further significance to this point is the level at which government expenditures are kept. If they increase, they will then tend to reduce the restraining impact of a progressive tax structure.

---

[6] The amount of redistribution that takes place is not great according to G. L. Bach and A. Ando, "The Redistributional Effects of Inflation," *Rev. Ec. & Stat.*, Feb. 1957, pp. 1–13.

A very interesting discussion of the impact of inflation on the distribution of income and on the distribution of wealth appears in JEC, *Empl., Growth, Price Levels*, SR, pp. 110–114.

[7] For a discussion of this problem see A. Smithies, "The Behavior of Money National Income under Inflationary Conditions," *Q. J. Ec.*, Nov. 1942, pp. 113–128, also reprinted in Smithies and Butters, eds., *Readings in Fiscal Policy*, Homewood, Ill.: Irwin for Am. Ec. Assoc., 1955, pp. 122–136.

The extent to which continual increases in prices result depends on the net impact of these five factors.

Cost-Push Inflation

We noted previously that there is wide disagreement about the causes of recent inflation in the United States. One of the more popular explanations for the price level increases of the last half of the 1950's has been the cost-push thesis. On the other hand, some economists have denied the existence of such a thing as cost-push, and argue that all inflations are basically of the demand-pull type.[8] We can construct a theoretical model in which cost-push inflation could occur, and in addition the evidence indicates that upward pressures on prices could so occur. We should very carefully note, though, that what can happen may not be the same as what has really happened. In reality, then, it is almost impossible to state accurately the causes of the increases in the price level in the last half of the 1950's. Furthermore, there is no reason why the basic elements of demand and cost inflation cannot be operating together at the same time. This makes it increasingly difficult to disentangle the price movements of this period.

There would certainly seem to be sufficient evidence that labor unions can exert upward pressures on wage rates which are independent of demand (that is, there is no excess demand).[9] In fact, the majority of the cost-push advocates have placed the blame directly on labor.[10] Recognition of some degree of power, however, does not necessarily spell out causes and effects for us. Nor does the fact that wage increases which are in excess of productivity increases for a given year or short period indicate that particular blame should be placed on unions.

Some Observations on Unions and Wages. Most labor economists are fairly well agreed that unions *do* affect wages. They tend to argue, however, that even though there have been abuses of power by certain

[8] See R. T. Selden, "Cost-Push versus Demand-Pull Inflation, 1955–57," *J. Polit. Ec.*, Feb. 1959; and R. J. Ball, "Cost Inflation and the Income Velocity of Money: A Comment," *J. Polit. Ec.*, June, 1960, pp. 288–296; Selden's reply on pp. 297–300, and Ball's rejoinder on p. 301. See also Selden's testimony before the JEC, *Empl., Growth, Price Levels,* H, Pt. 4, pp. 671–699 and 720–729.

[9] For a review of a good deal of the literature on union influences on wages see, Keiser, *Introductory Economics,* pp. 323–329.

[10] For a single example see the statement of Professor Fritz Machlup, JEC, *Empl., Growth, Price Levels,* H, Pt. 9A, pp. 2819–2832ff., especially p. 2823. During the hearings of the Senate Finance Committee in 1957 the statements of the members of the Eisenhower Administration and of the presidents of the Federal Reserve Banks, with few exceptions, placed the blame on labor unions. This has been the standard line of bankers, insurance companies, the NAM, and the Chamber of Commerce.

groups, unions have not been the major cause of price increases. The groups that have usually been accused of abusing their market positions have tended to be in the older craft unions, such as in the building trades (which have historically been criticized for their restrictive policies).

We should further note that giant unions alone cannot be associated with high wages. One is more likely to find a correlation between large unions, concentrated industries, and higher wages. Under such circumstances, it is possible for the oligopolistic firm to "pass on" wage increases because it has the market power to do so. (As we shall see later this has apparently happened in steel.) In addition, we find areas with strong unions but rather low wages (the ILGWU and dressmaking) because of a high degree of competition and no market power on the part of manufacturers. We would also expect to find industries with a high concentration ratio but weak unions and consequently low wages (as in the tobacco industry).[11]

It is not argued here that unions have been the main cause of recent inflation. Similarly, it is not argued that administered prices have been the main cause. What has been said thus far has been said to indicate that cost-push inflation is a distinct possibility. Its counterpart is administered price inflation which, also in and of itself, as noted, is not likely to be the sole cause of inflation. The fact that prices and wages are both primarily administered prices is explicitly recognized here.

We have noted previously that fiscal and monetary policies which are pushed far enough may eliminate or stop cost inflation of this type. But there is reason to believe that these would have to be pushed so far that unemployment would increase, profits would decline, and the rate of growth would fall. (Furthermore, all this may result and prices may still increase.) Some advocates of cost-push inflation have argued that it is not necessary to push fiscal-monetary policies this far. They argue that if wages and prices increase, and the money supply is not increased at the same time, aggregate demand will be reduced, unemployment will result, and wage increases will be stopped. On the other hand, many economists have seriously questioned (1) the extent to which a small increase in the price level will reduce demand, and (2) the argument that a small increase in unemployment will restrain wage-price increases.

The Mark-Up Thesis

A large group of economists believes that American corporations are very cost-oriented, and that they attempt to compute costs and then add

[11] For more on these issues see the excellent statements by A. Reese in JEC, *Rel. Prices to Ec. Stabil. & Growth*, P, pp. 660ff., and Lloyd Ulman, E. C. Budd, G. H. Hildebrand, O. A. Ornati, and others in JEC, *Empl., Growth, Price Levels*, H, Pt. 8.

to these costs a certain mark-up which (in many cases, at least) will provide them with a given "target return" on invested capital or sales.[12] Mark-up pricing, which is a type of administered price setting, in connection with certain other factors, is often used as a plausible explanation for recent inflationary movements.[13] Union activities are usually integrated into the mark-up theory by the assumption that labor is interested in wage increases which will match increases in the CPI. (It would not be un-realistic to assume that labor wants and expects a gradual increase in its standard of living also—regardless of how much productivity increases.) It is assumed by the mark-up theorists that an autonomous upward shift in either wages or prices can initiate the inflationary process.

As Ackley and others have pointed out, the mark-up approach "places the emphasis where unions and businessmen place it, not on the level of prices *per se*, nor on supply and demand, but on the preservation of 'fair' relationships between buying prices (including the cost-of-living), and selling prices (including wage rates)."[14] Ackley feels that when demand is higher, the mark-up tends to be higher, about equal to cost increases, and less (but not by too much) when demand is low and costs are up.[15] A similar pattern can be expected with reference to wage increases but the correlation between wage increases and profit increases is by no means exact.

Advocates of the mark-up thesis point out that, if the demands of both labor and business add up to more than 100 percent of the national

[12] There is no attempt here to cover the literature on this subject but see R. F. Lanzillotti, "Pricing Objectives in Large Companies," *Am. Ec. Rev.*, Dec. 1958; J. M. Blair, "Administered Prices: A Phenomenon in Search of a Theory," *Am. Ec. Rev.*, May 1959, pp. 431–450; and G. Ackley, "Administered Prices and the In-flationary Process," same source, pp. 419–430; and Lanzillotti in JEC, *Empl., Growth, Price Levels*, H, Pt. 7, pp. 2237–2262ff. See also Musgrave, *Theory of Public Finance*, pp. 426, 469.

See also F. D. Holzman, "Income Determination in Open Inflation," and James Duesenberry, "The Mechanics of Inflation," both in *Rev. Ec. & Stat.*, May 1950, pp. 150–158, and 144–149, respectively. These articles contain models of markup and both markup and demand inflation.

[13] See the article by J. P. Lewis in JEC, *Rel. Prices to Ec. Stabil, & Growth*, P, pp. 620ff. See also, in the same source, the article by G. Ackley, pp. 619–636, Ackley's article cited in the last footnote, and his *Macroeconomic Theory*, pp. 452-459. Ackley's book contains an excellent chapter on "The Theory of Inflation."

[14] Ackley, JEC, *Rel. Prices to Ec. Stabil. & Growth*, P, p. 629.

[15] The pattern of raising prices during recovery periods can be clearly seen in the steel industry.

As an illustration of the mark-up system T. F. Patton of Republic Steel said in May 1961 (as steel production was expanding) that a company cannot maintain "reasonable profit margins unless there is some compensating price increase." *The New York Times*, May 27, 1961, p. E1.

income, price increases will result. That is, if labor seeks a wage increase to match an increase in the cost of living, business firms raise their product prices to maintain their mark-ups, labor seeks another wage increase to offset the increase in the cost of living, business increases prices because costs increased again—the result can be an unending spiral, once started. If every business firm and every labor union attempts to maintain its mark-up, any price increase can become cumulative. This is because one firm's price increase tends to be a cost increase to other firms which may be passed on any number of times. Similarly, wage increases are cost increases. Furthermore, even when sales are made directly to consumers the same process may operate because the CPI then increases and labor fights for wage increases to offset this. One important offsetting force comes from productivity increases. But here again if all the productivity increase goes to profits and wages, prices will still continue to increase, given the foregoing conditions (an upward increase in some cost, autonomously created or due to excess demand in some product, which will be continuously passed on via price markups and wage increases to offset increases in the CPI). Finally, if the various groups attempt to raise their mark-ups, or raise their shares of the productivity increase (and the total claims are greater than the productivity increase), the inflationary trend will also continue.

One of the more important points those subscribing to the mark-up thesis make is that it is not particularly important where the price increase started, or who is to blame initially; what is important is the *process* by which the price (and wage) increases occur.

Mark-Ups and Excess Demand

Ackley has spelled out how both demand and mark-up factors can operate together in the inflationary process.[16] It is true that many agricultural and raw material prices are set under competitive conditions. Increases in food prices due to increases in demand show up rapidly in the CPI (because they receive a heavy weight in the CPI). Labor unions may attempt to raise wages to offset this increase in the cost of living. This raises business costs and results in price increases to maintain mark-ups, and we are off on our price increase binge once again. We have here, then, an example of the interaction of both excess demand and mark-up inflation. Excess demand in agricultural and raw material products makes the problem of mark-up inflation worse, a comment that applies with greater meaning to excess aggregate demand. Ackley has stated that "there is no sharp dichotomy between cost inflation operating only below

---

[16] This is done in considerable detail in his "Administered Prices and the Inflationary Process," *Am. Ec. Rev.*, May 1959.

some magic point of full employment and demand inflation operating only beyond it."[17] He has also gone so far as to claim that "whether aggregate demand is excessive or deficient, the problem needs to be analyzed in administrative, that is, essentially political, terms, and on the price as well as the wage side."[17] (The reader should be reminded that some reasonable arguments may be set forth justifying some degree of stability in prices and wages. The policy problem here, as with the degree of competition we attempt to maintain in the economy, is how to define "reasonable" price stability.)

Bottleneck and Sectoral Shift Inflation

Business cycle analysts have long recognized that during periods of rapid expansion in the economy not all industries will expand at the same rate. The result is that a large backlog of orders (excess demand) occurs in certain lines, with the further result that inflation results. This was no doubt one of our problems in the period immediately following World War II. Actual production declined, but expenditures increased at a rate at which it was virtually impossible for business to convert from war to peacetime production. It is, of course, also true that this would have been a period of excess demand even if astronomical reconversion rates has been realized.

Another explanation of inflation related to the mark-up theory previously noted which has received some considerable attention in recent years is the "sectoral shift thesis." Charles L. Schultze has developed this approach more fully than anyone else.[18] We should note, however, that there are many aspects to Schultze's approach besides shifts in demand from one sector to another. The similarity between Schultze's and Ackley's approaches will also become apparent.

Dr. Schultze's objective was to offer a reasonable explanation for the inflation of 1955–1957. It is his contention that, for the overall period, neither excessive aggregate demand nor overall pressure from wages on prices offers an acceptable explanation of the inflation of the period. Schultze recognizes (1) the downward rigidity and upward flexibility of prices and wages and the fact that price increases in certain sectors where demand is increasing are not offset by decreases in prices or wages in the contracting sectors; (2) the fact that the foregoing procedure will result in an increase in the price level; and (3) the relative insensitivity of prices

----

[17] *Ibid.*, p. 429.

[18] See JEC, *Empl., Growth, Price Levels*, SP No. 1. A summary of Schultze's study is presented in JEC, *Empl., Growth, Price Levels*, H, Pt. 7, pp. 2172–2205. See also Schultze's *Prices, Costs, and Output for the Postwar Period: 1947–57*, Washington, D.C.: CED, 1960, and JEC, *Empl., Growth, Price Levels*, SP No. 17.

and wages to the state of demand, and the possibility of a continuous upward spiral in prices due to (a) mark-ups and (b) wage demands to match cost-of-living increases (as discussed in the previous section).

Professor Schultze notes that excess demand can occur in particular sectors of the economy where there will likely be a general rise in materials and labor costs. Other industries are affected by this because the prices of the materials they purchase will rise. Wages in the excess demand industries will be bid up, which will cause an increase in wages in other industries because large wage differentials will bring a loss of labor, dissatisfaction, and reduced productivity. (This spread of wage costs may, in fact, raise unit wage costs more in the sectors or industries not experiencing excess demand, even though wages rise less, because productivity will tend to rise less rapidly in the less rapidly expanding industries.) Schultze's study shows that wage increases were approximately the same in all industries even though some industries expanded output by 12 percent and others reduced output by 6 percent, and employment increased by 1.8 percent in the former and declined by 9.1 percent in the latter industries.[19] Schultze's is not the only study that found such results; a United Nations study of several industrialized nations also found a "systematic tendency for the average wage increase to equal the increase in the most rapidly expanding industries." It warrants repeating that the spread of these wage increases from excess demand sectors to other sectors accentuates the increases in prices of semifabricated materials and components, which are passed on to the final stages of production and on to finished goods.[20]

As we have noted earlier in the text, price increases of this type become cumulative. This is so because of the downward rigidity of prices and wages: Reallocations of resources come by price increases that are not offset by equal price reductions. The result of this rachet effect is a secular upward drift in the price level as long as productivity gains are less than mark-up and wage demands.

Another factor that has shown its head in recent years is the importance of overhead or fixed costs. In recent years they have become a rapidly increasing proportion of total costs; this development played a role in the inflation of 1955–1957. During the 1955–1957 period investment outlays expanded significantly, but aggregate demand and output only moderately. Hiring of overhead employees was accelerated: 50 percent of the total rise in unit costs was due to higher salary costs per unit, and an additional 20 percent was caused by rising depreciation. The increases in productivity

---

[19] See the table in JEC, *Empl.*, *Growth*, *Price Levels*, H, Pt. 7, p. 2175.

[20] If the firm attempts to maintain a straight percentage profit, it will be capitalizing on a wage increase.

during 1956 and 1957 were low; or, more accurately, output per production worker increased sharply but not enough to offset the increase in overhead labor input costs (and the wage and salary increases).[21] Had output increases been larger, productivity increases would also have been larger, and unit costs would have been lower. Business firms were forced (by their standards) to increase prices to cover these cost increases.

Schultze does not deny that excess demand was important during this period. He does argue, however, that it was only for a short period during late 1955 that excessive aggregate demand existed. He further notes that there was a correlation between the sectors with the largest increases in demand and the largest increases in prices. The particular area in which this occurred (except for automobiles and steel) was in capital goods and associated industries where prices rose by 15 percent compared with an average of 4 percent for all other industries. Furthermore, prices in industries in which most of the inflation occurred rose substantially more than wage costs. Other industries experienced wage cost increases which were proportionately more than prices.

Uneven Growth Rates and Inflation: Profits and Wage Contracts

To the extent that our rate of growth fluctuates unnecessarily, we may have parallel and unnecessary increases in prices. Fluctuations in the level of federal expenditures, and other policies of the federal government, for example, have actually contributed to the instability of our economy. (Examples are given in Chapter 22.) These fluctuations, due to changes in the level of federal expenditures or other causes, bring (1) greater speculation in inventories and more of the sudden surges in demand that we should like to avoid, (2) greater possibilities of bottlenecks, and (3) greater fluctuations in profits and therefore in wages and prices.

Significant increases in the size of profits like those that occurred in 1955 bring with them a natural increase in wage demands. To expect otherwise would require the expectation that Walter Reuther and George

---

[21] The trend toward an increasing proportion of nonproduction workers has apparently continued since Schultze's study was done. Not only have they increased but their earnings are substantially higher than those of factory workers. See *Chase Manhattan Bank Newsletter*, Nov.–Dec. 1961.

Along similar lines some interesting data were presented to the JEC during its hearings on the *Jan. 1962. Ec. Rept. Pres.* by Walter Reuther. His data show that wage costs of factory production and maintenance workers per unit had been declining almost steadily since 1958(1), and that productivity increases more than offset increased wages. See also the very interesting table which gives unit wage cost and unit salary cost for the period 1953 to 1961 by quarters on p. 740.

See also R. P. Mack, "Inflation and Quasi-Elective Changes in Costs," *Rev. Ec. & Stat.*, Aug. 1959, and the previously cited SP Nos. 1 and 17.

Meany will slap General Motors executives on the back exclaiming, "Glad you fellows are doing so well. Keep up the good work. We don't want any of it!" The facts of life are that, in such a period, basic wage rates do go up. Further, if the firm wants a long-term contract, it must pay a price to get it, usually the promise of automatic wage increases for the next few years. If, however, the rate of growth of output is seriously slowed down, as it was in 1956, 1957, and 1958, anticipated and planned productivity increases do not materialize and the automatic wage increases are not justified in terms of productivity increases. The real villain is not the union, although a comparison of wage increases and productivity increases in 1956, 1957, and 1958 may so indicate; rather, the difficulty lies in the initial fluctuations in profits and (more so) in the succeeding inadequate rate of growth in the economy. Again, when the contractual wage increases occur, costs are up and prices are increased. These new wage rates, as per our discussion, are spread throughout the economy. The settling of wage contracts, under conditions of fluctuating profits, might serve the interests of society better if what is granted the union in periods of high profits is a percent of those high profits.[22] The firm, then, is not stuck with high basic wage rates when profits decline, and will not experience such large increases in costs (because of inadequate growth in output and productivity) which it feels it must pass on in the form of higher prices.

There is considerable evidence indicating that pattern bargaining, with the steel or automobile industries usually making the bargains during the postwar period, has been especially important in the industries with higher concentration ratios and strong unions. The key bargain in 1955 was in the automobile industry where profits were high and the settlement included a 3-year contract with an annual improvement factor of $2\frac{1}{2}$ percent, an automatic cost-of-living clause, plus fringes estimated at about 12 cents per hour. ("Profits before taxes represented a 46 percent return on stockholders' equity; profits after taxes were 21 percent."[23]) In 1955 the steel contract was reopened, profits were again high (27 percent before taxes and 13.5 percent after) and a wage increase of 15 cents per hour was negotiated. The 1956 settlement in steel was very favorable to the steel union, and automatic increases were provided for in 1957 and 1958 under

---

[22] Such a profit-sharing plan should also increase labor's interest in increased efficiency. American Motors has introduced such a program.

Some condemn profit-sharing plans on ideological grounds. Such a contention may, however, really be a false issue because the wage increases will no doubt accompany higher profit levels, in which case the "pure" capitalist is still better off with a profit-sharing plan.

[23] JEC, *Empl., Growth, Price Levels*, SR, p. 154.

a 3-year contract. Other industries followed this pattern in negotiations carried out in both 1955 and 1956. The basic importance of these settlements is that automatic increases for 1957 and 1958 were provided for in automobiles, farm equipment, meatpacking, electrical equipment, aircraft, steel, aluminum, copper, bituminous coal, railroads, and other industries. Wage (and therefore cost) increases in these years of low economic growth were set in 1955 and 1956, and they were not offset by productivity increases.[24]

Other Factors in Price Increases

The Steel Industry. In some respects the pattern of inflation in the steel industry has been different from that of other industries although the impact of the price and wage increases followed the pattern noted previously. A study of the steel industry by Otto Eckstein and Gary Fromm[25] showed a direct rise in the price of steel from 1951 to 1958 of 37 percent as compared with 9 percent for all commodities less farm and food products. The authors concluded that these direct effects plus indirect effects on the costs of other products in which steel is used accounted for about 40 percent of the increase in the WPI since 1947 and over 50 percent since 1953. Not only is the level of steel prices important to the level of costs and prices in other industries; wage settlements in steel have likely set the pattern for other industries such as copper, aluminum, and fabricated metal products.

Professors Eckstein and Fromm have placed the responsibility for this development directly on the shoulders of management, the steelworkers union, and the government. In this industry there is strong market power among the firms and within the union. Management was apparently willing to pass on wage increases, and was at times encouraged to do so by the government (in 1956 in particular). The authors further point out that the steel companies attempted to raise profit margins not only to maintain (or perhaps even increase) its share of income gains in the economy, but also to create additional internal sources of funds to finance expansion. Further, the wage settlements of 1955 and 1956 were carried out in an atmosphere of high profits, high output, and optimistic expectations for the future. Although wage increases have been large, productivity increases have been only average. Two other factors have also played a role in steel price increases—higher taxes and larger depreciation charges. Finally, the authors carefully point out that the increases in neither wages nor prices in steel can be reasonably explained by demand factors alone.

---

[24] An extended analysis is to be found in *ibid.*, pp. 150–158.
[25] JEC, *Empl., Growth, Price Levels*, SP No. 2.

Demand was generally not excessive, although it was high enough and inelastic enough to enable the steel firms to raise prices.[26]

A similar study has been done of the steel industry, with many similar but some dissimilar results, by the father of the concept of administered prices, Gardiner Means.[27] Means, for example, has concluded that from 1953 to 1961 three-quarters of the increase in steel prices was due (directly or indirectly) to the widening of profit margins and only one-quarter due to increased labor costs. Means further claimed that at 1953 prices and wages an operating rate of 80 percent of capacity would have yielded a return on capital after taxes of about 8 percent, whereas at 1959 prices and wage rates the same operating rate would have yielded about 16 percent return. He further maintains that the breakeven point for U.S. Steel in 1953 was around 50 percent of capacity, but in 1959 around 30 percent.[28]

The Machinery Industry.[29] The inflation of machinery prices from 1955 to 1958 was second only to that of steel prices, "machinery and motive products" rising some 16.7 percent or about one-fifth of the total rise from 1954 to 1958. In this sector, however, the cause was quite clearly the growth of demand: expenditures on plant and equipment, output trends, new and unfilled orders, and overtime hours are all consistent with the demand hypothesis. Although some carryover of the increase in steel prices is to be expected and reflected in machinery prices, material costs did not rise enough to cause the sharp rise in machinery prices which

[26] They point out that during peak periods demand no doubt aided the price increase. But the price trend was steadily upward even when demand was not strong; further, prices failed to decline during large cutbacks in production when demand declined sharply. *Ibid.*, p. 33.

The reader should be warned that there is no complete agreement on the stability of administered prices during periods of declining demand. See M. J. Bailey, "Administered Prices in the American Economy," in JEC, *Rel. Prices to Ec. Stabil. & Growth*, P, pp. 89–105; G. Stigler, "Administered Prices and Oligopolistic Inflation," *J. Bus.*, Jan. 1962, pp. 1–13; and the caustic comments of Professors Bailey and Selden on the previously cited papers of Ackley and Blair, *Am. Ec. Rev.*, May 1959, pp. 459–461 and 454–457. The reader of these articles and comments will note that not only matters of fact but also very important issues of theory are involved here.

There is no doubt that price shading goes on during periods of a decline in demand. But it is also irrefutable that adjustments are made in production to maintain prices (in steel, automobiles, etc.). One of the important issues is the size of the price concessions.

[27] See G. Means, *Industrial Prices and Their Relative Inflexibility*, 74th Cong., 1st Sess., Senate Document No. 13, Jan. 1935.

[28] See Mean's testimony in JEC, *Jan. 1962 Ec. Rept. Pres.*, H, pp. 365ff., and Means, *Pricing Power and the Public Interest*, New York: Harper, 1962.

[29] See JEC, *Empl., Growth, Price Levels*, SP No. 3. Summaries of both papers Nos. 2 and 3 are included in the *Staff Report*, Chapter 5. The 30 percent figure seems quite low.

did occur. Neither can unit wage costs be blamed, for demand pressure in this sector did not lead to higher wage increases in this sector, or the setting of a pattern for other sectors as one would expect under the Schultze thesis.[30] On the other hand, gross profit margins rose 52 percent in electrical machinery and 32 percent in nonelectrical machinery, compared with an increase of only 12 percent in manufacturing as a whole.[31]

It is particularly appropriate to conclude this section with a quote from the *Staff Report*.

Since steel and machinery together accounted for close to two-thirds of the 1955–58 increase in the wholesale price index, other than farm and food, it is clear that neither "demand-pull" nor "market power" is in itself a sufficient explanation of the creeping inflation of that period.[32]

Wage Behavior. Considerable evidence indicates that the wage increases of the immediate postwar and Korean War periods were caused primarily by demand forces.[33] The wage increases following the year 1955 are not so easily explained. An analysis of wages in manufacturing, mining, and railroads showed that (1) changes in hourly earnings were not significantly related to changes in employment (annual or for subperiods), (2) changes in wages and output were not closely related, and (3) changes in wages and in productivity per production worker man-hour were not related. On the other hand, it was found that profits (as a rate of return on equity) and the degree of competition were related to wage changes, especially after 1951.[34] No general correlation between union strength and wage changes was found although in some industries union power is no doubt important, as noted previously and in the following. Furthermore, wage increases provided for in contracts may go into effect when output or the rate of productivity increase have declined.

There is little doubt, as noted earlier, that in some sectors unions can and have autonomously raised wages. At various times this has been true in mining and railroads in the face of a decline in employment in both industries. There is strong reason to believe, again as noted previously,

---

[30] JEC, *Empl., Growth, Price Levels*, SP No. 3, pp. 56, 61.

[31] JEC, *Empl., Growth, Price Levels*, SR, p. 124.

[32] *Ibid.*, p. 127. The sharp increase in the prices of building materials was closely tied to the large expansion of 1955, which indicates that in this area also demand factors were operating.

[33] *Ibid.*, pp. 136–144,

[34] See *ibid.*, p. 147, and JEC, *Empl., Growth, Price Levels*, SP Nos. 9 and 15.

These conclusions were based on a study of 19 manufacturing industries, which is not a wide basis. Further, "in mining and railroads. . . the relationship of wages to profits did not appear and concentration ratios were not available."

that conditions are favorable to the exercise of market power in the construction industry—(1) the high degree of skill involved, (2) the sale of skills in local markets, (3) local bargaining (and interlocal rivalry), and (4) possible controls on entry (via limited apprenticeships, etc.). No doubt in construction both demand and market power have been important factors.

Summary

The foregoing is not intended to be a definitive statement on the causes of inflation. An attempt has been made only to discuss the various possible explanations, emphasizing those that appear to be the most plausible.

Aggregate demand played a role in overall inflation in the immediate postwar period, during the Korean War, and in late 1955. Thereafter demand in certain sectors (such as machinery) was important. But also important were the long-term wage contracts signed in 1955 and 1956 and the profit levels of that period. Of further significance have been pattern-setting key wage negotiations, business mark-up practices, the transmission of cost increases throughout the economy, the desire to raise prices to raise retained earnings for expansion, and the increase in business fixed costs. Finally, the market power of both business and unions, and the downward rigidity of wages and many prices have all been important factors (though not always at the same time). At the heart of our analysis seem to be demand pressures, the conditions of wage settlements, mark-ups, market power, and variations in productivity.

POLICY

Excess Demand, Cost-Push, Investment, and Direct Controls

Economists who have offered these explanations for the post-1955 inflation are almost unanimously agreed that tight fiscal-monetary policy is not the proper policy prescription. If the cause of inflation is clearly excess aggregate demand, then a tight fiscal-monetary policy is very appropriate. If, however, other factors such as long-term wage increases and increases in overhead costs, are the problem, then the result of using such a policy may be slower growth, or even inflation itself because of a failure of output to grow rapidly enough to increase productivity so that contractual wage increases may be absorbed, and fixed costs spread over a greater quantity.

We should further note that even in cases where excess demand is clearly the problem, if the process was initiated by an increase in investment spending it may be doubtful that the usual tight fiscal-monetary policy will have much effect on this sector. In fact, an overly restrictive policy may be necessary to control investment. This problem will be dealt with in greater detail in Chapter 19.

Dealing with this type of inflation is not easy. In an economy such as ours there will always be sufficient flexibility in the monetary system to accommodate the types of price increase we have listed. Complete control of prices and wages would, of course, do the job, but at a tremendous administrative and economic cost. The cost of such a program would be high relative to the return, which would consist of the avoidance of a yearly price level increase of $1\frac{1}{2}$ to 2 percent.

We have noted previously that economists often argue that the use of direct controls leads automatically to complete price and wage control in the economy. This point is debated, and it must be admitted that partial control does not necessarily mean that complete controls will follow. Galbraith, for example, argues that controls could be effectively used on a limited basis.[35]

The usual fiscal controls to deal with the level of demand were dealt with in Chapters 8 and 9, specific fiscal controls were discussed in Chapters 12, 13, and 16, and monetary controls were discussed in Chapter 17.[36] Other fiscal and monetary controls are covered in Chapter 19. Some degree of overlapping between this and other chapters occurs, but here we attempt to stick to policies aimed at mark-up pricing and administered wage problems.

Antitrust and Business and Labor

One of our difficulties is the market power of both business firms and unions. To reduce the market power of business firms many have suggested more effective antitrust enforcement. The maintenance of a reasonable degree of freedom of entry into American industry, and therefore a reasonable degree of competition, is a highly desirable social-political-economic goal because it provides for some degree of protection for the consumer, reduces the possibility of collusive practices and higher prices, the possibility of monopoly profits, the possibility of firms refusing to utilize the latest type of capital equipment, and the possibility of suppression of new products. The gains to be realized by enforcement of the antitrust laws are nothing to be scoffed at or belittled. The revelations of

[35] Galbraith, *The Affluent Society*, Boston: Houghton Mifflin, 1958, p. 247. A. G. Hart, on the other hand, argues that it is futile to use direct controls to combat creeping inflation, that the countries which have used them have dropped them, and that creeping inflation is less of an evil than direct controls. JEC, *Empl., Growth, Price Levels*, H, Pt. 9A, p. 2891.

[36] For more on the use of selective tax policy to negate wage and profit demands see Musgrave, *The Theory of Public Finance*, pp. 426, 469–471.

the extent of price gouging by certain firms of consumers and others in recent (or past) antitrust cases should testify to the need for such laws. On the other hand, the exact effect of antitrust enforcement on the price level cannot always be predicted; a higher degree of competition will likely introduce greater price instability into the economy; and, finally, it does not appear that stronger action in this direction is about to be undertaken in our society.[37] There should be little reason to doubt the importance of several decades of enforcement of the antitrust laws in the American economy (even though enforcement cannot be classified as "strict"), but it is perhaps unrealistic to expect too much help from this policy in combating creeping inflation. Furthermore, cost increases may result in price increases that are inflationary but do not result from increased profits and are not in conflict with the antitrust laws (in the opinion of many, at least).[38]

A corollary of the proposal that the antitrust laws be more vigorously applied to business is that they also be used to break up unions. Many labor economists argue that to do this may worsen the situation because the substitution of several for a few unions may result in greater interunion rivalry, higher wage demands, and more strikes with their concomitant losses. Foreign experience tends to substantiate this point of view. Finally, much labor union power is a derivative of the market power of the business firms with which the unions deal. The major exceptions to this may be the construction unions, which operate in local markets. No one has come up with a proposal of how to deal with this problem fairly.[39]

A Wage-Price Commission?

For these reasons many have concluded that some other type of government intervention is necessary—in fact, inevitable.[40] There is no attempt

[37] T. J. Kreps in JEC, *Empl., Growth, Price Levels*, SP No. 22, p. 42, states unequivocally that "giant enterprise. . . has grown irrevocably beyond the point of no return," and that "both atomization and surrender are impracticable." Kreps discusses many of the thorny problems of antitrust policy. The reader may find his discussion of the industrial and economic base of fascism interesting.

[38] Ruth Mack, *Am. Ec. Rev.*, May 1960, p. 175. It could still be argued, however, that the power to pass on the price increase demonstrates market power.

[39] Current coverage of labor unions under the antitrust laws, past court decisions, and recommendations are presented in JEC, *Empl., Growth, Price Levels*, H, Pt. 7, pp. 2068–2081 (from the Attorney General's National Committee of 1955). See pp. 2108ff. for the details of 20 cases from 1953 to 1959 of illegal labor union activity.

[40] See, for example, J. P. Lewis, "The Problem of Price Stabilization: A Progress Report," *Am. Ec. Rev.*, May 1959, pp. 311ff., and JEC, *Rel. Prices to Ec. Stabil. & Growth*, P, pp. 391–393. See also G. Ackley, "A Third Approach to the Analysis and Control of Inflation," *ibid.*, p. 634; R. Musgrave, *ibid.*, p. 606; and Ben Lewis, JEC, *Jan. 1962 Ec. Rept. Pres.*, H, p. 379, and "Economics by Admonition," *Am. Ec. Rev.*, May 1959, pp. 394–398.

to draw any inferences here, but it is interesting to notice that both John P. Lewis and Gardner Ackley have made proposals for intervention and both were appointed to President Kennedy's CEA.

Noting that some degree of price stability has many advantages and yet that the economy has a built-in inflationary bias, Lewis points out that the approach of economists should not be doctrinaire. That is, they should not assume that some intervention involves a rejection of the market mechanism. "Present pricing practice already is an amalgam of many institutional effects, some private and some public, some old and some new, and there is no reason to decide suddenly that further tinkering is impossible or would be calamitous."[41] Furthermore, Lewis argues that labor and business are not likely to rid themselves of the inflationary bias inherent in their wage-price practices without government intervention.

Professor Ackley has proposed the establishment of a Wage and Price Commission for the purpose of:

1. Formulating general standards for noninflationary wage and price decisions
2. Collecting the information necessary to apply these standards to particular strategic proposed increases of wages and prices, and
3. Making public its findings.[42]

Ackley's commission would have

the power of subpena, an adequate economic staff, and the authority, even, to require temporary postponement of specific wage and price increases pending the Commission's study. I do not see the commission as having any authority to establish legal maximum wages or prices, but merely that of expressing in as concrete terms as possible its dispassionate and documented judgments as to what the general objective of price stability might seem to require in the settlement of specific issues.

Eckstein's and Musgrave's proposals are basically the same.[43] Other

[41] J. P. Lewis, "The Problem of Price Stabilization: A Progress Report," *op. cit.*, pp. 315–316.

[42] G. Ackley, "A Third Approach to the Analysis and Control of Inflation," *op. cit.*, p. 634.

Several European countries have taken steps in the direction, and beyond. See, for example, O.E.C.D., *Policies for Price Stability*, 1962; O.E.E.C., *The Problem of Rising Prices*, May 1961; O.E.C.D. Country Studies; *Incomes Policy: the Next Step*, United Kingdom White Paper, 1962; and "Policy Statement of Chancellor to the German Parliament," Oct. 1962. Surveys of institutional arrangements for dealing with this problem are readily accessible in JEC, *Empl., Growth, Price Levels*, SP No. 11, and "Incomes Policies," *The O.E.C.D. Observer*, Jan. 1963, insert (unnumbered pages).

[43] Both have supported fact-finding boards in key industries. Musgrave's proposal appears in the source cited in footnote 40 and Eckstein's in the source cited in footnote 45.

proposals have called for annual labor-management-White House conferences on wage and price problems.[44] Others still feel that behind-the-scenes government intervention is best in spite of the fact that when it has been used it has had inflationary results.[45]

Throughout the 1950's the major policy pursued in an attempt to contain inflation was the issuance of exhortations to business and labor to behave themselves. Finally, in the January 1962 *Economic Report of the President* the CEA laid down guidelines for noninflationary price and wage behavior. The general guide was for wage rate increases "in such industry to be equal to the trend rate of overall productivity increase." Price reduction is called for if the industry's rate of productivity increase exceeds the overall rate, and "appropriate" price increases "if the opposite relationship prevails." The CEA very carefully added several important qualifications and exceptions to its general rule.[46]

The first real challenge to the Kennedy Administration came during the steel negotiations of 1962. The steelworkers' union was apparently convinced to keep its wage and fringe increases in line with productivity increases, and it was apparently understood that there would be no increase in steel prices. However, after the contract was signed U.S. Steel and other firms announced a price increase which they promptly retracted under threats of antitrust prosecution, being cut off from government contracts, and the public indignation which the President was able to arouse. Since this approach can be used only infrequently time only will tell whether the next step will be the establishment of a wage and price commission as many have predicted.

We do not want to end this chapter without pointing out that the future may not be as dark as our discussion may imply. In the first place, the post-1955 price increases should be kept in the proper perspective. There was, indeed, a very large shift in demand (investment increased by a full 25 percent). Furthermore, from our experience and the many excellent studies of this period, we should have learned something about the interrelationships among the relative roles of profits, wage increases (especially those provided for by long-term contracts), productivity increases, price mark-ups, the rate of growth, and fiscal-monetary policy. A somewhat higher but even growth rate may actually be conducive to greater price

[44] Another unique proposal is that of A. P. Lerner, JEC, *Empl.*, *Growth*, *Price Levels*, H, Pt. 7, pp. 2262–2266. See also Walter Reuther's proposal in JEC, *Jan. 1961 Ec. Rept. Pres.*, H, pp. 121, 145.

[45] See O. Eckstein's statement in JEC, *Jan. 1962 Ec. Rept. Pres.*, H, pp. 380–385.

[46] See pp. 188–190 of Jan. 1962 *Ec. Rept. Pres.* A useful list of policy suggestions will also be found in C. E. Lindblom, "Labor Policy, Full Employment, and Inflation," in Max F. Millikan, ed., *Income Stabilization for a Developing Democracy*, New Haven: Yale Univ. Press, 1953, pp. 538–546.

stability. Finally, our record on price stability has been considerably better than that of most other industrial nations.[47] Even though our growth rate has generally been lower, it is highly probable that we could have had greater growth and similar price behavior.

[47] During the years 1953–1959 only France turned in a better performance relative to the CPI (and in the case of France exchange rate changes would have to be considered). From 1959 to 1962 only Belgium and France did better. From 1953 to 1959, relative to the WPI, every country except the U.K. did better than the U.S., but from 1959 to 1962 the U.S. had the best record with no price increases. The comparisons are for the major European countries plus Japan. The complete data can be found in *Jan. 1963 Ec. Rept. Pres.*, p. 105.

19

The Public Debt, Fiscal Control,
and Economic Stability

One of the effects of Keynesian theory has been the general acceptance among economists of the use of both deficits and surpluses to counteract, respectively, depression, and inflation. There is some feeling, however, that excessive attention has been paid to the expansionary aspects of debt creation and that the effects of the debt itself have been slighted or passed off with the assumption and contention that there is neither an economic burden nor transfer effect, or that these effects are not generally serious. In this chapter we briefly review the argument over the burden of the debt, and the problem of simultaneously attaining both full employment and stable prices on the one hand and fiscal control on the other. (Selected data on the debt can be found in Table 19-1.)

A REVIEW OF THE BURDEN-TRANSFER ARGUMENT

The "Traditional" Point of View and the "New Orthodoxy"

The traditional approach, which may also be classified as that of the British classical economists, assumes that a valid analogy between private and public debt can be made: that debt, whether private or public, is impoverishment and can rapidly lead to bankruptcy; that the burden of the debt is passed on to our children who must be taxed to pay for it; that there is also an interest burden, which must be paid by means of higher taxation; and that such interest payments can involve both a redistribution of income (from taxpayers to bondholders) and a deflationary impact; that the imposition of additional taxes to pay interest will

Table 19-1. Selected Data on the Federal Debt

Year	Gross Public Debt[a] (Billions of Dollars)	Per Capita[a]	Gross Interest[b] (Billions of Dollars)	Gross Interest as a Percent of Federal Expenditures[c]	Calendar Year Net Interest[d] (Billions of Dollars)	Net Interest as a Percent of GNP	Net Public Debt[e] (End of Year) (Billions of Dollars)	Net Public Debt as a Percent of GNP
1945	258.7	1,848.60	3.6	3.7	—	—	252.7	118
1946	269.4	1,905.42	4.7	7.8	3.9	1.8	229.7	110
1947	258.3	1,792.05	5.0	12.7	4.2	1.8	223.3	96
1960	286.3	1,586.07	9.2	11.9	7.1	1.4	241.0	46
1962	304.0	1,622.09	9.2	10.5	6.7	1.2	256.8	46

[a] *Statistical Abstract of the United States*, 1961, p. 389. 1962 data from *Surv. Current Bus.*, Feb. 1963, pp. 5–12. Data as of June 30 for years prior to 1962; 1962 data as of end of 1962.

[b] *Ibid.*, p. 366.

[c] *Ibid.*, p. 389. Based on total federal expenditures not reduced by the amounts of interfund transactions representing interest payments and certain other payments to the Treasury. 1962 data from *Surv. Current Bus.*

[d] *Jan. 1963 Ec. Rept. Pres.*, p. 242.

[e] *Ibid.*, p. 234. Some would deduct from this figure the amount of federal debt held by Federal Reserve Banks, which in 1962 amounted to about $31 billion. Other data on the ownership of the federal debt can be found in *ibid.*, p. 236, or in any issue of the *FR Bull.*

adversely affect investment; that debt financing in itself is inevitably inflationary;[1] and that government debt is unproductive.

Advocates of the "new orthodoxy"[2] answer these arguments as follows: First, there is no need for the federal government ever to go bankrupt, because it can pay off currently maturing debt by selling new debt to others (or to the same individuals), and because it has the power to print money to pay off the debt should it need to. To do so under conditions which created or aggravated inflation would, of course, be irresponsible. Second, the real burden of government borrowing and spending activity falls during the period in which it is done. The burden is the use of resources for public purposes which could have been used for private purposes. In addition, it is argued that if less than full employment prevails there is no real burden since the resources would have gone unused. Furthermore, there need be no future interest burden under depression conditions since the expenditures can be financed through printing money.[3] The usual example given to demonstrate the point that the debt burden is contemporaneous is that the debt incurred during war (and the human and other resources) could have been used to produce goods useful to society rather than to produce goods which would be "shot up" on the battlefield.

Third, although the debt may not be retired in the present generation and may instead be passed on to the next generation, it is also true that if the debt is paid off in the next generation this same generation receives the payment. The succeeding generation inherits the debt, but it also inherits the bonds which represent the claims against the debt. It is generally conceded, however, that repayment of the debt could involve some problems of income redistribution through the tax-and-transfer process. It is further also generally recognized by advocates of the "new"

[1] The arguments have been summarized here from A. P. Lerner, "The Burden of the National Debt," in *Income, Employment, and Public Policy, Essays in Honor of Alvin H. Hansen*, New York: Norton, 1948, pp. 255–261. For another excellent summary and evaluation of the classical view of the balanced budget and national debt see J. Burkhead, "The Balanced Budget," *Q. J. Ec.*, May 1954, reprinted in Smithies and Butters, eds., *Readings in Fiscal Policy*, Homewood Ill.: Irwin for Am. Ec. Assoc., 1955.

[2] This label is used here for convenience only—it is not strictly correct. The views of Malthus and Carl Dietzel were strikingly antitraditional. See W. F. Stettner, "Carl Dietzel, Public Expenditures and the Public Debt," in *Income, Employment, and Public Policy, Essays in Honor of Alvin H. Hansen* pp. 276–299.

See also C. S. Shoup, "Debt Financing and Future Generations," *The Ec. J.*, Dec. 1962, pp. 887–898. Shoup notes Ricardo's argument that a burden can be passed on to the next generation in the form of a smaller stock of capital.

[3] James M. Buchanan, the leading defender of the argument that the burden of the debt is passed on, accepts this argument.

theory of the public debt that interest payments may involve some income redistribution. Some more extreme antitraditionalists, however, argue that it is not necessary to pay the interest with new taxes, that more debt can be sold to raise funds to make interest payments.[4]

Fourth, while it is true that government expenditures may be wasteful, it is not true that they are necessarily unproductive as the supporters of the traditional approach typically argue. This argument was disposed of in Chapter 1 and requires no further comment here.

Fifth, it is not necessarily true that tax rates must continuously increase in order to pay the interest on the debt. An increasing absolute size of the public debt could be serviced with a constant or declining tax rate as long as taxable income is expanding at a sufficiently high rate.[5]

Sixth, the difference between an internally and an externally financed debt should be pointed out. When the debt is held by foreigners, a real burden can be imposed because, when they demand payment, they may take it in the form of actual goods and services. This is production lost to our society.

Seventh, the impact of taxes on investment can be greatly diminished if 100 percent deductibility of losses against profits is provided for.[6] There is the further question of what the level of investment would be without the increase in debt during a deflationary period. As far as the alleged deflationary effect of tax collections to make interest payments are concerned, this can be offset by tax rate reduction, printing money, or additional borrowing to pay the interest.

The supposedly inflationary impact of debt creation is not in itself a valid objection to an expanding debt. With idle resources in the economy, which is the primary reason for incurring debt instead of increasing taxes, there should be no reason to be concerned over inflation (unless the

[4] This is Lerner's position; "The Burden of the National Debt," *op. cit.*, pp. 257–258, and his "Functional Finance and Federal Debt," *Social Research*, Feb. 1943, reprinted in Smithies and Butters, eds., *op. cit.*, pp. 468–478. E. Domar, whose article "The 'Burden of the Debt' and the National Income," *Am. Ec. Rev.*, Dec. 1944, represents the modern approach, assumes that interest charges will be paid for by taxes. Domar's article also appears in Smithies and Butters, eds., *op. cit.*, pp. 479–501, and in his *Essays in the Theory of Economic Growth*, New York: Oxford Univ. Press, 1957.

See also Seymour Harris, *National Debt and the New Economics*, New York: McGraw-Hill, 1947, especially Chapters 4 and 5; C. C. Abbott, *The Federal Debt: Structure and Impact*, New York: Twentieth Century Fund, 1953; and the Committee on Public Debt Policy, *Our National Debt: Its History and Meaning Today*, New York: Harcourt, Brace, 1949.

[5] See E. Domar, *op. cit.*

[6] See both of Lerner's articles and Richard Musgrave and Evsey Domar, "Proportional Income Taxation and Risk Taking," *Q. J. Ec.*, May 1944.

transfer of resources from private to public uses is not easily accomplished). No less an advocate of the "Keynesian" viewpoint than the originator of the concept of functional finance, Abba P. Lerner, has noted that "there is no need to assume these limitations so long as Functional Finance is on guard against inflation, for it is the fear of inflation which is the only rational basis for suspicion of the printing of money."[7]

The Revisionist Theory

In recent years there has been a resurgence of interest in the argument concerning the burden of the public debt.[8] Much of the recent material on the problem is complex, if not even esoteric. In essence, however, this approach maintains that the national debt can be a burden on the economy, that the analogy between public and private debt is valid, and that its real cost is (or, in the more moderate approaches, can be) passed on to future generations. It should be noted that many of the arguments of this school apply to (1) special cases and (2) special definitions of such terms as generations, burden, etc., and (3) that they sometimes tend to stress the effects of financial rather than real factors.[9]

An Antirevisionist View

Even the most extreme critics of the British classical theory of the debt recognize that there still may be "significant problems" of an internal national debt.[10] It is recognized, for example, that problems involved in the payment of interest may involve a redistribution of income. To this we might add that there are problems of making certain that the size of the debt at any time does not have an inflationary effect.

It is further true that debt creation may possibly have effects which last

[7] Lerner, "Functional Finance and the Federal Debt," in Smithies and Butters, eds., *op. cit.*, p. 476.

[8] See J. M. Buchanan, *Public Principles of Public Debt*, Homewood, Ill.: Irwin, 1958; W. G. Bowen, R. G. Davis, and D. H. Kopf, "The Public Debt: A Burden on Future Generations?," *Am. Ec. Rev.*, Sept. 1960, pp. 701–706. See also Musgrave, *The Theory of Public Finance*, New York: McGraw-Hill, 1959, Chapter 23; and J. E. Meade, "Is the National Debt a Burden?," *Ox. Ec. P.*, June 1958, and Feb. 1959.

For refutations or partial criticisms of the Buchanan, Bowen et al., and Meade theses see the reviews of Buchanan's book by E. R. Rolph, *Am. Ec. Rev.*, March 1959, pp. 183–185; A. H. Hansen, *Rev. Ec. & Stat.*, June 1959, pp. 377–378, and *Economic Issues of the 1960's*, New York: McGraw-Hill, 1960, Appendix C (on Meade and Buchanan); and A. P. Lerner, *J. Pol. Ec.*, April 1959, pp. 203–206. Reviews of the Bowen et al., thesis can be found in the *Am. Ec. Rev.*, March 1961 (by W. Vickrey, T. Scitovsky, and J. R. Elliott), pp. 132–139; and Lerner, *Rev. Ec. & Stat.*, May 1961.

[9] But Buchanan's study contains valuable source material.

[10] Lerner, "The Burden of the National Debt," *op. cit.*, p. 256.

beyond the present generation or are wholly realized during the next generation. What if the debt is used for the purpose of producing consumption goods in the present generation? Clearly the effect may be to use up both natural and capital resources so that the next generation has less of both.

On the other hand, what if the debt is used to build schools and colleges that (1) provide capital goods (public) which will be used by both the present and future generations, (2) raise the level of scientific, engineering, and technological knowledge, which renders significant returns in its own right, and which further (3) create additional investment outlets, maintain growth, and enlarge the stock of capital? Or assume that the debt is used simply to subsidize the construction of private capital. Assume further that had the debt not been contracted and an investment in human capital not been made, or private investment not subsidized, the level of investment would have been lower (because of a lack of innovations to be exploited, etc.). Clearly, in this case, the next generation will benefit from the expansion of debt in the present period.

It is, of course, also true that the creation of debt and consequent expenditure on consumption only benefits primarily if not wholly the present generation and does little for the next generation. The result in this case, as noted, may be the unnecessary using up of a nation's natural resources. But there are many possible qualifications to this contention, too. Resources are a function of technology, and the use of certain resources now may not mean deprivation for the next generation. Nonetheless, there may be a burden on the next generation in the sense that private capital is used up or is less than it otherwise would have been.

It is further true that even if present government expenditures are financed by taxes and *no debt is incurred*, there will be greater or lesser benefits to both present and future generations depending on how the money is spent by the government. It may again be spent on the equivalent of consumption goods which "unreasonably" (however this is to be defined) use up resources, or it may be spent on public capital which has the effect of raising the standard of living of both the present *and* the next generation. Also, if the expenditure subsidizes the creation of private capital which extends to the next generation, then both generations again benefit.[11] Furthermore, is not an unfair burden assumed by the present generation if it is taxed to pay for a project which clearly benefits the next several generations?

[11] The imposition of the tax may affect either consumption or investment. The impact on investment is discussed in F. Modigliani, "Long-Run Implications of Alternative Fiscal Policies and the Burden of the National Debt," *The Ec. J.*, Dec. 1961, p. 740. This article is highly recommended.

Professor Modigliani has pointed out that the method of financing the debt may also determine whether any burden is passed on to the next generation.[12] If full employment prevails and the government borrows funds which would have flowed into investment, then investment declines and the next generation is worse off because it has less private capital. To follow such a policy and avoid inflation, however, involves a highly effective monetary policy—a transfer of funds from private investment to public expenditure. Furthermore, the mere replacement of private investment by government expenditures does not necessarily harm the next generation. A comparison must be made between the nature of the private investment which would have taken place and the nature of the public expenditure. Perhaps it is a comparison of private investment in new tools for bigger tail fins on automobiles versus productivity-increasing aid to education (etc.). Furthermore, Professor Modigliani's argument assumes that the private investment would have occurred had not the funds been preempted by government debt.[13]

CONFLICTS BETWEEN THE GOALS OF FISCAL CONTROL, STABILIZATION, AND EFFICIENCY

The Annually Balanced Budget

The principle of the annually balanced budget receives widespread support because (1) it is held to be of neutral impact, (2) it is a simple and straightforward technique for imposing fiscal discipline, (3) it is considered important as a technique of minimizing both federal functions and expenditures,[14] (4) unbalanced budgets are felt to be inflationary and therefore to lower the purchasing power of the dollar, (5) the analogy detween public and private budgets is felt to be valid, and (6) its advocates argue that the alternative set forth by economists (the cyclically balanced budget) is politically impossible to realize.

The advocates of the annually balanced budget maintain that the use of the cyclically balanced budget theory results in "undesirable," wasteful, extravagant, and inflationary government borrowing and expenditures, and that the deficits but not the surpluses result. They maintain that the

---

[12] *Ibid.*, p. 738.

[13] There is the further question of how one defines a generation and how long capital lasts. If the real measure of burden of the debt is the loss in private capital, as Modigliani argues, then one must assume that the current reduction in capital cannot be "caught up." How realistic is this in view of today's rapid depreciation of capital goods? (Again, all this assumes full employment and a substitution of government for investment expenditure.)

[14] See the very interesting article by A. Smithies, "The Balanced Budget," *Am. Ec. Rev.*, May 1960, pp. 301–309. See also Burkhead, "The Balanced Budget," *op. cit.*

Congress is too reluctant to raise taxes for the purpose of realizing a surplus during periods of prosperity. They argue, in effect, that the government has not imposed sufficient discipline on its own policies to realize a balanced budget over the cycle—that countercyclical fiscal policy results in a secular upward trend in expenditures.

Critics of the annually balanced budget, however, can point out the many serious shortcomings of a rigid adherence to this policy. (1) As we noted in Chapter 9, the balanced budget is not necessarily neutral in its effect.[15] The balanced budget may have an expansionary, restrictive, inflationary, or deflationary effect. (2) Annual balance can in itself lead to waste and inefficiency. Many activities (research, development, construction, foreign aid, etc.) require expenditures over a period of several years, and cutting off appropriations in the middle of a project is sheer waste. Deferring payments to contractors for the purpose of realizing a balanced budget and instead paying them interest to get them to accept a later payment is pure stupidity.[16] (3) The fact that the budget is balanced leaves people with the impression that the government is well-managed, which may be seriously misleading if the balance is attained by means of cutting off badly needed programs, the rejection of very valuable new programs, back-door financing techniques, etc. (4) The conflict between the balanced budget and stabilization goals can be serious. (5) The annually balanced budget may not meet the needs of the economy as far as economic growth is concerned.[17]

[15] See Chapter 9 or H. M. Somers, "Federal Expenditure and Economic Stability: The Fallacy of the Balanced Budget," JEC, *Fed. Exp. Pol.*, P, pp. 412–419.

[16] Smithies, "The Balanced Budget," *op. cit.* The discussion in Smithies is very good.

[17]*Ibid.* S. M. Cohn, in criticizing the extent to which politicians cling to the concept of the annually balanced budget, has said: "For the life of me, I cannot imagine why so many people believe the maiden of an annually balanced budget can still be so virtuous. She has cried 'rape' so often that an impartial judge would certainly have much reason to wonder about her willingness." At the time Dr. Cohn was attached to the Bureau of the Budget. *Ibid.*, p. 333.

In commenting on the fact that the great years for Great Britain fell in the period from the Glorious Revolution of 1688 and ending with World War II, and that during this period her public debt grew steadily (she had budget deficits in 2 out of 3 years), Paul Samuelson quotes from Thomas Babington Macaulay, who wrote in 1840:

"At every stage in the growth of that debt the nation has set up the same cry of anguish and despair. At every stage in the growth of that debt it has been seriously asserted by wise men that bankruptcy and ruin were at hand. Yet still the debt went on growing; and still bankruptcy and ruin were as remote as ever . . . .

"The prophets of evil were under a double delusion. They erroneously imagined that there was an exact analogy between the case of an individual who is in debt to another individual and the case of a society which is in debt to a part of itself . . . . They made no allowance for the effect produced by the incessant progress of every

Although there has been much room for improvement in the fiscal policies followed throughout the postwar period, in many respects they have not been so terribly bad. In spite of the religious defense of the balanced budget, it is still true that recession deficits have been accepted by the Congress. Further, there have been periods of surpluses even though they have not offset the deficits.[18] In addition, the postwar period has been one of many crises—the Berlin crisis, the Marshall Plan, the "Truman Doctrine," the Korean War, Sputnik, etc. These crises have resulted in expenditure increases which have made it difficult to handle the budget. Finally, it is possible that more surpluses would have been realized had the full employment surplus problem been dealt with earlier. The attempt to balance the budget at a level substantially below full employment, under the conditions of the time, played havoc with the surpluses which could have been realized, and with the goals of full employment and more rapid economic growth.

Proposals to Achieve Fiscal Discipline

Smithies' Proposal. Professor Smithies has proposed certain changes which he believes "should have the same disciplinary value as balance from the point of view of the Congress and the executive departments."[19] He recommended the following: (1) The President's budget should be part of a comprehensive program with an analysis of goals and the instruments to be used in the realization of these goals. (2) The President should recommend a deficit, surplus, or balanced budget, depending on conditions in the economy. It is this proposal which Professor Smithies feels will exert fiscal discipline and control. He further points out that the Joint Economic Committee, the Appropriations Committee, and the Ways and Means Committee must cooperate among themselves and with the President. (3) The program of the President should differentiate between long- and short-run programs and policies. The former should have continuity but they should be subject to yearly reconsideration and revision. Further, revenue and expenditures should be estimated within the framework of full employment. (4) Countercyclical considerations should be dealt with separately. Smithies is extremely critical of the use of lower taxes to counteract recessions because they are not raised later, although he will accept automatic tax reductions (subject to Presidential

---

experimental science, and by the incessant efforts of every man to get on in life. They saw that the debt grew; and they forgot that other things grew as well . . . ." As cited in Am. Bankers Assoc., *A Symposium on Economic Growth,* New York, 1962, pp. 85–86.

[18] See Table 21-3.

[19] Smithies, "The Balanced Budget," *op. cit.,* p. 306.

veto),[20] which are automatically increased at a later point in the business upturn. Although Professor Smithies' proposals would score well on stabilization grounds, it is still difficult to see how they would meet the requirements of fiscal control.

Musgrave's Proposal. We noted previously that Professor Musgrave divides the budget of the government into three parts: the Allocation, Distribution, and Stabilization Branches. These three problems are dealt with separately. Society decides on the type of income distribution it desires and taxes and transfers income in order to secure this distribution; the Stabilization Branch uses transfers or taxes to secure full employment; and the Allocation Branch imposes taxes for the purpose of securing resources for the further purpose of producing public goods. It will be noted that the Allocation Branch finds it necessary to tax to secure resources because full employment is assumed. Except for certain circumstances,[21] the Allocation budget is balanced (even though the total budget may not be because of the need for a deficit or surplus in the Stabilization Branch). If Professor Musgrave's scheme is followed, taxes, as imposed by the Allocation Branch, are an index of opportunity cost. If people decide they want more by way of public goods or services, *they must be willing to pay for them.* The scheme therefore has fiscal discipline built into it.

Musgrave is among the first to recognize that Congress and the Administration are unlikely to rush to adopt his budget proposals. Under circumstances in which the Stabilization and Allocation functions are not separated and a deficit is called for for stabilization purposes, taxes may no longer serve as an index of opportunity cost. The fact that a deficit is needed may lead the public to feel that more public goods or services can be had cost-free. On the other hand, the requirement of a surplus can bring about the attitude that public services are more expensive than they really are. Dissatisfaction with paying taxes for both stabilization and allocation purposes creates this attitude, the result of which might be the provision of inadequate public services. In his scheme, Professor Musgrave attempts to avoid both these distortions which prohibit taxation from properly pricing public services.

Balancing the Budget over the Business Cycle. In addition to the annually balanced budget, the longer-run balancing of the budget has also been proposed. This proposal has been a direct result of the Keynesian

---

[20] *Ibid.*, pp. 306–309.

[21] Musgrave notes that annual balance is not necessary because the cost of durable goods or of services which last over a period of time can be paid for over their useful lives. See *The Theory of Public Finance*, pp. 16, 522, and 558.

approach to fiscal policy and is probably the most widely supported among economists. For the budget to be balanced over the cycle requires that the cycle be perfectly symmetrical; that is, the required surpluses should exactly equal the required deficits. We have noted the arguments of the advocates of the annually balanced budget—that balancing over the cycle brings many more deficits than surpluses and results in a secular upward increase in government expenditures, waste, and inflation, etc. Equally important, however, as Professor Musgrave points out, is the fact that persistent inflationary or deflationary trends can result in a permanent over- or underpricing of public services.

The CED Proposal. The Committee for Economic Development has proposed that tax rates be set such that at full employment a budget surplus is realized. The CED and other proposals have generally accepted the principle of deficits during periods of less than full employment and surpluses during periods of full employment. They further propose that expenditures be kept relatively constant and that the deficits and surpluses occur as a result of the built-in flexibility of the tax structure. Fiscal discipline is imposed by virtue of the fact that increases in public services come about only if tax rates are raised enough to raise revenue by an equal amount at the full employment level.[22]

The CED's proposal has been criticized on several grounds. (1) It may still result in an over- or underpricing of public services. (2) Built-in flexibility is simply not sufficient to counteract recession or inflation in the economy. Discretionary policy is also needed (see Chapter 16).[23] (3) The fact that when full employment is reached the budget will be in balance (or have a surplus) is no assurance that full employment itself will automatically be realized.[23] Those arguments against the use of formula flexibility apply equally here. It is extremely difficult to legislate the proper policy ahead of time; to do so assumes a degree of clairvoyance as far as the causes of future problems are concerned. Furthermore, tendencies toward secular inflation or secular deflation may require relatively continuous surpluses or deficits.

The Marginally Balanced Budget. Professor Musgrave has noted that the discipline objective could be satisfied by means of an overall deficit or surplus, but a balance at the margin. If the public decided that it wanted greater public services it could have them as long as their costs were

[22] For criticisms of the CED proposal see Musgrave, *The Theory of Public Finance*, pp. 523–524; A. Hansen, *Monetary Theory and Fiscal Policy*, New York: McGraw-Hill, 1949, pp. 176–180; and W. W. Heller, "CED's Stabilizing Budget After Ten Years," *Am. Ec. Rev.*, Sept. 1957.

[23] Musgrave, *Theory of Public Finance*, p. 524.

matched by an equal increase in tax revenue. For stabilization purposes, however, the amount by which tax revenue must increase or decrease in line with changes in public tastes must be greater than the change in government spending because of the balanced budget multiplier. Finally, the use of the marginally balanced budget assumes that the proper surplus or deficit has already been included in the overall budget, which may or may not be the case. It is still possible that government services may be over- or underpriced.

Of the preceding rules for attaining both fiscal discipline and stabilization goals there seems little doubt that Musgrave's scheme is the best. It, suffers however, from the serious shortcoming of having to overcome some rather serious political barriers. Professor Musgrave, under the circumstances, unenthusiastically accepts as a compromise the cyclically balanced budget. He would prefer, however, to educate the voters into

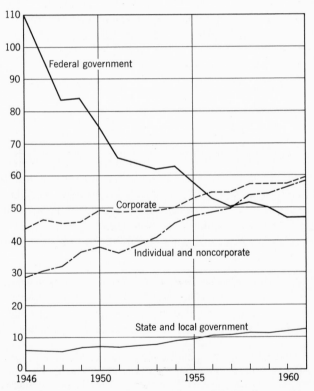

Figure 19-1. Net public and private debt as a percent of GNP. State and local government figures are for June 30 of each year. *Source:* JEC, *Ann. Rept.*, 1962, p. 40.

accepting the principle that proper expenditure determination and a flexible stabilization policy are not incompatible.[24]

The Debt Ceiling. An attempt to introduce fiscal discipline has also taken the form of a statutory limit on the size of the federal debt. It is obvious, however, that unless immediate and sufficient action is taken to increase the debt limit this policy will fail miserably on stabilization grounds. Marshall D. Robinson claims unequivocally that it has failed because it has (1) jeopardized long-run defense policy, (2) frustrated compensatory policy, (3) seriously interfered with the proper debt management policy, (4) induced and encouraged budgetary subterfuge, and (5) raised the cost of financing the government. As Dr. Robinson notes, the debt ceiling has not really helped us face up to the problems of financing public services.[25] Finally, as Robinson and other economists have long noted, an increase in business activity is accompanied by increases in debt. (The reader is referred to the discussion of the relationships between debt, surpluses, and deficits in the business and federal government sections in Chapter 15.) It is one way by which the saving of certain groups is borrowed and respent by other groups. It is further a way by which the money supply is expanded as borrowers secure funds from commercial banks. On balance, public and private debts have tended to increase by about 10 percent of the GNP per year. This is a long-term figure and naturally the actual rate will vary, tending to be greater the greater the rate of growth.[26] (See Figure 19-1.)

OTHER FACTORS AFFECTING THE PUBLIC DEBT

The long-term or secular characteristics of the economy will, whether or not a countercyclical fiscal policy is pursued, have an influence on the growth of the public debt. If secular inflation due to a high level of demand is the trend which is to dominate the economy, then a series of surpluses will be called for. On the other hand, if secular stagnation becomes the dominant trend in the economy, a series of deficits will be called for if no other policy action is effective.

Hansen's name is connected with the secular stagnation thesis, and he has been considerably criticized (by some) for ever having mentioned it. A close reading of Hansen's work will show, however, that he did not

[24] *Ibid.*, p. 525.
[25] M. D. Robinson, *The National Debt Ceiling*, Washington, D.C.: The Brookings Institution, 1959, Chapters 4 and 6.
[26] *Ibid.*, pp. 77–86. Robinson's short study is both interesting and informative. Along these same lines see the excellent article by Stettner, *op. cit.*

accept secular stagnation as an inevitable development.[27] Furthermore, the slowing down in the rate of growth of the population, the settlement of the West and the closing of the frontier and investment outlets, the absence of new products which could be exploited, the increasing rate at which investment was becoming more and more capital saving, and the fear that the average propensity to consume would decline—all these factors well describe the situation during the 1930's.[28]

Finally, we might note that if stagnation should become our major economic problem it could take several different forms. We may have stable stagnation, in which, the rate of growth of the public debt would be the same as that of income and the public debt as a percent of the GNP would tend to be constant, as would also generally be interest payments on the debt. In the case of decreasing stagnation, the rate of growth of debt would decline, and the ratio of interest payments to income would decline. In the case of increasing stagnation the ratio of debt to income would increase and the tax rate would have to be increased to pay the higher interest (whose ratio to income would increase).[29]

[27] See Hansen's *Fiscal Policy and Business Cycles*, New York: Norton, 1941, pp. 13–47, esp. pp. 38–47; and also B. Higgins, "Concepts and Criteria of Secular Stagnation," in *Income, Employment, and Public Policy, Essays in Honor of Alvin H. Hansen*, Chapter 4, and Higgins' *Economic Development*, New York: Norton, 1959, Chapter 7.

[28] See Musgrave, *The Theory of Public Finance*, pp. 498–500. Musgrave points out the method by which the classical economists also anticipated stagnation. See also B. Higgins, "Concepts and Criteria of Secular Stagnation," *op. cit.*, and particularly his *Economic Development*, Chapter 3.

[29] Musgrave, *The Theory of Public Finance*, pp. 499–500.

20

Improving Stabilization Policy

In this chapter we shall survey techniques and methods by which economic policies that are aimed at stabilization and growth may possibly be made more effective. Certain of these techniques have already been discussed in other contexts and will require little additional comment; this is particularly true of fiscal policies.

This chapter is divided into three sections. The first deals with the problem of overall stabilization policy, coordination of various monetary and credit policies and of monetary and fiscal policy, the issue of the independence of the Federal Reserve, and proposals for improving relations between the Federal Reserve and the Treasury Department. The second section deals with other suggestions for monetary policy, and the third section presents a summary of suggestions for improving fiscal policy.[1] Although certain proposals apply to both monetary and fiscal policy, there will be an attempt to avoid repetitious recommendations.

THE COORDINATION OF FISCAL AND MONETARY POLICY

The Need for Coordination

Under most circumstances, it does not make much sense to pursue one type of policy in one branch of government or agency and a contrary policy in another branch or agency. This, however, does not mean it has not been done. The fact that the Federal Reserve, the Treasury, and federal credit agencies follow divergent policies at any one time may be due (on one level) to ignorance of the goals of the others, refusal to take time to find out what the others are doing, outright obstinacy, the failure of the Administration to develop and carry out an explicit policy, or, in the case of the Federal Reserve, the political independence of the agency.

In 1956–1957 the Federal Reserve was attempting to restrict the growth

[1] Suggestions for improving debt management policy were included in Chapter 17.

449

of the money supply and raise interest rates, while the Treasury was at the same time issuing short-term securities. Whether or not the economy was better off because of this particular Treasury action is, of course, not the point; the lack of cooperation between the Treasury and the Federal Reserve was (given current debt management theory) lamentable. The Treasury's apparent explanation for its policy was its reluctance to interfere with "private enterprise," but during early 1958 (when the Federal Reserve was attempting to ease monetary policy during the recovery from the recession) the Treasury sold some $19 billion in long- and intermediate-term securities to the possible exclusion of current or later private placements. We should again emphasize that the specific debt management policies followed will vary (as noted in Chapter 17) and that it is the lack of cooperation and the inconsistencies with the then accepted theory of debt management that interest us at this point.

Similarly, the effectiveness of the policy of the Federal Reserve has been reduced by the actions and policies of the many federal credit agencies. During periods when the Federal Reserve has been placing pressure on member bank reserves, these agencies have been expanding their loans and guarantees. Other cases could be cited in which the same score or so of federal agencies have gone their own respective ways. One of the difficulties in these agencies is the piecemeal approach taken by the Congress in allocating the funds of certain agencies by special acts. Under these circumstances, it is difficult to achieve coordination unless the Chief Executive assumes the role of overall policy determination and coordination, and is aided in this by appropriate legislative action. As matters now stand, the Treasury Department does not have the legislative authority to coordinate and/or control these lending and loan-insuring activities. Each agency head generally reports to the President and must adhere to his policy, except where there are other explicit congressional directions. Similarly, there are no provisions for cooperation between these agencies and the Federal Reserve on matters affecting money and credit.[2] It has been reported, however, that the Bureau of the Budget encourages cooperation with the Federal Reserve on an individual agency basis through informal voluntary talks.[3]

The Issue of the Independence of the Federal Reserve

Cooperation among the federal credit agencies themselves, between these agencies and the Treasury, and between the agencies and/or the

---

[2] See COF, S, *Investigation Finan. Cond.*, H, Pt. 1, pp. 569–572.

[3] *Ibid.*, p. 572. For a short description of an attempt at cooperation within all the appropriate government agencies and coordination with the FR, see *ibid.*, Pt. 2, pp. 1144–1145.

Treasury and the Federal Reserve concern three different but related problems. (A fourth problem of coordination is between the state and local and federal governments.) It is with the problem of the independence of the Federal Reserve that we are now concerned.

During World War II the policy of the Federal Reserve was subverted to the mobilization interests of the federal government and the policy of the Treasury Department—the Federal Reserve supported the war effort by supporting the price and sales of government securities. This policy existed until the so-called accord of 1951, when the Federal Reserve once more became an independent arm of the government. Under the Eisenhower Administration, and also under the Kennedy Administration, meetings between the Federal Reserve and the Treasury Department were a regular occurrence.[4]

In answer to the following question, Secretary of the Treasury Anderson replied as noted. "Does the Treasury participate in the formulation of monetary policy? If so, in what ways? Is any such participation sufficient to insure coordination of monetary, budgetary, and debt management policies for achieving public economic policy objectives?"

The Treasury does not, of course, participate directly in the formulation of monetary policy. The Federal Reserve System is an agency created by and responsible to the Congress. Independence of Federal Reserve from the executive branch, in principle and in practice, is highly desirable.

Nevertheless, the necessity for coordination of national economic policies is recognized, and to this end a number of informal arrangements have been established for exchange of ideas and information. When occasion warrants, the President, the Chairman of the Board of Governors . . . , the Secretary of the Treasury, the Chairman of the Council of Economic Advisers, and the economic assistant to the President meet for an informal discussion of economic trends and developments.

. . . The Chairman of the Board of Governors and I usually have lunch together each Monday. On each Wednesday, the Under Secretary for Monetary Affairs and several members of the senior Treasury staff usually join the Chairman of the Board of Governors, plus at least one other Board member, and their senior staff people for lunch. At these meetings there is a free interchange of ideas and information concerning the state of the economy, credit and debt management problems, and other matters of mutual interest. In addition, we confer frequently on many occasions, either in person or by telephone.

. . . So long as there is basic agreement as to our national economic objectives and as to the means of achieving these objectives, these informal arrangements would appear to be sufficient for insuring the necessary degree of coordination between debt management and monetary policies. Any attempt to formalize relationships between the Federal Reserve and the executive would run the

[4] According to the *Jan. 1963 Ec. Rept. Pres.* (p. 159), the Chairman of the CEA, the Secretary of the Treasury, and the head of the Budget Bureau meet "periodically" with the Chairman of the Board of Governors.

serious risk of impairing the independence of the monetary authorities. Indeed, complete centralization of authority over monetary, budgetary, and debt management policies is impossible—and, in my judgment undesirable—under our form of government.[5]

The assumption of cooperation in goals and techniques of the first sentence of the last paragraph is crucial. The following question naturally arises in the mind of the interested observer: What happens when the Federal Reserve and the Treasury cannot agree on the policy to be pursued? Whose interests should dominate—those of the Treasury or those of the Federal Reserve? Such an event did take place in April of 1956, and other such events took place later. The Board of Governors took further restrictive steps (an increase in the discount rate) which were opposed by Secretaries Humphrey, Mitchell, and Weeks, and also by Dr. Arthur Burns, the Chairman of the CEA. The Administration on this occasion and others had been criticized for not making clear what it expected from the Federal Reserve by way of monetary policy.[6] In fact, the attitude of the Eisenhower Administration was that even if it seriously disagreed with the Federal Reserve it should not in any way attempt to coerce the Federal Reserve into accepting its point of view. In its eyes the independence of the Federal Reserve was sacred.[7] In this respect Chairman Martin has

[5] JEC, *Empl., Growth, Price Levels*, H, Pt. 6C, pp. 1720–1721. See also Pt. 6A, p. 1135.

[6] See JEC (Subcom. on Economic Stabilization), *Monetary Policy, 1955–56*, Hearings (Dec. 10 and 11, 1956). p. 79; and *Conflicting Official Views on Monetary Policy: April, 1956*, Hearings (June 12, 1956), 1956. For an explicit and strong statement denying that the Federal Reserve has a right to "enforce its own will" by a former Chairman of the Board of Governors, see the statement of Marriner Eccles before the Joint Committee on the Economic Report (Subcom. on Monetary, Credit, and Fiscal Policies—the Douglas Committee), Nov. 22, 1949.

The sentiment of economists on the so-called independence of the Federal Reserve is not known, although a few have in recent years proposed reform. Warren L. Smith, who has certainly done some fine work in the field of monetary policy, has gone all the way and argued that the FR Board should be replaced by a single administrator who should serve at the pleasure of the President. *Am. Ec. Rev.*, May 1962, p. 310. See also Smith's comments in JEC, *Rel. Prices to Ec. Stabil. & Growth*, H, pp. 350–356.

Representative Patman's views, which have included the charge that FR expenditures have been extravagant and should be audited by the Government Accounting Office, can be found in JEC, *Empl., Growth, Price Levels*, H, Pt. 6A, pp. 1472ff., and JEC, *1962 Ann. Rept.*, pp. 31–32.

[7] See Eisenhower's statement in JEC, *Monet. Pol.: 1955–56*, H, p. 79. Secretary of the Treasury Anderson said that "public statements of disagreement with current monetary policy, which presumably would be for the purpose of enforcing a change in policy, would be inappropriate." JEC, *Empl., Growth, Price Levels*, H, Pt. 10, p. 3333.

stated that if the Administration and the Federal Reserve could not agree on policy, the Federal Reserve should and would go its own way, which is exactly what it did in April of 1956.[8] With an Administration in power holding this attitude, Chairman Martin could make comments like this. Under the Kennedy Administration, however, which presumably was willing to "challenge" the Federal Reserve, it is not known whether Mr. Martin would talk and act in this manner. There may come a day when the issue will have to be settled once and for all.

Proposals for Federal Reserve-Treasury Cooperation

At present, when the Administration is held responsible for both the level of prices and the level of employment under the Employment Act and by the public (at the polls), such a situation as now exists seems, indeed, incongruous. Various recommendations have, therefore, been made to bring about a more effective coordination of fiscal and monetary policies. These recommendations have included the following proposals or suggestions: (1) the informal relationships (meetings, luncheons, etc.) established between the Federal Reserve and the Administration as under Presidents Eisenhower and Kennedy are sufficient; (2) the Administration should set forth in the *Economic Report of the President* its expectations regarding monetary policy; (3) proposals for a committee which would include the appropriate monetary and fiscal agents of the government; (4) the establishment of a national economic council; (5) the creation of a new department of finance which would include both the Treasury and the Federal Reserve; and (6) the simple proposal that the Board of Governors be made directly responsible to the President.

The Need for Monetary Coordination, the Shortcomings of the Informal Cooperation Theory, and Criticisms of the Present Organization of the Federal Reserve System

It is possible that past and current informal arrangements may prove satisfactory and that FR policies will reflect the views of the Administration. On the other hand, it is also equally possible that the Federal Reserve will go its own way (as it has in the past) when the Administration which is in power refuses to challenge the Federal Reserve. There is absolutely no reason to expect that such a development may not occur again. It is of further interest to note that (technically) the Federal Reserve is responsible to Congress, but at the same time the Administration, in the eyes of many, has the "moral" responsibility of securing monetary cooperation. The Administration is further charged with the responsibility of securing full employment, economic growth, price stability, and a balance of

[8] COF, S, *Investigation Finan. Cond.*, H, Pt. 3, pp. 1361–1363, and Pt. 7, p. 2181.

international payments. No one would deny the necessity of carrying out the appropriate monetary policy in the attainment of these goals, yet the Administration is virtually powerless (under current laws) to effectuate monetary cooperation.

There are other reasons why many economists have felt that some change should be made in the administrative setup of the Federal Reserve to make it a more responsible agent in democratic society. Many have felt that it is too dominated by bankers (or bankers and business). The people on whom the system draws are too closely associated with the banking community and its point of view and interests. Such a background gives too narrow a point of view to those who are responsible for making decisions of a more general economic character and which affect not just the banking and business communities but rather the whole of society.

The Board is supposed to represent a few interest groups,[9] and the System's original purpose was the accommodation of business and banking. But it is now recognized that the Federal Reserve no longer has as its major purpose the accommodation of business. It is now concerned with broad national stabilization objectives, and the current interest group make-up has a serious omission of representation by other major groups (mainly labor) which are greatly affected by its policies. Despite this, however, the truth of the matter is that we do not need a board representing various groups but rather a board which is highly qualified to develop monetary policy. But as long as the interest group basis is retained and labor is simultaneously eliminated, union groups will continue to be suspicious of what it feels is an institutional bias toward "sound money" in preference to economic growth and higher levels of employment.

The banker-business domination accusation is even more appropriately directed toward the regional Board of Directors of each Federal Reserve Bank. These boards are almost exclusively dominated by bank and big business interests, and their memberships look like a *Who's Who* of American industry.[10] The make-up of the Boards of Directors, however, may not be particularly significant since it would, under present circumstances, be possible and reasonable to completely abolish these boards; they are not really necessary.

[9] The President, in appointing the Board, is to do so on the basis of "fair representation of financial, agricultural, industrial, and commercial interests, and geographical divisions of the country."

[10] See M. D. Reagan, "The Political Structure of the Federal Reserve System," *Am. Polit. Sci. Rev.*, March 1961, reprinted in JEC, *Rev. Ann. Rept. FR, 1960*, H, pp. 133–146. A "pedigree" of the directors and a criticism of the present system can be found in E. Miller, *Rev. Ec. & Stat.*, Nov. 1961, pp. 380–384. For a criticism of the banker pointer of view of the FR see K. Brunner and A. Meltzer, *Banking*, March 1964, pp. 49–50. They also claim "that after 50 years, the Federal Reserve has not yet provided a rational basis for policy making."

Even though several Reserve Bank presidents have been professional economists, they have also been accused of having too narrow a point of view and interest-group association and bias. But here the problem is somewhat more serious because the presidents are either members of the Open Market Committee or (if not members) sit in on OMC meetings. While the Board of Governors dominates the OMC, if the Board should split the Federal Reserve Bank presidents would determine the vote.

There is, then, a serious question of the public accountability of the Federal Reserve Bank presidents and even of the Board of Governors, whose legal accountability to the Congress amounts to little by way of direct control since the System is financially independent of the Congress. Federal Reserve accountability to the Congress is more mythical than real, and furthermore constitutes an extremely poor administrative setup anyway. Such considerations, along with the secrecy and mysticism that surround Federal Reserve actions, have led John Kenneth Galbraith to state that Federal Reserve independence "reflects . . . the belief that monetary policy is the highly professional prerogative of the financial community. As such, it must be protected from the crude pressure of democratic government."[11]

Many of the recommendations for reform within the Federal Reserve have concerned the make-up of the Open Market Committee. In particular, since the Reserve Bank presidents serve on this committee, the issue has turned on how much power the regional bank presidents should have on the OMC and also the extent to which regional interests per se should be represented on the OMC. It would seem that the need for regional emphasis has passed, that open market operations are national rather than regional, and that it is questionable whether the Reserve Bank presidents (who are neither appointed by, nor accountable to, the Congress or the President) should have any vote at all.[12]

Another problem that has created demands for reform is the very size of the Board of Governors itself. In relations with the Treasury, the President, and the CEA and other agencies, the Chairman *is* the Board. In addition, many have questioned the wisdom of a structure in which the Federal Reserve Bank presidents may receive almost three times the salary of a Board member. Finally, some have asked questions about the

---

[11] *The Affluent Society*, Boston: Houghton Mifflin, 1958, p. 227.

[12] For more detailed discussions of these problems, issues, and proposed reforms see Reagan, *op. cit.*; George L. Bach, *Federal Reserve Policy-Making*, New York: Knopf, 1950; E. A. Goldenweiser, *American Monetary Management*, New York: McGraw-Hill, 1951; and JCER, *Monetary Policy and the Management of the Public Debt*, 1952 (Patman) and *Monetary, Credit and Fiscal Policy*, 1949 (Douglas).

qualifications of some Board members themselves, thus implying that few have been outstanding in any way.[13]

The Proposals for Change

The Present Arrangement Again. We noted that it is quite possible that the informal arrangements of the past may allow for and achieve effective cooperation between fiscal and monetary policy. We also noted the circumstances under which the informal arrangement has failed and may again break down. It is also true, of course, that the adoption and pursuance of an extreme policy on the part of the Federal Reserve would result in rapid congressional censure or actual legislative-administrative change. The facts of life are that the Federal Reserve cannot get too far out of step. It is further probably true that no important changes in the political structure of the Federal Reserve are likely to occur in the immediate future despite sound economic and political reasons for the change. If American history teaches us anything at all, it is that there will be no extreme changes unless there should be another serious crisis in the economy.

Including Monetary Policy in the Economic Report. The idea underlying the requirement that the Administration present a policy expectation or proposal relative to monetary policy is that any disagreement would become public. In such a case both the Administration and the Federal Reserve would find it necessary to defend their policy proposals, which the Federal Reserve does not have to do under present circumstances. Their failure to do so raises some serious questions about public accountability and bureaucratic responsibility in a democracy.[14]

Interdepartmental and Interagency Committees. Advisory committees of various sorts were used by President Eisenhower (the Advisory Board on Economic Growth and Stability, for example). On August 21, 1962, President Kennedy established the Cabinet Committee on Economic Growth. It is chaired by the Chairman of the CEA, and its purpose is to

[13] Former Chairman of the Board of Governors Eccles states that "I have felt that the Open Market Committee should be composed of those people who were appointed by the President and who were confirmed by the Senate, and whose salary is fixed by the Senate. They have a direct responsibility to Congress," JEC, *State Ec. & Pol. Full Empl.*, H, p. 525.

[14] In 1959 and 1960 Rep. H. Reuss and Sen. J. Clark introduced bills which would (1) require the President to make recommendations concerning monetary policy, (2) require the Board, if it disagrees, to explain why, through the President, to the Congress. See Committee on Banking and Currency (Senate), *Employment Act Amendments*, Hearings (Feb. 24–26, 1960), 1960; and Committee on Government Operations (House), *Amending the Employment Act of 1946*, Hearings (March 25, 26; April 9, 1959), 1959. The Board of Governors opposed this and other aspects of the bills. See the Senate hearings, pp. 8–10.

serve as a "focal point for concentrating the Government's interests and activities on the growth objective."[15] This committee's work was supplemented by that of the Interagency Growth Study Committee, also chaired by a member of the CEA and responsible "for developing and supervising an integrated program of studies of U.S. economic growth."[16] The extent of cooperation achieved by such committees is highly dependent on the spirit of cooperation of its members and the committee leadership. In other words, there is no assurance that a consensus can be arrived at, or that commitments will be made.

After Arthur Burns stepped down as its chairman, the Advisory Board on Economic Growth and Stability reportedly declined significantly in importance. We have already noted the possible difficulties in the use of the committee or informal meeting system to secure coordination between the Treasury and the Federal Reserve. It is probably nonetheless true that the use of the committee system within government and the informal system between the Treasury and the Federal Reserve is better than nothing, and further that (pending some crisis) these techniques will be the ones used in the immediate future.

A National Economic Council. Dr. Burns (also a former Chairman of the CEA) has suggested that the Advisory Board be continued and there be added periodic meetings of the Board with department and agency heads at the highest level in government and chaired by the President. Such an organization would, in Burns' opinion, "carry a weight in decisions on basic economic policies that would be fully comparable to that of the National Security Council in its sphere."[17] It is interesting to note (1) that Burns himself recognized that the Advisory Board was created because of "the want of regular governmental machinery," and (2) that the Advisory Board apparently declined in importance upon Burns' departure. The type of leadership such an organization has is of obvious importance, as noted. Without adequate leadership the committee system may break down, as apparently happened in this case.

The conclusion to be drawn is not necessarily that such an organization should be formalized by an act of Congress; even a formal agency may be relegated to a secondary role if the President so determines. We should note, however, that a legislative act bringing together as many credit

---

[15] *Jan. 1963 Ec. Rept. Pres.*, p. 61.

[16] *Ibid.*, p. 160.

[17] Arthur F. Burns, *Prosperity Without Inflation*, New York: Fordham Univ., 1957, pp. 86–87. Burns describes the operation of the Advisory Board and the establishment of another, higher-level committee to deal with problems of economic policy.

agencies as possible would still serve the purpose of assuring that a reasonably consistent financial policy would be pursued by the government. A further advantage would be the efficiency in having a single agency or department head deal with the Federal Reserve rather than several, as apparently has been the usual policy. It is generally recognized that such a Council should have something equivalent to cabinet status.

Various other proposals have been made for a federal National Economic Council. Such a Council should, according to many proposals, be the counterpart to the National Security Council. Some have proposed that it draw up 5- and 10-year economic blueprints setting forth production goals (including consumption, investment, growth rates, etc.), with annual modifications as conditions so dictate. The responsibility for the coordination of fiscal and monetary policies should fall on the Council.[18]

Equally important to some observers would be the presentation of such a council's blueprint and annual budget to the Joint Economic Committee. The Joint Economic Committee accordingly should be elevated to such a status that it would examine the coherent program, and its reaction should govern the actions of other congressional committees which pass on economic matters. The Joint Economic Committee, in other words, should take an overall look at the budget, and other congressional committees would be expected to follow its recommendations. This does not mean, of course, that the Joint Economic Committee should make decisions relative to the proper role of the federal government, the allocation of resources between private and public uses, and the like; these questions should be decided at the ballot box. It could, however, propose the most efficient ways in which these goals could be effectuated in coordination

---

[18] See the statement of R. V. Gilbert, "Economics for Cold War," JEC, *Rel. Prices to Ec. Stabil. & Growth*, C, p. 229. We are obviously skipping over the many complicated administrative problems such a proposal would involve. Presumably, however, such a council would have as its primary responsibility the development of policy rather than the enforcement of administrative rules and detail.

For other suggestions for the establishment of a National Economic Council see Warren L. Smith's comments in *ibid.*, Hearings, pp. 347–351; Walter Reuther in JEC, *Jan. 1962 Ec. Rept. Pres.*, H, p. 780; N. H. Jacoby in JEC, *Empl., Growth, Price Levels*, H, Pt. 1, pp. 67, 76; A. Smithies in G. Colm, ed., *Employment Act: Past and Future*, Washington D.C.: NPA, 1956, pp. 157–162. Smithies feels strongly that the present departmental and agency separation of fiscal and budgetary functions should be maintained. He further feels that under no circumstances should the independence of the Federal Reserve be sacrificed. He does, however, accept the establishment of a National Economic Council, chaired by the President, for the sole purpose of assisting the President in the determination of fiscal and credit policies. See also George L. Bach's proposal (*op. cit.*, pp. 186–207), which goes into considerable detail but which is somewhat more restricted than the others discussed here.

with the goals of price stability, growth, and full employment.[19] It has been further proposed that the National Economic Council be granted price, wage, and allocation authorities, particularly for use on a standby basis.

These suggestions are controversial to varying degrees, especially since anything that hints at national economic planning would be widely criticized in our society. This would be particularly true of grants of power over prices, wages, and resources. Further problems would be encountered in an attempt to reduce the prerogatives of the various congressional committees.

It is true that the last several years have been ones of relative price stability and the need for additional public policies or innovations in the techniques of public intervention may not seem so imperative. Nonetheless, it was only in the spring of 1962 that the late President Kennedy intervened when the steel industry attempted to increase prices, and his Administration has been deeply involved in contract negotiations in many industries. Furthermore, there is little reason to assume that we have seen the end of creeping inflation. In view of all this, it is indeed likely that new institutional arrangements will be asked for to deal with these problems. So, while proposals such as those discussed here may appear idealistic, future developments may show that there may be good reason to consider them thoroughly ahead of time.

A New Department of Finance. Various proposals have been made to establish an entirely new Department of Finance and incorporate in this single agency the fiscal, monetary, and lending functions of the government. This new Department of Finance would replace (or incorporate) existing agencies, including both the Treasury and the Board of Governors. Most such proposals recommend that this department include the functions of the Board of Governors and the Open Market Committee, bank chartering and supervision, and the financial policies of the government credit agencies (but not their operating duties). Professor Lawson's proposal provides for the continued separate agency status of both the CEA and the Bureau of the Budget, although close cooperation would be expected if not required. His proposal seeks a technique for securing an overall view of the total credit picture. He would expect such a department to act as "banker" to the operating agencies of the government, and the Finance Secretary, with Presidential sanction, would make recommendations to

[19] In this respect see G. Colm, ed., *The Employment Act: Past and Future*, pp. 79ff., and 154.

The interested reader may want to examine Ingvar Ohlsson, "The Swedish National Budget," in JEC, *Economic Policy in Western Europe*, 1959, pp. 265–75, reprinted from *Skandinaviska Banken Quarterly Review*, Oct. 1957, pp. 100–107.

Congress, which would accept or ignore them. Lawson further claims that his proposal would contain fiscal-monetary conflicts within a single operating department where they could be resolved in a manner employed by all executive departments. In short, Lawson maintains that all the financial activities of the government would be brought into clear focus so that responsibility and authority would be vested in one body with final authority over monetary and fiscal matters, subject to Presidential supervision and congressional review.[20]

Board of Governors Directly Responsible to the President. One way in which many of the objections to the current modus operandi could be met is by making the Board of Governors of the Federal Reserve directly responsible to the President. The Chairman would be appointed by the President and would report to him. He would argue his case on a basis equal to that of the Treasury Department. The advantages of such a program would be similar to those of the establishment of a new Department of Finance.

There is the further question here of degree of Presidential control. The Board may be retained in its present form but the Chairman appointed by the President, as President Kennedy proposed in 1962, and as the banking legislation of 1935 apparently intended.[21] Or, the entire Board may be replaced by a single head, which is certainly feasible. If it were decided that the head should serve at the will of the President, then the Chief Executive would have complete control and responsibility. It has also been recommended that the system be streamlined by reducing the Board of Governors to a three-man board, and introducing shorter terms (6-year terms, one expiring every 2 years).[22] Under this system as compared with the immediately preceding proposal, Presidential control obviously would be less but still would be significantly greater than it is at the present time.

Summary and Conclusion

We have noted that the federal government is held responsible for the level of employment, economic growth, and price stability; that the original organization of the Federal Reserve assumed a much more limited role than it now must carry out; and that it is necessary to coordinate both fiscal and monetary policies. It is a bit incongruous to hold the Administration responsible for these policies and not give it the appropriate tools

[20] Eric Lawson, "A New Department of Finance," *J. Finance*, March 1953, pp. 1–9.

[21] Kennedy proposed, in addition, that the terms of the other members begin and end in odd years instead of even years, and that the salaries of the Board of Governors be raised.

[22] Bach (*op. cit.*, pp. 186–230) has suggested this.

to carry out its responsibilities, or give it assurance that monetary policy will be compatible with its goals. The battle for independence of the Federal Reserve really makes little sense in today's world. There is no more reason for the determination of fiscal policy to be subjected to the ballot box and monetary policy not. There is nothing sacred, mystical, or supernatural about either fiscal or monetary policy.[23]

Probably the most potent argument in favor of independence of the Federal Reserve is the argument that an independent agency is more likely to pursue anti-inflationary measures than an agency directly responsible to the electorate. It is, of course, also true that the fiscal policy which is adopted can partially offset any given monetary policy. If it cannot, then it follows that the Congress and Administration would directly and publicly challenge the Federal Reserve.

We should note that banking groups widely support the independence of the Federal Reserve. The same is true of the business world but to a slightly lesser degree. (One head of General Motors has on at least one occasion publicly condemned the Reserve's tight money policy.) Whenever any group exerts or holds power and authority (and in some cases merely prestige, as do the Reserve Bank directors), or can in some manner identify itself with these things, it is reluctant to give them up—as are the bankers. There is, furthermore, little reason to believe that members of the banking community are our best-qualified individuals to determine policy (especially when their own profits are related to this policy). And finally, the very argument of the banking community that the Federal Reserve is the major defender of the value of the dollar (price stability was its major goal throughout the 1950's) is itself the very reason why the Federal Reserve should be a separate agency *within* government to present this point of view on an equal basis with other agencies and other equally important points of view rather than obstinately to go-it-alone. By all the standards of this society there is little to support an organization that has characteristics, to a greater or lesser degree, of arbitrariness, special interest group orientation,[24] and undemocratic representation.

It is a bit of an anomaly that the very conservative groups which condemn arbitrary federal and central power are staunch defendants of the independence of the Federal Reserve. Control over monetary policy has become perhaps one of the conservatives' last vestiges of power as

---

[23] In other industrialized countries the central bank is government controlled. For a survey of treasury-central bank relationships in foreign countries see JCER, *General Credit Controls, Debt Management, and Economic Mobilization*, 1951, Appendix I, pp. 79–98. See also JEC, *Economic Policy in Western Europe*, 1959.

[24] The Congress was ultimately incensed over the Business Advisory Council. See the Keiser article on the BAC in *The Western Political Quarterly* for June 1958.

far as national economic policy is concerned. What would their attitude be if the Federal Reserve were similarly independent and dominated by a group of loose money people? Would they still call its independence sacred?

Various proposals have been considered here to achieve a higher degree of coordination of the federal government's and the Federal Reserve's policy. All have the same goals although consistent policy action will not automatically result from all of them, especially from the committee system. Although they all have common goals they tend to fall into two main categories—those which propose to make the Federal Reserve an integral part of government and those which do not. The Department of Finance proposal attempts to solve the problems of the independence of the Federal Reserve and of a common credit policy *within* government simultaneously. It would be possible, of course, to bring unified credit policy within government and still maintain an independent Federal Reserve System.

The proposal that the Federal Reserve be made directly responsible to the President may be more palatable to some than the integration of the Federal Reserve into a Finance Department. There may be some fear that the department head may have a bias toward the interests of the Treasury division. Proposals aimed at streamlining the Federal Reserve and reducing the special interest orientation of the Reserve Bank Boards of Directors and the lack of public accountability of Reserve Bank presidents who help determine public policy—all these proposals are logical and sound irrespective of the future of the Federal Reserve.[25]

Finally, the obsession of Chairman Martin and other members of the Open Market Committee with the goal of price stability is another reason for greater public control.

OTHER SUGGESTIONS FOR MONETARY POLICY

There is little doubt that, although periods of recession were periods of easier monetary policy, the predominant goal of the Federal Reserve throughout the 1950's was the realization of a stable value for the dollar. Such a goal is, of course, highly desirable, but if the wrong tools are used

[25] The undemocratic nature of the present organization of the Federal Reserve, the problems of banker influence (and of the regulated being regulated by themselves), of policy coordination, etc., have all been recognized by the Commission on *Money and Credit*, Englewood Cliffs: Prentice-Hall, 1961. It proposed that the board be given full control over the discount rate, the Board be reduced to 5 members with 10-year terms, the terms of the Chairman and Vice-Chairman be parallel with that of the President, and that the Open Market Committee be abolished and its functions performed by the Board of Governors.

to attain the goal there may well be undesirable side effects. There is little question that monetary policy can retard any inflationary tendency if it is pushed far enough, although it is also possible that before this point is reached, a tight money policy may result in higher prices because unit costs are higher and because the rate of economic growth is not high enough to realize potential productivity gains.

It is highly likely that there were several major elements at work in the price increases of the middle and late 1950's:[26] (1) the level of demand; (2) shifts in the composition of demand and a consequent increase in prices and wages in the expanding but not the contracting industry; (3) the investment boom; (4) the very high profits of 1955 which were used as the basis of contractual increases in wages, which in turn were not covered by increases in productivity during 1956 and 1957 because of the retardation of the growth rate; (5) the instability in the level of federal government expenditures; and (6) price and wage rigidities, administered prices and wages, and price and wage mark-ups.

When prices and wages are downwardly rigid and a shift in the composition of demand results in an increase in the average price level, general monetary controls, unless vigorously pursued, are close to being useless. It is furthermore true that the very tight money policy of this period did little in fact to restrain the investment boom of 1955–1957, nor did it do much to restrain the tremendous upsurge in the demand for automobiles in 1955. It is even possible that the impact may have come instead during the 1956–1958 period when the GNP grew little (and productivity also grew but very little) and recession finally set in. These upward surges in investment demand tend to feed on themselves to such a point that increases in final demand cannot catch up with them. In addition to the inflationary results of such expansions in investment demand, there is then the additional threat of excess capacity creating recessions.

It seems rather clear that increases in consumer credit like those that financed the large increase in demand for automobiles in 1955 can be controlled. Consumer credit controls can be used to restrain any fairly sudden and unwanted expansions in consumption, and also to restrain possible explosions in investment that would result if consumption were not so restrained.

Controls over plant and equipment expenditures and inventories are fraught with more difficulties than controls over consumer credit and mortgage credit. While there may be a lagged effect of higher interest rates on investment, the delay of one year is of little help when the need to restrain investment is now. Warren L. Smith has suggested that the elimination of the interest rate deductibility from the corporate income

[26] See Chapter 19.

tax, and measures forcing business firms to reduce retained earnings and therefore rely more on borrowing would make corporations more sensitive to the rate of interest.[27] These proposals, of course, do nothing to reduce the lag problem in monetary policy.

Some experts have recommended that selective controls be applied to life insurance companies and other large holders of corporate securities as a technique for controlling the flow of funds into fixed investment. Others have suggested the use of fiscal controls, such as variable depreciation allowances or variable corporate income taxes, but these devices introduce a high degree of uncertainty into business decisions.[28] There are also the variable tax credit, tax-free reserve fund, and the use or nonuse of high initial depreciation allowances. (See Chapter 13.)

Extreme fluctuations in inventory investment also cause considerable instability in the economy. Various devices have again been suggested to control investment in inventory, such as a variable secondary reserve requirement in the form of government securities for commercial banks, but again agreement on the impact is far from uniform.

It would seem then, that effective control over consumer credit could be realized. The same would be true for residential construction; that is, interest rate ceilings could be removed but variable controls over downpayments and maturities of mortgages would be effective. It would appear to be wise public policy to establish these controls on a standby basis.

The problem of controlling fixed and inventory investment is, unfortunately, not so easy to handle. Some individuals have expressed a willingness to restrain consumer expenditures and more or less let investment go ahead.[29] But this may not be a satisfactory solution for at least two reasons: (1) The rate of increase in investment expenditure may so greatly exceed the capacity of the capital goods industries that further serious increases in prices *and* costs result; and (2) the level of investment demand will likely be unsustainable. Others have advocated the use of direct "moral suasion" to contain a capital boom, but this approach is equally questionable. The truth of the matter is that no one has as yet

---

[27] W. L. Smith, JEC, *Empl. Growth, Price Levels*, SR, pp. 397–398. Smith also mentions other problems which would be encountered.

[28] *Ibid.*, p. 398. Walter Heller has proposed that variable depreciation be closely studied. See JEC, *Empl., Growth, Price Levels.*, H, Pt. 9A, pp. 2997ff. C. L. Schultze has suggested the same (p. 2220).

On the use of selective controls generally, see A. Smithies, "Uses of Selective Credit Controls," F. W. Paish, "Monetary Policy and the Control of the Postwar British Inflation," and A. G. Hart, "Making Monetary Policy More Effective," all in The American Assembly, *United States Monetary Policy*, New York: Columbia Univ. Press, 1958.

[29] For an expression of this point of view, see R. A. Gordon in JEC, *Empl., Growth, Price Levels*, H, Pt. 8, p. 2981.

proposed an acceptable fiscal or monetary device for exerting greater control over investment. On the other hand, there is good reason for us to do so, and for us to explore the experience of other countries that use these special devices.

The use of selective controls has received widespread support from economists appearing before the Joint Economic Committee.[30] They have pointed out that we should use "the rifle more and the shotgun less," that many general controls may have very bad selective effects, and that foreign countries which have experienced greater success with monetary controls have often relied more on selective than general controls. It seems that greater study, consideration, and experimentation should be given selective controls, especially those which would apply to investment. The structure of our economy, its rigidities, the inability of general controls to affect price increases—all these factors point to the need for greater use of selective controls, and perhaps also antitrust policy.

IMPROVING FISCAL POLICY

Throughout the text we have noted certain changes suggested by various economists to improve the effectiveness of fiscal policy. We can, at this point, briefly review these suggestions and discuss in somewhat more detail those we previously skimmed over. Various proposals for improving fiscal policy include:

1. Granting discretionary authority to the President to vary personal income tax rates both up and down.

[30] Support can be found in the testimony, papers, and statements of economists before the JEC, in its hearings, etc., on *Rel. Prices to Ec. Stabil. & Growth* and *Empl., Growth, Price Levels.* In the former (C) see the comments of Smithies (p. 614) and Eckstein (p. 373); and in the latter those of R. A. Gordon (Pt. 9A, pp. 2962–2981), Musgrave (Pt. 9A, p. 2762ff), Heller (Pt. 9A, pp. 2997–2998), Smithies (Pt. 7, pp. 2439–2440), and Schultze (Pt. 7, pp. 2220–2221). See also in COF, S, *Investigation Finan. Cond.*, C, the statements of J. W. Angell (p. 542), G. Haberler (p. 617), M. W. Lee (pp. 642–643), R. A. Lester (p. 662), H. C. Wallich (p. 700), and C. R. Whittlesey (p. 704). See also Seymour Harris' summary in Pt. 7, p. 2183. Harris notes Secretary of the Treasury Humphrey's opposition to the use of selective controls on the grounds that (1) no one is smart enough to run this economy from Washington, or tell all Americans what they should do, (2) he would trust Americans to limit their borrowing themselves and decide themselves (individually) on the proper rate of economic growth, and (3) he dislikes arbitrary controls.

The most complete study of consumer credit controls, their impact, etc., of recent years is that of the Board of Governors of the FR System, *Consumer Installment Credit*, 6 vols., Washington, D.C.: Government Printing Office, 1957. See also E. Zupnick, "Consumer Credit and Monetary Policy in the United States and the United Kingdom," *J. Finance*, May 1962, and the many articles cited in W. L. Smith's chapter in JEC, *Empl., Growth, Price Levels*, SR.

2. Variable depreciation allowances to control investment, and/or the use and withdrawal of sizable initial depreciation allowances.
3. Variable tax credit allowances to control investment.
4. The use of tax-free reserve funds as in Sweden.
5. Greater use of the national income and product account budget to reflect more accurately the impact of the federal budget.
6. Use of budget expenditure plans for periods greater than 1 year, with some degree of Presidential discretion in the use of funds.
7. Reorganization of congressional committees so that a view of total budget expenditures and receipts is secured.

Warren L. Smith points out how clumsy our budgetary process is compared with that of the British. "... The British budget is a comprehensive financial plan covering both expenditures and taxation, and the budget as a whole is formulated with a view to its effect on the economy."[31] Barring only a major political crisis the budget as presented is accepted and quickly acted on without significant change. Finally, the budget is presented after the fiscal year to which it applies has started. This permits the government to keep its plans more nearly in line with the apparent needs of the economy. (Other proposals for improving the budgetary process appear in Chapter 14.)

8. Abandonment of attempts to balance the budget at levels considerably beneath full employment, and tax reduction so as to avoid a large full employment surplus,[32] unless, of course, there is a need to contain an excessive aggregate demand.
9. The use of explicit, quantitative (1) potential employment and production levels and (2) likely employment and production levels by the CEA and in the President's *Economic Report*.
10. The spelling out of specific steps to be undertaken by the Administration to attain full employment.
11. The spelling out of further specific steps to be taken if the full employment goal is not realized.
12. The inclusion in the *Economic Report of the President* of what the Administration expects by way of monetary policy.
13. Improving the system of unemployment compensation.
14. Considering the feasibility of better coordination of state-local and federal expenditure and tax programs, and the possible use of variable grants-in-aid to render state and local expenditures more anticyclical.

[31] W. L. Smith, "The Report of the Commission on Money and Credit, "*Am. Ec. Rev.*, May 1962, p. 304.
[32] The relative use of tax reduction or expenditure increase would depend on one's list of priorities.

15. More careful consideration of the impact of sudden changes in federal expenditures so as to eliminate government-caused recessions as in 1953–1954, to reduce the government's contribution to recessions as in 1957–1958, or to reduce pressures on prices.

16. Attempts to attain a smooth growth rate rather than one characterized by wide cyclical swings. The latter creates additional inflationary pressures by creating (1) more bottlenecks, and (2) wide swings in profits, which may in turn result in higher wage rates and higher contractual wage rates for subsequent years which may not be justified by future increases in productivity due to the failure of the economy to expand.

17. The establishment of a Wage and Price Commission of some sort to deal particularly with creeping inflation.[33]

Economists differ on the extent to which they would have the federal government implement employment and production goals. It is probably true that a substantial majority of those interested in stabilization policy feel that the CEA should issue quantitative employment and production goals. (This, of course, could be a function of their interest in full employment but, as noted previously, there is considerable reason for believing that this was the intent of the Employment Act.) Some feel that general figures should be issued while others feel that the figures should be broken down into components reflecting ranges of consumption and investment trends.[34] The expectation is that the CEA would have to work closely with industry and union advisory groups.[35] The end result is the establishment of a national economic budget which shows what the capacity of the economy is, and the contribution of each sector and breakdowns within sectors. A common proposal is for a 5-year projection, which is to be accompanied by a budget covering the same period of time.[36]

[33] The Clark-Reuss bills proposed that the President, directly or through any Federal agency he designates, hold public hearings on actual or proposed price or wage increases, and issue factual summaries and (when advisable) advisory statements.

[34] Recent proponents of such approaches include W. Reuther (see JEC, *Jan. 1961 Ec. Rept. Pres.*, H, pp. 108ff., and p. 124) and L. Keyserling. (See JEC, *Empl., Growth, Price Levels*, Pt. 1, pp. 151ff. See the projections of Keyserling's organization on p. 187.)

[35] A similar approach is used in France. A good summary of the French technique by Pierre Massé, head of the French government's national economic planning commission, is to be found in the NPA's *Looking Ahead*, Jan. 1963. The extent to which planning has contributed to France's prosperity, and the applicability of their techniques to our economy, are open questions.

[36] See H. C. Sonne, "The Employment Act, 1946–1961," *Looking Ahead*, NPA, Feb. 1961.

These proposals are tied to other activist proposals. That is, estimates are made of the potential for the various major sectors, and then estimates are made for what is likely to happen in these sectors. If the latter estimates indicate that a decline or an inadequate increase is likely, then alternative methods for raising consumption, investment, or government purchases would be considered. At this point, the usual fiscal-monetary controls would be available. Gerhard Colm has proposed that several alternative projections be made, accompanied by the programs contemplated by the government in each case and their probable impact on both consumption and investment.[37] The development of the techniques of national economic budgets was enhanced by the war production needs of World War II, defense needs during and following the Korean War, in several European countries by the Marshall Plan,[38] and under the auspices of the United Nations.[39]

Other proposals, omitted from our list but discussed previously in the text, have been made. (1) Hansen and others, for example, have called for the use of formula-flexible stabilizers, including such things as an automatic reduction (or increase) in tax rates as unemployment reached certain points, automatic increases in unemployment compensation, etc. (See Chapter 16.) (2) In 1962 President Kennedy requested standby authority to increase public works under given conditions. (See Chapter 16.)[40] (3) Proposals have been made which could slightly increase the built-in flexibility of the personal income tax. (See Chapter 16.) (4) Many economists urge acceptance by the Congress and the public of the difference between a deficit by default (a passive deficit) and a deliberate, expansionary (active) deficit, and (5) acceptance by the Congress of the value of a countercyclical policy, and the value of rapid action to avoid both depression and inflation tendencies.

It is not expected, of course, that the Congress is about to pass very many (if any) of these suggested reforms. One area which may be capable of receiving greater legislative support, and which is very important in the antirecession toolbox, is unemployment insurance.

Although the system of unemployment compensation is often cited as one of our first lines of defense against recessions, the system has come

---

[37] In JEC, *Fed. Exp. Pol.*, P, pp. 439ff.

On this subject see NPA, *National Budgets for Full Employment*, Pamphlets No. 43 and 44, April, 1945; and G. Colm, "National Economic Budgets," Bulletin of the Central Bank of Venezuela. The interested reader might also want to read about the planning techniques in both Britain and France.

[38] See R. Ruggels, *National Income Accounting and Its Relation to Economic Policy*, Economic Cooperation Administration, Paris, 1949.

[39] See Colm, *op. cit.*

[40] JEC, *Jan. 1963 Ec. Rept. Pres.*, H, p. 8.

under considerable fire in recent years for (1) not having expanded its coverage rapidly enough, (2) not having raised payments to high enough levels, and (3) for having been financially insolvent. The results of a study by Richard A. Lester of Princeton University (for the years 1948 to 1959) show that (1) only about 20 percent of the wage loss from total unemployment is offset by the regular state and railroad programs;[41] (2) the inclusion of all public programs (including extraordinary ones) raises this figure to only 23 percent;[42] (3) the rate of compensation for both total and partial unemployment appears to have been relatively constant over the 12-year period, expansions in coverage and benefit duration apparently being offset by lags in the maximum benefits paid weekly; (4) the percent of the total jobless who are insured significantly affects aggregate compensation rates, as one would expect, but especially serious is the fact that "at times and especially in the second year of a recession, a fairly high percentage of the unemployed are not subject to unemployment compensation;" (5) those who are unemployed because of recessions do not appear to be compensated at a rate higher than those unemployed for seasonal, frictional, and technological reasons; and (6) the range of compensation rates among the various states is such that some states pay twice as much as other states.[43]

The criticism of the financial insolvency of state unemployment programs is based on the fact that in recent recessions the federal government has had to make loans to states in order to enable them to extend their unemployment compensation payments beyond the regular time periods. The importance of the temporary program was reflected in the fact that in August of 1958 approximately one-third of the insured receiving payments were under the temporary program.[44] This summary of the results of Professor Lester's study indicates that there has been little if any relative improvement in the state unemployment compensation programs

[41] The figure is 15 percent if the wage loss from partial unemployment is included.

[42] And 18 percent if the wage loss from partial unemployment is included.

[43] R. A. Lester, "The Economic Significance of Unemployment Compensation, 1948–1959," *Rev. Ec. & Stat.*, Nov. 1960, pp. 349–371. See also his "Financing of Unemployment Compensation," *Industrial and Labor Relations Rev.*, Oct. 1960, pp. 52–67, and "Implications of Labor Force Developments for Unemployment Benefits," *Q. Rev. of Ec. and Bus.*, May 1961, pp. 47–56.

For labor's point of view see *Labor's Ec. Rev.*, April 1958. This article is extremely critical of the erosion of the employment tax rate under the system of experience rating. Professor Hart pointed out some years ago, as Lester does in the first article cited, that the experience rating system is procyclical.

Comments by Walter Reuther can be found in JEC, *Jan. 1961 Ec. Rept. Pres.*, H, p. 116.

[44] Based on a chart which appeared in *The New York Times*, March 8, 1959.

during the postwar period. His study seems to indicate that the system has merely held its own relative to wage and price increases.

Some economists, as we have noted, have called for automatic increases in unemployment compensation payments after the unemployment rate reaches a certain level. This proposal is, in effect, a type of formula-flexible stabilizer. One such proposal is made by Professor Galbraith in his *Affluent Society* when he proposes that unemployment compensation payments be cyclically graduated and dependent on the number unemployed.

Finally, we should repeat the point which was previously noted in this and other chapters—that new institutional devices may have to be developed to deal with so-called creeping inflation. While it is possible that a more even growth rate may be more conducive to general price stability and new policies may not be needed, it is also possible that creeping inflation will reappear on the scene in the future. Former President Kennedy's approach, while successful in the steel episode, is unlikely to be effective in very many additional cases. The President, most observers feel, can only use the prestige of his office to secure ends of this type on infrequent occasions.

PART VI

History of Fiscal Policies

21

History of Fiscal Policy:
1930 to 1952

Since accounts of the history of fiscal policy are available elsewhere[1] we shall only survey the more important actions and results with an attempt to evaluate policy decisions. The next two chapters are divided into four major sections—fiscal policy during (1) the 1930's, (2) World War II, (3) the immediate postwar period and the Korean War period, and (4) the 1953–1962 period. This chapter discusses the first three periods; and Chapter 22, the last period.

[1] Before 1940 see A. H. Hansen, *Fiscal Policy and Business Cycles*, New York: Norton, 1941, chapter 4; P. B. Trescott, "Some Historical Aspects of Federal Fiscal Policy, 1790–1956," in JEC, *Fed. Exp. Pol.*, P, pp. 60–83; L. H. Kimmel, *Federal Budget and Fiscal Policy, 1789–1958*, Washington, D.C.: Brookings Institution, 1959; E. C. Brown, "Fiscal Policy in the Thirties: A Reappraisal," *Am. Ec. Rev.*, Dec. 1956, pp. 857–79; S. Harris, ed., *American Economic History*, New York: McGraw-Hill, 1961, Chapter 5; G. Colm, "Fiscal Policy and the Federal Budget," Chapter 5 in Max F. Millikan, ed., *Income Stabilization for a Developing Democracy*, New Haven: Yale Univ. Press, 1953; G. Colm, *Essays in Public Finance and Public Policy*, New York: Oxford Univ. Press, 1955, Chapters 6–10, the last of which is reprinted from Millikan; H. H. Villard, *Deficit Spending and the National Income*, New York: Farrar & Rinehart, 1941; and K. D. Roose, "The Role of Net Government Contribution to Income in the Recession and Revival of 1937-8," *J. Finance*, March 1951, pp. 1–18.

After 1940 see Kimmel, Harris, and Trescott, and E. C. Brown, "Federal Fiscal Policy in the Postwar Period" in R. E. Freeman, ed., *Postwar Economic Trends in the United States*, New York: Harper, 1960, Chapter 5; A. H. Hansen, *The American Economy*, New York: McGraw-Hill, 1957, Chapters 2, 5, 6, and 7, and Paul J.Strayer, *Fiscal Policy and Politics*, New York: Harper, 1958. With two exceptions there was no attempt to include journal articles. Latecomers are W. Lewis, Jr., *Federal Fiscal Policy in the Postwar Recessions*, Washington, D.C.: Brookings Inst. 1962, and A. E. Holmans, *United States Fiscal Policy*, 1945–1959, London: Oxford Univ. Press 1961.

THE DEPRESSION YEARS

There is no need to repeat here the details of the catastrophic decline in the economy which followed the 1929 stock market crash.[2] Enough of the story can be told by the statistics on the unemployment rate found in Table 21-1. Table 21-2 shows the changes in GNP, consumption, investment, all government purchases, and federal expenditures and revenues during the depression years. All data are in current dollars. (Federal government data are on a fiscal year basis.) The fact that a

Table 21-1. Unemployment Rate 1929–1962 United States (in Percent)

Year	Rate	Year	Rate	Year	Rate
1929	3	1941	9.9	1953	2.9
1930	9	1942	4.7	1954	5.6
1931	16	1943	1.9	1955	4.4
1932	24	1944	1.2	1956	4.2
1933	25	1945	1.9	1957	4.3
1934	22	1946	3.9	1958	6.8
1935	20	1947	3.9	1959	5.5
1936	17	1948	3.8	1960	5.6
1937	14	1949	5.9	1961	6.7
1938	19	1950	5.3	1962	5.6
1939	17.2	1951	3.3	1963	5.5 (Aug.)
1940	14.6	1952	3.1		

Sources: Data for 1929 to 1938 from Trescott, *op. cit.*, p. 75; for 1939 to 1960 from *Business Statistics*, 1961 edition, p. 61; and for other years from *Economic Indicators*, June 1963.

serious decline in both investment and consumption occurred during the early 'thirties and recovered at a tortuously slow rate is shown by the data in the table. Government purchases do not appear to have been very helpful, but in real terms they did increase, as noted in Table 21-4.(p.480)

Somewhat more complete data are found in Table 21-3 on a national income account basis; note here that federal expenditures (column 5) increased from $2.6 billion in 1929 to $2.8 billion in 1930 to $4.2 billion in 1931, and then dropped to $3.2 billion in 1932. The impact of the federal government during both 1929 and 1930, however, was on the restrictive side, for there was a surplus in each year. Even though the federal budget was quite expansionary with a $2.1 billion deficit in 1931,

[2] An interesting narrative stressing the financial aspects, is that of J. K. Galbraith, *The Great Crash—1929*, Cambridge: Houghton-Mifflin, 1954.

the deficit was decreased in both 1932 and 1933. In fact, there was a sizable decline (about 25 percent) in federal expenditures in 1932. The year 1934 saw a significant increase in expenditures (and receipts) and the realization of a deficit of $2.9 billion. The following year (1935) expenditures were approximately the same but there was an increase in receipts which lowered the deficit to $2.6 billion. The year 1936 saw a

Table 21-2. Important Historical Statistics, United States (Billions of Current Dollars)

	Calendar Years				Fiscal Years		
	1	2	3	4	5	6	7
Year	GNP	Consump-tion	GPDI	Gov't Purchases	Federal Expend.	Federal Revenues	Deficit or Surplus
1929	$104	$79	$13.0	$9	$2.9	$3.8	$0.9
1930	91	71	8.0	9	3.1	4.0	0.9
1931	76	61	4.0	9	4.1	3.2	−1.0
1932	59	49	0.3	8	4.8	2.0	−2.7
1933	56	46	1.0	8	4.7	2.1	−2.6
1934	65	52	2.0	10	4.5	3.1	−3.3
1935	73	56	5.0	12	6.3	3.8	−2.4
1936	83	63	7.0	12	7.6	4.2	−3.5
1937	91	67	10.0	12	8.4	5.6	−2.8
1938	85	65	5.0	13	7.2	7.0	−0.1
1939	91	68	7.0	13	9.4	6.6	−2.9
1940	101	72	10.0	14	9.6	6.9	−2.7

Source: Trescott, *op. cit.*, p. 75.

large expansion in expenditures and receipts, but the deficit rose to − $3.5 billion. In 1937, however, there was a cutback in expenditures and a large increase in taxes (an increase in revenue of 40 percent!) with a consequent sizable decline in the deficit to almost nothing. This year and the year 1938 were years of a serious setback from the recovery as shown in the income statistics for 1938 in Table 21-2. In 1938 expenditures were increased and receipts declined to bring a deficit of $2 billion. There was some expansion of expenditures, revenues, and the deficit ($2.2 billion) in 1939. In 1940 expenditures and revenues continued to increase, but the deficit declined to $1.4 billion. (The reader should note that the figures cited are in current dollars.)

Extremely little was done on the part of state and local governments (column 9, Table 21-3) to help the economy. True, they did run deficits from 1929 to 1932, but they were small to start with and they became smaller in each subsequent year when they should have become larger. To some extent, the federal government deficits did not have a net impact but rather partly offset the increasingly restrictive character of state and

Table 21-3. Government Receipts and Expenditures in the National Income Accounts, 1929–1961 (Billions of Current Dollars)

	Total Government			Federal Government			State and Local Government		
	1	2	3	4	5	6	7	8	9
Calendar Year	Re-ceipts	Expendi-tures	Surplus or Deficit (−) on Income and Product Account	Re-ceipts	Expendi-tures	Surplus or Deficit (−) on Income and Product Account	Re-ceipts	Expendi-tures	Surplus or Deficit (−) on Income and Product Account
1929	11.3	10.2	1.0	3.8	2.6	1.2	7.6	7.7	−0.1
1930	10.8	11.0	−0.3	3.0	2.8	0.3	7.8	8.4	−0.5
1931	9.5	12.3	−2.8	2.0	4.2	−2.1	7.7	8.4	−0.7
1932	8.9	10.6	−1.7	1.7	3.2	−1.5	7.3	7.6	−0.2
1933	9.3	10.7	−1.4	2.7	4.0	−1.3	7.2	7.2	(a)
1934	10.5	12.8	−2.4	3.5	6.4	−2.9	8.6	8.1	0.5
1935	11.4	13.3	−2.0	4.0	6.5	−2.6	9.1	8.5	0.6
1936	12.9	15.9	−3.0	5.0	8.5	−3.5	8.6	8.1	0.5
1937	15.4	14.8	0.6	7.0	7.2	−0.2	9.1	8.4	0.7
1938	15.0	16.6	−1.6	6.5	8.5	−2.0	9.3	8.9	0.4
1939	15.4	17.5	−2.1	6.7	9.0	−2.2	9.6	9.6	0.1
1940	17.7	18.5	−0.7	8.6	10.1	−1.4	10.0	9.2	0.7
1941	25.0	28.8	−3.8	15.4	20.5	−5.1	10.4	9.0	1.3
1942	32.6	64.0	−31.4	22.9	56.1	−33.2	10.6	8.8	1.8
1943	49.2	93.4	−44.2	39.3	86.0	−46.7	10.9	8.4	2.5
1944	51.2	103.1	−51.9	41.0	95.6	−54.6	11.1	8.4	2.7
1945	53.2	92.9	−39.7	42.5	84.8	−42.3	11.6	9.0	2.6
1946	51.1	47.0	4.1	39.2	37.0	2.2	13.0	11.1	1.9
1947	57.1	43.8	13.3	43.3	31.1	12.2	15.5	14.4	1.1
1948	59.2	51.0	8.2	43.4	35.4	8.0	17.8	17.6	0.3
1949	56.4	59.5	−3.1	39.1	41.6	−2.5	19.6	20.2	−0.6
1950	69.3	61.1	8.2	50.2	41.0	9.2	21.4	22.4	−1.0
1951	85.5	79.4	6.1	64.5	58.0	6.4	23.5	23.8	−0.3
1952	90.6	94.4	−3.9	67.7	71.6	−3.9	25.5	25.4	0.1
1953	94.9	102.0	−7.1	70.3	77.7	−7.4	27.4	27.1	0.3
1954	90.0	96.7	−6.7	63.8	69.6	−5.8	29.1	30.1	−0.9
1955	101.4	98.6	2.9	72.8	68.9	3.8	31.7	32.7	−1.0
1956	109.5	104.3	5.2	77.5	71.8	5.7	35.2	35.7	−0.5
1957	116.3	115.3	1.0	81.7	79.7	2.0	38.6	39.6	−1.0
1958	115.1	126.6	−11.4	78.5	87.9	−9.4	42.0	44.1	−2.1
1959	129.3	131.6	−2.2	89.4	91.2	−1.8	46.5	46.9	−0.4
1960	139.1	137.2	1.9	96.0	92.8	3.3	49.2	50.6	−1.4
1961[b]	143.6	149.8	−6.2	97.9	101.4	−3.6	52.3	55.0	−2.7
1962[b]	158.2	161.0	−2.8	108.2	109.9	−1.7	57.7	58.8	−1.1

Source: Jan. 1962 Ec. Rept. Pres. p. 275. Federal grants-in-aid to State and local governments are reflected in federal expenditures and state and local receipts and expenditures. Total government receipts and expenditures have been adjusted to eliminate this duplication. Data for Alaska and Hawaii included beginning 1960.
[a] Less than $50 million.
[b] Preliminary estimates by Council of Economic Advisers.

local finance. This is true even though the state and local governments ran deficits because the size of their deficits were declining. Furthermore, state and local governments started running surpluses in 1933 (or thereabouts) which continued throughout the 1930's and afterward.

We recall that the ideology prevailing in 1929 was that the government was not to assume the responsibility for economic stability, welfare, or relief, and that the government that interfered the least was the best government. We should further recall that the size of the federal budget expenditures was only one-third of that of the state and local governments combined. Nonetheless, the Hoover Administration incurred sizable deficits in both 1931 and 1932. Not until 1934 did the Roosevelt Administration match Hoover's largest deficit. Hoover was greatly disturbed by these deficits and he did succeed in reducing federal expenditures by $1 billion in 1932. Hoover felt that it was necessary to balance the budget as a prerequisite to recovery, that failure to do so would prolong the Depression, that federal borrowing would retard recovery, that our most patriotic action would be not to request aid from the government, and that direct federal financing of relief would be "cold and distant charity." In 1931 he recommended a tax increase, and for fiscal 1934 a manufacturers' excise tax. He further felt that an unbalanced budget would be inflationary and would indicate that the government was irresponsible, and that to urge otherwise was outright immoral.[3] All this was part of the ideology of the time, but it certainly did not go unchallenged; there were many vociferous and respected dissenters.[4]

We should not think that a significant change occurred with the inauguration of Franklin D. Roosevelt in 1933, however. The facts show that (1) the New Deal never really tried deficit spending, (2) the New Deal policies were a long way from bringing us completely out of the Depression, (3) Roosevelt shared the views of his predecessor and did not even partially accept deficit theory until at least 1937.

Roosevelt was elected on a platform that condemned the rising tide of government expenditures and Hoover deficits (doesn't this sound familiar?), agreed with Hoover that a balanced budget was a prerequisite for recovery, claimed the Hoover Administration was extravagant, and argued that above all the federal budget must be balanced![5] In an economy drive aimed at balancing the budget, Roosevelt proceeded to reduce the pay of federal employees and veterans' payments. It is true, however, that expansionary programs (public works, relief, etc.) were undertaken, and that these were to have an avowed expansionary impact, but only with respect to "emergency" expenditures. These programs were looked on as of an emergency type to help the unemployed, and sight was never lost of the goal of an ultimately balanced budget. There was, however, a rapid realization that the budget would not be balanced, and there was somewhat

---

[3] See Kimmel, op. cit., pp. 144–153, 163, 167.

[4] See the interesting survey of the opinions and statements of economists and others who dissented from the "conventional wisdom" in ibid., pp. 152–161, 171–174.

[5] See ibid., pp. 164–169, and Trescott, op. cit., pp. 76–77.

less concern than Hoover had shown over the overwhelming necessity for an annually balanced budget.[6]

Kimmel and John H. Williams claim that it was not until the 1937–1938 depression that Roosevelt seriously expressed an interest in using deficits as a device for the direct expansion of the economy rather than merely for relief and as a concomitant to aid the unemployed until recovery came spontaneously from the private economy.[7] It was at this time that the most explicit statements were made of fiscal theory and that sizable increases were made in expenditures for WPA, PWA, etc. Prior to this time the Administration felt that it was only temporarily abandoning its goal of an annually balanced budget. Its actions were primarily intended to fill the gap until the economy got on its feet on its own. Furthermore, major emphasis in the early years was placed on the restrictive NRA program, agricultural aid, and some monetary experiments.[8] Of course, the impact of Keynes' theoretical justification for government expenditures could not have come until after the publication of his book in 1936.[9]

E. Cary Brown[10] has provided the most significant study showing that fiscal policy during the 1930's was neither tried nor very expansionary. Professor Brown computed the potential GNP for the years 1929 through 1939. He then attempted to measure whether fiscal policy was more or less expansive or more or less contractive at the given full employment level of demand. In other words, he attempted to measure the shift in demand attributable to fiscal policy as a percent of full employment income.

Brown's study showed that in only two years was the direct effect of all the government's fiscal policies on full employment aggregate demand relatively greater than in 1929. The two years were 1931 and 1936, which were years of special veteran's payments, strongly opposed by both Hoover and Roosevelt. In three years (1930, 1932, and 1939) the expansionary effect was above that of 1929 but not by a lot, in two years (1934 and 1935) it was about the same, in two years (1933 and 1937) it was much less, and in one year (1938) slightly less. Furthermore, the trend of the direct expansionary effects of fiscal policy during the 1930's was downward. Brown also found that the state and local governments' fiscal policy was roughly neutral from 1934 on, and that federal government

[6] Kimmel, op. cit., pp. 175–183, and Trescott, op. cit., pp. 76–77.

[7] Kimmel, op. cit., pp. 183–190; and Williams, "The Implications of Fiscal Policy for Monetary Policy and the Banking System," Am. Ec. Rev. (Proc.), March 1942; and Colm in Millikan, ed., op. cit., p. 216.

[8] Kimmel, op. cit., pp. 184–221.

[9] He did make recommendations along these lines prior to this date, however.

[10] In "Fiscal Policies in the 'Thirties: A Reappraisal," Am. Ec. Rev., Dec. 1956. See also Hansen, Fiscal Policy and Business Cycles, pp. 83–95.

activities in most years barely offset the contractive effects of the state and local governments. The major problem was that all levels of government increased their *tax structures* significantly. Government purchases expanded practically every year but tax yields at full employment also increased at least an equal amount. (See Figure 15-2.) *During most years of the Depression the tax structure was such that it would have yielded a tax surplus or balanced budget at full employment.* Of course, the tax surpluses were not realized because full employment was never realized, but this fact served only to disguise the real impact and real restrictive nature of the tax structure.[11]

Brown noted that the 1932 Revenue Act about doubled the full employment tax yield. This was the basis for the tax structure up to World War II. All rates were raised, especially those on middle and lower income groups. Exemptions were greatly cut, normal and surtax rates were pushed up steeply, a tax credit for low income groups was dropped, estate tax rates were raised, new and higher excise taxes were imposed, and corporate taxes were raised somewhat (throughout the whole period). Social security taxes went into effect in 1937, and state and local governments imposed or raised general sales and excise, personal, corporate, and gasoline taxes.[12]

Although it may be easy to exaggerate the impact of business confidence on investment decisions and such exaggerations may sometimes amount to nothing less than economic blackmail aimed at achieving the success of a privileged political party, and although such an effect is less likely to occur today (unless rather serious threats are made against the business community),[13] it is nonetheless true that the attitude of the Roosevelt Administration toward the business community, the congressional exposures of abuses in the securities markets and of holding companies, etc., the reforms undertaken by Roosevelt (which Keynes advised Roosevelt to undertake *after* recovery had been achieved, but which may not have been possible after the recovery since the crisis may have passed), the

[11] E. C. Brown, "Fiscal Policies in the 'Thirties: A Reappraisal," *op. cit.*, pp. 863–868.

[12] *Ibid.*, pp. 868–869. See also A. F. Burns, *Prosperity Without Inflation*, New York: Fordham Univ. Press, 1957, pp. 28–29; and G. Colm and F. Lehmann, "Public Spending and Recovery in the United States," *Social Research*, May 1936.

A summary of rate changes in the individual and corporate income taxes, and excise and other taxes, since 1913 can be found in many public finance texts, or in National Industrial Conference Board, *The Economic Almanac* (1958), New York: Crowell, 1958, pp. 438–441. See also Figure 15-2.

[13] It is very likely that the effect of Kennedy's handling of the steel price hike in early 1962 on business confidence and investment has been grossly exaggerated. Had investment opportunities been plentiful it is hard to believe that they would not have been pursued.

Table 21-4. Gross National Product or Expenditure, in 1961 Prices, 1929–61

Year	Total Gross National Product	Personal Consumption Expenditures				Gross Private Domestic Total	New Construction		
		Total	Durable Goods	Non-durable Goods	Services		Total	Residential Non-farm	Other
1929	209.8	142.8	15.7	70.6	56.5	42.4	25.5	10.2	15.3
1930	190.3	134.3	12.5	67.2	54.6	29.1	18.9	6.0	13.0
1931	175.9	130.2	10.8	66.8	52.5	18.0	13.3	5.0	8.3
1932	149.8	118.5	8.2	61.5	48.7	5.2	7.4	2.5	4.9
1933	146.3	115.7	8.0	59.7	48.0	5.7	5.6	1.9	3.8
1934	160.3	121.6	9.1	63.7	48.8	9.9	6.3	2.2	4.1
1935	175.6	129.1	11.3	67.2	50.5	18.7	8.2	3.6	4.6
1936	200.5	142.1	13.9	74.9	53.3	25.9	11.5	5.4	6.1
1937	210.9	147.1	14.6	77.5	55.1	31.7	13.8	5.8	7.9
1938	201.5	144.6	11.8	78.8	54.0	18.8	12.3	6.0	6.3
1939	218.1	152.7	14.1	83.0	55.7	26.2	14.7	8.0	6.8
1940	236.8	160.8	16.2	86.8	57.8	34.6	16.5	8.6	7.9
1941	275.8	171.4	18.7	92.6	60.1	43.7	18.5	9.2	9.3
1942	315.3	167.9	11.5	94.5	61.9	22.4	9.5	4.2	5.3
1943	355.2	172.3	9.9	97.4	65.0	13.5	5.4	2.0	3.3
1944	381.1	178.6	9.1	101.7	67.8	15.0	5.9	1.7	4.2
1945	373.8	190.9	10.4	109.7	70.9	20.8	8.2	2.2	6.0
1946	325.4	213.8	20.5	116.4	76.9	50.8	21.1	8.6	12.5
1947	324.9	217.4	24.6	113.9	78.9	50.8	24.2	11.3	12.9
1948	337.5	221.6	26.0	113.7	82.0	59.4	27.5	13.4	14.1
1949	338.3	227.3	27.8	115.0	84.4	47.4	27.1	13.2	13.9
1950	366.5	241.0	34.0	118.1	88.9	66.9	33.1	18.2	14.9
1951	396.5	243.2	30.8	120.3	92.1	69.3	31.6	15.1	16.5
1952	411.7	249.6	30.1	124.4	95.1	60.9	31.5	15.0	16.5
1953	430.6	261.5	35.0	128.0	98.5	61.6	33.5	16.0	17.5
1954	422.0	265.0	34.3	129.1	101.6	59.1	36.0	18.1	18.0
1955	455.1	284.7	41.9	135.7	107.2	75.0	41.0	21.3	19.7
1956	464.8	294.2	40.2	140.9	113.0	74.6	39.2	19.1	20.2
1957	473.6	302.1	40.8	143.4	117.9	70.0	38.6	18.0	20.6
1956	466.1	304.7	37.6	144.2	122.9	59.2	37.6	19.1	18.6
1959	497.3	322.4	43.3	150.2	128.9	73.5	41.4	22.8	18.6
1960	511.1	332.7	44.2	153.4	135.1	73.0	41.1	21.1	20.0
1961[c]	521.2	339.2	42.3	155.6	141.2	69.5	41.8	21.3	20.5

Source: Jan. 1962 Ec. Rept. Pres., pp. 208–209.
 [a] Net of government sales.
 [b] Not available separately.
 [c] Preliminary.

actions interpreted by the business community to constitute a redistribution of income, the extremely (but not wholly warranted) antagonistic attitude of the business community toward the Roosevelt Administration, the fight over social security, the bitter feelings engendered by the fight over packing the Supreme Court—all these factors did little to restore investment. Nonetheless, we can seriously challenge the statement that had businessmen had their own way on all these matters the economy would have recovered more rapidly. Modern income analysis has no way of measuring the confidence factor in the business cycle, but it may be true that recovery would have been less or later without outside influences.[14]

If any lessons are to be learned from the Depression experience, they are that (1) tax decreases and expenditure increases must be of sufficient

[14] Burns, op. cit., would not agree with this.

(Billions of Dollars, 1961 Prices)

Investment

				Government Purchases of Goods and Services			
		Net Exports		Federal			
Producers' Durable Equipment	Change in Business Inventories	of Goods and Services	Total	Total[a]	National Defense[a]	Other	State and Local
13.5	3.4	1.1	23.4	3.8	NA[b]	NA	19.7
10.7	−0.6	0.9	25.9	4.3	NA	NA	21.6
7.2	−2.5	0.4	27.3	4.7	NA	NA	22.6
4.3	−6.5	0.2	25.9	4.9	NA	NA	21.0
4.5	−4.4	−0.3	25.2	6.7	NA	NA	18.5
6.1	−2.4	−0.1	28.8	8.8	NA	NA	20.0
8.2	2.3	−1.3	29.2	8.5	NA	NA	20.6
11.2	3.2	−1.5	34.0	13.1	NA	NA	21.0
12.7	5.3	−0.9	32.9	12.3	NA	NA	20.7
8.8	−2.3	1.6	36.5	14.6	NA	NA	22.0
10.3	1.1	1.0	38.2	14.0	3.4	10.6	24.2
13.3	4.9	1.9	39.5	16.7	6.0	10.7	22.8
15.6	9.6	0.2	60.5	39.1	31.8	7.3	21.4
9.0	3.9	−2.3	127.3	107.8	102.3	5.5	19.5
8.4	−0.3	−6.0	175.4	157.6	154.8	2.9	17.7
11.1	−2.0	−6.1	193.6	176.2	173.1	3.1	17.4
15.5	−2.8	−4.8	166.8	149.0	147.0	2.1	17.8
19.6	10.1	5.0	55.8	35.9	28.1	7.8	19.9
26.4	0.2	9.5	47.2	24.6	16.1	8.5	22.5
27.6	4.2	3.1	53.4	29.1	16.7	12.4	24.3
24.1	−3.8	3.8	59.9	32.2	19.4	12.8	27.7
25.9	7.9	1.4	57.2	27.5	20.1	7.4	29.7
26.7	11.0	3.6	80.4	50.0	43.3	6.7	30.4
26.5	2.9	2.6	98.7	67.8	59.2	8.6	31.0
27.4	0.8	0.4	107.1	74.8	63.2	11.6	32.3
25.3	−2.2	2.3	95.6	60.5	52.0	8.5	35.0
27.4	6.6	2.5	92.9	55.4	47.4	8.0	37.5
30.3	5.0	4.3	91.8	53.0	46.4	6.6	38.7
29.9	1.5	5.7	95.8	55.0	48.7	6.3	40.8
23.6	−2.1	1.5	100.6	56.6	47.7	8.9	44.0
25.9	6.2	−0.3	101.6	55.8	47.6	8.2	45.8
27.5	4.4	3.7	101.8	53.8	45.7	8.1	48.0
25.7	2.0	4.0	108.6	57.2	48.6	8.5	51.4

magnitude to restore economic activity to a high level, (2) fiscal and other policies should be as consistent as possible so as not to be self-defeating, (3) state and local policies should be coordinated with national policy, (4) public understanding and public support should be secured,[15] (5) the public should understand that action will be taken and continued if necessary, (6) the recovery program should be bipartisan, (7) a little bit of pump-priming will not be sufficient to offset such a large decline nor will it set the ball rolling so that recovery will occur spontaneously and quickly, and (8) a permanent increase in the federal debt may be inevitable.

THE WAR YEARS

The most important experience that validates the potency of fiscal policy is that of World War II. In 1939 the unemployment rate was 17.2

---

[15] See Colm in Millikan, ed., *op. cit.*, p. 217.

482

percent, in 1940 it was 14.6 percent, in 1941 it was 9.9 percent, in 1942 it was 4.7 percent, in 1943 it was 1.9 percent, and in 1944 it reached an all-time low of 1.2 percent. (See Table 21-1.) These were very significant changes. The explanation is to be found in the rapid increase in federal government expenditures, and their maintenance at high levels, in the years 1941 through 1945. (See Table 21-3.) These were years of massive federal expenditures, massive deficits, and massive increases in the public debt. The deficits in current dollars were, for the years 1941 through 1945, $5.1 billion, $33.2 billion, $46.7 billion, $54.6 billion, and $42.3 billion, respectively. (See Table 21-3.) The impact on the GNP (in constant dollars) is shown in Table 21-4.

Federal government receipts in the national income accounts for the war years are shown in Table 21-3, column 4. It is clear that they also rose very rapidly, but that they still lagged far behind federal expenditures. Tax rates were raised or credits reduced on the individual income tax in each year. Some idea of the importance of these tax changes becomes obvious when one considers that only 4 million paid the individual income tax in 1939 while 42 million persons paid it in 1944. Rates were also raised rather steeply on corporate profits. During the early days of the war, taxes were not increased rapidly because it was thought it would not be conducive to rapid increases in production and employment. At this time, however, work relief programs were drastically reduced and public works projects were cut back. As the production of war goods was raised to a high level, tax rates were significantly increased. Nonetheless, these increases in taxes were neither sufficient to avoid very large deficits nor to absorb the rapid growth of purchasing power which was much greater than the level of production of consumer goods. It was necessary, therefore, to rely strongly (if not mostly) on controls over production and consumption. Rationing and controls over the allocation of resources, prices, and wages were necessary.[16]

A good part of the postwar inflation can be traced directly to the fiscal and monetary policies followed during the war (and to the policy of supporting the prices of government securities after the war). A large supply of excess liquidity was created during the war which was monetized and spent after the war (or made many consumers willing to spend a high percent of their current incomes after the war).

It is generally agreed that a higher level of taxes during the war would have greatly helped alleviate the inflation of this period and the years immediately following. It is not entirely clear, however, how high the

[16] For examples of the subtle techniques used by private interests to enhance their own incomes by virtual economic blackmail, see Strayer, *op. cit.*, pp. 29–39 and 43–48.

tax rates could have been pushed before they would have adversely affected incentives. It is doubtful, though, that we were near this point. The use of some type of compulsory saving (in war bonds redeemable at a time to be determined, but not in excess, say, of 10 years) would perhaps have offset the disincentive effects of higher tax rates. Higher tax rates would not have eliminated the need for controls over the allocation of resources and rationing (which was necessary on an equity basis). It is also true that there was a reluctance to impose higher taxes (than were already being used) on low-income groups, especially a regressive sales tax. On pure stabilization grounds this was not a wise policy decision.

THE IMMEDIATE POSTWAR PERIOD, THE 1948–1949 RECESSION, AND THE KOREAN WAR

The Period of Reconversion

As the war came to an end, the fear of another depression was the most important factor governing the thinking of legislators and economists as they peered into the future. Extensive congressional hearings were held and investigations were made of what might happen after the war ended, the Employment Act of 1946 was passed, economists predicted deflation and unemployment, easy money policies were planned, outstanding government contracts were settled on a basis highly favorable to business, and price controls were discontinued on November 9, 1946. The Revenue Act of 1945 (November 8) provided a major tax reduction which was to begin in 1946 and was estimated to be at the rate of $6 billion per year (in current prices). The excess profits tax was repealed, the corporate income tax rate reduced from 40 to 38 percent, personal taxes were reduced, a scheduled increase in the social security tax was postponed, and rebates were given on the excess profits tax.[17]

Both consumers and business entered the postwar transition period with a high degree of liquidity.[18] Furthermore, both businessmen and consumers were optimistic and willing to spend. In Table 21-4 we see

[17] On these matters, see E. C. Brown, "Federal Fiscal Policy in the Postwar Period," in R. E. Freeman, ed., *op. cit.*, p. 149; Strayer, *op. cit.*, pp. 48–55; and R. Blough, *The Federal Taxing Process*, New York: Prentice-Hall, 1952. Both the Brown and Strayer sources cover this period. The Brown chapter, though, was written with an attempt to provide a detailed study of fiscal policy during this period and is highly recommended. A very comprehensive study of the whole postwar period is that of A. E. Holmans, *United States Fiscal Policy, 1945–1959*, London: Oxford Univ. Press, 1961. See also the Kimmel study previously cited, and Bert C. Hickman, *Growth and Stability of the Postwar Economy*, Washington, D.C.: Brookings Institution, 1960.

[18] For a discussion of this and related matters see A. H. Hansen, *The American Economy*, pp. 28–30.

that in constant dollars the GNP declined rather sharply in 1946 and 1947 during the period of reconversion. The decline in the economy, however, was not as serious as the data may indicate since the unemployment rate rose to only 3.9 percent in each year. The rest of the story is told in Tables 18-1 and 18-2; the Consumer Price Index rose from 62.7 to 77.8, and the Wholesale Price Index from 61.3 to 96.5 from 1945 to 1947. In view of this development the tax rebate and tax reduction programs adopted in 1945 were inappropriate. Had the Administration known what was to happen after the war there is little doubt that more deflationary policies would have been advocated. The policies adopted were based on erroneous forecasts of a serious decline. As it was, the federal government realized a surplus of $2.2 billion in 1946, $12.2 billion in 1947, and $8 billion in 1948. (See Table 21-3.) The state and local governments also ran surpluses during these years, but at a rapidly declining rate ($1.9, $1.1 and $.3 billion, respectively). Brown has stated that these federal surpluses were "a truly remarkable achievement."[19] A major factor in the achievement of these surpluses was the maintenance of the tax rate structure (after the 1945 cuts) and the large drop in expenditures. (From $84.8 billion in 1945 to $37 billion in 1946 to $31.1 billion in 1947, and back up to $35.4 billion in 1948. See Table 21-3.)

It is of interest to note that in constant dollars the automatic stabilizers did not work well during this period. That is, in constant dollars the increase in revenue from the personal and corporate income taxes rose little from 1946 to 1948. Other taxes actually fell off in revenue yield in real terms.[20]

Since the Republican Congress was intent on cutting taxes in this period, considerable credit has been given the Truman Administration for resisting these pressures, vetoing tax cuts, and fighting for the retention of current rates and the extension of wartime excises. The Administration called for budget surpluses to fight inflation and to reduce the national debt (although it would have been better for the federal government to hold the funds itself, or reduce only that part held by the Federal Reserve). A special session of Congress was even called in late 1947 for the purpose of fighting inflation, although the Congress took no action. The pressure for tax cuts was great, however, and Truman did give in somewhat in his January 1948 *Economic Report*.[21] The Revenue Act of 1948 cut personal income and estate taxes by $5 billion per year over a Presidential veto. This was quite inappropriate because the economy was still expanding rapidly. The

---

[19] E. C. Brown, "Federal Fiscal Policy in the Postwar Period," *op. cit.*, p. 151.
[20] *Ibid.*, p. 152.
[21] He suggested a $4 billion reduction in the personal income tax, but an equivalent increase in corporate taxes. The net effect would no doubt have been expansionary.

justification in Congress was that such a reduction was necessary to fight inflation by increasing the incentive to work and thereby increase supply.[22]

The 1948–1949 Recession and the Korean War

The Truman Administration was very slow to realize that a recession was under way in late 1948 and early 1949. To some extent this was due to some lag in statistics and perhaps also the difficulty in switching from almost three years of fervent public advocation of anti-inflationary programs to antirecession programs.[23] It had proposed in January 1949, another anti-inflationary program of tax increases and a higher surplus. The CEA was not unaware of the slowdown in the economy, but it apparently had some difficulty choosing between anti-inflationary and antirecession policies when both appeared to be necessary. As things turned out, the tax reduction bill of 1948 constituted the proper action although passed on the basis of the wrong analysis. It did alleviate the severity of the recession, but its passage at this time was highly fortuitous.

In Table 21-5 we see that (in constant dollars) the GNP dipped slightly in 1948(1), rose significantly in 1948(2), slowed in its rate of increase in 1948(3) and 1948(4), and then dropped in 1949(1) and 1949(4). From 1949(4) to 1950(1), there was a rather sharp increase which continued until 1953(3), when a decline set in again. The decline of 1948–1949 was not terribly serious in production terms, but in terms of the unemployment rate it was fairly sharp. The rate of unemployment for 1948 was 3.8 percent; for 1949 it was 5.9 percent, and for 1950 it was 5.3 percent.

Although the Administration by mid-1949 (in the *Midyear Economic Report*) recognized that there had definitely been a slowdown in the economy, it offered little by way of tax reduction as a remedial policy. In its *Midyear Economic Report* (1949) it did call for but did not get upgrading, expanding the coverage, and the extension of the period of coverage of unemployment compensation, higher social security benefits, and longer RFC loans. President Truman further publicly accepted a deficit, which in itself was a highly significant break with tradition.[24] Despite this, emphasis was soon laid on the undesirable[25] budget deficit of the period, and even as

---

[22] E. C. Brown, "Federal Fiscal Policy in the Postwar Period," *op. cit.*, pp. 151–155; Strayer, *op. cit.*, pp. 56–61; Hickman, *op. cit.*, pp. 51–71; Kimmel, *op. cit.*, pp. 240–244; and Holmans, *op. cit.*, pp. 45–101. Holmans has a very complete discussion of the fiscal politics of the period.

[23] W. Lewis Jr. adds also that compensatory fiscal policy was less accepted at this time. *Op. cit.*, pp. 92–105.

[24] W. Lewis, Jr., *op. cit.*, p. 117.

[25] E. C. Brown argues that the deficit was "grudgingly accepted," but W. Lewis, Jr., argues that it was accepted and defended as proper policy by the President but not by the Secretary of the Treasury.

Table 21-5. Gross National Product or Expenditure, Seasonally Adjusted Quarterly Totals at Annual Rates, in Billions of Constant (1954) Dollars, 1947–1963 (1)

Line		1947					1948				
		I	II	III	IV	Year	I	II	III	IV	Year
1	Gross national product	278.4	280.4	282.9	287.2	282.3	286.4	293.3	295.6	297.3	293.1
2	Personal consumption expenditures	192.5	196.1	196.9	197.0	195.6	198.1	199.0	199.4	200.6	199.3
3	Durable goods	21.8	23.1	23.5	24.7	23.3	24.0	24.8	25.2	24.3	24.6
4	Nondurable goods	104.7	106.4	105.8	104.3	105.3	105.3	104.9	104.3	105.8	105.1
5	Services	65.9	66.5	67.5	68.0	67.0	68.9	69.3	69.9	70.4	69.6
6	Gross private domestic investment	40.6	39.3	39.2	46.4	41.5	47.4	50.7	51.3	49.5	49.8
7	New construction	18.4	18.3	20.2	22.3	19.9	22.0	23.1	23.0	22.2	22.7
8	Residential nonfarm	8.6	8.2	9.6	11.6	9.6	11.4	12.0	11.6	10.6	11.4
9	Other	9.9	10.0	10.5	10.7	10.3	10.7	11.2	11.5	11.6	11.2
10	Producer's durable equipment	21.5	21.6	21.6	22.1	21.7	22.8	22.6	22.5	23.3	22.8
11	Change in business inventories—total	0.6	-0.5	-2.5	2.0	-0.1	2.7	4.9	5.8	4.1	4.4
12	Nonfarm only	1.4	1.8	-0.3	2.9	1.4	1.9	3.1	4.1	3.0	3.0
13	Net exports of goods and services	8.5	8.7	8.8	6.2	8.0	2.9	1.7	1.4	1.9	2.0
14	Gov't purchases of goods and services	36.8	36.3	38.0	37.6	37.2	37.9	42.0	43.5	45.3	42.1
15	Federal	19.6	18.7	20.0	19.1	19.4	19.2	22.9	24.1	25.6	22.9
16	State and local	17.2	17.6	18.0	18.5	17.8	18.7	19.1	19.4	19.7	19.2

Line	1949 I	1949 II	1949 III	1949 IV	1949 Year	1950 I	1950 II	1950 III	1950 IV	1950 Year	1951 I	1951 II	1951 III	1951 IV	1951 Year	1952 I	1952 II	1952 III	1952 IV	1952 Year
1	291.5	290.3	295.6	293.0	292.7	302.7	312.0	325.6	331.6	318.1	334.0	340.0	346.3	346.9	341.8	349.6	349.3	352.6	362.3	353.5
2	199.9	203.6	204.8	209.0	204.3	210.7	214.2	225.6	217.0	216.8	222.3	214.5	217.5	219.8	218.5	220.0	222.7	223.8	230.2	224.2
3	23.7	26.0	27.1	28.5	26.3	29.0	29.8	37.3	32.2	32.1	33.0	27.8	28.1	27.7	29.2	27.0	28.4	27.0	31.6	28.5
4	105.9	106.4	105.6	107.3	106.3	107.9	108.9	111.9	108.1	109.2	112.0	109.2	110.9	112.7	111.2	113.2	114.1	115.8	116.7	115.0
5	70.4	71.2	72.1	73.2	71.7	73.8	75.4	76.3	76.7	75.5	77.2	77.6	78.6	79.4	78.2	79.8	80.2	81.0	81.9	80.8
6	41.9	35.8	39.8	36.4	38.5	46.2	53.8	56.5	66.3	55.9	59.1	62.7	57.7	51.9	57.7	52.7	46.0	49.5	53.2	50.4
7	21.3	21.4	22.5	23.9	22.3	25.3	27.3	28.3	28.0	27.4	27.6	26.2	25.6	25.3	26.0	25.7	25.8	25.7	26.5	26.0
8	10.1	10.3	11.5	12.8	11.2	14.0	15.5	16.5	15.4	15.5	14.8	12.9	12.0	12.1	12.9	12.4	12.6	12.8	13.4	12.8
9	11.2	11.1	11.0	11.1	11.1	11.3	11.8	11.8	12.6	11.9	12.8	13.4	13.5	13.2	13.2	13.3	13.2	13.0	13.1	13.2
10	21.0	20.4	19.3	18.5	19.8	18.2	21.1	23.0	22.8	21.3	21.5	22.0	22.3	22.2	22.0	22.5	22.9	20.0	21.8	21.8
11	-0.4	-6.0	-2.0	-6.0	-3.6	2.7	5.4	5.2	15.5	7.2	10.0	14.5	9.8	4.5	9.7	4.6	-2.7	3.8	4.9	2.6
12	0.4	-4.6	-0.8	-5.4	-2.6	2.4	4.8	4.1	14.5	6.5	9.2	13.7	9.2	3.9	9.0	4.0	-3.3	3.3	4.7	2.2
13	3.4	3.4	2.8	0.9	2.6	1.1	0.6	-0.7	0.0	0.2	0.0	1.8	3.6	3.6	2.2	3.5	2.8	-0.2	-1.1	1.2
14	46.3	47.4	48.2	46.8	47.2	44.6	43.5	44.2	48.3	45.1	52.5	61.1	67.6	71.6	63.3	73.4	77.7	79.5	80.0	77.7
15	25.6	25.8	25.9	23.8	25.3	21.1	20.0	20.7	24.7	21.6	28.8	36.9	43.3	47.4	39.3	49.1	53.2	55.2	55.3	53.3
16	20.7	21.6	22.4	23.0	21.9	23.6	23.5	23.5	23.6	23.5	23.8	24.1	24.2	24.1	24.1	24.3	24.5	24.4	24.7	24.5

(Continued)

Table 21-5 (*Continued*)

Line		1953					1954				
		I	II	III	IV	Year	I	II	III	IV	Year
1	Gross national product	368.9	373.2	370.2	363.9	369.0	360.4	359.5	362.1	370.1	363.1
2	Personal consumption expenditures	234.0	236.2	236.0	234.1	235.1	233.4	236.4	239.0	243.2	238.0
3	Durable goods	33.0	33.5	33.7	32.1	33.1	31.2	32.2	32.4	33.9	32.4
4	Nondurable goods	118.1	119.2	118.1	117.7	118.3	117.4	118.6	119.8	121.5	119.3
5	Services	82.8	83.6	84.1	84.3	83.7	84.9	85.6	86.8	87.9	86.3
6	Gross private domestic investment	52.8	53.0	51.0	45.4	50.6	46.9	47.0	48.9	52.2	48.9
7	New construction	27.1	27.6	27.6	27.8	27.6	27.9	28.9	30.2	31.5	29.7
8	Residential nonfarm	13.6	13.8	13.5	13.5	13.6	13.7	14.8	15.8	16.9	15.4
9	Other	13.5	13.8	14.1	14.3	14.0	14.2	14.1	14.4	14.6	14.3
10	Producers' durable equipment	23.1	22.2	22.6	22.2	22.5	21.5	20.9	20.7	19.9	20.8
11	Change in business inventories—total	2.6	3.2	0.7	-4.6	0.5	-2.5	-2.9	-2.0	0.8	-1.6
12	Nonfarm only	3.2	4.1	1.5	-4.3	1.1	-2.6	-3.4	-2.7	0.1	-2.1
13	Net exports of goods and services	-0.8	-1.1	-1.2	-0.5	-0.9	-0.1	0.9	0.6	2.4	1.0
14	Gov't purchases of goods and services	83.0	85.1	84.4	84.9	84.3	80.1	75.2	73.6	72.2	75.3
15	Federal	57.9	60.0	58.8	58.7	58.8	53.1	47.7	45.5	43.9	47.5
16	State and local	25.1	25.1	25.6	26.2	25.5	27.0	27.5	28.1	28.3	27.7

Sources: OBE, USDC. *U.S. Income and Output*, 1958, pp. 124–125; and *Surv. Current Bus.*, July 1962. p. 9; June 1963, p. S-2.

Line	1955 I	1955 II	1955 III	1955 IV	1955 Year	1956 I	1956 II	1956 III	1956 IV	1956 Year	1957 I	1957 II	1957 III	1957 IV	1957 Year
1	382.2	389.5	397.5	401.1	392.7	399.6	400.4	401.4	407.1	402.2	407.9	409.3	409.1	401.2	407.0
2	248.7	253.7	259.9	261.8	256.0	262.7	262.9	262.7	266.6	263.7	268.5	269.3	272.9	270.4	270.3
3	37.9	39.0	41.5	39.9	39.6	38.8	37.5	36.8	38.4	37.9	38.7	37.7	38.5	37.6	38.1
4	121.6	124.3	126.7	128.9	125.4	130.0	130.3	129.7	130.8	130.2	131.6	132.3	134.4	132.4	132.7
5	89.2	90.4	91.7	92.9	91.0	93.9	95.0	96.3	97.4	95.6	98.2	99.3	100.0	100.3	99.4
6	58.5	62.3	63.9	65.2	62.5	64.5	62.8	62.8	62.5	63.1	59.3	59.5	58.4	54.0	57.8
7	33.5	34.0	34.2	33.7	33.9	33.2	32.7	32.7	32.7	32.8	32.7	31.9	32.1	32.5	32.3
8	18.3	18.5	18.2	17.6	18.2	16.8	16.4	16.1	16.2	16.4	15.7	15.0	15.2	15.9	15.5
9	15.2	15.5	16.0	16.1	15.7	16.3	16.4	16.6	16.5	16.4	16.9	16.9	16.9	16.6	16.9
10	20.3	21.7	23.7	24.4	22.5	24.4	24.6	24.9	25.1	24.8	25.2	24.3	24.0	22.7	24.1
11	4.7	6.5	6.0	7.1	6.1	6.9	5.5	5.2	4.6	5.6	1.5	3.3	2.3	−1.3	1.4
12	3.9	5.8	5.4	6.6	5.4	7.0	5.8	5.1	4.2	5.5	0.5	1.8	0.8	−2.7	0.1
13	1.5	0.4	1.2	0.7	0.9	0.3	2.5	2.9	4.0	2.4	4.6	5.1	3.7	2.0	3.9
14	73.4	73.1	72.6	73.5	73.2	72.1	72.3	73.1	74.0	72.9	75.5	75.4	74.1	74.8	75.0
15	44.3	43.4	42.9	43.6	43.5	41.6	41.6	42.3	42.7	42.0	43.4	43.4	42.3	41.8	42.7
16	29.2	29.7	29.7	29.9	29.7	30.4	30.7	30.8	31.3	30.9	32.1	31.9	31.8	33.0	32.3

(Continued)

Table 21-5 (Continued)

Line		1956 I	1956 II	1956 III	1956 IV	1956 Year	1957 I	1957 II	1957 III	1957 IV	1957 Year	1958 I	1958 II	1958 III	1958 IV	1958 Year
1	Gross national product	398.8	398.9	400.2	405.5	400.9	409.6	410.0	411.0	403.8	408.6	393.0	395.2	402.9	413.6	401.3
2	Personal consumption expenditures	263.2	263.7	263.4	266.9	264.3	268.9	270.4	273.4	272.1	271.2	268.9	270.9	274.4	278.7	273.2
3	Durable goods	38.9	38.0	37.1	38.2	38.0	38.9	38.5	39.0	37.7	38.5	34.9	34.7	35.1	37.5	35.5
4	Nondurable goods	130.2	130.3	129.7	130.9	130.3	131.7	132.2	133.8	132.7	132.6	131.4	132.3	134.3	135.2	133.3
5	Services	94.2	95.3	96.7	97.8	96.0	98.3	99.7	100.7	101.8	100.1	102.6	104.0	105.1	106.1	104.4
6	Gross private domestic investment	62.8	61.5	61.4	61.3	61.7	59.8	59.3	58.9	54.1	58.1	46.8	45.8	48.1	54.7	49.0
7	New construction	32.7	32.6	32.3	31.8	32.3	31.9	31.7	31.7	31.6	31.8	31.0	30.2	30.6	32.1	31.1
8	Residential nonfarm	16.6	16.5	16.0	15.7	16.2	15.5	15.2	15.2	15.3	15.3	15.4	15.3	16.2	17.7	16.2
9	Other	16.1	16.1	16.3	16.0	16.1	16.4	16.5	16.5	16.3	16.5	15.6	14.9	14.5	14.4	14.8
10	Producers' durable equipment	24.3	24.7	25.2	25.5	25.0	25.4	24.8	24.9	23.6	24.6	20.4	19.1	18.8	19.5	19.4
11	Change in business inventories	5.8	4.1	3.9	4.0	4.5	2.5	2.8	2.3	-1.0	1.6	-4.6	-3.4	-1.3	3.1	-1.5
12	Nonfarm	6.4	5.0	4.3	3.9	4.9	1.8	1.7	1.3	-2.0	0.7	-5.5	-4.3	-2.1	2.4	-2.4
13	Farm	-0.6	-0.8	-0.4	0.1	-0.4	0.7	1.1	1.0	0.9	1.0	0.9	0.9	0.8	0.7	0.8
14	Net exports of goods and services	0.9	2.2	3.1	3.8	2.5	5.0	4.2	3.8	2.2	3.8	0.4	-0.2	0.2	-1.1	-0.2
15	Exports	20.6	22.0	23.4	23.5	22.4	25.2	24.7	24.7	23.0	24.4	21.0	21.3	21.8	21.6	21.4
16	Imports	19.7	19.7	20.2	19.7	19.8	20.2	20.5	20.8	20.8	20.6	20.7	21.5	21.6	22.7	21.6
17	Gov't purchases of goods and services	71.8	71.5	72.1	73.5	72.3	75.8	76.0	74.8	75.4	75.5	77.0	78.6	80.2	81.2	79.3
18	Federal	41.8	40.9	41.5	42.5	41.7	44.0	44.0	42.8	42.3	43.2	43.2	44.4	44.9	45.4	44.5
19	State and local	30.0	30.6	30.7	31.0	30.6	31.9	32.1	32.1	33.1	32.2	33.8	34.2	35.3	35.8	34.8

Line	1959 I	1959 II	1959 III	1959 IV	1959 Year	1960 I	1960 II	1960 III	1960 IV	1960 Year	1961 I	1961 II	1961 III	1961 IV	1961 Year	1962 I	1962 II	1962 III	1962 IV	1962 Year	1963 I
1	421.7	434.0	427.6	431.1	428.6	440.9	442.3	439.7	437.7	440.2	433.9	443.9	450.4	463.4	447.9	467.4	470.8	471.6	477.7	471.9	482.7
2	283.6	289.1	291.0	291.9	288.9	295.6	299.7	299.1	298.8	298.3	298.2	302.5	306.0	310.6	304.3	313.9	319.9	319.0	322.8	318.2	325.3
3	39.6	41.6	42.0	40.8	41.0	42.4	43.0	41.8	41.8	42.2	39.0	41.3	41.7	44.4	41.6	44.1	44.6	44.6	47.6	45.2	47.9
4	136.8	139.1	139.3	139.8	138.7	140.6	142.3	141.9	140.7	141.4	141.5	142.3	144.4	144.9	143.3	147.0	148.1	149.5	149.3	148.5	150.4
5	107.2	108.4	109.8	111.3	109.2	112.6	114.5	115.4	116.3	114.7	117.7	118.8	120.0	121.4	119.4	122.8	124.1	125.0	126.0	124.5	127.0
6	59.5	67.2	58.0	62.0	61.7	66.7	61.5	58.6	55.8	60.7	50.0	56.5	60.4	64.1	57.8	63.3	64.1	62.4	62.8	63.3	63.4
7	33.8	35.3	34.9	33.6	34.4	34.6	34.2	34.0	34.3	34.3	33.0	34.3	35.6	36.1	34.8	34.6	36.7	37.2	36.8	36.5	35.5
8	19.4	20.6	19.7	18.5	19.5	18.6	18.2	18.1	17.8	18.2	16.5	17.4	18.8	19.7	18.2						
9	14.4	14.7	15.2	15.2	14.9	16.0	16.0	15.9	16.5	16.1	16.5	16.9	16.7	16.4	16.6						
10	20.1	21.7	21.8	21.8	21.4	22.6	23.3	22.7	22.2	22.7	20.1	20.2	21.3	22.7	21.1	22.8	23.8	24.0	24.8	23.8	25.0
11	5.6	10.2	1.3	6.6	5.9	9.6	4.0	1.9	-0.7	3.7	-3.0	2.0	3.5	5.4	2.0	5.9	3.7	0.8	1.3		3.0
12	5.5	10.2	1.4	6.6	5.9	9.4	3.7	1.6	-1.0	3.4	-3.2	1.9	3.4	5.3	1.8						
13	0.0	-0.1	-0.1	0.0	-0.0	0.2	0.2	0.3	0.3	0.3	0.2	0.2	0.1	0.1	0.1						
14	-2.3	-3.1	-2.0	-1.1	-2.1	0.2	1.0	1.5	3.3	1.5	3.5	1.7	0.7	1.4	1.8	1.3	0.7	-0.3	0.5	0.5	0.5
15	20.9	21.2	22.9	22.7	21.9	24.0	25.1	25.0	25.6	24.9	25.7	24.4	25.1	26.2	25.3						
16	23.2	24.4	24.9	23.8	24.1	23.8	24.0	23.5	22.3	23.4	22.2	22.7	24.4	24.8	23.5						
17	80.9	80.9	80.6	78.3	80.1	78.4	80.0	80.5	79.9	79.8	82.2	83.3	83.3	87.2	84.0	88.9	89.2	90.5	91.6	89.9	93.4
18	44.4	44.4	44.3	42.4	43.9	42.0	42.9	42.7	41.8	42.3	42.9	44.4	44.1	46.7	44.5	48.3	48.6	49.0	49.3	48.7	50.7
19	36.5	36.4	36.3	35.9	36.2	36.4	37.1	37.8	38.1	37.4	39.2	38.9	39.2	40.5	39.4	40.6	40.6	41.5	42.3	41.2	42.7

late as January, 1950, Truman recommended a tax bill which would have had the effect of a net tax increase of $1 billion. It should be noted, however, that the proposed budget still had a deficit. There was an increase in federal expenditures at this time which helped reduce the severity of the recession. Federal purchases of goods and services increased sharply throughout most of 1948. (See Table 21-5.) From 1948 to 1949 federal expenditures were up by $6.2 billion (a sizable increase) but not because of stabilization considerations; the increases were largely the result of rising international tensions. The automatic stabilizers did help maintain income, but again they did not represent discretionary stabilization policy decisions. The federal budget deficit for 1949 was $2.5 billion and that of the state and local governments $0.6 billion.

In sum, discretionary fiscal policies had little to do with the recovery,[26] but one observer has defended the actions taken by the Administration on the grounds of the difficulty of breaking with tradition, the lag in statistics, the difficulty of switching policy, and the uncertainty concerning defense and international commitments.[27] The expenditure increases and the tax reductions of 1948 were fortuitous.

The economy was well on its way to recovery when the Korean War started in June of 1950. [From 1949(4) to 1950(1) the increase in the GNP was $7 billion, from 1950(1) to 1950(2) it was $9.3 billion, and from 1950(2) to 1950(3) it was $11.6 billion in constant dollars.] After the Korean War started the President sent a message to Congress explaining the increases in revenue needed to match the expected increases in federal expenditures. Actually his tax message of January 1950 had initiated work on a tax bill which at that time provided for about a $1 billion increase. It was because of this early start in tax legislation that a significant tax increase was accomplished within a very short time. Truman's messages and statements were transmitted in late July, and the Revenue Act of 1950 became effective on October 1, 1950, providing for approximately $4.5 billion in increased revenues. Shortly afterward (January 3, 1951) an excess profits tax was passed, again with considerable speed since work was not started until November 15, 1950, and since the tax was strongly opposed and bitterly contested in the Congress. It raised revenue by $3.3 billion. On October 22, 1951, the Revenue Act of 1951 was passed providing a further increase in revenue of $5.7 billion. (Truman had requested a $10 billion increase.)

All together these three bills raised revenue by about $13.5 billion. The

[26] Federal credit policies in the housing industry were important in the sharp increase in this area during 1949. E. C. Brown, "Federal Fiscal Policy in the Postwar Period," op. cit., p. 158, and W. Lewis, Jr., op. cit., pp. 122–123.

[27] W. Lewis, Jr., op. cit., pp. 124–127.

fiscal policy recommendations of the Truman Administration were very appropriate, and the action of the Congress was helpful but not necessarily sufficient in view of the large increase in federal expenditures which was to take place.[28] In restraining inflation some help came from price and wage controls; a decline in the consumption ratio; the decline in inventory accumulation; the FR-Treasury "Accord" of March 1951, and a more restrictive monetary policy; other selective controls; and the slack in the economy at the time the Korean War started.

In current prices federal government expenditures increased from $41.0 billion in 1950 to $58.0 billion in 1951, to $71.6 billion in 1952 and to $77.7 billion in 1953. Receipts rose from $50.2 billion in 1951 to $64.5 billion in 1951, to $67.7 billion in 1952, and to $70.3 billion in 1953. The surplus for 1950 was $9.2 billion and for 1951 $6.4 billion; in 1952 there was a deficit of $3.9 billion.

From 1950 to 1951 the WPI moved up sharply (by 9.9 points), only to fall by 2.7 points in 1952 and another 1.3 points in 1953. The CPI moved up from 83.8 in 1950 to 90.5 in 1951, to 92.5 in 1952, and to 93.6 in 1953. (See Tables 18-1 and 18-2.) The sharp increases in the CPI and the WPI took place in late 1950. The CPI, however, did increase about 4 points from February 1951 to February 1952.[29] Most of the early price increases were caused by increases in consumption and inventories since government expenditures were not yet raised greatly and since government orders, which normally have an impact prior to the payment for goods, were not yet of large enough scale to be significant.[30] The consumer buying spree of July 1950 created rather severe shortages (temporarily) of sugar, nylon stockings, and other goods. Again, the rather rapid tax legislation of the period helped restrain demand and inflation. In fact, as noted, the WPI actually declined from 1951 to 1954.

[28] For descriptions of the details of the tax recommendations, the arguments over tax legislation in the Congress and elsewhere, and the details of the various tax bills, see Brown, "Federal Fiscal Policy in the Postwar Period," *op. cit.*, pp. 159–163, and Holmans, *op. cit.*, pp. 123–149. The same and other important data and information can be found in the January and Midyear *Economic Reports of the President*, the *Annual Reports of the Secretary of the Treasury*, and Hearings of the JEC, the House Ways and Means Committee, and the Senate Finance Committee.

[29] BLS, U.S. Department of Labor, *Consumer Prices in the U.S., 1953–58*, n.d., p. 95.

[30] But note the interpretation of M. Weidenbaum, "The Economic Impact of the Government Spending Process" *Univ. of Houston Bus. Rev.*, Spring 1961, p. 39.

22

History of Fiscal Policy:
1953 to 1963

THE 1953-1954 RECESSION

Although there was a slight lull in early 1952 the rest of the year saw a continuing expansion in the GNP. This expansion continued until the third quarter of 1953 when a decline set in; its bottom was reached in 1954(2), and the next upturn in the GNP was achieved in 1954(3).

The Eisenhower Administration came into office in January 1953 with a determination to slash the high level of government spending and high taxes.[1] Of overriding importance, however, was the realization of a balanced budget. The alleged immorality of deficit spending permeated the message and speeches of Eisenhower and his Cabinet officers throughout his two terms. Immediate action was undertaken in an effort to cut federal spending. The impact, however, did not show up in the national income accounts until later, as we see in Table 21-5 (in constant dollars), when there was a $5.6 billion drop in federal purchases of goods and services in 1954(1), an additional $5.4 billion drop in 1954(2), a further drop of $2.2 billion in 1954(3), and another of $1.6 billion in 1954(4). The total drop from 1953(4) to 1954(4) was just short of a whopping $15 billion.[2] Some of the impact was no doubt felt earlier than 1954(1) because of the cancellation of orders which occurred and because of the fact that payments lag behind the initial impacts of placing of orders. The most important single factor in the recession was this cutback in federal purchases of goods and services. (The further tightening of a monetary policy which was already tight during the first four months of 1953 did not help matters.)

---

[1] Newspaper coverage of the campaign gives one a good taste of how strongly Eisenhower felt about these issues.

[2] On this matter, see B. C. Hickman, *Growth and Stability of the Postwar Economy*, Washington, D.C.: Brookings Institution, 1960, Chapter 9.

It is true that some tax cuts were made in 1953 (and again in 1954), but apparently they were based on commitments Eisenhower had made at an earlier date and not on the prevailing recession conditions, contrary to later contentions of the CEA and Administration spokesmen.[3] In other words, the tax cuts were again fortuitous. Furthermore, they were relatively light when compared with the cut in expenditures, and there was a deliberate attempt to maintain the current tax structure. (The excess profits tax, which was scheduled to expire on June 30, 1953, was extended. The attempt to move up by 6 months the reduction in income taxes scheduled for December 31, 1953, was successfully fought by the Administration. Eisenhower later recommended that the latter cut, and the similarly scheduled cut in excises, be allowed to occur with no knowledge whatever of whether the needs of the economy at that future date would be for a deflationary policy.)[4] This attempt to get on top of the budget nonetheless also involved an almost complete lack of consideration of the impact of a drastic cut in federal purchases.

The repeal of the excess profits tax and the reduction in personal income tax rates were realized on December 31, 1953. As we have noted, this was fortuitous—previously recommended in May 1953 before it was clear that a recession was to occur. The scheduled (January 1, 1954) increase in social security taxes was opposed by the Administration but went into effect, an attempt to repeal the tax on movie admissions was vetoed, and the Administration unsuccessfully opposed the Excise Tax Reduction Act of 1954. The latter reduced revenues by $1 billion, but the social security tax increase raised revenue by about $1.3 billion. The effect of these actions was almost neutral.

The most important action taken by the Administration was again one that would have been taken regardless of the recession and was aimed primarily at overall reform of the tax structure rather than at raising consumption. This was the Internal Revenue Code of 1954, which made a long list of changes in the tax laws (many with no public hearings). Accelerated depreciation was introduced as were the dividend credit, extended depletion allowances to many new minerals and resources,

---

[3] E. C. Brown, "Federal Fiscal Policy in the Postwar Period," in R. E. Freeman, ed., *Postwar Economic Trends in the United States*, New York: Harper, 1960, p. 168 (and footnotes) discusses this in detail.

[4] In early 1953 the Administration and Chairman Martin of the FR were extremely fearful of inflationary developments although they could provide little or no evidence to substantiate their opinions. The date of Eisenhower's tax message was May 20, 1953. In this same message, he recommended several substantial cuts in Truman's budget proposal for fiscal 1954 which Congress promptly accepted and to which they added a few of their own. See A. E. Holmans, *United States Fiscal Policy, 1945–1959*, London: Oxford Univ. Press, 1961, pp. 203–210.

increased allowable deductions for medical expenses, and some deductions for retirement income and child care for working mothers. The revenue reduction of this bill was some $1.4 billion, while that for the excess profits tax repeal and personal income tax reduction was expected to be some $5.0 billion. Total expected revenue reduction was then about $7.4 billion, against which must be deducted the $1.3 billion increase in social security taxes. This and the role played by the automatic stabilizers were important in cushioning the decline.[5] But little in these reductions was truly discretionary even though it is true that had inflation been a threat the scheduled and previously agreed upon tax cuts could likely not have occurred.

The tax reductions of 1954 were not achieved without considerable debate and controversy. Some congressmen, a few economists, and the unions favored action which would lower taxes on middle and lower income groups and were very critical of the "trickle-down theory." These efforts to raise consumption were again successfully resisted by Congress and the Administration. Again, little credit goes to discretionary fiscal policy. The tax cuts that did occur only partially offset the expenditure declines. Most of the credit should go to the automatic stabilizers. In addition, the loosening of monetary policy was probably instrumental in the steep rise in nonfarm residential construction during 1954.

RECOVERY AND DECLINE: 1955–1958

The economy moved rapidly after the upturn in 1954(3). In 1954(2) the GNP in constant dollars was running at an annual rate of $359.5 billion; in 1954(2) it was up to $389.5 billion. The recovery that began in 1953(3) continued until 1955(4). In 1956(1) there was a slight drop of $1.5 billion in the GNP rate, but a slow upward trend continued from this period until 1957(3). During this period of 8 quarters, the economy moved sideways. (We were in a period of "rolling readjustment"! See Table 21-5.) The unemployment rate dropped from 5.3 percent in January 1955 to 3.6 percent in December 1955. The rate had been as low as 3.3 percent in August and 3.2 percent in September and October.[6] The unemployment rate averaged 4.2 percent for 1956, 4.3 percent for 1957, and 6.8 percent for 1958. By December of 1957 the rate had increased to 5 percent. It increased to 7.6 percent in August 1958, when it began to decline, but not with a consistent trend.

The CPI was very stable throughout 1955, rising only .4 point from January to December. During 1956, however, it rose 3.8 points, during

[5] E. C. Brown, op. cit., pp. 166ff.
[6] Jan. 1956 Ec. Rept. Pres., p. 183.

1957 it rose 1.4 points, and during 1958 it rose .2 point.[7] The WPI rose .4 point in 1955, 3.0 points in 1956, 2.8 points in 1957, and 1.4 points in 1958. (See Table 18-1.)

Consumption increased fairly rapidly throughout 1954 and 1955 up to 1956(1), but leveled off for the first three quarters of 1956. It rose during the last quarter and somewhat thereafter but at a slow rate until 1957(3) when it dropped by $2.5 billion. Gross private domestic investment also rose throughout 1954, jumped up steeply during 1955 and began a gradual decline in 1956(1). Federal government purchases declined throughout 1954, were fairly constant throughout 1955, and the first half of 1956, but rose slightly in the second half of 1956 and early 1957 [$1.5 billion from 1956(4) to 1957(1)] and then declined again. Our net exports of goods and services expanded from $.1 billion in 1954(1) to $2.4 billion in 1954(4). It wavered between $.4 and $1.5 billion during 1954, dropped to $.3 billion in 1956(1), and rose continuously to $5.1 billion in 1957(2), from which point it dropped again. (See Table 21-5.)

There was a shift from a federal deficit of $5.8 billion in 1954 to a surplus of $3.8 billion in 1955—a very abrupt shift. The surplus in 1956 was higher at $5.7 billion and declined to $2.0 billion in 1957. There was an increase in state and local government purchases, and they also ran deficits from 1954 to 1961. The recovery, then, was helped by the automatic stabilizers, fortuitous tax cuts, and increases in consumption, investment, the net foreign balance, and state and local purchases (and the accompanying deficit). The federal deficit, which was primarily caused by the automatic stabilizers and the fortuitous tax decreases helped greatly, but the federal government's discretionary policy was of little help.

We noted that the price level increased throughout the years 1955 to 1958 (and thereafter). What fiscal action was taken to offset this? Very little; reliance was placed on the automatic stabilizers and the maintenance of the existing tax structure, a tight monetary policy, and exhortations to business and labor to be "good boys" and not pursue their own self-interests. It appears, then, that the Administration does not deserve a very high grade for its antirecession policy in 1953–1954 or for its anti-inflation policy during the subsequent recovery. It should be noted, however, that it did succeed in postponing scheduled cuts in both excise and corporate income taxes, and it did successfully resist attempts to lower taxes during 1955 and 1956. In addition, there was lack of agreement on the causes and cures of the inflation of this period. Its resistance of a tax cut in 1957, after the economy had moved virtually sideways for 7 successive quarters and after the unemployment rate climbed above 4 percent, was not so commendable. It is accurate to state that tax and expenditure actions

[7] *Consumer Prices in the United States, 1953–58*, p. 41.

and recommendations undertaken or proposed during this period were measured primarily against budgetary considerations (the goals of lower taxes and reduced government bureaucracy and expenditures) rather than against stabilization considerations. One can support the argument that the Administration was not permanently attached to the usual Republican dogmas of an annually balanced budget, etc., for it is true that a deficit was accepted and that if the 1953–1954 recession had become more serious the Administration planned to undertake large-scale public works, but it is rather difficult to contend that it had moved very far away from this position.

It is not always easy to differentiate between the extent to which a fiscal conservative (1) voices conservative economic dogma because he feels politically obligated to do so but believes and acts otherwise, and (2) voices the conservative dogma and believes it but acts otherwise for pure political reasons. An excerpt from the Eisenhower budget message of January 1956 seems to be somewhat compromising:

> Under conditions of high peacetime prosperity such as now exist we can never justify going further into debt to give ourselves a tax cut at the expense of our children. So in the present state of our financial affairs I earnestly believe that a tax cut can be deemed justifiable only when it will not unbalance the budget, a budget that makes provision for some reduction, even though modest, in our national debt. . . .
>
> Over the long term, a balanced budget is a sure index of thrifty management— in home, business, or in the Federal government. When achievement of a balanced budget is long put off in a business or at home, bankruptcy is the result. But in similar circumstances a government resorts to inflation of the money supply. This inevitably results in a depreciation of the value of money and an increase in the cost of living.[8]

The qualifying phrase "over the long term" certainly leads to an acceptance of a cyclically rather than an annually balanced budget. This should please economists for it does show progress in the acceptance of fiscal policy. On the other hand, to argue that taxes should be cut only when we run a surplus is, if fiscal theory has any validity at all, grossly absurd! Eisenhower has been justifiably criticized on this basis, even though a close reading indicates that he felt that taxes should be cut during prosperity only if such action does not unbalance the budget and still retains some surplus for debt repayment. The acceptance of the cyclically balanced budget implies acceptance of recession deficits. The statement can also be criticized on the basis that a surplus is a prerequisite to a tax cut. Under conditions of prosperity Eisenhower's advice would tend to be inflationary.

[8] From *The New York Times*, Jan. 6, 1956.

It could also be criticized for its analogy between private and public debt, and its assumption that deficits are inflationary.

The budget message for fiscal 1958 was sent to Congress in January of 1957. President Eisenhower eventually found that his budget was to be later condemned on several occasions by high Administration officials (the Secretary of the Treasury and his Deputy) and the Chairman of the Board of Governors of the Federal Reserve. It was in this context that Secretary Humphrey came forth with his famous words that if we did not cut the budget (and he said it could and should be cut by the Congress) and reduce the unbearable tax burden, we would have "a depression that will curl your hair."[9] Such criticism of their own budget was, indeed, rather strange procedure, aside from the other implications of Humphrey's comment. Eisenhower, too, followed through on Humphrey's advice by ordering a new examination to see where *he* could cut *his* budget. The Democratic Congress, to say the least, was obliging.

It was also during 1957 that the Administration pursued a drive for economy within its own departments. Apparently a major reason for this was that expenditures were pushing close to the debt limit and the Administration was stubbornly determined not to request that its upper limit, which was temporary, be continued (presumably because such action would be fiscally irresponsible, would adversely affect the government's financial integrity, etc.). There were, accordingly, rather severe cutbacks in defense orders and even some postponement of payments which threatened the solvency of many business firms. The fact that the Treasury resorted to techniques of borrowing money not subject to the legal debt limit did not reduce the severity of the cutbacks and payments postponement.[10]

In October 1957 the launching of Sputnik caused many individuals to question the wisdom of the severe cutbacks in defense expenditures: How much had the Eisenhower Administration cut meat rather than fat from the defense program? It should be remembered, however, that the Democratic Congress had sharpened its knife, too. Eventually there was general agreement that an increase would have to be made in the defense program; Eisenhower noted that consideration of an annually balanced budget should not preclude a deficit if needed to attain the proper level of defense spending.

[9] *The New York Times*, Jan. 17, 1957. Eisenhower was reluctant to support his own budget and willing, in some ways, at least, to let Congress cut it. See the discussion in Holmans, *op. cit.*, pp. 262–267, and W. Lewis, Jr., *Federal Fiscal Policy in the Postwar Recessions*, Washington, D.C.; Brookings, 1962, pp. 188–192.

[10] For discussions of those problems see E. C. Brown, *op. cit.*, pp. 174–176, and W. Lewis, Jr., *op. cit.*, pp. 195ff. and note 12, p. 196.

The recession of 1957–1958 was no doubt partially caused by the cut-backs in defense orders during the second half of 1957. But inventory liquidation set in in 1957(1) after inventories (nonfarm) themselves had been at low levels throughout the preceding 3 quarters. This liquidation continued until 1958(4). Nonfarm residential construction, which had risen to high levels in 1954 and 1955, declined (because of tight money) to a lower level throughout 1956 and 1957, then turned up significantly in the third and fourth quarters of 1958. Producers' durable equipment, which had increased by $4.1 billion (annual rate) from 1955(1) to 1955(4), leveled off in 1956 and 1957 between $24 and $25 billion (annual rate) and then dropped off in 1957(4) to $22.7 billion and to an average rate of $19.4 billion in 1958. It is also probably significant that the change in consumption during the first three quarters of 1956 was practically zero. It did increase at an annual rate of $3.9 billion in 1956(4) but again changed very little during 1957. Although it dropped in 1958(1) its rate of increase in 1958 was greater than in 1957, which fact means that it played an important role in the recovery. The decline in capital investment during 1958 was no doubt related to the failure of consumption to grow in 1956 and 1957. While cutbacks in defense orders played a role in this recession, their role was not as significant as in the 1953–1954 recession.

The most significant debate thus far over the use of a discretionary tax cut occurred during the 1957–1958 recession. Well-known and widely-respected economists, especially from academic circles, publicly called for a cut in taxes to spur consumption. It seemed for a while that Congress was willing, for the first time, to follow an enlightened fiscal policy to combat a recession, for there was also much agitation within its own chambers for the tax cut. (Some members of the Administration also favored a tax cut.) Again, however, the argument bogged down in debates over where the cuts should be made (to stimulate saving and investment or to stimulate consumption, excise or income tax reduction, the corporate income tax or accelerated depreciation, how effective the tax cut would be in getting people to spend their money, how "inflationary" the tax cut would be, etc.). After Congress returned from its Easter vacation in mid-April the enthusiasm for a tax cut died down.[11]

The President's January 1958 budget recommendation for fiscal 1959 included an increase in defense expenditures of close to $1 billion and an increase of $100 million to upgrade education, which had been under rather severe fire from many quarters after Sputnik. Several other reductions were suggested in expenditures for grants-in-aid to states for public assistance and hospitals and for veterans' benefits, and also recommended

[11] See E. C. Brown, *op. cit.*, pp. 176–178.

was an end to special aid to local school districts that experienced large enrollment increases because of federal programs in their districts. A sizable increase in postage rates was also recommended, and the administrative budget was to have a surplus of almost a half billion dollars. There was an assumption that the decline would be short-lived, and little expectation that fiscal policy would or should be called on to combat the decline. In fact, references were made to the use of a marginally balanced budget to cover the cost of increased defense expenditures.[12] It was clear at this time that the economy was in a recession, but it was not at all clear how deep the recession would become, or how long it would last. An unjustified assumption was made of the future course of the economy and of a budget surplus, and an emasculated version of the fiscal policy proposed was presented.

A major action taken during 1958 was to speed up expenditures on programs already under way or for which funds had already been allocated, and to move ahead some expenditures scheduled for 1959. Payments under grant-in-aid projects were speeded up, and refunds from tax return overpayments were also speeded up. Unemployment compensation payments were extended (but the states were to repay funds borrowed from the federal government), which added some $0.5 billion to personal income. A bill was passed (and signed, but only under protest) in which VA and FHA housing credit terms were eased and additional funds were made available. Another bill was passed to lift legal limitations on the rate of use of funds under the interstate highway program and to provide additional funds (for later years, however); again the President signed it only reluctantly. Eisenhower further pocket-vetoed a depressed-areas aid bill, a bill establishing grants-in-aid for municipal airports, and vetoed but later accepted a modified version of a rivers and harbors bill in late June of 1958. These discretionary programs added some $1 to $1.5 billion of expenditures to the economy, and even some of these small programs were opposed by the Administration. Furthermore, much of the expenditure was merely borrowed from the near future. Excessive reliance was again placed on the automatic stabilizers, and faith was placed in confidence as the most important factor in raising the level of aggregate demand. A tax cut was still considered ineffective or fiscally irresponsible because it would result in an unbalanced budget.[13]

The unemployment statistics included in Table 22-1 for 1958 when the tax debate was under way perhaps speak for themselves. In January of 1958, after the rate of unemployment had increased for 5 successive months and was to increase five times in the next 8 months (with no

[12] See *Jan. 1958 Ec. Rept. Pres.*, p. 49.
[13] E. C. Brown, *op. cit.*, pp. 178–182; Holmans, *op. cit.*, pp. 273–287.

declines) the Administration was calling for a small surplus in the administrative budget and reductions in nondefense expenditures. The gradual realization that a budget deficit was unavoidable prompted some observers to point out the inefficacy of deficits to stimulate demand. Others were just plain shocked at the thought of a terribly large deficit (which turned out to be $2.8 billion in fiscal 1958 and a grand $12.4 billion in fiscal 1959).[14] The $12.4 billion deficit must, indeed, have been a deep shock to

Table 22-1. Recent Unemployment Rates (Seasonally Adjusted Percent)

	1957	1958	1959	1960	1961	1962	1963
Jan.	4.2	5.7	6.0	5.3	6.6	5.8	5.8
Feb.	4.0	6.4	5.8	4.8	6.8	5.6	6.1
March	3.9	6.7	5.7	5.5	6.9	5.5	5.6
April	3.9	7.3	5.2	5.1	6.9	5.5	5.7
May	4.1	7.3	5.0	5.1	7.0	5.5	5.9
June	4.3	7.3	5.0	5.4	6.9	5.5	5.7
July	4.2	7.5	5.2	5.5	6.9	5.4	5.6
Aug.	4.2	7.5	5.4	5.8	6.8	5.7	5.5
Sept.	4.5	7.2	5.5	5.7	6.8	5.6	
Oct.	4.6	6.9	5.8	6.3	6.7	5.3	
Nov.	5.1	6.1	5.8	6.2	6.1	5.8	
Dec.	5.2	6.3	5.5	6.8	6.0	5.5	

Source: Various issues of the CEA's *Economic Indicators.* Depending on the source or issue these figures vary slightly because of changes in official definitions.

the defenders of fiscal integrity. It would be interesting to know what the deficits would have been had a prompt reduction in income taxes been made early in the recession (or even in late 1956).

Not only have the fiscal policies of 1958 come under heavy fire; so have the compilation and presentation of data. E. Cary Brown has accused the Administration of refusing to inform the public properly and accurately by releasing incomplete statistics, using or ignoring seasonal adjustments as the political needs dictated, including empty statements on fiscal policy in the *Economic Reports* (and he has attacked their assumption of omniscience and their self-justification), and of deliberately misleading the public.[15]

[14] These are from the CEA's *Economic Indicators*, Oct. 1962, and are for "budget receipts and expenditures." For the cash budget the figures were $−1.5 and $−13.1 billion.

[15] E. C. Brown, *op. cit.*, pp. 182–183.

On January 13, 1961, the Bureau of the Budget issued a Staff Report entitled *Federal Fiscal Behavior During the Recession of 1957–58.*[16] This last-minute report was presented presumably to record what went on during this recession for the benefit of the new Administration. In his letter of transmittal, Maurice H. Stans, Director of the Bureau of the Budget, some of whose political speeches since that time have shown nothing but utter ignorance of the most elementary aspects of fiscal policy, stated that "The fiscal actions of the Government which gave the biggest boost to the economy in 1958 were the built-in stabilizers. . . ."[17] This, of course, is an incorrect and most misleading assertion (even though it was unintended) since the words "fiscal actions" imply that direct discretionary action was undertaken.[18] Stans also cited the seriousness of the budget deficit, the fact that "many of the deliberate countercyclical actions" made a small contribution or were poorly timed, and inferred that long-range improvements should be made in the unemployment compensation system "which would prevent the periodical need for emergency action involving unexpected drains on the Federal budget."[19] Proposals were made to extend coverage and establish a federal loan fund,[20] but this writer is not aware of further concrete recommendations for long-range improvement in the system by Eisenhower, and he certainly had plenty of time to make them between 1958 and January 1961.[21] It is of further interest to note the ardent defense of, and claims for, Eisenhower's fiscal policies in 1958 and then read in this report of Stans' Staff that discretionary actions were of extremely little help, and further that some policies utilized were unsound. This report does show, however, the inadequacy of present discretionary actions open to the Chief Executive. The report further shows that most of the work in offsetting the impact of the recession was done by the automatic stabilizers.

[16] Bureau of the Budget, Executive Office of the President, Washington, D.C.

[17] *Ibid.*, p. i.

[18] The first sentence on p. 1 is equally misleading even though it is later qualified.

[19] Bureau of the Budget, *op. cit.*, p. ii. In "Government by Credit Card" in *The Commercial and Financial Chronicle* (June 28, 1962), p. 20, Stans raised the socialist cry and stated that ". . . as we continue on this course of economic recklessness and fiscal brinkmanship, we are playing Russian roulette with our freedoms and our destiny."

[20] W. Lewis, Jr., *op. cit.*, p. 153.

[21] S. Harris, *American Economic History*, New York: McGraw-Hill, 1961, p. 158, has made the following rather harsh but humorous statement: "Grant's views on fiscal policy in the 1870's were more advanced than those of another great general almost 100 years later." In fairness to General Eisenhower, however, it appears that he has finally been won over by his critics. In November 1962, he did come out for a tax cut, and without the usual Republican qualification which would reduce the expansive impact of the tax cut—that expenditures be reduced. His qualification was that they be not increased.

Table 22-2. Federal Government Receipts and Expenditures, 1957–1959
(Calendar Years, Billions of Dollars, Seasonally Adjusted Annual Rates)

	1957		1958				1959	
	July– Sep. (peak)	Oct.– Dec.	Jan.– March (trough)	Apr.– June	July– Sep.	Oct.– Dec.	Jan.– March	Apr.– June
Federal gov't receipts	82.5	79.7	75.4	76.5	79.4	83.1	87.6	91.9
Personal tax and nontax receipts	37.6	37.4	36.2	36.3	37.1	37.4	39.0	40.1
Corporate profit tax accruals	20.2	18.1	15.3	16.1	18.1	21.0	21.7	24.1
Indirect business tax and nontax accruals	12.3	12.0	11.7	12.0	11.7	12.1	12.6	12.8
Contributions for social insurance	12.4	12.2	12.2	12.1	12.5	12.6	14.3	14.8
Federal gov't expenditures	79.9	80.6	83.5	87.4	90.0	91.4	90.1	90.9
Purchases of goods and services	50.0	49.4	50.6	51.8	53.7	54.3	53.3	53.7
Nat'l defense	(45.0)	(44.0)	(44.4)	(44.6)	(44.9)	(45.5)	(45.9)	46.4)
Other (less sales)	(5.0)	(5.4)	(6.3)	(7.2)	(8.7)	(8.8)	(7.4)	(7.3)
Transfers to persons	16.0	17.2	18.3	20.4	21.0	20.6	20.1	20.3
Unemployment compensation								
Regular and temp. state programs	(1.7)	(2.4)	(3.1)	(4.0)	(4.0)	(3.7)	(2.6)	(2.0)
Temp. extended unemployment compensation	—	—	—	(.2)	(.8)	(.5)	(.3)	(.2)
OASI	(7.5)	(7.8)	(7.9)	(8.6)	(8.7)	(8.8)	(9.4)	(10.2)
Other	(6.8)	(7.0)	(7.3)	(7.6)	(7.5)	(7.6)	(7.8)	(7.9)
Transfer payments, foreign (net)	1.2	1.4	1.2	1.3	1.2	1.6	1.5	1.4
Grants-in-aid to state and local gov'ts	4.2	4.2	4.8	5.4	5.6	6.0	6.6	6.7
Highways	(1.1)	(1.3)	(1.8)	(2.2)	(2.4)	(2.6)	(3.1)	(3.1)
Other grants	(3.1)	(2.8)	(3.0)	(3.2)	(3.2)	(3.4)	(3.5)	(3.4)
Net interest paid	5.8	5.7	5.6	5.5	5.5	5.7	6.0	6.2
Subsidies less current surplus of gov't enterprises	2.8	2.6	2.9	3.0	3.0	3.0	2.7	2.6
Surplus or deficit (−)	2.6	−0.9	−8.1	−10.9	−10.6	−8.2	−2.5	1.0
Gross national product	448.3	442.3	432.0	436.8	447.0	461.0	473.1	487.9
Personal income	355.6	354.1	353.2	355.9	364.7	368.1	374.7	384.5
Corporate profits before tax	43.8	39.4	32.8	34.4	38.8	44.9	46.4	51.7
Unemployment (millions of persons)	2.9	3.4	4.4	4.9	5.0	4.5	4.0	3.5

Source: Bureau of the Budget, *Federal Fiscal Behavior During the Recession of 1957–58.* This table is on the national income and product account basis, compared to selected measures of economic activity.

Table 22-3. The Fiscal 1959 Deficit

		(billions)
I. Effect of built-in stabilizers		
1. Automatic decreases in revenues		$4.8
2. Automatic increases in expenditures		1.3
II. Effect of discretionary actions (expenditure increases)		1.5
III. Other noncountercyclical actions		
Increase in farm price support payments	$2.6	
Increase in defense spending	1.0	
Nonenactment of postal rate increase	.7	
Other	1.8	6.1
Total amount by which actual excess of payments exceeded original estimates		$13.7

Source: Bureau of the Budget, *op. cit.,* p. 2.

According to the Budget Bureau study the built-in stabilizers accounted for almost 80 percent of the change in the deficit during the period in which the GNP declined. The swing was from a $3 billion (annual rate) surplus in 1957(3) to a deficit of $8 billion in 1958(1) in the income and product account. The drop in the GNP was about $16 billion (annual rate).[22] In fiscal 1959 the impact of the various automatic, discretionary, and other policies which helped create a budget deficit of $13.7 billion (consolidated case basis) are shown in Table 22-3.

Table 22-2 contains some very interesting data on the behavior of tax receipts and expenditures during the recession and the following recovery. We see the following trends: (1) Federal receipts dropped $7.1 billion from the peak to the trough but recovered very rapidly especially during the recovery. They increased by $12.2 billion in a year and by $16.5 billion in five quarters (average figures). (2) The drop in corporate income tax collections vastly overshadowed the decline in the personal income tax, excises, or social security taxes, but the personal income tax and social security tax[23] collections increased rapidly during the recovery. (3) Federal expenditures, especially unemployment compensation with small increases in OASI payments and grants-in-aid, played a fairly important role early in the recovery. These expenditures increased by only $6.6 billion in a year, and by $7.4 billion over the same 5 quarters noted.

Also of interest and use is the Bureau's rating of various counter-cyclical policies utilized during the 1957–1958 recession.[24] See Table 22-4.

RECOVERY AND RECESSION AGAIN: 1959–1961

In 1958(3) the GNP turned up by $2.2 billion (annual rate) although unemployment for this quarter averaged 7.4 percent. In 1958(4) the GNP rose further by $7.7 billion (annual rate) but the unemployment rate still averaged 6.4 percent. Further significant increases in the GNP occurred during the first 6 months of 1959, and then the GNP declined in 1959(3) because of the steel strike. It recovered in 1959(4), but not to its previous peak, jumped up by $9.8 billion in 1960(1), then moved up slightly by $1.4 billion in 1960(2), from which point it declined until 1961(2). The rate of unemployment fluctuated considerably in early 1960, but in the months following May a definite upward trend set in. It is significant to note that at no time during the recovery from the 1957–1958 recession did the rate of unemployment fall below 5 percent.

[22] Bureau of the Budget, *op. cit.*, p. 10.
[23] Coverage was extended and the rate increased in 1958.
[24] Bureau of the Budget, *op. cit.*, p. 27.

Table 22-4. Tentative Rating of the Major Countercyclical Policies Employed in the 1957–1958 Recession

	Relative Economic Impact[a]	Efficiency—Impact per Dollar of Immediate Federal Outlay or Income	Reversi- bility
Built-in stabilizers			
Receipts			
Individual income taxes	large	good	good
Corporation income taxes	large	fair to good	good
Excise taxes	large	fair to good	good
Expenditures			
Unemployment trust fund, withdrawals by states	large	good	good
Other unemployment programs	medium	good	good
Discretionary actions			
Administrative			
Construction speedup, direct federal public works	medium	good	poor
Encouragement of faster private and state-local construction activities	small	good	fair
Advance procurement (fiscal 1958)	small	good	good
Speedup in tax refunds	medium	good	good
Liberalization of FHA and VA housing rules and speedup in processing FHA applications	medium	good	poor
Release of reserves in various FNMA special assistance programs	medium	good	good
Liberalization, farm housing loans	small	fair	poor
Emphasis on labor surplus areas in letting of contracts	small	good	good
Involving congressional action			
Temporary extended unemploy- ment compensation	large	good	good
FNMA special assistance	medium to large	poor	good
Reduction in FHA and VA downpayment requirements	medium to large	good	poor
Advance procurement (fiscal 1959)	small	good	good
Federal-aid highways ABC	large	fair	fair
Interstate and other	small	fair	poor

Source: Bureau of the Budget, *op. cit.*

[a] Relative economic impact in this tabulation is really a combination of size and speed of economic impact. A designation "large" in column 1 means that, by the end of fiscal 1959, the impact on the economy is judged to have totaled anywhere from about $200 million up. A designation "small" means an economic impact of less than $20 or $30 million by the end of fiscal 1959. In some cases the classification has to be made on a subjective or arbitrary basis.

Important factors in the recovery were the increase in consumption, the switch from inventory liquidation to inventory accumulation, an increase in residential construction, and a $1 billion increase in federal purchases from 1958(2) to 1958(4). Producers' durable equipment expenditures increased slightly, finally getting up to $23.3 billion (annual rate) in one quarter [1960(2)], which was still $2.2 billion below the 1956 peak.

Although there were official denials (the presidential election was forthcoming) another recession set in during the second half of 1960. An upturn in the GNP did not come until 1961(2). The rate of advance was significant during each quarter during 1961, but, while the GNP still increased throughout 1962,[25] it was moving at a snail's pace. The slow rate of growth was reflected in an unemployment rate that dropped below 5.5 percent for only 2 months during 1962.

A word about prices. The WPI rose .1 point from 1959 to 1960 and dropped .4 point from 1960 to 1961. The CPI, from 1957 to 1958, rose 2.7 points, from 1958 to 1959 by .8 point, from 1959 to 1960 by 1.6 points, from 1960 to 1961 by 1.1 points, and from 1961 to 1962 by 1.2 points. (See Tables 18-1 and 18-2.)

Five factors apparently played a significant role in the decline that came in 1960. In the first place, federal purchases declined by $2 billion from 1959(1) to 1959(4), and changed little throughout 1960. (State and local government expenditures rose, however.) Residential construction declined from a high of $20.6 billion (annual rate) in 1959(2) to $17.8 in 1960(4). Inventories fluctuated sharply because of the anticipated steel strike during 1959, but declined sharply throughout 1960. An extremely tight money policy was pursued throughout 1959. Even with a rate of unemployment of 5 percent and over throughout 1959, banks were heavily in debt to the Federal Reserve. Mr Martin was determined to restrain any inflationary boom before it got started this time. Finally, fiscal policy was tight, as shown in the full employment surplus.

Whether or not the economy was entering another recession was an issue in the 1960 presidential election. It was not until the third quarter of the year, however, that the GNP was on its way down and it was clear that a recession was under way. This information was not available until October. Successive increases in the rate of unemployment, however, occurred several months before the election. At any rate, Kennedy and other Democrats hammered away on the theme that the growth of the American economy had for several years been much too slow, as indeed, it had been.

[25] Up to and including the third quarter at least. It picked up in 1962(3) and 1963(1).

The 1960–1961 recession, however, was rather short-lived. The GNP declined for only three quarters, turning up in 1961(2). Consumption dropped very little [$1.5 billion from 1960(2) to 1961(1)], residential construction dropped from $18.6 to $16.5 billion from 1960(1) to 1961(1), producers' durable equipment dropped from $23.3 to $20.1 billion from 1960(2) to 1961(2), net exports increased significantly [from $−3.1 billion in 1959(2) to $.2 billion in 1960(2), to $3.5 billion in 1961(1)], and federal purchases of goods and services were fairly level but turned up in 1961(1), 1961(2), and 1962(4). (All data in constant dollars at annual rates.)

In 1962 the GNP continued to increase but the rate of increase during 1962(3) was slow. From 1962(2) to 1962(3) personal consumption continued to increase but gross private domestic investment dropped slightly. Net exports were down, but federal purchases of goods and services increased.

We noted that the 1960–1961 recession was short-lived. This statement should not slight over the high rate of unemployment that prevailed *before* the recession set in, or the high rate of unemployment that existed *after* recovery.

Eisenhower's January 1960 budget estimates for fiscal 1961 anticipated continued economic expansion and a budget surplus of $4.2 billion (even though unemployment in November was 5.8 percent, in December 5.5 percent, and in January, 1960, 5.3 percent). At the time of the midyear economic review (October 1960) the estimated surplus declined to $1.1 billion, and by January 1961 it had declined to an expected $0.1 billion. In the January 1961 budget for fiscal 1962 expenditures of $80.9 billion were proposed and revenues were estimated at $82.3 billion, for a surplus of $1.5 billion. This assumed a rapid increase in economic activity and some tax increases. Again, unemployment was high at the time this budget was proposed—well over 6 percent—but a restrictive budget was still proposed.[26] In terms of the full employment surplus the budget was even more restrictive. These two budgets represent very poor fiscal policy in light of the high level of unemployment. This is especially so since the Administration could no longer use the inflation argument as an excuse for inaction.

RECOVERY 1961–1963

What about President Kennedy's fiscal policies? Kennedy talked the expansionist's line during the 1960 election, and he further surrounded himself with economists who favored an active, expansionary fiscal policy.

[26] Data from JEC, *Jan. 1961 Ec. Rept. Pres.*, H, pp. 504–506.

On assuming office, Kennedy proposed a temporary extension of unemployment insurance, aid to depressed areas, aid to dependent children, easier credit terms to stimulate construction, and other programs in education, highways, natural resources, improvements in social security, and medicare. He stated in his February 2 (1961) message that if later conditions dictated additional measures would be proposed (presumably a tax cut).

The report of the CEA to the Joint Economic Committee was comprehensive, straightforward, and honest.[27] The CEA estimated that the programs proposed at this time would add at least $3 billion to the budget during the first year after enactment. The estimate of David Bell, Director of the Bureau of the Budget, was $2.3 billion.[28] Bell pointed out that these proposals would not unbalance Eisenhower's budget for fiscal 1962 since this $2.3 billion increase was less than Eisenhower's planned surplus of $1.5 billion plus $900 million of increased revenues which would be forthcoming as a result of the increased economic activity which would result from the Kennedy proposals. He pointed out, however, that Eisenhower's estimates of both revenue and the cost of proposed expenditures were too low. The revised estimate including all the President's proposals except for defense yielded a deficit of $2.2 billion.[29] The budget deficit for fiscal 1961 in the national income accounts was $2.2 billion, $3.9 billion in the administrative budget,[30] and $2.3 billion in the cash budget.[31]

Kennedy's programs enacted in 1961 included temporary unemployment compensation, aid to dependent children, more liberal social security benefits, the Housing Act of 1961, a raise and extension of the minimum wage, and the Area Redevelopment Act. National defense expenditures were raised $4.5 billion over the level included in the January 1961 budget.[32] The net effect of these programs was perhaps $6.2 billion[33] (all the recommendations of President Kennedy were not realized), and the economy did respond rapidly throughout calendar 1961. An important factor in this recovery then was the rate of increase in federal purchases, which increased from $42.9 billion in 1961(1) to $46.7 billion in 1961(4) in constant dollars, at the annual rate, and the increase in state and local purchases. The most important federal action to resist the decline in the

---

[27] Ibid., pp. 290–419. The CEA appeared before the Committee on March 6, 1961.

[28] Ibid., p. 505. Data are apparently on the administrative budget basis.

[29] Ibid., p. 507.

[30] Economic Indicators, Oct. 1962, p. 31.

[31] Ibid., p. 32.

[32] Helen B. Junz, "Expansion of Government Programs During Fiscal Year 1962," Surv. Current Bus., Nov. 1961, p. 8.

[33] My estimate.

economy was the increase in defense spending. Not a whole lot was done by way of a countercyclical program otherwise.

The projections of economic developments in 1962 by the CEA were highly optimistic. GNP was estimated at $570 billion, a $50 billion gain over 1961. The President requested a standby program of public works to counteract unemployment, discretionary authority to cut income taxes, a permanent strengthening of unemployment insurance, a tax credit for investment, and a retraining act.[34] The President's recommendations for fiscal 1963 were estimated to increase budget expenditures by $3.4 billion over those estimated for fical 1962. The proposed administrative budget showed a surplus of $.5 billion, the cash consolidated budget a surplus of $1.8 billion, and the national income account budget a surplus of $4.4 billion.[35]

We have already noted that the economy slowed down considerably in 1962. Instead of reaching a GNP of $570 billion, the actual level turned out to be $553.9 billion. But neither the Budget Bureau Director[36] nor the Chairman of the CEA[37] ruled out the possibility of a slower rate of growth during calendar 1962. Hence the emphasis on flexible and discretionary tax authority, standby public works, an improved unemployment compensation system, etc.

Some members of the Joint Economic Committee were doubtful that a $570 billion GNP would be reached.[38] When it became clear by 1962(3) that the rate of growth had declined, considerable agitation developed for a tax cut. This and most of the other important fiscal policy changes President Kennedy asked for were not granted. Again, the issue became entangled in an argument over whether the tax cut should be temporary or of the reform type. Kennedy postponed his decision until the July data were available and then in a television broadcast in August stated that he had decided against a tax cut at this time,[39] but he promised a tax cut in January, 1963, and at that time also to propose tax reforms. During this period the Chamber of Commerce advocated a tax cut (but with a reduction in federal expenditures); so did Eisenhower (in November), the AFL-CIO, the CED, the Vice-Chairman of Morgan Guarantee Trust, a former President of the Federal Reserve Bank of New York (Allan Sproul), David Rockefeller (President of the Chase Manhattan Bank; he proposed a tax cut of $8 to $10 billion), and certain Cabinet officials. Presumably

[34] A complete list of legislative recommendations can be found in JEC, *Jan. 1962 Ec. Rept. Pres.*, H, p. 8.

[35] *Ibid.*, pp. 76–79.

[36] *Ibid.*, p. 81.

[37] *Ibid.*, p. 16.

[38] *Ibid.*, *passim*, and JEC, 1962 *Ann. Rept.*, pp. 37–38.

[39] It was extremely doubtful that Congress would have gone along in any case.

they thought taxes should be cut in January, 1963. In November of 1962 the President's Advisory Committee on Labor-Management Policy advocated a $10 billion tax cut. The issue was still clouded by reform considerations, however, which meant that long congressional hearings would be held.[40]

Kennedy's programs for fiscal 1963[41] were not very expansionary; certainly they were inadequate to lower the rate of unemployment to the Administration's interim level of 4 percent by mid-1963. Kennedy's attempt to appear fiscally responsible made him determined to have a balanced budget for fiscal 1963. In fact, in November of 1961 he ordered federal agencies to cut their programs, lay off personnel, etc. This was done in spite of the previous and later (January 1962 *Economic Report of the President*) statements of the CEA on the dangers of the full-employment surplus, which for fiscal 1963 was expected to be some $9 or $10 billion. It was no wonder that 1962 turned out to be a disappointment.

Some have argued that it was politically necessary for President Kennedy not to pursue a tax cut in early 1961 and mid-1962, and to pursue a balanced budget in fiscal 1963. They claim that if the President were to propose a massive expansionary program (and the tax cuts it entails), he would be charged with fiscal irresponsibility, which would in turn endanger his other programs and general congressional support.[42] It seems a bit harsh, however, to state that "it is the President's task to weigh the losses of Congressional and public support associated with the charge of fiscal irresponsibility against the losses associated with excessive employment in 1962–64." To claim that "economists would do well, also, to consider the political issues" was little encouragement to the 4.2 million then unemployed. The proponents of this policy should perhaps be reminded that the President can do much in his position to lead and rally support, that all the voters are not incapable of understanding the full employment surplus concept, and that there are far-flung social and other implications to the current rate of unemployment other than the economic ones. Much of Kennedy's fiscal policy did not differ substantially from that of Eisenhower (in impact at least). President Kennedy's problem, however, was not the same as that of his predecessor—a failure to understand economics. It was his inability to see the proper legislation through the

[40] Members of the Cabinet who had proposed a tax cut included Dillon (Treasury), Hodges (Commerce), and Wirtz (Labor). The CEA was in favor of a cut, as demonstrated by their analyses and statements, as were other nongovernment economic advisers to the President.

[41] It should be recalled that the major government influences in the recovery was the increase in defense expenditures.

[42] Seymour Harris of Harvard and Paul Samuelson of M.I.T. take this position. See "Economic Policy for 1963: A Symposium," *Rev. Ec. & Stat.*, 1962, pp. 3–4.

Congress due to the fiscal concepts Congress still adheres to, the committee system in Congress, or his desire to appear fiscally responsible (in 1962), or to really push legislation, or too strong a political orientation, or to other factors. We should also note, though, that much of the conservative and business criticism of President Kennedy was quite irrational. He gave businessmen faster depreciation write-offs, one tax cut and laid the groundwork for another, high levels of profits, and one of the longest periods of recovery in the postwar period.

SUMMARY AND CONCLUSION

If one attempts to measure postwar fiscal policy against that of the 1930's certainly the improvements appear significant. But most of these improvements have involved institutional changes rather than deliberate changes at the time a switch in policy was called for—the automatic stabilizers, unemployment compensation, and so on. The policies of 1945 were not appropriate, although there was a definite error in forecasting and statistical data were not as readily available as now. The tax reduction programs of 1948 and 1953–1954 were fortuitous and not motivated by countercyclical considerations. They were primarily of the structural reform type.

The Republican Administration was eager not to appear as the party of unemployment and hence eager to restore full employment during the 1953–1954 recession. Nonetheless, they did little to fight the recession by way of a deliberate discretionary policy. Similarly, little was done during the 1957–1958 recession, and there was an official denial that one was under way in late 1960. In fact, in the 1957–1958 recession a tax cut, aside from possibly being fiscally immoral, was condemned on the grounds that its adoption would have precluded the "demonstration of the economy's inherent recuperative powers. We would have helped develop a philosophy that tax relief was necessary to pull us out of the downturn. Also, a tax cut would have increased our present deficit and our public debt, and with them the danger of inflationary pressures in the future."[43] With our present knowledge of economics there is neither a need nor an excuse for making such assumptions or drawing such conclusions about the performance of the economy, the impact of the debt, or the result of a deficit.

Increases in public spending were equally denounced in 1958. According to Eisenhower, those who advocated pump-priming schemes did not have faith in free enterprise and American individualism. These comments about "free spending" during recessions, the sacred nature of the annually

[43] JEC, *Jan 1959 Ec. Rept. Pres.*, The statement was made by Secretary of the Treasury Anderson.

balanced budget, the immorality of an increase in the public debt, the ineffectiveness of a deficit, and the inability to distinguish between a deliberate deficit to counteract a decline and one by default, which results from a failure to take action to counteract the decline—all these biases and prejudices only detract from an honest and objective policy discussion and development. Individuals who mouth such comments are really performing a disservice to the country. In their minds, however, they are convinced they must spread the dogma, the ideology, the religion.

Except for the speeding up of expenditures or programs already established, little was done in 1960 to combat the decline. In his January 1961 budget for fiscal 1962, Eisenhower planned on a $4.2 billion surplus in spite of a then high level of unemployment. Kennedy raised expenditures after he entered office, but it should be recalled that the big boost was in defense purchases. Furthermore, the economy was helped some by both the Berlin crisis of 1961 and the Cuban crisis in 1962. Although fiscal policy must be subverted to the needs of national defense, we do not look forward to a stablization policy based primarily on crises or defense needs. In 1962 Kennedy attempted to balance the budget again in the face of a high level of unemployment. This move was apparently primarily political, as noted previously.

The increase in taxes during the Korean War probably represents the best example of intelligent use of discretionary tax changes. On the other hand, the reduction in government expenditures following the Korean War of some $15 billion was done with no real consideration for its impact on the economy.

The automatic stabilizers have played a much more important role in cushioning economic declines than has discretionary fiscal policy. Although they cushion declines, they do not do much to counteract inflationary movements.

Lest the reader feel that little progress has been made in fiscal understanding, we should note that considerable progress has taken place since the 1930's. The Employment Act has been passed and accepted by both parties, automatic deficits during recessions have been accepted by both parties, and there have been no strong efforts to raise taxes during recessions to balance the budget; some enlightened business organizations (such as the CED) have attempted to spread economic understanding, the Chamber of Commerce has recommended tax cuts (November 1962) of $10 billion (but with a reduction in expenditures too) and has also recommended use of the cash consolidated rather than the administrative budget.[44] General Eisenhower has advocated a tax cut (with expenditures

[44] *The New York Times*, Western edition, Nov. 22, 1962.

held at their current level),[45] some Congressmen show a profound under-standing (but others a profound ignorance) of the implications of modern economic analysis, and the Joint Economic Committee has produced some top-notch economic studies.

Nonetheless, the old dogma that budgets should be balanced annually and that deficits are in themselves and automatically inflationary is perhaps still the dominant one. It is certainly still believed by a great many politicians and Congressmen and a large portion of the press.[46] Unless there is a substantial change in congressional attitudes and a crisis to justify increases in defense expenditures, the outlook for fiscal policy and the whole economy in the next recession is rather dim. On the other hand, because of the progress that has been made, and the wide support tax cuts received in late 1962 and 1963 from diverse groups, it is very likely that sufficient groundwork has been laid for a tax cut to help counteract the next decline. Finally, the 1964 tax reduction will be watched carefully by economists and others for its impact on economic growth, employment, and the price level. Even though some of its thunder may have been stolen by its anticipation in 1963 it will still be regarded as a test of fiscal policy.

[45] *Ibid.*, Nov. 19, 1962, p. 15. The full article was run a few days before this date.

[46] See almost any editorial of the *Wall Street Journal*. This statement is not meant to detract from what is otherwise good reporting in this paper; it refers primarily to its editorial policy.

Index

Abbott, C. C., 438
Abramovitz, Moses, 197n, 200n, 201n
Accelerated depreciation, 259 ff.
  advantages of, 259–261
  countercyclical, 271–272
  criticisms of, 261–264
Acceleration principle, 103–105, 366–373
Achinstein, Asher, 380n, 404n
Ackley, Gardner, 86n, 88n, 94n, 130n, 172n, 184n, 406n, 420, 421, 422, 431n, 432
Adams, Walter, 260n
Administered prices, 23, 420n
Administrative budget, 287–290
Advisory Board on Economic Growth and Stability, 458
Advisory Committee on Labor-Management Policy, 511
American Bankers Association, 16
American Farm Bureau Federation, 16
Anderson, Robert, 389, 451, 452n
Anderson, T., 349n
Ando, A., 417n
Angell, James W., 380n, 465n
Annually balanced budget, 441–443
Anti-inflationary policy, 135–136
Antitrust, and inflation, 430
Area Redevelopment Act of 1961, 341, 509
Ascheim, Joseph, 16n, 385n
AFL-CIO, 4, 194
Automatic stabilizers, 317–318, 374–378
Automation, employment and, 330 ff., 341–342

Average propensity to consume, 84, 360 ff.
Ayres, C. E., 196n

Bach, George L., 16n, 394n, 399n, 400n, 417n, 455n, 458n, 460n
Bailey, M. J., 427n
Bailey, S. K., 74n
Balanced budget, 169
  expansionary, 185
  restrictive, 185
Balanced budget multiplier, 142–143
Balance of international payments, economic goals and, 20–22
Ball, R. J., 418n
Barrit, D. P., 259n
Bator, Francis M., 50, 61n, 66n
  on government expenditures, 56–57
Baumol, W. J., 270n
Bell, David, 293n, 509
Bell-Gemmill thesis, 22
Beveridge, Sir William, definition of full employment, 39
Bird, R. M., 259n
Black, J., 259n
Blair, J. M., 420n
Blough, R., 483n
Bodenhorn, D., 258n
Bottleneck inflation, 422
Bowen, H. R., 74n
Bowen, W. G., 439n
Brazer, Harvey, 274n
Bronfenbrenner, Martin, 416n
Brown, E. Cary, 249n, 258n, 263, 265, 314n, 375n, 376, 473n, 478–479, 483n, 484n, 485n, 492n,

515